# Graphics Programming with
# VISUAL BASIC™

*Robert Stewart*

201 West 103rd Street
Indianapolis, Indiana 46290

*To Sandra and her little boy, Rupert.*

## Copyright © 1995 by Sams Publishing

### FIRST EDITION

All rights reserved. No part of this book shall be reproduced, stored in a retrieval system, or transmitted by any means, electronic, mechanical, photocopying, recording, or otherwise, without written permission from the publisher. No patent liability is assumed with respect to the use of the information contained herein. Although every precaution has been taken in the preparation of this book, the publisher and author assume no responsibility for errors or omissions. Neither is any liability assumed for damages resulting from the use of the information contained herein. For information, address Sams Publishing, 201 W. 103rd St., Indianapolis, IN 46290.

International Standard Book Number: 0-672-30509-7

Library of Congress Catalog Card Number: 94-66637

98 97 96 95      4 3 2 1

Interpretation of the printing code: the rightmost double-digit number is the year of the book's printing; the rightmost single-digit, the number of the book's printing. For example, a printing code of 95-1 shows that the first printing of the book occurred in 1995.

*Composed in AGaramond and MCPdigital by Macmillan Computer Publishing*

*Printed in the United States of America*

## Trademarks

All terms mentioned in this book that are known to be trademarks or service marks have been appropriately capitalized. Sams Publishing cannot attest to the accuracy of this information. Use of a term in this book should not be regarded as affecting the validity of any trademark or service mark.

Visual Basic is a trademark of Microsoft Corporation.

**Publisher**
Richard K. Swadley

**Acquisitions Manager**
Greg Wiegand

**Managing Editor**
Cindy Morrow

**Acquisitions Editor**
Grace Buechlein

**Development Editors**
Angelique Brittingham
Brad Jones

**Software Development Specialist**
Keith Davenport

**Production Editors**
Sandra Doell
Mary Inderstrodt

**Copy Editors**
Chuck Hutchinson
Tonya Simpson

**Editorial Coordinator**
Bill Whitmer

**Editorial Assistants**
Carol Ackerman
Sharon Cox
Lynette Quinn

**Technical Reviewer**
K.L. Murdock

**Marketing Manager**
Gregg Bushyeager

**Assistant Marketing Manager**
Michelle Milner

**Cover Designer**
Timmy Amrhein

**Book Designer**
Alyssa Yesh

**Director of Production and Manufacturing**
Jeff Valler

**Imprint Manager**
Kelly Dobbs

**Manufacturing Coordinator**
Paul Gilchrist

**Production Analysts**
Angela D. Bannan
Dennis Clay Hager
Mary Beth Wakefield

**Graphics Image Specialists**
Jason Hand
Clint Lahnen
Dennis Sheehan
Jeff Yesh

**Page Layout**
Elaine Brush
Charlotte Clapp
Mary Ann Cosby
Judy Everly
Robert Falco
Aleata Howard
Shawn MacDonald
Jill Tompkins
Dennis V.B. Wesner

**Proofreading**
Mona Brown
Michael Brumitt
Cheryl Cameron
DiMonique Ford
George Hanlin
Kimberly K. Hannel
Kim Mitchell
Brian-Kent Proffitt
Beth Rago
Erich Richter
SA Springer
Suzanne Tully

**Indexers**
Bront Davis
Craig Small

# Overview

|   | Introduction | xv |
|---|---|---|
| 1 | Basic Beginnings | 1 |
| 2 | The Artisan Program | 49 |
| 3 | Bézier Curves | 103 |
| 4 | The Artisan Program—Procedures C - N | 135 |
| 5 | The Artisan Program—Procedures N - Z | 175 |
| 6 | The Animator Program | 209 |
| 7 | Multi-Search and Replace | 241 |
| 8 | API Drawing Programs | 271 |
| 9 | Fountain Blends | 295 |
| 10 | The Mini-Bézier Curve Program | 319 |
| 11 | The Rounded Corners Program | 343 |
| 12 | The Text Alignment Program | 359 |
| 13 | The Join Nodes Program | 395 |
| 14 | The Scaling and Printing Program | 417 |
| 15 | ArtAPI | 441 |
| A | Artisan .BAS Files | 525 |
| B | Windows NT, Windows 95, and Higher | 551 |
| C | The Companion Disk | 559 |
|   | Index | 563 |

# Contents

| | Introduction | xv |
|---|---|---|
| 1 | **Basic Beginnings** | 1 |
| | Working with Circles | 4 |
| |     Selecting a Color with Which To Draw | 8 |
| |     The ColorBar | 9 |
| |     The Cls (Command1_Click) Button | 9 |
| |     Clicking the Mouse on the Form | 10 |
| |     Selecting a Drawing Option | 11 |
| | Calculating the Radius of a Circle | 11 |
| |     Pythagorean Theorem | 11 |
| | The Finished Product | 12 |
| | Calculating Radians for Arcs, Pies, and Pie Slices | 14 |
| | Summarizing the *Line* and *Circle* Statements | 15 |
| |     The *Line* Statement | 15 |
| |     The *Circle* Statement | 16 |
| | Using the *Pset* Statement | 17 |
| |     Choosing a Drawing Function Button | 23 |
| |     Clicking the Mouse on the Form | 23 |
| |     The *SineCosine* Procedure | 24 |
| | Calculating with Sin (sine) | 25 |
| | Calculating with Cos (cosine) | 26 |
| |     The *Box_Pset* Procedure | 26 |
| |     The *Bresenham* Method | 27 |
| |     The *Circle_Pset* Procedure | 29 |
| |     The *Circle_sin_cos* Procedure | 30 |
| |     The *Circle_Sqr* Procedure | 30 |
| |     The *Dash_Pset* Procedure | 31 |
| |     The *Fill_Line* Procedure | 32 |
| |     The *Fill_Pset* Procedure | 33 |
| |     The *Grid_Pset* Procedure | 34 |
| |     The *Line_Pset* Procedure | 34 |
| |     The Visual Basic *Point* Statement | 35 |
| |     Summary of the *Pset* Statement | 37 |
| | Using Object Movement | 37 |
| |     Clicking the Cls Button | 41 |
| |     Selecting a Movement Button | 42 |
| |     The *Form_MouseDown* Event | 43 |
| |     The *Form_MouseMove* Event | 45 |

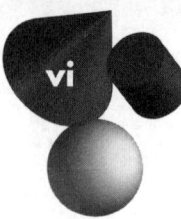

# Graphics Programming with Visual Basic

| | | |
|---|---|---|
| | The *Form_MouseUp* Event | 47 |
| | Summary of the *Movetest* Program | 48 |
| | Summary | 48 |
| **2** | **The Artisan Program** | **49** |
| | Importing or Exporting Filters | 51 |
| | Page Setup, Ruler, and Margin Printing Measurements | 51 |
| | What You See Is What You Get (WYSIWYG) | 51 |
| | Screen, Printer, and Resolutions | 52 |
| | Getting the Program in Sync | 52 |
| | AutoRedraw at Startup | 53 |
| | The Learning Process | 53 |
| | Program Speed and Picture Boxes | 54 |
| | The Tool Buttons Picture Box | 55 |
| | The Color Bar Palette | 56 |
| | The Scrollbar Controls | 58 |
| | The Status Area Frame | 58 |
| | The Menu Area | 58 |
| | File Menu | 61 |
| | Edit Menu | 61 |
| | Arrange Menu | 62 |
| | Color Menu | 62 |
| | Color Palette Submenu | 62 |
| | The Mouse Events | 62 |
| | Defining Variables, Arrays, and Structures | 70 |
| | Data Types | 71 |
| | User-Defined Data Type Variables | 72 |
| | Declaring Variables for the Artisan Program | 73 |
| | Default Form Loading Values at Startup | 81 |
| | Positioning the Control on the Artisan Form | 84 |
| | Selecting a Drawing Tool for the Toolbox | 86 |
| | Pushing in a Button when the Form is First Started | 88 |
| | Clicking the Desktop with a Tool | 88 |
| | Dragging or Moving the Mouse on the Desktop | 89 |
| | Completing the Drawing | 91 |
| | Lines to Bézier Curves | 93 |
| | Typing Characters on the Desktop | 94 |
| | Redrawing Text on the Desktop | 95 |
| | The *Bounding Box MouseDown* Procedure | 96 |
| | Performing the Actual Drawing on the Desktop | 97 |
| | Giving the New Object a Reference Number | 99 |
| | Summary | 101 |

## Contents

**3   Bézier Curves**     **103**
    Plotting the Points of a Bézier Curve ............................................. 109
    The *deCasteljau* Dividing Formula ................................................. 113
    Stretching the Curve by its Handles ............................................... 114
    Redrawing the Bézier's Levers ........................................................ 114
    Storing the Curve's New Coordinate Points ................................. 116
    The Second Bézier Handle for a Curve ......................................... 117
    Converting a Line to a Curve ......................................................... 119
    Grabbing a Curve ............................................................................ 121
    Erasing the Curve's Image Before a Move .................................... 124
    Building a Bounding Box for the Curve ....................................... 125
    Visual State of Lever Lines on a Curve ......................................... 126
    Stretching a Bézier Curve ............................................................... 129
  Summary ................................................................................................ 133

**4   The Artisan Program—Procedures C–N**     **135**
    Assigning Outlines and Fills to Objects ........................................ 136
    The ARTISAN.INI File .................................................................. 138
    Finding an Object Using a Marquee ............................................. 139
    Clicking the Mouse on an Object .................................................. 141
    Drawing Page Guidelines ............................................................... 144
    Positioning Stretch Handles Around an Object ........................... 145
    Reversing the Handle Positions on a Flipped Object .................. 149
    Preparing an Object To Be Stretched ............................................ 151
    Stretching an Object ....................................................................... 155
    Scrolling the Graphics on the Desktop ......................................... 158
    Changing the Thickness of an Object's Outline .......................... 160
    The Artisan Program's Main Menu Selections ............................ 162
    Deleting a Single Object from the Desktop ................................. 163
    Preparing for File Menu Option .................................................... 164
    Deleting All Objects on the Desktop ............................................ 165
    The Color Menu Item Option ....................................................... 166
    Changing Colors in the Color Palette ........................................... 166
    Calculating Mouse Moves ............................................................. 167
    Moving Objects on the Desktop .................................................. 168
    Position Nodes Around an Object ................................................ 169
    Removing Nodes and Handles from the Desktop ....................... 171
    Removing the Fill Color of an Object .......................................... 172
  Summary ................................................................................................ 172

**5   The Artisan Program—Procedures N–Z**     **175**
    Moving an Object by Its Node ...................................................... 176
    Moving a Line Object's Node ....................................................... 178
    Updating a Line Object After a Node Move ............................... 180

# Graphics Programming with Visual Basic

|   |   |   |
|---|---|---|
|   | Using the Popup Paint Tool To Fill an Object | 180 |
|   | Extracting Color Value from the .INI file | 182 |
|   | Creating Perfect Circles | 183 |
|   | Placing Text on the Desktop in Visual Basic | 183 |
|   | Rescaling the Interior Coordinates of Nodes and Handles | 185 |
|   | The Ruler's Mouse Events | 186 |
|   | Drawing Each Ruler's Slide Line | 188 |
|   | Drawing the Inch Marks in Each Ruler | 189 |
|   | Writing Values to the ARTISAN.INI File | 192 |
|   | Placing an Object to the Front or Back of All the Others | 193 |
|   | Redrawing All Objects on the Desktop | 195 |
|   | Redrawing the Underlying Page | 199 |
|   | Sending the Images to the Printer | 201 |
|   | Using a Zoom Tool | 203 |
|   | Rescaling the Desktop's ViewPort | 206 |
|   | Summary | 207 |
| **6** | **The Animator Program** | **209** |
|   | Default Values at Startup | 220 |
|   | Scaling a Picture Box for 3-D Animation | 221 |
|   | Starting the 3-D Animation Process | 222 |
|   | Calculating the 3-D Animation | 224 |
|   | Using the Arrows to Move the Object | 226 |
|   | Toggling the Movement On and Off | 230 |
|   | The Grid Control in the Animator Program | 230 |
|   | Viewing Different Angles of the 3-D Object | 232 |
|   | Opening or Saving a Data File | 233 |
|   | Saving the Data File | 234 |
|   | Opening and Displaying the Data | 235 |
|   | Updating New Values in a Data File | 236 |
|   | Moving the 3-D Object Using Scroll Values | 237 |
|   | Typing New Values for the Data | 237 |
|   | Summary | 239 |
| **7** | **Multi-Search and Replace** | **241** |
|   | Variables Used Within this Program | 249 |
|   | Positioning the Controls at Startup | 250 |
|   | Adding an Item to a Code List | 250 |
|   | Selecting an Item in Either List Box | 252 |
|   | Removing Items from the List Boxes | 253 |
|   | Tools Used to Edit Text | 253 |
|   | Editing the Items in the List Boxes | 254 |
|   | How to Cut, Copy, and Paste the Text | 255 |
|   | Opening or Saving a Text File | 256 |

|   | Opening a Text File .................................................................... 260 |  |
|---|---|---|
|   | Searching and Replacing Items ....................................................... 261 |  |
|   | Saving the Text File ...................................................................... 263 |  |
|   | The Text Spacing Text .................................................................. 265 |  |
|   | Summary ............................................................................................ 269 |  |
| 8 | **API Drawing Programs** | **271** |
|   | The Declaration Section of the APIdraw Program ........................ 275 |  |
|   | Clicking an API Function Button ..................................................... 279 |  |
|   | The Form's Mouse Events ................................................................. 280 |  |
|   | Painting via the *FloodFill* Function ................................................. 283 |  |
|   | The API Drawing Functions ............................................................. 284 |  |
|   | 32-Bit API Drawing Functions ......................................................... 292 |  |
|   | Summary ............................................................................................ 293 |  |
| 9 | **Fountain Blends** | **295** |
|   | Structures to Hold the Colors ........................................................... 297 |  |
|   | The Palette Program's Declarations ............................................. 301 |  |
|   | The *Form_Resize* Routine ........................................................... 302 |  |
|   | The Two Main Color Palettes ...................................................... 302 |  |
|   | Selecting a Color from the Palette ............................................... 304 |  |
|   | Enabling the Fountain Fill Controls ............................................ 306 |  |
|   | The API Color Palette .................................................................. 307 |  |
|   | Viewing the Range of a Color's Value ......................................... 308 |  |
|   | Displaying a Pure Color Palette ................................................... 308 |  |
|   | Creating a Custom Palette ........................................................... 309 |  |
|   | *PALETTE* and *PALETTEENTRY* .................................................. 310 |  |
|   | Using Dithered Colors in the Palette ........................................... 311 |  |
|   | Painting Each Palette Color ......................................................... 312 |  |
|   | The Fountain Fill Button ............................................................. 313 |  |
|   | Using *RGB* Color Values to Build a Palette ................................ 314 |  |
|   | Changing Colors with the Scrollbars ........................................... 315 |  |
|   | Painting a Complex Object with a Fountain Fill ......................... 316 |  |
|   | Summary ............................................................................................ 317 |  |
| 10 | **The Mini-Bézier Curve Program** | **319** |
|   | Variable Names for the 16-Bit Bézier Curve Program ...................... 323 |  |
|   | Calculating the Curve's Points .......................................................... 325 |  |
|   | Plotting the Curve Points ................................................................... 325 |  |
|   | Drawing the Line on the Form .......................................................... 329 |  |
|   | Erasing the Curve's Image Before a Move ......................................... 331 |  |
|   | Resetting Values to Start a New Curve .............................................. 332 |  |
|   | Bézier Handle #1 ................................................................................ 333 |  |
|   | Redrawing Levers for Handle #1 .................................................. 334 |  |
|   | Rescaling Handle #1 ..................................................................... 335 |  |

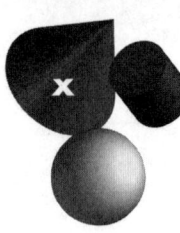

# Graphics Programming with Visual Basic

| | | |
|---|---|---|
| | Bézier Handle #2 | 335 |
| |    Redrawing Levers for Handle #2 | 335 |
| |    Rescaling Handle #2 | 337 |
| | Grabbing a Curve by Its Nodes | 337 |
| |    Rescaling Node #1 | 339 |
| |    Moving the Curve's Node #2 | 339 |
| | Converting a Line to a Curve | 341 |
| | Summary | 341 |
| **11** | **The Rounded Corners Program** | **343** |
| | How to Use the Program | 344 |
| |    Declarations and Startup Values | 348 |
| |    The Form's Mouse Events | 349 |
| |    Drawing a Rounded Rectangle Using the *Basic* Procedure | 351 |
| |    Using the *Step* Keyword to Round a Shape | 353 |
| |    Choosing a Drawing Option | 354 |
| |    Using the *Stretcher* Procedure to Draw a Rounded Rectangle | 355 |
| |    Using the Scrollbar Controls | 356 |
| | Summary | 357 |
| **12** | **The Text Alignment Program** | **359** |
| |    Line Spacing (Leading) | 360 |
| |    Letter Spacing (Width) | 361 |
| | The TxtAlign Program | 363 |
| |    Manually Setting Text in Visual Basic | 365 |
| | Summary of the TxtAlign Program | 367 |
| | Using the APItext Program | 367 |
| |    Declarations and Structures for the APItext Program | 372 |
| |    Default Startup Values | 373 |
| |    Adding Carriage Returns to API Text | 375 |
| |    Adding Attributes to the *TextOut* Function | 378 |
| |    Placing Text Using the *ScaleLeft* Property | 380 |
| |    Displaying the *FontLog* Attributes | 381 |
| |    Using the API Text-Alignment Function | 382 |
| |    Displaying the Text Metrics of a Font | 382 |
| | Summary of the APItext Program | 384 |
| | The DrawText Program | 384 |
| |    Variable Names and Startup Values | 387 |
| |    Drawing Text Using the *DrawText* Function | 389 |
| |    API Text Drawing and Text Height | 391 |
| | Summary of the DrawText Program | 393 |
| | Summary | 393 |

| | | |
|---|---|---|
| **13** | **The Join Nodes Program** | **395** |
| | How the Program Works .................................................................... 396 | |
| | Variable Names and Startup Values ................................................... 400 | |
| | The Mouse Events ............................................................................. 402 | |
| | Drawing the Polyline Segments ......................................................... 404 | |
| | Filling a Complex Object with Color ................................................ 406 | |
| | Using a Node to Edit the Shape ........................................................ 407 | |
| | Moving Connected Line Segments ................................................... 409 | |
| | Adding More Picture Box Nodes ...................................................... 411 | |
| | Loading All Nodes Around an Object .............................................. 412 | |
| | Drawing the Final Shape ................................................................... 413 | |
| | API Functions in the Join Nodes Program ....................................... 414 | |
| | Summary............................................................................................ 415 | |
| **14** | **The Scaling and Printing Program** | **417** |
| | Variable Names and API Functions ............................................. 421 | |
| | Drawing the Shapes on the Picture Box ...................................... 422 | |
| | Drawing the Objects .................................................................... 422 | |
| | Manually Scaling the Printer's Page ............................................. 423 | |
| | API Printing ................................................................................. 424 | |
| | Summary of the PrintAPI Program ................................................... 426 | |
| | The Scaltest Program ......................................................................... 426 | |
| | Declarations and Startup Values .................................................. 431 | |
| | The Picture Box Mouse Events.................................................... 432 | |
| | Aligning Scaling Values at Startup ............................................... 434 | |
| | The Zoom API Menu .................................................................. 435 | |
| | The Zoom Basic Menu ................................................................ 437 | |
| | Rescaling the Picture Box Control ............................................... 438 | |
| | Summary............................................................................................ 439 | |
| **15** | **ArtAPI** | **441** |
| | Handles and Nodes ...................................................................... 442 | |
| | Scaling and the Zoom Tool .......................................................... 442 | |
| | Desktop and Printer API Graphics .............................................. 442 | |
| | The Graphical API Functions in the ArtAPI Program ................ 443 | |
| | Major Changes in this ArtAPI Program ...................................... 443 | |
| | New Picture Box Control ............................................................ 443 | |
| | Old Controls Switched to Procedures ......................................... 444 | |
| | Other Changes ............................................................................. 444 | |
| | New Polyshape Procedures .......................................................... 445 | |
| | *To_Front_Back* Routines ............................................................. 446 | |
| | API Scaling and Winprint ........................................................... 447 | |
| | The Test Button ........................................................................... 447 | |
| | The Zoom Tool ............................................................................ 447 | |

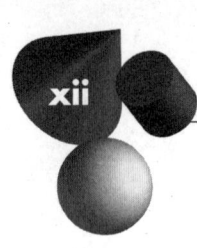

New Declaration for the ArtAPI Program ........................................ 455
Converting a Polyline to Curves ....................................................... 457
The Artwork Mouse Events .............................................................. 459
Redrawing the Polyshape on the Desktop ....................................... 461
The *Pnode* Image Control's *Tag* Properties ...................................... 464
Updating a Curve's Coordinates ....................................................... 469
Moving the Objects ........................................................................... 475
API Drawing Functions ..................................................................... 476
Finding the Outline of an Object ..................................................... 478
Calculating a Bounding Box for a Polyshape ................................. 479
Opening and Saving a Polyshape File ............................................. 480
Moving a Polyshape Object ............................................................. 481
The Polyshape's Nodes (*Pnodes*) .................................................... 483
Editing a Curve on a Polyshape ....................................................... 491
Drawing each Curve on a Polyshape ............................................... 497
Closing a Polygon Shape .................................................................. 499
Drawing a Polyline Shape ................................................................ 501
Editing a Polyline Shape ................................................................... 502
Loading and Positioning *Pnodes* on a Polyshape ........................... 504
Reloading *Pnodes* on a Polyshape ................................................... 506
After a Polyshape Segment is Edited ............................................... 508
Resizing and Stretching a Polyshape ............................................... 509
Using the Test Button ....................................................................... 510
Moving an Object to the Front or Back ........................................... 511
Selecting an Object by Its Outline Image ....................................... 513
Drawing all Objects onto the Desktop ............................................ 515
Printing all Objects ........................................................................... 520
Summary ................................................................................................. 523

**A   Artisan .BAS Files                                                              525**
The ART3_7.BAS File ............................................................................ 526
The ART3_7.BAS file Global Declarations ...................................... 526
The ARTFONT.BAS File Global Declarations ............................... 530
Assigning Color to the Palette ......................................................... 533
Assigning Colors to Objects ............................................................. 534
Artisan1 *Text* Form ................................................................................ 535
Summary of the *Text* Form .................................................................. 542
Artisan *NodeEdit* Form ......................................................................... 542
Artisan *ColorPalette* Form .................................................................... 543
Values Used in the Palette Form ..................................................... 544
Summary of the *Palette* Form .............................................................. 550

| | | |
|---|---|---|
| **B** | **Windows NT, Windows 95, and Higher** | **551** |
| | GDI32 Paths | 552 |
| | GDI32 *StrokePath* | 553 |
| | GDI32 *StrokeAndFillPath* | 553 |
| | GDI32 *FillPath* | 553 |
| | GDI32 *GetPath* | 553 |
| | GDI32 *SelectClipPath* | 554 |
| | GDI32 *PathToRegion* | 554 |
| | GDI32 *WidenPath* | 554 |
| | GDI32 Drawing Functions | 554 |
| | GDI32 *AngleArc* | 554 |
| | GDI32 *ArcTo* | 555 |
| | GDI32 *SetArcDirection* | 555 |
| | GDI32 *CloseFigure* | 555 |
| | GDI32 *PolyBezier* | 555 |
| | GDI32 *PolyBezierTo* | 555 |
| | GDI32 *PolyDraw* | 556 |
| | GDI32 *EnumEnhMetaFile* | 556 |
| | GDI32 *MaskBlt* | 556 |
| | GDI32 *PlgBlt* | 556 |
| **C** | **The Companion Disk** | **559** |
| | Installing the Companion Disk Files | 560 |
| | **Index** | **563** |

# Acknowledgments

I would like to thank Grace Buechlein for her patience and her efforts in organizing and coordinating the materials in this book.

I would also like to thank Brad Jones and Angelique Brittingham, the development editors, for their work in developing the manuscript, and for their many suggestions, inquiries, and discussions during the development of the manuscript.

Mary Inderstrodt and Sandra Doell deserve special thanks for the editorial work that they contributed to the manuscript. Thanks also to the other people at Sams Publishing who helped in the creation of this book.

I would also like to thank K.L. Murdock, the technical editor, who ensured that all the listings in the book and on the disk executed properly.

Finally, I would like to thank Sandra Guinan of Truro, Nova Scotia, for editing during the initial stages of this book.

# About the Author

Robert W. Stewart, of Barrie, Ontario, began his career as a graphic artist nearly sixteen years ago. His experience includes work in the advertising and newspaper publishing industries in Canada. His expertise is in computer programming and desktop publishing. He currently is an independent consultant and installs custom, networked-based graphical production systems. Robert resides in Toronto, Ontario, Canada.

# Introduction

*Graphics Programming with Visual Basic* covers graphical tools and their Visual Basic programs. This book discusses the code used to create simple drawing tools. For the most part, these tools were written using simple Basic programming statements. This book explains how you can emulate high-end drawing tools that were once only possible to create through language programs such as C++. These programs should be considered starting points, not end products. You can examine the possibility of incorporating parts of these programs in your own programs. I hope you find these routines beneficial in advancing your Visual Basic programs.

## Program Descriptions

The following sections contain information on the programs that are presented throughout this book.

## The Begin Program in Chapter 1

Chapter 1 shows several ways you can use the Basic `Line` and `Circle` statements, which are the standard graphics functions in all Basic languages. This chapter gives examples so you can understand better the `Step` keyword for `Line` statements and `Start` and `End` positions for circles and arcs.

## The Pset Program in Chapter 1

Chatper 1 also shows several examples of Basic's `Pset` statement, as well as the fundamentals of graphics algorithms.

## The MoveTest Program in Chapter 1

There are dozens of ways to move an object across the screen using a mouse. Chapter 1 shows three simple routines to help you understand better the principles involved.

## The Artisan Program in Chapter 2

Artisan is a mini-drawing program that uses fundamental drawing tools: shape, zoom, line, circle, box, and text tools, as well as a pointer. The rest of the program is merely cosmetic. Though the controls work, they are set up only for visual appeal. For instance, the rulers do indeed scale, but their measurements are not set for universal measurement. This program mostly uses `Basic` statements to draw graphics. (The ArtAPI program in Chapter 15 uses more elaborate codes and tools using Windows API function.) You should, however, examine the Artisan program because many of the routines in the ArtAPI program in Chapter 15 are located in the Artisan program of Chapter 2.

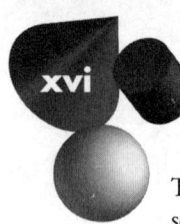

**Graphics Programming with Visual Basic**

The Artisan program is covered in Chapters 1 through 4. This book first shows the declaration section and forms so you can get an understanding of the variables and controls used in each program. Because all drawing is done in the Artwork picture box control, its events are shown first. Then this book discusses the BoundingBox procedures, which are extensions of the MouseDown, MouseMove, and MouseUp Artwork picture box events.

## The Artisan Program in Chapter 3

Chapter 3 shows the Bézier curve controls. They currently use seven procedures calls to execute several stages of calculating, drawing, and moving a Bézier curve. Once you are familiar with each procedure, you can combine some routines to shorten the procedure list (even though this is unnecessary).

## The Artisan Program in Chapter 4

Chapter 4 shows control events and procedures alphabetical order, starting with C (ColorBar picture box events) and continuing through N (the N_H_Clear procedure).

## The Artisan Program in Chapter 5

Chapter 5 lists the final procedures and control events, starting with N (Node picture box events) and continuing through Z (Zoom procedures).

## The Animator Program in Chapter 6

This chapter shows a basic formula to illustrate the fundamentals of wireframe animation modeling.

There are many add-on features for the Animator program. After you are familiar with the program, you can add three more picture controls to perform front, top, and side views, or to construct wireframe objects from another viewing plane. You also can capture each cell to a bitmap and then string the cells together using a script to perform real-time animation. The professional version of Visual Basic 3.0 has a PicClip VBX control that can accomplish this feat.

## The Multi-Search and Replace Program in Chapter 7

Multi-Search and Replace is what every word processor needs built in. I have sold more of these simple search-and-replace text editors than any other program I have designed. It uses a very simple Loop routine so you can search and replace multiple listings of words with one click of a button. It was so simple that I almost didn't write it because I thought the big boys would surely include this basic feature in their word programs. Not!

# Introduction

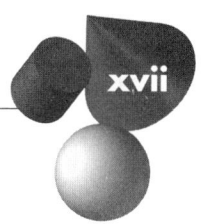

## The API Drawing Functions in Chapter 8

If you decide to use Windows API drawing functions in your program, you can use a handy little tool that I have included that shows you the basics of most, but not all, API graphical calls. Take special note of the `PtInRect`, `FloodFill`, and `Ellipse` functions.

## The Fountain Blends Program in Chapter 9

If you have a VGA card that can display 256 or more colors, Chapter 9 can give you a good view of pure blended or fountain fill colors. This chapter shows how to convert 255-percent `RGB` color values to 100-percent values, display any color within a color palette, blend shades of color between two colors, create a 256+ pure custom or dithered palette display, and fill complex objects with blended or fountain fill colors.

## The Mini-Bézier Program in Chapter 10

The Mini-Bézier program uses the same code structure that the Artisan program does to draw Bézier curves. I have included this mini-version so you can easily see how I draw Bézier curves using fixed, plotted points. Pre-plotted curves use two procedures that you may not need when using a recursive Bézier curve procedure. Either way, the algorithm is the same, and the speed is slightly faster using the pre-plotted routine.

## The Rounded Corners Program in Chapter 11

In the APIdraw program, you can use the API `RoundedRect` function to draw a rectangle with rounded corners. If you try to move this object using the same calls, the objects goes in and out of draw modes and flickers. Chapter 11 shows you how to draw the same shape using the Basic `Line` and `Circle` statements to draw flicker-free rounded rectangles.

## The Text Alignment Program in Chapter 12

Visual Basic provides you with simple ways to print text to a form. Windows API text functions are limited when you want to manipulate text such as high-end illustration packages. There is no easy solution without getting into the text's `Glyph` outline and designing your own text module in which the code explanation could virtually exceed the length of this book. This chapter shows you three simple ways to align text: left, right, or center of where you place the `MouseDown` insertion point.

## The Join Nodes in Chapter 13

This is the heart and soul of all drawing packages. It was not included in the Artisan program in Chapter 2 since you must have a direct goal for what you want your nodes and objects to do. The Artisan program was designed to avoid API function calls and to use standard Basic language. You reach the Basic language drawing threshold when it comes to filling complete objects. You then must resort to using `PSet` or `Line` statement loops to fill complex objects (since the Basic `Paint` statement has been put to rest in Windows). At this point, you must dive into Windows API drawing library. The source code used for this program is both simple and still required for using a host of variable holders. You can get very deep into code when you add breakable objects nodes and Bézier curve connections. This book's first chapter deals with the variables and arrays you must plan out before you start a drawing program.

## The PrintAPI and Scaltest Programs in Chapter 14

PrintAPI is a small, simple program that tests your printer against Windows API graphic functions. Using API calls, the program draws a box, circle, and line on a standard letter page. You can send a graphic to your printer and then adjust the device (monitor or printer) scaling by adding additional code. The second program, Scaltest, has various methods to scale a window region using both basic and API methods. You also should run the APIscale program, located in the 16MISC directory of the companion disk, to view an example of scaling (zooming) a marquee object within a window.

## The ArtAPI Program in Chapter 15

ArtAPI is a reworked version of the Artisan program in Chapter 1. The difference is that this program uses the Windows API drawing functions to replace the standard Basic language statements. A full description starts at the introduction of this chapter. Be sure you have read about the Artisan program in Chapter 1 and the Join Nodes program in Chapter 13 before venturing into the ArtAPI program.

## Appendix A

Appendix A contains the global variable listings for the Artisan program, as well as the text and palette forms used in the program.

## Appendix B

Appendix B contains information about Windows NT, Windows 95, and higher.

## Appendix C

Appendix C contains additional information on programs in the 16MISC directory supplied with the companion disk. Code explanations for these additional programs appear within the Visual Basic code forms of each program. These programs show working examples of the following:

- How to create custom ribbon bars and buttons
- How to create custom cursors within Visual Basic 2.0 and 3.0
- How to create tab-like dialog forms
- How to position and scale forms and their controls at runtime

# Introduction

- How to add menu items to other programs
- How to display bitmap images using little or no resources
- How to use DPI-printing of form or control images that use custom scaling dimensions
- How to creating Visual Basic and API viewports
- And more...

## The Graphical User Interface (GUI)

A graphical user interface like Windows is similar to Basic graphical statements because it uses underlying code to create graphical objects. Windows includes an API library of language functions that you can access to go above and beyond the standard Basic statements. The last version of Basic in the DOS operating system had some 200 functions, while the Windows API library has well over 1,000. In the graphical library alone, you have a wide variety of ways to make simple lines and circles more robust—without writing long routines to achieve the same result when using Basic. However, you must have some knowledge about how these lines and circles (or other objects) are placed on your monitor screen. After you fully understand this, you can undertake the advanced features found in the Windows API, which are reviewed in later chapters.

## The Basics and Windows

You have a giant head start in developing Windows programs using Visual Basic. The latest version now has more than 400 Basic statement interpretations. Combine these with the API functions mentioned previously, and you can create some powerful applications. Visual Basic may not win any awards for execution speed; but for fast development of Windows programs, Visual Basic wins hands down.

## Machine Code, Interpreters, and Compilers

There are two flavors of computer languages: low level and high level. The low-level languages usually are referred to as machine code or assembly language. The base level is machine code, which talks directly to the CPU using hexadecimal terms. The next step up is the assembly language, which uses abbreviated machine routines to make working with the CPU more bearable.

A high-level language is the next step up. High level is just a phrase and does not refer to how advanced you are with using the language. You shouldn't feel hesitant to step into these languages. Visual Basic can be called a high-level language that falls into the category of *interpreted* languages. On the flip side, there are varieties of C, Pascal, and similar language packages that use high-level compiling. The difference is that an interpreted program like Basic translates each statement to the underlying machine code to which the CPU then operates. The Visual Basic language needs a separate file to translate subroutines to machine code. This file is called VBrun, and the internal translator code is referred to as *P-code* interpretation. Your programs, therefore, are not truly 100-percent compiled .EXE files.

### Graphics Programming with Visual Basic

A compiled language (such as C) is sent to an assembly program, which creates a completely finished machine code. Though similar in action as the P-code interpretation, the compiled code runs circles around an interpreted language as far as speed is concerned. The interpreted code reads each Basic command statement, along with the input code, and then executes each line one at a time. The compiled code, however, is simply compiled into a single translation.

## What You Should Know Before You Start

Chapter 1 should give you an understanding of how the screen coordination's system works when using simple graphics statements. You will also be given a refresher course on trigonometry (that may give you flashbacks of old mathematics lessons in school). Luckily, there will not be a quiz after this section.

A short summary of each line of code is explained after each source code listing. In these summaries, the first few words of each code line are in **`bold monospace`** typeface and are followed by an explanation.

You should already be familiar with the fundamentals of Visual Basic. This book assumes that you are beyond the beginner's level of using the product. Some parts of the book review the fundamentals to ensure that you understand the basics; however, it is best if you already have a basic understanding of Visual Basic.

## The Programs

Great care was taken to make sure all programs work. Many of the programs have been written using standard functions and subroutines.

Many computers were used to test the code. These computers include the following: i386sx 16, 386AMD40, i486DX33, 486DCLcyrix, and Pentium 60.

Because of the graphical nature of these programs, a resolution higher than the standard VGA was needed. Most graphics programs are created for super VGA monitors. All the program forms in this book were designed to run on SVGA monitors at 800 by 600 resolution.

The code has been included on the accompanying disk for all the programs presented. Additional programs have also been included. See Appendix C for information on what is included on the disk with this book.

# CHAPTER 1

# Basic Beginnings

# Basic Beginnings

This chapter presents the Begin program (Figure 1.1), which is geared for beginners. The Begin program will help you understand the roots of graphical statements. Once you have a grasp of the code structures needed to place a simple line or circle object on your monitor screen, you will be able to understand better the inner workings of Basic and Windows graphical environments. The `Line` and `Circle` statements are essential in understanding the underlying structure of graphics. A window in Windows, for instance, is made up of lines and/or circles that form rectangular or elliptical shapes.

**Figure** 1.1.
*The Begin program.*

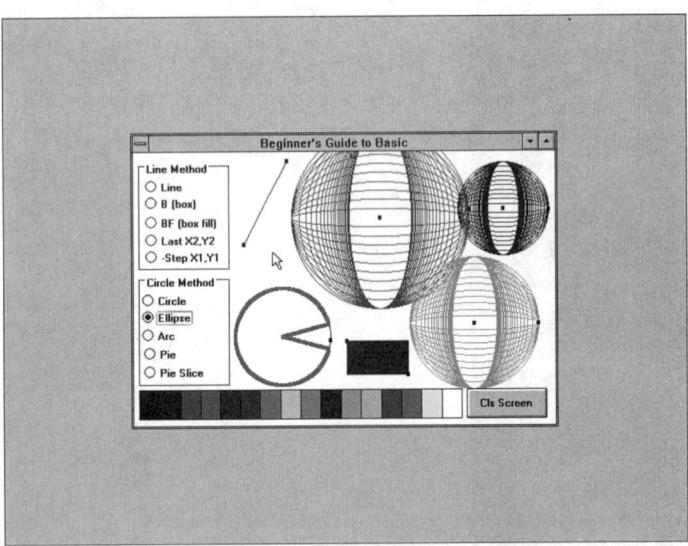

| Line Method | Circle Method |
|---|---|
| Line (X1,Y1)-(X2, Y2) | R = Radius, C = Color |
| Line - Step (X2, Y2) | S = Start, E = End, A = Aspect |
| Line - (X2, Y2) | Circle (X, Y), R |
| Line (X1,Y1) - Step (X2, Y2) | Circle (X, Y), R, C, S, E, A |

**Options:**

**C = Color, B = Box outline**
**BF = Box filled will color**

Line (X1, Y1)-(X2, Y2), Color

Line (X1, Y1)-(X2, Y2), C, B

Line (X1, Y1)-(X2, Y2), C, BF

See Figure 1.2 for examples of drawing basic objects.

**Figure 1.2.**
*Drawing basic lines, outline boxes, filled boxes, circles, ellipses, arcs, pies, and pie slices.*

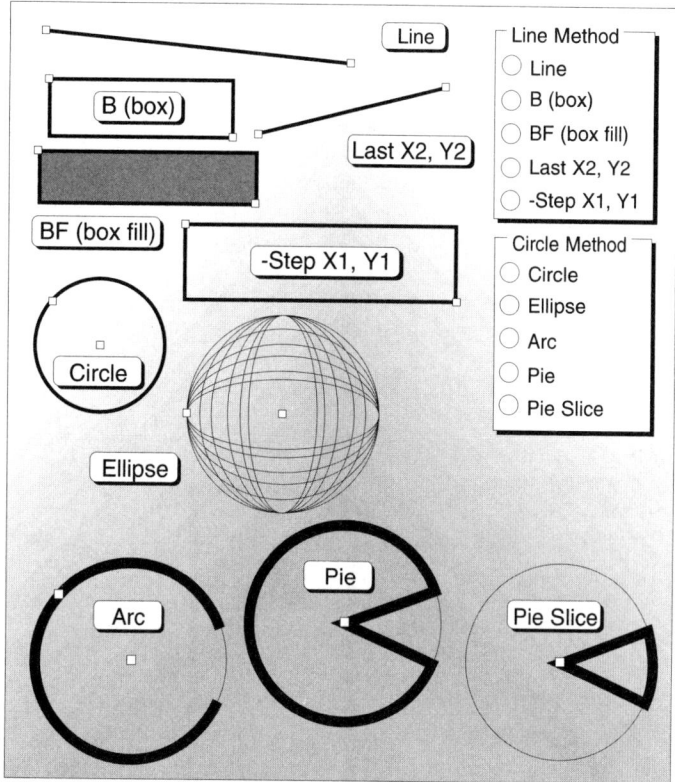

In Visual Basic, the Control.Left and Top properties place the control's top-left corner on the form's grid coordinate that reflects the current ScaleMode of the form.

Unfortunately, Visual Basic controls do not have a right or bottom property. To place a control's bottom-right corner position you must use its width and height properties. Furthermore, if you ever tried to center a control on a form you probably wished there was a form or control center property as well. Basic's Line statement, on the other hand, has a screen coordinate setting known as (X1,Y1)-(X2,Y2).

If you draw a box shape using the Line statement and start near the upper-left corner of your form and finish near the lower-right corner of the form, you could say the box has a left/top and right/bottom coordinate setting. In reality, the X1, Y1 coordinate indicates the starting point of the box shape and the X2, Y2 coordinate indicates the end point. A box shape has four corners, so there are four possible start and end point scenarios.

1. (left, top) - (right, bottom)
2. (right, top) - (left, bottom)
3. (right, bottom) - (left, top)
4. (left, bottom) - (right, top)

# Basic Beginnings

A line or box can start and end anywhere on the screen using an X, Y grid coordinate pattern. The X, Y coordinate system is based on a starting origin of 0,0, beginning at the upper-left corner of the screen. Positive X values increase toward the right of the origin while positive Y values increase toward the bottom of the screen. Imagine that X represents the columns of a grid and Y the rows. You can read this invisible grid from left to right. It should be pointed out, however, that Visual Basic and API scaling methods can be used to place the upper-left 0,0 origin anywhere and can be used to switch the direction in which the X and/or Y grid runs. This may be useful if you need to use negative (Cartesian) Y positions below the 0,0 origin, for example.

Figure 1.3 shows the basic left-top and bottom-right values of the three Line statements. It is not written in stone that you must use the variable names (X1,Y1);(X2,Y2) as temporary placement holders for these objects. Most programs in this book use (W,N);(E,S) (West, North, East, South) to get a better grasp of the location of an object's corners.

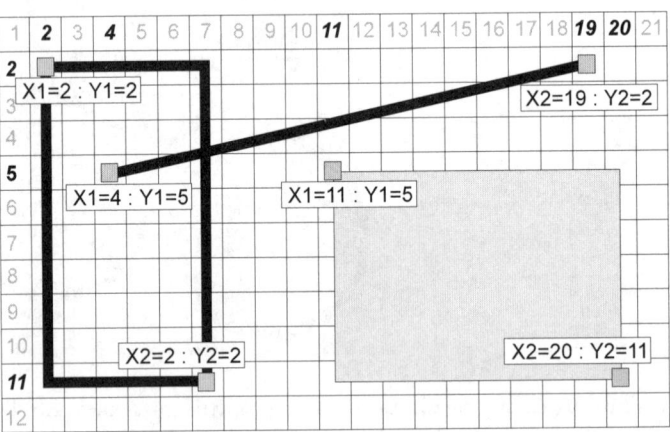

**Figure 1.3.**
*The left-top and bottom-right values of the three Line statements.*

The bold numbers in Figure 1.2 running left to right on the top of the grid indicate the current X positions of the objects, while the bold numbers running top to bottom on the left side of the grid show the current Y positions of the objects within the X and Y grid.

## Working with Circles

The size of a circle is determined by the length of its radius. The two black dots in Figure 1.4 represent the current (X1,Y1);(X2,Y2) coordinates of the radius. The X1,Y1 point represents the center of the circle while the X2,Y2 point represents a position on the outer edge of the circle's circumference. If a line were drawn from the X1,Y1 point to the X2,Y2 point, the length of this line would be the circle's radius.

**Figure 1.4.**
*How to find the radius of a circle using the Pythagorean theorem.*

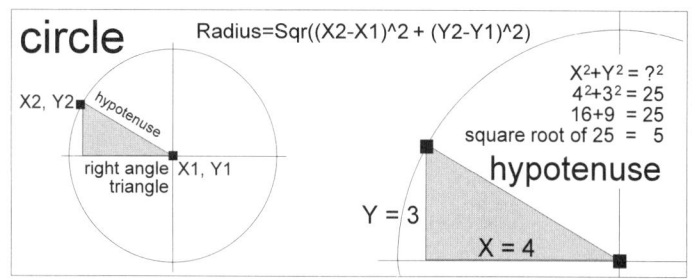

When the radius line is at an angle, you need a formula to find the radius' line length. The formula to calculate a circle's radius is called the *Pythagorean theorem*. The sloping radius line is the *hypotenuse*. The Pythagorean theorum states that "The square of the hypotenuse is equal to the sum of the squares of both sides." In layman terms, you first must find the horizontal length from X2 to X1 plus the vertical length from Y2 to Y1. Multiply each of these values by their lengths, which is fairly easy because both of these distances are right-angled (horizontal and vertical). Add the two lengths together and then find the square root of the total lengths. The section later in this chapter titled "Calculating a Circle's Radius," explains this theory.

The Begin program's form and control properties are listed in Table 1.1.

**Table 1.1.** The Properties of the `Begin` form.

*Object: Form*
*Object Name: Begin*

| | | | | |
|---|---|---|---|---|
| Height | = 5040 | Left | = | 210 |
| ScaleMode | = 3 'Pixel | Top | = | 1125 |
| Width | = 7455 | | | |

*Object: Frame*
*Object Name: Frame2*

| | | | | |
|---|---|---|---|---|
| Caption | = "Circle Method" | Height | = | 1905 |
| Left | = 90 | Top | = | 2070 |
| Width | = 1590 | | | |

*Object: OptionButton*
*Object Name: Option1*

| | | | | |
|---|---|---|---|---|
| Caption | = "Pie Slice" | Height | = | 285 |
| Index | = 9 | Left | = | 90 |
| Top | = 1530 | Width | = | 1275 |

*continues*

## Table 1.1. continued

**Object: OptionButton**
**Object Name: Option1**

| Caption | = "Pie" | Height | = 285 |
| Index | = 8 | Left | = 90 |
| Top | = 1215 | Width | = 1275 |

**Object: OptionButton**
**Object Name: Option1**

| Caption | = "Arc" | Height | = 285 |
| Index | = 7 | Left | = 90 |
| Top | = 900 | Width | = 1275 |

**Object: OptionButton**
**Object Name: Option1**

| Caption | = "Ellipse" | Height | = 285 |
| Index | = 6 | Left | = 90 |
| Top | = 585 | Width | = 1275 |

**Object: OptionButton**
**Object Name: Option1**

| Caption | = "Circle" | Height | = 285 |
| Index | = 5 | Left | = 90 |
| Top | = 270 | Width | = 1275 |

**Object: CommandButton**
**Object Name: Command1**

| Caption | = "Cls Screen" | Height | = 510 |
| Left | = 5805 | Top | = 4050 |
| Width | = 1410 | | |

**Object: PictureBox**
**Object Name: ColorBar**

| Height | = 510 | Left | = 90 |
| ScaleMode | = 0 'User | Top | = 4050 |
| Width | = 5640 | | |

**Object: Frame**
**Object Name: Frame1**

| Caption | = "Line Method" | Height | = 1860 |
| Left | = 90 | Top | = 135 |
| Width | = 1590 | | |

**Object: OptionButton**
*Object Name: Option1*

| | | | |
|---|---|---|---|
| Caption | = "-Step X1,Y1" | Height | = 285 |
| Index | = 4 | Left | = 90 |
| Top | = 1530 | Width | = 1275 |

**Object: OptionButton**
*Object Name: Option1*

| | | | |
|---|---|---|---|
| Caption | = "Last X2,Y2" | Height | = 285 |
| Index | = 3 | Left | = 90 |
| Top | = 1215 | Width | = 1275 |

**Object: OptionButton**
*Object Name: Option1*

| | | | |
|---|---|---|---|
| Caption | = "BF (box fill)" | Height | = 285 |
| Index | = 2 | Left | = 90 |
| Top | = 900 | Width | = 1275 |

**Object: OptionButton**
*Object Name: Option1*

| | | | |
|---|---|---|---|
| Caption | = "B (box)" | Height | = 285 |
| Index | = 1 | Left | = 90 |
| Top | = 585 | Width | = 1230 |

**Object: OptionButton**
*Object Name: Option1*

| | | | |
|---|---|---|---|
| Caption | = "Line" | Height | = 285 |
| Index | = 0 | Left | = 90 |
| Top | = 270 | Width | = 1185 |

Listing 1.1 declares all variable name holders for values you need to store during the running of the Begin program. If you are a beginner and unfamiliar with the concept of variables, a short explanation can be found at the beginning of Chapter 2, "The Artisan Program."

**Listing 1.1.** Declaration section of the Begin form.

```
Declarations
Dim CurrentOption As Integer
Dim X1, Y1, X2, Y2 As Integer
Dim Radius
Dim Lcolor As Long
Dim NextPoint As Integer
Const PI = 3.141593 'the value of PI
```

## Basic Beginnings

**NOTE** This book is organized in such a way that a line-by-line explanation follows each program's events or procedure source code. The **bold monospace** type that begins each explanation represents the first few keywords of the actual source code line.

**CurrentOption:** Saves the Index number of the current option button selected. There are 10 option buttons with index numbers ranging from 0 to 9. This makes it easy to figure out which option button the user has selected. A Select Case statement in the Form_MouseUp event matches the indexed option button to the object you want to draw.

**X1, Y1, X2, Y2:** These variables save the two screen point positions when you perform a MouseDown event on the form.

**Radius:** This variable saves the radius of a circle when calculated by the Pythagorean theorem. At present you do not have to save this value because the value is only used in a single procedure event.

**Lcolor:** Stores the hexadecimal color number value to display the outline or fill color of the line or circle. You use a Long variable data type when saving hexadecimal color values. Refer to the start of Chapter 2 for an explanation of variable types and values.

**NextPoint:** Toggles the variable on/off between mouse down events within the code.

**NOTE** All event and procedure codes immediately follow the declaration section. The event or procedure source code listings are in alphabetic order. If a section of source code becomes very complex, a further explanation is included within the block of text.

## Selecting a Color with Which To Draw

**Listing 1.2.** The Colorbar_MouseDown event.

```
Sub ColorBar_MouseDown (Button%, Shift%, X!, Y!)
    Lcolor = ColorBar.Point(X, Y)
End Sub
```

**LColor = ColorBVar.Point(X, Y):** The Point statement returns the hexadecimal color value of the selected color in the color palette. This will only work with solid colors since dithered colors are made up of several combinations of colors. The Point statement returns a single color pixel value. With a dithered color, the single pixel may not be the desired color. The 16 colors used in the color palette are the standard QBColor — the standard solid Basic language color values (0 through 15). The Artisan program in Chapter 2 shows you how to select higher color values, be they solid or dithered.

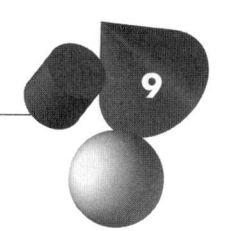

## The ColorBar

The color palette is a picture box. When its interior is scaled to 16 units across and 1 unit high, it is divided into 16 equal rectangular cells, in which you can place a color. ColorBar_Paint, presented in Listing 1.3, draws the color palette and dividing color lines of the color palette.

**Listing 1.3.** The ColorBar_Paint event.

```
Sub ColorBar_Paint ()
    ColorBar.Scale (0, 0)-(16, 1)
        For I = 0 To 15
            ColorBar.Line (I, 0)-(I + 1, 1), QBColor(I), BF
            If I Then ColorBar.Line (I, 0)-(I, 1)
        Next I
End Sub
```

> **For I = 0 to 15:** For every value of I, starting at 0 and continuing through 15, do the following:
>
> > **ColorBar.Line:** Fill all 16 block units of the ColorBar with a QBColor starting at 0 and ending at 15.
> >
> > **If I Then:** Draw a thin black dividing line between each color block.

## The Cls (*Command1_Click*) Button

The Command1_Click button erases all images on the form so you can begin a new drawing operation. Listing 1.4 presents the Command1_Click, which erases any images from the form.

**Listing 1.4.** The command1_click subroutine.

```
Sub Command1_Click ()
    Cls
End Sub
```

Listing 1.5 presents the Form_Load event, which sets the default values of variables at startup.

**Listing 1.5.** The Form_Load subroutine.

```
Sub Form_Load ()
    NextPoint = False
    Lcolor = QBColor(5)
End Sub
```

**B**asic Beginnings

## Clicking the Mouse on the Form

The Form_MouseDown event sets the start position of the object you have selected to draw. Using a Select/Case statement with the Case set from 0 to 9, set the drawing's start coordinates.

The Begin, Pset, and MoveTest programs all use Select/Case blocks to trigger coding events. In some control events, a Select/Case statement may seem unnecessary but is included so you can add additional coding cases if you want to. In some Select/Case blocks, coding routines that are similar are repeated rather then grouped into a single procedure. Therefore, you can cut and paste that block of code for your own use.

See Listing 1.6 for the Form MouseDown subroutine.

Listing 1.6. Form_MouseDown sets the initial values needed for drawing an object.

**Listing 1.6. The Form_MouseDown subroutine.**

```
Sub Form_MouseDown (Button%, Shift%, X As Single, Y As Single)
If NextPoint = False Then
    Select Case CurrentOption
        Case 0 To 9 'Line, Box, Box Filled
        X1 = X: Y1 = Y
        DrawWidth = 4: PSet (X1, Y1): DrawWidth = 1
End Select
End If
End Sub
```

**If NextPoint = False Then:** You want to stop every second mouse down event from working so you can set the X1, Y1 screen positions on the first mouse down event. You then set the final X2, Y2 screen positions on every second mouse up event. Each time the mouse up is triggered, it uses the Not operation (in the second-to-last line of the the Form_MouseUp event in Listing 1.8) to toggle the True and False (on/off) values back and forth.

**Select Case CurrentOption:** The Select/Case statement is not necessary but is available if you want to add other options that may not use these code statements.

**X1 = X: Y1 = Y:** Sets the first line screen points or the center position of a circle.

**DrawWidth = 4: Pset (X1,Y1): Drawwidth = 1:** Set the drawing width to 4 pixels wide, then draw a point at the location where the mouse was clicked down. Finally, reset the drawing width to its default value of 1 pixel wide.

## Selecting a Drawing Option

Selecting an option button enables the performance of a drawing routine that matches the option button's index number with the `Select/Case` expression when a mouse event is triggered on the form. The `Select/Case` test expression used in the form's mouse event is the value of the `CurrentOption` variable. The `Option1_Click` event in Listing 1.7 sets the `CurrentOption` variable to match the option button's assigned index number.

**Listing 1.7. The `Option1_Click` event.**

```
Sub Option1_Click (Index As Integer)
    CurrentOption = Index
End Sub
```

When you select an option button, the variable called `CurrentOption` changes to hold the option button's `Index` number.

## Calculating the Radius of a Circle

You can calculate the radius of a circle by finding the length of the longest side of a right triangle. The longest side of a triangle is called the hypotenuse.

If you were to place the starting point of the hypotenuse at the center point of a circle then the end point would represent the circle's outline. The length of the hypotenuse is equal to the radius of the circle. The hypotenuse of a right triangle is always opposite the right angle.

## Pythagorean Theorem

The square of the hypotenuse is equal to the sum of the squares of the two sides. If the two smaller sides of a right triangle were 3 and 4 units in length, the unknown hypotenuse would equal 5.

`( 3 x 3 ) + ( 4 x 4 ) = ? x ?`

this is shortened to:

`9 + 16 = ? x ?`

you know that 9 + 16 = 25, so simply ask "what value times itself = 25?". The answer to the previous question is 5, which is the square root of 25.

The longest side of a right triangle in this case equals 5, which is called the hypotenuse and is equivalent to the radius of the circle.

**B**asic Beginnings

## The Finished Product

After you set the second screen point (X2,Y2), the mouse up event triggers the drawing of your object. It may seem like the same type of line or box shape is drawn even when you have selected a completely different line drawing option button. In fact, you are drawing the same line object but using alternative line drawing methods.

The Line statement has several optional parameters that you can add to the Line statement, thus varying the way a line or box is drawn. The Step keyword is one example of a optional parameter that can be used to draw a line relative to values stored in the CurrentX and CurrentY properties of the control or relative to the X and Y of the opposite end of the line.

Most people use the Step keyword to draw a continuous complex line known as a *polyline*. It may, however, be more convenient in some case to mix and match Line statements to get the desired line pattern. A good example of mixed line drawing can be found in the Tabs program, directory 16MISC of the companion disk.

**Listing 1.8.** The Form_MouseUp event, which draws the finished object onto the form.

```
Sub Form_MouseUp (Button%, Shift%, X As Single, Y As Single)
X2 = X: Y2 = Y
If NextPoint = True Then
    Select Case CurrentOption
      Case 0 'Line
            Line (X1, Y1)-(X2, Y2), Lcolor
      Case 1 'Box
            Line (X1, Y1)-(X2, Y2), Lcolor, B
      Case 2 'Box Filled
            Line (X1, Y1)-(X2, Y2), Lcolor, BF
      Case 3 'From Last X2, Y2
            Line -(X2, Y2), Lcolor
      Case 4 'Add a Step From First
            Line -Step(X2 - X1, Y2 - Y1), Lcolor, B
      Case 5 'Circle
            Pythagorean = (X2 - X1) ^ 2 + (Y2 - Y1) ^ 2
            Hypotenuse = Sqr(Pythagorean)
            Radius = Hypotenuse
            Circle (X1, Y1), Radius, Lcolor
      Case 6 'Ellipse
            Radius = Sqr((X2 - X1) ^ 2 + (Y2 - Y1) ^ 2)
            For Aspect = 0 To 3 Step .1
                Circle (X1, Y1), Radius, Lcolor, , , Aspect
            Next Aspect
      Case 7 'Arc
            Radius = Sqr((X2 - X1) ^ 2 + (Y2 - Y1) ^ 2)
            RadianStart = 15 * (PI / 180)
            RadianEnd = 345 * .017453
            StartPt = RadianStart: EndPt = RadianEnd
            Circle (X1, Y1), Radius: DrawWidth = 4
            Circle (X1, Y1), Radius, Lcolor, StartPt, EndPt
            DrawWith = 1
```

```
      Case 8 'Pie
           Radius = Sqr((X2 - X1) ^ 2 + (Y2 - Y1) ^ 2)
           RadianStart = -15 * (PI / 180)
           RadianEnd = -345 * .017453
            StartPt = RadianStart: EndPt = RadianEnd
           Circle (X1, Y1), Radius: DrawWidth = 4
           Circle (X1, Y1), Radius, Lcolor, StartPt, EndPt
           DrawWith = 1
      Case 9 'Pie Slice
           Radius = Sqr((X2 - X1) ^ 2 + (Y2 - Y1) ^ 2)
           RadianStart = -345 * (PI / 180)
           RadianEnd = -15 * .017453
           StartPt = RadianStart: EndPt = RadianEnd
           Circle (X1, Y1), Radius: DrawWidth = 4
           Circle (X1, Y1), Radius, Lcolor, StartPt, EndPt
           DrawWith = 1
     End Select
DrawWidth = 4: PSet (X2, Y2): DrawWidth = 1
End If
     NextPoint = Not NextPoint
End Sub
```

**X2 = X: Y2 = Y:** These values set the second screen coordinate that represents the line's end point, or the opposite corner of a box, or the radius point of a circle.

**If NextPoint = True Then:** You only want the following Select/Case statements to be triggered on every second mouse up event. Each time the mouse up is triggered, it uses the Not operator to toggle the True and False.

**Select Case CurrentOption:** The CurrentOption value is equal to the index number of the option button you selected. This was set in the Option1 button's click event as CurrentOption = Index.

**Case 0:** You selected the Line option button (index 0).

**Line (X1,Y1)-(X2,Y2), Lcolor:** draws a line starting at the X1,Y1 screen position to the X2,Y2 screen position. Option: Use the Lcolor value to set the line's color.

**Case 1:** You selected the Box option button (index 1).

**Line (X1,Y1)-(X2,Y2), Lcolor, B:** Draw a box starting at the X1,Y1 (corner) screen position to the X2,Y2 (opposite corner) screen position. **Options :** Use the Lcolor value to set the outline color of the box. Use B to specify a box shape.

**Case 2:** You selected the Box Filled option button (index 2).

Same as above (Case 2) except the Line Option is BF to specify a box filled shape.

**Case 3:** You selected the From Last X2,Y2 option button (index 3).

**Line -Step(X2, Y2), Lcolor:** Draws a line from the last point (PSet statement).

**Case 4:** You selected the Step button (index 4).

**Line -Step(X2 -Y1, Y2 - Y1).Lcolor, B:** Another way to draw a box shape using the Step option keyword. It simply adds the distance from the first point drawn (Pset in mouse down event) to form the shape.

**B**asic Beginnings

**Case 5:** You selected the Circle button (index 5).

**Pythagorean:** Calculate the two shorter sides of a right triangle.

**Hypotenuse:** Calculate the square root of the sum of the squares from above.

**Radius:** The Hypotenuse is equivalent to the radius of the circle.

**Circle (X1,Y1), Radius, Lcolor, , ,Aspect:** Finally, you draw the circle using X1,Y1.

**Case 6:** You selected the Ellipse button (index 6).

**Radius:** This is a simplified calculation of those found in **Case 5** from above.

**For Aspect = 0 To 3 Step .1:** Change the Aspect value of each circle in the loop by increasing this value by .1. See **Circle Method** in Visual Basic's reference guide.

**Case 7:** You selected the Arc button (index 7).

**RadianStart: RadianEnd:** Radian values of a 360-degree circle. Radians start at the 3 o'clock position, which equals 0. Use a radian value between -6.2831853. and +6.2831853.

**Case 8:** You selected the Pie button (index 8).

**RadianStart, RadianEnd:** To specify a pie or pie slice shape using the Circle statement, assign negative values to both the Start and End place holders.

**Case 9:** You selected the Pie Slice button (index 9).

**RadianStart, RadianEnd:** To specify a pie or pie slice shape using the Circle statement, assign negative values to both the Start and End place holders.

**DrawWidth = 4: Pset (X1,Y1): Drawwidth = 1:** First set the drawing width to 4 pixels wide, then draw a point at the location where the mouse was clicked down. Finally, reset the drawing width back to its default value of 1 pixel wide.

**NextPoint = Not NextPoint:** This toggles the variable NextPoint on and off from False to True, True to False, False to True, and so on. This will make sure the X1,Y1 values are set on the first mouse down, mouse up events and the X2,Y2 values are set on the second mouse down, mouse up events.

## Calculating Radians for Arcs, Pies, and Pie Slices

A circle's start and end points, when drawing an arc, pie, or pie slice, are measured in radians. A radian is a circle's central angle, which intercepts an arc of a length equal to the radius of the circle. The following expressions illustrate the relationship of the radian and a circle:

**PI** = 3.14159 : **2 * PI** = 6.28318 : **Circle** = 360 degrees

**Radian** = 360 / 2 * PI : **Radian** = .017453

**Degree** = 1 / .017453 : **Radians** = 57.29577 Degrees

**Arcs and Pies in Visual Basic** = 2 * PI or approximately .017453 * 360 degrees

When drawing an arc, pie, or pie slice, the 0 radian value is always at the 3 o'clock position. The Circle statement's start and end values (radian) can be between -6.2831853 and +6.2831853. The circle is always drawn in a clockwise fashion. The use of negative and positive values on the start and end radian values affects the way the circle will appear (e.g. circle, arc, pie, pie slice). Refer to the Circle statement in the Visual Basic language reference guide for further details.

## Summarizing the *Line* and *Circle* Statements

The Begin program has shown the basic fundamentals of Visual Basic's Line and Circle statements. The starting plot position of each graphic is constructed on the mouse down of the form. The actual drawing of the graphic is constructed during the form's mouse up events.

## The *Line* Statement

The construction of the Line statement can be broken down in the following manner:

1. A line is placed on an X,Y coordinate grid with the default 0,0 origin located at the upper-left corner of the form or graphical container control (e.g. picture box).

2. A simple line is derived by plotting the start and end coordinates of the line. The start point is considered in generic terms as X1, Y1. The end point is considered in generic terms as X2, Y2. The start and end points are plotted on the grid as follows:
   X1 is a plotted point on an X-axis coordinate (grid running left to right).
   Y1 is a plotted point on a Y-axis coordinate (grid running top to bottom).
   X2 is a plotted point on a grid running left to right (horizontally).
   Y2 is a plotted point on the grid running top to bottom (vertically).
   A simple formula is: Line (X1,Y1)-(X2,Y2) or (horizontal, vertical)-(horizontal, vertical).

3. A Line statement can have several options attached to it. The Step keyword option can be used to continue a line from the CurrentX, CurrentY position. The CurrentX and CurrentY positions are defaulted to upper-left corner of a form or graphical container control with the origin being 0,0 (horizontal, vertical).

   The CurrentX and CurrentY settings change when the following graphic methods are implemented:

   Circle: The center of the circle object.

   Cls, EndDoc, and NewPage: Reset to coordinate 0,0.

   Line: The end point of the line.

   Print: The next print position.

   Pset: The point drawn.

   A simple formula is Line -Step (X2,Y2) or last CurrentX, CurrentY (horizontal, vertical).

**Basic Beginnings**

If the Step keyword is placed between the X1,Y1 and X2,Y2 coordinates, the line is continued from its starting point (X1,Y1) and ends at the given distance supplied by X2,Y2. A simple formula is

Line (X1, Y1) -Step (X2,Y2)

or

(X1 horizontally, Y1 vertically) - (distance from X1 horizontally, distance from Y1 vertically).

4. A line can be changed to a box shape by adding the B or BF options. The B option makes an outline of a box shape only if the current FillStyle equals 1 (the default), which makes the box's fill color transparent1; otherwise, the box is filled with a solid color or pattern.

The BF option makes a fill box using the current ForeColor of the form or graphical container control.

## The *Circle* Statement

The construction of the Circle statement can be broken down in the following manner:

1. A circle is placed on an (X,Y) coordinate grid with the default (0,0) origin located at the upper-left corner of the form or graphical container control (e.g. picture box).

2. A simple circle is derived by plotting its center point (X1,Y1). The center coordinate of the circle is plotted on the grid as follows:

   X1 is a plotted point on the X-axis.

   Y1 is a plotted point on the Y-axis.

   The circle statement must also contain a radius value. The radius is the distance measured from the center point (X1,Y1) of the circle to the circle's arc (half the circle's diameter).

   A simple formula is Circle (X1,Y1), 50 or (horizontal center pt., vertical center pt.), radius.

3. A Circle statement can have several options attached to it. The Step keyword option can be used to place a circle at the CurrentX, CurrentY position. The CurrentX and CurrentY positions are defaulted to the upper-left corner of a form or graphical container control with the origin being 0,0 (horizontal, vertical).

   The CurrentX and CurrentY settings change when the following graphic methods are implemented:

   Circle: The center of circle object.

   Cls, EndDoc, and NewPage: Reset to coordinate 0,0.

   Line: The end point of the line (X2,Y2).

   Print: The next print position.

Pset: The point drawn.

A simple formula is `Circle Step (X2,Y2)` or last `CurrentX, CurrentY` - (horizontal center pt., vertical center pt).

Take note that, unlike with the `Line` statement, a hyphen (-) is not used in the circle's `Step` keyword.

5. Other options of a `Circle` statement must run in consecutive order after the radius value. If you don't use an additional option, you must include a comma (,)at each option position that resides before the option argument you are inserting.

The order of additional circle options are

`Circle (X1,Y1) , Color`: RGB value (for example, &H255) or QBColor (0 to 15) value of circle.

`Circle (X1,Y1) , , start , end`: Radian value a partial arc, pie, pie slice, or ellipse shape. A radian value is between -6.2831853 and +6.2831853. The 3 o'clock position is 0.

`Circle (X1,Y1) , , , , Aspect`: A ratio between the horizontal or vertical diameter of the circle. The default ratio is one, which yields a perfect circle. Whole plus fractional values (for example, 1.01 and higher) yield a longer vertical ellipse. Fractional point values (for example, .01 and higher) yield a longer horizontal ellipse.

# Using The *Pset* Statement

You can use the `Pset` statement to set a pixel point on an object to a specified color. The object refers to a form, picture box, or printer. This Pset program shows how lines and curves can be created from mathematical algorithms. The Basic language must go through many interruptions to actually draw the points of a line or circle. For this reason, `Pset`'s capability of drawing a complex object is rather slow. (See Figure 1.5.)

| **Pset Method** | **Keywords** |
|---|---|
| `Pset (X,Y)` | Step: `CurrentX` and `CurrentY` |
| `Pset (X,Y),QBcolor(4)` | **Options** |
| `Pset Step (X,Y), QBcolor(value)` | Color: `RGB` or `QBcolor` |

The use of the `Pset` method in Visual Basic can be very useful in your programs. Beside the obvious use of placing a single colored pixel on the form or graphical container, you can substitute it as a `CurrentX, CurrentY` pointer. It can also be used to make custom dotted lines and dithered patterns. The `Pset` program in this chapter shows you how to offset `print` statements as in the printed numbers in the clock face example (Listing 1.12). The `Fill_Pset` procedure simulates a floodfill of color within a shape, while the `Line_Fill` demonstrates the speed difference between the two procedures. Though the `Pset` method can be useful in many routines, it does not get any awards for pure speed.

## Basic Beginnings

**Figure 1.5.**
*How to use the* Pset *method in ways other than drawing a dot.*

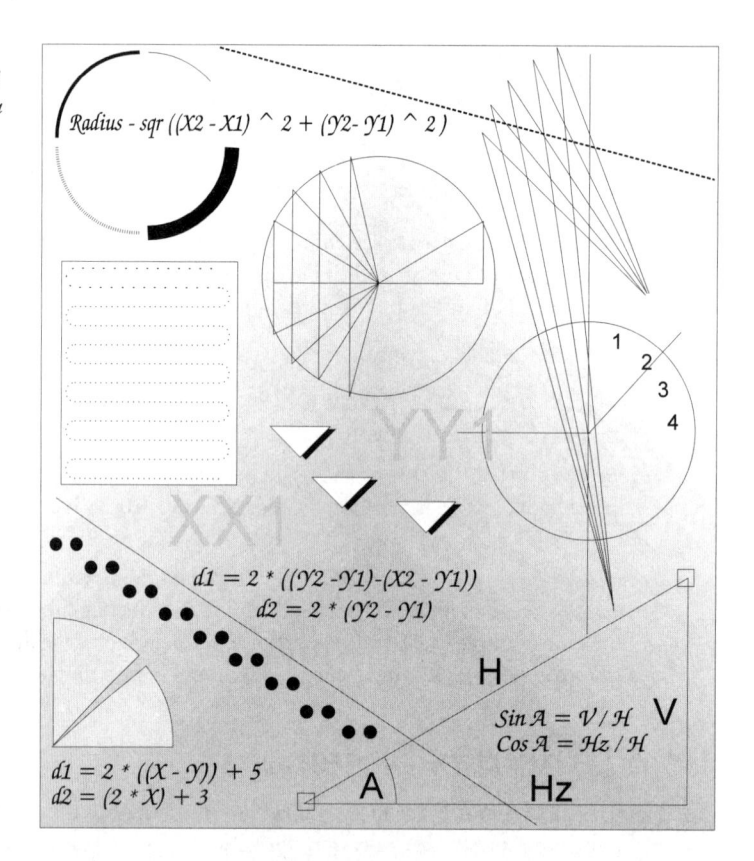

*Radius - sqr ((X2 - X1) ^ 2 + (Y2- Y1) ^ 2 )*

$d1 = 2 * ((Y2 -Y1)-(X2 - Y1))$
$d2 = 2 * (Y2 - Y1)$

$Sin A = V / H$
$Cos A = Hz / H$

$d1 = 2 * ((X - Y)) + 5$
$d2 = (2 * X) + 3$

The following list describes each of the command buttons in the Pset program:

- Circle sin/cos: Draws a circle in quarter-arc sections using the Sine, Cosine, and Pset methods.
- Circle Pset: Draws a circle in a counter-clockwise direction using the Sine, Cosine, and Pset methods.
- Circle Sqr: Draws a circle in quarter-arc sections using the Sqr (square root) function and Pset method.
- Line Pset: Draws a simple horizontal line using the Pset method.
- Dash Pset: Draws a dotted horizontal line using the Pset method.
- Box Pset: Draws a small box shape using the Pset method.
- Grid Pset: Draws a grid pattern using the Pset method.
- Fill Pset: Draws a fill pattern using the Pset method.

- `Line Pset`: Draws the same fill pattern as in the previous "Fill Pset" using the `Line` method (compare performance speeds).
- `Brensenham Line`: Draws a set of lines within a 45-degree arc using the `Pset` method.
- `Brensenham 360`: Draws a set of lines within a 360-degree arc using the `Pset` method.
- `Sine/Cosine`: Draws a rotating clock hand using the `Sine` and `Cosine` functions, and uses the `Pset` method to position numbers on the clock face.
- `Sine Cosine 2`: Draws various pie charts using a routine similar to the one explained in the preceding `Sine/Cosine`.

Finally, clicking the right mouse button at any time will draw a moving circle shape that bounces off randomly placed button controls. The `Pset` program's form and control properties are listed in Table 1.2.

**Table 1.2.** The properties of the `Pset` form.

*Object: Form*
*Object Name: Form1*

| Caption | = "Pset Drawing" | Height | = 6630 |
| Left | = 225 | ScaleMode | = 3 'Pixel |
| Top | = 1185 | Width | = 7455 |

*Object: CommandButton*
*Object Name: Command1*

| Caption | = "Sine / Cosine 2" | Height | = 510 |
| Index | = 12 | Left | = 0 |
| Top | = 5760 | Width | = 1770 |

*Object: CommandButton*
*Object Name: Command1*

| Caption | = "Sine / Cosine" | Height | = 510 |
| Index | = 11 | Left | = 0 |
| Top | = 5280 | Width | = 1770 |

*Object: Frame*
*Object Name: Frame1*

| Caption | = "Addition values" | Height | = 1575 |
| Left | = 1860 | Top | = 0 |
| Visible | = 0 'False | Width | = 1575 |

*continues*

**T**able 1.2. continued

*Object: OptionButton*
*Object Name: Option1*

| Caption | = "change X , Y" | Height | = 210 |
| Index | = 3 | Left | = 60 |
| Top | = 1200 | Width | = 1395 |

*Object: OptionButton*
*Object Name: Option1*

| Caption | = "change Y" | Height | = 210 |
| Index | = 2 | Left | = 60 |
| Top | = 900 | Width | = 1215 |

*Object: OptionButton*
*Object Name: Option1*

| Caption | = "change X" | Height | = 210 |
| Index | = 1 | Left | = 60 |
| Top | = 600 | Width | = 1215 |

*Object: OptionButton*
*Object Name: Option1*

| Caption | = "circle" | Height | = 210 |
| Index | = 0 | Left | = 60 |
| Top | = 300 | Value | = -1 'True |
| Width | = 1215 | | |

*Object: CommandButton*
*Object Name: Command1*

| Caption | = "Bresenham 360" | Height | = 510 |
| Index | = 10 | Left | = 0 |
| Top | = 4800 | Width | = 1770 |

*Object: CommandButton*
*Object Name: Command1*

| Caption | = "Bresenham Line" | Height | = 510 |
| Index | = 9 | Left | = 0 |
| Top | = 4320 | Width | = 1770 |

*Object: CommandButton*
*Object Name: Command1*

| Caption | = "Fill Line" | Height | = 510 |
| Index   | = 8           | Left   | = 0   |
| Top     | = 3840        | Width  | = 1770 |

*Object: CommandButton*
*Object Name: Command1*

| Caption | = "Fill Pset" | Height | = 510 |
| Index   | = 7           | Left   | = 0   |
| Top     | = 3360        | Width  | = 1770 |

*Object: CommandButton*
*Object Name: Command1*

| Caption | = "Circle Sqr" | Height | = 510 |
| Index   | = 2            | Left   | = 0   |
| Top     | = 960          | Width  | = 1770 |

*Object: CommandButton*
*Object Name: Command1*

| Caption | = "Grid Pset" | Height | = 510 |
| Index   | = 6           | Left   | = 0   |
| Top     | = 2880        | Width  | = 1770 |

*Object: CommandButton*
*Object Name: Command1*

| Caption | = "Box Pset" | Height | = 510 |
| Index   | = 5          | Left   | = 0   |
| Top     | = 2400       | Width  | = 1770 |

*Object: CommandButton*
*Object Name: Command1*

| Caption | = "Dash Pset" | Height | = 510 |
| Index   | = 4           | Left   | = 0   |
| Top     | = 1920        | Width  | = 1770 |

*Object: CommandButton*
*Object Name: Command1*

| Caption | = "Line Pset" | Height | = 510 |
| Index   | = 3           | Left   | = 0   |
| Top     | = 1455        | Width  | = 1770 |

*continues*

## Table 1.2. continued

**Object: CommandButton**
**Object Name: Command1**

| Caption | = "Circle Pset" | Height | = 510 |
|---|---|---|---|
| Index | = 1 | Left | = 0 |
| Top | = 480 | Width | = 1770 |

**Object: CommandButton**
**Object Name: Command1**

| Caption | = "Circle sin/cos" | Height | = 510 |
|---|---|---|---|
| Index | = 0 | Left | = 0 |
| Top | = 0 | Width | = 1770 |

Figure 1.6 shows the Pset program, and Listing 1.9 shows variable names required for Pset.

**Figure 1.6.**
*The Pset program.*

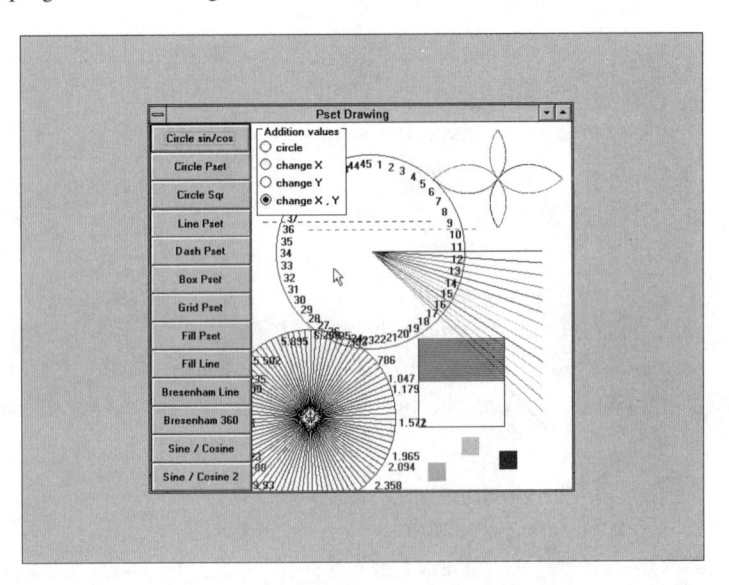

**Listing 1.9. Variable names needed for the Pset program.**

```
Declarations
Dim CurrentButton As Integer
Dim X1, Y1, X2, Y2 As Integer
Dim Yvalue, Xvalue As Integer
```

## Choosing a Drawing Function Button

To draw an object on the desktop, select a button, position the mouse on the form, and click. See Listing 1.10 for the `Command1 Click` event.

**Listing 1.10.** The `Command1_Click` event.

```
Sub Command1_Click (Index As Integer)
    Cls
    CurrentButton = Index
If Index < 2 Then Frame1.Visible = True Else Frame1.Visible = False
End Sub
```

**Cls**: Erase the last image that appears on the form.

**CurrentButton = Index**: Store the index number assigned to the button control. This will tell other events or procedures which button you have selected.

**If Index < 2 Then Frame1.Visible**: When you select the button indexed as 0 or 1, a frame control with drawing options buttons appears on the desktop.

## Clicking the Mouse on the Form

The `Form_MouseDown` event is presented in Listing 1.11. This event branches off to a drawing procedure that is associated with the button you selected.

**Listing 1.11.** The `Form_MouseDown` event.

```
Sub Form_MouseDown (Button%, Shift%, X As Single, Y As Single)
Tag = "Right Mouse"
If Button = 2 Then Exit Sub 'Bouncing Ball
If Command1(0).Left > 4 Then Exit Sub
Cls: ForeColor = QBColor(14 * Rnd)
Select Case CurrentButton
    Case 0
        Circle_sin_cos X, Y
    Case 1
        Circle_Pset X, Y
    Case 2
        Circle_Sqr X, Y
    Case 3
        Line_Pset X, Y
    Case 4
        Dash_Pset X, Y
    Case 5
        Box_Pset X, Y
    Case 6
        Grid_Pset X, Y
```

*continues*

**Listing 1.11. continued**

```
    Case 7
        Fill_Pset X, Y
    Case 8
        Fill_line X, Y
    Case 9
        X1 = X: Y1 = Y: X2 = X1 + 200: Y2 = Y1
        Bresenham X, Y
    Case 10
     X1 = X: Y1 = Y: X2 = X1 + 200: Y2 = Y1
    Bresenham_360 X, Y
    Case 11
        SineCosine X, Y
End Sub
```

**Tag = "Right Mouse":** If the right mouse button is clicked, all 13 buttons are randomly placed on the form and a circle shape bounces off the control within the form. To return the screen to its original appearance, the Do/Loop statement in Listing 1.24 requires the form's tag to read Right Mouse.

**Case 0 to 11:** You selected the button whose index number matched one of these Case statements. Each of the 10 cases branches off to the specified procedure and each carries the current value of X and Y along to the indicated procedure.

## The *SineCosine* Procedure

The SineCosine procedure presented in Listing 1.12 is a good example of the Sine (sin) and Cosine (cos) functions. You can get some pretty bizarre patterns by changing the values of X, Y or any number values of the A, B, C, D, E, F, and/or G variables. The SineCosine2 procedure is the place to play with the aforementioned variable settings.

The SineCosine procedure shows how to offset the printing of numbers using the Pset statement. You should also be able to get a grasp on how the Sine and Cosine methods work with angles. The SineCosine and SineCosine2 procedures should give you a better understanding when you come to the Animator program in Chapter 6, which uses the Sin and Cos statements extensively. Listing 1.12 presents the SineCosine procedure. SineCosine draws a needle guage using Sine and Cosine values.

**Listing 1.12. The SineCosine event.**

```
Sub SineCosine (X As Single, Y As Single)
Cls: DrawMode = 13
Circle (X, Y), 110, QBColor(4)
DrawMode = 6: Noon = 1
For R = 0 To 90 'to rotations
    A = Noon * .13819   'radians
    B = Sin(A)
    C = Cos(A)
    D = B * 100
```

```
        E = C * 100
        F = D + X
        G = (-1) * E + Y
        Line (X, Y)-(F, G)
            For delay = 1 To 8000: Next delay 'delay speed
        Line (X, Y)-(F, G) 'remark out to see divisions
        PSet (F - 10, G - 6): PSet (F - 10, G - 6)
            If Noon < 46 Then Print Noon
        Noon = Noon + 1
Next R
DrawMode = 13
End Sub
```

Both `SineCosine` and `SineCosine2` use the same algorithms. (The procedure `SineCosine2` is not listed in this chapter.)

**For R = 1 To lines**: The number of lines to drawn in a clockwise fashion.

**A = Noon * degrees**: We are going to make `degrees` equal a fraction divisible by a complete radian circle (6.2831853). By increasing the value of `Noon` (12 o'clock position) by 1 for each loop, we will get equal measurement as we go clockwise around the clock face.

**B = Sin(A)**: We now sine the radian value that A represents.

**C = Cos(A)**: We will also cosine the radian value that A represents.

**D = B * 100**: In our case, 100 represents the horizontal width (aspect) of the clock. Changing this number makes the clock face wider.

**E = C * 100**: In our case, 100 represents the vertical height (aspect) of the clock. Changing this number makes the clock's face higher.

**F = D + (X + 0)**: Adding the value of D to the X coordinate (center of clock) gives us the horizontal end position of the clock's arm: Changing the 0 value makes the arm horizontally oblong.

**G = (-1) * E + (Y + 0)**: Adding the value of E to the Y coordinate (center of clock) gives the vertical end position of the clock's arm: Changing the 0 value makes the arm vertically oblong. If you multiply E by (-1), the clock rotates clockwise. If you remove (-1), the clock travels counter-clockwise, starting at the 6 o'clock position.

**Line (X, Y)-(F, G)**: Draws the clocks arm.

**Noon = Noon + 1**: Increases the time count by one.

**Next R**: Repeats all of the above to calculate the next move of the clock's arm.

# Calculating with Sin (sine)

The sine of a right triangle is the ratio of the opposite side to the hypotenuse. The hypotenuse is the long sloping side, while the opposite side is usually the vertical side of the right triangle.

If the angle were named A, the vertical side were named Vert, and the hypotenuse were named Hyp, the sine of A would be

```
Sin A = Vert / Hyp
```

or A would equal the vertical height of the triangle divided by the long slope of the triangle.

## Calculating with Cos (cosine)

The cosine is calculated from the ratio of two sides of a right triangle. The ratio is the length of the side adjacent the angle divided by the length of the hypotenuse. In most cases, the adjacent side refers to the horizontal side of the right triangle.

If the angle were named A and the horizontal side were Horiz and the hypotenuse were named Hyp, the cosine of A would be

```
Cos A = Horiz / Hyp
```

or A would equal the horizontal length of the triangle divided by the long slope of the triangle.

## The *Box_Pset* Procedure

The `Box_Pset` procedure presented in Listing 1.13 draws a small box shape by using nested loops to make each individual pixel point travel left to right, then right to left, while climbing vertically up the screen. It may not seem too amazing because a `Line` statement can make a box shape faster. However, you will see this method used in Chapter 4 in order to find a given color value within a wide array of colored pixels. Stay tuned.

**Listing 1.13.** The `Box_Pset` procedure.

```
Sub Box_Pset (X As Single, Y As Single)

    For R = -10 To 10 Step 1
        For RR = -10 To 10 Step 1
            PSet (X + R, Y + RR)
        Next RR
    Next R
End Sub
```

**For R = R -10 To 10 Step 1:** This is the first part of a nested `Loop`. The `For/Next` statement counts from -10 through to 10 in single steps of one. This turns on 20 columns of pixels in single steps after the inner loop turns on 20 rows or pixels in each column.

**For RR = -10 To 10 Step 1:** This is the second part of nested `Loop`. The `For/Next` statement also counts from -10 through 10 in single steps of one. This will turn on 20 rows of pixels in single steps.

**Pset (X + R, Y + RR):** Turns on each individual pixel according to the column and row location specified in the next Loop routines.

**Next RR:** The inner Loop is completed first.

**Next R:** The outer Loop is then increased by one step, and the inner Loop repeats itself. X has shifted by one column, and the Y places the next column of pixel screen points.

## The *Bresenham* Method

In some examples in this section, you place individual pixels to form a circle or sloping line. When using Sin or Cos to find an angular slope we must deal in fractional numbers. These decimal numbers, known as *floating points*, can slow the computer considerably. The best method to speed up calculating is to use *integer numbers* (whole numbers) whenever possible.

The *Bresenham algorithm* is one such method for placing pixel points on the screen to form a sloping line. Most Basic line and circle statements use a derivative of these methods to calculate these shapes. You may find it best to search your main library to find the multitude of line and curve equations that are based on this method. The sample shown here is at its base stage, which draws a line from 0 to negative 45 degrees only. Listing 1.14 presents the Bresenham procedure, which demonstrates an Integer formula to draw a slopped line.

**Algorithm:**
```
d1 = 2 * ((Y2 - Y1)-(X2 - X1))
d2 = 2 * (Y2 - Y1)
```
**Comparison:**
```
If D < 0 Then
Y of Pset remains the same
If D > = 0 then Y of Pset is increased by 1.
```

See Listing 1.14 for the Bresenham procedure.

**Listing 1.14.** The Bresenham **procedure.**
```
Sub Bresenham (X As Single, Y As Single)
    For N = 0 To 14
        D = 0: Y = Y1
        d1 = 2 * ((Y2 - Y1) - (X2 - X1))
        d2 = 2 * (Y2 - Y1)
            For R = X1 To X2
                If D < 0 Then D = D + d2 Else D = D + d1: Y = Y + 1
            PSet (R, Y), QBColor(N)
        Next R
    Y2 = Y2 + 12
    Next N
End Sub
```

# Basic Beginnings

The Bresenham formula from Listing 1.14 can only calculate within a 45-degree, right-angled space. In order to make the sloping lines appear in a complete 360-degree area, we can scale our drawing area into eight quadrants and repeat the formula for each of the four sections.

The Bresenham_360 procedure in Listing 1.15 uses basically the same Bresenham formula presented in Listing 1.14 except that the X and Y values are switched around.

**Listing 1.15. The Bresenham_360 procedure.**

```
Sub Bresenham_360 (X As Single, Y As Single)
For Pattern = 1 To 4  'the first four horizontal sections
    X1 = X: Y1 = Y: X2 = X + 200: Y2 = Y
Select Case Pattern  'Choose statements could replace this Select Case
    Case 1
        Angle = 1: Length = 200: S = 1
    Case 2
        Angle = -1: Length = 200: S = 1
    Case 3
        Angle = 1: Length = -200: S = -1
    Case 4
        Angle = -1: Length = -200: S = -1
End Select
        For N = 0 To 14
            D = 0: YY = Y1
            d1 = 2 * ((Y2 - Y1) - (X2 - X1))
            d2 = 2 * (Y2 - Y1)

            For R = X To X + Length Step S
            If D < 0 Then D = D + d2 Else D = D + d1: YY = YY + Angle
            PSet (R, YY), QBColor(N)
        Next R
    Y2 = Y2 + 14
    Next N
Next Pattern
'''''''''''''''''''''''''''''''''''''''''''''
'the four vertical sections, same code except Y values replace some X values
For Pattern = 5 To 8
    X1 = X: Y1 = Y: X2 = X + 200: Y2 = Y
Select Case Pattern
    Case 5
        Angle = 1: Length = 200: S = 1
    Case 6
        Angle = -1: Length = 200: S = 1
    Case 7
        Angle = 1: Length = -200: S = -1
    Case 8
        Angle = -1: Length = -200: S = -1
End Select

For N = 0 To 14
    D = 0: YY = X1
    d1 = 2 * ((Y2 - Y1) - (X2 - X1))
    d2 = 2 * (Y2 - Y1)

        For R = Y To Y + Length Step S   'Y replaces X value
```

```
            If D < 0 Then D = D + d2 Else D = D + d1: YY = YY + Angle
            PSet (YY, R), QBColor(N)         'R and YY are reversed
        Next R
    Y2 = Y2 + 14
Next N
Next Pattern
End Sub
```

**For Pattern = 1 To 4**: The Bresenham formula is repeated four times, creating a 360-degree line revolution. Refer to the `Bresenham` procedure presented in Listing 1.14 for details on how the Bresenham formula works.

## The *Circle_Pset* Procedure

You are going to draw a circle without using the `Circle` statement. As explained at the beginning of this program, the `Pset` method is relatively slow compared to Basic's `Circle` statements. The `Pset` procedure that draws circles and rotating lines, however, can be used to find the `radian` (57.3), `degree` (360), `cos` (cosine), `sin` (sine), `tan` (angle), and/or `atn` (arc tangent) of a circle or line angle. This may be useful if you use a `Gage.VBX` and what to show or place the `Gage.VBX` needle with one of the aforementioned values. The `Circle_Pset` procedure presented in Listing 1.16 shows a radical way to set circles points.

**Listing 1.16.** The `Circle_Pset` procedure.

```
Sub Circle_Pset (X As Single, Y As Single)
PI = 3.141593
X1 = X: Y1 = Y
R = 75
For A = 0 To 2 * PI Step 0.9 / R
    Y = (R - Yvalue) * Sin(A)
    X = (R - Xvalue) * Cos(A)
    PSet (X1 + X, Y1 - Y)
        If Option1(0).Value = True Then Yvalue = 0: Xvalue = 0
        If Option1(1).Value = True Then Yvalue = Yvalue + .2
        If Option1(2).Value = True Then Xvalue = Xvalue + .6
        If Option1(3).Value = True Then Xvalue = Xvalue + .6: [IC:CCC]
    Yvalue = Yvalue + .3
Next A
End Sub
```

**PI = 3.141593:** The value of PI.

**X1 = X : Y1 = Y:** Used to set the offset value from the center of the circle.

**R = 75:** Sets the radius of the circle. You may want to set this with the mouse as explained in the Begin program in the previous section.

**For A = 0 To 2 * PI Step 0.9 / R:** The A represents the entry list of the sine and cosine tables. Going from 0 (3 o'clock position) to 360 degrees (2 * PI) we will make a circle. The Step keyword spaces the angle points apart; changing this value spaces the points apart or places more than one point on top of the other. The latter will slow the drawing of the circle considerably.

**Y = R * Sin(A): X= R * Cos(A):** This gives you the value to add from the circle's X1, Y1 center.

The additional Yvalue and Xvalue are values set by pressing an Option1 button. Change these values to test offset placements of pixel points.

**PSet (X1 + X, Y1 - Y):** We know now the distance from the center to place the pixel so we add them to X1 and Y1 screen position values, which are the center of the circle.

**Next A:** Go back to the beginning and do it all over again.

## The *Circle_sin_cos* Procedure

The Circle_sin_cos procedure presented in Listing 1.17 is the same routine as in the preceding Circle_Pset statements, but we divide PI by two. This divides the circle into four equal sections. We can then draw any section we wish. Remark Out (') any one of the four Pset code lines to draw only partial circle sections.

**Listing 1.17.** The Circle_sin_cos procedure, which shows a circle set by quadrant sectioning.

```
Sub Circle_sin_cos (X As Single, Y As Single)
PI = 3.141593 : X1 = X: Y1 = Y :R = 75
    For A = 0 To PI / 2 Step .9 / R
        Y = R * Sin(A) : X = R * Cos(A)
        PSet (X1 + X, Y1 - Y), QBColor(1)
        PSet (X1 - X, Y1 - Y), QBColor(2)
        PSet (X1 + X, Y1 + Y), QBColor(3)
        PSet (X1 - X, Y1 + Y), QBColor(4)
    Next A
End Sub
```

**Y = R * Sin(A) : X = R * Cos(A):** The Yvalue and Xvalue can be added to offset values when an Option1 button is selected. Change these values to test offset placements of pixel points.

## The *Circle_Sqr* Procedure

When creating a circle using the root of its radius, you cannot set side by side pixels to the farthest left and right of the circle's diameter. This is due to the formula's mathematics on the value of Y, which decreases in size in correlation to the number of repeats in the For/Next statement. The Circle_Sqr procedure in Listing 1.18 draws a circle by using a square root formula.

**Listing** 1.18. The `Circle_Sqr` procedure.

```
Sub Circle_Sqr (X As Single, Y As Single)
XCenter = X: YCenter = Y
R = 75
    For XX = R To 0 Step -1
        Y = Sqr(R ^ 2 - XX ^ 2)
        PSet (Xcenter + XX, YCenter - Y)
        PSet (Xcenter + XX, YCenter + Y)
        PSet (Xcenter - XX, YCenter + Y)
        PSet (Xcenter - XX, YCenter - Y)
    Next
End Sub
```

**Xcenter = X: Ycenter = Y:** Represents the center of the circle. Same as X1, Y1.

**R = 75:** Sets the radius of the circle. You may want to set this with the mouse events.

**For XX = R To 0 Step -1:** The value of XX equals the offset radius from the center of the circle. The value R in this case starts at 75 and continues down to 0. The step value of -1 makes the counter reverse.

**Y = Sqr(R ^ 2 - XX ^ 2):** The location of Y is what changes to place each pixel of the circle. We use the longest side of a right triangle formula to get the length of the ever changing hypotenuse end point. When we find the square root of the changing right triangle's hypotenuse, we will not have every Y outline position, which make this formula unusable for complete circle outlines.

**Pset:** The calculation above gives the placement of a quarter circular arc. By changing the XX and Y values from negative to positive, and vice versa, you can mirror the quarter sections to make a whole circle.

**Next:** Go back to the For statement and do it all over again.

## The *Dash_Pset* Procedure

Visual Basic only comes with a limited amount of dotted or dashed lined options. By changing the Dash and Pixel For/Next lengths, you can get a variety of different line styles. Listing 1.19 illustrates this with the Dash_Pset procedure. Dash_Pset draws a dotted line by setting pixels.

**Listing** 1.19. The `Dash_Pset` procedure.

```
Sub Dash_Pset (X As Single, Y As Single)
X1 = X: Y1 = Y
PSet (X1 - 1, Y1)
    For DASH = 1 To 20
        For Pixel = 1 To 5
        PSet Step(1, 0)
    Next Pixel
PSet Step(5, 0), BackColor
Next DASH
End Sub
```

**X1 = X: Y1 = Y:** Not needed if you replace X1 and Y1 in the PSet statement to just X and Y.

**PSet (X1, Y1):** Sets the start position of the dotted line you want to make.

**For DASH = 1 to 20:** The first, or outer, loop of a nested loop routine.

**For Pixel = 1 to 5:** The second, or inner, loop of a nested loop.

**PSet Step(1, 0):** Draws a single pixel, one pixel length in front of the last point placed.

**Next Pixel:** Repeats the For DASH loop until five pixels are placed to form a dash line.

**PSet Step (5, 0), BackColor:** Sets the next Dash line start position 5 pixels ahead of the last point set.

**Next DASH:** Go back and do it all over again.

## The *Fill_Line* Procedure

Visual Basic does not have the Paint statement that DOS Basic programs have. The Paint statement is able to fill areas of a screen like a paint brush. The Windows Application Programming Interface (*API*) library has several ways to paint simple rectangles or complex areas. You will get plenty of examples of the API drawing functions as you proceed through this book. In the meantime, the Fill_Pset procedure (Listing 1.21) shows you a rather slow way, similar to the DOS Basic Paint statement, to fill an area. For demonstration purposes, a simple Line statement loop in the Fill_Line procedure is used to duplicate the same painting effect used in the Fill_Pset procedure. The Fill_line procedure is presented first in Listing 1.20.

**Listing 1.20.** The Fill_Line, which challenges Fill_Pset procedure for speed.

```
Sub Fill_line (X As Single, Y As Single)
Line (X, Y)-(X + 100, Y + 100), QBColor(4), B
    For RR = 1 To 50 Step 2
        Line (X + 1, Y + RR)-(X + 100, Y + RR)
    Next RR
End Sub
```

**Line (X, Y) - (X,+100,Y + 100), QBColor(4), B:** Draws a red rectangular box.

**For RR = 1 To 50 Step 2:** The For/Next statement counts from 1 to 50 in steps of two, thus spacing Y coordinates two pixels units apart.

**Line (X + 1, Y + RR)-(X + 100, Y + RR):** Draw each line inside the red rectangle. If you remove the Step 2 keyword in the For/Next statement, the upper half of the box will be solid.

## The *Fill_Pset* Procedure

The `Fill_Pset` procedure in Listing 1.21 uses a routine that draws individual pixels as straight lines. The pixel line goes from left to right and always looks ahead to the next pixel's colors. If the next pixel in the path is of a color other than the color of the box shape's outline, see the following:

1. The pixel line moves up a distance that was assigned to the variable called `Spacing`.
2. The pixel line now moves in the opposite direction (right to left).
3. This process is repeated until the boundary area is filled with the pattern.

If the pixel line gets the chance to travel past the form's boundary, you must break the program or it will lay down pixels off screen until it reaches the integer length maximum. To prevent pixels from travelling off the screen in the `Fill_Pset` procedure (shown in Listing 1.21), the `NextX` and `CurrentX` values are examined during the loop.

**Listing 1.21.** The `Fill_Pset` procedure draws a winding fill pattern by setting pixels.

```
Sub Fill_Pset (X As Single, Y As Single)

Line (X - 50, Y - 50)-(X + 50, Y + 50), QBColor(4), B

CurrentX = X: NextX = X + 49
CurrentY = Y: NextY = Y
N = -1: Spacing = 2

Do

  If Point(CurrentX + N, CurrentY) = QBColor(4) Then
    NextX = NextX - N: NextY = NextY - Spacing
    Direction = Not Direction
    If Direction = 0 Then N = -1 Else N = 1
  End If

  If NextY <= (Y - 50) Or NextY >= (Y + 50) Then Beep: Exit Do
  If CurrentX < 0 Or CurrentX > ScaleWidth Then Exit Do

  PSet (NextX, NextY), QBColor(1): NextX = CurrentX + N

Loop
End Sub
```

**Line (X - 50, Y - 50)-(X + 50, Y + 50), QBColor(4), B:** Draws a red rectangular box.

**N = -1:** The value of N represents the direction in which to count. Negative 1 counts in decending order and a positive 1 counts in an ascending order. The value is switched for positive to negative to control the direction the line is travelling in.

**Spacing:** Change this value to control the pixel line spacing. Positive values make the pixels travel upward while negative values make the pixels travel downward.

**Do:** Continue doing the following statements forever.

**If Point(CurrentX + N, CurrentY) = QBColor(4) Then:** If the pixel point directly in front of the currently set pixel is the color red, you must change directions because you have reached the border of the red box.

**NextX = NextX - N: NextY = NextY - Spacing:** The `NextX` and `NextY` variables represent the next pixel point coordinate that will be turned on.

**Direction = Not Direction:** The Direction variable value will be toggled `True` or `False` every time the pixel line touched the box's edge.

**If Direction = 0 Then N = -1 Else N = 1:** If the Direction variable is toggle to `False` (0) then the pixels will travel from right to left. If the Direction variable is toggled to `True` (-1) then the pixels will travel from left to right.

**If NextY : If CurrentX:** If the pixel travels more than the specified distances, the loop is stopped and the procedure ends.

**Pset (NextX, NextY):** Set each individual pixel point according to values of `NextX`, `NextY`. Try changing the `QBColor(1)` value to read `QBColor (Rnd * 15)` to see each individual color placed within the box shape.

**NextX = CurrentX + N:** Add or subtract to advance the next pixel position.

**Loop:** Continue looping forever unless the above condition is true.

## The *Grid_Pset* Procedure

The `Grid_Pset` procedure presented in Listing 1.22 is basically the same routine as `Box_Pset` except the positions and `Steps` between each are greater to space the `Pset` point out. This is a good short routine to add grid spots to your programs.

**Listing 1.22. The `Grid_Pset` procedure.**

```
Sub Grid_Pset (X As Single, Y As Single)
    For R = -90 To 90 Step 15
        For RR = -90 To 90 Step 15
            PSet (X - R, Y - RR)
        Next RR
    Next R
End Sub
```

## The *Line_Pset* Procedure

The `Line_Pset` procedure presented in Listing 1.23 is as simple as it gets. When drawing a line using the `Pset` statement, you can see how slow this is compared to the `Line` statement. However, you may want to show a slow expanding line in some cases.

**Listing 1.23.** The `Line_Pset` procedure.

```
Sub Line_Pset (X As Single, Y As Single)
Y1 = Y
    For R = X To X + 200
        PSet (R, Y1)
        Y1 = Y1 + 0
    Next R
End Sub
```

**For R = X To X + 200:** For each value of R starting at the present X mouse down position, continue up 200 pixel units in length.

**Pset (R, Y1):** Set each individual pixel point along the X axis (left to right).

**Y1 = Y1 + 0:** By changing the value of Y1, you get an angular line, but unless it is a 45-degree angle, the pixel's points appears crooked. A simple formula for angular lines is continuously dividing the start and end points by 2. This is not integer-dependent and is even slower than what you see now.

# The Visual Basic *Point* Statement

The `Point` statement is similar to the `Pset` statement except instead of drawing a pixel, the `Point` statement returns the RGB color of the pixel at the X and Y coordinate specified. If the X and Y coordinates specified are outside the form or any control resides at the X and Y coordinate, the `Point` statement returns a value of -1. The `Form_MouseUp` event in Listing 1.24 demonstrates using the `Point` statement. When the right mouse button is clicked, the `Point` statement continuously checks to see whether the pixel immediately in front of a moving circle object equals -1. If the pixel value does equal -1, the moving circle has touched a button control or the borders of the form. The circle shape then moves in the opposite direction and continues bouncing off any object it encounters.

**Listing 1.24.** Finding the color value of a pixel.

```
Sub Form_MouseUp (Button As Integer, Shift As Integer, X As Single, Y As Single)
    Yvalue = 0: Xvalue = 0
''''''''''''''''''''
If Button = 2 Then 'Bouncing Ball
    color = -1: r = 10      'radius
    X1 = 1: Y1 = 1: Cls     'distance/angle
    X = ScaleWidth - 20     'starting point
    Tag = ""                'escape from loop flag
For r = 0 To 12
  Command1(r).Left = (Rnd * ScaleWidth \ 2)
Next r
  Do
    If Point(X + r, Y) = color Or Point(X - r, Y) = color Then
        X1 = -X1
    End If
    If Point(X, Y + r) = color Or Point(X, Y - r) = color Then
        Y1 = -Y1
```

# Basic Beginnings

```
        End If
    X = X + X1
    Y = Y + Y1
        Circle (X, Y), r, QBColor(4)   'red
            For rr = 1 To 1000: Next rr 'speed
        Circle (X, Y), r, QBColor(15) 'white
    DoEvents 'check for button click to exit loop
        If Tag = "Right Mouse" = True Then
            For r = 0 To 12
                Command1(r).Left = 4
            Next r
            Exit Do
        End If
    Loop
End If
End Sub
```

**Yvalue : Xvalue**: Reset the default start coordinates.

**If Button = 2 Then**: If the right mouse button is clicked then do the following code statements.

**color = -1: r = 10**: The color the `Point` statement will search for will be -1 and the radius of the circle shape will be 10 pixels.

**X1 = 1: Y1 = 1: Cls**: Increasing or decreasing the `X1` or `Y1` values will change the distance and angle the circle travels.

**X = ScaleWidth - 20**: The coordinate the circle will start from.

**Tag = ""**: A flag used to escape from the following loop routine.

**Command1(r).Left**: Randomly place all 13 buttons on the form.

**Do**: Continue doing the following block of code statements until one of the 13 buttons is pressed.

**If Point(X + r, Y) = color**: Check the value of the pixel immediately in front of the moving circle. If the pixel value is -1 then change the direction the circle is moving.

**Circle (X, Y), r, QBColor(4)**: Draw a red circle.

**For rr = 1 To 1000**: Controls the speed the circle moves.

**Circle (X, Y), r, QBColor(15)**: Erase the red circle.

**DoEvents**: Check to see if one of the 13 buttons has been clicked.

**If Tag = "Right Mouse"**: Clicking one of the 13 buttons will change the form's tag to `"Right Mouse"`. This will inform the loop routine to stop drawing the circle and exit the mouse up event.

**Loop**: Continue the `Do/Loop` until a button is clicked.

## Summary of the *Pset* Statement

The Pset statement can be used to set in many forms other than the simple setting a point on an object to a specific color. Pset can replace the CurrentX and CurrentY statements to align print text. However, a single dot will appear on your screen or page if you do not turn the drawing style to invisible or set the pixel color to match the background color.

Several programs in this book demonstrate setting adjustable ruler numbers using the Pset method. It should also be mentioned that by setting the DrawWidth property of your form or graphical container control, you can increase the size of the dot being displayed.

Similar to the Line and Circle statements, the Pset method can use the Step keyword. The rules are the same as explained in the section titled "Summarizing the Line and Circle Statements" of the Begin program earlier in this chapter. A simple formula is: Pset Step (X1,Y1) or last CurrentX, CurrentY - (horizontal, vertical) Take note that unlike the Line statement a hyphen (-) is not used in the Pset's Step keyword.

## Using Object Movement

This section deals with several ways to move your drawing from one part of the screen to another in a drag and drop fashion. In the Visual Basic Reference Guide, "Responding to Mouse Events", you are given an example of positioning a control with the mouse. However, this example only centers the control on the current X and Y position of the mouse while it is being moved. Most illustration programs can move an object from the point the mouse touches, thus giving a smooth illusion of the object being moved. Figure 1.7 illustrates how to make an object appear to move across the screen.

Several ways to achieve smooth movement effects are shown in this section, including moving several objects at once while objects are still visible on the screen. Because of the amount of work needed to redraw an object as it is being moved, you should only move an outline of the object. If you need to move a full color illustration and still be able to see it as it is being moved, you will need to resort to Window's API screen capturing functions. If you are using Visual Basic 4.0, the PaintPicture method can be used to transfer screen and picture images.

PaintPicture is similar to the Windows BitBlt or StretchBlt API function. Examples of the BitBlt API can be found in the Invert, C-clip, and VB-clip programs within the 16MISC directory of the companion disk.

**B**asic Beginnings

**F**igure 1.7.
*An object appears to move across the screen.*

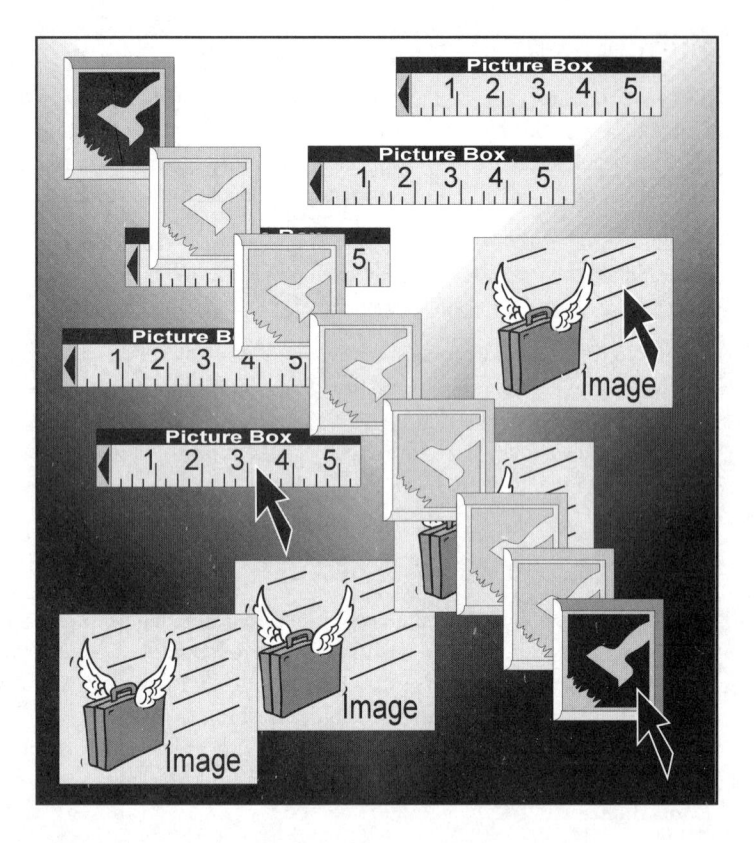

The Movetest program's form and control properties are listed in Table 1.3.

**T**able 1.3. The Properties of the Movetest form.

*Object: Form*
*Object Name: Movetest*

| | | | |
|---|---|---|---|
| Caption | = "Moving objects" | DrawMode | = 6 'Invert |
| Height | = 4950 | Left | = 720 |
| ScaleMode | = 3 'Pixel | Top | = 1845 |
| Width | = 6975 | | |

*Object: CommandButton*
*Object Name: Command1*

| | | | |
|---|---|---|---|
| Caption | = "Exit" | Height | = 435 |
| Index | = 12 | Left | = 4140 |
| Top | = 4140 | Width | = 1395 |

*Object: CommandButton*
*Object Name: Command1*

| Caption | = "T/B Stretch" | Height | = 435 |
| Index | = 11 | Left | = 2760 |
| Top | = 4140 | Width | = 1380 |

*Object: CommandButton*
*Object Name: Command1*

| Caption | = "Slide Stretch2" | Height | = 435 |
| Index | = 10 | Left | = 1380 |
| Top | = 4140 | Width | = 1395 |

*Object: CommandButton*
*Object Name: Command1*

| Caption | = "Slide Stretch1" | Height | = 435 |
| Index | = 9 | Left | = 0 |
| Top | = 4140 | Width | = 1380 |

*Object: CommandButton*
*Object Name: Command1*

| Caption | = "Blank" | Height | = 435 |
| Index | = 8 | Left | = 4140 |
| Top | = 3720 | Width | = 1380 |

*Object: CommandButton*
*Object Name: Command1*

| Caption | = "L/R Stretch" | Height | = 435 |
| Index | = 7 | Left | = 2760 |
| Top | = 3720 | Width | = 1395 |

*Object: CommandButton*
*Object Name: Command1*

| Caption | = "Slide T / B" | Height | = 435 |
| Index | = 6 | Left | = 1380 |
| Top | = 3720 | Width | = 1380 |

*Object: CommandButton*
*Object Name: Command1*

| Caption | = "Slide L / R" | Height | = 435 |
| Index | = 5 | Left | = 0 |
| Top | = 3720 | Width | = 1395 |

*continues*

**T**able 1.3. continued

*Object: CommandButton*
*Object Name: Command1*

| | | | |
|---|---|---|---|
| Caption | = "Move Objects" | Height | = 435 |
| Index | = 4 | Left | = 5520 |
| Top | = 0 | Width | = 1395 |

*Object: CommandButton*
*Object Name: Command1*

| | | | |
|---|---|---|---|
| Caption | = "XY Move" | Height | = 435 |
| Index | = 3 | Left | = 4140 |
| Top | = 0 | Width | = 1380 |

*Object: CommandButton*
*Object Name: Command1*

| | | | |
|---|---|---|---|
| Caption | = "Cls Screen" | Height | = 855 |
| Left | = 5520 | Top | = 3720 |
| Width | = 1395 | | |

*Object: CommandButton*
*Object Name: Command1*

| | | | |
|---|---|---|---|
| Caption | = "Offset shift" | Height | = 435 |
| Index | = 2 | Left | = 2760 |
| Top | = 0 | Width | = 395 |

*Object: CommandButton*
*Object Name: Command1*

| | | | |
|---|---|---|---|
| Caption | = "Center shift" | Height | = 435 |
| Index | = 1 | Left | = 1380 |
| Top | = 0 | Width | = 1380 |

*Object: CommandButton*
*Object Name: Command1*

| | | | |
|---|---|---|---|
| Caption | = "Draw Box" | Height | = 435 |
| Index | = 0 | Left | = 0 |
| Top | = 0 | Width | = 1395 |

Figure 1.8 shows a screen shot of the MoveTest program, and Listing 1.24 shows the variable names of MoveTest.

**Figure 1.8.**
*A screen shot of the MoveTest program.*

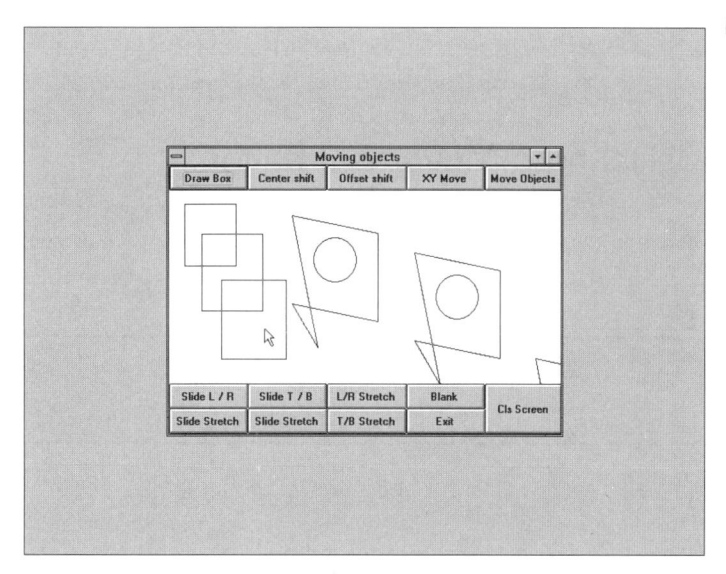

**Listing 1.24.** The variable names used in the Movetest program.

```
Declarations
Dim X1, Y1, X2, Y2 As Integer
Dim XX1, YY1, XX2, YY2 As Integer
Dim ShiftX, ShiftY As Integer
Dim WB, NB, EB, SB As Integer
Dim N As Integer
Dim CurrentButton As Integer
```

**X1, Y1, X2, Y2 : XX1, YY1, XX2, YY2:** Temporary bounding box position values.

**ShiftX, Shift Y:** Stores to offset needed to move the object.

**WB, NB, EB, SB:** Corner bounding box positions (West, North, East, South).

**N:** Holds an offset skewing value.

**CurrentButton:** Stores the index of the currently selected button.

## Clicking the Cls Button

The ClsBtn_Click event resets all the default values used in the program. This routine is presented in Listing 1.25.

**Listing 1.25.** The ClsBtn_Click event.

```
Sub ClsBtn_Click ()
    Cls
    X1 = 0: Y1 = 0: X2 = 0: Y2 = 0
    XX1 = 0: YY1 = 0: XX2 = 0: YY2 = 0
End Sub
```

**B**asic Beginnings

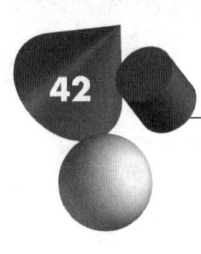

**Cls:** Clears the screen; erase all images.

**X1, Y1, X2, Y2:** Resets the values for the next move.

## Selecting a Movement Button

Clicking a button stores the currently selected movement option. This is done with the `Command1_Click` event presented in Listing 1.26. Figure 1.9 illustrates the main button functions.

**Listing 1.26.** The `Command1_Click` event.

```
Sub Command1_Click (Index As Integer)
    CurrentButton = Index
    If Index = 12 Then End
End Sub
```

**CurrentButton:** Equals the currently selected button.

**Figure 1.9.**
*The main button functions.*

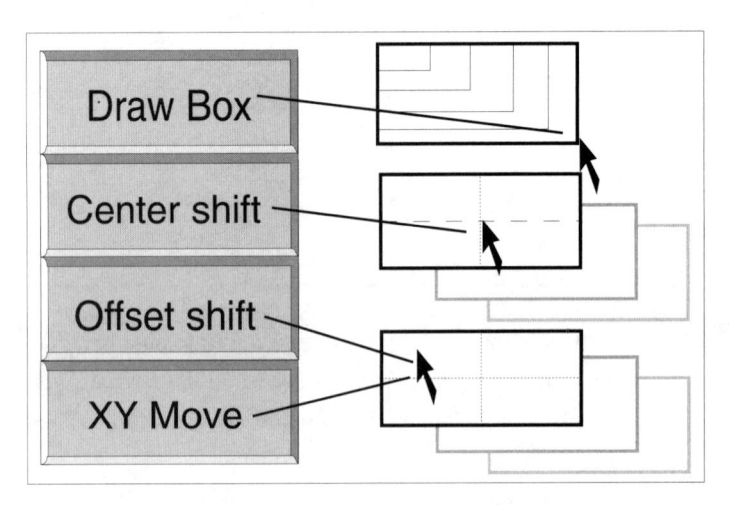

DrawMode **Property**

Settings

1. Black Pen
2. notMergePen
3. Mask Not Pen
4. Not Copy Pen
5. Mask Pen Not
6. Inverse
7. Xor Pen
8. Not Mask Pen
9. Mask pen
10. Not Xor Pen

| | | | |
|---|---|---|---|
| 11. | Nop | 14. | Merge Pen Not |
| 12. | Merge Not Pen | 15. | Merge Pen |
| 13. | Copy pen | 16. | White Pen |

## The *Form_MouseDown* Event

When moving an object, we change drawing modes so the first object we draw is erased by the next mouse move call. When a drawing statement is placed in a mouse move event, it continuously draws the object for every movement of the mouse. In normal mode (13) you would literally draw thousands of these objects if you move the mouse from one side of the form to the other. By drawing the same object on top of the first, you can get the illusion of animation. One way of doing this is to set the draw mode to Inverse (6), which draws in the reverse of the pixel it is placed on top of. If the object is a black outlined box for example, drawing the same box on top of it would erase it since the inverse of black pixels are white pixels, which is also the color of the background. Note: DrawMode (7) X_or is used for erasing objects that have multiple background colors. Listing 1.27 presents the Form_MouseDown routine, which initializes the bounding box and mouse positions.

**Listing 1.27. The** Form_MouseDown **event.**

```
Sub Form_MouseDown (Button%, shift%, X As Single, Y As Single)
Drawmode = 6
Select Case CurrentButton
    Case 0 'Draw Box
        Cls
        X1 = X: Y1 = Y: X2 = X1: Y2 = Y1
    Case 1 'Center Box on mouse
        XX1 = 0: YY1 = 0: XX2 = 0: YY2 = 0 'reset
    Case 2 'Shift box position with mouse
        ShiftX = X - ((X1 \ 2) + X2 \ 2)
        ShiftY = Y - ((Y1 \ 2) + Y2 \ 2)
        XX1 = ShiftX: YY1 = ShiftY
    Case 3 'Move box from X and Y offset
        XX1 = X: YY1 = Y
        WB = X1: NB = Y1: EB = X2: SB = Y2
    Case 4 'Move multi objects
        Cls
        N = 20 'Skew
        X1 = X: Y1 = Y: X2 = X1: Y2 = Y1
        Line (X1, Y1)-Step(100, 0 + N)
        Line -Step(0, 100)
        Line -Step(-100, 0 - N)
        Line -Step(30, 50)
        Line -Step(-30, -150)
        Circle (X1 + 50, Y1 + 50), 25
    Case 5 To 12 'Other effects
        XX1 = X: YY1 = Y
```

*continues*

## Basic Beginnings

**Listing 1.27.continued**

```
        WB = X1: NB = Y1: EB = X2: SB = Y2
End Select
End Sub
```

**DrawMode = 6:** Changes the drawing mode to `Inverse`.

**Select Case CurrentButton:** Depending on which button you selected do the following:

**Case 0:** Sets the temporary corner values of the box to all equal the current X and Y mouse position.

**Case 1:** Resets the box position, mouse position offsets back to the default of 0.

**Case 2:** The variable ShiftX finds the horizontal center of the box while variable ShiftY finds the vertical center of the form. When a box is displayed on the form, this formula finds the exact center position of the box. This formula could be written as ShiftX = X - (X1 + X2) \ 2, but adding X1 and X2 when using Twip ScaleMode could overflow the ShiftX integer. The ShiftX and ShiftY integers would have to be declared as a double data type, which requires additional memory.

**XX1, YY1:** Saves the ShiftX and ShiftY values to use as offsets in the mouse move event.

**The XX1 and YY1 set** Temporary placeholders for the current X and Y positions.

**WB = X1: NB = Y1: EB = X2: SB = Y2:** Most of the programs in this book use W, N, E, S variable names to store the bounding box's corner positions. This is because the X1, Y1, X2, Y2 variable holders are almost always used for temporary placement of X and Y values.

**Case 4:** This case block draws a circle within a multi-line object. We first draw the image on the mouse down event to erase or set a new image. Using the `Inverse` `DrawMode` the image will be set to Black and then to White continuously with every mouse move. This will give the illusion of a moving object.

**Case 5 to 12:**

These are the same values that are set in **Case** block 3.

> **NOTE**
>
> The principle of moving an object on screen using the mouse down, mouse move, and mouse up events is discussed in detail in Chapter 2, "The Artisan Program," in Listing 2.7.
>
> If you use some of these formulas to move a Visual Basic control, you do not need to add the X2 or Y2 values because Visual Basic draws the control itself, thus taking care of X2, Y2 values.

# The *Form_MouseMove* Event

The mouse move event controls the positioning of the object from the mouse as it is being dragged across the form. The key is to add an offset value that is the XCenter variable value for the XYmove routine or ShiftX, ShiftY if you use the Center Shift or Offset Center routines. The offset represents the distance from the bounding box's X1, Y1 - X2,Y2 original center coordinate before the move minus the X,Y position of the mouse pointer. *Bounding box* is a term given to an area that completely surrounds the object in question. The bounding box is rectangular in shape and is measured in the same way as a Line statement box.

> **NOTE** A bounding box is (X1,Y1) - (X2,Y2), (left, top) - (right, bottom), *or* (W, N) - (E, S).

A simpler approach to calculating the offset is used in the XYmove routine. During the mouse down event XYmove stores the X,Y mouse down coordinates and the corner positions of the bounding box. During the mouse move event, XYmove subtracts the distances moved from the original values. This can be seen in the Form_MouseMove procedure presented in Listing 1.18. The Form_MouseMove procedure draws the bounding box according to the mouse's movement.

**Listing 1.28.** The Form_MouseMove **event.**

```
Sub Form_MouseMove (Button%, X As Single, Y As Single)
If Button Then
    XCenter = XX1 - X: YCenter = YY1 - Y
    ShiftX = X - ((X1 \ 2) + X2 \ 2)
    ShiftY = Y - ((Y1 \ 2) + Y2 \ 2)

Select Case CurrentButton
    Case 0       'Draw box
        Line (X1, Y1)-(X2, Y2), , B
          X2 = X
          Y2 = Y
        Line (X1, Y1)-(X2, Y2), , B
    Case 1 To 2 'Center shift & Offset shift -Mouse
        Line (X1, Y1)-(X2, Y2), , B
        X1 = (X1 - XX1) + ShiftX
        Y1 = (Y1 - YY1) + ShiftY
        X2 = (X2 - XX1) + ShiftX
        Y2 = (Y2 - YY1) + ShiftY
        Line (X1, Y1)-(X2, Y2), , B
    Case 3       'XY Move -Mouse
        Line (WB, NB)-(EB, SB), , B
        WB = X1 - XCenter
        NB = Y1 - YCenter
        EB = X2 - XCenter
        SB = Y2 - YCenter
        Line (WB, NB)-(EB, SB), , B
    Case 4       'Move Object - Mouse
        Line (X1, Y1)-Step(100, 0 + N)
```

*continues*

## Listing 1.28. continued

```
        Line -Step(0, 100)
        Line -Step(-100, 0 - N)
        Line -Step(30, 50)
        Line -Step(-30, -150)
        Circle (X1 + 50, Y1 + 50), 25
        X1 = X : Y1 = Y
        Line (X1, Y1)-Step(100, 0 + N)
        Line -Step(0, 100)
        Line -Step(-100, 0 - N)
        Line -Step(30, 50)
        Line -Step(-30, -150)
        Circle (X1 + 50, Y1 + 50), 25
    Case 5      'Slide Left/Right
        Line (WB, NB)-(EB, SB), , B
        WB = X1 - XCenter
        EB = X2 - XCenter
        Line (WB, NB)-(EB, SB), , B
    Case 6      'Slide Top/Bottom
        Line (WB, NB)-(EB, SB), , B
        NB = Y1 - YCenter
        SB = Y2 - YCenter
        Line (WB, NB)-(EB, SB), , B
    Case 7      'Left/Right Stretch
        Line (WB, NB)-(EB, SB), , B
        NB = (Y1 - Y) - (YCenter - YY1)
        WB = X
        Line (WB, NB)-(EB, SB), , B
    Case 8
        'Test your own here
    Case 9      'Slide Stretch (L/R)
        Line (WB, NB)-(EB, SB), , B
        WB = X
        NB = Y
        EB = X2 - XCenter
        Line (WB, NB)-(EB, SB), , B
    Case 10     'Slide Stretch (T/B)
        Line (WB, NB)-(EB, SB), , B
        WB = X
        NB = Y
        SB = Y2 - YCenter
        Line (WB, NB)-(EB, SB), , B
    Case 11     'Top / Bottom Stretch
        Line (WB, NB)-(EB, SB), , B
        WB = (X1 - X) - (XCenter - XX1)
        SB = Y
        Line (WB, NB)-(EB, SB), , B
    Case 12
        'Test your own here
End Select
End If
End Sub
```

**If Button Then:** Continue only if a mouse button is held in during a drag.

**XCenter = XX1 - X : YCenter = YY - Y:** If the Center Shift button (index 1) was selected, the box is centered at the mouse pointer, and the halfway points of the box are adjusted to center the box in the direction of the drag. Hence, if the XX1, YY1 offsets value equal 0 at the mouse down event, the box is centered at the mouse pointer.

If the Offset Shift button (index 2) was selected, the box is also centered at the mouse pointer but is then shifted back to it original position by the added XX1, YY1 offsets.

**ShiftX, ShiftY:** This is the same formula found in the mouse down event that calculates the center position of the object's bounding box.

**Select Case CurrentButton:** Depending on which button you select, do the following:

**Case 0:** Draw the box. See the ArtWork_MouseMove event in Chapter 2 for details on how a movable box image is drawn.

**Case 1 To 2:** If the Center Shift button (index 1) is selected, you want to center the box at the current position of the mouse pointer. The box will always be centered on the pointer as you drag the mouse. If the Offset Shift button (index 2) is selected, you want to move the box from its present place without centering it on the mouse pointer, yet have it follow the mouse pointer. You do this by stating an offset value from the center of the present box to the position of the mouse pointer. These offsets are the XX1 and YY1 values in the mouse down event. The Artisan program uses this method.

**Case 3:** The XY Move button (index 3) performs the same actions as the Offset Shift button. However, the formula is different in that it does not need to calculate any offsets during the mouse down event. If you want to store the new position values you must do so in the Mouse up event. This makes for a shorter code routine. The ArtAPI program in Chapter 15 uses this method.

**Case 4:** Simply draw the objects twice; the second image erases the first, and so forth. You must first draw the objects in the mouse down event or a procedure connected to a mouse down call. This method is used for drawing poly-shaped objects in the ArtAPI program in Chapter 15.

**Case 5 To 12:** These case block routines show some of hundreds of ways to move an object. Most position values are interchangeable to perform the same drawing functions.

# The *Form_MouseUp* Event

After you drop the object, you must reset all bounding box positions and do a general clean up of variables. The Form_MouseUp routine presented in Listing 1.29 resets all bounding box position values.

**Listing 1.29.** The `Form_MouseUp` event.

```
Sub Form_MouseUp (Button %, Shift%, X As Single, Y As Single)
Select Case CurrentButton
    Case 3, 5 To 12
        X1 = WB: Y1 = NB: X2 = EB: Y2 = SB
    Case 4
        X1 = 0: Y1 = 0: X2 = 0: Y2 = 0
        XX1 = 0: YY1 = 0: XX2 = 0: YY2 = 0
End Select
End Sub
```

**Case 3, 5 To 12:** These Case block routines use the XY Move approach to move the bounding box. We need to update the box's positions at the mouse up event when using this formula.

**Case 4:** Rest all values in the routine because they can interfere with the other code in the program.

## Summary of the *Movetest* Program

The Movetest program has one extra blank command button indexed as number 8. As you can see, there are several buttons dedicated to sliding the graphic on a vertical or horizontal plane. The routines for doing this can be interchangeable with other routines. You can also switch X, Y variables, offset values, etc. and return the same results. The blank command button can be used to insert a mixer of routines to see the resulting movement of the object across the screen.

## Summary

The important thing to remember in this chapter is the term *bounding box*. Almost all programs included in this book use a bounding box structure in some way to move, stretch, flip, and adjust objects on the desktop. To refresh you in on the bounding box principle:

1. A bounding box is an invisible rectangular shape that encloses the entire graphic on the screen.

2. A bounding box's sides are usually referred to as the left, top, right, bottom or W, N, E, S or X1, Y1, X2, Y2.

> **NOTE** In this book, you will mainly use the variables W, N, E, and S to mean West, North, East, and South. In addition, X1, Y1, X2, and Y2 are used as temporary placeholders for other graphical methods used in the same programs. The Windows API Rect structure (to be discussed in Chapter 8 and Chapter 15) uses the terms left, top, right, and bottom.

# CHAPTER 2

# The Artisan Program

# The Artisan Program

The Artisan program is a small drawing package that uses Visual Basic language statements to create circles, ellipses, boxes, lines, and Bézier curves. (Figure 2.1 shows a screen shot of the Artisan program.) The goal during Artisan's design stage was to use Basic statements whenever possible and to avoid Windows API functions. The ArtAPI program, explained in Chapter 15, takes most of the Basic coding routines and converts them to the API graphical functions. In some cases, the codes in Chapter 15 are reworked to show shortcuts (First, you should understand the principles from this chapter.)

**F**igure 2.1.
*Screen shot of the Artisan program.*

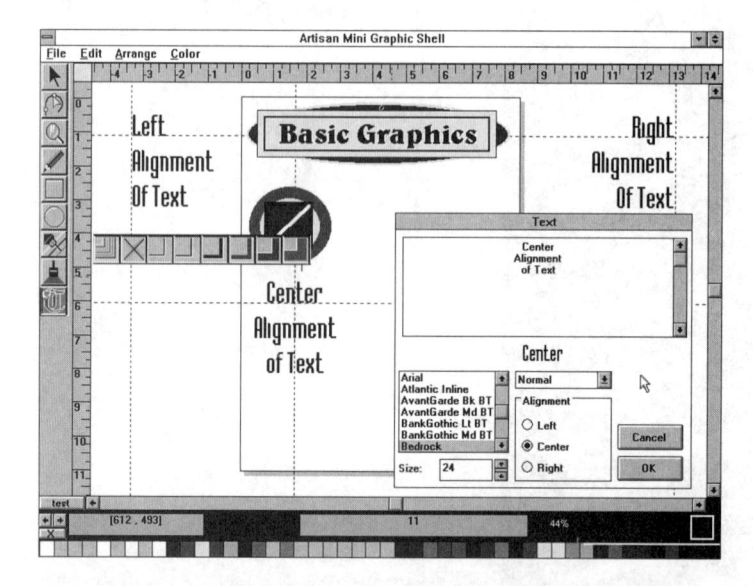

> **NOTE** API stands for Application Programming Interface. The API is a set of functions that is a part of the Windows operating system but can be accessed by other applications; thus, the API function's call routines are external to Visual Basic.

The following graphical features are excluded because they aren't practical within the Visual Basic language. Some of these functions (listed in the following sections) are either too long to incorporate in a single book form or are better suited for Windows API functions.

## Importing or Exporting Filters

*Filters* are program codes that decipher the code structure of other commercial product's graphics files. In most cases, such files are binary files that are made when you save a graphics file to disk. Because this is a competitive world, such information is rarely shared freely with other vendors. The only alternative is to break the application's original binary code structures yourself through trial and error or license the importing or exporting code from the source or a third party. Most software companies take pride in having the largest selection of importing and exporting filters—and rightly so.

In Visual Basic, you can import and export bitmap (.BMP), Windows metafile (.WMF), and text (.TXT) files easily. This is standard fare and is explained in detail in Visual Basic's reference guide. You also can use several API function calls to manipulate (stretch, rotate, and clip) bitmap files.

The Visual Basic knowledge-based help files already include examples of these graphic procedures, so there is no need to include these function calls in this program. In addition, you can purchase third-party custom controls that import and export a wide variety of images.

## Page Setup, Ruler, and Margin Printing Measurements

The page setup size in this program is defined in the Update Desktop procedure and uses rough calculations based on a screen resolution of 800×600. The page is simply a rectangular box drawn using Basic's Line statement. The distances are measured outward from the exact center of the desktop. To change the size of the page, change the Line statement's start and end points. Using a variable replacement for these values, you can build any page size you like. If, however, you use a different screen driver, the page doesn't display properly because all measurements are made in pixel widths, which can vary from monitor to monitor (device to device). This is where the API function GetDeviceCaps comes in handy; it is explained later in this chapter, "Default Form Loading Values at Startup."

## What You See Is What You Get (WYSIWYG)

Windows can tell you how many pixels per inch the device (monitor or printer) can display and the current resolution it uses. Once you have this information, you can calculate the proper page sizes, ruler measurements, printer image margins, and the appropriate scales needed to fine-tune your program.

The key is to calculate a WYSIWYG table in a procedure. The `Select/Case` statement is a good example of this: You use variable placeholders to change any measurements or scaling properties. You also have to take into consideration any user-defined scaling used in a desktop or other containers. The rulers used in this program are a good example of this, because the ruler guidelines and scrolling routines were built around a 800×600 screen resolution. Changing resolution to 640×480 throws the alignment of these features off, as will the changing of the `Left`, `Top`, `Width`, `Height`, and `Scaling` properties of the main desktop area.

## Screen, Printer, and Resolutions

The last thing to consider is the capability to print what you have drawn. Think of the printer as a second monitor to which you transfer your images. The printer, like a second monitor, can have a different screen size. Because the desktop page size is centered in a picture container, you can send an image to the printer in the same manner. Use simple math to calculate the center of the printer's printing area and place the screen image there. In most cases, however, this image will appear small because most printer's image areas are scaled like a very large monitor. You can compensate for this by subtracting the difference of the screen graphics container scale with that of the printer's scale. By adding or subtracting the printer scale top, left, width, or height, you can place the image anywhere on the printer's page and size the image to what the printer can handle.

## Getting the Program in Sync

Device scaling and screen driver resolution play a major part in keeping your program in sync with itself, as well as with any other devices it works with. For this reason, it might be best to use Windows Device API functions to handle compatibility with other hardware devices. Using Windows API device functions can be confusing to some because of logical and device coordination terms. This book uses such functions in later chapters, but for now you can manually set all printer and screen positions by using simple mathematics.

The Artisan program is in a condense form, which aids in better workability. Even with limited features, it contains more than 40 Visual Basic objects and 34 main procedures.

The declaration section has several dozen array structures to hold the image information, and this can grow higher as you start adding features. For all the previously listed reasons, the program was not set up to adhere to screen resolutions other than 800×600. Otherwise, API device procedures would get rather lengthy.

> **NOTE** Because of the large size of the Artisan Program, this chapter along with the following three are dedicated to covering its details.

## AutoRedraw at Startup

In Visual Basic, each picture box has two bitmap images associated with it. The first is the actual screen image, which can be clipped to prevent drawing outside the control's border area or within the control's internal dimensions. The second image is stored in memory if the control's AutoRedraw property is set to true. If, for example, a dialog box were to appear over your drawing, Visual Basic would restore your original drawing once the dialog box was hidden. Visual Basic does this by calculating and swapping image areas back and forth from the memory (persistent) bitmap to the screen image of the control.

The main desktop drawing area in this program is a picture box control that is called Artwork. The Artwork picture box images are updated each time an object is drawn or moved to a new location within the Artwork control. Normally, updating any graphics images in a picture box control is handled through the control's Paint event. However, since you can move objects in this program, the Paint event can be triggered unnecessarily during mouse movement events causing image flickering and slow performance. You can bypass the Artwork's Paint events completely by drawing all images in a procedure called UpDateObjects.

The AutoRedraw property for the Artwork picture box is set to True every time the UpdateObjects procedure is called to redraw the desktop page and objects. For scrolling purposes, the Artwork picture box control is sized to almost twice the monitor's screen area. AutoRedraw preserves a memory (persistent) image of the entire internal picture box control area so it can replace any images that are clipped during scrolling. This requires 1.5 MB of memory to store a bitmap image of the Artwork picture. Clipping the persistent bitmap image to save memory is unavailable because AutoRedraw uses in-house features that define the entire control's internal measurements as the memory bitmap.

> **CAUTION** If you get the message Cannot create AutoRedraw, you do not have the required 1.5 MB of memory. You will then have to Remark Out (') the ArtWork.AutoRedraw statements, get more memory, or resize the actual Artwork picture box to fit your screen's dimensions. If you use the latter method, the rulers and scrollbar scaling routines will have to be rewritten. Use the Scaltest program (see Chapter 14) first to find suitable solutions when making major resizing and scaling changes.

## The Learning Process

The Artisan program is a drawing program that uses almost all of the Visual Basic language statements and purposely avoids using Windows API functions when possible. Although it can accomplish a lot, it has its limits. The goal is to experiment with Artisan and then use the Scaltest program in Chapter 14, "The Scaling and Printing Program," as the shell to build your own graphics desktop. Once you understand the basic principles of drawing packages, you can add different procedures from the programs supplied with this book. You can then mix and match API drawing codes from the ApiDraw program presented in Chapter 8, "API Drawing Programs," or the programs presented in Chapter 15, "ArtAPI," for example, as well as the Basic language codes from the Artisan program to customize your own programs.

To shorten the procedures and array list, this program does not join or group objects. Chapter 13, which discusses the Join Nodes program, gives you an explanation of how this is done—as does Chapter 15, which covers an API version of this program.

The Zoom tool supports only two modes of Zoom because all text is placed on the desktop using the Print statement. This book explains later why there is a limitation of WYSIWYG text using the print statements in Visual Basic. Later in this book, you'll see how to use the Scaltest program to fine-tune control scaling and zoom tool values to your liking. Finally, if your monitor or printer is not responding to correct visual alignment, there might be scaling and monitor resolution conflicts. The Scaltest program, discussed in Chapter 14, uses the same Visual Basic object names, scaling properties, and procedures as the Artisan program. You should fine-tune the Scaltest program to your liking before making changes in the Artisan program.

## Program Speed and Picture Boxes

After you draw an object, little white boxes appear at the start and end of each line or curve segment that make up the object's shape. These are called *nodes* and are used to edit the appearance of the shape. However, you are limited to moving only line and curve object in this program with the attached nodes. A curve object is called a *Bézier* curve and has additional levers attached to the start and end points of the curve. These levers have little black boxes attached to them, called *handles*. They are used to adjust the curve's appearance. In the ArtAPI program in Chapter 15, you advance one step further by learning to edit complicated polyshapes using the node and handle picture box controls.

Probably the most noticeable event in slow performance is the repositioning of the handles and nodes around a highlighted object; all handles and nodes used in this program are Visual Basic picture boxes. Using these types of controls helps save lots of code writing for mouse events. The downside is that each control must be set to invisible, moved, rescaled, and finally made visible again whenever an object is selected. If a zoom tool were omitted from the program, the rescaling of picture boxes could also be omitted. Forms, picture boxes, and printers are the only objects that can use Visual Basic's Scale methods. The ArtAPI program, explained in Chapter 15, replaces many picture box controls with image controls that have less property attributes; thus, they appear faster. Additional coding must be used to align the internal mouse movement of the image controls to match the scale of the Artwork picture box.

Another solution is to simulate a control that can respond to mouse events. An example of this can be found in the Tabs program, located in the 16MISC directory of the companion disk that accompanies this book.

# The Tool Buttons Picture Box

The Tool Buttons make up a single bitmap image of a toolbox displayed in a picture box control. A tool is used to draw a shape and perform a task such as painting or changing the shape's outline width. For example, to draw a box, select the tool with a picture of a box icon on it. Next, start drawing your box by positioning the mouse on the desktop; then click the left mouse button. With the mouse button still held down, drag the mouse and a box shape will appear. When the mouse button is released, the box shape is set and completed. You also can use the button that looks likes a paintbrush icon to fill the box with a color.

The bitmap toolbox image can be found in the BITMAPS directory on the companion disk supplied with this book. You can edit the appearance of each tool by using any BMP painting software or the Paint program supplied with Microsoft Windows. The listing that follows describes each tool's function, starting with the top tool button.

The ToolButtons control on the left side of the screen has the following features:

- The *pointer tool* for selecting and highlighting objects or moving objects to a different screen location. You can use the pointer tool to draw a marquee (drag the mouse so a dotted box appears) around an object that you want to select. However, this program does not select multiple objects. You also use the pointer tool to stretch a single object and to pull a guideline from the rulers. Pressing the spacebar triggers the pointer tool when another tool is currently selected. The program does not stretch objects; this is best done using a custom font engine that extracts the fonts GlyphOutline (a polygon or Bézier outline of each character) for text manipulation. The standard API Text functions can make fonts wide, narrow, thick, thin, and rotated; however the functions do not mirror or inverse the font images.

- The Bézier tool (shape tool) for converting a line to a Bézier curve, or vice versa. You also can use this tool to move either end point of a line by dragging one of the line's end node point. This tool is the heart and soul of drawing programs and can be used to manipulate any object's node. However, the Bézier tool does not move nodes attached to boxes, circles, or text objects. This program, also, does not join or group objects. Chapter 13, "The Join Nodes Program," deals with this subject and shows you how to manipulate complex objects attached by nodes.

> **NOTE** A *node point* is where a little white box connects the end or start coordinate of an object.

# The Artisan Program

- The *zoom tool* for viewing the page and objects at different scalings. Chapter 14 shows examples of using this type of tool in multiple zoom magnifying. When scaling text in multiple zoom ranges, Visual Basic usually rounds the text point sizes to quarter values. This conflicts with the WYSIWYG approach to graphics. Most drawing programs use their own font-creating engines in the form of custom .DLL files. It is possible to create a font engine using Windows `GyphOutline` API function, but this requires advance font, B-spline curve, and memory management techniques. This book, however, does not deal with font specifics.
- The *line tool* for drawing straight lines. You may want to use API functions to draw lines—or for that matter any other object. Chapter 8 and Chapter 13, give examples of API drawing functions. In this case, the API `LineTo` function works best for freehand curve or straight line drawing.
- The *box tool* for drawing rectangular or square boxes. If you want to round the corners of a box using the nodes, refer to Chapter 11, "The Rounded Corners Program," or Chapter 8 for details.
- The *circle tool* (ellipse tool) for drawing circular and elliptical objects. The API `Ellipse` function is better-suited to handle this job. This API function already incorporates a perfect circle function. See Chapter 8 for a good example of this.
- The *outline tool* for changing the color or removing an outline of an object.
- The *fill tool* (paint tool) for painting the interior of a circle or box object in this program. This is where Basic language bails out of the graphics statements for complex objects. The old Basic `Paint` statement has been put to rest by Microsoft. The easiest way to use fills is with Windows API `FloodFill` functions or with the API `PolyFillMode` and `Polygon` functions. Windows API library also has a host of rectangular and elliptical painting functions. (See Chapter 8 for more information on API graphical functions).
- The *text tool* for displaying text on the page or desktop. As explained previously, Visual Basic has limitations when printing text. The APItext program covered in Chapter 12, "The Text Alignment Program," can be modified in code to change the height, width, and rotation of text. However, the APItext program also has limitations. For true text manipulation, you need to convert the fonts `GyphOutline` to poly segments, which is advanced font technology and is not dealt with in this book.

## The Color Bar Palette

The color bar palette is a picture box that displays a variety of side-by-side colors. The palette is located on the bottom of the screen. It displays additional colors when you use the left and right scroll button controls to the left side of the color palette. When you scroll, each new color that appears is processed through the `ColorBar` picture box `Paint` event. This example is a modified version of the IconWorks example supplied by Visual Basic. By placing the color updates in the `Paint` event, as is done in the Artisan program, the scrolling speed of the palette is slowed down. Refer to Chapter 15 for an alternative way to speed palette scrolling.

The color bar picture box control involves the following events:

- When a box or circle object is selected, you can fill it with color by clicking the left mouse button in a color from the color bar palette.
- When a box, circle, or line object is selected, you can change the outline color by clicking the right mouse button in a color from the color bar palette.
- The *color scroll* control located below the Test button scrolls the color bar palette left or right, as shown in Figure 2.2. The color values used in the palette are the same color values documented in the IconWorks example supplied with Visual Basic. If you want to change these values, refer to the ColorBar procedure in Chapter 4. You also must make appropriate changes to the ARTISAN7.BAS file. (See Appendix A.)

**F**igure 2.2.
*The main Artisan form and its controls.*

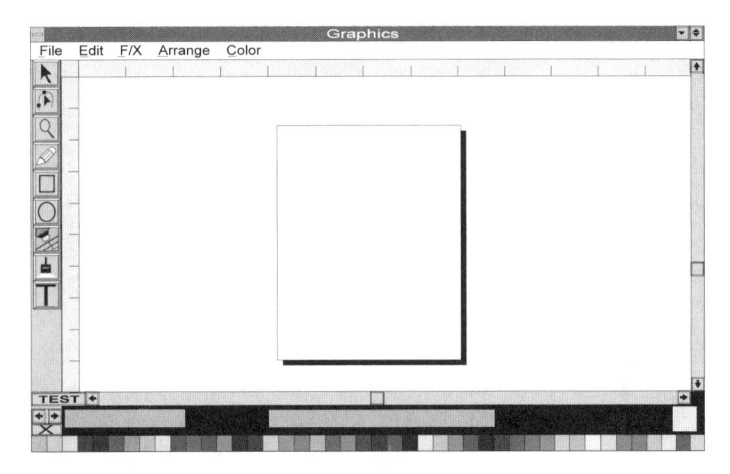

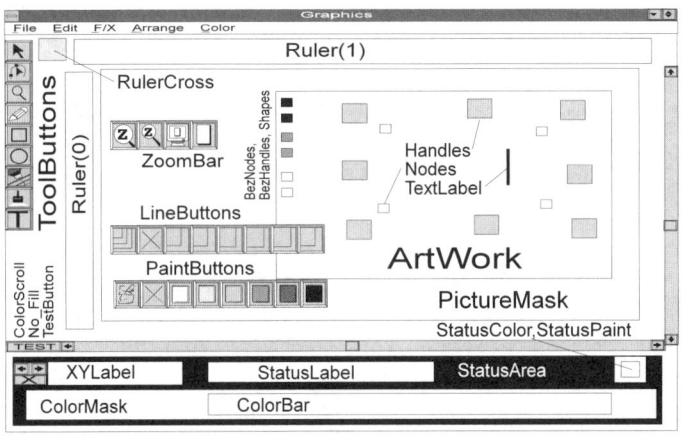

- Pressing the *no fill* (marked as an "X" character) button, which is located directly below the tools control, erases any fill color of a circle or box object that is currently selected.
- The *status color* picture box control, located at the bottom-right of the screen, displays the current outline color of an object. The next picture box, *status paint*, displays the current fill color of an object.
- The *test* button control can use this button to test future coding.

## The Scrollbar Controls

The scrollbar controls are standard vertical and horizontal scrolling controls in Visual Basic. They are used to pan (move) the desktop images left, right, top, and bottom within the physical viewing area of the Artwork picture box control.

The HScroll and VScroll controls have the following events:

- HScroll pans the desktop horizontally.
- VScroll pans the desktop vertically. Maximum and Minimum values are not adjusted to reflect a Zoom In or Zoom Out event. You can use the Scaltest program in Chapter 14 to fine-tune desktop scrolling features.

## The Status Area Frame

The *status area* displays the following information:

- The XYLabel control displays the current *x* and *y* positions of the mouse pointer on Artwork's desktop, as well as the *x* and *y* internal coordinates of any controls this container holds (for example, handles, nodes, BezHandles, and BezNodes). All measurements displayed are twips, which are then converted to pixel values.
- The StatusLabel control displays any information you want to show the user. StatusLabel.Caption = Format$(variable) is a standard call to this control. The StatusLabel can display the current object number, the twip measurement of a stretching bounding box, or the current font that was selected using the font dialog box.

## The Menu Area

The *menu area* is a standard Windows pull-down menubar in which you can open, save, and delete objects you have drawn. Menu areas have limited features because of the length of coding needed to achieve special effects or other features. The Artisan program includes some very useful alternatives to saving, opening, or printing graphics within your own programs. Most coding uses long formulas. Fancy loops or sophisticated array structures are eliminated, thus allowing even a beginner to easily understand the basic principles. For instance, the delete object option in the Edit menu erases the 30 attributes available for any shape you draw, such as the one coded in

Listing 2.1. However, it takes several lines of code to erase each attribute. As you advance in this book, it will become apparent that these attributes values can easily be stored in temporary variables. These variables can be used by inserting additional code to cut and paste the objects.

**Listing 2.1. Deleting an object from the desktop.**

```
Sub Menu_EditSelection_Click (Index As Integer)
Select Case Index
. Case 6 'DELETE
If B = 0 Then Exit Sub
If Node(0).Visible = True Then
. N_H_Clear
. FillValue(B) = 0: LineValue(B) = 0: OutLineColor(B) = 0
. PaintColor(B) = 0: LineWidth(B) = 1: FlagAlign(B) = 0
. OFFSET(B) = 0: TextSize(B) = 0: TextFont(B) = ""
. TextBold(B) = 0: TextItalic(B) = 0: CarriageCount(B) = 0
. Storedtext(B) = ""
. FlagBézier(B) = 0: FlagLine(B) = 0: FlagBox(B) = 0
. FlagCircle(B) = 0: FlagText(B) = 0
. P1X(B) = 0: P1Y(B) = 0: p2X(B) = 0: p2Y(B) = 0
. h1X(B) = 0: h1Y(B) = 0: h2X(B) = 0: h2Y(B) = 0
DeleteObject = True
XX1 = W(B): YY1 = N(B): XX2 = E(B): YY2 = S(B)
W(B) = 0: N(B) = 0: E(B) = 0: S(B) = 0
. UpdateObjects
. DeleteObject = False
End If
End Select
End Sub
```

See Listing 2.2 for the `To_Front_Back` procedure for the Artisan program from Chapter 5.

**Listing 2.2. The `To_Front_Back` procedure.**

```
Sub To_Front_Back (Index As Integer)
Dim PC As Long: Dim OLC As Long
Dim St As String: Dim TF As String
If Node(0).Visible = False Then Exit Sub
If Index = 0 And B = Total Then Exit Sub
If Index = 1 And B <= 1 Then Exit Sub
''''''store objects attributes
If FlagText(B) = B Then FT = 1
If FlagCircle(B) = B Then FC = 1
If FlagLine(B) = B Then FL = 1
If FlagBox(B) = B Then FB = 1
If FlagBézier(B) = B Then Bez = 1
OLC = OutLineColor(B): PC = PaintColor(B): LW = LineWidth(B)
Fill = FillValue(B): LV = LineValue(B): St = Storedtext(B)
TS = TextSize(B): TF = TextFont(B): TB = TextBold(B): TI = TextItalic(B)
FA = FlagAlign(B): OF = OFFSET(B): CR = CarriageCount(B)
W1 = W(B): N2 = N(B): E3 = E(B): S4 = S(B)
p1XX = P1X(B): p1YY = P1Y(B): p2XX = P2X(B): p2YY = p2Y(B)
h1XX = h1X(B): h1YY = h1Y(B): h2XX = h2X(B): h2YY = h2Y(B)
''''''End of every possible attribute
```

*continues*

## Listing 2.2. continued

```
If Index = 0 Then Last = Total - 1: First = 1 Else Last = 2: First = -1
For B = B To Last Step First: A = B + (First)
W(B) = W(A): N(B) = N(A): E(B) = E(A): S(B) = S(A)
P1X(B) = P1X(A): P1Y(B) = P1Y(A)
P2X(B) = P2X(A): p2Y(B) = p2Y(A)
h1X(B) = h1X(A): h1Y(B) = h1Y(A)
h2X(B) = h2X(A): h2Y(B) = h2Y(A)
OutLineColor(B) = OutLineColor(A)
PaintColor(B) = PaintColor(A)
LineWidth(B) = LineWidth(A)
FillValue(B) = FillValue(A)
LineValue(B) = LineValue(A)
Storedtext(B) = Storedtext(A)
TextSize(B) = TextSize(A)
TextFont(B) = TextFont(A)
TextBold(B) = TextBold(A)
TextItalic(B) = TextItalic(A)
FlagAlign(B) = FlagAlign(A)
OFFSET(B) = OFFSET(A)
CarriageCount(B) = CarriageCount(A)
If FlagText(A) = 0 Then FlagText(B) = 0 Else FlagText(B) = B
If FlagCircle(A) = 0 Then FlagCircle(B) = 0 Else FlagCircle(B) = B
If FlagLine(A) = 0 Then FlagLine(B) = 0 Else FlagLine(B) = B
If FlagBox(A) = 0 Then FlagBox(B) = 0 Else FlagBox(B) = B
If FlagBézier(A) = 0 Then FlagBézier(B) = 0 Else FlagBézier(B) = B
Next B

''''Reset objects attributes
If FT = 1 Then FlagText(B) = B Else FlagText(B) = 0
If FB = 1 Then FlagBox(B) = B Else FlagBox(B) = 0
If FC = 1 Then FlagCircle(B) = B Else FlagCircle(B) = 0
If FL = 1 Then FlagLine(B) = B Else FlagLine(B) = 0
If Bez = 1 Then FlagBézier(B) = B Else FlagBézier(B) = 0
OutLineColor(B) = OLC: PaintColor(B) = PC: LineWidth(B) = LW
FillValue(B) = Fill: LineValue(B) = LV: Storedtext(B) = St
TextSize(B) = TS: TextFont(B) = TF: TextItalic(B) = TB: TextItalic(B) = TI
FlagAlign(B) = FA: OFFSET(B) = OF
CarriageCount(B) = CR
W(B) = W1: N(B) = N2: E(B) = E3: S(B) = S4
P1X(B) = p1XX: P1Y(B) = p1YY: P2X(B) = p2XX: p2Y(B) = p2YY
h1X(B) = h1XX: h1Y(B) = h1YY: h2X(B) = h2XX: h2Y(B) = h2YY
UpdateObjects
End Sub
```

See Listing 2.3 for the To_Front_Back procedure for the ArtAPI program in Chapter 15.

## Listing 2.3. The To_Front_Back procedure.

```
Sub To_Front_Back (Index As Integer)
    If B = 0 Then Beep: Exit Sub
    If PolyShape(B) = B Then B = FirstPolyPt(B)

    Select Case Index
    Case 0 'To Front
```

```
        For Objectnumber = 1 To Total
            Z = DrawOrder(Objectnumber)
            If Z = B Then Exit For
        Next Objectnumber 'Objectnumber will highlighted object
    Temp = DrawOrder(Objectnumber)

    For Repeat2 = Objectnumber To Total
        NextA = Repeat2 + 1
        DrawOrder(Repeat2) = DrawOrder(NextA)
    Next Repeat2
    DrawOrder(Total) = Temp

    Case 1 'To back
        For Objectnumber = 1 To Total
            Z = DrawOrder(Objectnumber)
            If Z = B Then Exit For
        Next Objectnumber 'Objectnumber will highlighted object
    Temp = DrawOrder(Objectnumber)

        For Repeat2 = Objectnumber To 2 Step -1
        NextA = Repeat2 - 1
        DrawOrder(Repeat2) = DrawOrder(NextA)
        Next Repeat2
    DrawOrder(1) = Temp
    End Select
            UpdateObjects
End Sub
```

## File Menu

The File menu is the first menu item in the Artisan program. Clicking the mouse on the File menu will display the following options:

- The New menu option erases all variable arrays and starts a new drawing.
- The Open menu option in Visual Basic 3.0 and 4.0 versions of this program, a CMDialog box appears, enabling you to open an existing graphic. .ART is the default file extension.
- The Save and Save As menu options in Visual Basic 3.0 and higher use the CMDialog control, which enables you to save the present object you have drawn.
- The Exit menu option enables you to leave the program, but your present drawing will not automatically be saved.

## Edit Menu

The Edit menu is the second menu item in the Artisan program. Clicking the Edit menu will display the following options:

- The Delete menu option and the Delete key erase the currently selected object.

# Arrange Menu

The Arrange menu is the third menu item in the Artisan program. Clicking the Arrange menu will display the following options:

- The To Front menu option takes the currently selected object and moves it to the top of all objects currently displayed on the desktop.
- The To Back menu option takes the currently selected object and moves it to the bottom of the objects currently displayed.

# Color Menu

The Color menu is the fourth menu item in the Artisan program. Clicking the Color menu will display the following options:

- The Show Rulers menu option hides or displays the rulers.

# Color Palette Submenu

The Color Palette submenu is the second menu item of the Color menu in the Artisan program. Clicking the mouse on the Color Palette submenu will display the following options:

- The Edit palette menu option adds a new color to the present color bar palette. Use the RGB scrollbars to select a color and drag the color from the large picture box that displays the new color. The cursor changes to a Felt Marker icon. Drop the icon onto any current color row. The new color will appear on the color chart, as well as on the color bar palette.
- The Default Palette menu option loads the default color palette defined in the ARTISAN7.BAS file.
- The Custom Palette menu option loads the custom palette stored in the ARTISAN.INI file. This file is made only when you save a custom color file.
- The Save As Custom menu option writes the color values from the new palette to the ARTISAN.INI file. This will be the palette loaded in the future. You can erase or overwrite this file or use the default palette when needed.

# The Mouse Events

The mouse events are the actions you perform with your mouse. In this program, the left mouse down, double-click, and right mouse down events can trigger program procedures:

- The left mouse button enables you to select an object, move an object by dragging it, draw a marquee around a single object to select it, move a line or Bézier curve node, draw a box, circle, or line shape, drag a guideline from rulers, and select the fill color of an object.

- The left mouse button double-click enables you to show the Edit Node form when a line or curve is selected; the Bézier (shape) tool must also be selected. The Edit Node's option buttons can then be used to convert a line to a Bézier curve.
- The right mouse button opens a limited text editor when the text tool is selected, displays the last selected menu's submenu items, and selects the outline color of an object.

The Artisan program's form and control properties are listed in Table 2.1.

**Table 2.1.** The properties of the Artisan form and controls.

*Object: Form*
*Object Name: Artisan*

| | | | |
|---|---|---|---|
| BackColor | = &H00404040& | Caption | = "Artisan Mini Graphic Shell" |
| ForeColor | = &H00FFFFFF& | Height | = 7095 |
| Left | = 165 | ScaleMode | = 3 'Pixel |
| Top | = 1065 | Width | = 7260 |

*Object: CommonDialog*
*Object Name: CMDialog1*

| | | | |
|---|---|---|---|
| Left | = 0 | Top | = 4410 |

*Object: Picture Box*
*Object Name: RulerCross*

| | | | |
|---|---|---|---|
| BackColor | = &H0000FFFF& | Height | = 345 |
| Left | = 540 | Top | = 0 |
| Width | = 345 | | |

*Object: Picture Box*
*Object Name: StatusArea*

| | | | |
|---|---|---|---|
| Align | = 2 'Align Bottom | BackColor | = &H00000000& |
| BorderStyle | = 0 'None | ForeColor | = &H00FFFFFF& |
| Height | = 1455 | Left | = 0 |
| Top | = 4980 | Width | = 7170 |

*Object: Picture Box*
*Object Name: ColorMask*

| | | | |
|---|---|---|---|
| Height | = 435 | Left | = within StatusArea |
| ScaleHeight | = 27 | ScaleMode | = 3 'Pixel |
| Top | = within StatusArea | Width | = 7155 |

*continues*

## The Artisan Program

**T**able 2.1. continued

*Object: Picture Box*
*Object Name: ColorBar*

| | | | |
|---|---|---|---|
| Height | = 270 | Left | = within ColorMask |
| ScaleHeight | = 1 | ScaleMode | = 0 'User |
| Top | = within ColorMask | Width | = 6930 |

*Object: Picture Box*
*Object Name: StatusColor*

| | | | |
|---|---|---|---|
| BorderStyle | = 0 'None | Height | = 390 |
| Left | = within StatusArea | ScaleMode | = 3 'Pixel |
| Top | = within StatusArea | Width | = 450 |

*Object: Picture Box*
*Object Name: StatusPaint*

| | | | |
|---|---|---|---|
| BorderStyle | = 0 'None | Height | = 315 |
| Left | = within StatusColor | Top | = within StatusColor |
| Width | = 345 | | |

*Object: HScrollBar*
*Object Name: ColorScroll*

| | | | |
|---|---|---|---|
| Height | = 255 | LargeChange | = 80 |
| Left | = within StatusArea | Max | = 2000 |
| SmallChange | = 16 | Top | = within StatusArea |
| Width | = 510 | | |

*Object: CommandButton*
*Object Name: No_Fill*

| | | | |
|---|---|---|---|
| Caption | = "X" | Height | = 195 |
| Left | = within StatusArea | Top | = within StatusArea |
| Width | = 495 | | |

*Object: HScrollBar*
*Object Name: HScroll*

| | | | |
|---|---|---|---|
| Height | = 240 | LargeChange | = 100 |
| Left | = 810 | Max | = 200 |
| Min | = -200 | SmallChange | = 10 |
| Top | = 45 | Width | = 5985 |

*Object: CommandButton*
*Object Name: TestButton*

| | | | |
|---|---|---|---|
| Caption | = "test" | Height | = 285 |
| Left | = within StatusArea | Top | = within StatusArea |
| Width | = 780 | | |

*Object: Label*
*Object Name: XYLabel*

| | | | |
|---|---|---|---|
| Alignment | = 2 'Center | BackColor | = &H00FFFF00& |
| BorderStyle | = 1'Fixed Single | Height | = 390 |
| Left | = within StatusArea | Top | = within StatusArea |
| Width | = 1125 | | |

*Object: Label*
*Object Name: StatusLabel*

| | | | |
|---|---|---|---|
| Alignment | = 2 'Center | BackColor | = &H00FFFF00& |
| BorderStyle | = 1 'Fixed Single | Height | = 390 |
| Left | = within StatusArea | Top | = within StatusArea |
| Width | = 2775 | | |

*Object: Picture Box*
*Object Name: Ruler*

| | | | |
|---|---|---|---|
| BackColor | = &H00C0C0C0& | Height | = 4335 |
| Index | = 0 | Left | = 540 |
| Top | = 405 | Width | = 330 |

*Object: VScrollBar*
*Object Name: VScroll*

| | | | |
|---|---|---|---|
| Height | = 4725 | LargeChange | = 100 |
| Left | = 6930 | Max | = 250 |
| Min | = -250 | SmallChange | = 10 |
| Top | = 0 | Width | = 255 |

*Object: Picture Box*
*Object Name: Ruler*

| | | | |
|---|---|---|---|
| BackColor | = &H00C0C0C0& | Height | = 345 |
| Index | = 1 | Left | = 900 |
| ScaleHeight | = 315 | ScaleWidth | = 5985 |
| Top | = 0 | Width | = 6015 |

*continues*

Table 2.1. continued

*Object: Picture Box*
*Object Name: PaintButtons*

| | | | |
|---|---|---|---|
| Height | = 510 | Left | = 1035 |
| Picture | = Paint.BMP | ScaleMode | = 3 'Pixel |
| Top | = 3960 | Visible | = 0 'False |
| Width | = 3840 | | |

*Object: Picture Box*
*Object Name: ZoomBar*

| | | | |
|---|---|---|---|
| Height | = 510 | Left | = 1020 |
| Picture | = Zoom.BMP | ScaleMode | = 3 'Pixel |
| Top | = 1020 | Visible | = 0 'False |
| Width | = 1920 | | |

*Object: Picture Box*
*Object Name: LineButtons*

| | | | |
|---|---|---|---|
| Height | = 510 | Left | = 1035 |
| Picture | = Linetool.BMP | ScaleMode | = 3 'Pixel |
| Visible | = 0 'False | Width | = 3840 |

*Object: Picture Box*
*Object Name: PictureMask*

| | | | |
|---|---|---|---|
| BorderStyle | = 0 'None | Height | = 4245 |
| Left | = 945 | ScaleMode | = 3 'Pixel |
| Top | = 495 | Width | = 5865 |

*Object: Picture Box*
*Object Name: ArtWork*

| | | | |
|---|---|---|---|
| BackColor | = &H00FFFFFF& | BorderStyle | = 0 'None |
| ClipControls | = 0 'False | FontName | = "Arial" |
| FontSize | = 12 | Height | = 2325 |
| Left | = within PictureMask | Top | = within PictureMask |
| Width | = 3570 | | |

*Object: Picture Box*
*Object Name: ScaleBox*

| | | | |
|---|---|---|---|
| Height | = 330 | Left | = within Artwork |
| Top | = within Artwork | Visible | = 0 'False |
| Width | = 330 | | |

*Object: Picture Box*
*Object Name: Handle  8 indexed controls*

| | | | |
|---|---|---|---|
| BackColor | = &H000000FF& | BorderStyle | = 0 'None |
| Height | = 120 | Index | = 0 through 7 |
| Left | = within Artwork | MousePointer | = 2 'Cross |
| ScaleHeight | = 120 | ScaleWidth | = 120 |
| Top | = within Artwork | Visible | = 0 'False |
| Width | = 120 | | |

*Object: Picture Box*
*Object Name: BezNode2*

| | | | |
|---|---|---|---|
| BackColor | = &H0000C000& | BorderStyle | = 0 'None |
| Height | = 105 | Left | = with Artwork |
| ScaleHeight | = 105 | ScaleWidth | = 105 |
| Top | = within Artwork | Visible | = 0 'False |
| Width | = 105 | | |

*Object: Picture Box*
*Object Name: BezNode1*

| | | | |
|---|---|---|---|
| BackColor | = &H0000C000& | BorderStyle | = 0 'None |
| Height | = 105 | Left | = within Artwork |
| ScaleHeight | = 105 | ScaleWidth | = 105 |
| Top | = within Artwork | Visible | = 0 'False |
| Width | = 105 | | |

*Object: Picture Box*
*Object Name: BezHandle2*

| | | | |
|---|---|---|---|
| BackColor | = &H00FF00FF& | BorderStyle | = 0 'None |
| Height | = 105 | Left | = within Artwork |
| ScaleHeight | = 105 | ScaleWidth | = 105 |
| Top | = within Artwork | Visible | =  0 'False |
| Width | = 105 | | |

*Object: Picture Box*
*Object Name: BezHandle1*

| | | | |
|---|---|---|---|
| BackColor | = &H00FF00FF& | BorderStyle | = 0'None |
| Height | = 105 | Left | = within Artwork |
| ScaleHeight | = 105 | ScaleWidth | = 105 |

*continues*

**T**able 2.1. continued

| | | | |
|---|---|---|---|
| Top | = within Artwork | Visible | = 0 'False |
| Width | = 105 | | |

*Object: Picture Box*
*Object Name: Node 4 indexed controls*

| | | | |
|---|---|---|---|
| BackColor | = &H00000000& | BorderStyle | = 0 'None |
| Height | = 90 | Index | = 0 through 3 |
| Left | = within Artwork | ScaleHeight | = 90 |
| ScaleWidth | = 90 | Top | = within Artwork |
| Visible | = 0 'False | Width | = 90 |

*Object: Label*
*Object Name: Txt*

| | | | |
|---|---|---|---|
| AutoSize | = -1 'True | BackColor | = &H00FFFFFF& |
| BackStyle | = 0 'Transparent | BorderStyle | = 1 'Fixed Single |
| Height | = 480 | Left | = within Artwork |
| Top | = within Artwork | Visible | = 0 'False |
| Width | = 15 | | |

*Object: Shape*
*Object Name: Shape2*

| | | | |
|---|---|---|---|
| BackColor | = &H00FF0000& | BackStyle | = 1 'Opaque |
| BorderStyle | = 0 'Transparent | Height | = 105 |
| Left | = within Artwork | Top | = within Artwork |
| Visible | = 0 'False | Width | = 105 |

*Object: Shape*
*Object Shape1*

| | | | |
|---|---|---|---|
| BackColor | = &H00FF0000& | BackStyle | = 1 'Opaque |
| BorderStyle | = 0 'Transparent | Height | = 105 |
| Left | = within Artwork | Top | = within Artwork |
| Visible | = 0 'False | Width | = 105 |

*Object: Picture Box*
*Object Name: ToolButtons*

| | | | |
|---|---|---|---|
| AutoSize | = -1 'True | BackColor | = &H00C0C0C0& |
| BorderStyle | = 0 'None | DrawMode | = 6 'Invert |
| Height | = 4320 | Left | = 0 |
| Picture | = Toolbar.BMP | ScaleHeight | = 288 |

|  |  |  |  |
|---|---|---|---|
| ScaleMode | = 3 'Pixel | ScaleWidth | = 36 |
| Top | = 45 | Width | = 540 |

*Object: Menu*
*Object Name: Menu_File*
        = "&File"

*Menu_FileSelection*
  Caption     = "&New"      Index     = 0

*Menu_FileSelection*
  Caption     = "&Open..."      Index     = 1

*Menu Menu_FileSelection*
  Caption     = "&Save"      Index     = 2
  Shortcut    = +{F12}

*Menu_FileSelection*
  Caption     = "Save &As..."      Index     = 3
  Shortcut    = {F12}

*Menu_FileSelection*
  Caption     = "&Print"      Index     = 4

*Menu_FileSelection*
  Caption     = "E&xit"      Index     = 5

*Menu_Edit*
  Caption     = "&Edit"

*Menu_EditSelection*
  Caption     ="&Delete"      Index     = 6

*Menu_Arrange*
  Caption     = "&Arrange"

*Menu_ArrangeSelection*
  Caption     = "To &Front"      Index     = 0

*Menu_ArrangeSelection*
  Caption     = "To &Back"      Index     = 1

*Menu_ArrangeSelection*
  Caption     = "POPUP MENU"      Checked     = -1 'True
  Index       = 3

*continues*

# The Artisan Program

**T**able 2.1. continued

*Menu_Color*
   Caption       = "&Color"

*Menu_ColorSelection*
   Caption       = "&Color Palette"     Index      = 0

*Menu_Palette*
   Caption       = "&Edit Palette"      Index      = 0

*Menu_Palette*
   Caption       = "&Default Palette"   Index      = 1

*Menu_Palette*
   Caption       = "&Custom Palette"    Index      = 2

*Menu_Palette*
   Caption       = "Save As Custom"    Index      = 3

*Menu_ColorSelection*
   Caption       = "-"                      Index      = 1

*Menu_ColorSelection*
   Caption       = "Show &Rulers"      Checked    = -1 'True
   Index = 2

## Defining Variables, Arrays, and Structures

The following example defines an array with three elements:

```
Dim Varname(1 To 3)%
```

An *array* is a representation of a table stored in memory. Think of it as an indexed chart. You store your information in this chart by declaring the statement Dim followed by any letter or word that you choose to represent the subject. The chart heading is called the *variable*.

After the variable name, place the number of index arrays in parentheses, (). Each array entry is also a variable that can hold information. Think of each array element as a cell in your chart.

A single cell entry in a variable can hold only so much information before it requires a larger cell block. For this reason, you need to tell the variable what size cell is required to hold the information. The size of the cell is called the data type. The smallest data type you can use in a cell is called an *integer*. The following is an example:

```
Dim CH As Integer
```

In this example, CH can store any size value that is within the range of an integer. Visual Basic uses signed integer values that range between -32,768 and 32,767.

The following line enables you to store this value in the variable CH:

```
CH = 27425 + 5342
```

However, you cannot store the following value because it exceeds the integer's range by 1:

```
CH = 27425 + 5343
```

One byte can hold a value up to 255. An integer uses 2 bytes. These bytes are called the *low byte* and *high byte*. For example, low byte + (256×high byte) = the total value, or:

```
255 + (256 x 255) = 65535-32768 to 32767 = 65535
```

If you exceed the range of a data type, Visual Basic issues an overflow error. You must then store your variable in a larger cell. Larger data type cells are named long, single, double, currency, string, and user-defined (type).

## Data Types

Rather than type the data type's full name (for example, integer), you can use its short form after each Dim statement,

| *Data type* | *Size* |
| --- | --- |
| Integer % | 2 bytes |
| Long & | 4 bytes |
| Single ! | 4 bytes |
| Double # | 8 bytes |
| Currency @ | 8 bytes |
| String 4 bytes $ | *1 byte |

*Per character to approximately 65,535 (usually 63,000 characters)

Refer to the Visual Basic Language Reference Book Data Types for range values for each of the previously listed data types.

In short, integer and long are used for whole numbers, single and double for decimal points, string for text, and currency for money.

*Index arrays* are extensions of your indexed charts. This means you are to define more cell blocks under your variable name:

```
Dim Txt(1 to 200) As String
```

In this example, you can store up to 200 text entries under a chart heading called Txt. (1 to 200) defines the index number to which each text string is located.

The BoundingBox_MouseUp procedure, like the one used in Listing 2.4, uses this type of index array to store the attributes of almost every object drawn.

# The Artisan Program

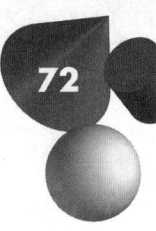

**L**isting 2.4. The `BoundingBox_Up` procedure.

```
Sub BoundingBox_Up (X1, Y1, X2, Y2)
If MoveMouse() = True Then
    Total = Total + 1: B = Total
    StatusLabel.Caption = Format$(B)

    LineWidth(B) = ArtWork.DrawWidth
    W(B) = X1: E(B) = X2: N(B) = Y1: S(B) = Y2
        Select Case CurrentTool
            Case PointerTool
                Exit Sub
        Case BézierTool
            Exit Sub
        Case ZoomTool
            Exit Sub
        Case LineTool
            FlagLine(B) = B
            Nodes
        Case BoxTool
            FlagBox(B) = B
            FillValue(B) = 1
            Nodes
        Case CircleTool
            FlagCircle(B) = B
            FillValue(B) = 1
            Nodes
        Case TextTool
            ' no code needed here
    End Select
End If
End Sub
```

Most variables declared for the Artisan program have an index array of (`Limit`), where `Limit` represents 1,000 elements. The last index is 999 because 0 counts as the name of the first cell.

## User-Defined Data Type Variables

User-defined type variables are similar to array variables except they have user-defined subheadings (subscripts) to retrieve or store data. You can use multiple subheads to define data. Most API graphics functions don't work unless you use a user-defined `Type` structure. These data types can point to the variable name and extract from a list of values. The following is a `Type` structure example:

```
Type PointAPI
. X As Integer
. Y As Integer
End Type
```

Normally, a declared variable such as `Dim DT As Integer` would give `DT` the capability to store any single integer value. If you changed the variable data type from `Integer` to a name such as `PointAPI` to read `Dim DT As PointAPI`, `DT` would could store two values. In this case, you call the two value holders *X* and *Y* and declare them as integers.

Rather than use X = 208, use DTs (*X*) value field = X, You now could assign 208 to DT like this:

```
DT.X = 208
```

The . point tells the program that a data field called x exists. Also, remember that you made a field called Y, so you could assign it a value:

DT.Y = 387

You must put a user-defined Type in the Declaration section of a module form (or a .BAS file).

## Declaring Variables for the Artisan Program

Listing 2.5 shows that the general Declaration section for the Artisan form is divided into three parts. You will need the ARTISAN7.BAS file (Appendix A) module declaration and procedures for global variable and constant values.

**Listing 2.5. Declaration section of Artisan's main form.**

```
Declarations
DefInt A-Z
Const Limit = 1000
Dim Draw As Integer
Dim FillValue(Limit) As Integer 'No Fill
Dim LineValue(Limit) As Integer 'No Line
Dim OFFSETx, OFFSETy, PtInRectBasic As Integer
Dim WIDE, HIGH As Integer 'Monitor Type
Dim PixelX, PixelY As Integer
Dim SSM As Single 'Side Scroll Move
Dim BSM As Single 'Bottom Scroll Move
Dim LastMove As Integer
Dim LastMenu As Integer
Dim FlagMove As Integer
Dim V As Integer 'Ruler Guide Lines
Dim TGL As Integer
Dim NewGuideLine As Integer
Dim GuideX(Limit) As Long
Dim GuideY(Limit) As Long
Dim Zoom As Integer 'Zoom Offsets
Dim NodeZoom As Integer
Dim Scaling As Integer
Dim OldSW As Double 'Scales
Dim OldSH As Double
Dim OldRH As Single 'Rulers
Dim OldRW As Single
Dim PerSW As Single 'Percentage of scales
Dim PerSH As Single
Dim Xstr As String, Ystr As String
Dim OutLineColor(Limit) As Long
Dim PaintColor(Limit) As Long
Dim LineWidth(Limit) As Integer
Dim TextX, TextY As Integer ' Text Values
Dim FlagAlign(Limit) As Integer
Dim OFFSET(Limit) As Integer
Dim TextSize(Limit) As Single
Dim TextFont(Limit) As String
Dim TextBold(Limit) As Integer
Dim TextItalic(Limit) As Integer
Dim Storedtext(Limit) As String
```

## The Artisan Program

Figure 2.3 shows some standard object attributes.

**F**igure 2.3.
*Some standard object attributes.*

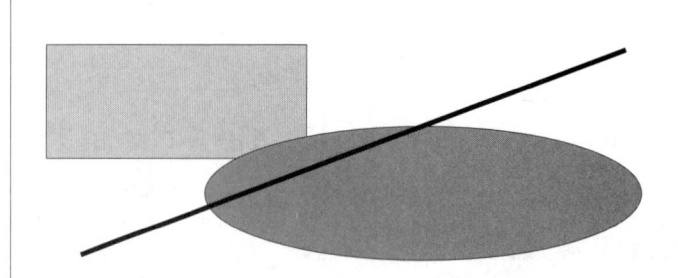

```
Variables used to store boxes, circles, and lines:
W, N, E, S = Bounding box dimensions
FlagBox, FlagLine, FlagCircle = Objects in bounding box
Radius, XCenter, YCenter, Aspect = Circle requirements
```

**DefInt A-Z:** Requires that all variables with the names A through Z be integer by default.

**Const Limit:** 1,000 objects or bounding boxes that can be drawn in this program before the index tables are full. You can increase this number; however, you may be restricted by Visual Basic's data limitations or memory.

**Draw:** True or false, used to skip UpdateObjects for quick redraw time.

**FillValue:** The FillStyle setting for each object, usually 0 (solid) or 1 (transparent).

**LineValue:** The DrawStyle setting for objects. Because DrawWidth cannot equal 0, an object with no outline must be set to DrawStyle 5 (invisible) to achieve the drawing style.

**OFFSETx, OFFSETy, PtInRectBasic:** Used with the MoveObject procedure.

**WIDE and HIGH:** Used to switch monitor resolution. VGA and SVGA are usually 96 pixels per inch.

**PixelX and PixelY:** Represent the TwipsPerPixelX and TwipsPerPixelY values as defined in the Visual Basic Reference language guide.

**SSM (side scroll move) and BBM** (bottom scroll move): Offsets used for scrollbars when moving Artwork and Rulers picture boxes.

**LastMove:** Tells which object last had handles visible when UpdateObjects loops to redraw all objects.

**LastMenu:** Tells what menu to show on a right mouse click. The last menu you selected will be shown when you click the right mouse button.

**FlagMove:** Tells the program you are moving an object so it will not draw a new object. This is a T/F (True/False) value.

**V (value), TGL (total guidelines), NewGuideLine, GuideX, and GuideY:** Used to store the X,Y positions of pulldown ruler guides.

**Zoom-PerSH:** Manual offsets used to rescale controls after a zoom.

**Xstr and Ystr:** String variables used to display the X,Y coordinates of the mouse as it moves around the screen.

**OutLineColor:** Color index of the color used to pen an outline around an object.

**PaintColor:** Color index of the color used to brush or fill the inside of an object.

**LineWidth:** Outline width of an object. LineWidth must be at least one unit in width for all objects; if an object has no outline, use LineValue to flag it as transparent.

**TextX and TextY:** Current X and Y positions used to draw the first line of text. These aren't really needed because CurrentX and CurrentY do the same thing. TextX and TextY are used as a safeguard only.

**FlagAlign:** Used to left-, center-, or right-align text. The values are 0 = left, 6 = center, and 2 = right alignment.

**OFFSET:** TextWidth value used so that FlagAlign will position correctly at the CurrentX and CurrentY of the text cursor.

**TextFont:** The font family name for each string typed in a bounding box.

**TextSize:** The point size of each string typed.

**TextBold:** Flags the text bold. Can be on or off.

**TextItalic:** Flags the text italic. Can be on or off.

**StoredText:** Stores the entire text string for each text object.

Figure 2.4 shows some standard text object attributes.

**Figure 2.4.**
*Standard text object attributes.*

### Attributes of this text if it had been typed on the screen

FlagAlign = 6 (centered); OFFSET = TextWidth \2
TextFont = Lydian; TextSize = 18 point
TextBold = True; TextItalic = False
StoredText = Stores the text string
W, N, E, S = Bounding box dimensions
PaintColor = Color of font
FlagText = Type of object in bounding box

# The Artisan Program

```
Dim B As Integer 'Current Object (Bounding Box)
Dim Total As Integer ' Total Number of Objects
Dim X1 As Long
Dim Y1 As Long
Dim X2 As Long
Dim Y2 As Long
Dim XX1 As Long
Dim YY1 As Long
Dim XX2 As Long
Dim YY2 As Long
Dim W(Limit) As Long 'West or Left
Dim E(Limit) As Long 'East or Right
Dim N(Limit) As Long 'North or Top
Dim S(Limit) As Long 'South or Bottom
Dim FlagBézier(Limit) As Integer
Dim FlagLine(Limit) As Integer
Dim FlagBox(Limit) As Integer
Dim FlagCircle(Limit) As Integer
Dim FlagText(Limit) As Integer
Dim Radius As Integer
Dim XCenter As Single
Dim YCenter As Single
Dim Aspect As Single
Dim SideRuler As Integer
Dim TopRuler As Integer
Dim X1Ruler As Integer
Dim Y1Ruler As Integer
Dim X2Ruler As Integer
Dim Y2Ruler As Integer
Dim DeleteObject As Integer
'Bézier Curve
Declare Function Polyline Lib "GDI" (ByVal hDC%, P As POINTS, [CI:CCC]
ByVal NUM_PTS%) As Integer
Const MAX_POINTS = 33
Dim P_Index(1 To MAX_POINTS) As POINTS
Dim BezErase As Integer
Dim ShowDotted As Integer
Dim P As Integer
```

**Dim B:** The main and most important variable in this program because it represents a number assigned to an object when it's first drawn. Every object is located within a bounding box (object), so I named this variable B (for box) to save on the amount of typing required.

**Dim Total:** The total of all bounding boxes that you have drawn. You use Total plus B to increase the total count of bounding box objects drawn to date.

**B = Total + 1:** This increases the number each time a new object is drawn. The next statement, Total = B, makes sure of this. If the third object you draw happens to be a rectangle, for example, all index headings associated with that object would equal B; all values would then be stored in index number 3. Examples of some attributes associated with rectangle number 3 are OutLineColor(3), PaintColor(3) and its position on the screen, (W(3), N(3), E(3), and S(3)).

**X1, X2, Y1, Y2, XX1, XX2, YY1, and YY2:** Temporary screen coordinates used to erase the last position of an object when it is moved to another location, or when drawing a new object.

**W, N, E, and S:** The next most important variables in this program. They represent the four position points of each bounding box that each object is within. W represents the west side of the box, N the north, E the east, and S the south. Each value represents the diagonal corners of each box, but this can be visually confusing. The values also can switch, depending on which direction you start (for instance, MouseDown to draw an object) and end (or, MouseUp), or when you flip an object.

**FlagBézier, FlagLine, FlagBox, FlagCircle, and FlagText:** TRUE or FALSE flags are used to update an object. If the fourth object you draw is a circle, for example, the FlagCircle index would be set to 4. Remember that B will equal 4 as soon as the fourth object is drawn. The UpDateObject procedure (Listing 2.6) uses these variable names to know which objects must be redrawn.

**L**isting 2.6. The flag names used in the UpDateObjects procedure.

```
Sub UpdateObjects ()
LastMove = B
ArtWork.DrawMode = Copy_Pen
ArtWork.DrawStyle = Solid
ArtWork.AutoRedraw = True
If Draw = True Then GoTo SkipErase
ArtWork.DrawWidth = 20
ArtWork.Line (W(B), N(B))-(E(B), S(B)), White, BF
ArtWork.Line (XX2, YY2)-(XX1, YY1), White, BF: B = 1
.. UpdateDeskTop
Do While B Total + 1
. ArtWork.DrawWidth = LineWidth(B)
. If LineValue(B) 0 Then ArtWork.DrawStyle = 5 Else
➥. ArtWork.DrawStyle = Solid
SkipErase:
Select Case B
. Case FlagCircle(B)
.. X1 = W(B): Y1 = N(B): X2 = E(B): Y2 = S(B)
.. ArtWork.DrawWidth = LineWidth(B)
.. GoodCircle = PerfectCircle(X1, Y1, X2, Y2)
.. ArtWork.FillColor = PaintColor(B):
.. ArtWork.FillStyle = FillValue(B)
.. ArtWork.Circle (XCenter, YCenter), Radius,
➥.. OutLineColor(B), , , Aspect
.. ArtWork.FillColor = 0: ArtWork.FillStyle = 1

. Case FlagLine(B)
.. ArtWork.Line (W(B), N(B))-(E(B), S(B)), OutLineColor(B)
. Case FlagBox(B)
.. If FillValue(B) = 1 Then GoTo SkipFill
.. ArtWork.Line (W(B), N(B))-(E(B), S(B)), PaintColor(B), BF
SkipFill:
.. ArtWork.Line (W(B), N(B))-(E(B), S(B)), OutLineColor(B), B
. Case FlagBézier(B)
.. p1.X = p1X(B): p1.Y = p1Y(B): p2.X = p2X(B): p2.Y = p2Y(B)
```

*continues*

## Listing 2.6. continued

```
..    h1.X = h1X(B): h1.Y = h1Y(B): h2.X = h2X(B): h2.Y = h2Y(B)
..    ArtWork.ForeColor = OutLineColor(B)
..    BezDraw
.   Case FlagText(B)
..    ArtWork.CurrentX = OFFSET(B): ArtWork.CurrentY = N(B)
..    SaveScaleLeft = ArtWork.ScaleLeft
..    ArtWork.ScaleLeft = -ArtWork.CurrentX + Scaling
..    ArtWork.FontName = TextFont(B)
..    ArtWork.ForeColor = PaintColor(B)
..    ArtWork.FontSize = TextSize(B) * TextPoint
..    ArtWork.FontBold = TextBold(B)
..    ArtWork.FontItalic = TextItalic(B)
..    wFlag = FlagAlign(B)
..    TA = SetTextAlign(ArtWork.hDC, wFlag)
..    ArtWork.Print Storedtext(B)
..    ArtWork.ScaleLeft = SaveScaleLeft
End Select
If Draw = True Then Draw = False:
➥..    ArtWork.AutoRedraw = False : B = LastMove: Exit Sub
.  B = B + 1
Loop
B = LastMove
.  ArtWork.AutoRedraw = False
.  ArtWork.DrawWidth = 1
.  ArtWork.DrawStyle = Solid
If DeleteObject = True Then Exit Sub
If CurrentTool = 1 Or CurrentTool = 2 Then Exit Sub
If SideRuler = True Or TopRuler = True Then Exit Sub
.  Handles
.  Nodes
End Sub
```

**Radius, XCenter, YCenter, and Aspect:** Values needed while making a circle or ellipsis using the `Circle` statement. An example is `Circle(XCenter, YCenter),Radius,,,Aspect`.

**SideRuler and TopRuler:** True or false if a ruling guideline is being pulled from one of the two rulers. If so, set the value to `True`, which disables drawing on-screen (which could occur with a `MouseMove` event). You also can use `Artwork.Enabled = False`.

**X1Ruler, Y1Ruler, X2Ruler, and Y2Ruler:** Temporary line position points for drawing a ruler guideline. These are used in the `Line` statement as are X1, Y1, X2, and Y2.

**DeleteObject:** Used to exit `UpdateObjects` so the handles and nodes are not displayed after an object is deleted.

**Declare Function Polyline:** An API Windows function to draw a line, similar to a `Line` statement using the `Step` keyword option or the `DRAW` statement in DOS versions of the BASIC language.

**Const MAX_POINTS:** The total number of points to store on a Bézier curve.

**P_Index:** The index that holds the Bézier points. Each curve's control points are stored using a `Type` variable called `POINTS`, which can group the X and Y coordinates to a single index number.

**BezErase:** A flag to erase the first image of Bézier curve when a move is in session.

**ShowDotted:** Toggles the display of the dotted Bézier handle lines. True shows dotted lines.

**P:** The starting point of indexed arrays. Use as a fail-safe error handler only.

Figure 2.5 shows the standard attributes for drawing a Bézier curve.

**Figure 2.5.**
*The standard attributes needed for drawing a Bézier curve.*

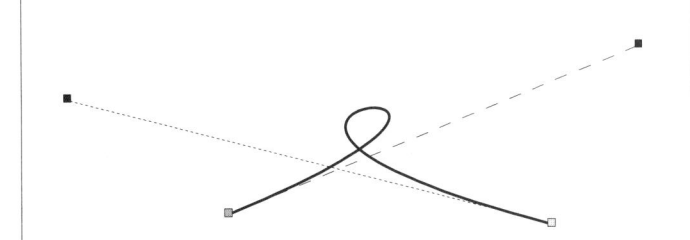

Variables used to store a Bézier curve:
p1, p2, h1, h2, = Four control points
q0, q1, q2, r0, r1, s0 = Temporary *deCasteljau* division
ShowDotted = Visible property of dotted handle lines
W, N, E, S = Bounding box dimensions

```
Dim p1 As POINTS 'Bézier control Points / Handles
Dim h1 As POINTS
Dim h2 As POINTS
Dim p2 As POINTS
Dim p1X(Limit) As Long
Dim p1Y(Limit) As Long
Dim p2X(Limit) As Long
Dim p2Y(Limit) As Long
Dim h1X(Limit) As Long
Dim h1Y(Limit) As Long
Dim h2X(Limit) As Long
Dim h2Y(Limit) As Long
Dim C1(1 To MAX_POINTS) As POINTS
Dim D1(1 To MAX_POINTS) As POINTS 'Curve Points
Dim D2(1 To MAX_POINTS) As POINTS
Dim D3(1 To MAX_POINTS) As POINTS
Dim E1(1 To MAX_POINTS) As POINTS
Dim E2(1 To MAX_POINTS) As POINTS
Const YELLOW = &HFFFF&
```

**p1, h1, p2, and h2:** The four control points of a Bézier curve. P1 = Bézier node point 1, P2 = Bézier node point 2, H1 = Bézier handle 1, and H2 = Bézier handle 2. They are stored in a data type called Points that holds the *X, Y* coordinate points. To get each value, use the structures P1.X, P1.Y, H1.X, H1.Y, P2.X, P2.Y, H2.X, and H2.Y. If node 1 (P1) used in the curve was located at X coordinate 1004 and Y at coordinate 2205, P1.X would equal 1004 and P1.Y, 2205. You cannot pass these values as

## The Artisan Program

arguments (such as `Sub BezDivide P1.X%, P1.Y%`) to a procedure in Visual Basic. You can, however, do this: `Dim P1 As Points`, and then have a `Sub`'s arguments look like that in the following example:

`Sub BezDivide (P1 As Points, Etc...)`

**p1X, p1Y, p2X, p2Y, h1X, h1Y, h2X, and h2Y:** These values are used to store the X and Y position, which reside in the POINTS type structure. You will need these values to update recursive Bézier curve points.

**D1, D2, D3, E1, E2, and C1:** The actual divided points of a Bézier curve. The most significant is C1, which is an actual curve point after each *deCasteljau* divide. (See Figure 2.6.) When 33 such points are calculated, the curve is plotted and you connect the dots or points using a `Line` statement or the API `Polyline` function. For more information, see the Bézier curve section in Chapter 3.

**Figure 2.6.**
*The order in which curve points are plotted.*

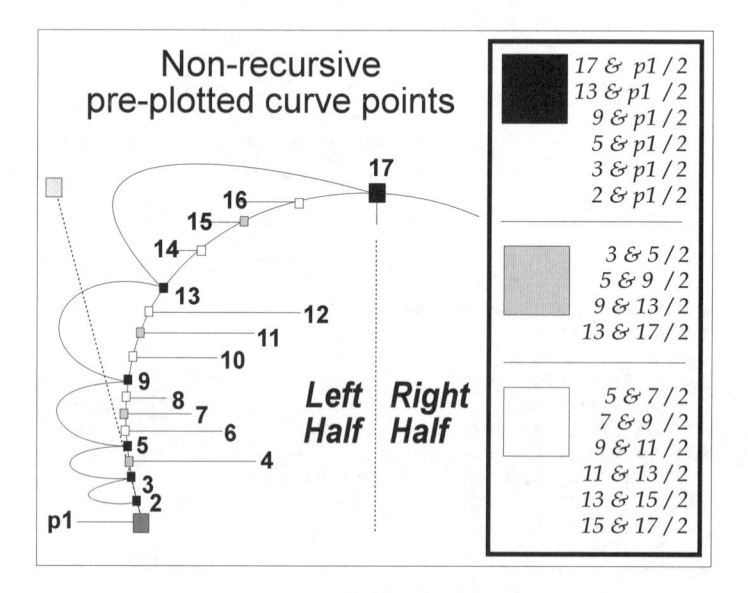

**Non-recursive pre-plotted curve points**

17 & p1 / 2
13 & p1 / 2
9 & p1 / 2
5 & p1 / 2
3 & p1 / 2
2 & p1 / 2

3 & 5 / 2
5 & 9 / 2
9 & 13 / 2
13 & 17 / 2

5 & 7 / 2
7 & 9 / 2
9 & 11 / 2
11 & 13 / 2
13 & 15 / 2
15 & 17 / 2

Left Half | Right Half

**Const Yellow:** The hexadecimal number for the color yellow. The dotted lines you see when moving a curve handle are cyan. The color yellow will appear cyan when the `DrawMode` is set to drawing pixels in `Xor` mode. The `Xor` mode will restore any background color that the dotted line may pass over as it is being moved.

> **NOTE** Each chart heading represents a variable name. The value of variable B assigns the index number (object number) and fills that cell (array) with the correct attribute value that belongs to that object. You could make one huge multidimensional array to handle everything or a large user-defined `Type` structure. API statements could also eliminate some of the arrays used in this program.

**F**igure 2.7.
*An example of seven objects' attribute arrays.*

| T | B | W | E | N | S | FLAG | FillValue | PaintColor | LineValue | OutLineColor | LineWidth |
|---|---|---|---|---|---|------|-----------|------------|-----------|--------------|-----------|
| 1 | 1 | 283 | 473 | 245 | 384 | FlagBox | True | StatusPaint | True | StatusColor | 1 |
| 2 | 2 | 652 | 924 | 522 | 619 | FlagLine | False | Not Used | True | Not Used | 4 |
| 3 | 3 | 311 | 650 | 570 | 679 | FlagCircle | True | StatusPaint | True | StatusColor | 2 |
| 4 | 4 | 826 | 961 | 251 | 525 | FlagBox | True | StatusPaint | False | StatusColor | 1 |
| 5 | 5 | 656 | 862 | 274 | 452 | FlagCircle | False | StatusPaint | True | StatusColor | 2 |

| T | B | W | E | N | S | FLAG | FillValue | PaintColor | LineValue | OutLineColor | LineWidth |
|---|---|---|---|---|---|------|-----------|------------|-----------|--------------|-----------|
| 6 | 6 | 403 | 696 | 428 | 510 | FlagText | True | StatusPaint | False | StatusColor | 1 |
|   |   | FlagAlign | OFFSET | TextFont | TextSize | TextBold | TextItalic | | StoredText | | |
|   |   | TA_Center | Wide \ 2 | Univ_Roman | 120 | True | False | | Label.Caption Text (Txt.Caption) | | |

| T | B | W | E | N | S | FLAG | FillValue | PaintColor | LineValue | OutLineColor | LineWidth |
|---|---|---|---|---|---|------|-----------|------------|-----------|--------------|-----------|
| 7 | 7 | 320 | 498 | 443 | 591 | FlagBezier | False | Not Used | True | StatusColor | 2 |
|   |   | p1.X | p1.Y | p2.X | p2.Y | h1.X | h1.Y | h2.X | h2.Y | | |
|   |   | 329 | 566 | 492 | 556 | 357 | 441 | 407 | 581 | | |

**F**igure 2.8.
*How seven objects would appear if you used the table values in Figure 2.6.*

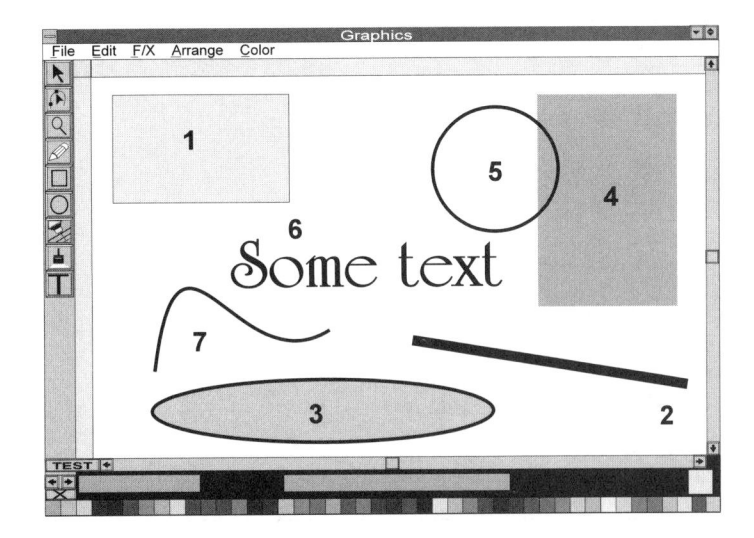

# Default Form Loading Values at Startup

Find out what type of monitor you are using so that all the controls are placed in the correct position when the form is first loaded or resized. I used a 15-inch SVGA monitor at 800×600 resolution—which is less than 12,000 twips wide—and a 19-inch Hercules type at 1664×1200 resolution, which is more than 19,000 twips wide.

A *twip* is 1,440 units per inch (1440\15, or 96); most VGA type monitors are 96 pixels per inch, whereas some dual-page monitors are 118 pixels per inch (roughly 1440\12, or 120). You can use less than 19,000 units as a base ScreenWidth for most VGA monitors. You also can resort to the API called GetDeviceCaps to find the logical pixels per inch using the index references—LogPixelsX and LogPixelsY.

The following is an example using API GetDeviceCaps:

```
Declare Function GetDeviceCaps% Lib "GDI" (ByVal hDC%, [CI:CCC]
ByVal nIndex%)
Const LOGPIXELSX = 88: Const LOGPIXELSY = 90
```

# The Artisan Program

Call the API `GetDeviceCaps` function with this sample statement:

```
X = GetDeviceCaps(Form1.hDC, LOGPIXELSX)
Y = GetDeviceCaps(Form1.hDC, LOGPIXELSY)
Print X: Print Y
```

**Listing 2.7.** Startup values when the program begins.

```
Sub Form_Load
PixelX = Screen.TwipsPerPixelX: PixelY = Screen.TwipsPerPixelY
WIDE = Screen.Width \ PixelX: HIGH = Screen.Height \ PixelY
 NewGuideLine = False
 ArtWork.FontSize = 12: Txt.FontSize = 12
Artwork.FontName = txt.FontName
 WindowState = 2
 TextPoint = 1
 PerSH = 1: PerSW = 1
 StatusColor.BackColor = Black
 LineWidth(B) = 1
 PenColor = Black
 MoveFlag = False
 LastMenu = 3
 Convert_Curve = False
 Convert_Line = False
 P = 1: B = 0: Total = 0
 ArtWork.Enabled = False
 ArtWork.BackColor = White
 ArtWork.FillColor = White
 ArtWork.FillStyle = TransParent
 VScroll.Value = 0: HScroll.Value = 0
 Color_INI
 Load TextForm
 KeyPreview = True
End Sub
```

For drawing purposes, it's best to use twips as the `ScaleMode` instead of pixels or other units of measure. However, most API routines require measurement in pixels. You can convert twips to pixels by dividing the twip units by 15 or 12, depending on your monitor type; or use the `TwipsPerPixelX` and `TwipsPerPixelY` methods.

**PIXELX and PIXELY:** `TwipsPerPixelX` and `TwipsPerPixelY` statements can accomplish the conversion and be used along with the `Screen.Width` and `Screen.Height` to get most monitors' pixels-per-inch value. If not, see the API `GetDeviceCaps` function.

**NewGuideLine:** A dotted ruling line that is pulled from the rulers. This line is used to count the number of ruling lines on-screen when updating objects.

**ArtWork.FontSize:** Sets the desktop default font size to 12 points.

**Txt.FontSize:** Sets the `TxtLabel`'s default font size to 12 points.

**WindowState:** Maximizes the main form to fit the entire screen.

**TextPoint:** Used to multiply the point size of text by a set factor during Zoom In or Zoom Out using the ZoomTool. During a Zoom In or Zoom Out, the TextPoint value is an approximate enlargement or reduction percentage. The true values are in one-thousand of a percent precision when used. Using the value 1 multiplies this offset by 1; hence, there is no change, as shown in Listing 2.8.

**Listing 2.8. Partial listing of the ZoomBar procedure.**

```
Sub ZoomBar_MouseDown (Button%, Shift%, X !, Y!)
Select Case CurrentZoom
. Case ZoomIn 'First Button
..  If Zoom_Out = True Or Zoom_In = True Then Beep: Exit Sub
..  ArtWork.AutoRedraw = True: ArtWork.Cls:
..  ArtWork.AutoRedraw = False
..  Scaling = 3750: Zoom_In = True: Zoom_Out = False
*** Approximate enlargement of text point size ***
..  Zoom = -48: NodeZoom = -21: TextPoint = 1.7
..  Txt.FontSize = Txt.FontSize * TextPoint
..  ZoomScale 2, 3750, 3750, -7500, -6375
. Case ZoomOut 'Second Button
..  If Zoom_Out = True Or Zoom_In = True Then Beep: Exit Sub
..  ArtWork.AutoRedraw = True: ArtWork.Cls:
..  ArtWork.AutoRedraw = False
..  Scaling = -5000: Zoom_In = False: Zoom_Out = True
*** Approximate reduction of text point size ***
..  Zoom = 65: NodeZoom = 28: TextPoint = .65
..  Txt.FontSize = Txt.FontSize * TextPoint
..  ZoomScale 2, -5000, -5000, 10000, 8500
. Case ZoomAll 'Third Button
. Case ZoomPage 'Fourth Button
..  ArtWork.AutoRedraw = True: ArtWork.Cls:
..  ArtWork.AutoRedraw = False
..  ArtWork.Scale: PerSW = 1: PerSH = 1
*** reset the TextPoint value to 1, normal text point size ***
..  Zoom = 0: NodeZoom = 0: TextPoint = 1
..  Scaling = 0: Zoom_In = False: Zoom_Out = False
'Note: Partial listing only !
. ZoomScale 2, 0, 0, 0, 0
End Select
End Sub
```

**PerSH and PerSW:** Used to divide scale units. A default value of 0 would trigger a Divide By Zero error.

**StatusColor.BackColor:** Initializes the pen color to black, which is the default.

**LineWidth(B):** Sets to value 1 at startup. Having LineWidth(B) equal 0 or less causes an error because this variable also sets the draw width. DrawWidth properties cannot be less than 1 in value.

**PenColor(0):** Initializes the pen index to 0 (or a runtime error will occur).

**MoveFlag:** No objects are currently being moved, so the value is set to False.

**LastMenu:** The Arrange menu is displayed when the right mouse is clicked.

**ConvertCurve:** No line is being converted to a curve, so you can turn this off.

**P = 1: B = 0: Total = 0:** Initializes the object number to 0 (resulting in no object).

**ArtWork.Enabled:** Means that the mouse will not interfere with the `Rulers_Paint` event.

**ArtWork.BackColor:** Means that the drawing area is set to paper white.

**ArtWork.FillColor and ArtWork.FillStyle:** Defaults for the first object drawn. For example, a box is filled with white and then set to transparent or hollow.

**VScroll.Value and HScroll.Value:** Means that the scrollbar tab is centered in each scroll.

**Color_INI:** Loads the default colors in the color bar palette.

**Load TextForm:** Puts the `TextForm` in memory because a large number of fonts in your system can slow down the program during runtime.

**KeyPreview:** Keyboard events are invoked for the form first then for the control that has the focus (for example, `KeyDown`, `KeyUp`, and `KeyPress`).

## Positioning the Control on the Artisan Form

The `Form_Resize` event shown in Listing 2.9 is used to position and size all the controls displayed when the program starts. The control being positioned is obvious by its generic name (for example, `Ruler(0)`, `Ruler(1)`, and `ToolButtons`). The `PictureMask` picture box is used as container control for the `Artwork` picture box. This enables scrolling of any pictures on the `Artwork` desktop. Masked controls are not visible when the form is made visible.

The `Move` statement used to reposition controls has the following structure:

*object*.Move Left, Top, Width, Height

**Listing 2.9.** `Form_Resize` repositions all controls on the Artisan form.

```
Sub Form_Resize ()
ToolButtons.ZOrder : StatusArea.ZOrder : ColorMask.ZOrder
'StatusArea picture box''''''
StatusArea.Visible = False
StatusArea.Move 0, 0, WIDE, 70
ColorMask.Move 0, 50, WIDE, 20
ColorBar.Move 0, 0, WIDE, 20
StatusColor.Move WIDE - 36, 20, 28, 28
StatusPaint.Move 2, 2, 24, 24
XYlabel.Move 36, 20, WIDE \ 5, 26
Statuslabel.Move (WIDE \ 2) - (Statuslabel.Width \ 2), 20, WIDE \ 3, 26
ColorScroll.Move 0, 20, 34, 17
No_Fill.Move 0, 37, 34, 13
TestButton.Move 0, 0, 56, 17
StatusArea.Visible = True
''''''''''''''''''''''''''''
ZoomBar.Move 64, ToolButtons.Top + 70, 128, 34
LineButtons.Move 64, ToolButtons.Top + 192, 256, 34
PaintButtons.Move 64, ToolButtons.Top + 224, 256, 34
PictureMask.Move -200, -250, WIDE + 400, HIGH + 400
ArtWork.Move 0, 0, PictureMask.Width, PictureMask.Height
```

```
RulerCross.Move 40, 0, 22, 22
Ruler(0).Move 40, PictureMask.Top, 22, PictureMask.Height 'Side Ruler
Ruler(1).Move PictureMask.Left, 0, PictureMask.Width, 22'Top ruler
Txt.Move 0, 0
ToolButtons.Move 0, 0, 40, HIGH
Vscroll.Move WIDE - 17, 22, 17, StatusArea.Top - 22
Hscroll.Move 56, 0, WIDE - 73, 17

ScaleBox.Move 3600, 3750, 330, 330
OldSW = ArtWork.ScaleWidth: OldSH = ArtWork.ScaleHeight
OldRW = 300: OldRH = 300

Ruler(0).Scale: Ruler(1).Scale
UpdateObjects
CurrentTool = 0
End Sub
```

**ToolButtons.ZOrder**: The ZOrder statements make the ToolButtons, StatusArea, and ColorMask controls appear on top of the desktop so they are not hidden by the rulers or the desktop drawing area.

While controls are resized, their visible properties can be set to False; so you do not see the disarray of positioning these controls. You should not make controls visible in Resize or Paint events because doing so will trigger the events to be called twice.

Figure 2.9 shows what the screen looks like after you run Form Resize.

**Figure 2.9.**
*After the* Form_Resize *is run, your screen should look like this illustration.*

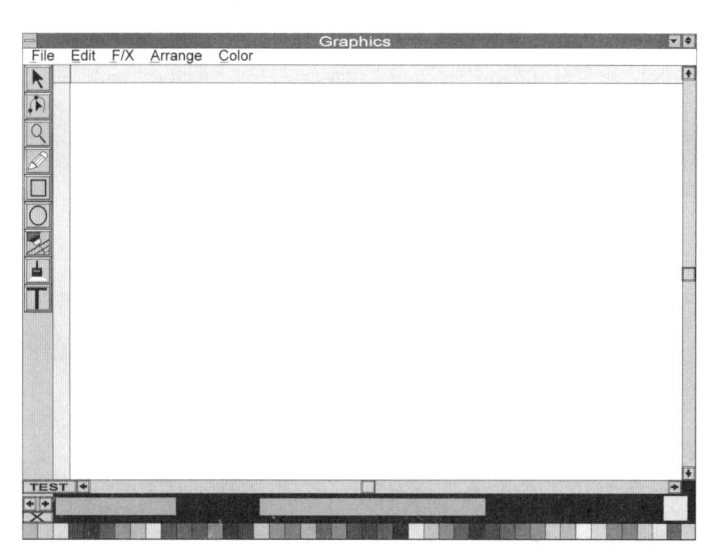

## Selecting a Drawing Tool for the Toolbox

The `ToolButtons` control lets you select a drawing tool. When you click a button, the image of the button is inverted to give the illusion of being pushed in. There are several ways to code for this effect; the Button program located in the 16MISC directory of the companion disk shows three examples.

The remainder of the `ToolButtons_MouseDown` code hides controls that might be visible when a different tool was selected. See Listing 2.10 for an example.

**Listing 2.10.** `ToolButton_MouseDown` changes a button's color so that the button appears pushed in.

```
Sub ToolButtons_MouseDown (Button%, Shift%, X As Single, Y As Single)
ArtWork.ForeColor = Black
ArtWork.MousePointer = 0
LastToolUsed = CurrentTool: NewTool = Y \ 32
 . If Y < 288 Then
 ..   ToolButtons.Line (0, CurrentTool * 32 + 1)-(31, CurrentTool * [CI:CCC]
 ..   32 + 31), , BF
 ..   ToolButtons.Line (0, NewTool * 32 + 1)-(31, NewTool * [CI:CCC]
 ..   32 + 31), , BF
 ..   CurrentTool = NewTool
 End If
Select Case CurrentTool
 . Case 1
 ...If BezHandle1.Visible Then Exit Sub
 ...If FlagBézier(B) = B Then ShowDotted = True: BezUpdate
 . Case 2
 ...ZoomBar.Visible = True
 . Case 6
 ...LineButtons.Visible = True
 . Case 7
 ..  PaintButtons.Visible = True
 . Case 8
 ..  ARTWORK.MousePointer = 2
End Select
If LastToolUsed = TextTool Then ReDrawText
If CurrentTool = 0 And Total > 0 Then
 . Nodes
 . Handles
Else
 . For R = 0 To 7
 ..  Handle(R).Visible = False
 . Next R
End If
If CurrentTool <> 1 And BezHandle1.Visible Then ShowDotted = [CI:CCC]
....False : BezUpdate
 . If CurrentTool <> 2 Then ZoomBar.Visible = False
 . If CurrentTool <> 6 Then LineButtons.Visible = False
 . If CurrentTool <> 7 Then PaintButtons.Visible = False
End Sub
```

**ArtWork.ForeColor:** ForeColor is the current pen's drawing color. It must always be reset to black before drawing another object. Otherwise, the new object's Outlinecolor would be the color last selected when using the ColorBar palette.

**LastToolUsed:** A flag to update the Paint event when the ZoomBar, LineButtons, and PaintButtons lose the focus after a tool selection is made.

**NewTool:** Y is the current Y mouse move position over the ToolButtons. Each icon drawing is 32 pixels high. The total number of icons (9) times their height (32) is 288. Y/32 returns the exact button number (0–9) of each button icon using this formula.

**CurrentTool = NewTool:** Is the current tool that performs the code associated with it. For example, if the box icon button were pressed, the mouse would be between Y values 128–160. The first Line statement inverses the last tool used to restore the look, and the next Line statement inverses the button icon picture for the reversed look. Finally, the CurrentTool = NewTool tells the following Select/Case CurrentTool statement which code to execute.

**Case 1:** BézierTool was selected. If the Bézier handle is visible, the dotted line connecting the handle to the Bézier node should be visible. Do nothing in this case. If the handle is not visible, the dotted line would be attached to nothing. If Showdotted line = True, call BezUpdate to erase the line.

**Case 2:** The ZoomBar currently isn't visible; so show it.

**Case 6:** The LineButtons currently aren't visible; so show them.

**Case 7:** The PaintButtons currently aren't visible; so show them.

**Case 8:** The TextTool was selected; so change the cursor to a cross shape.

The following section deals with the ToolButton_MouseDown event losing the focus of the ArtWork (if you were to click the ToolButton). For example, if the TextTool is selected and the end user has typed something on the desktop, you would need to update this text if you were to select another tool. Any handles or nodes that maybe visible would also have to be hidden.

**If LastToolUsed = TextTool:** Means that you probably have typed text; so you need to set all the types attributes using the ReDrawText procedure.

**If CurrentTool = 0 And Total > 0 Then:** You have selected the pointer tool; so highlight the current object by placing the nodes and handles around the object. Or, if you have selected a tool other than the pointer tool, there is no need to have the handles appear around the object.

**If CurrentTool <> (1):** Check to see if Bézier's dotted lines need erasing.

**If CurrentTool <> (2, 6, 7):** You need to hide the ZoomBar, LineButtons, and PaintButtons after you make a selection with one of them.

## Pushing in a Button when the Form is First Started

The `ToolButtons_Paint` event in Listing 2.11 draws an inverted box over the tool button you select. This will give the illusion that the button is pressed in.

Listing 2.11. Repainting an inverted tool button to restore its original look.
```
Sub ToolButtons_Paint ()
. ToolButtons.Line (0, CurrentTool * 32 + 1)-(31, CurrentTool *
➥....32 + 31), , BF
 End Sub
```

`CurrentTool` represents the selected drawing tool from the `ToolButtons` control. Every time you select a new tool, the `CurrentTool` value will equal the number that was assigned to that button's name. The button name and its value are listed in the general declaration section of the ARTISAN7.BAS file under the heading *Artisan's ToolPalette IDs*. The values range from 0 (top button) to 8 (bottom button).

## Clicking the Desktop with a Tool

When you click the Artwork picture box, nodes and handles will appear or disappear, depending on whether you touched an object or not. The program will then branch off to a procedure related to the currently selected tool. (See Listing 2.12.)

Listing 2.12. `Artwork_MouseDown` starts all drawing operations on the desktop.
```
Sub ArtWork_MouseDown (Button%, Shift %, X As Single, Y As Single)
ZoomBar.Visible = False
LineButtons.Visible = False : PaintButtons.Visible = False
If SideRuler = True Or TopRuler = True Then Exit Sub
If Button = Left_Button Then N_H_Clear
Select Case CurrentTool
. Case PointerTool
..   Find_Object X, Y
..   BoundingBox_Down X, Y
. Case BézierTool
..   If BezHandle1.Visible = True Then ShowDotted = False: BezUpdate
..   BoundingBox_Down X, Y
. Case LineTool To CircleTool
..   BoundingBox_Down X, Y
. Case TextTool
..   If Txt.Caption > "" Then Align = 0: ReDrawText
..   If Button = Left_Button Then

       txt.BorderStyle = 0
       Dim tm As TEXTMETRIC
       API = GetTextMetrics(Artwork.hDC, tm)
       Leading = (tm.tmExternalLeading + tm.tmInternalLeading) * PixelY
       txt.Left = X: txt.Top = Y - (txt.Height - Leading)
```

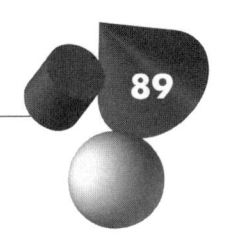

```
..    End If
End Select
If CurrentTool <> 1 Then BezNode1.Visible = False:
➥BezNode2.Visible = False
End Sub
```

If the `ZoomBar`, `LineButtons`, or `PaintButtons` are visible because of a `ToolButtons` selection and no selection is made in these popup tools, they must be hidden again. You also can put their visible properties in the `Lost_Focus` event.

> **If the SideRuler or TopRuler = True:** The user is pulling a ruler guide onto the page. Exit the subroutine, or the `PointerTool` will think you are drawing a marquee selection box.
>
> **CurrentTool:** The button currently selected in the `ToolButtons` control.
>
> **Case PointerTool:** The `Find_Object` procedure checks to see whether the mouse pointer was clicked within the bounding box of an object. If so, that procedure highlights the object by showing the nodes and handles.
>
> **BoundingBox_Down**: A routine that saves the current X and Y positions of the mouse click so drawing will start at these coordinates.
>
> **Case BézierTool:** If the handle of a Bézier curve is visible, the dotted line joining the handle and node is also visible. You need to erase this dotted line and hide the Bézier's handles and nodes if the user clicks on the Artwork desktop. Flag the dotted line to `False` and call `BezUpdate` to accomplish this feat.
>
> **Case TextTool:** Text is first placed on-screen inside a label control. Because a label is in Visual Basic's middle graphical layer, it cannot be sent to the back of a graphics method object. Therefore, you must convert the `Label.Caption` (the text you type) to graphical type. The `ReDrawText` procedure uses the `Print` statement to do this manually. In order to place the text at the correct text cursor position, you have to retrieve the leading and text height of the character being used. Using Visual Basic's `TextHeight` method will not retrieve the internal leading values, so the API `TextMetric` function is required. (Refer to Chapter 12, "The Text Alignment Program," for explanations on text properties.)
>
> **Txt.Left and Txt.Top**: Positions used to place the text on the desktop.

Finally, if the currently selected tool is the `BézierTool`, check to see whether the Bézier's nodes are visible. If so, make the nodes invisible.

## Dragging or Moving the Mouse on the Desktop

The `MouseMove` event will perform all move coordinate functions. It must also know if you are indeed drawing an object or dragging a ruler guideline from one of the two rulers. (See Listing 2.13.)

## The Artisan Program

**Listing 2.13.** `Artwork_MouseMove` calculates the mouse's coordinates.

```
Sub Artwork_MouseMove (Button%, Shift%, X As Single, Y As Single)
Xstr = Format$(X \ PIXELX, "000")
Ystr = Format$(Y \ PIXELY, "000")
XYLabel.Caption = "[" + Xstr + " , " + Ystr + "]"
RulerGuides Index, Button, Shift, X, Y
. If SideRuler = True Or TopRuler = True Then
.. GuideLines Index, X, Y
.. Exit Sub
. End If
If Button = Left_Button Then
. BoundingBox_Move Shift, X, Y
. X2 = X: Y2 = Y
. BoundingBox_Move Shift, X, Y
End If
End Sub
```

The X and Y positions are shown in the `XYLabel` located near the bottom-left of the screen. (See Figure 2.2.) You are working in twips, so dividing X and Y by the value of `PixelX`, `PixelY` gives you the caption in pixel units. This is the same as using `TwipsPerPixelX` and `TwipsPerPixelY`.

> **RulerGuides:** The routine that draws the moving lines in each ruler to give you a visual location of the position of the mouse's current X and Y positions.
>
> If the side `Ruler(0)` or top `Ruler(1)` were clicked, you call `GuideLines` to draw the dotted ruling lines on the page. Do this by dragging a ruler guideline from either ruler.
>
> **BoundingBox_Move:** Starts the graphical statements for the current drawing function (such as the `Box`, `Circle`, and `Line` functions). The `DrawMode` equals `Inverse` when the first image is drawn. Then, switch the starting *X, Y* (`MouseDown`) positions with X2 = X: Y2 = Y, which are the current mouse move X,Y positions. By forcing the start and end points to switch back and forth continuously, you draw two images for each mouse move, meaning that thousands of bounding boxes are drawn as you move the mouse. The `Inverse` property erases the second image of each move so that the illusion of a single stretching object is achieved. Remark out (') the `Inverse` statement and ensure that this is in progress. Remember to always draw the object first before switching the values. Otherwise, you may end up drawing thousands of invisible bounding boxes.

Figure 2.10 shows an elastic, drawn box.

**F**igure 2.10.
*An elastic, drawn box.*

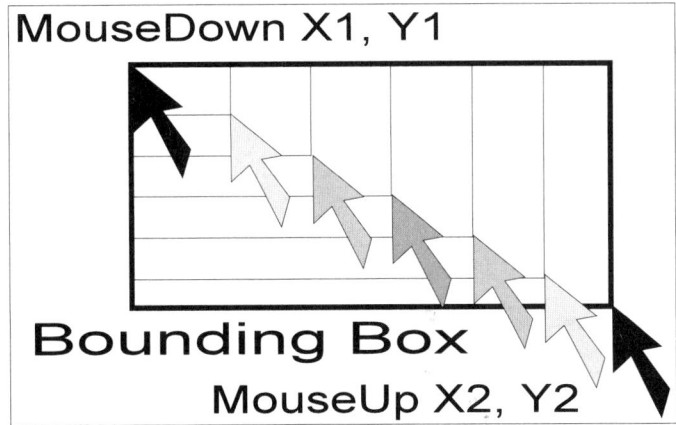

[Figure: Bounding box illustration showing MouseDown X1, Y1 at top-left and MouseUp X2, Y2 at bottom-right]

## Completing the Drawing

The MouseUp event draws the final object. If the right mouse button was clicked, a popup menu will appear that lists options available form the main menu of the Artisan form. (See Listing 2.14.)

**L**isting 2.14. `ArtWork_MouseUp` draws the final object on the desktop.

```
Sub Artwork_MouseUp (Button%, Shift%, X As Single, Y As Single)
If CurrentTool <> 8 Then ArtWork.MousePointer = 0
If SideRuler = True Or TopRuler = True Then
. Ruler_MouseUp Index, Button, Shift, X, Y
. Exit Sub
End If
If Button = Left_Button Then
. Select Case CurrentTool
.. Case PointerTool
....If FlagMove = True Then UpdateObjects:
➥....FlagMove = False: Exit Sub
....If Node(0).Visible Then Handles: Exit Sub
....If BezNode1.Visible Then Handles: Exit Sub
..... If MoveMouse() = True Then
......   ArtWork.Line (X1, Y1)-(X2, Y2), YELLOW, B
......   FindAllObjects X1, Y1, X2, Y2, X, Y
..... End If
. Case BézierTool
..  If MoveMouse() = True Then
....ArtWork.Line (X1, Y1)-(X2, Y2), YELLOW, B
```

*continues*

## The Artisan Program

**Listing 2.14. continued**

```
..   End If
.  Case ZoomTool
..     ''''''''''''''''''''''
.  Case LineTool To CircleTool
..   If MoveMouse() = True Then
....BoundingBox_Up X1, Y1, X2, Y2
....If B = Total Then Draw = True: UpdateObjects
..   End If
.  Case TextTool
..   Txt.BorderStyle = 1: Txt.Width = 15: Txt.Visible = True
.  End Select
ArtWork.DrawWidth = 1: ArtWork.DrawStyle = Solid
End If
If Button = 2 And Menu_ArrangeSelection(12).Checked
➥. And CurrentTool < 8 Then
..   Dim X_Y As POINTS : GetCursorPos X_Y
..   R = TrackPopupMenu(GetSubMenu(GetMenu(hWnd), LastMenu),
➥....0, X_Y.X, X_Y.Y, 0, hWnd, 0)
ElseIf CurrentTool = TextTool And Button = 2Then    Artwork.CurrentY = txt.Top
    TextForm.Show Modal
    If txt.Caption > "" Then ReDrawText

End If
End Sub
```

If Artwork's mouse pointer has been changed, put it back to its default setting.

If the side or top rulers have been clicked, finish drawing the dotted ruling guide line and then exit the subroutine.

If the mouse's left button was pressed, continue with the `Select/Case` statement; otherwise the right button (2) was clicked, and a popup menu will be displayed.

>   **Case PointerTool:** If the Shift key were pressed, you would be moving an object. Call `UpdateObjects` to draw the object at its new location. Turn the `FlagMove` off and then exit this routine so that no further drawing statements will execute.

If a standard node is visible, you have selected an object. Therefore, no `UpDateObjects` is required and you can exit the subroutine.

If a Bézier node is visible, you have just finished working on a curve; highlight it with the handles and exit the subroutine.

If you moved the mouse more than 45 twips in any direction, you have drawn a marquee around an object to select it. Call the `FindAllObjects` routine. See if any objects are located within the marquee area.

>   **Case BézierTool:** This is the same as `Case PointerTool`, except with no `FindAllObject` call. You could add a Bézier node call here to highlight nodes within a marquee.
>
>   **Case ZoomTool:** Reserved for future use, if needed.

**Case LineTool To CircleTool:** If the currently selected tool is a line, box, or circle tool, change the `DrawMode`. Switch it to normal (`Copy_Pen-13`). Call the `BoundingBox_Up` routine to draw the finished object to the desktop.

If the value of `B` (the current object) equals `Total` (all objects drawn to date), flag the variable `Draw` as `True`. `UpdateObjects` will then skip the `Loop` statement that redraws all objects. This speeds up the application.

> **NOTE** Having all objects redrawn each time in the `UpdateObjects` procedure can slow down the application. What you should do is redraw only the areas of the screen that have changed due to a stretch, zoom, or move. Visual Basic's clipping controls are not suited for this, and the `ArtWork_Paint` event could cause side effects if `AutoRedraw` comes into play on certain calls. You may want to write code that redraws only the objects in a given area.

**Case TextTool:** The caret (text cursor) used to show the start of the text insertion point is a label with its width set to 15 twips and its `BorderStyle` set to visible (1). As you type, the border is set to invisible (0), and the label expands as you continue typing. This gives the illusion that you are typing directly on the page. The label's position is set with the `Txt.Left` and `Txt.Top` values defined by the `MouseDown` event.

Artwork's `DrawWidth` is reset to 1 because it can be changed at any time by using the `LineButtons` tool, which sets outline drawing widths.

Artwork's `DrawStyle` is reset to solid (0) because it can be changed during a dotted line marquee selection.

If the right mouse button was clicked, show a popup menu. This routine is handled by the API `TrackPopUpMenu`. The location that the menu pops up is user-defined.

**GetCursorPos:** Finds the current position of your mouse. This API routine needs a user-defined `Type` structure, and all `X,Y` positions are sent in pixel screen units.

## Lines to Bézier Curves

If you double-click a line of Bézier curve and the current tool is the `BézierTool`, the `Node Editing` form is displayed in `Modal` state

> **NOTE** The user must make a button selection before continuing in `Modal` state.

# The Artisan Program

**Listing 2.15.** `Artwork_DlbClick` opens a node edit form to convert a line to Bézier curves.

```
Sub Artwork_DblClick ()
If FlagLine(B) = B Then NodeEdit!To_Line.Enabled = False :[CI:CCC]
..   NodeEdit!To_Curve.Enabled = True
If FlagBézier(B) = B Then NodeEdit!To_Curve.Enabled = False:[CI:CCC]
...NodeEdit!To_Line.Enabled = True
If CurrentTool = 1 Then NodeEdit.Show Modal Else Exit Sub
Select Case True
. Case Convert_Curve
..    FlagLine(B) = 0: FlagBézier(B) = B
..    BezErase = True: BezHandles
..    BezHandle1.Visible = True: BezHandle2.Visible = True
..    BezNode1.Visible = True: BezNode2.Visible = True
..    Convert_Curve = False: NodeEdit!To_Line.Enabled = True
. Case Convert_Line
..    FlagBézier(B) = 0: FlagLine(B) = B
..    BezNode1.Visible = False: BezNode2.Visible = False
..    W(B) = P1X(B): N(B) = P1Y(B)
..    E(B) = p2X(B): S(B) = p2Y(B)
..    Nodes
..    Convert_Line = False: NodeEdit!To_Curve.Enabled = True
..    UpdateObjects
End Select
End Sub
```

If you select the button called `To_Curve`, which flags `Convert_Curve` to `True`, the line's array flag (`FlagLine`) number is set to `0`. An object flagged `0` can't be drawn. The Bézier's array flag (`FlagBézier`) number is then set to whatever the line's flag index number was.

`BezErase` is then flagged `True`, and the line is converted to a curve with handles and nodes evenly positioned on the new curve by calling the `BezHandle` procedure.

All Bézier handles and nodes are invisible; so make them visible and then reset the `Convert_Curve` flag to its original setting of `False`.

Finally, if the outline color of the line was black, reset the value to reflect the current pen outline color.

## Typing Characters on the Desktop

When the text tool is selected and the cursor is placed on the page, you can type characters. The functions for formatting or deleting characters is very limited since a word-processor program is a book on its own. However, you should get general instructions on how to place and align text with the Artisan program.

You also can click the right mouse to display a simple font selection dialog box.

**Listing 2.16.** Artwork_KeyPress counts text lines as they are typed on the desktop.

```
Sub ArtWork_KeyPress (KeyAscii As Integer)
If CurrentTool = TextTool Then
  Select Case KeyAscii
    Case 13 'Return
      crCounter = crCounter + 1
    Case 8 'BackSpace
      If Txt.Caption = "" Then Exit Sub
      If Txt.Caption > "" Then
        If Mid$(Txt.Caption, Len(Txt.Caption)) = Chr(13) [CI:CCC]
          Then crCounter = crCounter - 1
Txt.Caption = Mid$(Txt.Caption, 1, Len(Txt.Caption) - 1): Exit Sub
      End If
  End Select
  Txt.Caption = Txt.Caption + Chr(KeyAscii)
  StatusLabel.Caption = Txt.FontName
  If Txt.Caption > "" Then Txt.BorderStyle = 0
End If
End Sub
```

**ArtWork_KeyPress:** If you are using the text tool, you first type text in the Txt label control. The Txt label control is opaque so it appears as though you are really typing on the desktop. The crCounter variable is used to count the carriage returns. This is necessary only for extracting each line when saving and opening a file. If you use a more elaborate file saving and opening routine (binary or sequential), you may not need this. The MID$ statement is used to erase characters or a carriage returns when the backspace key is used. Each Case expression (13 and 8) is the ASCII key values for Carriage Return and BackSpace.

## Redrawing Text on the Desktop

Text that appears on the desktop as you type is really inside the Txt label control. You must transfer this text on to the Artwork desktop when you are finishing typing. (See Listing 2.17.)

**Listing 2.17.** Artwork_LostFocus redraws the text characters.

```
Sub ArtWork_LostFocus ()

If CurrentTool = TextTool And txt.Caption <> "" Then ReDrawText
End Sub
```

If the user has started typing text in the Txt.Label and clicked a different control, hide the label and update the text with the ReDrawText procedure.

Figure 2.11 shows a line converted to a curve, the Node Edit form, and the Txt label control.

# The Artisan Program

**Figure 2.11.**
*A line converted to a curve, the* Node Edit *form, and the* Txt *label control.*

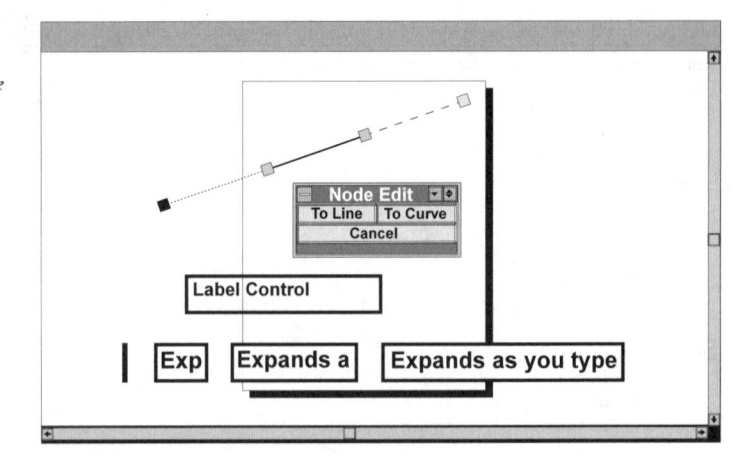

## The *Bounding Box MouseDown* Procedure

The Bounding Box_Down procedure shows how to move an object from a bounding box's center positions. This is one of several ways to move an object across the screen. Refer to the MoveTest program in Chapter 1 for other possible routines you could use.

**Listing 2.18.** BoundingBox_Down *stores an object's positions before drawing.*

```
Sub BoundingBox_Down (X As Single, Y As Single)
For R = -30 To 30 Step 15: For RR = -30 To 30 Step 15
. If ArtWork.Point(X - R, Y - RR) <> ArtWork.BackColor Then
..   FlagMove = True
..   XCenter = X - ((W(B) \ 2) + (E(B)) \ 2)
..   YCenter = Y - ((N(B) \ 2) + (S(B)) \ 2)
..   OFFSETx = XCenter: OFFSETy = YCenter: Exit For
. End If
'ArtWork.PSet (X - R, Y - RR) 'use To view point area
If FlagMove = True Then Exit For
Next RR: Next R
 X1 = X: Y1 = Y: X2 = X1: Y2 = Y1
 Radius = 0
 ArtWork.DrawMode = Inverse
. XX1 = W(B)
. YY1 = N(B)
. XX2 = E(B)
. YY2 = S(B)
End Sub
```

**For R = -30 To 30 Step 15:** You can move an object only if the object is within two pixels of the mouse pointer. You can calculate this distance by using Visual Basic's Point statement and increasing the X and Y values that it uses to find a color. A nested For/Next statement points to all pixels within the range of two pixels. (You can see this happen by using the Pset statement.) If Artwork's BackColor (white) is not found, use two Exit For statements to escape from the loops.

If an object were filled with a dithered color, the blank spaces between the color pixels in some dithered patterns could equal the desktop's `BackColor`. Using the `Point` statement in this fashion would not find the object.

> **FlagMove:** Means that the `Point` statement found a color other than white. Set the flag to `True` so you can move that object in the `BoundingBox_Move` procedure.
>
> **XCenter and YCenter:** Calculates the center position of the object's bounding box.
>
> **OFFSETx and OFFSETy:** These formulas alone would put the object dead center of the mouse pointer. Use these offsets as a way to re-offset the object's original positions in the `MoveObject` procedure.
>
> **X1, Y1, X2, and Y2:** Store the temporary upper-left and lower-right X and Y positions needed in graphical statements to draw an object.
>
> The radius is reset to `0` so it will not interfere with the `Circle` statement when a new circle object is drawn. This also prevents a runtime error during execution.
>
> **ArtWork.DrawMode:** Set to `Inverse` to create the illusion that only one object at a time is being drawn during the `MouseMove` event.
>
> **XX2, YY2, XX1, and YY1:** Temporary holders used to erase the last position of an object after the user stretches a bounding box using the `Handles` procedure or when moving the object to a new screen position.

---

### MouseMove *Function*

`MoveMouse` is a function that determines whether the mouse has moved a preset distance of pixels before any action is taken. If the mouse has moved the stated number of pixels, starting from the `X,Y` coordinate of the `MouseDown` event, the drawing of an object is commenced.

This procedure stops any unwanted drawing if the user happens to click the Artwork desktop without wanting to actually draw an object.

---

## Performing the Actual Drawing on the Desktop

As you drag the mouse, the bounding box `MouseMove` event draws the object. All graphics in the Artisan program use only Basic language graphical statements. The ArtAPI program in Chapter 15 is a reconstruction of the Artisan program using only Windows API drawing functions. You will find that mixing and matching these two types of drawing functions can help save programming time.

## The Artisan Program

**Listing 2.19.** `BoundingBox_move` draws the actual graphic.

```
Sub BoundingBox_Move (Shift As Integer, X As Single, Y As Single)
If CurrentTool = 0 And FlagMove = True And [CI:CCC]
....MoveMouse() = True Then MoveObject Button, [CI:CCC]
......   Shift, X, Y: Exit Sub
If Node(0).Visible = True Then Exit Sub
If MoveMouse() = True Then
. Select Case CurrentTool
..  Case PointerTool To BézierTool
....ArtWork.DrawMode = Xor_Pen
....ArtWork.DrawStyle = Dot
....ArtWork.Line (X1, Y1)-(X2, Y2), YELLOW, B
..  Case LineTool
....ArtWork.Line (X1, Y1)-(X2, Y2)
..  Case BoxTool
....ArtWork.Line (X1, Y1)-(X2, Y2), , B
..  Case CircleTool
....LastCircleGood = PerfectCircle(X1, Y1, X2, Y2)
....ArtWork.Circle (XCenter, YCenter), Radius, , , , Aspect
. End Select
End If
End Sub
```

**If CurrentTool = 0:** If the currently selected tool is the `PointerTool` and the `FlagMove` variable was set to `True` in the `BoundingBox_Down` procedure, you are going to move an object rather than draw one. In this case, exit the subroutine.

**If Node(0).Visible:** A standard node is visible, which means an object has been highlighted; so do not try to draw an object. Exit the subroutine.

**Select/Case:** Depending on the currently selected tool, do one of the following `Case` expressions:

**Case PointerTool To BézierTool:** Used to draw a marquee around an object. Turn the `DrawMode` to `Xor_Pen` (7). A marquee is a box with a dotted line border, so change the drawing style to a dotted line using `ArtWork.DrawStyle = Dot`.

The `Line` statement makes a box with a yellow-dotted border. When the color yellow is set to `Xor` mode, you get cyan (light blue) as the border color. When the object passes over another color, such as a green filled box, the line turns yellow within that area. The background color (green in this case) retains its color after the marquee passes over it.

**Case LineTool:** This statement draws a line only if the `B` option has been omitted in the statement.

**Case BoxTool:** This statement draws a box only if the `B` option has been included in the statement.

**Case CircleTool: LastGoodCircle:** A function call to a `PerfectCircle` procedure. This routine is the same as the one found in Visual Basic's IconWorks example. It returns values for `XCenter` and `YCenter`, which are needed in the circle statement. The API `ellipse` call can do the same thing without the `PerfectCircle` function.

Chapter **2**

## Giving the New Object a Reference Number

This is where all newly drawn objects are given an index number. The B variable controls what attributes are assigned to that object. The color of an object's outline, its outline width, the fill color used to paint the object, and the position of the object on-screen are just some of the attributes that can be assigned to the new object.

The value of B represents the current object's value. This number can be used to store attributes in any one of several indexed arrays.

The UpdateObjects procedure collects all the attributes whose indexes match the object's number, and then draws the finished object.

**Listing 2.20.** BoundingBox_Up sets the object index number of the graphic.

```
Sub BoundingBox_Up (X1, Y1, X2, Y2)
If MoveMouse() = True Then
. Total = Total + 1: B = Total
. StatusLabel.Caption = Format$(B)
. LineWidth(B) = ArtWork.DrawWidth
. W(B) = X1: E(B) = X2: N(B) = Y1: S(B) = Y2
.. Select Case CurrentTool
....Case PointerTool
....Exit Sub
.. Case BézierTool
....Exit Sub
.. Case ZoomTool
....Exit Sub
.. Case LineTool
....FlagLine(B) = B
....Nodes
.. Case BoxTool
....FlagBox(B) = B
....FillValue(B) = 1
....Nodes
.. Case CircleTool
....FlagCircle(B) = B
....FillValue(B) = 1
....Nodes
.. Case TextTool
....' no code needed here
. End Select
End If
End Sub
```

This is the most important procedure of the application. After each object is drawn, the bounding box, which holds the object inside, is given a number. This number is assigned to the variable B. The value of B controls every attribute that may be assigned to the object (such as a box, Bézier curve, or text).

# The Artisan Program

When the form loads, the value of B equals 0, the total number of objects drawn is 0, and you have a blank page. A variable called Total keeps track of all the objects you create.

B tells you which bounding box (object) you have highlighted and assigns that number to the index (cell) number for each attribute (such as flags, styles, or color) in an array. For instance, if the third object you drew was a circle, B would equal 3 and the outline width, color, fill, bounding box position, and values would be indexed in cell 3 of each attribute array.

**If MoveMouse = True:** You've moved the mouse far enough to start a drawing event. Otherwise, you've just clicked the mouse on the page.

**Total =Total + 1:** Increase the object count by one. Total will equal the total number of objects drawn to date.

**B = Total:** Assigns a number to the bounding box (object).

**LineWidth(B):** The LineWidth index entry will equal the current DrawWidth. Because a draw width cannot be 0, the LineWidth(B) value will prevent a runtime error.

**W(B), E(B), N(B), and S(B):** The corner points of each bounding box. X1, X2, Y1, and Y2 are used only as temporary coordinate placeholders. Assigning B to each of these variables tells the program to which bounding box the W, E, N, and S corner positions belong.

> **NOTE** The W, E, N, and S variables represent the west, east, north, and south points of the bounding box. Some API calls use a Rectangle type structure that uses the variable names right, left, top, and bottom. So the next logical references would be W, E, N, and S. They are easier to type and remember.

**Select Case CurrentTool:** This depends on which of the following tools is used.

**Case PointerTool:** You cannot draw any object with this tool; so exit the subroutine.

**Case BézierTool:** The Bézier curve drawing is handled by the DrawBézier procedure, and its bounding box is set by the BézierStore procedure; exit the subroutine.

**Case ZoomTool:** This tool is reserved for future use and has no code attached; so exit the subroutine.

**Case LineTool:** Inserts the object number (B) in the FlagLine index array so the program will know that the bounding box contains a line. Call Nodes to place a node on either end of the line.

**Case BoxTool:** Inserts the object number (B) in the FlagBox index array so the program will know the bounding box contains a box. It also inserts the object number (B) in the FillValue index array so the program will know whether the box is solid (0) or transparent (1). It also calls Nodes to place a node on each corner of the box.

**Case CircleTool:** Inserts the object number (B) in the FlagCircle indexed array so the program will know that the bounding box contains a circle. It also inserts the object number (B) in the `FillValue` indexed array so the program will know whether the circle is solid (0) or transparent (1). It also calls `Nodes` to place a node on the twelve-o'clock position of the circle.

**Case TextTool:** Text drawing is handled by the `DrawText` procedure; so you can exit the subroutine.

> **NOTE** Each chart heading (see Figure 2.12) represents an indexed array except for *B* and *T*. The variable *B* represents the currently selected or last-drawn object. The variable *T* represents the total number of objects drawn so far. If the third object drawn (*B* = 3) were a box, all chart headings associated with that box would also be indexed as 3. The `UpdateObjects` call would then rebuild an object by getting these stored values and pointing to the correct index number.

See Figure 2.12 for examples of objects that have been drawn.

**Figure 2.12.**
*Five objects that have been drawn so far.*

| T | B | W | E | N | S | FLAG | FillValue | PaintColor | LineValue | OutLineColor | LineWidth |
|---|---|---|---|---|---|---|---|---|---|---|---|
| 1 | 1 | 283 | 473 | 245 | 384 | FlagBox | True | StatusPaint | True | StatusColor | 1 |
| 2 | 2 | 652 | 924 | 522 | 619 | FlagLine | False | Not Used | True | Not Used | 4 |
| 3 | 3 | 311 | 650 | 570 | 679 | FlagCircle | True | StatusPaint | True | StatusColor | 2 |
| 4 | 4 | 826 | 961 | 251 | 525 | FlagBox | True | StatusPaint | False | StatusColor | 1 |
| 5 | 5 | 656 | 862 | 274 | 452 | FlagCircle | False | StatusPaint | True | StatusColor | 2 |

# Summary

You should now have a good idea of how the `Artwork` events and `BoundingBox` procedures work together to draw an object on the desktop. You aren't done yet, however. The next three chapters complete the discussion of the Artisan drawing program. Each chapter introduces you to new features. All these features use only Basic language statements.

The code in each event and function is designed in a long form; that is, this book avoids condensing routines in fancy loops, nested loops, and so forth. This will give you the opportunity to understand each routine's structures and apply code-condensing formulas in the future.

The ArtAPI program (with Windows API graphical functions) in Chapter 15 is a remake of the Artisan program. It contains some routines that have already been condensed from the longer versions in the next three chapters. However, you should not skip any chapter or go directly to Chapter 15 because the ArtAPI programs gets quite complicated at points. This is especially true when it comes to joining line and Bézier curves together and then editing them.

# CHAPTER 3

## Bézier Curves

# Bézier Curves

A *Bézier curve* is an algorithm for plotting flexible curve points along a stated path. It is named after the French mathematician Pierre Bézier and was developed as part of a computer-aided design system for the Renault automotive company. Today, most graphics design computer and printer language programs use the Bézier curve formula.

The Bézier's curve points can be constructed in several ways. Each curve has a start point and an end point, which this chapter calls P1 and P2. Each curve also has at least one or more control handles. A three-control-point Bézier curve is often called a B-spline curve. It uses control points P1 and P2, and one control handle. The type of Bézier curve this book uses has four control points, consisting of a curve's start point (P1), the curve's end point (P2), and two control handle points (H1 and H2). This type of Bézier curve is often referred to as a four-point Bézier spline curve. Figure 3.1 illustrates the points of the Bézier curve.

**Figure 3.1.**
*The deCasteljau division formula.*

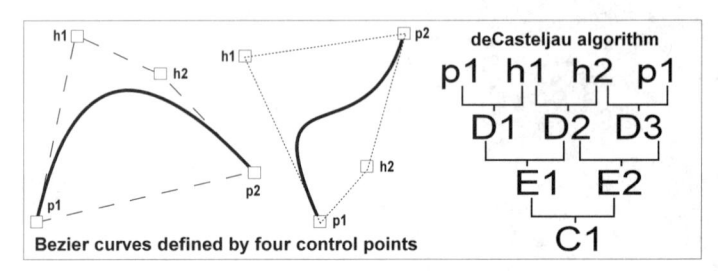

The following shows how to calculate a four-point Bézier spline:

$$P(u) = (1 - u)^3 P1 + 3u(1 - u)^2 H1 + 3u^2(1 - u) H2 + u^3 P2$$

You can simplify the calculation of a Bézier curve by using an algorithm known as the *deCasteljau* algorithm. By dividing the four Bézier curve control points (P1, P2, H1, and H2) by integers (whole numbers) over and over again, you can plot all the curve's segment points. Starting at point (P1), you draw straight lines to each of these plotted points in a connect-the-dots fashion. The last point of the curves is P2. The path of the curve depends on the placement of H1 and H2, called curve-control handles.

The *deCasteljau* algorithm is a simple formula for division that looks similar to a tree chart. You should always think of the curve's starting point (P1) as being affiliated with control handle number one (H1). The curve's end point (P2) is always related to control handle two (H2). The P1 and H1 control points are the left side of the curve, and the P2 and H2 control points are the right side. In the following example, the algorithm finds the halfway marks between the curves left-side control points, the two curve control handles, and the curve's right-side controls points. It then continues to find halfway marks between these calculated marks until the tree is down to its final possible division (C1), which is an actual point plotted on the curve.

The following formula finds the halfway points between the curve's control points and the halfway points between each of the previous halfway points:

```
(P1 + H1) / 2 = D1
(H1 + H2) / 2 = D2
(P2 + H2) / 2 = D3
(D1 + D2) / 2 = E1
(D2 + D3) / 2 = E2
(E1 + E2) / 2 = C1 (a point on the curve)
```

Figure 3.2 shows the first step of plotting the center segment point (C1) of a Bézier curve. The four Bézier control points are P1, P2, H1, and H2. Imagine a polygon shape connected by these four control points. The curve would always be inside this imaginary four-cornered container, regardless of the curve's shape.

**Figure** 3.2.
*A Bézier curve's dividing points.*

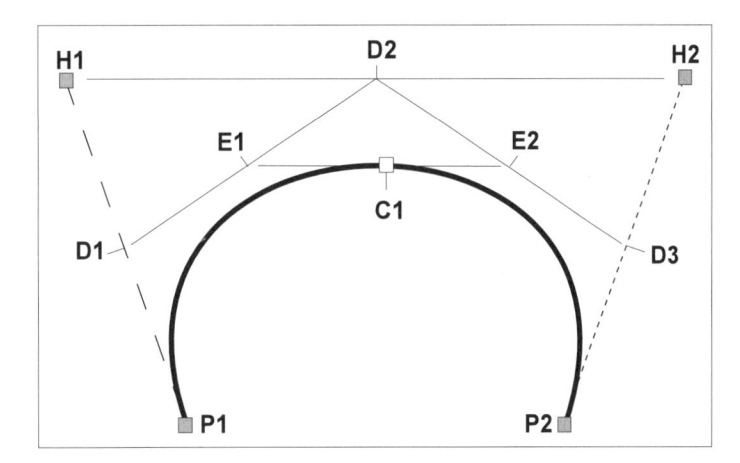

Using the *deCasteljau* algorithm, start with points P1 and H1. By adding the position of these two points and dividing by 2, you get the halfway point (D1):

D1 = ( P1 + H1 ) \ 2 = D1

Then add the positions of H1 and H2 and divide by 2. The result is D2.

Continue using this formula until you get the curve's segment point (C1). The first C1 position will always be the halfway or center point position of the rendered curve.

Figure 3.3 shows the center segment point of the curve (C1). To see how to plot a new segment point, you must look at the curve as if it were divided in half.

## Bézier Curves

**Figure 3.3.**
*A Bézier curve's left and right halves.*

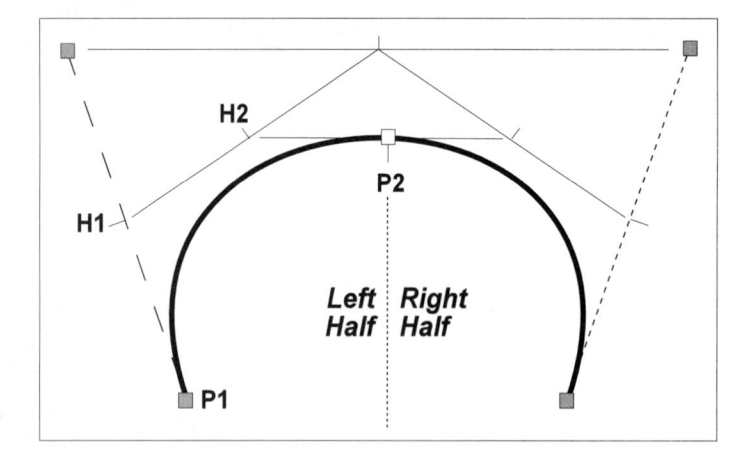

You store the position of point C1 in an array so you can rename this point P2. If you rotate this illustration clockwise about 45 degrees, you'll see what will happen.

Pretend that the center point (C1) is really the end point of the curve (P2) and the values of D1 and E1 are actually the two Bézier handles points (H1 and H2).

Figure 3.4 shows the same formula that was shown in Figure 3.2 to find the center segment of the left half of the curve. Rotate Figure 3.4 clockwise slightly and P1 and C1 become the new curve start and end points; repeat the steps in Figure 3.2. A vortex starts to happen, getting smaller and smaller as you get closer to control point P1. Each new C1 point will lie on the curve. If you go clockwise and then counter-clockwise, you get a recursive formula, which you repeat for each half of the curve.

**Figure 3.4.**
*Plotting the next point on the curve.*

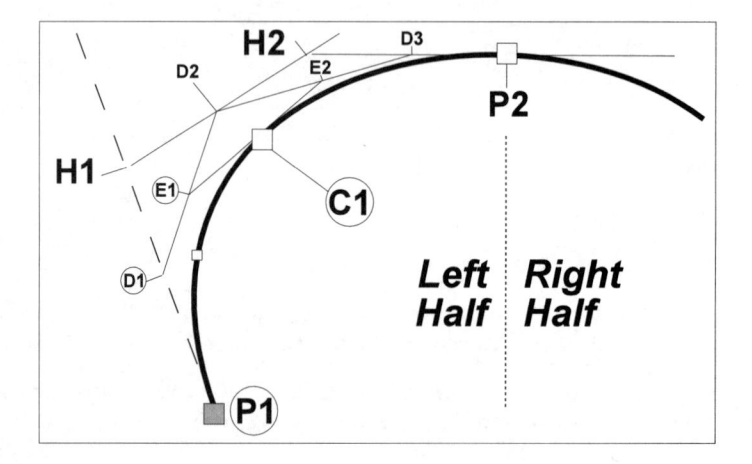

The Bézier curve has 32 points to plot. Each X,Y plot point is stored with a user-defined data type called POINTAPI, which has two subheadings called X and Y. (The POINTAPI user-defined data type is located in the ARTISAN7.BAS file.)

Each curve also has the original start and end points that the nodes are attached to, so 34 points make up a curve. Point P1 is the start of the curve, and P2 is the end of the curve. Figure 3.5 shows the curve points for the left side of a Bézier curve. Figure 3.6 shows the curve points for the right side of a Bézier curve.

**Figure 3.5.**
*The left half of a pre-plotted (user-defined) Bézier curve.*

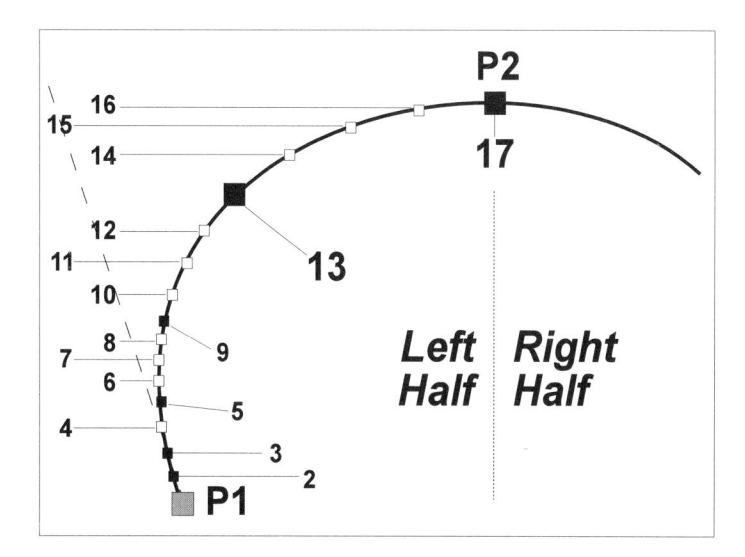

Curve point 17 holds the X and Y positions for the center of the curve since 34 / 2 = 17.

The BezDivide procedure contains a formula for division called the *deCasteljau* algorithm. The four values next to each BézierDivide call are *arguments*. The order of arguments for BézierDivide is as follows:

```
Sub BézierDivide (p1 as PointApi, h1 As PointApi, h2 As PointApi, p2 As PointApi)
```

You fool the BézierDivide subroutine into thinking that the four arguments you pass to it are the Bézier's node points p1 and p2 and handle points h1 and h2.

The BezDraw procedure, shown in Listing 3.1, then sends the two handles and new control points to the division formula in the BezDivide procedure (shown in Listing 3.2), which plots each curve point. The last calculations, C1(P).X and C1(P).Y, make up the actual curve point.

Finally, the BezDraw procedure takes all the 32 points that were stored in data array C1 and connects the dots using a Line statement (or Polyline) to give the illusion of a smooth curved line.

In Figure 3.6, the curve's right half is plotted by starting again with the center curve point, which is index 17 of array C1.

# Bézier Curves

**Figure** 3.6.
*The right half of a pre-plotted Bézier curve.*

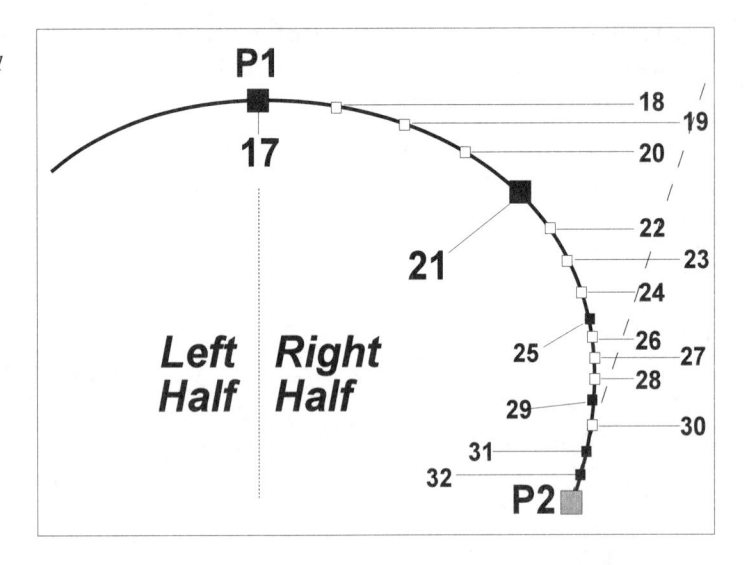

On the left side of the curve, points 2 through 16 are calculated and stored in the indexed data array `C1` using their curve position numbers as the index references.

On the right side of the curve, points 18 to 32 are calculated and stored in indexed array `C1` using their position points as the indexes in which to store them. The right side of the Bézier curve uses the right side curve dividing values to plot points. Note that this is not a true recursive division routine as found in most C language routines. The plots have been preplanned as to where they should go and in what order each point is calculated.

> **NOTE**
>
> The advantage of pre-plotted Bézier curve's is that the code executes faster since recursive routines double the number of curve points when calculating a smooth curve.
>
> The disadvantage is that you have to calculate each point manually, which adds an additional 32 lines of code to the procedure.

The finished curve's plots (`C1`) would have a data array as followed:

`C1(2), C1(3), C1(4), C1(5), C1(6), C1(7)....continuing on to finish at....C1(32).`

Each `C1` index number has two values stored inside: `X` and `Y`, as `POINTAPI`.

The `X` and `Y` coordinates for each `C1` index would be as followed:

`C1(2).X, C1(2).Y - C1(3).X, C1(3).Y,....continued on to finish at.... C1(32).X, C1(32).Y`

`C1(index).X` holds the logical X coordinate for its assigned curve point.

`C1(index).Y` holds the logical Y coordinate for its assigned curve point.

# Plotting the Points of a Bézier Curve

Here is a description of the variables used to plot a Bézier curve in the following BezDraw procedure.

The number following the variable P represents the index number that will be used to store each value generated by the *deCasteljau* algorithm.

P also represents the number given to the plotted points that make up the curve. Beginning from the curve's starting point (P1) and stopping at the curve's end point (P2), The curve's plot points are numbered 2 through 32. This would place the curve point numbered 17 on the center halfway mark of the curve.

You plot the left side of the curve first using the same dividing formula for each new curve plot. This gives you the curve points 2 through 16.

Next, plot the right side, which is basically a mirror of what you plotted on the left side. This gives you the curve points 18 through 32. Listing 3.1 shows the calculations for curve plots.

**Listing 3.1.** Calculating predefined argument curve plots to be divided.

```
Sub BezDraw
'''Left side of curve
P = 17: BézierDivide P1, h1, h2, p2
P = 13: BézierDivide P1, D1(17), E1(17), C1(17)
P = 9: BézierDivide P1, D1(13), E1(13), C1(13)
P = 5: BézierDivide P1, D1(9), E1(9), C1(9)
P = 3: BézierDivide P1, D1(5), E1(5), C1(5)
P = 2: BézierDivide P1, D1(3), E1(3), C1(3)
'''''
P = 4: BézierDivide C1(3), E2(3), D3(3), C1(5)
P = 7: BézierDivide C1(5), E2(5), D3(5), C1(9)
P = 6: BézierDivide C1(7), D1(7), E1(7), C1(5)
P = 8: BézierDivide C1(7), E2(7), D3(7), C1(9)
P = 11: BézierDivide C1(9), E2(9), D3(9), C1(13)
P = 10: BézierDivide C1(11), D1(11), E1(11), C1(9)
P = 12: BézierDivide C1(11), E2(11), D3(11), C1(13)
P = 15: BézierDivide C1(13), E2(13), D3(13), C1(17)
P = 14: BézierDivide C1(15), D1(15), E1(15), C1(13)
P = 16: BézierDivide C1(15), E2(15), D3(15), C1(17)
'''Right side of curve
P = 21: BézierDivide C1(17), E2(17), D3(17), p2
P = 25: BézierDivide C1(21), E2(21), D3(21), p2
P = 29: BézierDivide C1(25), E2(25), D3(25), p2
P = 31: BézierDivide C1(29), E2(29), D3(29), p2
P = 32: BézierDivide C1(31), E2(31), D3(31), p2
'''''
P = 30: BézierDivide C1(29), D1(31), E1(31), C1(31)
P = 27: BézierDivide C1(25), D1(29), E1(29), C1(29)
P = 28: BézierDivide C1(29), E2(27), D3(27), C1(27)
P = 26: BézierDivide C1(25), D1(27), E1(27), C1(27)
P = 23: BézierDivide C1(21), D1(25), E1(25), C1(25)
P = 24: BézierDivide C1(25), E2(23), D3(23), C1(23)
P = 22: BézierDivide C1(21), D1(23), E1(23), C1(23)
P = 19: BézierDivide C1(17), D1(21), E1(21), C1(21)
```

*continues*

# Bézier Curves

### Listing 3.1. continued

```
P = 20: BézierDivide C1(21), E2(19), D3(19), C1(19)
P = 18: BézierDivide C1(17), D1(19), E1(19), C1(19)
If FlagPrinter = 2 Then GoTo PrintToPage
If ArtWork.AutoRedraw = False Then ArtWork.DrawMode = Inverse
ArtWork.DrawStyle = Solid
'P_Index(1).X = p1.X \ PIXELX
'P_Index(1).Y = p1.Y \ PIXELY
    'For P = 2 To 32
        'P_Index(P).X = C1(P).X \ PIXELX
        'P_Index(P).Y = C1(P).Y \ PIXELY
    'Next P
'P_Index(33).X = p2.X \ PIXELX
'P_Index(33).Y = p2.Y \ PIXELY
'NUM_PTS = 33
'R = Polyline(ArtWork.hDC, P_Index(1), NUM_PTS)
''''''''''''''''''''''''''''''''''''''''''''''''
ArtWork.PSet (P1.X, P1.Y)
    For P = 2 To 32
        ArtWork.Line -(C1(P).X, C1(P).Y)
    Next P
ArtWork.Line -(p2.X, p2.Y)
Exit Sub
PrintToPage:
Printer.PSet (P1.X, P1.Y)
    For P = 2 To 32
        Printer.Line -(C1(P).X, C1(P).Y)
    Next P
Printer.Line -(p2.X, p2.Y)
Exit Sub
End Sub
```

> **Left side:** P is a temporary integer that passes the index number of arrays D1, D2, D3, E1, E2, and C1. It also represents the order in which the points are placed on a curve. They start at BezNode1 (p1) and count up 32 more points until finally connecting to point 33, which is BezNode2 (p2).

You fool BézierDivide into thinking that the four arguments you will pass to it are the Bézier's node points P1 and P2 and the Bézier's handle points H1 and, H2.

The first block of six calculations divides the left side of the curve, as shown in the Figure 3.7 (the black nodes starting from 17). These curve points are stored as C1 (index number). Hence the first block of six points are stored in C1(17), C1(13), C1(9), C1(5), C1(3), and C1(2).

Now plot the remaining 10 points for the left side by finding the halfway point between the black nodes starting with points 3 and 5 (C1(3), C1(5)) and working your way back up. (See the gray nodes in Figure 3.7.) If there is a visual gap between a gray and black node, you'll find the halfway point between each of these points and plot another point (the white nodes in Figure 3.7).

**Figure 3.7.**
*The order in which curve points are plotted.*

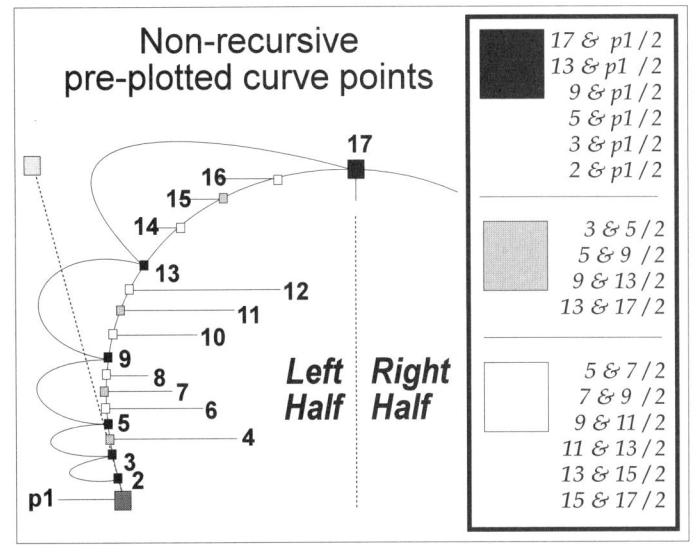

**Non-recursive pre-plotted curve points**

| | |
|---|---|
| ■ (dark) | 17 & p1 / 2 |
| | 13 & p1 / 2 |
| | 9 & p1 / 2 |
| | 5 & p1 / 2 |
| | 3 & p1 / 2 |
| | 2 & p1 / 2 |
| ■ (gray) | 3 & 5 / 2 |
| | 5 & 9 / 2 |
| | 9 & 13 / 2 |
| | 13 & 17 / 2 |
| □ (light) | 5 & 7 / 2 |
| | 7 & 9 / 2 |
| | 9 & 11 / 2 |
| | 11 & 13 / 2 |
| | 13 & 15 / 2 |
| | 15 & 17 / 2 |

Left Half | Right Half

Look at the second block of statements starting with P = 4. Notice that the first argument C1 and the fourth argument, also C1, are pretending to be two Bézier node points. The two middle arguments are pretending to be the Bézier's control handles. What you are doing is creating a vortex of the same pattern used to create the first point (17) and swirling counter-clockwise to make the left side of the curve. The right side is created by repeating this vortex pattern but having it swirl clockwise, starting from point (17). Each repeated pattern gets smaller and smaller as it nears the end points. p1 is the start point for the left side, and p2 is the end point for the right side.

The Bézier curve is now ready to be displayed on your desktop. You have two ways to draw the Bézier curve. If you want to use the API Polyline function, remark out (') the five lines that currently use Basic's Line statement and then remove the remark out (') for the API Polyline section.

**PIXELX, PIXELY:** API's Polyline works only in pixel mode, so convert the twips to pixels. PIXELX and PIXELY were defined at Form_Load event.

**P_Index:** A temporary indexed array that holds both X and Y pointers defined by the POINTS type structure in the ARTISAN.BAS file.

**p1.X, p1.Y:** (BezNode1) The starting points of the curve.

**For P = 2 to 32:** Set P to the starting value or 2; end the counter at 32.

**P_Index(P).X = C1(P).X \ TPX:** Store each X coordinate of C1 (the curve point) in array P_index. The X points are in twips, so convert them to pixels by dividing the value by TwipsPerPixelX (TPX).

**P_Index(P).Y = C1(P).Y \ TPY:** Stores each Y coordinate of C1 (the curve point) in array P_Index. The Y points are in twips, so convert them to pixels by dividing the value by TwipPerPixelY (TPY).

## Bézier Curves

**Next P:** Go back to the For P statement and increase the value of P by 1. Repeat the previous lines of code until you have all 32 X, Y points are stored in P_Index.

**p2.X and p2Y:** (BezNode2) The end points of the curve.

**NUM_PTS = 33:** The array index size. This tells API the number of points to connect.

**R= Polyline (ArtWork.hDC, P_Index(1), NUM_PTS):** Call the API Polyline function and tells it to do the following:

- To draw in the Artwork picture box
- To start drawing at the X, Y points stored in P_Index, index number 1
- To stop drawing when it reaches the stored index number 33

**The LINE statement:** This is just as fast as the API Polyline statement, but with less typing.

**ArtWork.PSet:** Start the Line statement at P1 (BezNode1) by setting the currentX and currentY using the PSet statement.

**For...Next statement:** Continue the line using the C1 index array values.

**ArtWork.Line:** P2.X, P2.Y (BezNode2) are the end points of the curve.

---

The API Polyline function draws a series of lines. The lines are drawn starting with the first point and moving through to the last point specified. To use this function, you must create a user-defined point structure in a module (.BAS file). The point structure has the following form:

```
Type POINTAPI
    X As Integer
    Y As Integer
End Type
```

You can store the X and Y points of each line segment in the type variable called POINTAPI, like this:

```
Dim Pt(1 to N) As POINTAPI
Pt(1).X = 154 : Pt(1).Y = 276
Pt(2).X = 212 : Pt(2).Y = 280
```

An example follows:

```
Polyline(Pic.Hdc, Pt(1), 2)
```

The syntax for the preceding line is as follows:

Pic.Hdc is the control you want to draw into. Pt(1) is the starting point of the line. The number two is the number of points to draw.

# The *deCasteljau* Dividing Formula

Long division is used in Listing 3.2 to force the answers to integer values (as illustrated in Figure 3.8).

**Listing 3.2.** The *deCasteljau* formula in action.

```
Sub BézierDivide (P1 As POINTS, h1 As POINTS, h2 As POINTS, p2 As POINTS)
D1(P).X = (P1.X \ 2 + h1.X \ 2)
D1(P).Y = (P1.Y \ 2 + h1.Y \ 2)
D2(P).X = (h1.X \ 2 + h2.X \ 2)
D2(P).Y = (h1.Y \ 2 + h2.Y \ 2)
D3(P).X = (p2.X \ 2 + h2.X \ 2)
D3(P).Y = (p2.Y \ 2 + h2.Y \ 2)
E1(P).X = (D1(P).X \ 2 + D2(P).X \ 2)
E1(P).Y = (D1(P).Y \ 2 + D2(P).Y \ 2)
E2(P).X = (D2(P).X \ 2 + D3(P).X \ 2)
E2(P).Y = (D2(P).Y \ 2 + D3(P).Y \ 2)
C1(P).X = (E1(P).X \ 2 + E2(P).X \ 2)
C1(P).Y = (E1(P).Y \ 2 + E2(P).Y \ 2)
'ArtWork.DrawWidth = 4
'ArtWork.PSet (C1(P).X, C1(P).Y)
'ArtWork.DrawWidth = 1
End Sub
```

p1.X \ 2 + h1.X \ 2 can be shortened to (p1.X + h1.X) \ 2 and works fine in pixel mode; but for twips, p1.X + h1.X could surpass the maximum value that an integer can store (signed 32,767).

Always use the shift-right operator (\) to divide when using the *deCasteljau* formula. The (\) operator divides two numbers and returns an integer (whole number) result. If you were to use the (/) operator to divide, slow performance would result since the (/) operator divides two numbers and returns a floating-point (decimal) result. Floating-point results require unnecessary mathematic calculations by your computer's processor when you use the *deCasteljau* formula.

See Figure 3.8 for the tree sturcture of the *deCasteljau* algorithm.

**Figure 3.8.**
*The tree structure of the* deCasteljau *algorithm.*

```
D1(P).X = (P1.X + h1.X) \ 2     deCasteljau algorithm
D1(P).Y = (P1.Y + h1.Y) \ 2
D2(P).X = (h1.X + h2.X) \ 2      p1  h1  h2  p1
D2(P).Y = (h1.Y + h2.Y) \ 2
D3(P).X = (p2.X + h2.X) \ 2       D1  D2  D3
D3(P).Y = (p2.Y + h2.Y) \ 2
E1(P).X = (D1(P).X + D2(P).X) \ 2
E1(P).Y = (D1(P).Y + D2(P).Y) \ 2    E1   E2
E2(P).X = (D2(P).X + D3(P).X) \ 2
E2(P).Y = (D2(P).Y + D3(P).Y) \ 2        C1
C1(P).X = (E1(P).X + E2(P).X) \ 2
C1(P).Y = (E1(P).Y + E2(P).Y) \ 2
```

## Stretching the Curve by its Handles

The `BezHandle1_MouseDown` event (Listing 3.3) starts the process of redrawing the curve to give the illusion of movement as the curve is being reshaped.

**Listing 3.3.** The `MouseDown` event draws the Bézier curve using handle #1.

```
Sub BezHandle1_MouseDown (Button As Integer, Shift As Integer, X!, Y!)
XX2 = E(B): YY2 = S(B): XX1 = W(B): YY1 = N(B)
BezHandle1.Visible = False
BezNode1.BackColor = Blue: BezNode2.BackColor = Black
    BezMove
    BezDraw
End Sub
```

**XX2, YY2, XX1, and YY1:** Temporarily store the bounding box dimensions so you can erase the last curve position.

**BezHandle1:** First, make the current Bézier handle invisible. `AutoRedraw` can leave mouse turd (specs of pixel lines) on display. The Bézier nodes and handles are really picture box controls. The dotted lines that join the Bézier nodes to the handles are centered in the middle of each picture box. The dotted lines are drawn in `Xor_Mode`; overlapping these dotted lines with the picture boxes can trigger the mode to go out of sync.

**BezNode1.BackColor:** Change the colors of the nodes for a visual focus only.

**BezMove:** Call the procedure `BezMove` to draw the first curve. `BezMove` draws the first Bézier curve white in normal mode, and then `AutoRedraws` erases the old curve line. The `AutoRedraw` property slows the first movement of the curve considerably. You may want to improve this using another route. Be warned! I experimented with the `AutoRedraw`, and the first curve always left specs of curve behind, even though the coordinates were correct.

**BezDraw:** Start the *deCasteljau* algorithm. Draw this and any future curves in `Inverse` mode. This makes sure the curve line is black when the `MouseMove` event is triggered.

## Redrawing the Bézier's Levers

The lever is a dotted line that attaches to the handle and the curve's ending point. When you reshape a curve using one of its two handles, the levers must be redrawn also. (See Listing 3.4.)

**Listing 3.4.** Redrawing the Bézier curve when handle #1 is moved.

```
Sub BezHandle1_MouseMove (Button As Integer, Shift As Integer, X!, Y!)
OFBN = 45 + NodeZoom
Xstr = Format$(X \ PixelX, "000")
Ystr = Format$(Y \ PixelY, "000")
XYLabel.Caption = "[" + Xstr + " , " + Ystr + "]"
If Button Then
    BezDraw
```

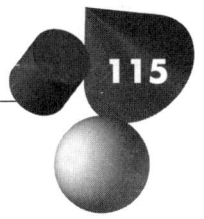

```
        ArtWork.DrawMode = 7: ArtWork.DrawStyle = 2
        ArtWork.Line (P1.X, P1.Y)-(h1.X, h1.Y), YELLOW
        ArtWork.Line (p2.X, p2.Y)-(h2.X, h2.Y), YELLOW
        h1.X = X
        h1.Y = Y
        Shape1.Left = h1.X - OFBN
        Shape1.Top = h1.Y - OFBN
        Shape1.Visible = True
        ArtWork.Line (P1.X, P1.Y)-(h1.X, h1.Y), YELLOW
        ArtWork.Line (p2.X, p2.Y)-(h2.X, h2.Y), YELLOW
        BezDraw
    End If
End Sub
```

**OFBN:** Offset for the Bézier's node (45 Twips is half Shape1's width). This places Shape1 in the center of X and Y (mouse pointer location) during the move.

**NodeZoom:** The value stated in the ZoomBar control to adjust the OFBN offset when the scale of Artwork desktop's view has changed due to a zoom in or zoom out.

**Xstr and Ystr:** The BezHandle is a separate picture box, so send the X and Y coordinates to XYlabel so correct coordinates will be displayed.

**If Button then:** If the mouse button is held in, continue.

**DrawBez:** Draw a curve in Inverse (6) DrawMode.

**ArtWork.DrawMode:** Change DrawMode to Xor (7) so the dotted lever lines can pass over other objects without erasing them.

**ArtWork.Line:** Draw the dotted lines. Yellow will appear cyan when in Xor mode. There are two different handles, so you must draw two separate lever lines.

**h1.X = X:** Switch the current X points for the illusion of moving.

**h1.Y = Y:** Switch the current Y points for the illusion of moving.

**Shape1.Left, Shape1.Top:** A Shape control is used to replace the BezHandle1 picture box control. If you moved the BezHandle1 control, the control would repeatedly bounce to its Left property to the current X coordinate. Additional code can be written to prevent this; but why bother? A Shape control works just fine. It saves on writing API Polyline or Basic Line statements to draw the little handle or node shapes.

**Shape1.Visible = True:** Since there are only two Shape controls used in this program, their locations might be unknown. Move them to their proper locations and then make them visible.

**BezDraw:** Draw a curve in Inverse (6) DrawMode. This will erase the last curve's image to give the illusion of movement.

## Bézier Curves

> **ScaleLeft Properties:** Set a new x position coordinate for a form, picture box, or printer object. The x (horizontal) position you state will start at the leftmost edge of the control. (ScaleLeft is the inside left coordination scale of the control.)
>
> **ScaleTop Properties:** Set a new y position coordinate for a form, picture box, or printer object. The y (vertical) position you state will start at the uppermost edge of the control. (ScaleTop is the inside top coordination scale of the control.)
>
> Using ScaleMode changes these settings. See the Visual Basic language reference for more details.

## Storing the Curve's New Coordinate Points

Once a curve has been stretched or moved to a new location, the coordinate points must be restored. All node and handles must be repositioned and the lever lines redrawn. (See Listing 3.5.)

Listing 3.5. Rescaling the Bézier's handles to the new locations.

```
Sub BezHandle1_MouseUp (Button As Integer, Shift As Integer, X !, Y !)
OFBN = 45 + NodeZoom
Shape1.Visible = False
BezHandle1.Move X - OFBN, Y - OFBN
BezHandle1.ScaleLeft = BezHandle1.Left
BezHandle1.ScaleTop = BezHandle1.Top
BezHandle1.Visible = True
ArtWork.DrawStyle = 0: ArtWork.DrawWidth = 1
    P1X(B) = P1.X: P1Y(B) = P1.Y
    p2X(B) = p2.X: p2Y(B) = p2.Y
    h1X(B) = h1.X: h1Y(B) = h1.Y
    h2X(B) = h2.X: h2Y(B) = h2.Y
    BézierStore
    UpdateObjects
P1.X = P1X(B): P1.Y = P1Y(B): p2.X = p2X(B): p2.Y = p2Y(B)
h1.X = h1X(B): h1.Y = h1Y(B): h2.X = h2X(B): h2.Y = h2Y(B)
ArtWork.DrawMode = 7: ArtWork.DrawStyle = 2
ArtWork.Line (P1.X, P1.Y)-(h1.X, h1.Y), YELLOW
ArtWork.Line (p2.X, p2.Y)-(h2.X, h2.Y), YELLOW
End Sub
```

**OFBN:** Offset for the Bézier's node (45 twips is half of Shape1's width). This places Shape1 in the center of X and Y (mouse pointer location) during the move.

**Shape1.Visible:** Hide the Shape control after the move.

**BezHandle1.Move:** Move the handle to its new coordinate.

**BezHandle1.ScaleLeft:** See BezHandle.ScaleTop.

**BezHandle.ScaleTop:** Rescale the picture box so the X and Y coordinates are the same as Artwork's. Since the BezHandle is a picture box within a picture box, its Left and Top properties are positioned using Artwork's internal scale. Making BezHandle1's ScaleLeft and ScaleTop equal its own left and top border positions would make the BezHandle1's internal X and Y coordinates equivalent to Artwork's scale.

**BezHandle1.Visible:** The handle was hidden during the MouseDown event but not moved. You must now move it to the curve's new location.

**ArtWork.DrawStyle:** You were using the dotted line mode, so this changes to the solid line mode.

**ArtWork.DrawWidth:** Make sure the drawing width is switched back to the default of 1.

**p1.X(B), p1Y(B), etc....:** Stores the handle and node points. Details of these array variables are explained in Listing 3.8.

**BézierStore:** Store the bounding box's new coordinate positions.

**UpdateObjects:** Redraw all the objects created to date.

**p1.X, p1.Y, etc....:** Reset the BezHandle and BezNode positions.

**ArtWork.DrawMode, ArtWork.DrawStyle:** You are going to make dotted lines again, so set DrawMode to Xor and change DrawStyle to Dot.

**ArtWork.Line:** Draw the final dotted lines for each lever connected to the curve.

# The Second Bézier Handle for a Curve

All BezHandle2 mouse events use the same formulas and routines as the previous BezHandle1 mouse events. You are now working with Bézier handle 2 and node point 2, so switch these names where applicable. (See Listing 3.6.)

**Listing 3.6.** Setting the Bézier curve when clicking handle #2.

```
Sub BezHandle2_MouseDown (Button As Integer, Shift As Integer, X!, Y!)
XX2 = E(B): YY2 = S(B): XX1 = W(B): YY1 = N(B)
    BezHandle2.Visible = False
BezNode2.BackColor = Blue: BezNode1.BackColor = Black
    BezMove
    BezDraw
End Sub
```

**BezHandle2:** Refer to the BezHandle1 MouseDown procedure in Listing 3.3 for details on the BezHandle2_MouseDown event.

See Listing 3.7 for how to redraw the Bézier curve after handle #2 is moved.

## Bézier Curves

**Listing 3.7. Redrawing the Bézier curve when handle #2 is moved.**

```
Sub BezHandle2_MouseMove (Button As Integer, Shift As Integer, X!, Y!)
OFBN = 45 + NodeZoom

Xstr = Format$(X \ PixelX, "000")
Ystr = Format$(Y \ PixelY, "000")
XYLabel.Caption = "[" + Xstr + " , " + Ystr + "]"

If Button Then
    BezDraw
    ArtWork.DrawMode = 7: ArtWork.DrawStyle = 2
    ArtWork.Line (P1.X, P1.Y)-(h1.X, h1.Y), YELLOW
    ArtWork.Line (p2.X, p2.Y)-(h2.X, h2.Y), YELLOW
     h2.X = X
     h2.Y = Y
    Shape2.Left = h2.X - OFBN
    Shape2.Top = h2.Y - OFBN
    Shape2.Visible = True
    ArtWork.Line (P1.X, P1.Y)-(h1.X, h1.Y), YELLOW
    ArtWork.Line (p2.X, p2.Y)-(h2.X, h2.Y), YELLOW
    BezDraw
End If
End Sub
```

**BezHandle2:** Refer to the BezHandle1 MouseMove procedure in Listing 3.4 for details on the BezHandle2_MouseMove event.

See Listing 3.8 for rescaling the Bézier's handles.

**Listing 3.8. Rescaling the Bézier's handles to the new location.**

```
Sub BezHandle2_MouseUp (Button As Integer, Shift As Integer, X !, Y!)
OFBN = 45 + NodeZoom
Shape2.Visible = False
BezHandle2.Move X - OFBN, Y - OFBN
BezHandle2.ScaleLeft = BezHandle2.Left
BezHandle2.ScaleTop = BezHandle2.Top
BezHandle2.Visible = True
ArtWork.DrawStyle = 0: ArtWork.DrawWidth = 1
P1X(B) = P1.X: P1Y(B) = P1.Y
p2X(B) = p2.X: p2Y(B) = p2.Y
h1X(B) = h1.X: h1Y(B) = h1.Y
h2X(B) = h2.X: h2Y(B) = h2.Y
BézierStore
UpdateObjects
P1.X = P1X(B): P1.Y = P1Y(B): p2.X = p2X(B): p2.Y = p2Y(B)
h1.X = h1X(B): h1.Y = h1Y(B): h2.X = h2X(B): h2.Y = h2Y(B)
ArtWork.DrawMode = 7: ArtWork.DrawStyle = 2
ArtWork.Line (P1.X, P1.Y)-(h1.X, h1.Y), YELLOW
ArtWork.Line (p2.X, p2.Y)-(h2.X, h2.Y), YELLOW
End Sub
```

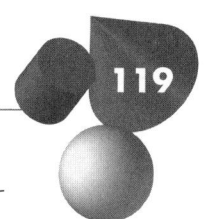

p1X(B), p1Y(B) through to h2X(B), h2Y(B) are where each Bézier curve's four control screen positions are stored (p1,p2,h1,h2).

```
p1X(B) = p1.X: p1Y(B) = p1.Y : p2X(B) = p2.X: p2Y(B) = p2.Y
h1X(B) = h1.X: h1Y(B) = h1.Y : h2X(B) = h2.X: h2Y(B) = h2.Y
```

The screen positions of box, line, and circle objects can easily be stored by using their bounding box's coordinates since their outlines actually touch their bounding box's outline. However, Bézier curve control points can reside within the bounding box area. For this reason, you must store each X and Y coordinate of the four curves controls (P1, P2, H1, and H2) after you have drawn the Bézier curve. The Bounding program in the 16MISC directory on the companion disk can help you understand this concept by demonstrating an endless number of possible curve control point coordinates within a randomly generated bounding box.

**BézierStore:** After the points are stored, you must calculate the position of the curve's bounding box by calling the BézierStore procedure, as shown in Listing 3.17. This procedure can find which of the curve's four on-screen control points are the farthest west, north, south, and east, and calculate a bounding box to fit around the curve object.

## Converting a Line to a Curve

The BezHandle procedure converts a line to a curve by adding the Bézier nodes and handles to the existing line.

Draw a line using the line tool (button 3) from the tool buttons. Select a line by using the pointer tool (button 1) or drawing a marquee around the line. Next, select the Bézier tool (button 2) and double-click the line.

A small form will appear that enables you to choose a button to convert the line to a curve.

The Artwork.Dlb_Click event then calls the BezHandle procedure to place the Bézier's nodes and handles on either end of the line. Finally, the FlagLine object number for the old line is switched to a FlagBézier. (See Listing 3.9.)

**Listing 3.9. Places the handles and dotted lines on a line.**

```
Sub BezHandles ()
OFBN = 45 + NodeZoom
    BezNode1.Move W(B) - OFBN, N(B) - OFBN
    BezNode2.Move E(B) - OFBN, S(B) - OFBN
 P1.X = W(B)
 P1.Y = N(B)
 p2.X = E(B)
 p2.Y = S(B)
'''''''''''''
ArtWork.DrawMode = 7: ArtWork.DrawStyle = 2
HalfLeft = (E(B) + W(B)) \ 2
HalfTop = (S(B) + N(B)) \ 2
```

*continues*

## Bézier Curves

**Listing 3.9. continued**

```
BezHandle1.Left = (W(B) + HalfLeft) \ 2 - OFBN
BezHandle1.Top = (N(B) + HalfTop) \ 2 - OFBN
BezHandle2.Left = (E(B) + HalfLeft) \ 2 - OFBN
BezHandle2.Top = (S(B) + HalfTop) \ 2 - OFBN
BezHandle1.ScaleLeft = BezHandle1.Left
BezHandle1.ScaleTop = BezHandle1.Top
BezHandle2.ScaleLeft = BezHandle2.Left
BezHandle2.ScaleTop = BezHandle2.Top
BezNode1.ScaleLeft = BezNode1.Left
BezNode1.ScaleTop = BezNode1.Top
BezNode2.ScaleLeft = BezNode2.Left
BezNode2.ScaleTop = BezNode2.Top
 ReScale 'If a zoom tool is to be used in program
h1.X = BezHandle1.Left + OFBN
h1.Y = BezHandle1.Top + OFBN
h2.X = BezHandle2.Left + OFBN
h2.Y = BezHandle2.Top + OFBN
P1X(B) = P1.X: P1Y(B) = P1.Y
p2X(B) = p2.X: p2Y(B) = p2.Y
h1X(B) = h1.X: h1Y(B) = h1.Y
h2X(B) = h2.X: h2Y(B) = h2.Y
ArtWork.Line (P1.X, P1.Y)-(h1.X, h1.Y), YELLOW
ArtWork.Line (p2.X, p2.Y)-(h2.X, h2.Y), YELLOW
End Sub
```

**OFBN:** Offset for Bézier Handle1 and Bézier Handle2. (45 twips are half the handle's width.) OFBN places the handle lever in the center of h1 and h2.

**ArtWork.AutoRedraw:** Turn this off because you do not want to capture an image of this process.

**BezNode1.Move, BezNode2:** Replace the two standard line nodes with Bézier nodes.

**p1.X, p1.Y, p2.X, p2.Y:** These values represent the start and end points of the curve, so make them equal to the values (which were previously stored in W(B), N(B), S(B), and E(B)) of the start and end points of the line.

**Artwork.DrawMode:** Add dotted lines that join the BezHandles to the BezNodes, which are drawn in Xor mode. Also change the DrawStyle to Dots.

**HalfLeft, HalfTop:** You have to calculate the halfway mark of the line, so place the handles near the center positions of the line.

**BezHandle1.Left, BezHandle1.Top:** See BezHandle2.Left, BezHandle2.Top.

**BezHandle2.Left, BezHandle2.Top:** This is where you place the handles.

**BezHandle1.ScaleLeft (Top), BezHandle2.ScaleLeft (Top):** See BezNode1.ScaleLeft (Top), BezNode2.ScaleLeft (Top).

**BezNode1.ScaleLeft (Top), BezNode2.ScaleLeft (Top):** Rescale the Bézier's two handles and two nodes to reflect Artwork's internal X, Y coordinate scale.

**Rescale:** If a zoom tool were used, you would need to reflect the previous scaling to that of the zoom in or zoom out scale of the desktop.

**h1.X, h1.Y, h2.X, and h2.Y:** The handles are now positioned correctly, so pass their X, Y coordinates to variables that will hold the two handle's present positions.

**p1X(B), p2X(B), h1X(B), h2X(B), and so on:** Now store all four Bézier control points to the indexed arrays that keep track of which points belong to which Bézier curve.

**ArtWork.Line:** Finally, draw the dotted lever lines that join the two Bézier nodes to the two Bézier handles.

When you double-click a line with the Bézier tool (button 3), the NodeEdit form appears in the middle of the screen. If the currently selected object is a line, choose the To Curve option button. If the currently selected object is a curve, choose the To Line option button. Figure 3.9 illustrates what a line would look like after the user had chosen to convert it to a curve.

The two end points are the Bézier curve's nodes, and the two middle points are the Bézier curve's handles. You could add extra controls to the NodeEdit form to perform other tasks such as deleting, breaking, and joining nodes. This program, however, does not edit curves.

**F**igure 3.9.
*A line being converted to a curve.*

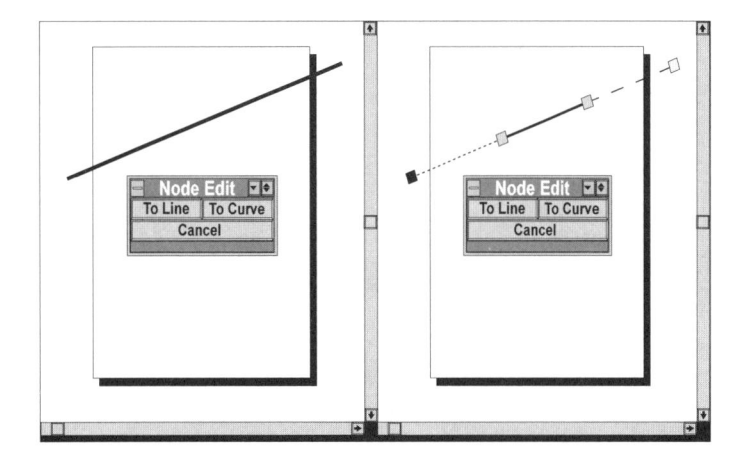

# Grabbing a Curve

The nodes located on either end of a curve object are called BezNode1 and BezNode2. You can move a curve using either one of these Bézier nodes.

The BezNode1 mouse event routines are based on the BezHandle routines (starting at Listing 3.3), except you also must move the handle (BezHandle1) that is attached to the BezNode1 while moving the curve. (See Listing 3.10.)

## Bézier Curves

**Listing 3.10. Setting the curve when clicking the Bézier's node #1.**
```
Sub BezNode1_MouseDown (Button As Integer, Shift As Integer, X!, Y!)
XX2 = E(B): YY2 = S(B): XX1 = W(B): YY1 = N(B)

BezNode1.BackColor = Blue: BezNode2.BackColor = Black
    X1 = p1.X: Y1 = p1.Y
    XX1 = X: YY1 = Y
    P = 1
End Sub
```

**X1, Y1:** Temporarily store the current node's position before any moving.

**XX1, YY1:** Determine whether you actually moved the node or just highlighted it.

The `BezNode1 MouseMove` event is based on the `BezHandle1 MouseMove` routines. Refer to Listing 3.4 for any further explanation of code in Listing 3.11.

**Listing 3.11. Redraws the Bézier curve when Bézier node #1 is moved.**
```
Sub BezNode1_MouseMove (Button As Integer, Shift As Integer, X!, Y !)
OFBN = 45 + NodeZoom
Xstr = Format$(X \ PixelX, "000")
Ystr = Format$(Y \ PixelY, "000")
XYLabel.Caption = "[" + Xstr + " , " + Ystr + "]"
If Button Then
    If X = XX1 And Y = YY1 Then XX1 = 0 And YY1 = 0: Exit Sub
        If P = 1 Then
            P = 0: BezHandle1.Visible = True:
            BezHandle2.Visible = True: BezMove
            BezDraw
        End If
BezDraw
ArtWork.DrawMode = 7: ArtWork.DrawStyle = 2
ArtWork.Line (P1.X, P1.Y)-(h1.X, h1.Y), YELLOW
ArtWork.Line (p2.X, p2.Y)-(h2.X, h2.Y), YELLOW
 P1.X = X
 P1.Y = Y
 h1.X = (X - X1) + h1X(B)
 h1.Y = (Y - Y1) + h1Y(B)
BezHandle1.Left = h1.X - OFBN
BezHandle1.Top = h1.Y - OFBN
    Shape1.Left = P1.X - OFBN
    Shape1.Top = P1.Y - OFBN
    BezNode1.Visible = False: Shape1.Visible = True
    ArtWork.Line (P1.X, P1.Y)-(h1.X, h1.Y), YELLOW
    ArtWork.Line (p2.X, p2.Y)-(h2.X, h2.Y), YELLOW
BezDraw
End If
End Sub
```

**X = XX1 and Y = YY1:** Equals true if you clicked a node but did not move it. This prevents the Bézier node from moving a few pixels positions.

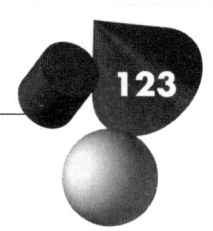

**If P = 1 Then:** P will be true for every newly converted curve. You need to call the BezMove procedure only once to erase the old line and start drawing a Bézier curve.

Making P = 0 makes the procedure skip this block of statements since the block of statements needs executed only once:

h1.X = (X - X1) + h1X(B) : h1.Y = (Y - Y1) + h1Y(B):

These calculations move the handle the same distance the node is moved. Y equals the current Y position of the mouse as it moves. Y1 is the starting position of the move (node position.) By subtracting these two values and adding the handle position before each move, the calculation will always put the handle the same distance from the node.

The BezNode1_Mouse_Up event is based on the BezHandle1_Mouse_Up routines. Refer to Listing 3.5 for any further explanation of code within Listing 3.12.

**Listing 3.12. Rescales the Bézier's handles to the new location.**

```
Sub BezNode1_MouseUp (Button As Integer, Shift As Integer, X!, Y!)
OFBN = 45 + NodeZoom
If X = XX1 And Y = YY1 Then XX1 = 0 And YY1 = 0: Exit Sub
BezNode1.Move X - OFBN, Y - OFBN
BezNode1.ScaleLeft = BezNode1.Left
BezNode1.ScaleTop = BezNode1.Top
Shape1.Visible = False: BezNode1.Visible = True
BezHandle1.ScaleLeft = BezHandle1.Left
BezHandle1.ScaleTop = BezHandle1.Top
X1 = P1.X: Y1 = P1.Y
    P1X(B) = P1.X: P1Y(B) = P1.Y
    p2X(B) = p2.X: p2Y(B) = p2.Y
    h1X(B) = h1.X: h1Y(B) = h1.Y
    h2X(B) = h2.X: h2Y(B) = h2.Y
UpdateObjects
P1.X = P1X(B): P1.Y = P1Y(B): p2.X = p2X(B): p2.Y = p2Y(B)
h1.X = h1X(B): h1.Y = h1Y(B): h2.X = h2X(B): h2.Y = h2Y(B)
ArtWork.DrawMode = 7: ArtWork.DrawStyle = 2
    ArtWork.Line (P1.X, P1.Y)-(h1.X, h1.Y), YELLOW
    ArtWork.Line (p2.X, p2.Y)-(h2.X, h2.Y), YELLOW
BézierStore
End Sub
```

BezNode2 mouse events are not listed in this chapter, Refer to the source code for the Artisan program that comes on the companion disk.

The BezNode2 mouse event routines are based on the BezHandle routines (starting at Listing 3.3). You also have to move the handle BezHandle2 (that is attached to the BezNode2) while moving the curve.

The BezNode2_MouseDown, BezNode2_MouseDown, and BezNode2_MouseDown events use the same formulas and routines as the BezNode1 mouse events. The only difference is that the P1 and H1 values are changed to reflect the P2 and H2 values.

## Bézier Curves

## Erasing the Curve's Image Before a Move

The routine in Listing 3.13 is called to draw the first Bézier curve when a handle or node is moved. When a curve is positioned, it is drawn by the `UpdateObjects` procedure, which draws it in normal `Copy_Pen` (13) mode. The image of the curve is preserved using the `AutoRedraw` function. When editing or moving a curve, erase this preserved image of a curve from your screen.

**Listing 3.13.** Erases the old image of the curve and dotted handle lines.

```
Sub BezMove ()
ArtWork.DrawMode = 7: ArtWork.DrawStyle = 2
ArtWork.Line (P1.X, P1.Y)-(h1.X, h1.Y), YELLOW
ArtWork.Line (p2.X, p2.Y)-(h2.X, h2.Y), YELLOW
If BezErase = True Then
    ArtWork.AutoRedraw = True
    ArtWork.DrawStyle = 0: ArtWork.DrawMode = 13
    ArtWork.Line (P1.X, P1.Y)-(p2.X, p2.Y), QBColor(15)
    ArtWork.AutoRedraw = False: BezErase = False
Else
    ArtWork.AutoRedraw = True
    ArtWork.DrawMode = 16
    ArtWork.DrawWidth = 1
    ArtWork.PSet (0, 0)
    BezDraw
    ArtWork.DrawWidth = 1
    ArtWork.AutoRedraw = False
End If
ArtWork.DrawMode = 7: ArtWork.DrawStyle = 2
ArtWork.Line (P1.X, P1.Y)-(h1.X, h1.Y), YELLOW
ArtWork.Line (p2.X, p2.Y)-(h2.X, h2.Y), YELLOW
End Sub
```

**ArtWork.DrawMode:** The dotted lever lines that join the handles and nodes are drawn in Xor mode over the previous lever.

**If BezEraze = True Then:** This flag is set when you first convert a line to a curve. You need to draw a straight white line to erase it.

**Else:** The curve does not resemble a straight line, so change the DrawMode to White (16) in preparation to draw a white curve.

**ArtWork.Pset (0,0):** Switching back and forth with Visual Basic's DrawMode while AutoRedraw is true can switch modes on you with no warning! You can fix this by sending any graphical statement to the form, which will then refresh the drawing mode. A Pset statement is a good example: set the pixel well off the viewing area or port (0,0 in this case). This trick works equally well with Windows graphical API functions that go in and out of DrawModes regularly.

**BezDraw:** Draw the Bézier curve.

**ArtWork.Line:** Finally, reset the dotted lines you previously erased.

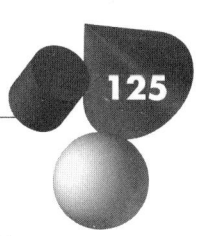

# Building a Bounding Box for the Curve

The BézierStore procedure checks all possible positions the curve's nodes and handles could be in. It then stores only the four coordinates that match each handle and node that are at furthest points to enclose the curve.

An array sorting function can do this with less code. If you have Visual Basic 3.0 or higher, the Choose statement would shorten the routine. Nested loops also can be used to condense the code. The BézierStore shows you the routine in its four-section format so you can get an idea on what it needs to do. (See Listing 3.14.)

**Listing 3.14.** Calculating the new bounding box of a curve.

```
Sub BézierStore ()
If P1.X <= h1.X And P1.X <= h2.X And P1.X <= p2.X Then W(B) = P1.X
If h1.X <= P1.X And h1.X <= h2.X And h1.X <= p2.X Then W(B) = h1.X
If h2.X <= P1.X And h2.X <= h1.X And h2.X <= p2.X Then W(B) = h2.X
If p2.X <= P1.X And p2.X <= h1.X And p2.X <= h2.X Then W(B) = p2.X
If P1.Y <= h1.Y And P1.Y <= h2.Y And P1.Y <= p2.Y Then N(B) = P1.Y
If h1.Y <= P1.Y And h1.Y <= h2.Y And h1.Y <= p2.Y Then N(B) = h1.Y
If h2.Y <= P1.Y And h2.Y <= h1.Y And h2.Y <= p2.Y Then N(B) = h2.Y
If p2.Y <= P1.Y And p2.Y <= h1.Y And p2.Y <= h2.Y Then N(B) = p2.Y
If P1.X >= h1.X And P1.X >= h2.X And P1.X >= p2.X Then E(B) = P1.X
If h1.X >= P1.X And h1.X >= h2.X And h1.X >= p2.X Then E(B) = h1.X
If h2.X >= P1.X And h2.X >= h1.X And h2.X >= p2.X Then E(B) = h2.X
If p2.X >= P1.X And p2.X >= h1.X And p2.X >= h2.X Then E(B) = p2.X
If P1.Y >= h1.Y And P1.Y >= h2.Y And P1.Y >= p2.Y Then S(B) = P1.Y
If h1.Y >= P1.Y And h1.Y >= h2.Y And h1.Y >= p2.Y Then S(B) = h1.Y
If h2.Y >= P1.Y And h2.Y >= h1.Y And h2.Y >= p2.Y Then S(B) = h2.Y
If p2.Y >= P1.Y And p2.Y >= h1.Y And p2.Y >= h2.Y Then S(B) = p2.Y
End Sub
```

**BézierStore:** This routine searches through the data arrays of the four controls points of the Bézier curve, which are as follows:

        p1.X, p1.Y (BezNode1)
        h1.X, h1.Y (BezHandle1)
        h2.X, h2.Y (BezHandle2)
        p2.X, p2.Y (BezNode2)

When BézierStore finds the farthest points West, North, East and South, it will store these values in W(B), N(B), E(B), and S(B). These final values are used to border the objects with a bounding box.

Figure 3.10 shows six curves, each with different coordinates of BezHandles and BezNodes. Since you have an infinite number of ways to place these four curve control points, you must find a way to relocate the bounding box after each curve is made.

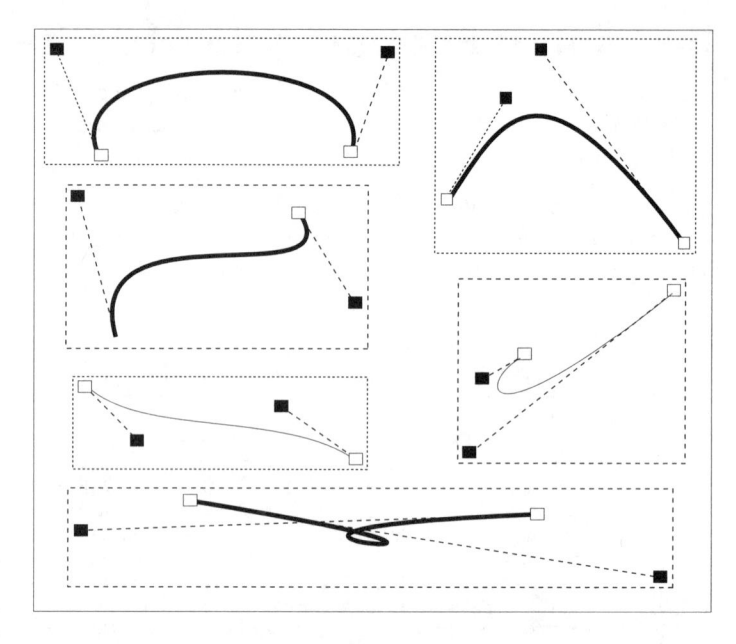

**Figure 3.10.**
*Several scenarios for* W, N, E, *and* S *values.*

## Visual State of Lever Lines on a Curve

The vstate variable flag is very important and can get confusing at times. vstate toggles the visible properties of the Bézier nodes and handles on and off. This is necessary for visual appearance when the Bézier curve loses the focus due to any one of the following:

- Selecting another tool
- Choosing a color
- Scrolling the artwork
- Clicking the desktop outside of the curve's bounding box

See Listing 3.15 for resetting a scaling and a curve's handle lines.

**Listing 3.15. Resets scaling and dotted handle lines of a curve.**

```
Sub BezUpdate ()
OFBN = 45 + NodeZoom
P1.X = P1X(B): P1.Y = P1Y(B)
p2.X = p2X(B): p2.Y = p2Y(B)
h1.X = h1X(B): h1.Y = h1Y(B)
h2.X = h2X(B): h2.Y = h2Y(B)
BezHandle1.Left = h1.X - OFBN: BezHandle1.Top = h1.Y - OFBN
BezHandle2.Left = h2.X - OFBN: BezHandle2.Top = h2.Y - OFBN
BezNode1.Left = P1.X - OFBN: BezNode1.Top = P1.Y - OFBN
BezNode2.Left = p2.X - OFBN: BezNode2.Top = p2.Y - OFBN
BezHandle1.ScaleLeft = BezHandle1.Left
BezHandle1.ScaleTop = BezHandle1.Top
```

```
BezHandle2.ScaleLeft = BezHandle2.Left
BezHandle2.ScaleTop = BezHandle2.Top
BezNode1.ScaleLeft = BezNode1.Left
BezNode1.ScaleTop = BezNode1.Top
BezNode2.ScaleLeft = BezNode2.Left
BezNode2.ScaleTop = BezNode2.Top
Shape1.Left = h1.X - OFBN: Shape1.Top = h1.Y - OFBN
Shape2.Left = h2.X - OFBN: Shape2.Top = h2.Y - OFBN
ReScale ''' If ZoomTool Used
ArtWork.DrawMode = 7: ArtWork.DrawStyle = 2
ArtWork.Line (P1.X, P1.Y)-(h1.X, h1.Y), YELLOW
ArtWork.Line (p2.X, p2.Y)-(h2.X, h2.Y), YELLOW
ArtWork.DrawStyle = 0
If ShowDotted = False Then VState = False Else VState = True
BezHandle1.Visible = VState: BezHandle2.Visible = VState
If Not CurrentTool = 1 Then VState = False Else VState = True
BezNode1.Visible = VState: BezNode2.Visible = VState
If CurrentTool = 1 Then N_H_Clear Else Nodes
End Sub
```

**OFBN:** Offset for BezHandle1 and BezHandle2 plus BezNode1 and BezNode2. (45 twips are half of each control's width.) This establishes each control's center point.

**p1.X, p1.Y, p2.X, p2.Y:** These values represent the start and end points of the curve. The indexed arrays p1X(B), p1Y(B), and so on, currently store the values needed for each curve.

**h1.X, h1.Y, h2.X, h2.Y:** These values represent the values of the two Bézier handles. The indexed arrays h1X(B), h1Y(B), and so on, currently store the values needed for each curve.

Figure 3.11 shows that ShowDotted is true and the nodes are visible, Figure 3.12 shows that it is false and the nodes are visible, and Figure 3.13 shows that ShowDotted is false, with no nodes.

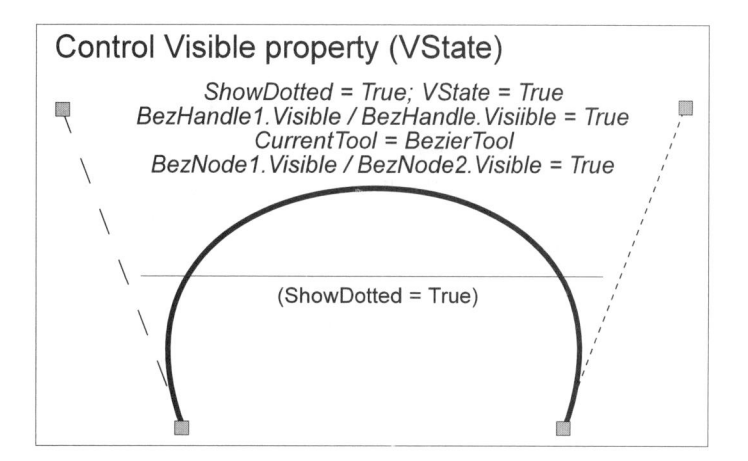

**Figure 3.11.**
*True, nodes visible.*

Control Visible property (VState)

ShowDotted = True; VState = True
BezHandle1.Visible / BezHandle.Visiible = True
CurrentTool = BezierTool
BezNode1.Visible / BezNode2.Visible = True

(ShowDotted = True)

# Bézier Curves

**Figure 3.12.**
*False, nodes visible.*

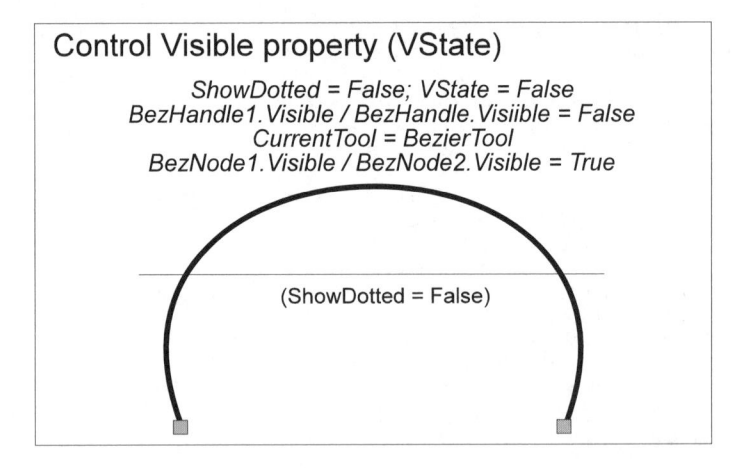

```
Control Visible property (VState)

    ShowDotted = False; VState = False
BezHandle1.Visible / BezHandle.Visiible = False
           CurrentTool = BezierTool
   BezNode1.Visible / BezNode2.Visible = True




                    (ShowDotted = False)
```

**Figure 3.13.**
*False, no nodes.*

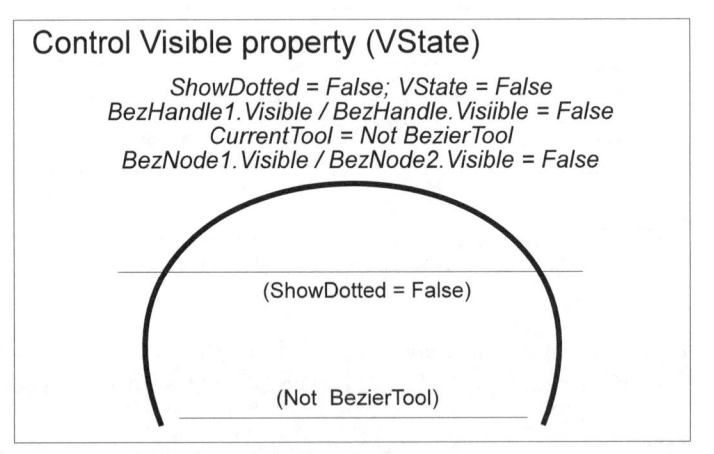

```
Control Visible property (VState)

    ShowDotted = False; VState = False
BezHandle1.Visible / BezHandle.Visiible = False
         CurrentTool = Not BezierTool
  BezNode1.Visible / BezNode2.Visible = False




                    (ShowDotted = False)


                    (Not  BezierTool)
```

This `BezUpdate` procedure (Listing 3.18) is called to display or hide the Bézier's handles, nodes, and the dotted line that connects each control. This depends largely on when the curve loses the focus. (For example, the user has the curve selected but then selects a different drawing tool.) There are only four picture box controls used in this program to represent the handles and nodes. When the curve is selected, you must relocate these controls to the proper curve. You also must rescale the interior dimensions of each node and handle so they are in sync with Artwork's picture box current scale.

**BezHandle1.Left (Top, ScaleLeft, ScaleTop), and so on:** Perform the previously mentioned duties. The two `Shape` controls can be moved at this time also.

**ArtWork.Line:** Draw the dotted lines that connect each handle and node. This makes the dotted lines visible or invisible, depending on their last visual state on the screen.

> **NOTE** You must be able to hide or show the handles or nodes, depending on what the user's last action was (losing the focus or gaining the focus).

Figures 3.11, 3.12, and 3.13 show possible visual states (VState) of a curve, depending on the value of the flag Showdotted. If your currently selected tool is not the BézierTool, the BezNodes must be hidden.

If the current tool is the Bézier tool, clear the standard nodes and stretch handles; if a tool other than the Bézier tool is currently selected, show only the standard nodes.

Standard nodes are white nodes that appear only on box and line shapes. Stretch handles are eight little red boxes that appear around an object's bounding box after it has been drawn. The stretch handles are used to expand or shrink the drawn image.

## Stretching a Bézier Curve

> **CAUTION** Divide by Zero is a common error if any handle's or node's X and Y positions are equal to another's.
>
> Twip mode reduces this possibility greatly, but it is poor programming to let this to occur at all.
>
> Divide by Zero happens when you try to divide one value (numerator) by zero (denominator). Suppose that during runtime, the value of X and the value of X1 ended up being the same. For instance, the statement 354 \ (X - X1) would be 354 \ 0. A Divide by Zero error will cause the program to stop.
>
> The BezStretch procedure makes no effort to stop a Divide by Zero error because it uses basic mathematics. However, it is still difficult to get a Divide by Zero error in this procedure.

Figure 3.14 shows the variables and formula to stretch or flip a Bézier curve.

## Bézier Curves

**Figure 3.14.**
*Stretching or flipping a Bézier curve.*

The BezStretch procedure in Listing 3.16 shrinks, expands, or flips a curve on the desktop. The stretch is performed only on the sides of the bounding box that are being expanded or shrunk. The sides of the bounding box that remain stationary during the stretch act as anchors and the points within the bounding box (the nodes) act as boats that drift away from the anchors. Boats (nodes) drift further away from the anchor even more. This effect gives a uniform elastic feel to stretching of images.

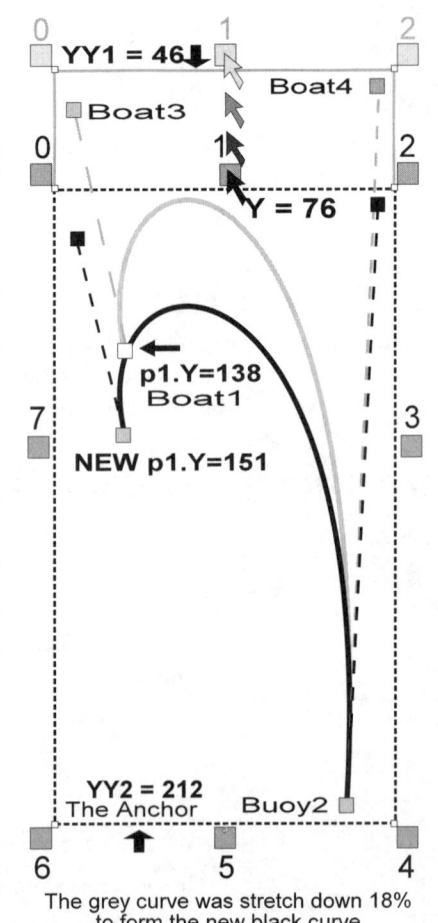

YY1 = 46
Boat4
Boat3
Y = 76
p1.Y=138
Boat1
NEW p1.Y=151
YY2 = 212
The Anchor    Buoy2

The grey curve was stretch down 18% to form the new black curve

(Y−YY1) / (YY2−YY1)
(76−46) / (212−46)
(30) / (166) = .18072
18.1%
18.1% = percentage

((YY2−p1.Y) * Percentage) + p1.Y
((212−138) * 18.1) + 138
(.74 * 18.1) + 138
(13.394) + 138
(13) + 138 = 151
151 = p1.Y

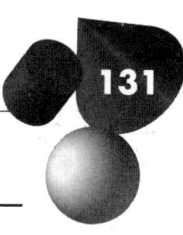

**L**isting 3.16. Calculating new coordinates of a curve when stretched.
```
Sub BezStretch (Index As Integer, Button As Integer, Shift As Integer, X!, Y!)
Select Case Index
    Case 0, 1, 2, 4, 5, 6
      pt1 = P1Y(B): pt2 = p2Y(B): hd1 = h1Y(B): hd2 = h2Y(B)
    Case 3, 7
      pt1 = P1X(B): pt2 = P2X(B): hd1 = h1X(B): hd2 = h2X(B)
End Select
If pt1 = pt2 And hd1 = hd2 Then
W(B) = XX1: N(B) = YY1: E(B) = XX2: S(B) = YY2: Exit Sub
End If
Boat1 = pt1: Boat2 = pt2: Boat3 = hd1: Boat4 = hd2
'''''''''''''''''''''''''''''''''''''''''''''''
Select Case Index
    Case 0, 1, 2
      percentage! = (Y - YY1) / (YY2 - YY1): ANCHOR = YY2
    Case 3
      percentage! = (X - XX2) / (XX1 - XX2): ANCHOR = XX1
    Case 4, 5, 6
      percentage! = (Y - YY2) / (YY1 - YY2): ANCHOR = YY1
    Case 7
      percentage! = (X - XX1) / (XX2 - XX1): ANCHOR = XX2
End Select
Boat1 = ((ANCHOR - Boat1) * percentage!) + Boat1
Boat2 = ((ANCHOR - Boat2) * percentage!) + Boat2
Boat3 = ((ANCHOR - Boat3) * percentage!) + Boat3
Boat4 = ((ANCHOR - Boat4) * percentage!) + Boat4
If Index = 3 Or Index = 7 Then GoTo Xpoint Else GoTo Ypoint
Xpoint: 'Stretch from middle side Handles
p1.X = Boat1: P1X(B) = Boat1: p2.X = Boat2: P2X(B) = Boat2
h1.X = Boat3: h1X(B) = Boat3: h2.X = Boat4: h2X(B) = Boat4
BézierStore
Exit Sub
Ypoint: 'Stretch from middle top and bottom Handles
p1.Y = Boat1: P1Y(B) = Boat1: p2.Y = Boat2: p2Y(B) = Boat2
h1.Y = Boat3: h1Y(B) = Boat3: h2.Y = Boat4: h2Y(B) = Boat4
If Index = 1 Or Index = 5 Then BézierStore: Exit Sub
'''''''''''' Stretch from corner Handles ''''''''''''
pt1 = P1X(B): pt2 = P2X(B): hd1 = h1X(B): hd2 = h2X(B)
Boat1 = pt1: Boat2 = pt2: Boat3 = hd1: Boat4 = hd2
Select Case Index
    Case 0, 6
      percentage! = (X - XX1) / (XX2 - XX1): ANCHOR = XX2
    Case 2, 4
      percentage! = (X - XX2) / (XX1 - XX2): ANCHOR = XX1
    Case Else
      BézierStore
      Exit Sub
End Select
Boat1 = ((ANCHOR - Boat1) * percentage!) + Boat1
Boat2 = ((ANCHOR - Boat2) * percentage!) + Boat2
Boat3 = ((ANCHOR - Boat3) * percentage!) + Boat3
Boat4 = ((ANCHOR - Boat4) * percentage!) + Boat4
p1.X = Boat1: P1X(B) = Boat1: p2.X = Boat2: P2X(B) = Boat2
h1.X = Boat3: h1X(B) = Boat3: h2.X = Boat4: h2X(B) = Boat4
BézierStore
End Sub
```

## Bézier Curves

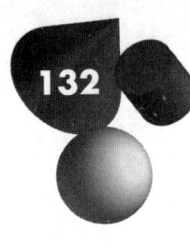

**Select Case Index:** There are eight indexed array handles (red boxes) located around a selected curve. Their index numbers start at 0—the upper-left red box—and continue clockwise to (red box) index number 7.

**Case 0, 1, 2, 4, 5, 6:** If you are stretching the curve using one of these red boxes (top row 0, 1, 2 or bottom row 4, 5, 6), the temporary variables `pt1`, `pt2`, `hd1`, and `hd2` will hold the Y coordinates of the curve's two handles and nodes.

**Case 3, 7:** If you are stretching the curve using the two red boxes at the sides of the curve (between boxes 0 and 6 on the left and between boxes 2 and 6 on the right), do the same as previously, but use the curve's X coordinate.

**If pt1 = pt2 And hd1 = hd2 Then:** The curve resembles a straight line horizontally or vertically. It cannot be stretched, so exit the subroutine.

**Boat1 = pt1 : Boat2 = pt2 : Boat3 = hd1 : Boat4 = hd2:** Temporarily store the four Bézier control points. These are called boats because they float to new positions when you stretch the curve's bounding box.

**Select Case Index:** Depending on which red box you use, go to one of the following matching `Case` expressions.

**percentage!:** Calculate the percent the bounding box has moved. It uses floating-point (decimal-point) accuracy so it is marked as a `Single` (!) variable type.

**Case 0, 1, 2:** One of the red boxes (top row) is used to stretch the bounding box.

**Case 3:** The red boxes (middle right) are used to stretch the bounding box.

**Case 4, 5, 6:** One of the red boxes (bottom row) is used to stretch the bounding box.

**Case 7:** The red boxes (middle left) are used to stretch the bounding box.

**Boat1 = ((ANCHOR - Boat1) * percentage!) + Boat1:** A sample formula is
((YY2 - p1.Y) * Percentage!) + p1.Y.

YY2 is the ANCHOR because it does not move (a fixed bounding box position). p1.Y is BOAT1 because it floats down to a new position during the stretch. Percentage! uses one of the bounding box's current position and the Y mouse move position from the formula (Y - YY1) / YY2 - YY1) to calculate the percentage of how much the bounding box enlarged or shrank. p1.Y was the original BOAT1 position just before this calculation.

**If Index = 3 or Index = 7 then:** If you are using the middle-right box (index 3) or the middle-left box (index 7), the curve can be stretched only horizontally (X-axis), so go to the line marked Xpoint.

**Else:** You are using any one of the other boxes to stretch the curve. Go to the line marked Ypoint.

**Xpoint:** You have successfully stretched the curve horizontally, so store the four new coordinate points of the curve. The new positions will be saved and stored using the BézierStore procedure.

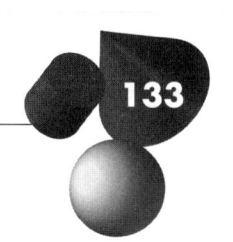

**Ypoint:** You have successfully stretched the curve vertically, so store the four new coordinate points of the curve. The new positions will be saved and stored using the BézierStore procedure. Exit this procedure only if you used the vertical stretching handles.

You are stretching the curve both horizontally and vertically using the corner stretch handles. Recalculate the horizontal *X* axis using the same routines (used previously) but with new values.

> **NOTE** You can combine most of the axis stretch routines from the Bézier Stretch procedure to shorten the overall code. Listing 3.16 is shown here in long form so you'll understand the algorithm. The ArtAPI program in Chapter 15 uses a reworked version of this procedure in its polyStretch procedure to stretch multiconnected poly shapes.

# Summary

You worked with some large calculations and a big variety of variable names in this chapter. The Bézier curve procedures can be difficult to follow the first time. Chapter 10 shows a Mini-Bézier curve program that uses the same variable-naming and routines used in this chapter. Since the Mini-Bézier program is a stand-alone application, it does not need to take into account all the other desktop functions that may occur in a real drawing package.

You should practice with the Mini-Bézier program in Chapter 10 before trying to make changes to either the Artisan program or to the ArtAPI program in Chapter 15.

If you want to shorten all the Bézier curve procedures, you can experiment with recursive Bézier routines. Recursive routines are implemented in almost all drawing and text-conversion programs written in C.

Recursive Bézier curves are easier to write in C because of the way C can point to arrays and track their positions as the *deCasteljau* algorithm calculates each curve point. The Recursive Bézier curve gets its name by calling the BezDivide (*deCastlejau* formula) procedure repeatedly, by having its own procedure statement, BezDivide(p1, D1, E1, C1, leftcounter) and BezDivide(C1, E1, D3, p2, rightcounter), placed after the *deCastlejau* formula. The trick is to break out of the endless loop after each of the curve's points have been plotted. The number of plotted points on the curve depends on the number of cursive loops that are performed.

# CHAPTER 4

# The Artisan Program—Procedures C–N

# The Artisan Program—Procedures C–N

This chapter explains the Artisan program's procedures alphabetically listed C through N. Some of the routines to examine include the ColorBar palette events, which can be used to assign outline and fill colors to an object. Other procedures and events you will find in this chapter include the following:

The FindAllObjects procedure is a routine similar to the BezierStore procedure in Listing 3.17 in Chapter 3, "Bézier Curves." When you marquee an object by drawing a dotted box around it with the pointer tool, this routine scans all bounding box coordinates and selects (highlights) the first object that is within the marquee area.

The FindObject procedure is very similar to the FindAllObjects procedure except it only selects (highlights) the bounding box your mouse pointer is within. In Chapter 15, "The ArtAPI Program," you will use a more sophisticated approach, where the object is only highlighted if you touch the object's outline shape.

The Guidelines procedure is a simple routine that uses oversized Line statement boxes to give the illusion that you are dragging page-guiding lines from either ruler.

The Handle, Handles, and HandleReverse procedures all act together to reposition stretch boxes around an object. Stretch boxes are little red boxes that are used to rescale the size of an object.

The positioning of nodes (little white boxes that connect object coordinate points) around line and box objects is looked at in the Nodes procedure. Finally, this chapter ends with a procedure called N_H_clear, which is used to clear or hide nodes and handles off the desktop.

## Assigning Outlines and Fills to Objects

To change the outline (border) color of an object, you select a color from the ColorBar palette using the right mouse button. To change the fill (paint) color of an object, select a color from the ColorBar palette using the left mouse button.

The outline color is then stored in a variable called PenColor. If you are filling an object with color, the color value is stored in the BrushColor variable. The ARTISAN7.BAS file contains a global procedure called Update_Mouse_Colors that grabs the correct colors, which are stored in an array called Colors. The Update_Mouse_Color procedure is a revised version from the Iconworks example included with Visual Basic.

The code listing for the Update_Mouse_Color procedure is located at the end of the ARTISAN7.BAS module listing in Appendix A.

## Chapter 4

**Listing 4.1.** `ColorBar_MouseDown` finds the color value you selected.

```
Sub ColorBar_MouseDown (Button%, Shift%, X!, Y!)
    If (X >= 0) And (X <= 47) Then Update_Mouse_Colors Button, X, Y
End Sub
```

The picture box named `ColorBar` has its `ScaleWidth` set to 48. The box was divided into equal parts by the `Display_Color_Palette` procedure located in the ARTISAN7.BAS file, which is as follows:

```
ColorBar.Scale (0, 0)-(48, 1)
For I = 0 To 47
ColorBar.Line (I, 0)-(I + 1, 1), Colors(I), BF
If I Then ColorBar.Line (I, 0)-(I, 3)
Next I
```

Clicking your mouse on a color will call `Update_Mouse_Colors` (ARTISAN7.BAS file). The mouse's X position is rounded to a whole number (`Fix`) and represents the color's index number to search for in the array called `Colors`. All indexed colors in array `Colors` are in hexadecimal form.

Some examples of hexadecimal color values are `16777215`, `14737632`, and `12632319`.

The preceding numbers are the hexadecimal values of the first three color values defined in the general declaration section of ARTISAN7.BAS, titled "default color palette values." All numbers are spliced together to generate the 48 colors within the `ColorBar` picture box during the `Form_Load` event.

**Listing 4.2.** `ColorBar_MouseUp` stores and then displays the selected color.

```
Sub ColorBar_MouseUp (Button%, Shift%, X!, Y!)
If Node(0).Visible = False Then Exit Sub
Select Case Button
    Case Right_Button
        OutLineColor(B) = PenColor
    Case Left_Button
        PaintColor(B) = BrushColor: FillValue(B) = 0
End Select
UpdateObjects
End Sub
```

**If Node(0).Visible:** If the nodes are visible, exit the mouse event.

**Case Right_Button:** If you select a color using the right mouse button, you are changing the object's outline color.

**Case Left_Button:** If you select a color using the left mouse button, you are changing the object's fill color.

**UpdateObjects:** Redraw all the objects so the color change takes effect.

## The Artisan Program—Procedures C–N

**Listing 4.3.** The `ColorBar_Paint` event calls a module procedure to repaint every color.
```
Sub ColorBar_Paint ()
    Display_Color_Palette ColorBar
End Sub
```

`Display_Color_Palette ColorBar` reloads all the colors within the palette if the form is moved or hidden. The `ColorBar` argument points to the name of the picture box control because other controls with different names also use this procedure. The ArtAPI program in Chapter 15 moves this call out of the `Paint` event so scrolling of the color palette bar is speeded up.

**Listing 4.4.** A horizontal scrollbar control is used to display all colors in the palette.
```
Sub ColorScroll_Change ()
    ColorBar.Move ColorScroll.Value
End Sub
```

The `ColorScroll_Change` event moves the `ColorBar` left or right, producing the illusion that the `ColorBar` is stationary while the colors seem to scroll.

**Figure 4.1.**
*Artisan's Color Palette indexes.*

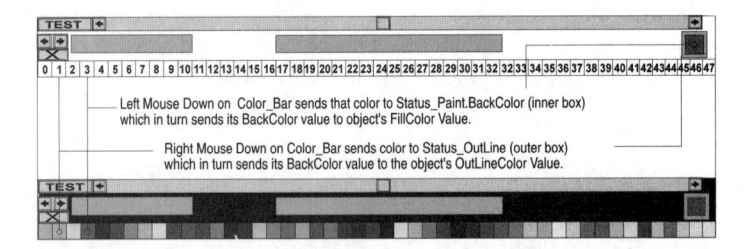

## The ARTISAN.INI File

The `Color_INI` procedure uses a Window's API routine that writes the hexadecimal color values to the ARTISAN.INI file. These are the only values that are written to the .INI file. Several programs (such as VB-clip and C-clip) in the 16MISC directory on the companion disk write form and button positions to .INI files for their own use. They show different styles of splicing values together to save repeated calls to the .INI files.

**Listing 4.5.** Extracting the color value numbers from an .INI file.
```
Sub Color_INI ()
    ColorString = Space$(144)
R = GetPrivateProfileString(KEY_NAME, KEY_ENTRY + "1",
➥BAS_PALETTE1, ColorString, Len(ColorString), INI_FILENAME)
PaletteBarColors ColorString, 0
R = GetPrivateProfileString(KEY_NAME, KEY_ENTRY + "2",
➥BAS_PALETTE2, ColorString, Len(ColorString), INI_FILENAME)
PaletteBarColors ColorString, 16
R = GetPrivateProfileString(KEY_NAME, KEY_ENTRY + "3",
➥BAS_PALETTE3, ColorString, Len(ColorString), INI_FILENAME)
```

```
PaletteBarColors ColorString, 32
End Sub
```

**ColorString:** A 144-character buffer is reserved to pass each color value string.

**GetPrivateProfileString:** API function that reads a user-defined .INI file.

If a custom .INI file is not found, the function will use the default color values that are located in the ARTISAN7.BAS file within Appendix A.

**PaletteBarColors:** The ColorBar values are stored in the Colors array. The key routines here are the numbers 0, 16, and 32, which are used to count the three separate blocks of color values. The best way to see how this is performed is to single step through this procedure using the F8 key or single step ribbon bar icon.

# Finding an Object Using a Marquee

A *marquee* is a moving dotted outline of a box that you draw with the pointer tool. You use a marquee to select an object on the desktop by drawing a dotted line box shape around the object.

The FindAllObjects procedure finds every bounding box on your desktop by looping through every position object coordinate value available. Normally, you would search only the region of the marquee area, but this would add yet another array to store region boundaries. Remember that this is only a sample program.

There are several different Loop routines in this book. In order to help you understand this better, I have shown the loops in this procedure in their long form.

Another example of loops can be found in the ZoomBar event called ZoomAll, which finds all the objects using a two-level loop. Yet another loop routine you may want to consider is a nested loop, which can be difficult to follow at times but can speed the search routine considerably. You can find an example of a nested loop search in the Array Sorter program in the 16MISC directory of the companion disk.

**Listing 4.6.** The FindAllObjects procedure searches for objects within a marquee outline.

```
Sub FindAllObjects (X1%, Y1%, X2%, Y2%, X!, Y!)
CopyX1 = X1: CopyX2 = X2: CopyY1 = Y1: CopyY2 = Y2
If X2 > X1 And Y2 > Y1 Then X1 = CopyX1: X2 = CopyX2
➥: Y1 = CopyY1: Y2 = CopyY2'NW >SE
If X2 > X1 And Y1 > Y2 Then X1 = CopyX1: X2 = CopyX2
➥: Y1 = CopyY2: Y2 = CopyY1'SW >NE
```

*continues*

### Listing 4.6. continued

```
If X1 > X2 And Y1 > Y2 Then X1 = CopyX2: X2 = CopyX1
➥: Y1 = CopyY2: Y2 = CopyY1'SE >NW
If X1 > X2 And Y2 > Y1 Then X1 = CopyX2: X2 = CopyX1
➥: Y1 = CopyY1: Y2 = CopyY2'NE >SW
I = Total
Do While I > 0
If E(I) >= W(I) And S(I) >= N(I) Then West = W(I): East = E(I)
➥: North = N(I): South = S(I) 'NW > SE
If E(I) >= W(I) And N(I) >= S(I) Then West = W(I): East = E(I)
➥: North = S(I): South = N(I) 'SW > NE
If W(I) >= E(I) And N(I) >= S(I) Then West = E(I): East = W(I)
➥: North = S(I): South = N(I) 'SE > NW
If W(I) >= E(I) And S(I) >= N(I) Then West = E(I): East = W(I)
➥: North = N(I): South = S(I)'NE > SW
If X1 <= West And Y1 <= North And X2 >= East And Y2 >= South
➥Then B = I: Handles: Nodes
I = I - 1
Loop
End Sub
```

The `FindAllObjects` routine can find every object that is currently drawn on the desktop. It is used when you use the pointer tool to draw a marquee around an object to select it. Drawing a marquee around several objects will only highlight the last object drawn since there is no procedure to group or join objects in this program.

**CopyX1, CopyX2, CopyY1, CopyY2:** Temporary holders to compare values.

**If X2 > X2 And Y2 > Y1 Then:** Determine where the marquee box was started. The white arrows in the illustration below show four possible start points.

**I = Total:** Temporarily store the `Total` number of objects drawn to date.

**Do While:** Loop through the following code statement until all object coordinates have been found.

**If E(I) >= W(I) And S(I) >= N(I) Then:** Loop through every bounding box position and find the correct order of East, West, North, and South.

It is possible that the original W, N, E, S values could be reversed if the object had been flipped, so that the If/Then statements search every possible angle. If the previously listed coordinates are within the marquee area, handles and nodes are placed around the object that resides within the marquee area.

When drawing a marquee around an object, the corner X1,Y1 and X2,Y2 box coordinates can be reversed or switched, depending on which direction you drag the mouse when first initializing the marquee.

In Figure 4.2, the white arrows show four possible ways to draw a marquee using the pointer tool. X1 and Y1 represent the marquee box's corner value at the MouseDown event. Each marquee box is dragged diagonally until you release the mouse (MouseUp event), which stores the X2,Y2 marquee corner positions.

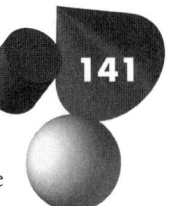

The black arrows in Figure 4.2 show how a simple line can be flipped continuously. Each time you flip the line's bounding box, the west, north, east, and south screen positions flip also.

**Figure 4.2.**
*Drawing a marquee using the pointer tool.*

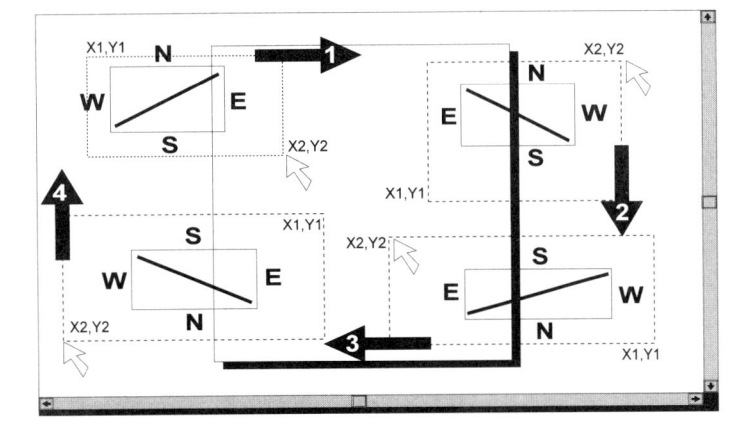

## Clicking the Mouse on an Object

The FindObject procedure highlights or selects the object on which you click the mouse pointer. This procedure, however, has a drawback in that the object will also be highlighted if you click anywhere within the object's bounding box. This may be all you need for your particular program to drag or select an object. If, however, you need to select an object by its outline shape, refer to the ArtAPI program in Chapter 15 for an example of object outline selecting.

To find the bounding box of an object, the FindObject procedure searches through all coordinate values in the W, N, E, S arrays. The Windows API has a function for doing this called PtInRect.

The API PtInRect function can be used as an alternative routine to find bounding boxes. To do this, you will need to build a user-defined type structure that can store each of the bounding box's four corners, similar to the W, N, E, S arrays used in this program.

The following code snippet is an example of user-defined Type.

```
Type Rect
    Left(1 to N) As integer
    Top(1 To N) As Integer
    Right(1 To N) As Integer
    Bottom(1 To N) As Integer
End Type
```

# The Artisan Program—Procedures C–N

The APIdraw program in Chapter 8 shows an example of the PtInRect function searching for Type Rect bounding boxes.

**Figure 4.3.**
*The ruler guidelines are actually dotted outline boxes.*

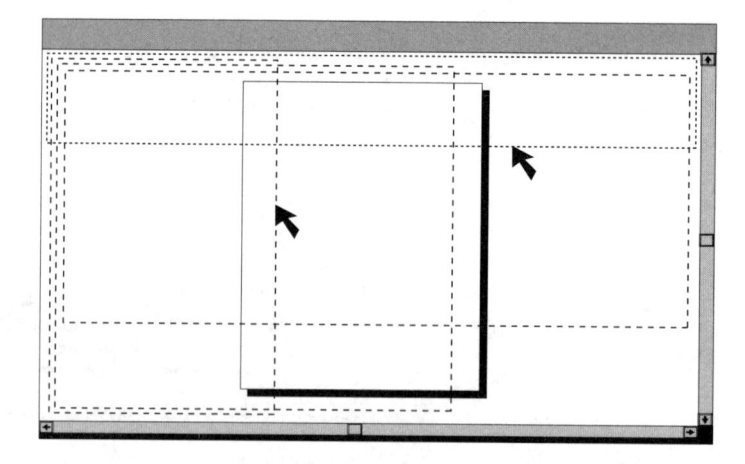

**Listing 4.7.** Searching for a bounding box under the mouse position.

```
Sub Find_Object (X As Single, Y As Single)
R = TGL
Do While R > 0  '''Find GuideLines
If X < (GuideX(R) + 30) And X > (GuideX(R) - 30) Then
    ArtWork.DrawMode = Xor_Pen: ArtWork.DrawStyle = Dot
    ArtWork.AutoRedraw = True
    ArtWork.Line (-5000, -5000)-(GuideX(R), 24000), YELLOW, B
    ArtWork.AutoRedraw = False: X = -5000: SideRuler = True: V = R
    Exit Sub
End If
If Y < (GuideY(R) + 30) And Y > (GuideY(R) - 30) Then
    ArtWork.DrawMode = Xor_Pen: ArtWork.DrawStyle = Dot
    ArtWork.AutoRedraw = True
    ArtWork.Line (-5000, -5000)-(24000, GuideY(R)), YELLOW, B
    ArtWork.AutoRedraw = False: Y = -5000: TopRuler = True: V = R
    Exit Sub
End If
R = R - 1
Loop
''''''''''Find Bounding Box
I = Total
Do While I > 0
If S(I) >= N(I) And E(I) >= W(I) Then West = W(I): East = E(I)
➥: North = N(I): South = S(I) 'NORMAL
If N(I) >= S(I) And W(I) >= E(I) Then West = E(I): East = W(I)
➥: North = S(I): South =N(I) 'DIAGONAL
If N(I) >= S(I) And W(I) <= E(I) Then West = W(I): East = E(I)
➥: North = S(I): South =N(I) 'top/bottom
If S(I) >= N(I) And W(I) >= E(I) Then West = E(I): East = W(I)
➥: North = N(I): South = S(I) 'side to side
If X >= West And X <= East And Y >= North And Y <= South
➥Then Exit Do
    I = I - 1
```

```
    Loop
If I = 0 Then PtInRectBasic = False: Exit Sub
    B = I: PtInRectBasic = True
    StatusLabel.Caption = Format$(B)
    Artisan.StatusColor.BackColor = OutLineColor(B)
    Artisan.StatusPaint.BackColor = PaintColor(B)
    Nodes
End Sub
```

In the `Find_Object` procedure, if the mouse is clicked on a dotted guideline (see Figure 4.3), the guideline will be erased so it can be moved to another position.

Dotted guidelines are really dotted boxes. If you could see the outermost edges of Artwork's drawing area, which are hidden, they would look similar to the guideline illustrated in Figure 4.3.

**R = TGL:** R equals the total number of guidelines drawn so far.

**Do While:** Loop through the total of all guidelines drawn to date.

**If GuideX(R) = X Then:** GuideX(number) stored the X coordinate of the dotted guideline. This is similar to the way we stored bounding box positions. The R variable represents the index number that holds the guideline's X coordinate. If the mouse is found to be on the X position during the Loop, the following codes statements within the If/Then expression are executed until the Exit Sub statement is encountered:

> **ArtWork.DrawMode:** You are going to move a guideline, so change DrawMode to Xor and start drawing using dotted lines (Dot DrawStyle)
>
> **ArtWork.AutoRedraw:** You must erase the current guideline you are about to move.
>
> **ArtWork.Line:** Draw a new line over the old one to erase it.
>
> **ArtWorkAutoRedraw:** You erased the line, so now turn off AutoRedraw.
>
> **X = 0:** Set the X coordinate to 0 to draw the line as you move and hold down the mouse button.
>
> **SiderRuler = True:** Flag the SideRuler variable on so the Artwork's MouseMove event will perform the drawing using the GuideLines routine.
>
> **Exit Sub:End If:** The job is done, so leave this procedure.

The following code statements work similarly to the FindAllObjects routine, the difference being the If statements near the bottom of the code. After looping through all the possible bounding box positions, it calculates if the mouse's X and Y positions are within any object's bounding box frame. It is important to note that it finds the actual bounding box and not the objects shape. Clicking outside a circle shape, for example, will still highlight the object because the circle is within a rectangular bounding box. (See Figure 4.4.)

> **B = I:** If the routine found an object, the current bounding box number is represented by B, which is the object's assigned index number.

## The Artisan Program—Procedures C–N

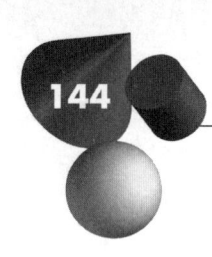

**PtInRectBasic:** See the `MoveObject` procedure in Listing 4.27 for details.

**StatusLabel:** Show the object's index number in the label control.

**ArtWork.Status:** Update the current color of the object in the `Status Area`.

**Nodes:** You just highlighted a bounding box, so show the object's nodes and exit.

**Figure 4.4.**
*Manually finding bounding box positions.*

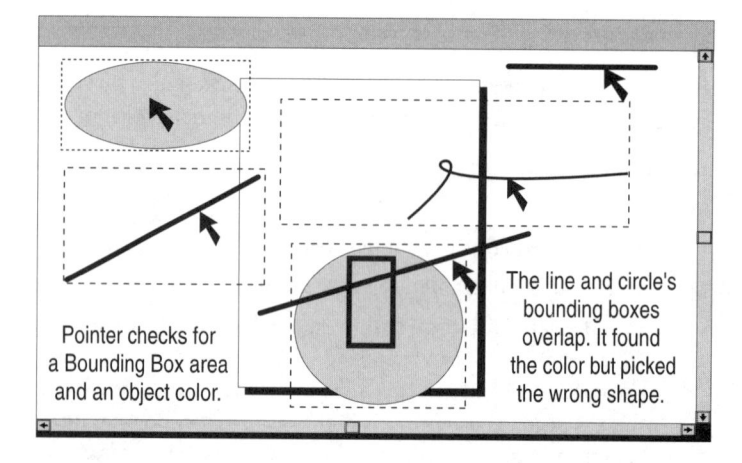

Pointer checks for a Bounding Box area and an object color.

The line and circle's bounding boxes overlap. It found the color but picked the wrong shape.

## Drawing Page Guidelines

Guidelines are used in desktop applications to visually align text or objects on the desktop. Guidelines can be set up so the baseline of text or the edges of the graphical object snap or cling to the dotted guidelines for easier alignment. This program does not include a "snap to guideline" feature, but you can get a general idea of how to perform this by examining the guideline section of the `Find_Object` procedure in Listing 4.7. The `FindObject` procedure can find the coordinates of a guideline. You could then use a similar routine to snap the object's bounding box to the X or Y coordinate of a guideline during a `MouseMove` event on the `Artwork` picture box.

**Listing 4.8. Guidelines are pulled away from either ruler.**

```
Sub GuideLines (Button As Integer, X As Single, Y As Single)
ArtWork.DrawStyle = 2
ArtWork.DrawMode = 7
If SideRuler = True Then 'Side Ruler
    ArtWork.Line (-5000, -5000)-(X2, Y2), YELLOW, B
    X2 = X
```

```
    Y2 = 40000
    ArtWork.Line (-5000, -5000)-(X2, Y2), YELLOW, B
End If
If TopRuler = True Then 'Top Ruler
    ArtWork.Line (-5000, -5000)-(X2, Y2), YELLOW, B
    X2 = 40000
    Y2 = Y
    ArtWork.Line (-5000, -5000)-(X2, Y2), YELLOW, B
End If
End Sub
```

The GuideLines procedure draws the dotted lines that you pull from the side ruler (Ruler(0)) or the top ruler (Ruler(1)).

**ArtWork.DrawStyle:** Guidelines are dotted in style, so make them so.

**ArtWork.DrawMode:** Guidelines can pass over objects, so change the DrawMode to Xor so the objects on the desktop will not be erased.

**If SideRuler = True Then:** You are dragging a guideline from the side ruler.

> **NOTE** The guidelines are really boxes, so draw a dotted box using this standard formula for drawing moving box objects.

**If TopRuler = True Then:** You are dragging a guideline from the top ruler.

When pulling a guideline from the side ruler or top ruler, we use 40000 as the Y2 value. This makes sure the guideline (which is really a dotted box) is still visible when the zoom tool is used. If the Y2 value is set too low, you will see the actual edges of the dotted box appearing on the desktop area when scrolling. If the value is set too high, you may get an overflow error for exceeding the variable data limits.

It is possible to create the moving guideline using the Visual Basic Line method rather than the Box option line method. The Line method, however, is extremely slower at redrawing the guideline as it is being moved when the length of the line is very long.

## Positioning Stretch Handles Around an Object

The next several pages deal with handles. It is important to remember that there are several different types of handle events and procedures. The following is a short description of each:

**Handle:** A picture box control that is the actual red box you see on the screen when an object is selected. This Handle is an indexed control consisting of eight picture boxes numbered 0 through 7.

**Handles:** A procedure that places the eight little picture boxes around an object's bounding box. (In this program, the handles are red in color.)

# The Artisan Program—Procedures C–N

**HandlesReverse:** A procedure that places the eight little picture boxes around an object's bounding box that has been previously flipped.

**BezHandle1:** A picture box control that is used to move Bézier curves only.

**BezHandle2:** A picture box control that is used to move Bézier curves only.

*NOTE* As shown in Figure 4.5, the handles are offset from bounding box corner positions. These positions, which are stored as W(B), N(B), E(B), and S(B), are also equal to the center position of each corner's white node. The white nodes are 90 twips wide, so the center of each node is at the 45 twip mark. Handles located on the left half of the bounding box are placed using their width (120 twips) plus the offset of 45 twips. Handles on the left side of the Bounding Box use the offset of 45 twips only.

**Figure 4.5.**
*The size of the handles.*

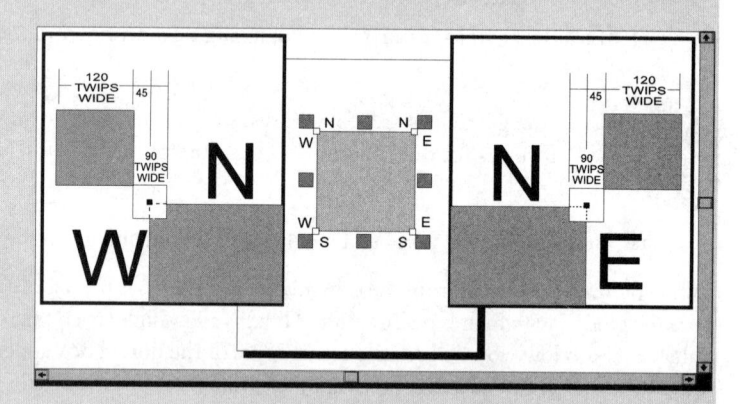

In the Artisan program, the eight little red controls that are placed around each object are the Handle picture boxes. When displayed onscreen they are slightly offset from the object's bounding box edges. This makes the object easier to see and the handles easier to grab when dealing with smaller objects.

Because a bounding box can be flipped, the coordinates can also be switched. For this reason, you need two procedures to place the eight red handle boxes. The Handles procedure is for normal offsets, and the HandlesReverse procedure is used when a bounding box's coordinates are flipped.

**Listing 4.9. Placing the eight stretch handles around the object.**

```
Sub Handles ()
BezNode1.Visible = False: BezNode2.Visible = False
Shape1.Visible = False: Shape2.Visible = False
If N(B) > S(B) And W(B) < E(B) Or S(B) > N(B) And W(B) > E(B)
➥Then HandlesReversed: Exit Sub
If S(B) > N(B) And E(B) > W(B) Then AA = -120: BB = 88
If N(B) > S(B) And W(B) > E(B) Then AA = 88: BB = -120
OSH = 44 + NodeZoom 'OFFSET Handles
    WC = W(B) - OSH: NC = N(B) - OSH:
    EC = E(B) - OSH: SC = S(B) - OSH
    MH = (WC \ 2 + EC \ 2)
    MV = (NC \ 2 + SC \ 2)
Handle(0).Left = WC + AA
Handle(0).Top = NC + AA
Handle(1).Left = MH
Handle(1).Top = NC + AA
Handle(2).Left = EC + BB
Handle(2).Top = NC + AA
Handle(3).Left = EC + BB
Handle(3).Top = MV
Handle(4).Left = EC + BB
Handle(4).Top = SC + BB
Handle(5).Left = MH
Handle(5).Top = SC + BB
Handle(6).Left = WC + AA
Handle(6).Top = SC + BB
Handle(7).Left = WC + AA
Handle(7).Top = MV
For R = 0 To 7
    Handle(R).ScaleLeft = Handle(R).Left
    Handle(R).ScaleTop = Handle(R).Top
    Handle(R).ScaleWidth = Handle(R).Width + Zoom
    Handle(R).ScaleHeight = Handle(R).Height + Zoom
    Handle(R).Visible = True
Next R
End Sub
```

**BezNode1, BezNode2:** Hide these Bézier curve controls if they are visible.

**Shape1, Shape2:** Hide these Bézier curve controls if they are visible.

**If statement:** If the object has been previously flipped, the bounding box coordination has reversed. Call the HandlesReverse procedure, which sets offset values to their opposite reverse values, and then exit this procedure.

Stretch handles are used to size objects in some page layout programs; the Visual Basic program put the handles directly on the bounding box of the objects. This can be accomplished very simply by placing the handles on the corner positions and dividing each corner by 2. Be aware that this method can make the handles get in the way of seeing your finished object's outline.

## The Artisan Program—Procedures C–N

**If S(B) > N(B) And E(B) > W(B) Then:** The direction in which the object's bounding box was originally drawn determines the correct `S`, `N`, `E`, `W` values; 120 and 88 are the width dimensions of the `Handle` and `Nodes`, respectively. The `Handle` picture box controls are positioned using their `Left` property. Placing handles on the right side of the bounding box, for instance, would mean you need an offset of only 44 twips.

**OSH = 44 + NodeZoom:** Each node is 88 twips wide and 88 twips high, so the value 44 represents the center of each node. Adding the 44 twip offset (distance) value will place each handle beside the adjacent node. The `NodeZoom` value is the additional offset (distance) value needed when you use the zoom tool to enlarge or decrease the viewing area of the desktop.

**WC, NC, EC, SC:** West corner, north corner, and so on. To place the middle horizontal and middle vertical handles, you divide by the corner handle coordinates starting at each handle's center (`OSH`) as follows:

`MH = (WC \ 2 + EC \ 2):`

Middle Horizontal handle = West Corner \ 2 + East Corner \ 2.

`MV = (NC \ 2 + SC \ 2):`

Middle Vertical handle = North Corner \ 2 + South Corner \ 2

> **Handle(Index number).Left:** Move each handle's left position.
>
> **Handle(Index number).Top:** Move each handle's top position.

*Abbreviations:*

WC = West Corner handle W(B)

NC = North Corner handle N(B)

EC = East Corner handle E(B)

SC = South Corner handle S(B)

MH = Middle Horizontal handles

MV = Middle Vertical handles

AA = -120 or 105 twips: BB = 105 or -120 twips

OSH = OffSet Handle: ZSH = Zoom Scale Handle

Changing the scale properties of Artwork's desktop can emulate zooming in or out on objects on the page.

Since all graphic objects are redrawn after a zoom, they will draw proportionally to the scale chosen, but `Handles`, `Nodes`, `BezHandles`, `BezNodes`, and text need special treatment. You are using separate `picture box` controls that reside within the `Artwork` picture box control. Because the desktop acts as a container for these controls, they must be rescaled individually. Once the controls are rescaled, you must compensate for any embedded `Offset` values that reside within your code. An example of this would be the `OSH` variable found in this procedure.

Handles and nodes only have their interiors rescaled, but the height and width of these controls must stay the same. The 44 twip Offset value for each handle, for instance, would not hold true after rescaling.

Visual Basic's ScaleLeft, ScaleTop properties have the following effects on the internal scaling dimensions of forms and picture boxes:

ScaleLeft changes the internal horizontal leftmost coordinates starting at the object's top left edge. ScaleTop changes the internal vertical topmost coordinates starting at the object's top edge. The default value for both properties is 0.

ScaleLeft and ScaleTop can be used with ScaleWidth and ScaleHeight to assign custom coordinates to a form or picture box controls.

ScaleWidth changes the internal horizontal scaling width. ScaleHeight changes the internal vertical scaling height. Positive settings make the coordinates increase from top to bottom and left to right. Negative settings make the coordinates increase from bottom to top and right to left.

A form or picture box's BorderWidth and BorderStyle properties affect the final internal dimensions of each. The border widths decrease the internal scaling space available for use.

## Reversing the Handle Positions on a Flipped Object

The HandleReverse routine is called from the Handles procedure only if the object's bounding box has been flipped in any direction. To see what happens if this procedure were not called, remark out ( ' ) the If/Then statement at the top of the Handles procedure. The result is that the handles align opposite to their Left and Top properties.

You could bypass this by having a function always determine the center of a control. You could also ask Microsoft to add extra properties to controls like Control.Right, Control.ScaleRight, Control.Center, Control.ScaleCenter. This would save us all the extra typing you must do, for instance, to center a form.

**Listing 4.10. Placing handles around a flipped object.**
```
Sub HandlesReversed ()
If N(B) > S(B) And W(B) < E(B) Then AA = 88: BB = -120  '
If S(B) > N(B) And W(B) > E(B) Then AA = -120: BB = 88  '
OSH = 44 + NodeZoom  'OFFSET Handles
WC = W(B) - OSH: NC = N(B) - OSH:
EC = E(B) - OSH: SC = S(B) - OSH
```

*continues*

## Listing 4.10. continued

```
        MH = (WC \ 2 + EC \ 2)
        MV = (NC \ 2 + SC \ 2)
Handle(0).Left = WC + BB
Handle(0).Top = NC + AA
Handle(1).Left = MH
Handle(1).Top = NC + AA
Handle(2).Left = EC + AA
Handle(2).Top = NC + AA
Handle(3).Left = EC + AA
Handle(3).Top = MV
Handle(4).Left = EC + AA
Handle(4).Top = SC + BB
Handle(5).Left = MH
Handle(5).Top = SC + BB
Handle(6).Left = WC + BB
Handle(6).Top = SC + BB
Handle(7).Left = WC + BB
Handle(7).Top = MV
For R = 0 To 7
    Handle(R).ScaleLeft = Handle(R).Left
    Handle(R).ScaleTop = Handle(R).Top
    Handle(R).ScaleWidth = Handle(R).Width + Zoom
    Handle(R).ScaleHeight = Handle(R).Height + Zoom
    Handle(R).Visible = True
Next R
End Sub
```

**If N(B) > S(B) And W(B) < E(B) Then:** Just reverse the AA and BB values. See the Handles procedure (Listing 4.9) for explanations of each code line.

**Handle(index number).Left:** The AA and BB values are switched.

**Handle(index number).Top:** The AA and BB values are switched.

*Abbreviations:*

WC = West Corner handle W(B)

NC = North Corner handle N(B)

EC = East Corner handle E(B)

SC = South Corner handle S(B)

MH = Middle Horizontal handles

MV = Middle Vertical handles

AA = -120 or 105 twips: BB = 105 or -120 twips

OSH = OffSet Handle: ZSH = Zoom Scale Handle

### Manually Drawing Handles

This chapter deals mainly with using Visual Basic's picture box controls as Handles and Nodes. Although these controls make programming faster, there is one drawback. They are slow in appearing on the desktop. One alternative is to draw the handles yourself, and then spend a considerable amount of time attaching codes to Artwork's desktop mouse events. Another approach is to use Image controls, which are explained in the introduction section of the ArtAPI program in Chapter 15.

The preceding code examples show the Handles and HandlesReverse code routines using Visual Basic's Line statement, thus eliminating picture box controls as handles.

This approach will save you the headache of rescaling the controls each time they are moved or when using the zoom tool. Unfortunately, you must add additional code in order for mouse events to be recognized.

**Example of drawing handles manually:**

```
Handle(0) = ArtWork.Line (WC + AA, NC + AA)-
➥(WC + AA + 105, NC + AA + 105), RED, BF
Handle(1) = ArtWork.Line (MH, NC + AA)-
➥(MH + 105, NC + AA + 105), RED, BF
Handle(2) = ArtWork.Line (EC + BB, NC + AA)-
➥(EC + BB + 105, NC + AA + 105), RED, BF
Handle(3) = ArtWork.Line (EC + BB, MV)-
➥(EC + BB + 105, MV + 105), RED, BF
Handle(4) = ArtWork.Line (EC + BB, SC + BB)-
➥(EC + BB + 105, SC + BB + 105), RED, BF
Handle(5) = ArtWork.Line (MH, SC + BB)-
➥(MH + 105, SC + BB + 105), RED, BF
Handle(6) = ArtWork.Line (WC + AA, SC + BB)-
➥(WC + AA + 105, SC + BB + 105), RED, BF
Handle(7) = ArtWork.Line (WC + AA, MV)-
➥(WC + AA + 105, MV + 105), RED, BF
```

## Preparing an Object To Be Stretched

When an object is stretched or moved to a new location, the object's image in the old location must be erased. One way to erase this image is to simply draw a box with a solid fill the same color as the desktop's BackColor and then redraw any other objects that may have been positioned in that area.

In the Handle_MouseDown event in Listing 4.11, XX1, YY1, XX2, and YY2 are the variables that hold the original positions of the object that is to be stretched or moved. These values are then used in a Line statement within the UpdateObjects procedure (Listing 4.12) to erase the area.

**Listing 4.11. Setting the stretch handle's moveable bounding box.**

```
Sub Handle_MouseDown (Index%, Button%, Shift%, X!, Y!)
If B = FlagText(B) Then Exit Sub
ArtWork.DrawMode = Xor_Pen
ArtWork.DrawWidth = 1
    N_H_Clear
    XX1 = W(B)
    YY1 = N(B)
    XX2 = E(B)
    YY2 = S(B)
ArtWork.Line (W(B), N(B))-(E(B), S(B)), YELLOW, B
End Sub
```

The three Handle mouse events are used to stretch the bounding box in any direction. Do not confuse these events with the Handles procedure that is used to place the Handle picture box controls around the bounding box.

**Listing 4.12. Redrawing the underlying page and all objects upon it.**

```
Sub UpdateObjects ()
LastMove = B
ArtWork.DrawMode = Copy_Pen
ArtWork.DrawStyle = Solid
ArtWork.AutoRedraw = True
If Draw = True Then GoTo SkipErase
ArtWork.DrawWidth = 20
ArtWork.Line (W(B), N(B))-(E(B), S(B)), White, BF
ArtWork.Line (XX2, YY2)-(XX1, YY1), White, BF: B = 1
        UpdateDeskTop
Do While B Total + 1
    ArtWork.DrawWidth = LineWidth(B)
    If LineValue(B) 0 Then ArtWork.DrawStyle = 5 Else
    ➥ArtWork.DrawStyle = Solid
SkipErase:
Select Case B
    Case FlagCircle(B)
        X1 = W(B): Y1 = N(B): X2 = E(B): Y2 = S(B)
        ArtWork.DrawWidth = LineWidth(B)
        GoodCircle = PerfectCircle(X1, Y1, X2, Y2)
        ArtWork.FillColor = PaintColor(B):
        ArtWork.FillStyle = FillValue(B)
        ArtWork.Circle (XCenter, YCenter), Radius,
        ➥OutLineColor(B), , , Aspect
        ArtWork.FillColor = 0: ArtWork.FillStyle = 1
```

```
      Case FlagLine(B)
          ArtWork.Line (W(B), N(B))-(E(B), S(B)), OutLineColor(B)
      Case FlagBox(B)
          If FillValue(B) = 1 Then GoTo SkipFill
          ArtWork.Line (W(B), N(B))-(E(B), S(B)), PaintColor(B), BF
SkipFill:
          ArtWork.Line (W(B), N(B))-(E(B), S(B)), OutLineColor(B), B
      Case FlagBezier(B)
          p1.X = p1X(B): p1.Y = p1Y(B): p2.X = p2X(B): p2.Y = p2Y(B)
          h1.X = h1X(B): h1.Y = h1Y(B): h2.X = h2X(B): h2.Y = h2Y(B)
          ArtWork.ForeColor = OutLineColor(B)
          BezDraw
      Case FlagText(B)
          ArtWork.CurrentX = OFFSET(B): ArtWork.CurrentY = N(B)
          SaveScaleLeft = ArtWork.ScaleLeft
          ArtWork.ScaleLeft = -ArtWork.CurrentX + Scaling
          ArtWork.FontName = TextFont(B)
          ArtWork.ForeColor = PaintColor(B)
          ArtWork.FontSize = TextSize(B) * TextPoint
          ArtWork.FontBold = TextBold(B)
          ArtWork.FontItalic = TextItalic(B)
          wFlag = FlagAlign(B)
          TA = SetTextAlign(ArtWork.hDC, wFlag)
          ArtWork.Print Storedtext(B)
          ArtWork.ScaleLeft = SaveScaleLeft
End Select
If Draw = True Then Draw = False:
          ↪ArtWork.AutoRedraw = False : B = LastMove: Exit Sub
      B = B + 1
Loop
B = LastMove
    ArtWork.AutoRedraw = False
    ArtWork.DrawWidth = 1
    ArtWork.DrawStyle = Solid
If DeleteObject = True Then Exit Sub
If CurrentTool = 1 Or CurrentTool = 2 Then Exit Sub
If SideRuler = True Or TopRuler = True Then Exit Sub
    Handles
    Nodes
End Sub
```

All objects are positioned within a bounding box. When you stretch an object, you are really stretching the bounding box. The procedure UpDateObjects (Listing 4.12) redraws the actual object's shape after you finish stretching it.

**ArtWork.DrawMode:** The bounding box can pass over other objects while it is being stretched, so change DrawMode to Xor so other objects are not erased during the stretching of the bounding box.

**ArtWork.DrawWidth:** The DrawWidth is set to 1.

**N_H_Clear:** Call this procedure to clear (hide) the nodes and the handles.

## The Artisan Program—Procedures C–N

You must now store the bounding box's present coordinates, which were stored in W(B), N(B), E(B), S(B). Use the temporary variable holders XX1, YY1, XX2, and YY2 to save the coordinates and then pass the values to the UpDateObject procedure. The UpDateObjects procedure will then erase the image in the old area, after the bounding box has been stretched to another location on the desktop.

> **XX1 = W(B):** Temporarily store the west side bounding box position.
>
> **YY1 = N(B):** Temporarily store the north side bounding box position.
>
> **XX2 = E(B):** Temporarily store the east side bounding box position.
>
> **YY1 = S(B):** Temporarily store the south side bounding box position.
>
> **ArtWork.Line:** Draw the present bounding box using the west, north, east, and south coordinate positions that were stored in the indexed arrays W(B), N(B), E(B), S(B). The color yellow used in the Line statement will be cyan (light blue) in color when the Xor mode is used.

**Figure 4.6.**
*The index numbers of each handle.*

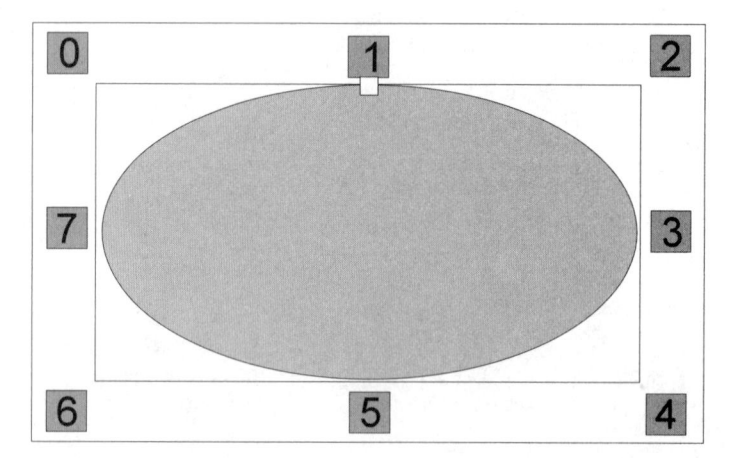

In Figure 4.6, each Handle is an indexed picture box control. No matter which way you stretch or flip the bounding box, each indexed handle ends up in its proper position. The Handles procedure (Listing 4.9) is used to move each handle to the proper location of the selected object. There are eight indexed picture box controls called Handle in this program; their index numbers are 0 to 7 going clockwise from the upper-left corner.

As illustrated in Figure 4.7, if Handle(3) were used to stretch the bounding box any distance to the right, the MouseDown event would first hide the nodes and handles. The original bounding box with the old circle inside (Figure 4.7) would also need to be erased. The old image coordinates are stored in XX1, YY1, XX2, YY2.

A box shape would then be drawn and as the mouse dragged the handle, a stretching bounding box would be shown.

The Handle_MouseMove event takes care of drawing the stretching bounding box and displays the bounding box's new width and height measurements in the StatusLabel control.

**Figure 4.7.**
*Stretching the bounding box with handle 3.*

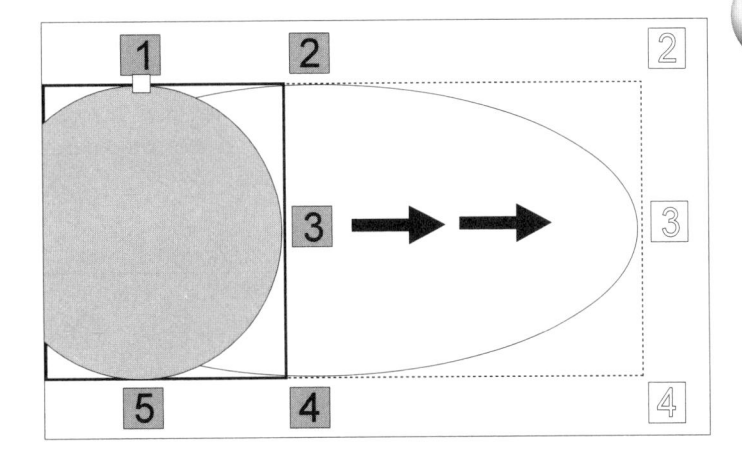

The Handle_MouseUp event updates the object within the bounding box after the stretch. If the object is a box, circle, line, or text, the procedure calls the UpdateObjects procedure (Listing 4.12) to redraw the object. If the object is a Bézier curve, the new points are calculated first in the BezStretch procedure (Listing 3.19) and then sent to the UpDateObjects procedure to be redrawn.

In Figure 4.8, the illustration shows a bounding box with the circle inside being stretched and flipped. The stretch starts at Handle(0) and is dragged to the bottom-right corner. After the stretch, the handles procedure relocates all the stretch handles as shown.

**Figure 4.8.**
*A stretched and flipped circle object.*

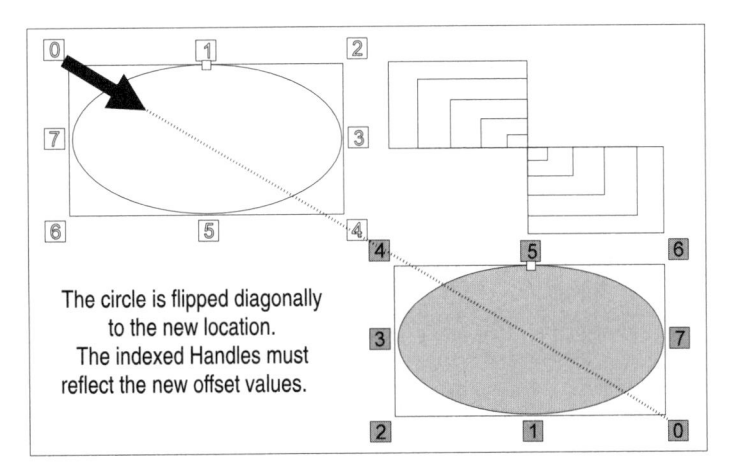

## Stretching an Object

The Handle mouse move event stretches the object's bounding box by increasing or decreasing the coordinate values W(B), N(B), E(B), and/or S(B).

Boxes, circles, and line objects are directly connected to the edges of their bounding box. This makes redrawing them in the UpdateObjects procedure (Listing 4.12) very simple. Bézier curves, on the other hand, reside within their bounding box so a separate procedure is used to reposition the four coordinate points of a curve.

Objects that are grouped or joined together would also need a procedure to established their bounding box's dimensions after a stretch. The `Poly_Stretch` procedure in the ArtAPI program uses a routine to update connected polyshape objects.

**Listing 4.13. Dragging and stretching the object's bounding box.**

```
Sub Handle_MouseMove (Index%, Button%, Shift%, X!, Y!)
If B = FlagText(B) Then Exit Sub
Xstr = Format$(X \ PixelX, "000") :
Ystr = Format$(Y \ PixelY, "000")
XYLabel.Caption = "[" + Xstr + " , " + Ystr + "]"
    RulerGuides Index, Button, Shift, X, Y
If Button Then
    ArtWork.Line (W(B), N(B))-(E(B), S(B)), YELLOW, B
    ArtWork.DrawStyle = Dot
Select Case Index
    Case 0
        Handle(0).MousePointer = 8
        W(B) = X :  N(B) = Y
    Case 1
        Handle(1).MousePointer = 7
        N(B) = Y
    Case 2
        Handle(2).MousePointer = 6
        E(B) = X :  N(B) = Y
    Case 3
        Handle(3).MousePointer = 9
        E(B) = X
    Case 4
        Handle(4).MousePointer = 8
        E(B) = X :  S(B) = Y
    Case 5
        Handle(5).MousePointer = 7
        S(B) = Y
    Case 6
        Handle(6).MousePointer = 6
        W(B) = X :  S(B) = Y
    Case 7
        Handle(7).MousePointer = 9
        W(B) = X
End Select
    ArtWork.Line (W(B), N(B))-(E(B), S(B)), YELLOW, B
End If
    BoxWidth = E(B) - W(B): BoxHeight = S(B) - N(B)
If Button Then StatusLabel.Caption = "Width " +
➥Format$(BoxWidth) + " " + "Height " + Format$(BoxHeight)
End Sub
```

**Xstr, Ystr:** A handle is a separate picture box control, so send the interior X, Y coordinates to XYLabel control it be displayed.

**RulerGuiders:** Call the RulerGuides procedure repeatedly to draw the page-position lines in each ruler.

**If Button Then:** If the mouse button is held down, continue.

**Select Case Index:** Execute the Case statement that equals the currently selected handle's index number. There are 8 handles indexed 0 through 7.

**ArtWork.Line:** Redraws a line over the top of the first line to erase it.

**ArtWork.DrawStyle = Dot:** The bounding box changes to a dotted rectangle when stretched.

**Case 0:** MousePointer will be NW-SE. The west and north sides can stretch freely.

**Case 1:** MousePointer will be N-S. The north side can stretch freely.

**Case 2:** MousePointer will be NE-SW. The east and south sides can stretch freely.

**Case 3:** MousePointer will be W-E. The west side can stretch freely.

**Case 4:** MousePointer will be NW-SE. The east and south sides can stretch freely.

**Case 5:** MousePointer will be N-S. The south side can stretch freely.

**Case 6:** MousePointer will be NE-W. The west and south sides can stretch freely.

**Case 7:** MousePointer will be W-E. The west side can stretch freely.

**ArtWork.Line:** Redraw the line over top of the last to Xor it.

**BoxWidth, BoxHeight:** The width and height of box as it is stretched. The StatusLabel control will display these dimensions.

Table 4.1 contains a breakdown of where each of the eight handles are positioned around the bounding box. Handle indexes are clockwise from top-left corner of the bounding box. Index numbers will match the Case expressions.

**T**able 4.1. Handle positions on a bounding box.

| Index | position |
|-------|----------|
| 0:    | Top left |
| 1:    | Top center |
| 2:    | Top right |
| 3:    | Right side |
| 4:    | Bottom right |
| 5:    | bottom center |
| 6:    | bottom left |
| 7:    | Left side |

In Figure 4.9, the thick, gray, outlined rectangle represents the XX1, YY1, XX2, YY2. This area will be erased after the circle object has been stretched to the new location that is represented by the dotted rectangular area. The old circle (solid gray circle) is erased in the UpdateObjects procedure using the following statement: Artwork.Line (XX2, YY2)-(XX1,YY1), White, BF. The border is set to 20 pixels wide during erasing.

**Figure 4.9.**
*Illustrates stretching a circle shape.*

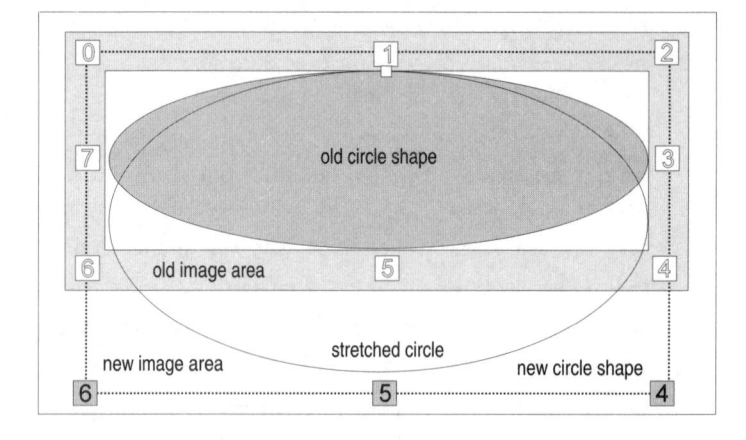

The `Handle_MouseUp` event calls the `UpdateObject` procedure (Listing 4.12) in order to redraw the object after it has been stretched.

**Listing 4.14. Updating the object's position after it has been stretched.**

```
Sub Handle_Mouseup (Index%, Button%, Shift %, X !, Y!)
If B = FlagText(B) Then Exit Sub
If FlagBezier(B) = B Then BezStretch Index, Button, Shift, X, Y
    UpdateObjects
    For R = 0 To 7
        Handle(R).MousePointer = 2
    Next R
End Sub
```

If the current object is a Bézier curve, the curve's four coordinate points must be updated before calling the `UpdateObjects` procedure (Listing 4.12) which will redraw all objects on the desktop after the Stretch is performed. All eight `Handle` picture box control's mouse pointers are then reset to a `Cross Hair` (2 mouse pointers).

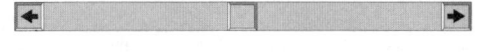

## Scrolling the Graphics on the Desktop

The `Hscroll` and `VScroll` scrollbar controls are used to move the desktop either vertically or horizontally. This is accomplished by having the `Artwork` picture box reside within another picture box control. The underlying picture box is called `PictureMask` and contains no code whatsoever. A control within a control acting as a container can be moved to any coordinate within the underlying container. If any part of the inside control (`Artwork`) is outside the actual viewing area of the underlying container (`PictureMask`), Visual Basic automatically clips the part of the image not visible. This makes scrolling any type of object very easy within Visual Basic.

Within each ruler are moving dotted lines that indicate the current mouse pointer desktop position. These ruler guidelines are drawn using the `RulerGuides` procedure (Listing 4.15). When you leave the `Artwork` picture box desktop area, the dotted ruler guidelines stop at the last position the mouse was at before leaving.

**Listing 4.15.** Drawing the ruler's internal guidelines.

```
Sub RulerGuides (Index%, Button As Integer, Shift As Integer, X !, Y!)
R0SL = Ruler(0).ScaleLeft 'Side Ruler
R0L = Ruler(0).Left - 5000: R0T = Ruler(0).Top - 5000
    R1ST = Ruler(1).ScaleTop 'Top Ruler
    R1L = Ruler(1).ScaleLeft - 15: R1T = Ruler(1).ScaleTop - 15
Ruler(0).Line (R0L, R0T)-(X1Ruler, Y1Ruler), Cyan, B 'Vert.
Ruler(1).Line (R1L, R1T)-(X2Ruler, Y2Ruler), Cyan, B 'Horz.
 X1Ruler = R0SL + 500 'Side Ruler.Width
        Y1Ruler = Y
        X2Ruler = X
 Y2Ruler = R1ST + 500 'Top Ruler.Height
Ruler(0).Line (R0L, R0T)-(X1Ruler, Y1Ruler), Cyan, B 'Vert
Ruler(1).Line (R1L, R1T)-(X2Ruler, Y2Ruler), Cyan, B 'Horz
End Sub
```

You need a way to keep sending a `MouseMove` event to each of the two scrollbar controls to erase the visible ruler guidelines when scrolling the desktop. You cannot add `MouseMove` events to scrollbar controls since they do not have `MouseMove` events.

To have the ruler guides erased, use the API `SendMessage` function. This API function can send a message to the Artwork `MouseMove` event telling it to perform a `MouseMove` event, thus triggering the code within.

**Listing 4.16.** Scrolling the desktop horizontally.

```
Sub HScroll_Change ()
ArtWork.Enabled = False
    Dim WM_MOUSEMOVE%
    WM_MOUSEMOVE% = &H200
API = SendMessageByNum(ArtWork.hWnd, WM_MOUSEMOVE%, 0, 0)
    ArtWork.Move -HScroll.Value, ArtWork.Top
    Ruler(1).Move ArtWork.Left - 200, Ruler(1).Top
    BSM = (HScroll.Value * PixelX) * PerSW
End Sub
```

**ArtWork.Enabled = False:** You will disable `Artwork` so no other events will be triggered.

**WM_MOUSEMOVE% = &H200:** The API `SendMessage` function has a very long list of messages it can send to forms and controls. The messages are stored in a API library file and are accessed by sending a hexadecimal reference value to the API `SendMessage` function. To trigger a mouse move event to a control that can receive one, the hexadecimal value is `&H200`.

**API = SendMessageByNum:** API messages can be sent by a text or numeric value. You are sending a numeric value, so use an alias name for the procedure (SendMessageByNum) since the arguments (numeric values) as declared as non-string values. The SendMessage function must be declared in a Module file. In this program, the declaration is located in the ARTISAN7.BAS file as

```
Declare Function SendMessageByNum% Lib "User" Alias "SendMessage" (ByVal hWnd%,
    ByVal wMsg%, ByVal wParam%, ByVal lParam&).
```

Refer to "Calling Procedures in DLLs," in the Visual Basic Programmer's Guide, for an entire chapter outlining API function calls and considerations.

**ArtWork.Move:** Move (scroll) the Artwork desktop horizontally the distance indicated in the Hscroll small move or large move properties.

**Ruler(1).Move:** The rulers must also be moved to align with the artwork that has just moved. Another way to realign ruler marks without moving the ruler is demonstrated in the Ruler program in the 14SCALE directory of the companion disk. The Ruler program is a copy of the Scaltest program in Chapter 14, but uses yet another way to scale and align the desktop and rulers.

**BSM = (HScroll.Value * PixelX) * PerSW:** This value is needed only when you incorporate a zoom tool that rescales the desktop viewing area. It calculates the difference of scaling from the current view to the zoom view. The BSM value is then used in Ruler_Paint events to redraw the ruler marks in the new scale. BSM is an acronym for **B**ase **S**cale **M**ovement.

### Listing 4.17. Scrolling the desktop vertically.

```
Sub VScroll_Change ()
ArtWork.Enabled = False
    Dim WM_MOUSEMOVE%
    WM_MOUSEMOVE% = &H200
API = SendMessageByNum(ArtWork.hWnd, WM_MOUSEMOVE%, 0, 0)
    ArtWork.Move ArtWork.Left, -VScroll.Value
    Ruler(0).Move Ruler(0).Left, ArtWork.Top - 250
    SSM = (VScroll.Value * PixelY) * PerSH
End Sub
```

Refer to the Hscroll_Change procedure (Listing 4.16) for details on the code routine used in the previous Vscroll_Change event (Listing 4.17).

# Changing the Thickness of an Object's Outline

The LineButtons procedure is very straightforward. To change the thickness (width) of an object's outline, you first select the object and then select the outline button from the toolbar (seventh button from the top of the ToolButtons control).

**Listing 4.18.** `LineButton_Down` changes the outline width of an object.

```
Sub LineButtons_MouseDown (Button%, Shift%, X!, Y !)
If Node(0).Visible = False
         ➥Then LineButtons.Visible = False: Exit Sub
CurrentTool = 6: ToolButtons_Paint:
CurrentTool = LastToolUsed: ToolButtons_Paint
CurrentLine = X \ 32: LineButtons.Visible = False
Select Case CurrentLine
    Case LineColor
        ' ' ' ' ' ' ' ' ' ' ' ' '
    Case NoLine
        LineValue(B) = B
    Case HairLine
        ArtWork.DrawWidth = 1
    Case OnePt
        ArtWork.DrawWidth = 2
    Case TwoPt
        ArtWork.DrawWidth = 3
    Case FourPt
        ArtWork.DrawWidth = 5
    Case EightPt
        ArtWork.DrawWidth = 9
    Case TwelvePt
        ArtWork.DrawWidth = 13
End Select
LineWidth(B) = ArtWork.DrawWidth
If B = 0 Then Exit Sub
If Not CurrentLine = NoLine Then LineValue(B) = 0
    UpdateObjects
End Sub
```

**If Node(0).Visible:** First checks to see if `Node(0)` is visible. If the node is not visible, you have not selected any object so exit the procedure.

**CurrentTool:** Same routine used in `ToolButtons` procedure (Listing 2.10) to invert a button to make it look pushed or press in. The `ToolButton_Paint` event (Listing 2.11) will select the last drawing tool used.

**Select Case CurrentLine:** The button you selected in `LineTools` bar will match the one of the following `Case` expressions.

**Case:** These values are defined in the ARTISAN.BAS file; in short, they are the buttons reading left to right.

**Case LineColor:** Not connected, but you could connect it to the `PaletteBar` form and write a little code to change the object's outline color. For now, you can click with the right mouse button on the `ColorBar` control to achieve the same result.

**Case HairLine To Twelve Pt.:** Changes the outline width of any object except text to the given value.

**LineWidth(B):** Stores the value of the line width you selected. The `UpdateObjects` procedure (Listing 4.12) is used to redraw the object with the new outline. Do not set this value to zero (0) or a runtime error will occur. By default, all objects are given a

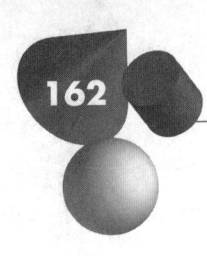

`DrawWidth` of 1. The outline of an object is redrawn by setting the `DrawWidth` property of `Artwork` to the value stored in `LineWidth(object number)`. `DrawWidth` will not accept a value of zero.

Objects with no outlines are given an invisible property using a flag variable called `LineValue(object number)`. If this value is true, the `DrawStyle` of the outline is set to invisible.

**If B = 0:** B represents the object's number. At startup, B equals 0 since no objects have been drawn. If this is the case, exit the procedure.

**If Not CurrentLine:** If any button other than the `NoLine` button was selected, flag `LineValue(B)` as a visible line to be redrawn in a solid `DrawStyle`.

The `LineButtons_MouseUp` event will set `Artwork`'s drawing width to 1 pixel so it is ready to draw a new object on the desktop.

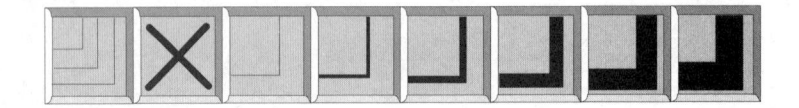

**Listing 4.19. Resetting the desktop default width.**
```
Sub LineButtons_MouseUp (Button%, Shift%, X !, Y!)
    ArtWork.DrawWidth = 1
End Sub
```

`ArtWork.DrawWidth = 1`: Reset the drawing width to the default of 1 pixel width.

## The Artisan Program's Main Menu Selections

Most menu items do not have any routine code attached except for the statement `LastMenu = Index`. This is used for the popup menu to display the last menu the user selected manually from the main menu captions. A popup menu is activated by clicking the right mouse button on the desktop at any time.

Menus that exclude `Case` blocks do not have code written for that menu item. This program is to be used as a starting point and does not implement special effect features.

**Listing 4.20. Moving an object to the front or back of all others.**
```
Sub Menu_ArrangeSelection_Click (Index As Integer)
Select Case Index
    Case 0
        To_Front_Back Index
    Case 1
        To_Front_Back Index
End Select
End Sub
```

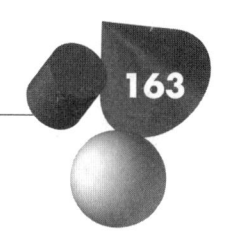

**Case 0:** Move the selected object to the front by calling the To_Front_Back procedure (Listing 5.15).

**Case 1:** Move the selected object to the back by calling the To_Front_Back procedure (Listing 5.15).

Refer to the To_Back_Front procedure in Chapter 5 for details on how an object is moved to the front or back of all other.

A quicker way to move an object to the front or back is demonstrated in the ArtAPI program, Chapter 15. However, if you only need to sort a few objects in your program, the bubble method of sorting objects in this chapter may better suit your needs.

## Deleting a Single Object from the Desktop

The program deletes an object by setting all of the object's assigned attributes to zero. The arrays that held these attribute settings are not resized and consume the same amount of memory as when the program was first initiated.

**Listing 4.21.** Deleting an object from the desktop.

```
Sub Menu_EditSelection_Click (Index As Integer)
Select Case Index
    Case 6 'DELETE
If B = 0 Then Exit Sub
If Node(0).Visible = True Then
    N_H_Clear
    FillValue(B) = 0: LineValue(B) = 0: OutLineColor(B) = 0
    PaintColor(B) = 0: LineWidth(B) = 1: FlagAlign(B) = 0
    OFFSET(B) = 0: TextSize(B) = 0: TextFont(B) = ""
    TextBold(B) = 0: TextItalic(B) = 0: CarriageCount(B) = 0
    Storedtext(B) = ""
    FlagBezier(B) = 0: FlagLine(B) = 0: FlagBox(B) = 0
    FlagCircle(B) = 0: FlagText(B) = 0
    P1X(B) = 0: P1Y(B) = 0: p2X(B) = 0: p2Y(B) = 0
    h1X(B) = 0: h1Y(B) = 0: h2X(B) = 0: h2Y(B) = 0
DeleteObject = True
XX1 = W(B): YY1 = N(B): XX2 = E(B): YY2 = S(B)
W(B) = 0: N(B) = 0: E(B) = 0: S(B) = 0
    UpdateObjects
    DeleteObject = False
End If
End Select
End Sub
```

**N_H_clear:** Hide all the nodes and handles that appear around the object to be deleted.

**FillValue(B) = 0: LineValue(B) = 0, etc.:** There are 26 attributes in total, but not all objects require that many in order to be drawn. Because the arrays that hold the attribute's values are not resized, the indexes in each attribute array that match the object's number already will contain a value of **0**. Setting an attribute index to **0** in an array that does not pertain to the object being deleted will have no effect on other objects on the desktop.

You may want to declare attribute arrays that are resizable if you need to save memory or if you need to store numerous objects. In this case, it is best to build multi-dimensional arrays that can be indexed into individual groups. You should visualize it much like a data program divided into separate fields of information. You may also want to consider using a `Type` structure in which the `Type` declared could be the objects' names (such as `Type circle`) and have every possible attribute for a circle listed in the `Type` structure.

**DeleteObject = True:** This is a flag that tells the `UpdateObject` (Listing 4.12) to not display the nodes and handles at their present locations because the object will no longer be there.

**XX1 = W(B): YY1 = N(B):** Temporarily store the bounding box positions of the object so the `UpdateObjects` procedure (Listing 4.12) can erase the image from the area.

**W(B) = 0: N(B) = 0:** Since the bounding box positions of the object are now temporarily stored, you are safe to erase the bounding box's dimensions.

**UpdateObject:** Redraw the objects on the desktop, minus the one you just deleted.

## Preparing for File Menu Option

If you are going to click the file menu caption, you most likely are going to open, save, or print the graphic. In this case, you must hide all nodes, handles, and popup tools.

**Listing 4.22. Updating the desktop's nodes and handles.**

```
Sub Menu_File_Click ()
LastMenu = 0 : N_H_Clear
If Txt.Caption > "" Then ReDrawText

    If BezHandle1.Visible = True Then
        ShowDotted = True: BezUpdate
        BezHandle1.Visible = False: BezHandle2.Visible = False
        BezNode1.Visible = False: BezNode2.Visible = False
        Shape1.Visible = False: Shape2.Visible = False
    End If
End Sub
```

**If Txt.Caption > "" Then ReDrawText:** It is possible that you have a text object currently selected as you select this menu item. In that case, you must redraw the text on the desktop before saving or printing the images.

If `BezHandles1` is visible, you have a Bézier curve selected. In this case you must hide all the curve's nodes and handles.

## Deleting All Objects on the Desktop

To delete an object, you must reset all of the object's attributes to 0. All objects are given a number starting at 1 for the first object and continuing as high as 1000.

Reassigning attributes of any object to 0 tells the program to assign this value to the index number associated with that object. This does not resize the indexed arrays for each attribute but resets them to their original values at startup, which is 0.

**Listing 4.23. Erasing all array value and objects.**

```
Sub Menu_FileSelection_Click (Index As Integer)


  Select Case Index
    Case 0 'New
  Erase FillValue, LineValue, OutLineColor, PaintColor, LineWidth
  Erase FlagAlign, OFFSET, TextSize, TextFont, TextBold, TextItalic
  Erase CarriageCount, Storedtext, W, E, N, S
  Erase FlagBezier, FlagLine, FlagBox, FlagCircle, FlagText
  Erase P1X, P1Y, P2X, p2Y, h1X, h1Y, h2X, h2Y
  Erase GuideX, GuideY
  p = 0: Total = 0: V = 0: B = 0: TGL = 0
      Artwork.DrawWidth = 1
      Artwork.DrawMode = 6: Artwork.DrawStyle = 0
      Artwork.AutoRedraw = True: Artwork.Cls
      UpdateObjects
    Case 1 'OPEN
      mnuFileOpen
    Case 2 To 3
      mnuFileSave
    Case 4 'Print
      WinPrint
    Case 5 'EXIT
      End
  End SelectEnd Sub
```

**Case 0 'New:** This erases all attributes assigned to every object that was drawn.

See Listing 4.21 for more information on deleting a single object from the desktop.

**Case 1 To 3:** Displays the CMDialog command dialog control. You can then save, save as, or open a file.

**Case 4:** You have selected the menu's Print option item. The WinPrint procedure will print all objects to your printer. WinPrint is set up to print only on 300-dpi printers. You can manually change the code very easily, however, to print at resolutions higher than 300 dots per inch.

**Case 5:** You have elected to end the program.

## The Color Menu Item Option

The `Color` menu item, when clicked, displays a menu that also includes a submenu for changing the colors within the color palette at the bottom of the screen.

The submenu selection items are listed in the `Menu_Palette_Click` event in Listing 4.25. The only other option in the `Color` menu is to hide the rulers.

**Listing 4.24.** Editing the color palette bar.

```
Sub Menu_ColorSelection_Click (Index As Integer)
Select Case Index
    Case 2 'Show rulers
Menu_ColorSelection(2).Checked = Not Menu_ColorSelection(2).Checked
        Y1Ruler = 0: X2Ruler = 0
        RulerCross.Visible = Not RulerCross.Visible
        Ruler(0).Visible = Not Ruler(0).Visible
        Ruler(1).Visible = Not Ruler(1).Visible
End Select
End Sub
```

The ruler's visible property is toggled off or on by using the Not operator. One of the easiest ways to toggle something on and off in Visual Basic is to use the Not operator.

A computer memory bit is similar to a light switch. The bit can be either on (value 1) or off (value 0). Because a bit can only have two values, 0 or 1, the bit is referred to as a binary number. The prefix *bi* means two.

When using the Not operator, values become opposites: true becomes false, or false becomes true. If the value is null it remains unchanged.

The NOT operator inverts the binary bit values of any variable as follows. (A bit can only be either, 0 or 1 in value.)

    0    becomes    1
    1    becomes    0

## Changing Colors in the Color Palette

The `ColorPalette` form is a modified version of the color palette found in Visual Basic's sample program, IconWorks. It has some additional features such as drag and drop color changing. You can use the RGB scrollbars in the `ColorPalette` form to create custom colors and then drag the new color onto the main palette display area. This will save the color onto a secondary palette, which is then saved in the ARTISAN.INI file.

Once you have changed the default color palette, the program will use the ARTISAN.INI palette information every time you start this program. To have the program use the default palette again at startup, you must erase the ARTISAN.INI file. The `ColorPalette` form is explained further in Appendix A.

**Listing 4.25.** Resetting the default color palette.

```
Sub Menu_Palette_Click (Index As Integer)
Select Case Index
    Case 0 'Show Color Palette
        ColorIndex = 0
        ColorPalette.Show
    Case 1 'Default Palette
        PaletteBarColors BAS_PALETTE1, 0
        PaletteBarColors BAS_PALETTE2, 16
        PaletteBarColors BAS_PALETTE3, 32
        Display_Color_Palette ColorBar
    Case 2
        Color_INI 'Custom Palette
        Display_Color_Palette ColorBar
    Case 3 'Save As Custom
        SaveColor_INI
End Select
End Sub
```

**Select Case:** Depending on which menu item you selected, do the following:

**Case 0:** Show the ColorPalette form.

**ColorIndex = 0:** Set the index value of the color array to the first color position. All the colors stored in the array will then be loaded into the ColorPalette's display palette.

**Case 1:** Load the default color palette.

**PaletteBarColor Bas_Palette1(2, 3):** Read the default hexadecimal color values from the ARTISAN.BAS file. See Appendix A to view this file.

**Case 3:** Save any custom colors you dragged into the main palette in the ARTISAN.INI file.

**Figure 4.10.**
*The ColorPalette form when displayed.*

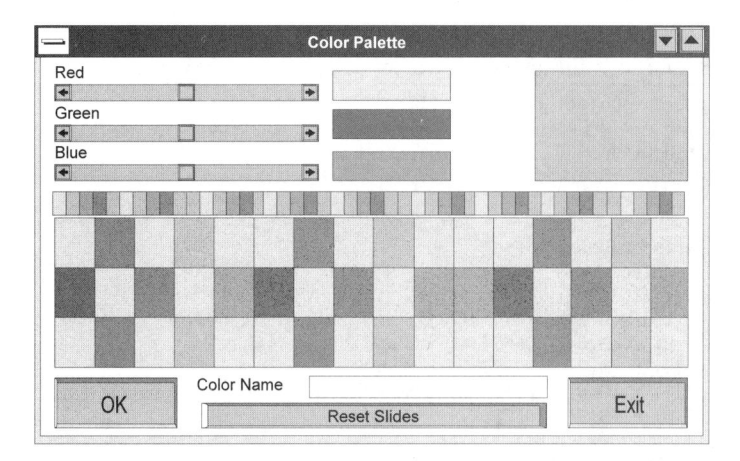

## Calculating Mouse Moves

The MoveMouse function returns True if the mouse has traveled a given distance on the desktop while the mouse's button is held in. Otherwise, it returns False. You use the function to stop unnecessary drawing of objects, if the user happens to just click the desktop for some unknown reason.

**Listing 4.26. Determining whether the mouse has moved a given distance.**
```
Function MoveMouse ()
If X1 > X2 + 45 Or X1 < X2 - 45 Or Y1 > Y2 + 45 Or Y1 < Y2 - 45 Then
    MoveMouse = True
Else
    MoveMouse = False
End If
End Function
```

> **If X1 > X2 + 45 Or X1 < X2 - 45 , etc. Then:** X1 and Y1 store the current X and Y positions of the Artwork's mouse down event. X2, Y2 store the X and Y values as the mouse moves. While the mouse button is held down, the mouse must move a preset distance before any object is drawn. The distance the mouse must travel before any action is taken is 45 twips or 3 pixels in any direction. You can change this number to any value for any direction you want to calculate.

## Moving Objects on the Desktop

The MoveObject procedure moves an object if the object's color is not equal to Artwork's BackColor. The object will be centered on the mouse pointer.

Objects are moved using one of the several methods that can be found in the Movetest program in Chapter 1. Objects are moved by clicking within their bounding box area. To move objects by clicking only their outline shapes, refer to the MoveObject procedure in Chapter 15.

**Listing 4.27. Moving an object using on-the-fly values.**
```
Sub MoveObject (Button%, Shift As Integer, X!, Y !)
If B = 0 Or PtInRectBasic = False Then Exit Sub
 N_H_Clear
 ArtWork.DrawMode = 7
 ArtWork.DrawWidth = 1
 'ArtWork.DrawStyle = Dot
 ArtWork.MousePointer = 5
 XCenter = X - ((W(B) \ 2) + (E(B)) \ 2))
 YCenter = Y - ((N(B) \ 2) + (S(B)) \ 2))
 ArtWork.Line (W(B), N(B))-(E(B), S(B)), YELLOW, B
 W(B) = (W(B) - OFFSETx) + XCenter
 N(B) = (N(B) - OFFSETy) + YCenter
 E(B) = (E(B) - OFFSETx) + XCenter
 S(B) = (S(B) - OFFSETy) + YCenter
 If FlagBezier(B) = B Then
    P1X(B) = (P1X(B) - OFFSETx) + XCenter
    P1Y(B) = (P1Y(B) - OFFSETy) + YCenter
    p2X(B) = (p2X(B) - OFFSETx) + XCenter
    p2Y(B) = (p2Y(B) - OFFSETy) + YCenter
```

```
    h1X(B) = (h1X(B) - OFFSETx) + XCenter
    h1Y(B) = (h1Y(B) - OFFSETy) + YCenter
    h2X(B) = (h2X(B) - OFFSETx) + XCenter
    h2Y(B) = (h2Y(B) - OFFSETy) + YCenter
 End If
 If FlagText(B) = B Then OFFSET(B) =
➥(OFFSET(B) - OFFSETx) + XCenter
    ArtWork.Line (W(B), N(B))-(E(B), S(B)), YELLOW, B
End Sub
```

**N_H_Clear:** Make all nodes and handles invisible.

**ArtWork.DrawMode, Wide, Style:** The bounding box changes to a dotted rectangle while it's being dragged. The mouse pointer is changed to an arrowhead (4) direction pointer.

**XCenter, YCeneter:** Calculate the center of the bounding box.

**W(B) = formula**: West side of the bounding box plus the center of the box before the move.

**N(B), E(B), S(B):** north side, east side, south side plus center position.

**If FlagBezier Then:** Same formula, except use a curve's four Bézier control points.

**If FlagText Then:** Sets the text alignment value to the new position. The indexed array OFFSET(text object number) holds the alignment offset that was defined in the procedure ReDrawText (explained in Listing 5.7).

**Figure 4.11.**
*Shows a circle being dragged to a new location.*

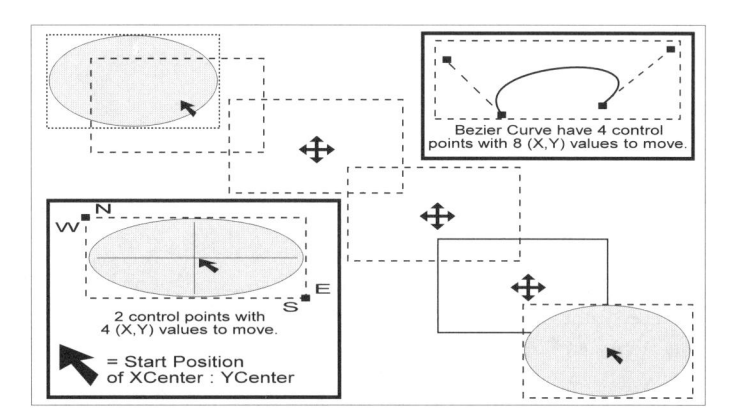

## Position Nodes Around an Object

The node procedure repositions nodes within the object selected.

Nodes are the little picture box controls that appear on an object's line and curve points. Nodes are used to change the shape of the object or to relocate a selected object to a new coordinate.

In this program, you can use a node to only relocate a line or a curve's end points. In the ArtAPI program in Chapter 15 you can use a node to change the shape of a multiline or curve object.

# The Artisan Program—Procedures C–N

**Listing 4.28. Positioning the nodes around an object.**

```
Sub Nodes ()
OSN = 45 + NodeZoom 'OFFSET Nodes
Select Case B
    Case FlagLine(B)
        Node(0).Left = E(B) - OSN : Node(0).Top = S(B) - OSN
        Node(2).Left = W(B) - OSN :  Node(2).Top = N(B) - OSN
        Node(0).Visible = True :  Node(1).Visible = False
        Node(2).Visible = True :  Node(3).Visible = False
    Case FlagBezier(B)
        Node(0).Left = P1X(B) - OSN :  Node(0).Top = P1Y(B) - OSN
        Node(1).Left = p2X(B) - OSN :  Node(1).Top = p2Y(B) - OSN
        Node(0).Visible = True :  Node(1).Visible = True
    Case FlagCircle(B)
        P = (W(B) + E(B)) \ 2
        Node(0).Left = P - OSN :  Node(0).Top = N(B) - OSN
        Node(0).Visible = True : Node(1).Visible = False
        Node(2).Visible = False : Node(3).Visible = False
    Case FlagBox(B)
        Node(0).Left = E(B) - OSN :   Node(0).Top = S(B) - OSN
        Node(1).Left = W(B) - OSN :   Node(1).Top = S(B) - OSN
        Node(2).Left = W(B) - OSN :   Node(2).Top = N(B) - OSN
        Node(3).Left = E(B) - OSN :   Node(3).Top = N(B) - OSN
            For R = 0 To 3
                Node(R).Visible = True
            Next R

    Case FlagText(B)
        Node(0).Left = W(B) + Zoom :  Node(0).Top = S(B) + Zoom
        Node(0).Visible = True
End Select
ReScale
End Sub
```

The `Nodes` procedure routine places the nodes on each end or junction point of a highlighted object (not to be confused with `BezNodes`, which are separate controls used to move a Bézier curve).

> **OSN:** Each node is 90 twips wide and high, so 45 represents the center position and is used as an offset to align each node correctly. `NodeZoom` is an additional offset used when a zoom tool rescales the viewing area.
>
> **Select Case:** B is the currently selected object's assigned number.
>
> **Case FlagLine(B):** Two nodes, one on either end of line object.
>
> **Case FlagBezier(B):** Two nodes, one on either end of curve.
>
> **Case FlagCircle(B):** One node on top of circle.
>
> **Case FlagBox(B):** Four nodes, one on each corner of box.
>
> **Case FlagText(B):** One node on bottom of first letter only in this program.

There are only four picture box controls used for nodes. Drawing programs use many nodes when objects are joined or for each character typed. You can add more node controls at runtime, but you will need a more structured code to keep things in check. See the Join Nodes program in Chapter 13 for an example of multiple nodes connected to a complex object.

The following is an example of adding nodes:

```
Static NodeIndex as Integer
NodeIndex = NodeIndex + 1
Load PictureBox(NodeIndex)
PictureBox(NodeIndex).Visible = True
```

Note that a new control is invisible by default.

> **NodeZoom:** You are using separate picture box controls as nodes and handles that reside within the Artwork picture box. Since the desktop acts as a container for these controls, they must be rescaled also.

Once the controls are rescaled, you must compensate for any additional offsets that reside within your code. An example of this would be the OSN variable found in this procedure. Handles and nodes have only their interiors rescaled, but the height and width of these controls must stay the same. The 44 twip offset for each handle, for instance, would not hold true after a zoom in or zoom out, since the scaling is changed from the original twip scale to a user-defined scale. The zoom tool adds an additional value to the variable NodeZoom to compensate for any new scaling dimensions.

**F**igure 4.12.
*The positioning of nodes around an object.*

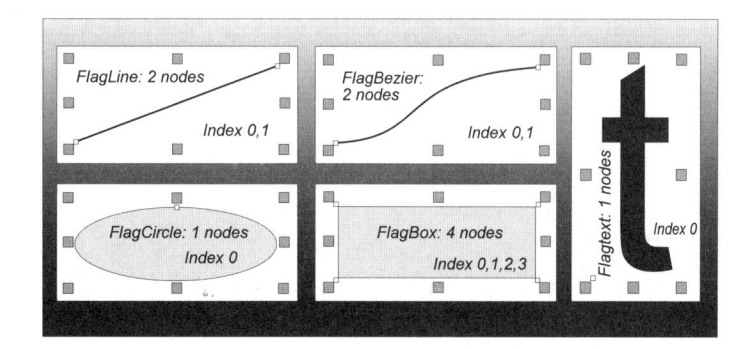

## Removing Nodes and Handles from the Desktop

The N_H_Clear procedure is about as simple as it gets. It simply hides the nodes and handles. (See Listing 4.29.)

**L**isting 4.29. Making the nodes and handles invisible.

```
Sub N_H_Clear ()
If B > 0 Then
    For R = 0 To 7
        Handle(R).Visible = False
    Next R
End If
 Node(0).Visible = False :   Node(1).Visible = False
 Node(2).Visible = False :   Node(3).Visible = False
End Sub
```

**For R:** Repeat counter starting at index 0 up to the last index 7.

**Handle(R):** Hide each of the eight handles.

**Node(0).Visible = False:** Hide each of the four nodes.

## Removing the Fill Color of an Object

The button that is marked with an "X" is the `No_Fill` command button. When an object that contains a fill color (a box or a circle) is selected, pressing this button will remove the fill color and make the object transparent again.

**Listing 4.30.** The "X" button removes the fill color from an object.

```
Sub No_Fill_Click ()
If B = FlagLine(B) Or Node(0).Visible = False Then Exit Sub
    FillValue(B) = 1
    UpdateObjects
End Sub
```

**If B = FlagLine(B):** If the object cannot contain a fill color, exit the event.

**FillValue(B) = 1:** Change the `FillValue` variable flag for the object to 1. This will change the `FillStyle` of `Artwork` to transparent (5) in the `UpdateObjects` procedure (Listing 4.12).

**UpdateObjects:** Redraw all objects on the desktop.

## Summary

The better part of this chapter dealt with the eight handle controls that are placed around an object after it is drawn. You can take advantage of the built-in mouse events for the eight picture box controls. However, you also have to deal with the fact that you must rescale these controls every time you change the interior scale of the Artwork picture box in which they reside. One way to overcome this is to replace the handle picture boxes by drawing handle shapes directly on the desktop. This means you would have to have additional procedures to perform the mouse events needed for the handle's mouse routines. This type of procedure structure is common when building drawing packages in a language like C. However, C language has more advantages when jumping from procedure to procedure. In Visual Basic, it would require a lot of work and a well-thought-out procedure structure to have all possible mouse routines for the desktop branch off from the main Artwork picture box's mouse events.

Another consideration when dealing with picture boxes as handles is the routine that actually places the handles around the object. In this program, you use offset values to place the handles slightly away from the object they are highlighting. A second procedure is used to reverse the offsets if the object is flipped around. What you may want to consider is a small function that calculates the interior center point of a handle and then uses only one procedure to place the eight handles around an invisible rectangular region. This is commonly used in Windows packages by taking advantage of the Windows API `Region` and `Rect` functions. This book does not go into any great detail about API `Region` and `Rect` functions because of the amount of functions available. The APIdraw program in Chapter 8 has some example of more widely used API functions.

# CHAPTER 5

# The Artisan Program—Procedures N–Z

# The Artisan Program—Procedures N–Z

This is the final chapter dealing with the Artisan program. In Chapter 5, you will look at the Artisan program's procedures alphabetically N through Z. One of the routines you will look at is the Node picture box mouse event, which is used to reposition or change the shape of objects.

A node is used to move a line that has already been placed on the artwork. You can add additional lines to a line you have already drawn. In this program, however, any additional lines are treated as separate objects; that is, they are not joined or grouped together as a single object. Also, the Node mouse events work only on nodes attached to lines or curves.

You could add additional code to have the nodes work with other object types (for example, creating rounded corners on a box or creating a pie or arc using the circle's node). Refer to the Join Nodes program in Chapter 10 or the ArtAPI programs in Chapter 15 for examples of connecting line and/or curve objects.

In professional illustration applications, nodes have the capability to connect and join objects, change the shape of elliptical objects to pie or pie slice shapes, round the corners of box shapes, and align text characters in various ways. Additional node features can add or delete nodes within object's shapes, and the list goes on.

You can add node features to your own programs. This book has several smaller graphic application programs that can get you started. Trying to rebuild a complete professional drawing package with Visual Basic, however, may be wishful thinking. You could almost certainly never keep up with new features that are continuously added to professional drawing packages, and Visual Basic's execution speed is slower compared to applications developed in C language. You must remember that the Artisan program is here to give you real world graphical application basics so you can enhance your own applications visually without having to rely too much on OCX and VBX custom controls.

## Moving an Object by Its Node

In the Artisan program, you can only move a line object using the node picture box controls. In the ArtAPI program in Chapter 15, you will be able to move complex objects that are joined together using lines or curves.

The two nodes attached to a line object can be used to move either end of a line to a new location when the Bézier tool is selected. You can also continue a new line object from the line's node you have just created. When drawing continuous lines in this manner, the lines will not be joined to one another and are treated as separate objects. The Join Nodes program in Chapter 13 demonstrates joining line objects.

**Listing 5.1.** Node_MouseDown erases the old line image.

```
Sub Node_MouseDown (Index%, Button%, Shift%, X!, Y!)
If Not FlagLine(B) = B And Not FlagBezier(B) = B Then Exit Sub
    OSN = 45 + NodeZoom
    Node(0).Visible = False: Node(2).Visible = False
ArtWork.DrawMode = Inverse
```

```
Select Case CurrentTool
    Case BezierTool
        ArtWork.DrawMode = 13
        ArtWork.AutoRedraw = True
        ArtWork.Line (W(B), N(B))-(E(B), S(B)), White
        ArtWork.AutoRedraw = False
        ArtWork.DrawMode = Inverse
        ArtWork.Line (W(B), N(B))-(E(B), S(B)), White
            If Index = 2 Then
                X1 = W(B): Y1 = N(B)
                X2 = E(B): Y2 = S(B)
                W(B) = E(B): N(B) = S(B)
            ElseIf Index = 0 Then
                X1 = E(B): Y1 = S(B)
                X2 = W(B): Y2 = N(B)
            End If
 XX2 = X2: YY2 = Y2: XX1 = X1: YY1 = Y1
    Case LineTool
        If Index = 0 Then X1 = Node(0).Left + [IC:CCC]
            OSN: Y1 = Node(0).Top + OSN
        If Index = 2 Then X1 = Node(2).Left +[IC:CCC]
            OSN: Y1 = Node(2).Top + OSN
        X2 = X1: Y2 = Y1
    End Select
End Sub
```

**If Not FlagLine(B) = B And Not FlagBezier(B) = B Then:** The currently selected object is not a line object, so exit the MouseDown event.

**OSN:** This represents the offset needed to align the center of the nodes. NodeZoom is an additional offset needed when you use the zoom tool.

**Node(0).Visible:** Hides the current node while you move a line segment.

**Node(2).Visible:** Hides the current node while you move a line segment.

**Select Case CurrentTool:** Go to the Case expression that equals the currently selected tool.

**Case BezierTool:** The Bézier tool is currently selected from ToolButtons.

**If FlagBezier(B):** If the currently selected object is a Bézier curve, show the Bézier's handles, a Bézier's nodes, and its connecting dotted lines using the BezUpdate procedure (Listing 3.18).

**If FlagLine(B) = B And Index = 2:** You can also use the Bézier tool to move a line to a different position. The illusion of drawing a moving line must have a fixed start point to perform this task. Otherwise, the line would start drawing at the opposite end of the line segment. The Nodes procedure (Listing 4.26) assigns two nodes, one for either end of the line. There are four node controls used in this program. A line object uses Node(0) and Node(2). If the current object is indeed a line object and the currently selected line node is indexed as (2), use the following coordinates:

X1 = W(B):Y1 = N(B) : X2 = E(B): Y2 = N(B)

**W(B) = E(B): N(B) = S(B):** Reverses the start and end positions of the line.

**ElseIf:** If the line node index number is (0), use the normal line coordinates.

`X1 = E(B): Y1 = S(B) : X2 = W(B): Y2 = N(B)`

**XX2, YY2, XX1, YY1:** Temporarily stores the line's original bounding box positions so you can erase the line's old image after you have moved one of the line's nodes.

**Case LineTool:** The currently selected tool in ToolButtons is the line tool.

**If Index = 0: If Index 1:** The line node is indexed as either (0) or (2), and drawing a new line will start from this indexed node. You must calculate the center of the current node so the new line's start point will attach to the current line's end point.

**Figure 5.1.**
*Dragging a line node.*

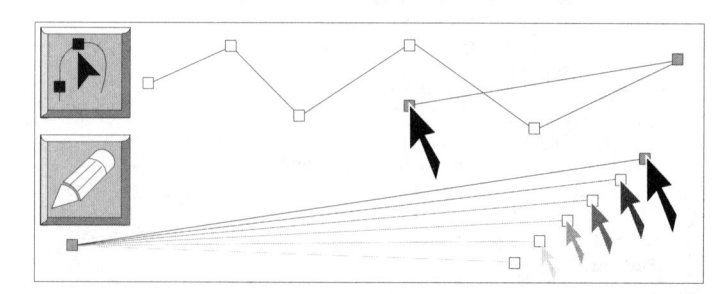

## Moving a Line Object's Node

The Node's mouse move event uses the Line statement to redraw the line as you move either of its two nodes.

**Listing 5.2.** The Node MouseMove event draws the line as it is moves.

```
Sub Node_MouseMove (Index%, Button%, Shift%, X!, Y!)
Xstr = Format$(X \ PIXELX, "000")
Ystr = Format$(Y \ PIXELY, "000")
XYLabel.Caption = "[" + Xstr + " , " + Ystr + "]"
If Not FlagLine(B) = B And Not FlagBezier(B) = B Then Exit Sub
If Button Then
    Select Case CurrentTool
        Case BezierTool
            If FlagLine(B) = B Then
                ArtWork.Line (X1, Y1)-(X2, Y2)
                X1 = X: Y1 = Y
                ArtWork.Line (X1, Y1)-(X2, Y2)
            End If
        Case LineTool
            ArtWork.Line (X1, Y1)-(X2, Y2)
            X2 = X: Y2 = Y
            ArtWork.Line (X1, Y1)-(X2, Y2)
    End Select
End If
End Sub
```

**If Not FlagLine(B) = B Then:** The currently selected object is not a line object, so exit the mouse move event.

**If Button Then:** If the mouse button is held in, continue.

**Select Case CurrentTool:** Go to the Case expression that matches the currently selected tool.

**Case BezierTool:** The Bézier tool is currently selected from ToolButtons.

**ArtWork.Line:** Use the standard formula for drawing a moving object.

**Case LineTool:** The line tool is currently selected from ToolButtons.

**ArtWork.Line:** Use the standard formula for drawing a moving object.

Figure 5.2 shows the effects of continuing a line from the last node position of each line segment using the LineTool. The star shape is not grouped as a single object but is made up of 10 separate line objects. This program does not join or group objects.

**Figure 5.2.**
*Continuing a line object from a node.*

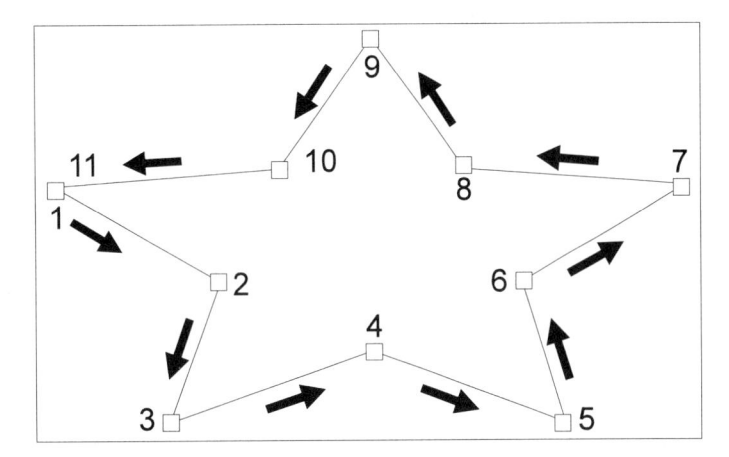

Figure 5.3 shows the effect of a node being relocated from its original star shape position as a result of the BezierTool. Because the star shape is not a single object, you must select one of the 10 line segments that make up the star in order to show the segment's two nodes.

**Figure 5.3.**
*Moving a line object's node.*

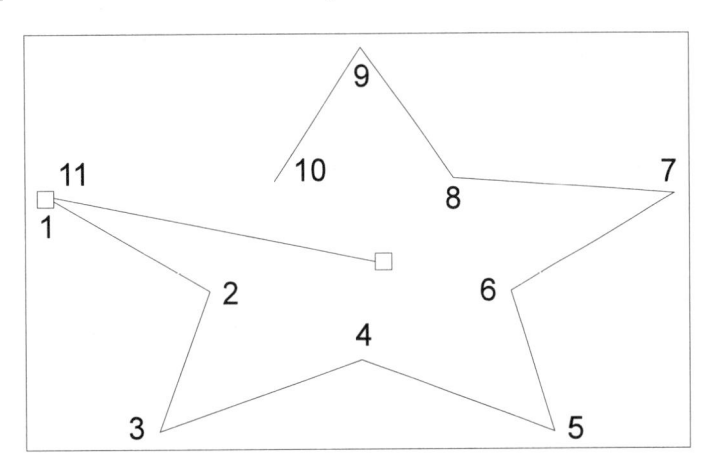

## Updating a Line Object After a Node Move

The Node's MouseUp event recalculates the line's bounding box positions after either of its two nodes have been moved.

**Listing 5.3.** The Node MouseUp event updates the new coordinates of the line.

```
Sub Node_MouseUp (Index%, Button%, Shift%, X!, Y!)
If Not FlagLine(B) = B And Not FlagBezier(B) = B Then Exit Sub
Select Case CurrentTool
    Case BezierTool
        W(B) = X1: N(B) = Y1: E(B) = X2: S(B) = Y2
        UpdateObjects
        Nodes
    Case LineTool
        ArtWork.DrawMode = Copy_Pen
        BoundingBox_Up X1, Y1, X2, Y2
        If B = Total Then Draw = True: UpdateObjects
End Select
End Sub
```

**If Not FlagLine(B) = B Then:** The currently selected object is not a line object, so exit the MouseUp event.

**Select Case CurrentTool:** Go to the Case that matches the currently selected tool.

**Case BezierTool: W(B), N(B), E(B), S(B):** Stores the new bounding box position of the line segment. Call the UpdateObjects procedure to redraw the line and then reposition the line's nodes to their new locations.

**Case LineTool:** The line tool is currently selected from ToolButtons.

**ArtWork.DrawMode:** Resets the drawing mode to normal.

**BoundingBox_Up:** You have made a new line object, so you must increase the total number of objects by 1. The BoundingBox_Up (Listing 2.20) procedure does all the calculations needed to increase the object count.

**If B = Total:** If the line is the new object, you only have to redraw the line and not all objects on the desktop. Flagging the Draw variable to true will make UpdateObjects draw only the new line object onto the desktop.

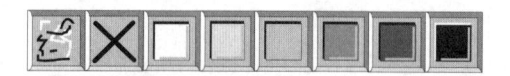

## Using the Popup Paint Tool To Fill an Object

The PaintButtons picture box contains a bitmap of a Color Fill button's image. To change the fill color of an object to a preset color, you simply click the fill button that has a picture image of the color you prefer. The code routine is similar to the way you selected a tool from the ToolButtons picture box control (Listing 2.10). All button bars in this program use bitmap images of buttons instead of Visual Basic's Command buttons. You may want to use image controls, which are faster and save resources, instead of picture box controls. Refer to the Buttons program in the 16MISC directory on the companion disk for alternative bitmap button image examples.

**Listing 5.4. Fills the selected object with color.**

```
Sub PaintButtons_MouseDown (Button%, Shift%, X!, Y!)
If Node(0).Visible = False Then PaintButtons.Visible = False: Exit Sub
CurrentTool = 7: ToolButtons_Paint: CurrentTool = LastToolUsed : ToolButtons_Paint
CurrentBrush = X \ 32: PaintButtons.Visible = False

Select Case CurrentBrush
    Case Palette

        CMDialog1.Color = PaintColor(B)
        CMDialog1.Flags = &H2& Or &H1&
        CMDialog1.Action = 3
        PaintColor(B) = CMDialog1.Color: FillValue(B) = 0
    Case NoFill
        No_Fill_Click
    Case WhiteBrush
        PaintColor(B) = &HFFFFFF: FillValue(B) = 0
    Case Brush10
        PaintColor(B) = &HE5E5E5: FillValue(B) = 0
    Case Brush20
        PaintColor(B) = &HCCCCCC: FillValue(B) = 0
    Case Brush50
        PaintColor(B) = &H7F7F7F: FillValue(B) = 0
    Case Brush70
        PaintColor(B) = &H4C4C4C: FillValue(B) = 0
    Case BlackBrush
        PaintColor(B) = &H0: FillValue(B) = 0
End Select
    UpdateObjects
End Sub
```

Refer to the routine used in `ToolButtons` mouse events (Listing 2.10) for an explanation on how the buttons are made to look pushed in.

**Select Case CurrentBrush:** One of the seven buttons you can press.

**Cases:** The brush color (fill color) you want to paint the object with. The `CurrentBrush` names (`Brush10`, `Brush20`, and so on) are global constants declared in the ARTISAN.BAS file, which is in Appendix A.

**Case Palette:** Displays the `CMDialog` common dialog control. When the `CMDialog` control appears, you can choose a custom color from the dialog form to fill the object.

**CMDialog1:** Refer to the Visual Basic Language Guide, "Common Dialog Control" and "Filters," for explanations of the CMDialog control's methods and properties values.

**Case NoFill:** Removes any fill color by calling the `No_Fill` click event button (Listing 4.30).

**All other Cases:** Changes the object's indexed color value to a new hexadecimal color value (this can be any value you choose). It then sets the object's `FillValue` flag variable to 0, which is used in `UpdateObjects` (Listing 5.16) to redraw the object in solid color.

## Extracting Color Value from the .INI file

The `PaletteBarColor` will take a grouped character string (in this case, hexadecimal color values) and assign each value to an indexed array called `Colors`. The string consists of 16 hexadecimal color values side-by-side, with a single space between each. The `ColorString`'s values are located in the ARTISAN.BAS declaration section (Appendix A) and are divided into three sections called `BAS_PALETTE1`, `BAS_PALETTE2`, and `BAS_PALETTE3`. If a custom color palette was defined in the ARTISAN.INI, the custom color values listed in the ARTISAN.INI are used to define the palette's colors.

**Listing 5.5.** `PaletteBarColors` extracts the color values from an .INI file.

```
Sub PaletteBarColors (ColorString$, FirstColor, RefreshPalette)
Start = 1
    For C = FirstColor To FirstColor + 15
        Colors(C) = Val(Mid$(ColorString, Start, 8))
        Start = Start + 9
    Next C
End Sub
```

**C =:** The index number to assign to each hexadecimal color value extracted.

**FirstColor =:** An argument passed from the `Color_INI` procedure (Listing 4.5). The `Color_INI` procedure passes the values, 0, 16, or 32, which represent the insertion point to start extracting each of the three groups of hexadecimal color values. The `FirstColor + 15` value will count 16 hexadecimal colors per group. When the `PaletteBarColor` procedure has finally been called three times by the `Color_INI` procedure, the color palette will have 48 colors in the color palette bar.

**Color(C) = Val(Mid$(ColorString$, Start, 8)):** The array called `Colors` will index each of the 48 colors (0 to 47). Each hexadecimal color value is 8 numeric characters long, so the Visual Basic `Mid$` string function will extract each hexadecimal color from the grouped numeric strings (`BAS_PALETTE1`, and so on).

**Start = Start + 9:** Each of the eight numeric character hexadecimal color values is separated by a single space. Making the start position in `Mid$` function increase by nine character spaces after each color extraction will position the next color extraction point correctly.

Chapter 5

## Creating Perfect Circles

The `PerfectCircle` function can also be found in Visual Basic's IconWorks example. I have included a modified version of this example since it uses only basic language statements to calculate the radius of a moving circle. However, the API `Ellipse` function can be used to eliminate the `PerfectCircle` function. An example of using the API `Ellipse` function on a moving circle object is demonstrated in the DrawAPI program in Chapter 8. The `ArtAPI` program in Chapter 15 uses the API Ellipse function also.

**Listing 5.6. Calculating the radius of a moving circle.**
```
Function PerfectCircle (X1, Y1, X2, Y2)
Xleg = Abs(X2 - X1)
    If Xleg <> 0 Then
    Yleg = Abs(Y2 - Y1)
    Aspect = Abs(Yleg / Xleg)
If Xleg >Yleg Then Radius = Xleg \ 2 Else Radius = Yleg \ 2
    XCenter = X1 + (X2 - X1) \ 2
    YCenter = Y1 + (Y2 - Y1) \ 2
 End If
        PerfectCircle = Xleg
End Function
```

**Xleg** =: The absolute value of the circle's bounding box's width.

**Yleg** =: The absolute value of the circle's bounding box's height.

**Aspect** =: The absolute aspect. If value equals 1, the circle is perfect.

**Radius** =: The center position of the bounding box's width or height.

**XCenter, YCenter** =: The center point of the circle's bounding box.

## Placing Text on the Desktop in Visual Basic

The `ReDrawText` procedure is used to redraw any text that you first type in the `Txt` label control or in the textbox controls in the `Text` form. The `ReDrawText` procedure will transfer the text strings to the desktop and assign the text an object number.

The `ReDrawText` procedure uses only the standard Visual Basic text properties to draw text. Therefore, you are very limited when controlling text. The Windows API text functions are superior to Visual Basic's. There are three small API text program examples in Chapter 12 that deal with API `TextOut` and `DrawText` functions.

**Listing 5.7. Drawing text objects on the desktop.**
```
Sub ReDrawText ()
If Txt.Caption > "" Then
Total = Total + 1: B = Total
CarriageCount(B) = crCounter: crCounter = 0
LineWidth(B) = ArtWork.DrawWidth
```

*continues*

## Listing 5.7. continued

```
FlagText(B) = B: FillValue(B) = 1
    TL = Txt.Left: TT = Txt.Top
    TW = Txt.Left + Txt.Width
    TH = (Txt.Top + Txt.Height)
    Txt.Visible = False
TextSize(B) = Txt.FontSize 'Size of Txt.Label Type
Storedtext(B) = RTrim(Txt.Caption)
TextFont(B) = RTrim(ArtWork.FontName)
TextBold(B) = ArtWork.FontBold
TextItalic(B) = ArtWork.FontItalic
If Align = 0 Then FlagAlign(B) = TA_LEFT:OS = 0
If Align = 6 Then FlagAlign(B) = TA_CENTER:OS = (Txt.Width / 2)
If Align = 2 Then FlagAlign(B) = TA_RIGHT:OS = Txt.Width
''''''''''''''''''''''''''''''''''''''
    ArtWork.AutoRedraw = True
    ArtWork.CurrentX = TL
    OFFSET(B) = ArtWork.CurrentX
    ArtWork.CurrentY = TT
    SaveScaleLeft = ArtWork.ScaleLeft
    ArtWork.ScaleLeft = -ArtWork.CurrentX + Scaling
    ArtWork.ForeColor = PaintColor(B)
    Artwork.FontName = TextFont(B)
    ArtWork.FontSize = TextSize(B)
    TextSize(B) = Txt.FontSize/TextPoint 'store as normal 44% size
    ArtWork.FontName = TextFont(B)
    ArtWork.FontBold = TextBold(B)
    ArtWork.FontItalic = TextItalic(B)
    wFlag = FlagAlign(B)
    TA = SetTextAlign(ArtWork.hDC, wFlag)
    ArtWork.Print Storedtext(B)
    ArtWork.AutoRedraw = False
    ArtWork.ScaleLeft = SaveScaleLeft
W(B) = TL - OS: E(B) = TW - OS: N(B) = TT: S(B) = TH
Txt.Caption = ""
End If
Txt.Visible = False
Txt.FontBold = False
Txt.FontItalic = False
Txt.Width = 15
    ArtWork.FontBold = False
    ArtWork.FontItalic = False
End Sub
```

The ReDrawText procedure is explained in a step-by-step format as follows:

1. Any text typed on-screen is placed within the label control called Txt.

2. The Txt.Caption is a new object; therefore, you increase the total by 1 and assign the text object that number.

3. Assign the text's new bounding box coordinates the same position values as those used in the text label's dimension size.

4. Store the Txt label's caption text in an indexed array called StoredText and the Visual Basic text attributes in the indexed arrays (TextSize, TextFont, TextBold, and TextItalic).
5. Redraw the text onto the desktop as follows:

    - Place text by using the Print statement, which needs to know the CurrentX and CurrentY of the text cursor that is being used to place the text. You are using a label control as a text cursor by setting the label's width to 1 pixel wide.
    - CurrentX equals the value of the label's Left property value, which is represented by the TL variable. CurrentY is equal to the label's Top property value, which is represented by the TT variable.
    - **SaveScaleLeft**: An embedded carriage return that appears in a text string will set the CurrentX value to scale 0. Thus, save the current ScaleLeft property value of Artwork picture box control.
    - **ArtWork.ScaleLeft = -ArtWork.CurrentX**: Reset Artwork's ScaleLeft property so the next line will be placed directly below the first. An additional value called Scaling is used when a zoom tool in used in the application.
    - Assign all the attributes of the text to be drawn.
    - **TextSize(B)**: Represents the point size of the text to be redrawn and must be resized if a zoom tool is used in your application. In this program, you are using a simplified way to do this by dividing the point size by a variable value TextPoint. The TextPoint variable value was calculated in the ZoomBar procedure (Listing 5.19). Refer to the introduction of the ArtAPI program in Chapter 15 for the most accurate mathematical text point conversion formulas. Also, when using API viewport functions to simulate a zoom feature, text can be automatically resized if redrawn using API graphical text functions. Refer to the Scaltest program in Chapter 14 for examples on API viewport scaling.
    - **wFlag = FlagAlign(B)**: Use the API alignment function to set the left, center, or right justifications. Refer to the TxtAlign programs in Chapter 12 for manual and API text alignment examples.
    - **ArtWork.Print Storedtext(B)**: Prints the stored text.
    - Reset Artwork's original ScaleLeft property and store the text's bounding box coordinates.

# Rescaling the Interior Coordinates of Nodes and Handles

The Rescale procedure is used to update the internal scaling of all nodes and handles after a zoom in or zoom out. The value of Zoom is calculated in the ZoomBar events.

## The Artisan Program—Procedures N–Z

**L**isting 5.8. Rescaling a container's controls after a zoom.

```
Sub ReScale ()
 BezHandle1.ScaleWidth = BezHandle1.Width + Zoom
 BezHandle1.ScaleHeight = BezHandle1.Height + Zoom
 BezHandle2.ScaleWidth = BezHandle2.Width + Zoom
 BezHandle2.ScaleHeight = BezHandle2.Height + Zoom
 BezNode1.ScaleWidth = BezNode1.Width + Zoom
 BezNode1.ScaleHeight = BezNode1.Height + Zoom
 BezNode2.ScaleWidth = BezNode2.Width + Zoom
 BezNode2.ScaleHeight = BezNode2.Height + Zoom
 ' ' ' ' '
 For R = 0 To 3
     Node(R).ScaleLeft = Node(R).Left
     Node(R).ScaleTop = Node(R).Top
     Node(R).ScaleWidth = Node(R).Width + Zoom
     Node(R).ScaleHeight = Node(R).Height + Zoom
 Next R
 For R = 0 To 7
     Handle(R).ScaleLeft = Handle(R).Left
     Handle(R).ScaleTop = Handle(R).Top
     Handle(R).ScaleWidth = Handle(R).Width + Zoom
     Handle(R).ScaleHeight = Handle(R).Height + Zoom
 Next R
 Zoom = 0
End Sub
```

**`BezHandle1.ScaleWidth =:`** Rescale all internal scale properties of the two `BezHandle` picture box control.

**`BezNode1.ScaleWidth =:`** Rescale all internal scale properties of the two `BezNode` picture box control.

**`Node(R).ScaleLeft =:`** Rescale all internal scale properties of the two `Node` picture box control.

**`Handle(R).ScaleWidth =:`** Rescale all internal scale properties of the two `Handle` picture box control.

## The Ruler's Mouse Events

The two rulers are picture box controls that display ruler marks in inch measurements. The ruler marks are set to the vertical and horizontal 0,0 marks of the upper-left corner of the page displayed on the desktop. Each ruler also displays a dotted rule guide line to indicate the current X and Y coordinates of the mouse pointer on the screen.

**L**isting 5.9. `Ruler_MouseDown` sets the new guideline from the ruler.

```
Sub Ruler_MouseDown (Index%, Button%, Shift%, X!, Y!)
If BezHandle1.Visible = True Then ShowDotted = False: BezUpdate
    NewGuideLine = True
    X2 = -5000: Y2 = -5000
If Index = 0 Then SideRuler = True: Exit Sub
If Index = 1 Then TopRuler = True: Exit Sub
End Sub
```

**If BezHandle1.Visible = True:** If a curve is selected as you are about to pull a ruler guide line from either ruler, you must update the curve before continuing.

**NewGuideLine = True:** Setting this variable flag to true indicates that you are pulling a new guideline onto the desktop. When this flag is set to false, you are simply moving a guideline already present on the desktop to a new location.

**X2 = -5000: Y2 = -5000:** Since you are drawing the guidelines in twip scales, you will make the length of each line drawn long enough to reach across the dimensions of the desktop area.

**If Index = 0 Then SideRuler = True:** The side ruler is indexed as Ruler(0). If this is the ruler you are pulling the guide line from, set the `SideRuler` variable flag to true. The `SideRuler` variable will tell the `GuideLines` procedure (Listing 4.8) to draw a vertical guide line.

**If Index = 0 Then TopRuler = True:** The side ruler is indexed as Ruler(1). If this is the ruler you are pulling the guideline from, set the `TopRuler` variable flag to true. The `TopRuler` variable will tell the `GuideLines` procedure (Listing 4.8) to draw a horizontal guideline.

**Listing 5.10. Drawing the guideline.**

```
Sub Ruler_MouseMove (Index%, Button%, Shift%, X!, Y!)
    Xstr = Format$(X \ PixelX, "000")
    Ystr = Format$(Y \ PixelY, "000")
XYLabel.Caption = "[" + Xstr + " , " + Ystr + "]"
        RulerGuides Index, Button, Shift, X, Y
    If Button Then GuideLines Index, Button, X, Y
End Sub
```

**Xstr = Format$:** The rulers are picture boxes separate form the `Artwork` desktop. Therefore, you send the mouse's X and Y coordinates to the `XYLabel` control to display the current X and Y coordinates of the mouse pointer.

The `RulerGuides` procedure draws the moving dotted lines within each ruler. If you press and hold the mouse button, the `GuideLines` procedure draws a dotted guideline on `Artwork`'s desktop as you drag the mouse.

**Listing 5.11. Calculating the new coordinates of the guideline.**

```
Sub Ruler_Mouseup (Index%, Button%, Shift%, X!, Y!)
X2 = X: Y2 = Y
    If NewGuideLine = True Then TGL = TGL + 1: V = TGL
    If SideRuler = True Then GuideX(V) = X2
    If TopRuler = True Then GuideY(V) = Y2
```

*continues*

## Listing 5.11. continued

```
NewGuideLine = False
ArtWork.DrawStyle = Solid
        UpdateObjects
SideRuler = False: TopRuler = False: ShowDotted = False
End Sub
```

**Figure 5.4.**
*A guideline being pulled from a ruler.*

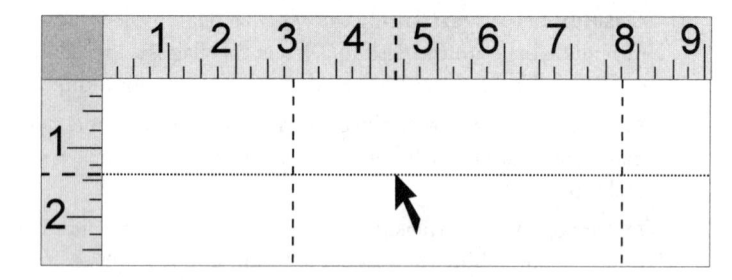

**If NewGuideLine:** The `Ruler_MouseDown` event flagged the `NewGuideLine` variable as `True`, so increase the total number of guidelines (TGL) on the page by 1.

The variable V represents the guide's assigned index number. This is the same as in the `BoundingBox_Up` procedure (Listing 2.20) when a new object is drawn (for example, `Total = Total + 1: B = Total`).

**GuideX(number) = X2:** Stores the vertical guideline's X coordinate so you can find it when you want to move the line to another screen position.

**GuideY(number) = Y2:** Stores the horizontal guideline's Y coordinate so you can find it when you want to move the line to another screen position.

**ArtWork.DrawStyle:** Changes the drawing style to `Solid`.

**UpdateObjects:** Redraws all objects on the desktop and then resets the `SideRuler` and `TopRuler` flags to off.

## Drawing Each Ruler's Slide Line

This `RulerGuides` routine draws the moving dotted lines in each ruler. The ruler slide line follows the mouse's current X and Y coordinates.

### Listing 5.12. Drawing the ruler slide lines.

```
Sub RulerGuides (Index%, Button As Integer, Shift As Integer, X!, Y!)
R0SL = Ruler(0).ScaleLeft 'Side Ruler
R0L = Ruler(0).Left - 5000: R0T = Ruler(0).Top - 5000
    R1ST = Ruler(1).ScaleTop 'Top Ruler
    R1L = Ruler(1).ScaleLeft - 15: R1T = Ruler(1).ScaleTop - 15
Ruler(0).Line (R0L, R0T)-(X1Ruler, Y1Ruler), Cyan, B 'Vert.
Ruler(1).Line (R1L, R1T)-(X2Ruler, Y2Ruler), Cyan, B 'Horz.
 X1Ruler = R0SL + 500 'Side Ruler.Width
```

```
        Y1Ruler = Y
        X2Ruler = X
 Y2Ruler = R1ST + 500 'Top Ruler.Height
Ruler(0).Line (R0L, R0T)-(X1Ruler, Y1Ruler), Cyan, B 'Vert
Ruler(1).Line (R1L, R1T)-(X2Ruler, Y2Ruler), Cyan, B 'Horz
End Sub
```

**R0SL:** (Ruler 0 ScaleLeft.)

**R0L, R0T:** (Ruler 0 ScaleLeft, ruler 0 Top.) The ruler's ScaleLeft and ScaleTop can change when you scroll the desktop vertically or horizontally. Therefore, use the ruler's current internal scale to start the ruler slide line drawing.

**R1SL:** (Ruler 1 ScaleLeft.)

**R1L, R1T:** (Ruler 1 ScaleLeft, ruler 1 Top.) The ruler's ScaleLeft and ScaleTop can change when you scroll the desktop vertically or horizontally. Therefore, use the ruler's current internal Scale to start the ruler slide line drawing.

**Ruler(0).Line: Ruler(1).Line:** The dotted ruler line is actually a dotted box. Three of the box's sides are outside the viewing area, so the one side you see appears as though it is a line. By assigning a negative value to the standard X1 and Y1 values, you won't see the outermost edges of the dotted box.

## Drawing the Inch Marks in Each Ruler

The Ruler_Paint event is a very clean, stripped-down, easy way to put ruler marks and numbers within a picture box or form. Once you understand how the Line statements use a recursive pattern in conjunction with the ruler's scale, you can change the measurement scale and appearance. The measure values used here are approximate, so you will need a calculator to accurately set WYSIWYG measurements.

**Listing 5.13.** Ruler_Paint draws inch marks within each ruler.

```
Sub Ruler_Paint (Index As Integer)
Ruler(0).Cls: Ruler(1).Cls
Ruler(0).DrawMode = 13: Ruler(1).DrawMode = 13
Ruler(0).DrawStyle = Solid: Ruler(1).DrawStyle = Solid
'''''''''''''''''''''''''''''''''
Ruler(0).ScaleLeft = 0: Ruler(0).ScaleWidth = 4: Num = -8
    For I = 300 To 15000 Step 576
        Ruler(0).Line (0, I)-(4, I)
        Ruler(0).Line (2, I - 288)-(4, I - 288)
        Ruler(0).Line (3, I - 144)-(4, I - 144)
        Ruler(0).Line (3, I - 432)-(4, I - 432)
        Ruler(0).PSet (-.5, I), Ruler(0).BackColor
        Num = Num + 1: Ruler(0).Print Num
    Next I
'''''''''''''''''''''''''''''''''
Ruler(1).ScaleTop = 0: Ruler(1).ScaleHeight = 4: Num = -12
    For I = 200 To 18000 Step 576
        Ruler(1).Line (I, 0)-(I, 4)
```

*continues*

# The Artisan Program—Procedures N–Z

## Listing 5.13. continued

```
        Ruler(1).Line (I - 288, 0)-(I - 288, 2)
        Ruler(1).Line (I - 144, 0)-(I - 144, 1)
        Ruler(1).Line (I - 432, 0)-(I - 432, 1)
        Ruler(1).PSet (I, 1), Ruler(1).BackColor
        Num = Num + 1: Ruler(1).Print Num
    Next I
'''''''''''''''''''''''''''''''''''
 Ruler(0).ScaleTop = ArtWork.ScaleTop
 Ruler(0).ScaleHeight = ArtWork.ScaleHeight
 Ruler(0).ScaleLeft = ScaleBox.Left + BSM
 Ruler(0).ScaleWidth = OldRW * PerSW
 Ruler(1).ScaleLeft = ArtWork.ScaleLeft
 Ruler(1).ScaleWidth = ArtWork.ScaleWidth
 Ruler(1).ScaleTop = ScaleBox.Top + SSM
 Ruler(1).ScaleHeight = OldRH * PerSH
'''''''''''''''''''''''''''''''''''
Ruler(0).DrawMode = Xor_Pen: Ruler(1).DrawMode = Xor_Pen
Ruler(0).DrawStyle = Dot: Ruler(1).DrawStyle = Dot
        XRuler = -5000: YRuler = -5000
        ArtWork.Enabled = True
End Sub
```

**Ruler(0).DrawMode:** The rulers use the Xor draw mode to draw the dotted ruler lines that follow the mouse's X and Y positions. Change it temporarily to the normal default of Copy_Pen in order to draw the inch marks.

**Ruler.DrawStyle:** Temporarily changes the drawing style to the default, which is Solid.

**Ruler(0).Scale:** The side ruler(0) is the same height as the internal dimensions of ArtWork's desktop. The top ruler(1) is the same width as ArtWork's desktop. You need to scale only the interior to accommodate the easy placement of each quarter-inch mark drawn with the Line statements.

**Num = -8:** Change this number to adjust the inch numbers to the next or previous inch mark. The higher the Num value is, the higher the inch number in the ruler.

**For I = 300 To 15000 Step 576:** Repeats the counter I, starting at 300 and continuing up to 15,000 twip units by intervals of 576. These values place the quarter-, half-, three-quarter, and one-inch marks on the ruler. You can fine-tune all measurements by changing the Step value. If you change the start number (300) and/or the end number (15,000), you can adjust the number of marks on the ruler; however, you will also have to fine-tune the Num variable and Step value. The Scaltest program in Chapter 14 uses the same Ruler_Paint procedure, so it is recommended that you experiment with these values in the Scaltest program.

Following are examples of line statements X1,Y1 and X2,Y2 values:

**Ruler(0).Line (0, I)-(4, I):** Represents the position of each one-inch mark on the ruler.

**`Ruler(0).Line (2, I - 288)-(4, I - 288):`** Represents the position of each three-quarter inch mark on the ruler.

**`Ruler(0).Line (3, I - 144)-(4, I - 144):`** Represents the position of each half-inch mark on the ruler.

**`Ruler(0).Line (3, I - 432)-(4, I - 432):`** Represents the position of each quarter-inch mark on the ruler.

The numbers 432, 288 and 144 are the twip distances between each mark on the ruler. To adjust these values, use numbers that are divisible with each other so the spacing is even throughout the ruler's length.

**`Ruler(0).PSet:`** Sets the X value to move the ruler number left or right. It also sets the Y value to move the ruler number up or down.

**`Ruler(0).Print I:`** Prints the ruler's inch number. It also advances the Num count by one number for each loop.

To set the proper alignment scaling of the rulers to match Artwork's, perform the following:

**`Ruler(n).Scale:`** Resets the two ruler's scales to reflect the `Artwork's` scale. The variables BSM, SSM, oldRW, oldRH, PerSW, and PerSH are offsets to add when using the zoom tool or when scrolling the desktop. These values can be found in the Hscroll_change or Vscroll_change events (Listing 4.14).

**`Ruler.DrawMode, DrawStyle, XRuler, YRuler:`** Resets all the ruler's properties back to what they were before for the Ruler_Paint event began.

**`XRuler: YRuler:`** Resets the ruler guide's X1 and Y1 drawing values.

**`ArtWork.Enabled = True:`** Artwork is disabled at startup so it will not interfere with the Ruler_Paint event.

When you draw ruler marks using the Line statement, you have to add spacing values between each mark (line) drawn. The placement of these offset values depends on whether the ruler is vertical or horizontal. An example is

```
Line ( X1, Y1 )-( X2, Y2 )
```

*Vertical ruler*

---

**X1** = Length of each ruler mark
**Y1** = Vertical distance between each ruler mark
**X2** = Right side of the ruler where the lines meet the ruler edge
**Y2** = Same spacing as Y1

*Horizontal ruler*

---

**X1** = Horizontal distance between each ruler mark.
**Y1** = Top of ruler where the lines meet the ruler edge
**X2** = Same spacing as X1
**Y2** = Length of each ruler mark

# Writing Values to the ARTISAN.INI file

At startup, the values used to display each color in the `ColorBar` palette are taken from the default listing in the ARTISAN7.BAS file. The color values are located on three lines under the subhead, "Default Color Palette Values."

**Listing 5.14. Extracting array colors and then writing them to an .INI file.**

```
Sub SaveColor_INI ()
For I = 0 To 2
    ColorString = ""
        For C = 0 To 15
            ColorString = ColorString + [IC:CCC]
            Format$(Colors(I * 16 + C), "00000000 ")
        Next C
    X = WritePrivateProfileString(KEY_NAME, KEY_ENTRY + [IC:CCC]
    Format$(I + 1), ColorString, INI_FILENAME)
Next I
End Sub
```

The following items happen before the color palette is loaded at runtime.

1. The Artisan `Form_Load` event (Listing 2.7) calls the `Color_INI` procedure (Listing 4.5).
2. The `Color_INI` procedure uses an API function to search for a custom .INI file. If one is not found, `Color_INI` uses default values located in the ARTISAN7.BAS file. The API function is as follows:

   ```
   GetPrivateProfileString(KEY_NAME, KEY_ENTRY + "1", BAS_PALETTE1,
       →ColorString, Len(ColorString), INI_FILENAME)
   ```

   KeyWord Names as defined in the ARTISAN7.BAS.bas file:

   Global Const KEY_NAME = "Artisan"

   Global Const KEY_ENTRY = "Colors Row"

   Global Const INI_FILENAME = "Artisan.INI"

   Default Color palette values as defined in the ARTISAN7.BAS file:

   Global Const BAS_PALETTE1 = "16777215 14737632 12632319...etc.

   Global Const BAS_PALETTE2 = "12632256 04210752 08421631...etc.

   Global Const BAS_PALETTE3 = "08421504 00000000 00000255...etc.

3. The `PaletteBarColors` procedure (Listing 5.5) is called three times to extract the values that have been stored in a buffer called `ColorString`. The values `0`, `16`, and `32` are arguments that will change the `FirstColor` variable used for counting each color.
4. The `Colors(C)` array now holds an index for each color ranging from index 0 to index 47.
5. Finally, the `ColorBar_Paint` event (Listing 4.3) calls `Display_Color_Palette`, (Appendix A) which scales the Picture Box control into 48 sections and assigns each color palette entry.

# Placing an Object to the Front or Back of All the Others

The To_Front_Back procedure switches the attributes of every object in order to move the object to the top or to the bottom of all other objects on the desktop. This routine is very long and really should be used when dealing with only a few objects in your projects. A much shorter To_Front_Back procedure is available in the ArtAPI program in Chapter 15. The ArtAPI approach reduces the amount of code needed to only a few lines. However, the nested loop routine may be confusing to beginners, and additional arrays must be implemented to redraw all objects in the correct order.

**Listing 5.15. Sending an object to the front or back of all others.**

```
Sub To_Front_Back (Index As Integer)
Dim PC As Long: Dim OLC As Long
Dim St As String: Dim TF As String
If Node(0).Visible = False Then Exit Sub
If Index = 0 And B = Total Then Exit Sub
If Index = 1 And B <= 1 Then Exit Sub
''''''store objects attributes
If FlagText(B) = B Then FT = 1
If FlagCircle(B) = B Then FC = 1
If FlagLine(B) = B Then FL = 1
If FlagBox(B) = B Then FB = 1
If FlagBezier(B) = B Then Bez = 1
OLC = OutLineColor(B): PC = PaintColor(B): LW = LineWidth(B)
Fill = FillValue(B): LV = LineValue(B): St = Storedtext(B)
TS = TextSize(B): TF = TextFont(B): TB = TextBold(B): TI = TextItalic(B)
FA = FlagAlign(B): OF = OFFSET(B): CR = CarriageCount(B)
W1 = W(B): N2 = N(B): E3 = E(B): S4 = S(B)
p1XX = P1X(B): p1YY = P1Y(B): p2XX = P2X(B): p2YY = p2Y(B)
h1XX = h1X(B): h1YY = h1Y(B): h2XX = h2X(B): h2YY = h2Y(B)
''''''''End of every possible attribute
If Index = 0 Then Last = Total - 1: First = 1 Else Last = 2: First = -1
For B = B To Last Step First: A = B + (First)
W(B) = W(A): N(B) = N(A): E(B) = E(A): S(B) = S(A)
P1X(B) = P1X(A): P1Y(B) = P1Y(A)
P2X(B) = P2X(A): p2Y(B) = p2Y(A)
h1X(B) = h1X(A): h1Y(B) = h1Y(A)
h2X(B) = h2X(A): h2Y(B) = h2Y(A)
OutLineColor(B) = OutLineColor(A)
PaintColor(B) = PaintColor(A)
LineWidth(B) = LineWidth(A)
FillValue(B) = FillValue(A)
LineValue(B) = LineValue(A)
Storedtext(B) = Storedtext(A)
TextSize(B) = TextSize(A)
TextFont(B) = TextFont(A)
TextBold(B) = TextBold(A)
TextItalic(B) = TextItalic(A)
FlagAlign(B) = FlagAlign(A)
OFFSET(B) = OFFSET(A)
CarriageCount(B) = CarriageCount(A)
```

*continues*

## The Artisan Program—Procedures N–Z

**Listing 5.15. continued**

```
If FlagText(A) = 0 Then FlagText(B) = 0 Else FlagText(B) = B
If FlagCircle(A) = 0 Then FlagCircle(B) = 0 Else FlagCircle(B) = B
If FlagLine(A) = 0 Then FlagLine(B) = 0 Else FlagLine(B) = B
If FlagBox(A) = 0 Then FlagBox(B) = 0 Else FlagBox(B) = B
If FlagBezier(A) = 0 Then FlagBezier(B) = 0 Else FlagBezier(B) = B
Next B

''''Reset objects attributes
If FT = 1 Then FlagText(B) = B Else FlagText(B) = 0
If FB = 1 Then FlagBox(B) = B Else FlagBox(B) = 0
If FC = 1 Then FlagCircle(B) = B Else FlagCircle(B) = 0
If FL = 1 Then FlagLine(B) = B Else FlagLine(B) = 0
If Bez = 1 Then FlagBezier(B) = B Else FlagBezier(B) = 0
OutLineColor(B) = OLC: PaintColor(B) = PC: LineWidth(B) = LW
FillValue(B) = Fill: LineValue(B) = LV: Storedtext(B) = St
TextSize(B) = TS: TextFont(B) = TF: TextItalic(B) = TB: TextItalic(B) = TI
FlagAlign(B) = FA: OFFSET(B) = OF
CarriageCount(B) = CR
W(B) = W1: N(B) = N2: E(B) = E3: S(B) = S4
P1X(B) = p1XX: P1Y(B) = p1YY: P2X(B) = p2XX: p2Y(B) = p2YY
h1X(B) = h1XX: h1Y(B) = h1YY: h2X(B) = h2XX: h2Y(B) = h2YY
UpdateObjects
End Sub
```

**If Node(0):** No object is selected, so exit this procedure.

**If Index = 0 And B = Total:** You have chosen to move the object to the front, but the object is already there so exit this procedure.

**If Index = 1 And B <= 1:** You have chosen to move the object to the back, but the object is already there so exit this procedure.

**If FlagText(B) = B Then FT = 1:** Find out the type of object being moved (circle, box, line). If the object type's flag equals B (object's assigned number) then you have a match.

**OLC = OutLineColor(B): PC = PaintColor(B), etc.:** Temporarily store any possible attribute the object might have been assigned.

**W1 = W(B), N2 = N(B), E3 =E(B), S(B) = S(B):** Temporarily store the object's current bounding box coordinates.

The next step is to determine the direction of the sort—ascending (to the front) or descending (to the back).

**If Index = 0 Then Last = Total - 1: First = 1 Else Last = 2: First = -1:** If the Menu index you selected equals 0, you move the object to the front. The variable called Last will equal the total number of objects minus 1, and the variable called First will equal 1.

**Else:** Moves an object to the back so the variable Last will equal 2, and the variable First will equal -1. Having a negative Step value (for example, -1) will make the For/Next statement count backwards; hence, the object moves to the back rather than the front.

**For/Next:** Performs the sorting loop.

**For B= B To Last Step First: A = B + (First):** For every object (B) starting at the current object (B) and continuing to the last object, do the following.

All values in each attribute array listed within the For/Next statement will be relocated to the next attributes index number in the array. The B value represents the current object's assigned index number. The A value will equal the next index number B + 1, ascending order, or B - 1, descending order.

**If FlagText(A) = 0 Then FlagText(B) = 0 Else FlagText(B) = B:** This will make sure each object is assigned its correct object flag name. The UpdateObject procedure (Listing 15.41) must know the flag name in order to redraw the correct object.

**Next B:** Repeat for the next object.

All the objects except the one you are moving have been updated. The last part of this procedure will place the selected object either to the front or back of all others.

**W(B), N(B), E(B), S(B):** Restore the object's original bounding box positions.

**p1X(B), p1Y(B), etc.:** If the object was a curve, restore the curve's four control points.

**OutLineColor(B), PaintColor(B), etc.:** Restore all the original attributes of the object.

**If T = 1:** The object was Text so, restore the flag. **Else:** turn flag off.

**If FT = 1 Then FlagText(B) = B Else FlagText(B) = 0:** At the top of this procedure you checked to see what type of object had been selected to move. Now restore the object's original flag name.

**UpdateObjects:** Redraws all the objects in the proper order.

## Redrawing All Objects on the Desktop

All objects on the desktop, as well as the underlying image of the page, are redrawn in the UpDateObjects procedure. When each object is created, it is given a flag name and object number in the BoundingBox_Up procedure (Listing 2.20). The object's assigned number will match the index entry within the array that represents the flag name (for example, FlagBox(B) and FlagCircle(B)). For instance, if the third object you created on the desktop were a circle, the index 3 of the FlagCircle array would contain the value 3 (FlagCircle(3)). All other flag name arrays index 3 position would have the value of zero (0).

A Do/Loop statement is used to count through all the objects (B) on the desktop. A Select/Case statement can then be used to find matches of the object number (B) with the index value of the flag name. In the ArtAPI program, Chapter 15, a similar UpdateObjects procedure uses the For/Next statement to count through all objects on the desktop rather than using a Do/Loop statement.

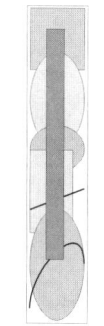

# The Artisan Program—Procedures N–Z

**L**isting 5.16. Redrawing the underlying page and all objects on it.

```
Sub UpdateObjects ()
LastMove = B
ArtWork.DrawMode = Copy_Pen
ArtWork.DrawStyle = Solid
ArtWork.AutoRedraw = True
If Draw = True Then GoTo SkipErase
ArtWork.DrawWidth = 20
ArtWork.Line (W(B), N(B))-(E(B), S(B)), White, BF
ArtWork.Line (XX2, YY2)-(XX1, YY1), White, BF: B = 1
        UpdateDeskTop
Do While B Total + 1
    ArtWork.DrawWidth = LineWidth(B)
    If LineValue(B) 0 Then ArtWork.DrawStyle = 5 Else [IC:CCC]
    ArtWork.DrawStyle = Solid
SkipErase:
Select Case B
    Case FlagCircle(B)
        X1 = W(B): Y1 = N(B): X2 = E(B): Y2 = S(B)
        ArtWork.DrawWidth = LineWidth(B)
        GoodCircle = PerfectCircle(X1, Y1, X2, Y2)
        ArtWork.FillColor = PaintColor(B):
        ArtWork.FillStyle = FillValue(B)
        ArtWork.Circle (XCenter, YCenter), Radius, [IC:CCC]
        OutLineColor(B), , , Aspect
        ArtWork.FillColor = 0: ArtWork.FillStyle = 1

    Case FlagLine(B)
        ArtWork.Line (W(B), N(B))-(E(B), S(B)), OutLineColor(B)
    Case FlagBox(B)
        If FillValue(B) = 1 Then GoTo SkipFill
        ArtWork.Line (W(B), N(B))-(E(B), S(B)), PaintColor(B), BF
SkipFill:
        ArtWork.Line (W(B), N(B))-(E(B), S(B)), OutLineColor(B), B
    Case FlagBezier(B)
        p1.X = p1X(B): p1.Y = p1Y(B): p2.X = p2X(B): p2.Y = p2Y(B)
        h1.X = h1X(B): h1.Y = h1Y(B): h2.X = h2X(B): h2.Y = h2Y(B)
        ArtWork.ForeColor = OutLineColor(B)
        BezDraw
    Case FlagText(B)
        ArtWork.CurrentX = OFFSET(B): ArtWork.CurrentY = N(B)
        SaveScaleLeft = ArtWork.ScaleLeft
        ArtWork.ScaleLeft = -ArtWork.CurrentX + Scaling
        ArtWork.FontName = TextFont(B)
        ArtWork.ForeColor = PaintColor(B)
        ArtWork.FontSize = TextSize(B) * TextPoint
        ArtWork.FontBold = TextBold(B)
        ArtWork.FontItalic = TextItalic(B)
        wFlag = FlagAlign(B)
        TA = SetTextAlign(ArtWork.hDC, wFlag)
        ArtWork.Print Storedtext(B)
        ArtWork.ScaleLeft = SaveScaleLeft
End Select
If Draw = True Then Draw = False: [IC:CCC]
        ArtWork.AutoRedraw = False : B = LastMove: Exit Sub
    B = B + 1
Loop
```

```
        B = LastMove
            ArtWork.AutoRedraw = False
            ArtWork.DrawWidth = 1
            ArtWork.DrawStyle = Solid
        If DeleteObject = True Then Exit Sub
        If CurrentTool = 1 Or CurrentTool = 2 Then Exit Sub
        If SideRuler = True Or TopRuler = True Then Exit Sub
            Handles
            Nodes
        End Sub
```

**LastMove = B:** Temporarily store the current object assigned number B in variable LastMove. If the objects are being redrawn due to using the To_Front_Back procedure (Listing 5.15), you highlight the object being moved with nodes and handles after all other objects have been redrawn. The LastMove variable will be used at the end of this procedure to assign nodes and handles to the last selected object.

**ArtWork.DrawMode:** Redraw objects in the default Copy_Pen drawing mode.

**ArtWork.DrawStyle:** Redraw objects in the default Solid drawing mode.

**If Draw = True Then GoTo SkipErase:** When the Draw flag is set to true, you have just drawn or stretched an object that is on top of all other objects, so there is no need to redraw all the objects below the topmost object. You can skip the Do/Loop statement and draw only the topmost object by going to SkipErase.

The next three lines are used to erase the last position of the object's bounding box.

**ArtWork.DrawWidth:** Set the bounding box border width to 20 pixels. This will ensure that any object that had a very wide outline will have its border outline erased.

**ArtWork.Line (W(B), N(B))-(E(B), S(B)):** The current object's bounding box dimensions. The area is erased by filling the box with the desktop color (white).

**ArtWork.Line (XX1,YY1)-(XX2,YY2):** If the object was moved to a new screen location or the object was stretched, erase the old image area by filling the box with the desktop color (white).

**UpdatePageSize:** The white page that is centered on the desktop is constructed by drawing two boxes. The first box is filled with black, and the other box is filled with white and shifted slightly to the left. This gives the illusion of a sheet of paper on the desktop. The drawing of the page is done in the UpDatePageSize procedure in Listing 5.17. You are now ready to redraw objects in the Artwork picture box control (the desktop).

**Do While B < Total + 1:** Loop through all objects on the desktop. Keep doing the loop until the object number is less than the total of all objects plus 1.

**ArtWork.DrawWidth = LineWidth(B):** Sets the width of each object you are about to draw.

**If LineValue(B) 0 Then:** If an object's LineValue variable equals 0, it tells you the object has no outline. You cannot set Artwork's DrawWidth to 0 in order not to draw an outline of an object. For objects with no outlines, you must set Artwork's drawing style to invisible (5).

**SkipErase:** Skips the Do/Loop statement if the Draw flag was set to true.

**Select Case B:** B represents the object's assigned number.

**Case FlagCircle(B):** The object is a circle, so the circle's bounding box dimensions, X1, Y1, X2, Y2, are passed to the PerfectCircle function (Listing 5.6) to recalculate the radius and center points of the circle.

**ArtWork.Circle:** Draw the circle using the values returned by the PerfectCircle procedure.

**Case FlagLine(B):** The object is a line, so simply use the Line statement to redraw it.

**Case FlagBox(B):** The object is a box, so use the Line statement's box options to redraw it. A solid box will be drawn if the objects FillValue variable equals 0. If the FillValue variable equals 1, it goes to the SkipFill code line and draws a box with no fill.

**Case FlagBezier:** The object is a Bézier curve; therefore, get the four stored control points of the curve. The BezDraw procedure (Listing 3.1) will redraw the curve.

**Case FlagText:** The object is text, so redraw the text string. Refer to the ReDrawText procedure (Listing 5.7) on how text is drawn in this program.

**ArtWork.CurrentX:** You are drawing text with Visual Basic's Print statement, so set the starting point of the text using the CurrentX and CurrentY statements. The CurrentX is stored by the ReDrawText procedure in an array called OffSet. The CurrentY is the north (top) coordinate of the text's bounding box.

**ArtWork.ScaleLeft:** When a text string is wrapped to the next line by an embedded carriage return, the CurrentX or starting point of the next line of text is set to 0. Change Artwork's ScaleLeft property temporarily to the first lines of the text's CurrentX position and subtract these values to align the text below.

**ArtWork.FontName:** The font name that the text object uses.

**ArtWork.ForeColor:** The font's color.

**ArtWork.FontSize:** The point size of the text used.

**ArtWork.FontBold:** A flag to determine whether the font has a Bold attribute.

**ArtWork.FontItalic:** A flag to determine whether the font has an Italic attribute.

**wFlag:** An API Windows flag used for setting left, center, or right alignment.

**TA = SetTextAlign:** An API function called to set the alignment properties. ArtWork.hDC is the name of the picture box you are using. wFlag is the API alignment of text.

**ArtWork.Print:** Prints the text string stored in the StoredText(B) array.

**ArtWork.Scale:** Resets the scale of Artwork to its original values.

**If Draw = True Then:** If the Draw variable flag was set as True, this procedure was to only redraw a single object and then exit. Turn the AutoRedraw off and make sure that the current object is assigned the value stored in LastMove.

**B = B + 1:** This makes the object number increase by 1, so you are ready to redraw the next object.

**Loop:** Repeat the `Do/While` statement block for the next object to be drawn.

**B = LastMove:** The loop has finally redrawn all the objects. If an object's bounding box was highlighted with handles or nodes before this procedure, tell the program so. The loop had changed the value of B, but you stored the original B variable in the LastMove variable at the beginning of this procedure. Make B equal the current object number once again.

**ArtWork. AutoRedraw:** Turns the AutoRedraw off.

**ArtWork.DrawWidth:** Resets the draw width back to the default of 1.

**ArtWork.DrawStyle:** Resets the draw style back to the default of Solid.

**If DeleteObject = True:** You deleted an object, so do not show the handles or nodes by exiting the procedure.

**If CurrentTool = the BezierTool:** You do not want to show the handles or nodes because a Bézier curve has its own BezHandles and BezNodes routines so exit the procedure.

**If either SideRule or TopRuler flags are True then:** Means that you were drawing a dotted guide line that needed to be updated. You do not want to show handles or nodes so exit the procedure.

**Handles:** If you have not exited by now, the object needs to show handles.

**Nodes:** You also need nodes around the object that displays handles.

## Redrawing the Underlying Page

This first part of the UpdateDeskTop procedure draws the page that appears in the center of the Artwork desktop. The second part of the UpDateDeskTop procedure redraws any dotted guide lines that may appear on the desktop. Guidelines are placed on the desktop by dragging them to the desktop from either ruler.

**Listing 5.17. Redrawing the guidelines and underlying page.**

```
Sub UpdateDeskTop ()
SW = ((ArtWork.Width) \ 2) * PixelX 'Redraw Page
SH = ((ArtWork.Height) \ 2) * PixelY
OS = 75
 ArtWork.DrawWidth = 1
    PageX1 = SW - (163 * PixelX) * 1
    PageY1 = SH - (212 * PixelY) * 1
    PageX2 = SW + (163 * PixelX) * 1
    PageY2 = SH + (212 * PixelY) * 1
    ArtWork.Line (PageX1 + OS, PageY1 + OS)-[IC:CCC]
           (PageX2 + OS, PageY2 + OS), GRAY, BF
    ArtWork.Line (PageX1, PageY1)-(PageX2, PageY2), White, BF
    ArtWork.Line (PageX1, PageY1)-(PageX2, PageY2), Black, B
```

*continues*

# The Artisan Program—Procedures N–Z

**L**isting 5.17. continued

```
' ' ' ' ' ' ' ' ' ' ' ' ' ' ' '
For R = 1 To TGL 'Redraw Any Guide Lines
    ArtWork.DrawStyle = Dot
    ArtWork.Line (-5000, -5000)-(GuideX(R), 24000), QBColor(1), B
    ArtWork.Line (-5000, -5000)-(24000, GuideY(R)), QBColor(1), B
Next R
        X2 = -5000: Y2 = -5000
ArtWork.DrawStyle = Solid
End Sub
```

**SW:** Represents your screen (monitor) width's center point.

**SH:** Represents your screen (monitor) height's center point.

**OS:** Represents an offset used to give a visual depth to the page you draw.

**ArtWork.DrawWidth:** The page that you'll draw has a one-pixel-wide border.

**PageX1 = SW - (163 * PixelX) * 1:** Equals the left edge of the page. If you are using a large monitor, you can change the * 1 multiplier to * 2.

**PageY1:** Equals the top edge of the page.

**PageX2:** Equals the right edge of the page.

**PageY2:** Equals the bottom edge of the page.

**ArtWork.Line #1:** Draws a solid, black box using the page dimensions from above with an offset (OS) to give a shadow effect to the page.

**ArtWork.Line #2:** Using the page dimensions with no offset; this draws a second box with a solid, white fill over the top of the back box.

**ArtWork.Line #3:** Draws a black border line around the white box.

Redrawing the guidelines:

**For R = 1 To TGL:** Repeats the counter R starting at 1 and then counts up to the total number of guidelines drawn so far. The variable TGL holds the total number of guidelines drawn to date.

**ArtWork.DrawStyle:** You will redraw the guidelines, which are dotted lines. So change the drawing style to Dot.

**ArtWork.AutoRedraw:** Turn AutoRedraw on if it is presently off.

**ArtWork.Line #1:** Redraws the vertical guideline.

**ArtWork.Line #2:** Redraws the horizontal guideline.

**Next R:** Repeats the process for the next set of guidelines, if any.

**ArtWork.DrawStyle:** Changes the drawing style back to Solid.

**Figure 5.5.**
*The placement of the desktop page.*

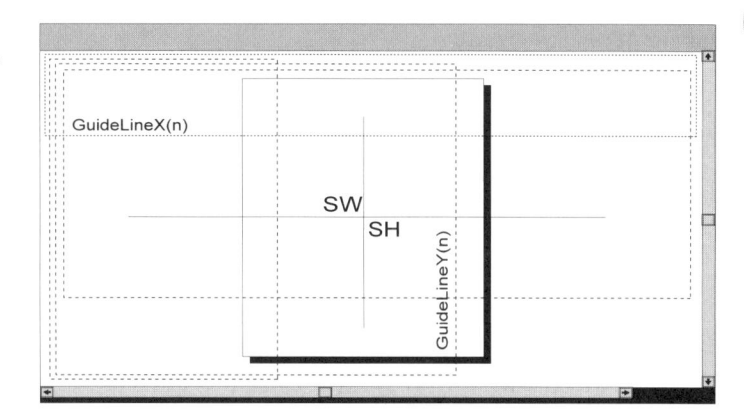

## Sending the Images to the Printer

The WinPrint procedure is similar to the UpdateObject procedure (Listing 5.16). The difference is that you display objects on the printer's page rather than on the monitor. For example, instead of drawing on Artwork's desktop (Artwork.Line (X1, Y1)-(X2, Y2)), you would change the statement to read (Printer.Line (X1, Y1)-(X2, Y2)).

**Listing 5.18.** The WinPrint procedure sends the objects to your printer.

```
Sub WinPrint ()
    On Error GoTo PrintErr:
CMDialog1.CancelError = True
CMDialog1.Flags = &H2& Or &H4& Or &H8& Or &H20&
CMDialog1.Action = 5
NumCopies = CMDialog1.Copies
Screen.MousePointer = 11
  For r = 1 To NumCopies

    PrinterScale = Printer.ScaleWidth 'Save scale for fontsize
    Printer.ScaleLeft = PageX1 'Left Margin
    Printer.ScaleTop = PageY1  'Top Margin
    Printer.ScaleWidth = (PageX2 - PageX1) 'Right Enlarge
    Printer.ScaleHeight = (PageY2 - PageY1)'Bottom Enlarge
B = 1
Do While B < Total + 1
 Printer.DrawWidth = LineWidth(B)
 If LineValue(B) > 0 Then Printer.DrawStyle = 5 Else Printer.DrawStyle = Solid
 Select Case B
  Case FlagCircle(B)
       X1 = W(B): Y1 = N(B): X2 = E(B): Y2 = S(B)
       GoodCircle = PerfectCircle(X1, Y1, X2, Y2)
       Printer.FillColor = PaintColor(B): Printer.FillStyle = FillValue(B)
       Printer.Circle (XCenter, YCenter), Radius, OutLineColor(B), , , Aspect
       Printer.FillColor = 0: Printer.FillStyle = 1
  Case FlagLine(B)
    Printer.Line (W(B), N(B))-(E(B), S(B)), OutLineColor(B)
```

*continues*

# The Artisan Program—Procedures N–Z

**Listing 5.18. continued**

```
  Case FlagBox(B)
    If FillValue(B) = 1 Then GoTo SkipFill2
    Printer.Line (W(B), N(B))-(E(B), S(B)), PaintColor(B), BF
SkipFill2:
    Printer.Line (W(B), N(B))-(E(B), S(B)), OutLineColor(B), B
  Case FlagBezier(B)
    p1.X = P1X(B): p1.Y = P1Y(B): p2.X = P2X(B): p2.Y = p2Y(B)
    h1.X = h1X(B): h1.Y = h1Y(B): h2.X = h2X(B): h2.Y = h2Y(B)
    Printer.ForeColor = OutLineColor(B): FlagPrinter = 2
    BezDraw
  Case FlagText(B)
    Printer.CurrentX = OFFSET(B): Printer.CurrentY = N(B)
    SaveScaleLeft = Printer.ScaleLeft
    Printer.ScaleLeft = -(OFFSET(B) - Printer.ScaleLeft)
    Printer.FontName = TextFont(B)
    PFontScale! = (PrinterScale) / (Printer.ScaleWidth)
    Printer.FontSize = TextSize(B) * PFontScale!
    Printer.FontBold = TextBold(B)
    Printer.FontItalic = TextItalic(B)
    Printer.ForeColor = PaintColor(B)
    wFlag = FlagAlign(B)
    TA = SetTextAlign(Printer.hDC, wFlag)
    Printer.Print Storedtext(B)
    Printer.ScaleLeft = SaveScaleLeft
End Select
'''''
B = B + 1
Loop
    Printer.EndDoc
Next r
    Screen.MousePointer = 0
    FlagPrinter = 0
Exit Sub
PrintErr:
    Screen.MousePointer = 0
    FlagPrinter = 0
    Exit Sub
End Sub
```

---

**CMDialog1:** Refer to the Visual Basic Language Guide, "Common Dialog Control" and "Filters," for explanations of the CMDialog control's methods and properties values.

**PrinterScale = Printer.ScaleWidth:** Save the current scale of the printer. When printing each line of text the printer's ScaleLeft is changed in the Select/Case FlagText section of this procedure. The PrinterScale variable will be used in the Select/Case FlagText section to reassign the proper scaling needed by the printer.

**Printer.ScaleLeft = PageX1:** The left margin value. Change this value to adjust or move the images closer or further away from the left edge of page.

**Printer.ScaleTop = PageY1:** The top margin value. Change this value to adjust or move the images closer or further away from the top edge of page.

**Printer.ScaleWidth = (PageX2 - PageX1):** The width of the page. Change this value to scale the images vertically.

**Printer.ScaleHeight = (PageY2 - PageY1):** The height of the page. Change this value to scale the images horizontally.

**Case FlagText(B):** The `FlagText` block is slightly different than the `UpdateObjects` procedure's method when displaying text. The `Printer.ScaleLeft` statement must now reflect the internal scale of the printer instead of the `Artwork` picture box's interior scale. The font size must be multiplied to reflect the true printed size in points. The best way to achieve this manually is to print some text on a page using Window's Write program and then compare the results with some text printed from this program. The ArtAPI program in Chapter 15 uses API text functions to bypass the manual way of scaling text point sizes. Refer to the introduction of the ArtAPI program for mathematical formulas that can be used to calculate text point sizes.

# Using a Zoom Tool

The `ZoomTool` procedure uses simple manual scaling to achieve two zoom viewing states (large or small). The API scaling functions are superior to Visual Basic's scaling methods and provide a greater range of scaling methods and accuracy. Take note, also, that the Zoom In and Zoom Out features shown here do not use exact measurements of scaling and are only rough percentages.

The APIscale program in the 16MISC directory on the companion disk shows an example on how to zoom into a selected area of the desktop. It also shows how to change the mouse pointer to a custom zoom tool icon when using Visual Basic version 3.0 and under.

Two other programs (Rulers and Scaltest) that use manual and API scaling features can be found in 14SCALE directory of the companion disk.

**Listing 5.19. Scales the desktop for a zoom effect.**

```
Sub ZoomBar_MouseDown (Button%, Shift%, X!, Y!)
CurrentTool = 2: ToolButtons_Paint:
CurrentTool = LastToolUsed: ToolButtons_Paint
CurrentZoom = X \ 32: ZoomBar.Visible = False: N_H_Clear
Select Case CurrentZoom
    Case ZoomIn 'First Button
        If Zoom_Out = True Or Zoom_In = True Then Beep: Exit Sub
        ArtWork.AutoRedraw = True: ArtWork.Cls:
        ArtWork.AutoRedraw = False
        Scaling = 3750: Zoom_In = True: Zoom_Out = False
        Zoom = -48: NodeZoom = -21: TextPoint = 1.7
        Txt.FontSize = Txt.FontSize * TextPoint
        ZoomScale 2, 3750, 3750, -7500, -6375
    Case ZoomOut 'Second Button
        If Zoom_Out = True Or Zoom_In = True Then Beep: Exit Sub
        ArtWork.AutoRedraw = True: ArtWork.Cls:
```

*continues*

## Listing 5.19. continued

```
        ArtWork.AutoRedraw = False
        Scaling = -5000: Zoom_In = False: Zoom_Out = True
        Zoom = 65: NodeZoom = 28: TextPoint = .65
        Txt.FontSize = Txt.FontSize * TextPoint
        ZoomScale 2, -5000, -5000, 10000, 8500
    Case ZoomAll 'Third Button
    X1 = W(1): Y1 = N(1) : X2 = E(1): Y2 = S(1)
        For I = 1 To Total
            If X1 > W(I) Then X1 = W(I)
            If Y1 > N(I) Then Y1 = N(I)
            If X2 < E(I) Then X2 = E(I)
            If Y2 < S(I) Then Y2 = S(I)
        Next I
        For I = 1 To Total
            If X1 > E(I) Then X1 = E(I)
            If Y1 > S(I) Then Y1 = S(I)
            If X2 < W(I) Then X2 = W(I)
            If Y2 < N(I) Then Y2 = N(I)
        Next I
ArtWork.Line (X1, Y1)-(X2, Y2), QBColor(4), B
    Case ZoomPage 'Fourth Button
        ArtWork.AutoRedraw = True: ArtWork.Cls:
        ArtWork.AutoRedraw = False
        ArtWork.Scale: PerSW = 1: PerSH = 1
        Zoom = 0: NodeZoom = 0: TextPoint = 1
        Scaling = 0: Zoom_In = False: Zoom_Out = False
        Txt.FontSize = 12
            For R = 0 To 7
                Handle(R).Scale
            Next R
            For R = 0 To 3
                Node(R).Scale
            Next R
        ArtWork.MousePointer = 1
        VScroll.Value = 0: HScroll.Value = 0
        ZoomScale 2, 0, 0, 0, 0
End Select
        StatusArea_Paint
    ToolButtons_MouseDown Button, Shift, X, Y
End Sub
```

**Select Case CurrentZoom:** One of the four possible zoom buttons you can choose.

**Case ZoomIn:** The first button from the left. Used to zoom in on the desktop.

**If Zoom_Out:** Stops you from zooming more than one step in the scale. Because all nodes and handles have to be rescaled when the ArtWork's scale is changed, you need a special function to calculate each percentage change so the nodes and handles align correctly after the zoom.

**ArtWork.AutoRedraw: Cls:** Erases the current bitmap image of the desktop from memory.

Now you can zoom by changing Artwork's scale. By increasing the left scale one-quarter of Artwork's normal (15000) ScaleWidth and decreasing the Artwork's normal ScaleWidth by half (7500), you increase the zoom percentage to around 25 percent and still maintain the images within the center of the screen (control).

You must maintain the correct aspect ratio for the ScaleHeight of Artwork. By increasing the top scale by one-quarter Artwork's normal (18000) ScaleHeight and decreasing the normal ScaleWidth by a multiple of .85, you proportionately scale the height of the image with the proper width percentage (assuming you are using an SVGA monitor).

**Scaling = 3750:** Represents the new ScaleLeft value of Artwork. The Scaling value is also needed to change the scaling offsets used by the rulers to reflect the new scale dimensions.

**Zoom:** The eight handles (red boxes) that surround a selected object also need to be rescaled. None of these controls increase or decrease in size during a zoom. They are separate controls on top of the objects you have drawn. Zooming in, for instance, increases the drawing's size and scale—but the handles retain their original size and scale. Therefore, you must calculate the percentage difference between Artwork's new scale and the handle control's interior scale. The Zoom variable represents the offset to add to each handle control.

**NodeZoom:** The offset added to each node control. See Zoom for details.

**TextPoint = 1.7:** Represents the percentage to increase any text point size to reflect the new scale of Artwork. Take note that the value 1.7 is an approximate percentage. Visual Basic rounds off point sizes to quarter values fractions (for example, 8.25 pts). Using a formula to get exact text point sizes will do us no good.

**ZoomScale 2:** Sends your new scaling dimension to this ZoomScale procedure (Listing 5.20) for rescaling.

**Case ZoomAll:** The third zoom button from the left will zoom all objects to fit on-screen. It is not operational or functional within this program and is best suited to use with API scaling functions. However, this routine shows how to find all objects drawn to date and then puts a box around them, which represents the zoom-in area you would like to enlarge. Once you have established a zooming method, you give the values of X1, Y1, X2, and Y2 as the new viewing port dimensions to scale.

**Case ZoomPage:** The fourth zoom button from the left. This button resets to the default view of a page.

**ArtWork.AutoRedraw:** Erases all images contained in `Artwork` with the `Cls` (clear screen) statement.

**Zoom: NodeZoom: etc.:** Resets all the values to normal.

**Handle(R): Node(R):** Resets all the handles and nodes to the normal scale.

**VScroll, HScroll:** Resets the scrolls to their center positions.

**ZoomScale 2:** Resets the normal scaling by sending zero values as arguments.

**ToolButtons_MouseDown:** Sends a click event to the Tool Buttons picture box so a tool will be highlighted.

## Rescaling the Desktop's ViewPort

The new scaling dimensions are sent as arguments (the four number values) in the `Zoom_In`, `Zoom_Out`, or `ZoomPage` routines of the `ZoomBar_MouseDown` event (Listing 5.19).

### Listing 5.20. Changing the desktop's scale.

```
Sub ZoomScale (Index%, ZLeft%, ZTop%, ZWidth%, ZHeight%)
 ArtWork.ScaleLeft = ArtWork.ScaleLeft + ZLeft
 ArtWork.ScaleTop = ArtWork.ScaleTop + ZTop
 ArtWork.ScaleWidth = ArtWork.ScaleWidth + ZWidth
 ArtWork.ScaleHeight = ArtWork.ScaleHeight + ZHeight
 NewSW = ArtWork.ScaleWidth: NewSH = ArtWork.ScaleHeight
 PerSW = NewSW / OldSW: PerSH = NewSH / OldSH
 BSM = BSM * PerSW: SSM = SSM * PerSH
 ' ' ' ' ' ' ' ' ' ' '
        Ruler(0).ScaleTop = ArtWork.ScaleTop
        Ruler(0).ScaleHeight = ArtWork.ScaleHeight
        Ruler(1).ScaleLeft = ArtWork.ScaleLeft
        Ruler(1).ScaleWidth = ArtWork.ScaleWidth
    Ruler(0).Refresh
    UpdateObjects
End Sub
```

**ArtWork.ScaleLeft = ArtWork.ScaleLeft + ZLeft:** Add or subtract the value of `ZLeft` to rescale the `Artwork` picture box's interior scale. After all controls have been scaled using the Zoom In or Zoom Out features, check the following events to see if they appear and work correctly:

- All nodes and handles should align correctly. If they don't, change the `Zoom` and `ZoomNode` values.
- When you move the desktop using the scrollbars, do the ruler guides align with the moving mouse pointer? Also, do the ruler guidelines align when you drag the mouse pointer? If they don't, change the `BSM` and `SSM` values in each `Scroll_Change` event (Listing 4.15). Figure 5.6 illustrates the correct and incorrect alignments.

**NewSW = ArtWork.ScaleWidth:** Store the new scale width and new scale height dimensions to calculate the PerSW and PerSH value in the next code line.

**PerSW = NewSW / OldSW: PerSH = NewSH / OldSH:** The PerSW (percentage of scale width) value and the PerSH (percentage of scale height) values are used to recalculate the scroll bars' present positions if the desktop was scrolled vertically or horizontally before the zoom. The values will also be sent to each ruler. If the scroll bars were not used then PerSW and PerSH will equal 1.

**BSM = BSM * PerSW: SSM = SSM * PerSH:** The BSM (base scroll movement) value and the SSM (side scroll movement) value are used to calculate the ScaleLeft and ScaleTop properties of each ruler after the zoom.

**Ruler(0).ScaleTop = ArtWork.ScaleTop:** Reset each ruler's scale to match the new scale of Artwork.

**UpdateObjects:** Redraw all the objects on the desktop in the new scale.

**F**igure 5.6.
*Correct and incorrect scaling.*

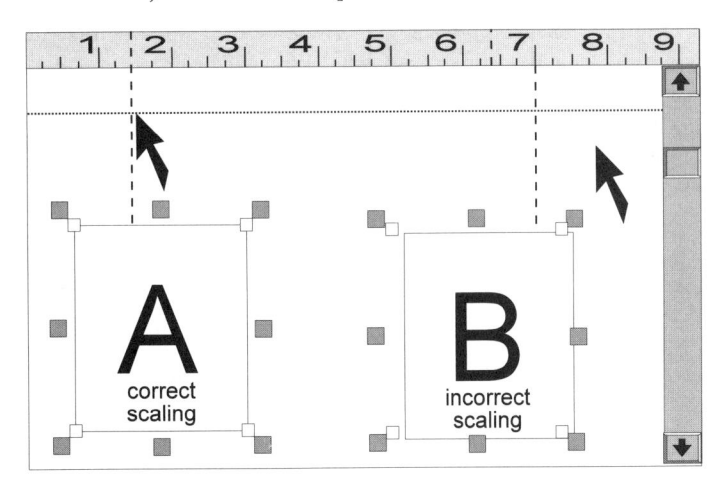

## Summary

The Visual Basic language has the capability to enhance your programs to new graphical heights. By using the mouse events with Line and Circle graphical statements, the Artisan program has simulated to a limited degree the beginnings of a drawing package. The Artisan program was not intended to be a full-featured illustration package. Its main intent is to show the basic principles of graphic illustration so you have the ability to incorporate simple mouse drawn and graphic repositioning techniques within your programs.

You should also be aware that all the routines used in the previous chapters could be used as alternative ways to make user friendly program interfaces. Here are just a few examples you may want to consider:

## The Artisan Program—Procedures N–Z

- The capability to enable the user to use the mouse to adjust a line or bar chart
- The capability to enable the user to type directly on the forms or controls
- The capability to manually shuffle, overlap, or move other controls or bitmap images

It should be pointed out that the DOS version of the Basic language had the Draw keyword, which is used to connect line objects. The DOS Draw keyword was replaced by the Visual Basic Line statement's Step keyword but excluded the Angle option, which made the rotation and skewing of objects very easy.

The Artisan program does not join line or curve objects together. This is not due to Visual Basic's Line or Curve statement's capability to connect end points. The Line and Circle statements have the Step, Start, and End keywords to manipulate their shapes. The problem with drawing connecting objects using only Visual Basic graphical language statements is that you cannot fill the shape with a color. Visual Basic language omitted the DOS Basic language Paint statement from its Windows product. In DOS Basic language, the Paint statement can be used to fill a shape, such as a triangle. This is where the Windows API graphical library takes over and gives you more power than any Basic program ever had. You will be introduced to some of these API functions in the upcoming chapters, and you will rebuild the Artisan program by way of the ArtAPI program in Chapter 15. You will be given examples of alternative ways to build Bézier curves, join complex objects, and set text in the chapter leading up to the ArtAPI program.

# CHAPTER 6

# The Animator Program

# The Animator Program

The Animator program (see Figure 6.1) is a simple wireframe, computer-aided design (CAD) application. It enables you to draw objects made up of line segments that are connected to each other. Animator is limited in its drawing capabilities since it only incorporates single line segment connects. However, modifying the line segment routines can yield advance results.

**Figure 6.1.**
*Screen shot in the Animator program.*

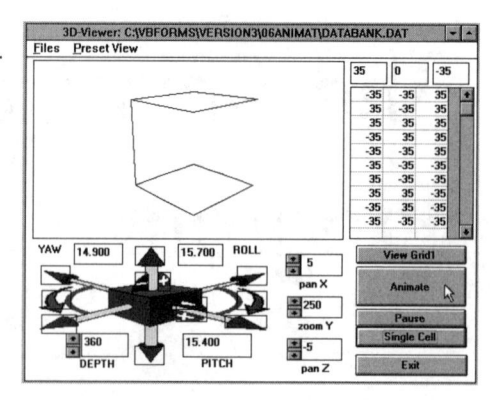

Each lines segment's start and end points are positioned in a three-dimensional viewing field. This field is called the *view port* and is represented in this program by a picture box control called `PictureCell`. The coordinate system used in this picture box has its X and Y zero coordinates located dead center on the control. Starting from the center of the picture box control (0,0 coordinate) and moving right, you get positive X coordinates; going left from center gives you negative X coordinates. To get positive Y coordinates, move up from the center; for negative Y coordinates, move down from the center. The `PictureCell` scale is shown in Figure 6.2.

**Figure 6.2.**
*The 2-D scale system. The Animator Program uses the Y axis as depth; thus the Z axis replaces the standard Y axis. X, Y, and Z axis systems also can have their negative and positive inner changeable. The Animator program's X, Y, Z axis system (known as the -Y left-handed system) is best suited for computing algorithms on slower computers.*

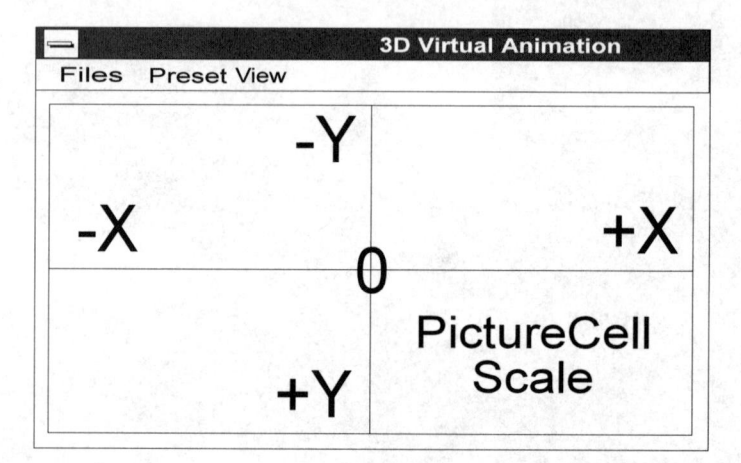

This 3-D coordinate system uses a new dimension called Z. The Z axis replaces the standard Y axis, which is vertical (top to bottom). The Y axis is now used for depth. Negative y coordinates are increased as images move toward you, and positive y coordinates increase as images move inward to the back of your monitor. A 3-D scale showing the X, Y, Z axes is shown in Figure 6.3.

**Figure 6.3.**
*The 3-D coordinate system.*

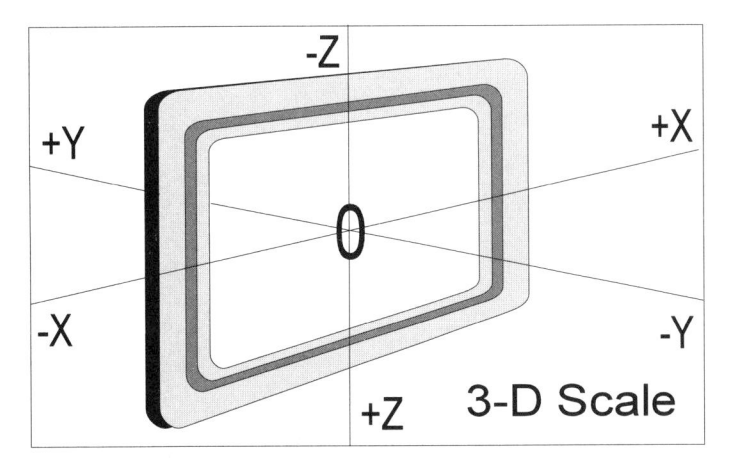

To better understand your new coordination system, picture a three-dimensional picture of a person's head facing you and floating dead center on your monitor. The zero X, Y, Z coordinates for each would be the at the center (inside) of person's head. The top of the head would be in the negative Z (vertical top), and the person's chin would be in the positive Z (vertical bottom). The nose would be negative Y, and the back of the head would be positive Y. Finally, the right side of the face (your perspective) would be the positive X side and the left side of the face would be negative X. This takes some time to get used to. Once mastered, however, you can place custom objects quite easily.

You can test the Animator program by opening a data file called DATABANK.DAT (located in the 06ANIMAT directory of the companion disk). The database file is a random-access file that stores each group of X, Y, and Z values in a separate field. The DATABANK.DAT file has the following ASCII values:

```
-35  -35  35  ^  35  -35  35  ^  35  35  35  ^  -35  35  35  ^  -35  -35  35
-35  -35  -35  ^  35  -35  -35  ^  35  35  -35  ^  -35  35  -35  ^  -35  -35  -35
```

The chevron (^) represents a single space and is used to show the separate X, Y, and Z fields.

After you load a database using the File menu's Open option, you can animate the object in several ways. One way is to press the Animate button, which rolls, pitches, and yaws the object continuously. Another way is to use the arrow controls, which move the object in the direction you select; hold the mouse down over an arrow. The third way is by using the scrollbar values to move the object.

# The Animator Program

The YAW value changes the wire object's compass heading and is similar to a merry-go-round movement (as viewed from above). Figure 6.4 illustrates the yaw movement.

**Figure 6.4.**
*The yaw movement.*

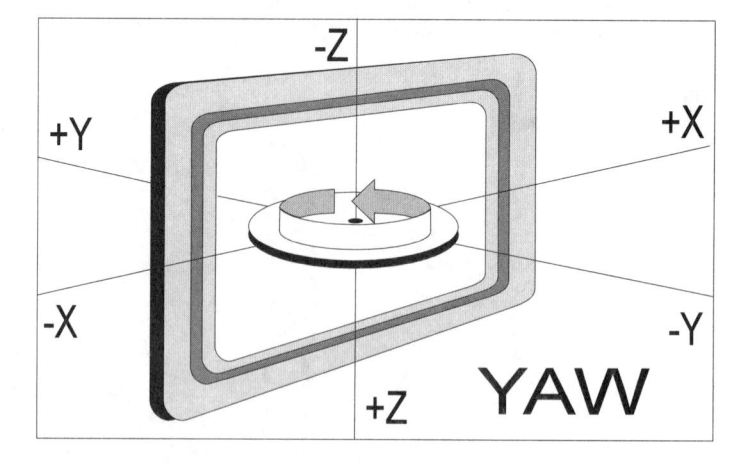

The ROLL value changes the wire object's clockwise and counter-clockwise positions and is similar to a tumbling dryer. Figure 6.5 illustrates the roll movement.

**Figure 6.5.**
*The roll movement.*

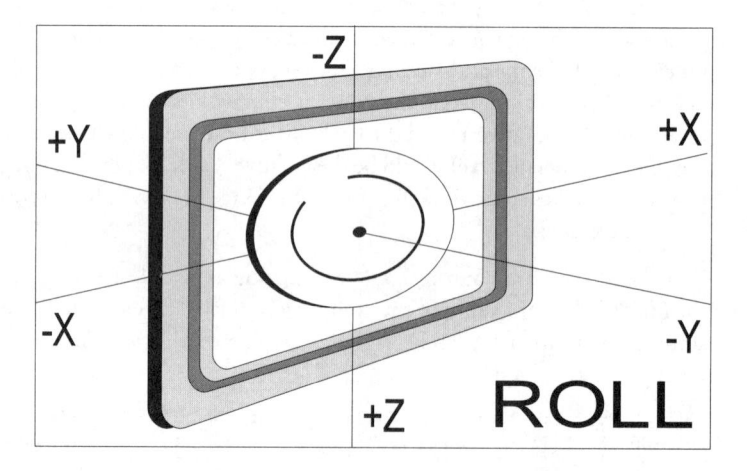

The PITCH value changes the wire object's nose position and is similar to the front view of a steamroller. Figure 6.6 illustrates the pitch movement.

**Figure 6.6.**
*The pitch movement.*

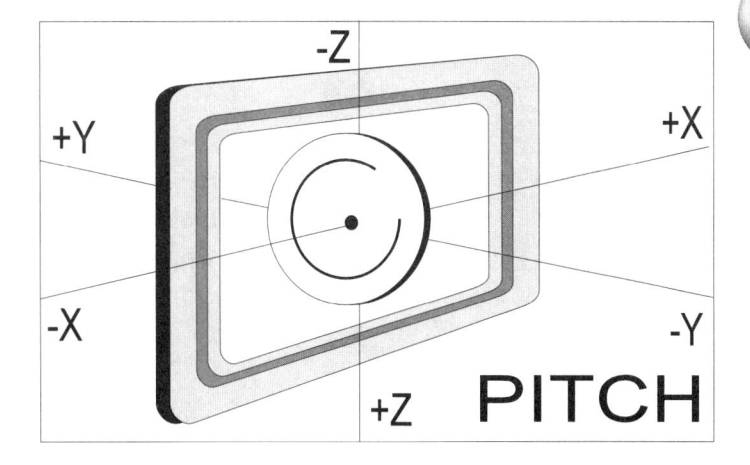

The X value is an object's width. The Y value is an object's depth. The Z value is an object's height.

All objects rotate in a circular motion, which is calculated in radian measurements. A complete circle is 360 degrees, which is equivalent to 0, or 6.28319 radians. See the `circle` statement in Visual Basic's reference guide for more details.

The Animator program's form and control properties are listed in Table 6.1.

**Table 6.1. The properties of the Animator form and controls.**

*Object: Form*
*Object Name: Viewer*

| | | | |
|---|---|---|---|
| Caption | = 3D Virtual Animation | Height | = 6165 |
| Left | = 75 | Top | = 1080 |
| Width | = 8010 | | |

*Object: CommandButton*
*Object Name: ViewButton*

| | | | |
|---|---|---|---|
| Caption | = "View Grid1" | Height | = 315 |
| Left | = 5820 | Top | = 3180 |
| Width | = 1935 | | |

*Object: Text Box*
*Object Name: XYZinput  3 indexed controls*

| | | | |
|---|---|---|---|
| Height | = 375 | Index | = 0 to 3 |
| Left | = above GRID1 | Top | = above GRID1 |
| Width | = 645 | | |

*continues*

**T**able 6.1. continued

*Object: Grid*
*Object Name: Grid1*

| | | | |
|---|---|---|---|
| Cols | = 3 | FixedCols | = 0 |
| FixedRows | = 0 | Height | = 2595 |
| HighLight | = 0 'False | Left | = 5700 |
| Rows | = 20 | ScrollBars | = 2 'Vertical |
| Top | = 480 | Width | = 2175 |

*Object: Picture Box*
*Object Name: Bit_map*

| | | | |
|---|---|---|---|
| AutoSize | = -1 'True | BorderStyle | = 0 'None |
| Height | = 2250 | Left | = 60 |
| Picture | = Pointer.BMP | Top | = 3120 |
| Width | = 4455 | | |

*Object: CommandDialog*
*Object Name:* CMDialog1

| | | | |
|---|---|---|---|
| Left | = 90 | Top | = 1665 |

*Object: Text Box*
*Object Name: ValueBox  4 indexed controls*

| | | | |
|---|---|---|---|
| Height | = 405 | Index | = 0 to 3 |
| Left | = within Bit_map | Top | = within Bit_map |
| Width | = 840 | | |

*Object: VscrollBar*
*Object Name: VScroll*

| | | | |
|---|---|---|---|
| Height | = 420 | Index | = 3 |
| Left | = 675 within Bit_map | Max | = 5000 |
| SmallChange | = 5 | Top | = 1575 within Bit_map |
| Value | = 360 | Width | = 255 |

*Object: Label*
*Object Name: Arrows  12 indexed controls*

| | | | |
|---|---|---|---|
| BackStyle | = 0 'Transparent | BorderStyle | = 1 'Fixed Single |
| Height | = 225 | Index | = 11 |
| Left | = within Bit_map | Top | = within Bit_map |
| Width | = 540 | | |

*Object: Label*
*Object Name: Labels*

| | | | |
|---|---|---|---|
| Alignment | = 2 'Center | Caption | = "DEPTH" |
| Height | = 225 | Index | = 3 |
| Left | = 765 | Top | = 1995 |
| Width | = 960 | | |

*Object: Label*
*Object Name: Labels*

| | | | |
|---|---|---|---|
| Alignment | = 2 'Center | Caption | = "PITCH" |
| Height | = 225 | Index | = 2 |
| Left | = 2745 | Top | = 1980 |
| Width | = 1200 | | |

*Object: Label*
*Object Name: Labels*

| | | | |
|---|---|---|---|
| Alignment | = 2 'Center | Caption | = "YAW" |
| Height | = 315 | Index | = 1 |
| Left | = 45 | Top | = 45 |
| Width | = 675 | | |

*Object: Label*
*Object Name: Labels*

| | | | |
|---|---|---|---|
| Alignment | = 2 'Center | Caption | = "ROLL" |
| Height | = 315 | Index | = 0 |
| Left | = 3510 | Top | = 45 |
| Width | = 675 | | |

*Object: CommandButton*
*Object Name: SingleCell*

| | | | |
|---|---|---|---|
| Caption | = "Single Cell" | Height | = 360 |
| Left | = 5820 | Top | = 4560 |
| Width | = 1950 | | |

*Object: VScrollBar*
*Object Name: VScroll*

| | | | |
|---|---|---|---|
| Height | = 375 | Index | = 2 |
| Left | = 4620 | Max | = 100 |
| Min | = -100 | SmallChange | = 5 |
| Top | = 4770 | Width | = 255 |

*continues*

**Table 6.1. continued**

*Object: VScrollBar*
*Object Name: VScroll*

| | | | |
|---|---|---|---|
| Height | = 375 | Index | = 1 |
| Left | = 4620 | Max | = 1000 |
| Min | = 100 | SmallChange | = 20 |
| Top | = 4050 | Value | = 250 |
| Width | = 255 | | |

*Object: Text Box*
*Object Name: XYZ*

| | | | |
|---|---|---|---|
| Alignment | = 1 'Right Justify | Height | = 375 |
| Index | = 2 | Left | = 4845 |
| Top | = 4770 | Width | = 735 |

*Object: Text Box*
*Object Name: XYZ*

| | | | |
|---|---|---|---|
| Alignment | = 1 'Right Justify | Height | = 375 |
| Index | = 1 | Left | = 4845 |
| Top | = 4050 | Width | = 735 |

*Object: Text Box*
*Object Name: XYZ*

| | | | |
|---|---|---|---|
| Alignment | = 1 'Right Justify | Height | = 375 |
| Index | = 0 | Left | = 4845 |
| Top | = 3330 | Width | = 735 |

*Object: CommandButton*
*Object Name: ExitBtn*

| | | | |
|---|---|---|---|
| Caption | = "Exit" | Height | = 360 |
| Left | = 5820 | Top | = 5040 |
| Width | = 1965 | | |

*Object: VScrollBar*
*Object Name: VScroll*

| | | | |
|---|---|---|---|
| Height | = 375 | Index | = 0 |
| Left | = 4590 | Max | = 100 |
| Min | = -100 | SmallChange | = 5 |
| Top | = 3330 | Width | = 255 |

*Object: CommandButton*
*Object Name: AnimateBtn*

| | | | |
|---|---|---|---|
| Caption | = "Animate" | Height | = 675 |
| Left | = 5820 | Top | = 3540 |
| Width | = 1935 | | |

*Object: CommandButton*
*Object Name: Pause*

| | | | |
|---|---|---|---|
| Caption | = "Pause" | Height | = 315 |
| Left | = 5820 | Top | = 4260 |
| Width | = 1935 | | |

*Object: Picture Box*
*Object Name: PictureCell*

| | | | |
|---|---|---|---|
| Height | = 3045 | Left | = 120 |
| ScaleMode | = 3 'Pixel | Top | = 45 |
| Width | = 5475 | | |

*Object: Label*
*Object Name: Labels*

| | | | |
|---|---|---|---|
| Alignment | = 2 'Center | Caption | = "pan Z" |
| Height | = 255 | Index | = 6 |
| Left | = 4620 | Top | = 5175 |
| Width | = 990 | | |

*Object: Label*
*Object Name: Labels*

| | | | |
|---|---|---|---|
| Alignment | = 2 'Center | Caption | = "zoom Y" |
| Height | = 315 | Index | = 5 |
| Left | = 4620 | Top | = 4455 |
| Width | = 990 | | |

*Object: Label*
*Object Name: Labels*

| | | | |
|---|---|---|---|
| Alignment | = 2 'Center | Caption | = "pan X" |
| Height | = 315 | Index | = 4 |
| Left | = 4575 | Top | = 3735 |
| Width | = 990 | | |

*continues*

**T**able 6.1. continued

*Object: Menu*
*Object Name: MENU_F*

| | | | |
|---|---|---|---|
| Caption | = "&Files" | | |

*MENU_Open*

| | | | |
|---|---|---|---|
| Caption | = "&New" | Enabled | = 0 'False' |
| Index | = 0 | Shortcut | = ^N |

*MENU_Open*

| | | | |
|---|---|---|---|
| Caption | = "&Open" | Index | = 1 |
| Shortcut | = ^O | | |

*MENU_Open*

| | | | |
|---|---|---|---|
| Caption | = "Save &As.." | Enabled | = 0 'False' |
| Index | = 2 | Shortcut | = ^A |

*MENU_Open*

| | | | |
|---|---|---|---|
| Caption | = "-" | Index | = 3 |

*MENU_Open*

| | | | |
|---|---|---|---|
| Caption | = "E&xit" | Index | = 4 |
| Shortcut | = ^X | | |

*MENU_P*

| | | | |
|---|---|---|---|
| Caption | = "&Preset View" | | |

*MENU_degrees*

| | | | |
|---|---|---|---|
| Caption | = "&0 degrees" | Index | = 0 |

*MENU_degrees*

| | | | |
|---|---|---|---|
| Caption | = "&45 degrees" | Index | = 1 |

*MENU_degrees*

| | | | |
|---|---|---|---|
| Caption | = "&Bird's Eye" | Index | = 2 |

Listing 6.1 shows the variable names used in Animator.

**Listing 6.1. The variable names used in this program.**

```
Declarations
Type AddrRecType
  XField As String * 4
  YField As String * 4
  ZField As String * 4
End Type


Global FileName As String
Global TempFile As String
Global AddrRec As AddrRecType   ' An address record.
Global PINPOINTS As Integer     ' Current number of records.
Global Continue As Integer
Global ButtonDown, Counter As Integer
Global NextRow As Integer
Global Untitled As String
```

**ANIMATE#.BAS:** Declarations are placed in a `Global` module called ANIMATE#.BAS. (See Appendix A.)

**AddrRec:** Holds the X, Y, and Z coordinates used in animation. These data fields represent the screen pixel positions and can be up to four digits long.

The ANIMATE#.BAS file has the following `Type` data structure for `AddrRec`:

```
Type AddrRec
        XField As String * 4
        YField As String * 4
        ZField As String * 4
End Type
```

**PINPOINTS:** The starting points of each X, Y, and Z field in a `Random` file.

The program extracts the values from the data file and assigns each to the grid control, so you can view each X, Y, and Z value in the grid's cell rows.

**Continue:** Flag used to continue animation after a pause or interrupt.

**ButtonDown, Counter:** Flags used to trigger user input `Scroll` values.

**NextRow:** Used in the grid control to assign values to the next row.

## Default Values at Startup

See Listing 6.2 for setting the default values at startup.

**Listing 6.2. Setting the default values at startup.**
```
Sub Form_Load ()
Viewer.Caption = "3D-Viewer: " & FileName
    XYZ(0).Text = "0"
    XYZ(1).Text = "250"
    XYZ(2).Text = "0"
        ValueBox(0).Text = "05.70"
        ValueBox(1).Text = "06.30"
        ValueBox(2).Text = "05.90"
        ValueBox(3).Text = "360"
End Sub
```

**TempFile:** Not used, but could represent a temp file for data saves.

**Viewer.Caption:** The form's title bar will read 3DViewer *temp filename* (where *temp filename* is the name of the temp file).

**XYZ(index number):** The default X, Y, and Z object placement values at startup.

**ValueBox(index number):** The default object's angle position values at startup. For example:

```
ValueBox(0)= YAW : ValueBox(1) = ROLL :

ValueBox(2)= PITCH : ValueBox(3) = DEPTH
```

Listing 6.3 shows how to center the form in the middle of the screen.

**Listing 6.3. Centering the form in the middle of the screen.**
```
Sub Form_Resize ()
If WindowState = 0 Then
    Viewer.Left = (Screen.Width - Viewer.Width) \ 2
    Viewer.Top = (Screen.Height - Viewer.Height) \ 2
End If
End Sub
```

See Listing 6.4 for closing the data file when exiting Animator.

**Listing 6.4. Closing the data file on exiting the program.**
```
Sub Form_Unload (Cancel As Integer)
        Close #1
End Sub
```

Figure 6.7 shows Animator's control names.

**Figure 6.7.**
*Animator's control names.*

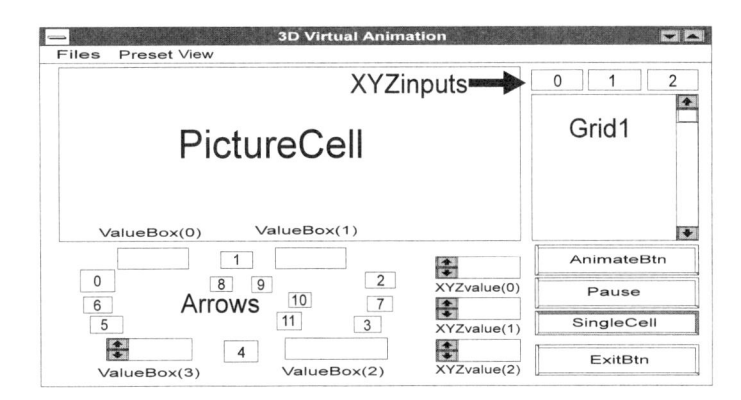

## Scaling a Picture Box for 3-D Animation

You scale the PictureCell picture box so the 0,0 coordinates are dead center.

Listing 6.5 shows how to program for drawing a crosshair dotted line on the viewport.

**Listing 6.5. Drawing the crosshair dotted line on the viewport.**

```
Sub PictureCell_Paint ()
PictureCell.Cls
X1 = PictureCell.ScaleWidth  \ 2
Y1 = PictureCell.ScaleHeight \ 2
X2 = PictureCell.ScaleWidth  \ 2
Y2 = PictureCell.ScaleHeight \ 2
    PictureCell.Scale (-X1, -Y2)-(X2, Y2)
X1 = PictureCell.CurrentX
Y1 = PictureCell.CurrentY
X2 = PictureCell.Width
Y2 = PictureCell.Height
PictureCell.DrawStyle = 2
    PictureCell.Line (X1, 0)-(X2, 0), QBColor(4)
    PictureCell.Line (0, Y1)-(0, Y2), QBColor(4)
SingleCell_Click
End Sub
```

**X1 = PictureCell.ScaleWidth \ 2**: Find the dead center point of the picture box control. The X1, X2 and Y1, Y2 are repeat values and are shown for clarity.

**PictureCell.Scale (-X1, -Y2)-(X2, Y2)**: Scale the picture box so the 0,0 coordinates of X and Y are dead center.

**PictureCell.Line (X1, 0)-(X2, 0), QBColor(4)**: The remainder of the code routine draws horizontal and vertical dotted red lines to form a cross pattern in the picture box.

# The Animator Program

Figure 6.8 shows the Animator form.

**Figure 6.8.**
*The Animator form.*

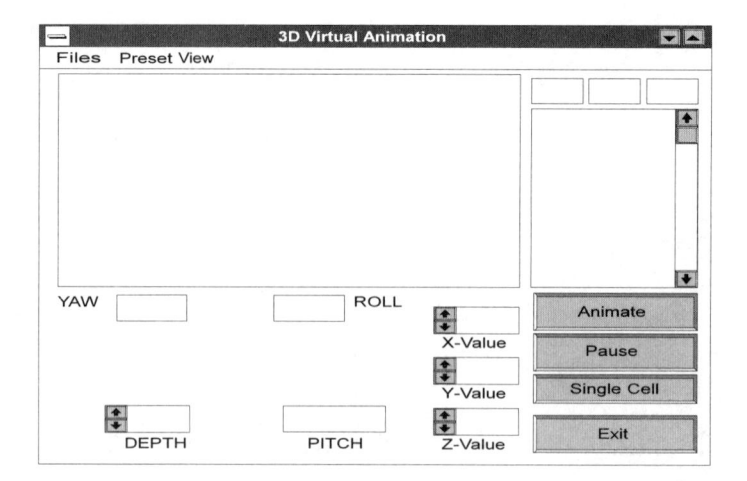

## Starting the 3-D Animation Process

After you create or load a data file, you start the animation by clicking the button labeled Animate. For display purposes, a preset radian movement value of .05 is used to move the object in all spinning directions. A `While/Wend` statement loops the object so that it spins indefinitely. To stop the object, press either the button labeled Pause or the button labeled Single Cell. (See Listing 6.6.)

**Listing 6.6. Starting continuous animation.**

```
Sub AnimateBtn_Click ()
If PINPOINTS = 0 Then Exit Sub
Grid1.Visible = False
Continue = True
Movement = .05
While Continue
    Yaw = Val(ValueBox(0).Text) + Movement
    Roll = Val(ValueBox(1).Text) + Movement
    Pitch = Val(ValueBox(2).Text) + Movement
        ValueBox(0).Text = Format$(Yaw, "00.00")
        ValueBox(1).Text = Format$(Roll, "00.00")
        ValueBox(2).Text = Format$(Pitch, "00.00")
    ANIMATION
    t = DoEvents()
Wend
End Sub
```

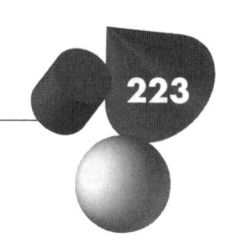

**If PINPOINTS:** Exit this routine if no X, Y, or Z values have been loaded in the grid control's cells.

**Continue:** If the pause button, single cell button, or one of the Vscrolls controls is pressed, the animation will temporarily halt. Setting Continue to True will restart the animation process.

**Movement = .05:** This represents the value to add to YAW, ROLL, and/or PITCH. This will make the animation move at a steady viewing speed. Increasing this value will make each additional redraw of the animate appear further apart. This will make the animation seem quicker but very jumpy, whereas decreasing this value will make each additional redraw closer together. This will make the animations appear to move very slowly.

> **NOTE** The Movement will not take effect if you remark out (') the (+ Movement) following the YAW, ROLL, and/or PITCH statements.

**While/Continue:** Starts a loop and doesn't stop until Continue equals False.

**YAW:** The amount the object will yaw or move like a compass (when viewed from the top). See Figure 6.3.

**ROLL:** The amount the object will move clockwise or counter-clockwise.

**PITCH:** The amount the object will pitch or move nose-up or nose-down (when viewed from the front). See Figure 6.5.

**ValueBox(Index).Text:** All yaw, roll, and pitch animation values are calculated using the values that are displayed in these text box controls.

**ANIMATE:** Call the Animate procedure (Listing 6.7) that calculates the data file.

**t = DoEvent:** In a loop using the While/Wend Statement, this statement processes the animation while the variable continue still equals true. The DoEvents statement yields execution so Microsoft Windows can process events. It will continue checking to see if any keyboard input or mouse clicks have been executed while the program is in a loop. If a DoEvents function were omitted from within this loop, you would be unable to stop the program and the animation would continue indefinitely.

## Calculating the 3-D Animation

The Animation procedure takes the X, Y, and Z coordinate values and draws a simple wireframe object using Visual Basic's Line statement. All lines are connected to each other, so in order to draw separate line objects, you need to enhance the code routine. One way to render separate objects is to insert data for each object being rendered. Then use a variable flag to turn the PictureCell's drawing mode to invisible (11) or its drawing style to invisible (5) when connecting two objects. The drawing or style modes would have to be turned on to draw the next object in the data file.

All data files are saved in the Random file format. You could use the Write# and Print# statements to save and retrieve data in a more visible ASCII character manner. You can use the Write# statement to insert commas between the X, Y, and Z coordinates and place quotation marks around strings, which could be used as flags. (See Listing 3.7.)

**Listing 6.7. The calculations to draw in a 3-D plane.**

```
Sub ANIMATION ()
PictureCell.DrawStyle = 0
PictureCell.Cls
LastRecord = PINPOINTS : r = 0
For i = 1 To LastRecord
    Yaw = Val(ValueBox(0).Text)   '05.70
    Roll = Val(ValueBox(1).Text)  '06.30
    Pitch = Val(ValueBox(2).Text) '05.90
    DEPTH = Val(ValueBox(3).Text) '360
SinYaw = Sin(Yaw): CosYaw = Cos(Yaw)
SinRoll = Sin(Roll): CosRoll = Cos(Roll)
SinPitch = Sin(Pitch): CosPitch = Cos(Pitch)
Grid1.Col = 0: Grid1.Row = r: X = Val(Grid1.Text)
Grid1.Col = 1: Grid1.Row = r: Y = Val(Grid1.Text)
Grid1.Col = 2: Grid1.Row = r: Z = Val(Grid1.Text)
    YawX = (CosYaw * X) - (SinYaw * Y)
    YawY = (SinYaw * X) + (CosYaw * Y)
    RollX = (CosRoll * YawX) + (SinRoll * Z)
    RollZ = (CosRoll * Z) - (SinRoll * YawX)
    PitchY = (CosPitch * YawY) - (SinPitch * RollZ)
    PitchZ = (SinPitch * YawY) + (CosPitch * RollZ)
PanX = Val(XYZ(0).Text)
PanY = Val(XYZ(1).Text)
Zoom = Val(XYZ(2).Text)
        Xaxis = RollX + PanX
        Yaxis = PitchY + PanY
        Zaxis = PitchZ + Zoom
sx = DEPTH * Xaxis \ Yaxis
sy = DEPTH * Zaxis \ Yaxis
If r = 0 Then PictureCell.PSet (sx, sy)
        PictureCell.Line -(sx, sy), QBColor(4)
r = r + 1
Next i
End Sub
```

**PictureCell.DrawStyle:** Draw each cell in a solid pen, which is the default pen style.

**LastRecord = PINPOINTS : r = 0:** The PINPOINTS variable represents the total number of grouped X, Y, and Z values in the data file. When you place X, Y, and Z value coordinates on the desktop, they represent a pinpoint coordinate for a line's start or end position in a 3-D space. Use the r variable to send the correct data to each row with the Grid control starting at row 0.

**For i = 1 To LastRecord:** For each data record field starting at 1 and ending at the last record (total number of pinpoints), do the following block of code statements.

**YAW:** The amount the object will move like a compass (when viewed from the top). (See Figure 6.4.)

**ROLL:** The amount the object will move clockwise or counter-clockwise. (See Figure 6.5.)

**PITCH:** The amount the object will move nose-up or nose-down (when viewed from the front). (See Figure 6.6.)

**Depth:** The world view from the viewer's eyes. (See Figure 6.3.)

The following statements calculate the sine and cosine of YAW, ROLL, and PITCH, which are expressed in radians. A full circle turn of 360 degrees is equivalent to 0, or 6.28319 radians. Refer to the Visual Basic Programmer's guide for further details on radian values.

**SinYaw:** Return the sine of YAW (compass-like) using the Sin function. The value is expressed in radians.

**CosYaw:** Return the cosine of YAW (compass-like) using the Cos function. The value is expressed in radians.

**SinRoll:** Return the sine of ROLL (clock-like), which is expressed in radians.

**CosRoll:** Return the cosine of ROLL (clock-like), which is expressed in radians.

**SinPitch:** Return the sine of PITCH (nose-up or nose-down), which is expressed in radians.

**CosPitch:** Return the cosine of ROLL (nose-up or nose-down), which is expressed in radians.

**Grid1.Col = 0: Grid1.Row = r: X = Val(Grid1.Text):** The X, Y, and Z coordinates are extracted from each of the Grid control's cells. Each group of X, Y, and Z values represent a pinpoint coordinate of the line's start or end point in 3-D space.

> **NOTE** The *X* coordination represents the left-to-right screen position. The *Y* coordination represents the depth (front-to-back) position. The *Z* coordination represents the top-to-bottom position. See Figure 6.2.

**YawX = (CosYaw * X) - (SinYaw * Y)**: The next six lines of code calculate `YawX`, `YawX`, `RollX`, `RollZ`, `PitchY`, and `PitchZ` in a trigonometry fashion. These right-angle calculations on the X, Y, and Z axes give you correct perspective points within 3-D space.

**PanX = Val(XYZ(0).Text)**: Pan or zoom values so the object can be moved along the screen's X, Y, and/or Z axes' paths.

**PanX:** Pan the object to the left or right.

**ZoomY:** Zoom the object in or out.

**PanZ:** Pan the object up or down.

**Xaxis = RollX + PanX:** Move the object along the X screen axis (pans left and right).

**Yaxis = PitchY + ZoomY:** Move the object along the Y screen axis (zooms in and out).

**Zaxis = PitchZ + PanZ:** Move the object along the Z screen axis (pans up and down).

**sx, sy:** Calculate the actual monitor's visual X and Y positions so you can draw the object using Visual Basic's `Line` statements.

**If r = 0 then:** You will use the `Line` statement's `Step` command to draw the object, which will connect each line to the last line drawn. You can use the `Pset` statement to make the first `sx` and `sy` positions of a line the current X and current Y coordinates.

**PictureCell.Line:** The `Step` command connects each new line to the end point of the last line drawn. Each line in the object is drawn in real time, which equals the speed of your computer. Screen flickering happens because each cell image is not saved in memory.

## Using the Arrows to Move the Object

When you hold the mouse on the arrow's label control, the object will move in the direction the arrow is pointing. The speed of the object's movement is controlled by the variables `Increments` and `Decrements`. By increasing the value of `Increments`, you can move the object a further or shorter distance along any of its X, Y, or Z axes paths. (See Listing 6.8.)

> **NOTE**
>
> If the increment number is increased in value, the object will appear to move faster.
>
> If the number is too large or you have a slow computer or slow screen refresh rate, the object's movement will appear jumpy. If the increment number is decreased in value, the object will appear to move more slowly along its axis path.
>
> If the number is too small or you have a slow compute or slow refresh rate, the object's movement will appear slow. `Decrements` move the object in the opposite direction.

**Listing 6.8. Moving the objects when the bitmap arrows are pressed.**

```
Sub Arrows_MouseDown (Index%, Button%, Shift%, X!, Y!)
Grid1.Visible = False
ButtonDown = True
Continue = True : Increments = -10 : Decrements = 10
Select Case Index
  Case 0 'Y positive
        ZoomOut = Val(XYZ(1).Text)
        While DoEvents() And ButtonDown
        XYZ(1).Text = Str$(ZoomOut): ZoomOut = ZoomOut + Decrements
        ANIMATION
     Wend
  Case 1 'Z negitive
        PanUp = Val(XYZ(2).Text)
        While DoEvents() And ButtonDown
        XYZ(2).Text = Str$(PanUp): PanUp = PanUp + Increments
        ANIMATION
     Wend
  Case 2 'X positive
        PanRight = Val(XYZ(0).Text)
        While DoEvents() And ButtonDown
        XYZ(0).Text = Str$(PanRight): PanRight = PanRight + Decrements
        ANIMATION
     Wend
  Case 3 'Y positive
        ZoomIn = Val(XYZ(1).Text)
        While DoEvents() And ButtonDown
        XYZ(1).Text = Str$(ZoomIn): ZoomIn = ZoomIn + Increments
        ANIMATION
     Wend
  Case 4 'Z positive
        PanDown = Val(XYZ(2).Text)
        While DoEvents() And ButtonDown
        XYZ(2).Text = Str$(PanDown): PanDown = PanDown + Decrements
        ANIMATION
     Wend
  Case 5 'X negative
        PanLeft = Val(XYZ(0).Text)
        While DoEvents() And ButtonDown
        XYZ(0).Text = Str$(PanLeft): PanLeft = PanLeft + Increments
        ANIMATION
     Wend
  Case 6 'YAW left
        Yaw = Val(ValueBox(0).Text)
        While DoEvents() And ButtonDown
        ValueBox(0).Text = Format$(Yaw, "00.000"): Yaw = Yaw + 0.1
        ANIMATION
     Wend
  Case 7 'YAW right
        Yaw = Val(ValueBox(0).Text)
        While DoEvents() And ButtonDown
        ValueBox(0).Text = Format$(Yaw, "00.000"): Yaw = Yaw - 0.1
        ANIMATION
     Wend
  Case 8 'Roll negative
        Roll = Val(ValueBox(1).Text)
        While DoEvents() And ButtonDown
```

*continues*

## Listing 6.8. continued

```
        ValueBox(1).Text = Format$(Roll, "00.000"): Roll = Roll + 0.1
        ANIMATION
    Wend
    Case 9 'Roll positive
        Roll = Val(ValueBox(1).Text)
        While DoEvents() And ButtonDown
        ValueBox(1).Text = Format$(Roll, "00.000"): Roll = Roll - 0.1
        ANIMATION
    Wend
    Case 10 'PITCH negative
        Pitch = Val(ValueBox(2).Text)
        While DoEvents() And ButtonDown
        ValueBox(2).Text = Format$(Pitch, "00.000"): Pitch = Pitch + 0.1
        ANIMATION
    Wend
    Case 11 'PITCH positive
        Pitch = Val(ValueBox(2).Text)
        While DoEvents() And ButtonDown
        ValueBox(2).Text = Format$(Pitch, "00.000"): Pitch = Pitch - 0.1
        ANIMATION
    Wend
End Select
End Sub
```

The following increase and decrement values are used to pan the object up or down on the Z axis and left or right on the X axis, or zoom in or out on the *Y* axis.

> **Increments:** This value is added to the XYZ textboxes to move the object 10 positive units along the X, Y and/or Z axes path.
>
> **Decrements:** This value is subtracted to XYZ textboxes to move the Object 10 negative units along the X, Y and/or Z axes path.

The following 0.1 values are used to increase or decrease the yaw, roll, or pitch of the object:

> **YAW = YAW + 0.1:** This value is added to the YAW value boxes to move the object (0.1) positive radian units (top view/compass-like) around the center axis.
>
> **YAW = YAW - 0.1:** This value is subtracted from the YAW value boxes to move the object (0.1) negative radian units (top view/compass-like) around the center axis.
>
> **ROLL = ROLL + 0.1:** This value is added to the ROLL value boxes to move the object (0.1) positive radian units(front view/clock-like) around the center axis.
>
> **ROLL = ROLL - 0.1:** This value is subtracted from the ROLL value boxes to move the object (0.1) negative radian units (front view/clock-like) around the center axis.
>
> **PITCH = PITCH + 0.1:** This value is added to the PITCH value boxes to move the object (0.1) positive radian units (front view/nose-up or nose-down) around the center axis.
>
> **PITCH = PITCH - 0.1:** This value is subtracted from the PITCH value boxes to move the object (0.1) negative radian units (front view/nose-up or nose-down) around the center axis.

Figures 6.9 and 6.10 show the bitmap arrows' values and coordinate paths. Figure 6.11 shows the placements of the X, Y, and Z values.

**F**igure 6.9.
*The bitmap arrows and the label control's index values.*

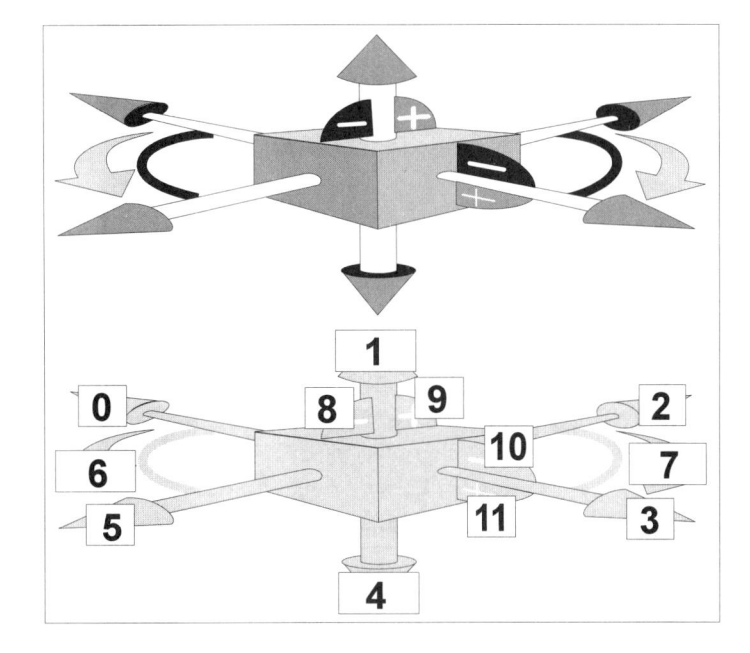

**F**igure 6.10.
*The bitmap arrows' coordinate paths.*

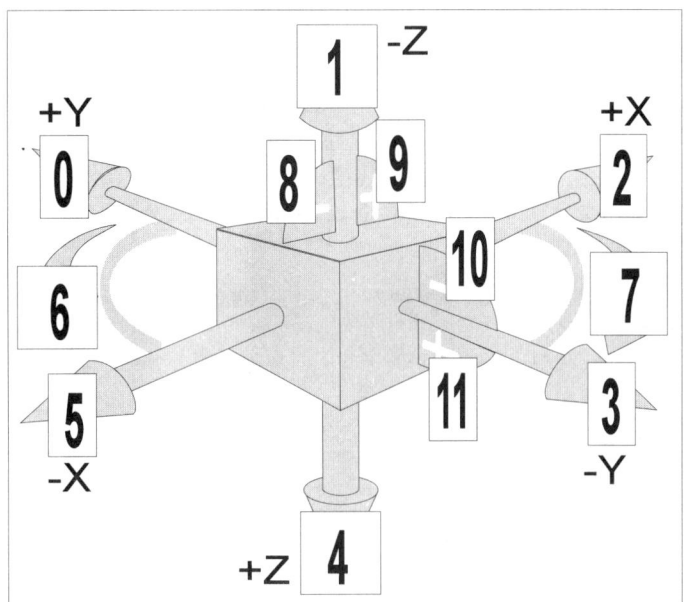

# The Animator Program

**Figure 6.11.**
*General placements of the X, Y, and Z values.*

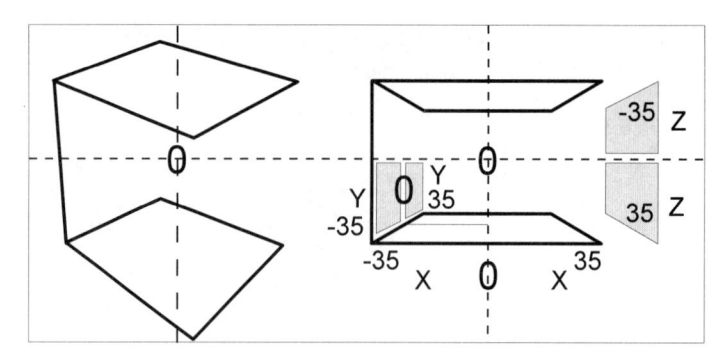

## Toggling the Movement On and Off

Each Case statement within the arrow's MouseDown event (Listing 6.9) is in a continuous loop until the variable ButtonDown is set to false. A DoEvents statement is also used within each Case statement to check the mouse events. When you release the mouse button, the ButtonDown variable is set to False and the loop is terminated.

**Listing 6.9. Toggling the movement of the object off.**

```
Sub Arrows_MouseUp (Index%, Button%, Shift%, X !, Y!)
    ButtonDown = False
End Sub
```

**ButtonDown:** Used to escape the While/Wend statements in Arrows_MouseDown.

## The Grid Control in the Animator Program

The grid control displays the X, Y, and Z data values in each of its rows. To input an X coordinate value into Grid1, use the first text box above the Grid1 control. Then press the spacebar to tab over to the next textbox to the right (Y coordinate value). Pressing the spacebar once again tabs you to the last text box (Z coordinate value).

Pressing the spacebar once more inserts all three X, Y, and Z values in the next available Grid1 row. Clicking any Grid1 cell with the right mouse button erases any data in that field or replaces it with the value typed in the corresponding XYZInput text box above the Grid1 control. (See Listing 6.10.)

**Listing 6.10. Removing the data from the grid control.**

```
Sub ClearGrid ()
    Grid1.SelStartCol = 0
    Grid1.SelStartRow = 0
        Grid1.SelEndCol = Grid1.Cols - 1
        Grid1.SelEndRow = Grid1.Rows - 1
Grid1.FillStyle = 1
```

*continues*

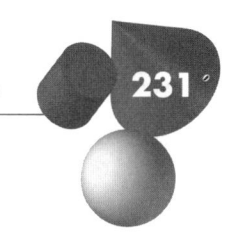

```
Grid1.Text = ""
    Grid1.FillStyle = 0
    Grid1.HighLight = False
        NextRow = 0
End Sub
```

The `ClearGrid` procedure removes the X, Y, and Z database values from the grid. The variable `NextRow` is reset to `0`, so the `ShowData` procedure (Listing 6.18) will insert any new data starting at the first row and column. The `Grid1` control is cleared when you open a new data file.

The `Grid1_MouseDown` event shows how to change `Grid1` cell text entries. (See Listing 6.11.) You can erase X, Y, or Z values by having no text appear in corresponding text boxes above `Grid1` or replace entries by typing a new value in the text boxes and selecting any cell in the corresponding column. The data is instantly saved to the file, so be careful. You also can experiment with `Drag` and `Drop` events to perform these duties.

**Listing 6.11.** Changing data values in the grid cells.

```
Sub Grid1_MouseDown (Button%, Shift%, X!, Y!)
If Button = 2 Then 'Right button only
    If PINPOINTS = 0 Then Exit Sub
    Continue = False: N = Grid1.Col
    If XYZInput(N).Text = "" Then XYZInput(N).Text = "0"
    If Grid1.Col = 0 Then Grid1.Text = XYZInput(0).Text :
        ↪AddrRec.XField = XYZInput(0).Text
    If Grid1.Col = 1 Then Grid1.Text = XYZInput(1).Text :
        ↪AddrRec.YField = XYZInput(1).Text
    If Grid1.Col = 2 Then Grid1.Text = XYZInput(2).Text :
        ↪AddrRec.ZField = XYZInput(2).Text
End If
End Sub
```

**N = Grid1.Col**: N equals the column number (0, 1, or 2) that you select.

**If XYZInput(N).Text = "" Then:** If there is no text in the corresponding text box above Grid1, the default X, Y, or Z value will be zero (0).

**If Grid1.Col = 0 Then:** Write the new value to the data file.

Listing 6.12 shows how to select all text characters in a text box control.

**Listing 6.12.** `HighlightText` selects data similar to a text editor.

```
Sub HighlightText (TextBox As Control)
    TextBox.SelStart = 0
    TextBox.SelLength = Len(TextBox.Text)
End Sub
```

**TextBox.SelStart = 0**: Insert the text cursor at the beginning of the text.

**TextBox.SelLength = Len(TextBox.Text)**: Select all of the text within the text box.

*continues*

## Viewing Different Angles of the 3-D Object

When you select the Preset View main menu item, you'll get three choices on how you would like to view the 3-D object. (See Listing 6.13.)

Listing 6.13. The `Menu_degrees_Click` event.

```
Sub MENU_degrees_Click (Index As Integer)
    XYZ(0).Text = "0"
    XYZ(1).Text = "250"
    XYZ(2).Text = "0"
Select Case Index
    Case 0 '0 degrees
        ValueBox(0).Text = "0.000"
        ValueBox(1).Text = "0.000"
        ValueBox(2).Text = "0.000"
        ValueBox(3).Text = "360"
    Case 1 '45 degrees
        ValueBox(0).Text = "05.70"
        ValueBox(1).Text = "06.30"
        ValueBox(2).Text = "05.90"
        ValueBox(3).Text = "360"
    Case 2
        If PINPOINTS = 0 Then Exit Sub
        BirdsEye.Show 1: Exit Sub
End Select
        SingleCell_Click
        XYZInput(0).SetFocus
End Sub
```

**Case 0 ' 0 degrees:** Resetting the YAW, ROLL, and PITCH to zero will display the image as a head on the front view.

**Case 1 '45 degrees:** Resetting the YAW, ROLL, and PITCH to the default startup values will display the image at roughly a 45-degree angle.

**Case 2 'Bird's eye view:** Open a second form that displays the front, side, and top views of the object on the screen. The code used to display these views is similar to the code used to open a data file (Listing 6.18). You omit one of either the X, Y, or Z coordinate values in order to show a front, side, or top view of the object.

The following is an example of how to show the side view of an object:

```
For i = 1 To PINPOINTS
    Grid1.Col = 1: Grid1.Row = r: X1 = Val(Grid1.Text)
    Grid1.Col = 2: Grid1.Row = r: Y1 = Val(Grid1.Text)
    If r = 0 Then Picture1(1).PSet (X1, Y1)
    Picture1(1).Line -(X1, Y1), QBColor(4)
    r = r + 1
Next i
```

Refer to the `Picture1_Paint` event of the `Animate2` form's source code. For details on the routine used to display an image from a data file, see Listing 6.18.

## Opening or Saving a Data File

This program opens files in Random mode and each X, Y, and Z value is treated as a separate data field. (See Listing 6.14.) Since the program saves files in Random mode, trailing spaces can be present in the field you delete. See Visual Basic's reference guide on Random file mode to see how to delete blank fields or rewrite the SaveData procedure (Listing 6.17) to use Binary access or Write # file modes.

Finally, you should always make a backup of all data files using the File menu's Save As option. This program uses the quick approach, the Kill statement, to destroy the old file information.

**Listing 6.14. Opening and saving a data file.**

```
Sub MENU_Open_Click (Index As Integer)
CMDialog1.Filter = "All Data Files (*.dat)¦*.dat"
CMDialog1.Flags = &H400& Or &H1000&
CMDialog1.CancelError = True
On Error GoTo ErrorHandler
Select Case Index
    Case 0 'New
        Continue = False
        Close #1: ClearGrid
        On Error Resume Next
        Kill "C:\Datatest.dat"
        PINPOINTS = 0: PictureCell.Cls
        Viewer.Caption = "3D-Viewer: " & TempFile
    Case 1 'Open
        CMDialog1.DialogTitle = "Open"
        CMDialog1.Flags = &H1000& Or &H400& Or &H800&
        CMDialog1.DefaultExt = "dat"
        CMDialog1.Action = 1
        Close #1: ClearGrid
        Filename = CMDialog1.Filename
        Viewer.Caption = "3D-Viewer: " & Filename
        ShowData
    Case 2 'Save As...
        CMDialog1.DialogTitle = "SAVE AS..."
        CMDialog1.Flags = &H800& Or &H400& Or &H2&
        CMDialog1.DefaultExt = "dat"
        CMDialog1.Action = 2
        Close #1: TempFile = CMDialog1.Filename
        Viewer.Caption = "3D-Viewer: " & TempFile
        SaveFILE
    Case 4 'Exit
    Close #1
        End
End Select
ErrorHandler:
SingleCell_Click
Exit Sub
End Sub
```

# The Animator Program

**CMDialog1.Filter =:** Refers to the Visual Basic language reference guide for details on file filters, flags, and file cancel error statements for the `CMDialog` control.

**Select Case Index:** Select the menu item that corresponds with its `Index` number.

**Case 0:** You have chosen the `New File` menu option.

**Continue = False:** Turn off any animation that may be happening on-screen.

**Close #1: ClearGrid:** If a data file is currently open, close it. Call the `ClearGrid` procedure (Listing 6.11) to erase the X, Y, and Z values from the `Grid1` control.

**On Error Resume Next:** If you cannot open or delete a file, continue on to the next code statement.

**Kill "C:\Datatest.dat":** If you are using a temporary file to store data, delete it.

**PINPOINTS = 0: PictureCell.Cls:** Reset the X, Y, Z field to 0 and erases any 3-D object image on the screen.

**Case 1:** You have selected the `Open` data file option. Do basically the same routine as in `Case 0` to reset the program. Then call the `ShowData` procedure (Listing 6.18) to open the file.

**Case 2:** You have selected the Save As new filename option. Do basically the same routine as in `Case 0` to reset the program. Then call the `SaveFile` procedure (Listing 6.17) to open the file.

**Case 4:** You have selected the Exit Program option.

**ErrorHandler:** If a file could not be saved or opened, exit the procedure.

**SingleCell_Click:** Forces a click event to occur on the `SingleCell` command button (Listing 6.19). This will draw the new data file to display the 3-D image.

See Listing 6.16 for how to pause the animation.

### Listing 6.16. Pausing the animation.

```
Sub Pause_click ()
    Continue = False
End Sub
```

## Saving the Data File

See Listing 6.15 for saving the data in the grid control to a file.

### Listing 6.15. Saving the data in the grid control to a file.

```
Sub SaveDATA ()
  PINPOINTS = PINPOINTS + 1

  AddrRec.XField = XYZInput(0).Text
  AddrRec.YField = XYZInput(1).Text
```

*continues*

```
    AddrRec.ZField = XYZInput(2).Text
If PINPOINTS = 1 Then Open TempFile For Random As #1 Len = Len(AddrRec)
Put #1, PINPOINTS, AddrRec
    Viewer.Caption = "3D-Viewer: " & TempFile
    XYZInput(0).SetFocus
End Sub
```

**PINPOINTS:** This variable is used to select a field position when writing to a Random file. It indexes the X, Y, Z coordinates in fields by using Visual Basic's Put statement.

**AddrRec.XField, AddrRec.YField, AddrRec.ZField:** These are the character strings that will be added to the data file. They can be up to four characters long and are defined by the Type AddrRec structure located in the ANIMATOR3.BAS file. Because you are working in pixel positions, no X, Y, or Z screen positions will need to be greater than four digits.

**Open:** Open the data file. Refer to Visual Basic's Open statement for details.

**Put #1:** Writes the data to the file. Only one file can be opened at any time, so call the file #1. The PINPOINTS variable points to a position (field) within the file to write the X, Y, and Z coordinate values.

**Viewer.Caption:** The form's caption will be 3-D Viewer *data filename* (where *data filename* is the name of the data file).

**XYZinput(0).SetFocus:** Set the text cursor in the first text box above Grid1.

## Opening and Displaying the Data

The ShowData procedure opens the data file and inserts each X, Y, and Z value into the Grid1 control. (See Listing 6.16.)

**Listing 6.16. Loading a data file into the grid control.**

```
Sub ShowData ()
PINPOINTS = 0
If Filename <> "" Then
MENU_Open(0).Enabled = True: MENU_Open(2).Enabled = True
    Open Filename For Random As #1 Len = Len(AddrRec)
    PINPOINTS = LOF(1) / Len(AddrRec)
Else
    Exit Sub
End If
For indexpos% = 1 To PINPOINTS
    If indexpos% <> 0 Then
        Get #1, indexpos%, AddrRec
        DataXYZ$ = RTrim(AddrRec.XField) & Chr(9) & [IC:CCC]
            RTrim(AddrRec.YField) & Chr(9) & RTrim(AddrRec.ZField)
        Grid1.AddItem DataXYZ$, NewColumn
        NewColumn = NewColumn + 1
        Grid1.ColAlignment(0) = 1: Grid1.ColAlignment(1) = 1
        Grid1.ColAlignment(2) = 1
    End If
Next indexpos%
End Sub
```

## The Animator Program

**PINPOINTS = 0:** Set the data file field position to 0.

**If FileName:** If you are loading a data file, this routine continues.

**MENU_Open:** The New and Save As... File menu options are grayed out, so enable them after a file has been loaded or data is entered in Grid1.

**Open:** Open a data file. Refer to Visual Basic's Open statement for details.

**PINPOINTS:** By dividing the data file's total length (LOF(1)) by each record field's length (Len(AddrRec)), you get the total number of individual record fields.

**For index% = 1 To PINPOINTS:** For each index record field starting at record field 1 to the total number of records fields, do the following block of code statements:

**Get #1:** Retrieve each X, Y, and Z record set from the data file.

**DataXYZ$:** If each X, Y, or Z value is less than four characters long, trim the excess (null) spaces away and append a tab character to each value. Inserting a tab character (Chr(9)) forces the X value into column 0 of the grid, the Y value in column 1, and the Z value in column 2.

**Grid1.AddItem:** Insert each X, Y, and Z value to the Grid1 control for viewing.

**NewRow:** Add a new row so that in the next set, a X, Y, and Z values can be added.

**Grid1.ColAlignment:** Right-align all the numbers so reading is easier.

**Next indexpos%:** Repeat the process until all the data is displayed in the Grid1 control.

## Updating New Values in a Data File

The SingleCell button is used to update new X, Y, or Z coordinate values entered into the Grid1 control. (See Listing 6.17.)

**Listing 6.17. Drawing a single cell image on the screen.**

```
Sub SingleCell_Click ()
If PINPOINTS = 0 Then Exit Sub
    Continue = False
    PictureCell.Cls
    ANIMATION
End Sub
```

**If PINSPOINTS = 0 Then:** No data file is loaded, so exit the procedure.

**Continue:** Stops any animation currently running.

**PictureCell.Cls:** Erase any object currently displayed.

**ANIMATION:** Call the Animation procedure (Listing 6.7) to draw a single cell image.

## Moving the 3-D Object Using Scroll Values

The X, Y, and Z axes positions of the object are displayed in the XYZ text boxes. You can change these values while the object is moving by selecting the scrollbar controls beside each XYZ textbox. The bitmap arrows also move and change the values displayed in the XYZ text boxes. (See Listing 6.18.)

**Listing 6.18. Changing the image's axis.**
```
Sub VScroll_Change (Index As Integer)
    Select Case Index
        Case 0
            XYZ(0).Text = Format$(VScroll(0).Value)
        Case 1
            XYZ(1).Text = Format$(VScroll(1).Value)
        Case 2
            XYZ(2).Text = Format$(VScroll(2).Value)
        Case 3
            ValueBox(3).Text = Format$(VScroll(3).Value)
    End Select
End Sub
```

**Case 0:** Pan a 3-D object to the left or right.

**Case 1:** Zoom a 3-D object in or out.

**Case 2:** Pan a 3-D object to the top or bottom.

**XYZ(i).Text:** Change the values of the object's X, Y, or Z axis, or the object's perceptive depth, using the scrollbar controls.

See Listing 6.19 for how to highlight text.

**Listing 6.19. Highlighting text as a text editor does.**
```
Sub XYZinput_GotFocus (Index As Integer)
    i = Index
    HighlightText XYZinput(i)
End Sub
```

**HighlightText XYZinput(i):** Highlight any text (X, Y, and Z position values) that appear in the three boxes above Grid1. This makes deleting input much easier.

## Typing New Values for the Data

The XYZinput text boxes are used to insert new data. There are more text boxes above the Grid1 control to input X, Y, and Z coordinate values. You can tab over to each text box by using the spacebar. (See Listing 6.20.)

# The Animator Program

> **CAUTION:** Using the spacebar while the last text box has the focus will write the data to the file.

**Listing 6.20.** Saving data by using the spacebar.

```
Sub XYZinput_KeyPress (Index As Integer, KeyAscii As Integer)
If KeyAscii >= Asc("0") And KeyAscii <= Asc("9") Or KeyAscii = &H20 Or [IC:CCC]
    KeyAscii = &H8 Or KeyAscii = Asc("-45") Then  Else KeyAscii = 0: Beep
If KeyAscii = &H20 Then  'spacebar
    Index = Index + 1
        If Index > 2 Then
            Index = 0
            DataXYZ$ = XYZInput(0).Text & Chr(9) & XYZInput(1).Text & [IC:CCC]
                Chr(9) & XYZInput(2).Text
            Grid1.AddItem DataXYZ$, NextRow
            NextRow = NextRow + 1
            SaveDATA
XYZInput(0).Text = "": XYZInput(1).Text = "": XYZInput(2).Text = ""
        End If
XYZInput(Index).SetFocus
KeyAscii = 0: MENU_Open(0).Enabled = True: MENU_Open(2).Enabled = True
End If
End Sub
```

**If KeyAscii >= Asc("0"):** Insert numeric characters into the text boxes.

**If KeyAscii = &H20:** If the spacebar is pressed, tab to the next XYZinput box above the Grid1 control.

**If Index > 2 Then:** You are at the third and last input box and have pressed the spacebar. The data in the three input boxes above Grid1 will be added into the Grid1 control using the following block of code statements

**DataXYZ$:** Store the X, Y, and Z input values and appends a tab Chr(9) to each value.

**Grid1.AddItem:** Insert each X, Y, and Z value to the Grid1 control for viewing.

**NewRow:** Advance to the next row in the Grid1 control.

**SaveData:** Call this routine to save your new X, Y, and Z values to the data file. Remove this line if you do not want any data to be written to the open file.

**XYZinput:** Clear all the input text boxes of X, Y, and Z values.

**XYZinput.(i).SetFocus:** Send the text cursor to the first input box so you can continue adding values (if you want to).

**KeyAscii:** Setting KeyAscii to 0 clears the buffer so you can resume new input values.

**MENU_Open.Enabled:** At startup, the New and Save As... File menu options are grayed out (disabled). You can now enable these options items.

## Summary

The Animator program is very simple in design and should help you design more advanced three-dimensional modeling applications.

You should consider applying rendering tools such as the drawing tools described in the Artisan program from Chapters 2 through 5. This way, you can use the mouse pointer to draw each segment of the 3-D model, without manually inputting the coordinates.

Try changing or switching the sine and cosine values in the Animation procedure. You will get objects that pulsate in and out or rotate in weird orbital paths. Change, switch, or insert offset values to the Line statement that renders the 3-D object so the lines will interloop within each other. Change the Line statement's QBColor(4) to QBColor(Rnd *14) in order to view each of the lines being rendered as it is animated.

Insert the object that was demonstrated in the TestMove program from Chapter 1 by replacing the Line statements with this code:

```
If r = 0 Then PictureCell.PSet (sx, sy)

PictureCell.Line -(sx, sy), QBColor(4)
PictureCell.Line (sx, sy)-Step(100, 0 + N)
PictureCell.Line -Step(0, 100)
PictureCell.Line -Step(-100, 0 - N)
PictureCell.Line -Step(30, 50)
PictureCell.Line -Step(-30, -150)
PictureCell.Circle (X1 + 50, Y1 + 50), 25
```

Experiment with various values in for the Movement variables in the AnimateBtn_Click event.

Finally, you have probably noticed that the images flicker a lot and that the screen refresh rate can be very slow. There is no quick and easy solution to these drawbacks within Visual Basic. Using API functions to paint the interiors of the image or draw the lines will slow the performance even more. The Basic language programs available in DOS can switch screen pages so animation can be achieved in real time. However, Windows requires a lot more overhead to generate its window images. However, help is on the way. Microsoft has introduced two new API libraries, called Win32G and WinG32.DLL, that cater to animation and game programmers. Refer to the WinGame program in the 16MISC directory of the companion disk for an example of the new WinG API functions. In order to use the new WinG functions, you must download the WinG SDK kit from the Microsoft WinMM library. The WinG SDK kit is free and contains all the required .DLL files.

# CHAPTER 7

# Multi-Search and Replace

# Multi-Search and Replace

Chapter 7 deals with text string manipulation. Text strings can be used as an integral part of graphical applications such as text illustration and desktop publishing. This book deals mainly with Visual Basic's graphical capabilities (lines, curves); however, the Multi-Search and Replace program has been included as a chapter to give you an insight into Visual Basic's string handling methods and functions. The text spacing example in this program shows how to align a line of text correctly within a picture box control using the Visual Basic `TextHeight` and `TextWidth` functions. In Chapter 12, you will be introduced to more advanced text properties using the Windows API text functions.

The Multi-Search and Replace program takes any ASCII text file and replaces multiple words with one push of a button. The program accomplishes this by using a simple loop to read each entry in the list box control holding the Search list. It then uses Visual Basic's select text (`Sel`) statements to highlight and change the text using the first entry of the adjacent list box holding the Replace list.

What makes Multi-Search and Replace different is the presence of the `Do/Loop` statement at the bottom of the `ReplaceCom` procedure (Listing 7.17). When the start position (`startpos`) variable equals 0, the cursor position has reached the end of the file. The procedure then selects the next item in the `Search` list box, continuing the loop until all of the items have been replaced from the `CodeLst2` (replace) list box.

The Multi-Search and Replace program designed for Visual Basic version 3.0 and higher uses the DMDialog.VBX in order to save and open text files. To use Multi-Search and Replace, do the following:

1. Type a word into the Search For text box.
2. Press the Add command button directly below the list box on the left side of the form, or press the Enter key.
3. Repeat the previous steps for the Replace With text box using the Add command button on the right side of the form. You can use the left- and right- arrow keys to set the focus on each text box.

> **NOTE** If you use the same search-and-replace lists often, you can add each list item in the `Form_Load` event using the list box's `ADDITEM` method. For example:
> ```
> CodeLst1.AddItem "Company".
>     CodeLst2.AddItem "Co."
> ```

Use the Kill One Listing button to delete a single search-and-replace match that you highlight within the List boxes.

The Kill Search List and Kill Replace List buttons delete entire listings from the corresponding list box.

The Replace button starts the search-and-replace process of the text file. After the search and replace is finished, save the text file using the Save As file menu option.

**Figure 7.1.**
*The form and its control names.*

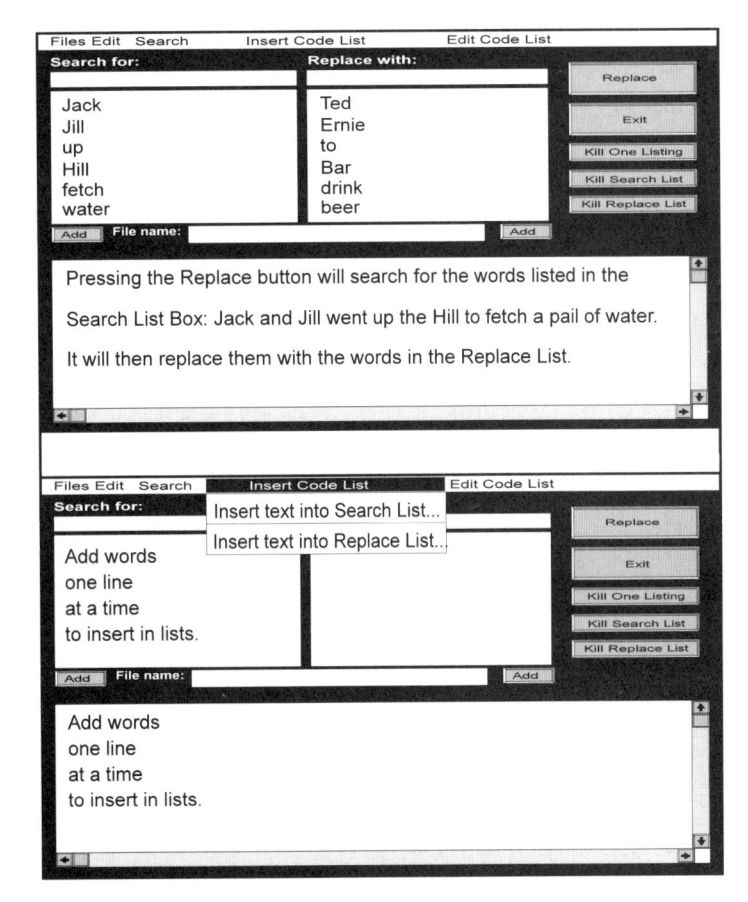

The search-and-replace program's form and control properties are listed in Table 7.1.

**Table 7.1. The properties of the search-and-replace form and controls.**

*Object: Form*
*Object Name: replace*

| | | | |
|---|---|---|---|
| Caption | = "MULTI-SEARCH & REPLACE" | Top | = 1080 |
| Height | = 7275 | Width | = 9690 |
| Left | = 105 | | |

*continues*

**Table 7.1. continued**

| | | | |
|---|---|---|---|
| *Object: Frame* <br> *Object Name: Frame1* | | | |
| BackColor | = &H00FF0000& | Top | = 90 |
| Height | = 3480 | Visible | = 0 'False |
| Left | = 90 | Width | = 9405 |
| *Object: CommandDialog* <br> *Object Name: CMDialog1* | | | |
| Left | = 8370 | | |
| Top | = 2925 | | |
| *Object: CommandButton* <br> *Object Name: AddBtn* | | | |
| Caption | = "Add" | Top | = 2970 |
| Height | = 285 | Width | = 735 |
| Index | = 1 | | |
| Left | = 6435 | | |
| *Object: CommandButton* <br> *Object Name: AddBtn* | | | |
| Caption | = "Add" | Top | = 2970 |
| Height | = 285 | Width | = 735 |
| Index | = 0 | | |
| Left | = 90 | | |
| *Object: CommandButton* <br> *Object Name: replacebtn* | | | |
| Caption | = "Replace" | Top | = 135 |
| Height | = 645 | Width | = 1815 |
| Left | = 7470 | | |
| *Object: CommandButton* <br> *Object Name: Exitbtn* | | | |
| Caption | = "Exit" | Top | = 855 |
| Height | = 645 | Width | = 1815 |
| Left | = 7470 | | |

*Object: CommandButton*
*Object Name: Deletebtn*

| Caption | = "Kill One Listing" | Top | = 1575 |
| Height | = 375 | Width | = 1800 |
| Index | = 0 | | |
| Left | = 7470 | | |

*Object: CommandButton*
*Object Name: Deletebtn*

| Caption | = "Kill Search List" | Top | = 2025 |
| Height | = 375 | Width | = 1800 |
| Index | = 1 | | |
| Left | = 7470 | | |

*Object: CommandButton*
*Object Name: Deletebtn*

| Caption | = "Kill Replace List" | Top | = 2475 |
| Height | = 375 | Width | = 1800 |
| Index | = 2 | | |
| Left | = 7470 | | |

*Object: Text Box*
*Object Name: SearchBox*

| Height | = 315 | Top | = 270 |
| Left | = 90 | Width | = 3480 |

*Object: Text Box*
*Object Name: ReplaceBox*

| Height | = 315 | Top | = 270 |
| Left | = 3690 | Width | = 3480 |

*Object: List Box*
*Object Name: codelst1*

| Height | = 2370 | Top | = 585 |
| Left | = 90 | Width | = 3480 |

*Object: List Box*
*Object Name: codelst2*

| Height | = 2370 | Top | = 585 |
| Left | = 3690 | Width | = 3480 |

*continues*

## Multi-Search and Replace

**T**able 7.1. continued

*Object: Label*
*Object Name: Labels*

| BackColor | = &H00FF0000& | Index | = 2 |
| Caption | = "File name:" | Left | = 990 |
| ForeColor | = &H00FFFFFF& | Top | = 2970 |
| Height | = 255 | Width | = 990 |

*Object: Label*
*Object Name: Labels*

| BackColor | = &H00FF0000& | Index | = 1 |
| Caption | = "Replace with :" | Left | = 3690 |
| ForeColor | = &H00FFFFFF& | Top | = 0 |
| Height | = 255 | Width | = 1215 |

*Object: Label*
*Object Name: Labels*

| BackColor | = &H00FF0000& | Index | = 0 |
| Caption | = "Search for :" | Left | = 90 |
| ForeColor | = &H00FFFFFF& | Top | = 0 |
| Height | = 255 | Width | = 1215 |

*Object: Label*
*Object Name: FileNameLabel*

| Height | = 330 | Top | = 2970 |
| Left | = 1980 | Width | = 4245 |

*Object: Text Box*
*Object Name: Textbox*

| Height | = 2895 | ScrollBars | = 3 'Both |
| Index | = 0 | Top | = 3660 |
| Left | = 90 | Visible | = 0 'False |
| MultiLine | = -1 'True | Width | = 9375 |

*Object: Menu*
*Object Name: Menu_File*

| Caption | = "&File" |

*Menu_FileSub*

| Caption | = "Open" |
| Index | = 0 |

*Menu_FileSub*

Caption = "Save As..."
Index = 1
Shortcut = {F2}

*Menu_FileSub*

Caption = "File Manager"
Index = 2
Shortcut = ^F

*Menu_FileSub*

Caption = "-"
Index = 3

*Menu_FileSub*

Caption = "Quit"
Index = 4
Shortcut = ^Q

*Menu_Edit*

Caption = "&Edit"

*Menu_EditSub*

Caption = "Cut"
Index = 0
Shortcut = ^X

*Menu_EditSub*

Caption = "Copy"
Index = 1
Shortcut = ^C

*Menu_EditSub*

Caption = "Paste"
Index = 2
Shortcut = ^V

*Menu_EditSub*

Caption = "-"
Index = 3

*continues*

**Table 7.1. continued**

*Menu_EditSub*
Caption = "Clear NotePad"
Index = 4

*Menu_Search*
Caption = "&Search"

*Menu_FindSub*
Caption = "Find"
Index = 0

*Menu_FindSub*
Caption = "Find Selected Text"
Index = 1
Shortcut = ^S

*Menu_FindSub*
Caption = "Replace"
Index = 2
Shortcut = ^R

*Menu_Insert*
Caption = "Insert Code Lists"

*Menu_InsertSub*
Caption = "Insert Text into Search List..."
Index = 0

*Menu_InsertSub*
Caption = "-"
Index = 1

*Menu_InsertSub*
Caption = "Insert Text into Replace List..."
Index = 2

*Menu_EditCodeS*
Caption = "Edit Code Lists"

*Menu_EditCodeSub*
Caption = "Edit Search List with NotePad"
Index = 0

*Menu_EditCodeSub*

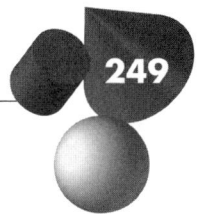

Caption     = "-"

Index       = 1

*Menu_EditCodeSub*

Caption     = "Edit Replace List with NotePad"

Index       = 2

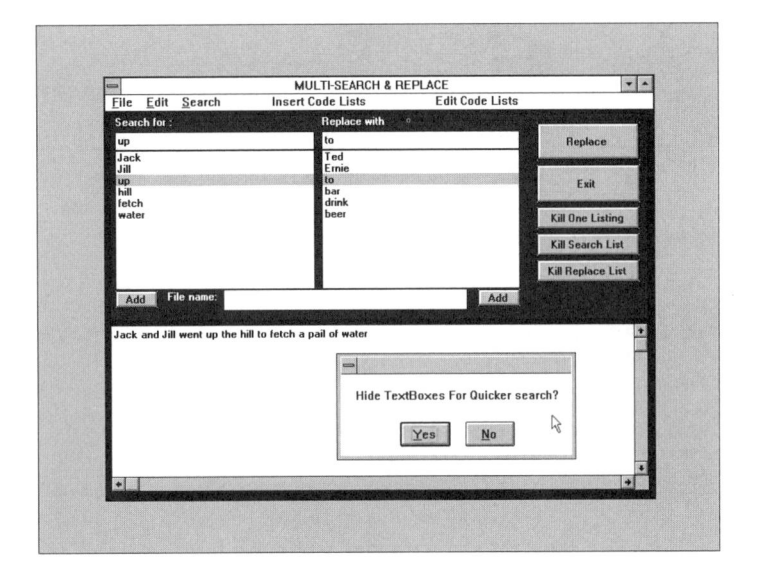

**Figure 7.2.**
*The Search for and Replace with list boxes.*

## Variables Used Within this Program

**Listing 7.1** The variable names declared at startup.

```
Declarations
Const BUFFER_SIZE = 16384
Dim Buffer As String 'file I/O buffer
Dim GlobalFilename As String
```

**Const Buffer_Size:** Used in the Opencom menu event to load a text file into the main text box control. In the Do/While loop, a block of 16,384 characters of text is grabbed during each loop until the end of the file is reached. Increasing this number may cause the buffer to overflow, decreasing the value causes flickering. Visual Basic's text box controls have slightly less than a 64KB character limitations.

# Multi-Search and Replace

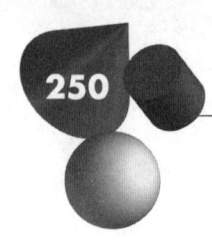

**Buffer As String:** Also used in the OpenCom menu event, it temporarily stores each block of text retrieved from the text file. When all the text is in the buffer, it is sent to the main text box to be displayed.

**Dim GlobalFilename As String:** Stores the name of text file you are opening.

## Positioning the Controls at Startup

The Form_Resize event in Listing 7.2 makes the controls on the form relocate proportionately to the form's dimensions. By grouping the controls within a frame control, less code is needed to move most controls.

**Listing 7.2. Repositioning the controls on the form.**

```
Sub Form_Resize ()
Pixel = Screen.TwipsPerPixelX
Pixel = Screen.TwipsPerPixelY
If WindowState = 1 Then Exit Sub
    Frame1.Top = 5
    Frame1.Left = 5
    Frame1.Width = (Replace.Width - 200) \ Pixel
TextBox(0).Top = Frame1.Height + 10
TextBox(0).Left = 5
TextBox(0).Height = (Replace.Height \ Pixel) -
        ➥(Frame1.Height + 60)
TextBox(0).Width = (Replace.Width - 200) \ Pixel
Frame1.Visible = True : Textbox(0).Visible = True
End Sub
```

**Pixel:** Convert the screen's twip width and height to pixel units. For most VGA type monitors, the variable Pixel equals 15.

**If WindowState = 1 Then Exit Sub:** If the form is minimized, exit this procedure.

## Adding an Item to a Code List

There are two buttons with the captions Add. The first button, indexed as 0, is used to insert the text you typed in the Search for text box into the corresponding Search list box. The second Add button is indexed as 1. It is used to insert the text you type in the Replace with text box into the corresponding Replace list box.

**Listing 7.3. Inserting the search or replace items into the list boxes.**

```
Sub Addbtn_Click (Index As Integer)
    Select Case Index
        Case 0
            If SearchBox.Text = "" Then Exit Sub
            CodeLst1.AddItem SearchBox.Text
```

```
            SearchBox.Text = ""
            SearchBox.SetFocus
        Case 1
            If ReplaceBox.Text = "" Then Exit Sub
            CodeLst2.AddItem ReplaceBox.Text
            ReplaceBox.Text = ""
            ReplaceBox.SetFocus
    End Select
End Sub
```

**Select Case Index:** Depending on which button you select, do the Case block that matches the index of the button.

**Case 0:** The Add button below the Search list box was selected.

**If Searchbox:** If no text has been typed in the Search for text box, exit this event.

**CodeLst1.AddItem:** Add the text displays in the Search For text box into the Codelst1 list box (Search list box).

**SearchBox.Text = "":** the Search for text is cleared from the text box.

**SearchBox.SetFocus:** Places the text cursor (caret) back into the Search for text box.

**Case 1:** The Replace button below the Replace list box was selected.

**If Replacebox:** If no text has been typed in the Replace with text box, exit this event.

**CodeLst2.AddItem:** Adds the text displays in the Replace for text box into the Codelst2 list box (Replace list box).

**ReplaceBox.Text= "":** The Replace with text is cleared from the text box.

**ReplaceBox.SetFocus:** Places the text cursor (caret) back into the Replace Box text box.

The Addbtn_GotFocus event makes the Add button the default button for the list you are editing. This makes it easier to insert items into the list boxes (by pressing the Enter key).

### Listing 7.4. Switching the focus between buttons.

```
Sub Addbtn_GotFocus (Index As Integer)
    Select Case Index
        Case 0
            addbtn(0).Default = True
        Case 1
            addbtn(1).Default = True
    End Select
End Sub
```

**addbtn(0).Default = True**: Send the current Add button as the default. When the Enter key is pressed, the Addbtn_Click event (Listing 7.3) is triggered.

## Selecting an Item in Either List Box

The `Codelst1` list box word must have a corresponding `Codelst2` list box word. If not, the items in the Search or Replace list will not match and the `CodeLst1_Click` event in Listing 7.5 will issue a message that informs you to correct one of the lists.

### Listing 7.5. Matching a Search word with a Replace word.

```
Sub codelst1_Click ()
If CodeLst1.ListCount <> CodeLst2.ListCount Then
    MsgBox "ONE OF YOUR LISTS IS LONGER THAN THE OTHER!"
    Exit Sub
End If
    SearchBox.Text = CodeLst1.Text
    ReplaceBox.Text = CodeLst2.Text
    CodeLst2.ListIndex = CodeLst1.ListIndex
    CodeLst2.SetFocus
End Sub
```

**If CodeLst1.ListCount:** If either the Search or Replace list is longer than the other, a warning message is displayed.

**SearchBox.Text:** Display the item you have highlighted in the Search box.

**ReplaceBox.Text:** Finds the matching indexed item in the Replace box.

**Codelst2.ListIndex, SetFocus:** Highlight the matching search and replace items.

The `codelst2_click` list box event in Listing 7.6 is similar to the `codelst1_click` event (Listing 7.5) except that you highlighted a replace item rather than a search item.

### Listing 7.6. Matching a replace word with a search word.

```
Sub codelst2_Click ()
If CodeLst1.ListCount <> CodeLst2.ListCount Then
    MsgBox "ONE OF YOUR LISTS IS LONGER THAN THE OTHER!"
    Exit Sub
End If
SearchBox.Text = CodeLst1.Text
    ReplaceBox.Text = CodeLst2.Text
    CodeLst1.ListIndex = CodeLst2.ListIndex
    CodeLst1.SetFocus
End Sub
```

**If CodeLst1.ListCount:** If either the Search or Replace list is longer than the other, a warning message is displayed.

**SearchBox.Text:** Displays the item you have highlighted in the Search box.

**ReplaceBox.Text:** Finds the matching indexed item in the Replace box.

**Codelst1.ListIndex, SetFocus:** Highlights the matching replace and search items.

## Removing Items from the List Boxes

The `Delete_Btn_Click` event in Listing 7.7 defines three buttons representing cases you can use to delete items within the list boxes. The button named Kill One Listing deletes both the search and replace items that you have highlighted in the list boxes. The Kill Search List button deletes all entries in the Search list box. The Kill Replace List deletes all items in the Replace list box.

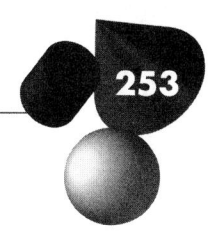

**Listing 7.7. Removing and deleting an item from the list.**

```
Sub Deletebtn_Click (Index As Integer)
Select Case Index
    Case 0
        If CodeLst1.Text = "" Or CodeLst2.Text = "" Then Exit Sub
        N = CodeLst1.ListIndex
        CodeLst1.RemoveItem (N)
        CodeLst2.RemoveItem (N)
        SearchBox.Text = "" : ReplaceBox.Text = ""
    Case 1
        CodeLst1.Clear : SearchBox.Text = ""
    Case 2
        CodeLst2.Clear : ReplaceBox.Text = ""
End Select
End Sub
```

**Select Case Index:** Depending on which button you choose, do the Case block that matches the index of the button you selected.

**Case 0:** You have pressed the Kill One Listing button.

**If CodeLst1.Text:** Exit the event if no items are present.

**N:** Represent the index number (highlighted item) you selected in both list boxes.

**CodeLst1.RemoveItem:** Delete the highlighted item.

**CodeLst2.RemoveItem:** Delete the highlighted item.

**SearchBox, ReplaceBox:** Remove any characters within the text boxes.

**Case 1:** You have pressed the Kill Search List button.

**Codelst1.Clear:** Removes all items from the Search for list box.

**Case 2:** You have pressed the Kill Replace List button.

**Codelst2.Clear:** Removes all items from Replace with list box.

## Tools Used to Edit Text

This section covers the various editing tools available within the menu selection items. Use the Search menu item to find a string within a text file that matches the characters you typed into the Search for text box control. Use the `Find Selected Text` option to continue the search for one word at a time. Both menu options use the `FindCom` procedure (Listing 7.8) to perform these duties.

## Multi-Search and Replace

**Listing 7.8. Finding a word within the text.**

```
Sub FindCom ()
Static curindex As Long
Dim Find As String
    Find = SearchBox.Text
    If Find = "" Then Exit Sub ' nothing to find
    curindex = InStr(curindex + 1, TextBox(0).Text, Find)
        If curindex > 0 Then
            TextBox(0).SelStart = curindex - 1
            TextBox(0).SelLength = Len(Find)
            TextBox(0).SetFocus
        Else
            MsgBox "No More Matching Strings"
        End If
End Sub
```

**Static curindex:** Store the cursor position within the text using the `InStr` function.

**Find As String:** Temporarily store the text for which you are searching.

**If Find = "" Then:** Exit this procedure if no text appears in the Search for text box.

**curindex = InStr:** (Current index position.) The `InStr` function returns the position of the first occurrence of the Search for text and then uses that position to search forward for the next occurrence of the word.

**Instr:** The `INSTR` function is defined as follows: 1. The position within the text from which to start the search. 2. The text copy you are searching. 3. The word you are searching for.

**If curindex > 0 then:** You found a matching word, so you will highlight it.

**TextBox(0).SelStart:** Place the cursor just before the word.

**TextBox(0).SelLength:** Highlight the word.

**TextBox.SetFocus:** Set the focus on the text box in case you want to type over, delete, or edit the word.

**Else:** There are no more matching strings to be found, so display a message.

## Editing the Items in the List Boxes

Use the Insert Code Listing and Edit Code Listing menu items to edit any Search or Replace list. You also can type a complete search or replace list in the main text box and then have all the items inserted into either list box. You must type each item on a single line and add a carriage return after each (by pressing the Enter key).

**Listing 7.9. Editing a Search or Replace list.**

```
Sub Menu_EditCodeSub_Click (Index As Integer)
Dim CL As String
Select Case Index
    Case 0 'Edit Search Code fields
```

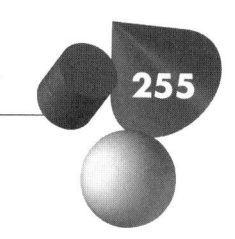

```
        TextBox(0).Text = ""
    For i = 0 To CodeLst1.ListCount
        CL = CodeLst1.List(i)
        TextBox(0).Text = TextBox(0).Text + CL + Chr$(13) + Chr$(10)
    Next
        CodeLst1.Clear
        SearchBox.Text = ""
    Case 2 'Edit Replace Code fields
        TextBox(0).Text = ""
    For i = 0 To CodeLst2.ListCount
        CL = CodeLst2.List(i)
        TextBox(0).Text = TextBox(0).Text + CL + Chr$(13) + Chr$(10)
    Next
            CodeLst2.Clear
            ReplaceBox.Text = ""
End Select
    TextBox(0).SetFocus
    SendKeys "%{HOME}"
End Sub
```

**Dim CL As String:** Store the list box text item.

**Select Case Index:** Depending on which list box you want to edit, do the following.

**Case 0:** You want to edit the Search for list box.

**TextBox(0).Text = "":** Clear the main text box of any character type or open file.

**For i = 0 To CodeLst.ListCount:** For every CodeLst1 item starting at index 0 and continuing up to the last CodeLst1 item, do the following:

**TextBox(0).Text = TextBox(0).Text:** This is the same as opening a file except each line is processed individually. You may want to use a buffer to stop the text from flickering. Add a carriage return and a line feed (CR/LF) so each code list item is flush left in the text box.

**Case 2:** You want to edit the Replace with list box.

The Case 2 block is basically the same routine as in Case 0 except you are dealing with the CodeLst2 list box rather than the CodeLst1 list box.

## How to Cut, Copy, and Paste the Text

Use the Edit menu item to cut, copy, or paste text within the text file. Perform all operations by using Windows Clipboard feature.

**Listing 7.10. Cutting, copying, or pasting text into the notepad.**

```
Sub Menu_Editsub_Click (Index As Integer)
Select Case Index
    Case 0 'Cut
        clipboard.SetText Screen.ActiveControl.SelText
        Screen.ActiveControl.SelText = ""
        SendKeys "{HOME}", 1
```

*continues*

## Multi-Search and Replace

**Listing 7.10. continued**

```
        Case 1 'Copy
            If Screen.ActiveControl.SelText <> "" Then
                clipboard.SetText Screen.ActiveControl.SelText, CF_TEXT
            End If
        Case 2 'Paste
            Screen.ActiveControl.SelText = clipboard.GetText()
        Case 4 'Clear TextBox
            TextBox(0).Text = ""
    End Select
End Sub
```

**Select Case Index:** Depending on what type of text edit you want, do the `Case` block that matches the index of the menu item.

**Case 0:** Cut the highlighted text to the clipboard.

**clipboard.SetText:** Use `Screen.ActiveControl` since you can cut text from the Search for, Replace with, or main text box. The `Screen.ActiveControl` keyword tells the clipboard what text control has the current focus so the clipboard can cut, copy, or paste to this text box control.

**SendKeys:** Send the text cursor to the HOME position.

**Case 1:** Copy the highlighted text to the clipboard.

**clipboard.SetText:** Same as cut (`Case 1`), but you specify that you are copying a text format by adding `CF_TEXT` to the end of the `SelText` statement.

**Case 2:** Paste the text stored in the clipboard to a text box.

**Screen.ActiveControl.SelText:** The `GetText` keyword retrieves any text that was cut or pasted in the clipboard.

## Opening or Saving a Text File

The `Menu_FileSub_Click` in Listing 7.11 uses the File menu item to open or save the text file that appears in the main text box. The Open menu option calls the `Opencom` procedure (Listing 7.14), and the Save As... option calls the `SaveCom` procedure (Listing 7.18). You also can switch to Windows File Manager to check the status of your file.

**Listing 7.11. Opening or saving a file.**

```
Sub Menu_FileSub_Click (Index As Integer)
Select Case Index
    Case 0 'Open
        Opencom
    Case 1 'Save As
        SaveCom
    Case 2 'File Manager
        Dummy = Shell("Winfile")
    Case 4 'Quit
        End
```

```
End Select
End Sub
```

**Select Case Index:** Depending on the file menu item you sleected, do the `Case` block that matches the index of menu item.

**Case 0:** You want to open a file.

**Opencom:** Call the `Opencom` procedure to display the `Openfile` box.

**Case 1:** You want to save a file under a new name.

**Savecom:** Call the `Savecom` procedure to display an input box.

**Case 2:** You want to see the Windows File Manager.

**Dummy = Shell("WinFile"):** Start the Windows File Manager so you can determine whether files have been saved properly.

**Figure 7.3.**
*Ilustrating the form's control names.*

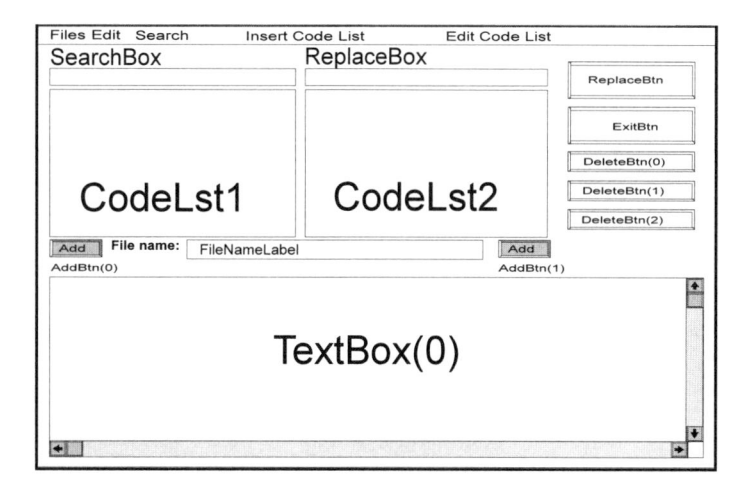

The `Menu_FindSub_Click` event in Listing 7.12 finds text that you enter into the Search for text box or any recurrence of a word you highlight in the main text box. The third option performs the search and replace of all items listed.

**Listing 7.12. Finding text within text.**

```
Sub Menu_FindSub_Click (Index As Integer)
Select Case Index
    Case 0 'Find
        FindCom
    Case 1 'Find Highlighted
        If TextBox(0).SelText <> "" Then
            SearchBox.Text = TextBox(0).SelText
        End If
        FindCom
    Case 2 'Replace
```

*continues*

## Multi-Search and Replace

### Listing 7.12. continued

```
        ReplaceCom
End Select
End Sub
```

**Select Case Index:** Depending on what menu option you choose, do the Code block that matches the index of the menu item's index..

**Case 0:** You want to find the text that you have typed it the Search for text box that matches any type or word in the main text box.

**FindCom:** Call the procedure that will find the word you are searching for in the text.

**Case 1:** You want to find all occurrences of the type or word that you have highlighted in the main text box.

**If TextBox(0).Text:** If no text has been highlighted in the main text box, default to the text that is displayed in the Search for text box.

**SearchBox.Text:** If text is highlighted in the main text box, find any recurrence of this string in the current file displayed.

**FindCom:** Call the procedure that will find the word you are searching for in the text.

**Case 2:** You want to search and replace any codes inserted in the Search for and Replace with lists. This is the same as pressing the big Replace button on the form.

The `Menu_Insert_Click` event helps you take words listed in the Notepad text box and insert them in either the Search for (`CodeLst1`) or Replace with (`CodeLst2`) list boxes. If you have a large list of search or replace words, you can edit the words as you would edit words in Windows Notepad files and then insert them in the appropriate list boxes.

### Listing 7.13. Inserting each line of text from the main text box into a list box.

```
Sub Menu_InsertSub_Click (Index As Integer)
If Not Right$(TextBox(0).Text, 1) = Chr$(10) Then
    MsgBox "YOU MUST HAVE A SINGLE RETURN ➥
            AT END OF TEXT!": Exit Sub
End If
Dim word As String
    Select Case Index
        Case 0 'Insert into Search field
While Not TextBox(0).Text = ""
    EndofWord% = InStr(1, TextBox(0).Text, Chr$(10))
    word = Left$(TextBox(0).Text, EndofWord%)
    TextBox(0).SelStart = 0
    TextBox(0).SelLength = Len(word)
    codes$ = Left$(TextBox(0).SelText, EndofWord% - 2)
    CodeLst1.AddItem codes$
    TextBox(0).SelText = ""
Wend
    Case 2 'Insert into replace field
While Not TextBox(0).Text = ""
        EndofWord% = InStr(1, TextBox(0).Text, Chr$(10))
```

```
            word = Left$(TextBox(0).Text, EndofWord%)
            TextBox(0).SelStart = 0
            TextBox(0).SelLength = Len(word)
            codes$ = Left$(TextBox(0).SelText, EndofWord% - 2)
            CodeLst2.AddItem codes$
            TextBox(0).SelText = ""
    Wend
End Select
End Sub
```

**If Not Right$(Text.Box(0).Text,1):** This routine uses a line-feed code (Chr$(10)) to find the end of each text line in the main text box. In order for the routine to work, you must insert the line feed character at the end of text line.

**MsgBox:** Tell the user to add the last line-feed character (Chr$(10)) by pressing the Enter key.

**word:** This represents the word or text line to insert in the code lists.

**Select Case Index:** Depending on which code list you want to place the main text into, the menu item's index will match the one of the following Case blocks.

**Case 0:** You want to insert the main text into the Search for list.

**While Not:** Loops the following code until all the text in the Notepad text box has been removed and inserted in the list box.

**EndofWord%:** This represents the line-feed position within each line of text. The Instr keyword function retrieves the starting position of the file, the text to search, and the character to look for.

**word:** This represents the word or string of text in each line of the main text box.

In the following group of statements you are going to highlight each line of text to extract.

**TextBox(0).SelStart:** You will place the text cursor at the very start of the line.

**TextBox(0).SelLength:** You highlight the entire length of the line.

**codes$:** Store the selected or highlighted text from the previous step.

Now you need to trim any carriage returns and line feeds that are embedded in each line. One way is to use the Visual Basic's Left$ statement. The Left$ statement takes two arguments. The first is the text that has been selected or highlighted. The second is the number of characters in the line minus the carriage return and line feed.

**Codelist1.AddItem:** Insert the selected or highlighted text line into the list box.

**TextBox(0).Seltext:** Clear the selected text so the next line can be set.

**Wend:** Repeat the loop process for the next line of text.

**Case 2:** You want to insert the main text into the Replace With list box. The Case 2 block is similar to the Case 0 scenario except you are inserting each text line into the Replace with list box.

## Opening a Text File

The Search and Replace program designed for Visual Basic 3.0 and higher uses the CMDialog.VBX to retrieve filenames.

**Listing 7.14. Opening a file in `Binary` mode.**

```
Sub Opencom ()

Dim F As String
 Dim BufNum As Integer
CMDialog1.Filter = "All Files (*.*)¦*.*¦Text Files(*.txt)¦*.txt"
CMDialog1.Flags = &H1000& Or &H800&
CMDialog1.CancelError = True
On Error GoTo BadFile
CMDialog1.FilterIndex = 2
CMDialog1.Action = 1
GlobalFilename = CMDialog1.Filename
    If GlobalFileName <> "" Then
        FilenameLabel.Caption = GlobalFileName
    Else
        Exit Sub
    End If
    F = FilenameLabel.Caption
    If F = "" Then Exit Sub
        On Error GoTo BadFile
    BufNum = FreeFile ' get next free buffer number
    Open F For Binary As #BufNum
    Textbox(0).Text = ""
    Do While Not EOF(BufNum)
        Buffer = Space$(BUFFER_SIZE)
        Get #1, , Buffer
        Textbox(0).Text = Textbox(0).Text + Buffer
    Loop
    Close #BufNum
    Textbox(0).Text = RTrim$(Textbox(0).Text) ' trims spaces
Exit Sub
'***********Error-handler**********
BadFile: Beep
    Exit Sub
End Sub
```

**Dim F As String:** This represents `FilenameLabel.Caption`, which equals the file's name.

**Dim BufNum As Integer:** This represents each file's unique file number.

**CMDialog1:** Refer to the Visual Basic Language Guide, "Common Dialog Control" and "Filters," for explanations of the CMDialog control's methods and properties values.

**If GlobalFilename:** When you select a file from the `OpenFile` form or CMDialog.VBX the file's name and path are stored in a global filename variable. If you close the `OpenFile` form without selecting a file, the global filename will not be issued. Therefore, you must exit the subroutine.

**If F = "" then Exit Sub:** No file was selected, so exit the subroutine.

**On Error Goto BadFile:** When an error occurs, go to the error-handler line called BadFile. This is a very condensed error handler that will not return messages such as Drive Door Open and Computer Meltdown. What it will do is let you try again after it resets the OpenBox.Caption.

**Open F For Binary As #BufNum:** Open the file you have selected in Binary mode (first bit to last bit) and gives the file a unique file number (usually file number 1).

**TextBox(0).Text = "":** Clear any text that may be present in the main text box.

**Do While Not EOF(BufNum):** Loop through the following routine until you have reached the end of the file (EOF).

**Buffer = Space$(BufferSize):** This represents a reserved buffer space, which is the size of the Buffer_Size value. Each block of text is processed in this buffer.

**Get #1, Buffer:** Grab a block of text from the file.

**TextBox(0).Text:** Put the block of text into the main text box.

**Loop:** Repeat the process until the entire text file is visible in the main text box.

**Close #BufNum:** Clear the text buffer's memory, thus closing the file.

**TextBox(0).Text:** Trim any extra blank spaces that may be present at the end of the file.

**Error Handler:** If the file failed to open, the computer will sound a beep. Add addition error-handling codes to suit you particular programming needs.

**Beep:** Sound a warning beep and exit this procedure.

# Searching and Replacing Items

Listings 7.15 through 7.17 deal with searching and replacing of all items within the code list boxes.

**Listing 7.15. Activating the Add button for a list box.**

```
Sub ReplaceBox_GotFocus ()
    addbtn(1).Default = True
End Sub
```

**addbtn(1).Default:** You can press the Enter key to insert a new item.

The ReplaceBtn_Click event in Listing 7.16 asks if you want to hide the notepad.

**Listing 7.16. Selecting the Replace button.**

```
Sub replacebtn_Click ()
If TextBox(0).Text = "" Then Exit Sub
    msg = "Hide TextBoxes For Quicker search?"
    Response = MsgBox(msg, 1, TextBoxes)
    If Response = 1 Then
        TextBox(0).Visible = False
    End If
ReplaceCom
    TextBox(0).Visible = True
```

*continues*

## Multi-Search and Replace

**Listing 7.16. continued**

```
    MsgBox "NO MORE MATCHING STRINGS", 64, "INFORMATION"
    Textbox(0).SetFocus
    SendKeys "^{HOME}"
End Sub
```

**If TextBox(0).Text:** Exit this subroutine if no text is visible in the Notepad text box.

When searching and replacing text, it is quicker to process a long list of search and replace words when the main text box is hidden. A visible text box sends the text cursor (caret) to the start of each word it is searching (SelStart). The procedure then highlights the text (SelLength) and scrolls the text if necessary. The graphical user interface (GUI) would have to process the visible screen actions. Furthermore, the text box scrollbars scroll the long text file vertically and/or horizontally, making the process extremely long. To overcome this, you can hide the main text box while the code is being processed.

**msg:** Ask the user if he or she would like the main text box hidden.

**Response:** Show the message with Yes and No option buttons.

**If Response =1:** Indicate a selection of Yes to hide the main text box.

**TextBox(0).Visible:** Hide the main text box.

**ReplaceCom:** Call the ReplaceCom procedure that is the heart of this program.

**TextBox(0).Visible:** If the text box was hidden, reshow it.

The ReplaceCom procedure in Listing 7.17 performs the actual searching and replacing of a word or list of words when the Replace button is clicked.

**Listing 7.17. The main search and replace code.**

```
Sub ReplaceCom ()
Dim Find As String, Replace As String
If CodeLst1.ListCount <> CodeLst2.ListCount Then Exit Sub

For i = 0 To CodeLst1.ListCount - 1
Do
   Find = CodeLst1.List(i)
   SearchBox.Text = Find
   Replace = CodeLst2.List(i)
   ReplaceBox.Text = Replace
   startpos = InStr(startpos + 1, Textbox(0).Text, Find)

   If startpos = 0 Then Exit Do
   Textbox(0).SelStart = startpos - 1
   Textbox(0).SelLength = Len(Find)
   Textbox(0).SelText = Replace

 Loop While startpos > 0

Next i
End Sub
```

**If CodeLst1.ListCount:** If one of the list box's total items is longer than the other list box's items, exit this procedure.

**For i = 0 To CodeLst1.ListCount - 1:** Repeat the next block of statements for each item in the Search for list box.

**Do:** Repeat the following block of statements.

**Find:** This represents a word or text from the CodeLst1 (Search for) list box.

**SearchBox.Text:** Displays each word during the search.

**Replace:** This represent a word or text from the CodeLst2 (Replace with) list box.

**ReplaceBox.Text:** Display each word during the replace.

**startpos = InStr:** Store the start position of each string search using the InStr function. The InStr function is explained here:

> startpos + 1: The beginning character position from which the InStr function will start each search.
>
> Textbox(0).Text: The text file to search.
>
> Find: The word to look for.

**If startpos = 0 Then Exit Do:** The search has reached the end of the file, and the Find word has been successfully replaced. Exit the Do/Loop routine. The trick is to place this code statement before the following SelText statements. This will ensure that no error message will be triggered if the text does not exist.

**TextBox(0).SelStart:** Position the text cursor just in front of the search word.

**TextBox(0).SelLength:** Select or highlight the word for which you are searching.

**TextBox(0).Seltext:** Replace the Search for text with the Replace with text.

**Loop While startpos > 0:** Continue to look for the Find word until you reach the end of the text.

**Next i:** Repeat the process for the next search-and-replace words in the list boxes.

## Saving the Text File

The SaveCom procedure presented in Listing 7.18 saves any text that appears in the main text box.

**Listing 7.18.** The SaveCom procedure saves the file in Binary mode.

```
Sub SaveCom ()
Dim BufNum As Integer
Dim i As Long

CMDialog1.Filter = "All Files (*.*)|*.*|Text Files(*.txt)|*.txt"
CMDialog1.Flags = &H2& Or &H800&
CMDialog1.CancelError = True
On Error GoTo BadFileName
CMDialog1.FilterIndex = 2
```

*continues*

# Multi-Search and Replace

**Listing 7.18. continued**

```
CMDialog1.Action = 2
GlobalFilename = CMDialog1.Filename
    If GlobalFileName <> "" Then
        FilenameLabel.Caption = GlobalFileName
    Else
        Exit Sub
    End If
    If (GlobalFileName <> "") Then
        On Error GoTo BadFileName
        BufNum = FreeFile ' get next free buffer number
        Open GlobalFileName For Binary As #BufNum

        For i = 1 To Len(Textbox(0).Text) Step BUFFER_SIZE
            Buffer = Mid$(Textbox(0).Text, i, BUFFER_SIZE)
            Put #BufNum, , Buffer
        Next i
        Close #BufNum
    End If
Exit Sub
'****************Error-Handler***************
BadFileName:
    Exit Sub
End Sub
```

**Dim BufNum As Integer:** This represents the unique file number.

**Dim i As Integer:** This represents the block of text to save.

**CMDialog1:** Refer to the Visual Basic Language Guide sections, "Common Dialog Control," and "Filters," for explanations of the CMDialog control's methods and property values.

**GlobalFileName:** This represents the path and filename to save.

**If (GlobalFileName <> ""):** If a path and filename is present, you can continue saving the file.

**On Error Goto BadFileName:** If an error occurs during the saving of the file, go to the line called BadFileName (error-handler).

**BufNum:** Get the next available, free file number.

**Open:** Open a file in Binary mode (first bit to last bit) with the path and filename (you chose) with a unique file number.

**For i = 1 To Len(TextBox(0).Text) Step Buffer_Size:** This saves a file. For every block of text starting at byte number 1 and continuing through to the last bit (length of text), you will collect text in blocks specified by the value of Buffer_Size.

**Buffer:** This represents each block of text to save. The Mid$ function includes the following:

(Textbox(0)): The text the Mid$ function looks at.

(i): The starting position of each buffer of text.

(Buffer_Size): How much text to put into the buffer.

**Put #BufNum, , Buffer:** Save each block of text to the file.

**Next:** Repeat the process to save the next block of text.

**Close #BufNum:** The file is now saved, so close it.

# The Text Spacing Text

The text spacing example used in the Multi-Search and Replace program deals with the Visual Basic TextWidth and TextHeight properties. When you click the menu item marked "Text spacing example," a picture box control fills the entire form area. Placing the mouse pointer anywhere within the picture box will automatically place the text cursor in the correct line spacing coordinate. The following menu item and controls are used to perform the text spacing:

1. Menu_txt: the menu item marked "Text spacing example."

2. Picture1: a picture box control that contains all the controls used by this example.

3. BUIF: a picture box control that is used to format the text that is typed (normal, italic, bold, and so on).

4. Label1: a label control that simulates a text cursor.

5. Timer1: a timer control that makes the text cursor blink on and off.

The Menu_txt event in listing 7.19 changes the form to a scaled-down text editor with limit features.

**Listing 7.19. Changing the form's appearance.**

```
Sub Menu_txt_Click ()
    Picture1.Cls 'erase old text images
    Picture1.Move 0, 0, ScaleWidth, ScaleHeight
    Menu_Edit.Visible = Not Menu_Edit.Visible
    Menu_EditCodeS.Visible = Not Menu_EditCodeS.Visible
    Menu_File.Visible = Not Menu_File.Visible
    Menu_Insert.Visible = Not Menu_Insert.Visible
    Menu_Search.Visible = Not Menu_Search.Visible
    Picture1.Visible = Not Picture1.Visible
    If Picture1.Visible Then
        Caption = "This is a Picture Box Control"
    Else
        Caption = "MULTI-SEARCH & REPLACE"
    End If
End Sub
```

# Multi-Search and Replace

**Picture1.Cls:** Erase any old text images.

**Picture1.Move:** Make the picture control the same size as the form.

**Menu_Edit.Visible:** Disable any all the menu items used by the search and replace example.

The `Picture1._MouseUp` event in Listing 7.20 will calulate the correct placement of the text cursor using the the `TextHeight` amd `TextWidth` methods.

### Listing 7.20. Calculating text line spacing.

```
Sub Picture1_MouseUp (Button As Integer, Shift As Integer, X As Single, Y As Single)
    Timer1.Enabled = True
Linecount = Y \ Picture1.TextHeight("")
    X1 = X
    Y1 = Picture1.TextHeight("") * Linecount
    Y2 = Picture1.TextHeight("")
    Label1.Move X1, Y1, 30, Y2
    Label1.Visible = True
    Picture1.CurrentX = X1: Picture1.CurrentY = Y1
End Sub
```

**Timer1.Enabled:** Start the timer to make the text cursor (label control) blink off and on.

**Linecount = Y \ Picture1.TextHeight(""):** Calculate how many lines of text can fit within the picture box.

**X1 = X:** Used to place the text cursor (label control) at the mouse pointer coordinate.

**Y1 = Picture1.TextHeight("") * Linecount:** The height of the text (includes leading) times the line count will place the text curor at the correct Y coordinate.

**Y2 = Picture1.TextHeight(""):** The height of text (includes leading) will make the text cursor the correct height.

**Label1.Move X1, Y1, 30, Y2:** Move the text cursor to the correct text line coordinate.

**Picture1.CurrentX = X1:** Change the picture box's `CurrentX` and `CurrentY` to reflex the text cursor's position.

The `Picture1.KeyPress` event in Listing 7.21 will display each character typed and then advance the text cursor to the next character position.

### Listing 7.21. Advancing the text cursor position.

```
Sub Picture1_KeyPress (KeyAscii As Integer)
   Label1.Visible = True: Timer1.Enabled = False
    If Chr(KeyAscii) = Chr(13) Then
        Y1 = Y1 + Picture1.TextHeight("")
        Picture1.CurrentY = Y1 'line feed
        Picture1.CurrentX = X1 'return
        Label1.Move X1, Y1, 30, Y2
        Exit Sub
```

```
      End If
      CursorX = Picture1.CurrentX    'save CurrentX
      Picture1.Print Chr$(KeyAscii) 'forces CurrentX to 0
      CharWidth = Picture1.TextWidth(Chr$(KeyAscii))
      Picture1.CurrentX = CursorX + CharWidth: Picture1.CurrentY = Y1
      Label1.Move Picture1.CurrentX, Y1, 30, Y2
      Timer1.Enabled = True
    End Sub
```

**Timer1.Enabled = False:** Turn the timer off so the cursor does not blink as text is typed.

**If Chr(KeyAscii) = Chr(13) Then:** The carriage return (Enter key) was pressed, so the CurrentY is advanced one text line and the CurrentX is left aligned to the the first text line. The text cursor (label control) is then advanced to the new text line position, and the key press event terminates.

**CursorX = Picture1.CurrentX:** Save the CurrentX coordinate so you can reset the cursor position after the following Print statement. The Print statement by default forces the CurrentX to the 0 coordinate when the Enter key (carriage return) is pressed.

**Picture1.Print Chr$(KeyAscii):** Print the character.

**CharWidth = Picture1.TextWidth(Chr$(KeyAscii)):** Get the width of the character just typed.

**Picture1.CurrentX = CursorX + CharWidth:** Advance the CurrentX coordinate the width of the character just typed.

**Label1.Move:** Relocate the text cursor to the character position.

**Timer1.Enabled = True:** Turn the timer back on so the text cursor will blink on and off.

The BUIF_MouseDown event in Listing 7.22 will change the current fonts attribute (normal, italic, bold, and so on).

**L**isting 7.22. Changing the font style.

```
Sub BIUF_MouseDown (Button As Integer, Shift As Integer, X As Single, Y As Single)
  X = Fix(X)
  BIUF.Line (X, 0)-(X + 1, 1), , BF
'''''''''''''''''
Select Case X
    Case 0  'Bold
      Picture1.FontBold = Not Picture1.FontBold
      B_Button = Not B_Button
    Case 1  'Italic
      Picture1.FontItalic = Not Picture1.FontItalic
      B_Button = Not B_Button
    Case 2  'Underline
      Picture1.FontUnderline = Not Picture1.FontUnderline
      B_Button = Not B_Button
End Select
End Sub
```

**BIUF.Line (X, 0)-(X + 1, 1), , BF:** Invert the bitmap image so the button appears pressed in.

**Select Case X:** The BUIF picture is scaled to 4 units wide, so the X coordinate will match the Case block that will toggle the bold, italic, and underline font attributes on or off when a button is selected.

The BUIF_MouseUp event in Listing 7.23 will display the CMDialog control so it is possible to change fonts and additional font attributes (size, color, etc.).

**Listing 7.23. Displaying the font dialog box.**

```
Sub BIUF_MouseUp (Button As Integer, Shift As Integer, X As Single, Y As Single)
  X = Fix(X)
    If Fix(X) = 3 Then
      BIUF.Line (X, 0)-(X + 1, 1), , BF
        CMDialog1.Flags = &H100 Or &H1& Or &H200& Or &H40000
        CMDialog1.FontName = Picture1.FontName
        CMDialog1.FontSize = Picture1.FontSize
        CMDialog1.FontBold = Picture1.FontBold
        CMDialog1.FontItalic = Picture1.FontItalic
        CMDialog1.FontUnderLine = Picture1.FontUnderline
        CMDialog1.FontStrikeThru = Picture1.FontStrikethru
        CMDialog1.Color = Picture1.ForeColor
        CMDialog1.Action = 4  'font dialog box
        Picture1.FontName = CMDialog1.FontName
        Picture1.FontSize = CMDialog1.FontSize
        Picture1.FontBold = CMDialog1.FontBold
        Picture1.FontItalic = CMDialog1.FontItalic
        Picture1.FontUnderline = CMDialog1.FontUnderLine
        Picture1.FontStrikethru = CMDialog1.FontStrikeThru
        Picture1.ForeColor = CMDialog1.Color
DoEvents
  If Picture1.FontBold = True Then B_Button = True Else B_Button = False
  If Picture1.FontItalic = True Then I_Button = True Else I_Button = False
  If Picture1.FontUnderline = True Then U_Button = True Else U_Button = False
  If B_Button = True Then BIUF.Line (0, 0)-(1, 1), , BF
  If I_Button = True Then BIUF.Line (1, 0)-(2, 1), , BF
  If U_Button = True Then BIUF.Line (2, 0)-(3, 1), , BF
End If
      Picture1.SetFocus
      Picture1.CurrentX = Label1.Left
End Sub
```

**CMDialog1:** Refer to the Visual Basic Language Guide sections, "Common Dialog Control," and "Filters", for explanations of the CMDialog font control's methods and properties values.

**If B_Button = True Then:** Reset the any inverted buttons on the BUIF picture box to match the current font attributes in use.

The BUIF_Paint event in Listing 7.24 will set the drawmode to inverted (6) and scale the picture box's scale to 4 units wide.

## Listing 7.24. Scaling the BUIF picture box.

```
Sub BIUF_Paint ()
    BIUF.DrawMode = 6  'Invert
    BIUF.Scale (0, 0)-(4, 1)
End Sub
```

> **BIUF.DrawMode:** Invert the drawing mode of the picture box.
>
> **BIUF.Scale:** Scale the interal coordinates of the picture box to 4 units wide by 1 unit high.

The `Timer1_Timer` event in Listing 7.25 toggles the visible property of the text cursor (label control) on and off. The text cursor will then be blinking.

## Listing 7.25. Making the text cursor blink.

```
Sub Timer1_Timer ()
    If Picture1.Visible = True Then
Label1.Visible = Not Label1.Visible
    End If
End Sub
```

> **Label1.Visible:** Toggle the label control's visible property on and off.

# Summary

The Multi-Search and Replace program uses most of the Visual Basic string methods and functions you can cross-reference when applying test string manipulation within your own programs. When using the Multi-Search and Replace program, the text file you will most likely save is the file on which you just performed the search and replace. However, you can save individual Search for lists or Replace with lists that you may use regularly. If you use the same lists on a regular basis, you can add the code automatically at startup. An example is replacing company, limited, state, and province names that needed to be abbreviated (for example, Co., Ltd., CA., and Ont.).

The text spacing example demonstrated how to easily space lines of text within a picture box control. You may want to add features to simulate a mini-word processor. However, you will most likely need to use Windows API functions in order to fine-tune leading, character spacing, and justification. The three text alignment programs in Chapter 12 demonstrate some of API text function available to Visual Basic.

The following example shows one possible method with which you can adjust the text cursor (label control) to be placed automatically between characters on the display. The following example requires a global array to be declared as `Dim tBuf(100) As String`:

Here is an example for the `Picture1_MouseUp` event:

```
    Timer1.Enabled = True
Linecount = Y \ Picture1.TextHeight("")
    X1 = X
```

# Multi-Search and Replace

```
        Y1 = Picture1.TextHeight("") * Linecount
        Y2 = Picture1.TextHeight("")
For R = 0 To 99
  If Fix(X) >= tBuf(R) And Fix(X) <= tBuf(R) + (tBuf(R + 1) - tBuf(R)) \ 2 Then
        Label1.Move tBuf(R), Y1, 30, Y2
        FoundChar = True: Exit For
    ElseIf Fix(X) >= tBuf(R) + (tBuf(R + 1) - tBuf(R)) \ 2 And Fix(X) <= (tBuf(R + 1))
Then
        Label1.Move tBuf(R + 1), Y1, 30, Y2
        FoundChar = True: Exit For
  End If
Next R
  If FoundChar = False Then Label1.Move X1, Y1, 30, Y2
        Label1.Visible = True
```

Here is an example for the `Picture1_KeyPress` event:

```
Static CursorX As Integer
Label1.Visible = True: Timer1.Enabled = False
    If Chr(KeyAscii) = Chr(13) Then
        Y1 = Y1 + Picture1.TextHeight("")
        Picture1.CurrentY = Y1 'line feed
        Picture1.CurrentX = X1 'return
        Label1.Move X1, Y1, 30, Y2
        Exit Sub
    End If
Static R As Integer
    CursorX = Picture1.CurrentX    'save CurrentX
    tBuf(R) = Fix(Label1.Left): R = R + 1
    Picture1.Print Chr$(KeyAscii) 'forces CurrentX to 0
    CharWidth = Picture1.TextWidth(Chr$(KeyAscii))
    Picture1.CurrentX = CursorX + CharWidth: Picture1.CurrentY = Y1
    tBuf(R) = Fix(Picture1.CurrentX)
    Label1.Move Picture1.CurrentX, Y1, 30, Y2
    Timer1.Enabled = True
End Sub
```

The text spacing example uses a label control to simulate a text cursor. It is possible to use the `Line` statement to draw the text cursor, but you must take into consideration that `CurrentX` and `CurrentY` values will change whenever the `Line` statement is implemented. The following code example shows one possible method in which you can use the `Line` statement to draw a text cursor.

Here is an example of `Line` statment cursor:

```
CursorX = Picture1.CurrentX    'save CurrentX
CharWidth = Picture1.TextWidth(Chr$(KeyAscii))
Picture1.Line (CursorX, Y1)-(CursorX + CharWidth, Y1 + Y2), Picture1.BackColor, BF
Picture1.CurrentX = CursorX: Picture1.CurrentY = Y1
Picture1.Print Chr$(KeyAscii) 'forces CurrentX to 0
Picture1.CurrentX = CursorX + CharWidth: Picture1.CurrentY = Y1
```

The previous examples are limited and take no consideration of storing or editing the text that is displayed. You may want to visit your local library to get material on computer word processing. Editing text displayed on the computer's monitor has been available since day one of the PC. Older computer library books I have come across have had enough information to get you on the right track.

# CHAPTER 8

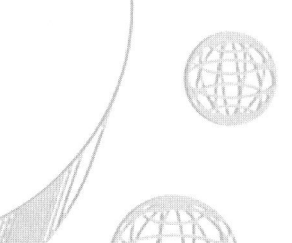

# API Drawing Programs

# API Drawing Programs

The API drawing function's form presented in Figure 8.1 can be used to access some of the most commonly used built-in API graphic language calls. Windows 16-bit operating system has three major Dynamic Link Library (.DLL) files that hold selected parts of the powerful Application Program Interfaces (API). For Windows 3.11, the files are located in the Windows system directory and are titled GDI.EXE, USER.EXE, and KRNL386(286).EXE. There are more than 1,000 API functions available in programming. The Microsoft SDK (Software Developer's Kit) includes full API reference material. The Microsoft Knowledge Base, available through Microsoft on CD or modem, has additional API reference material.

**Figure 8.1.**
*The API form and its controls.*

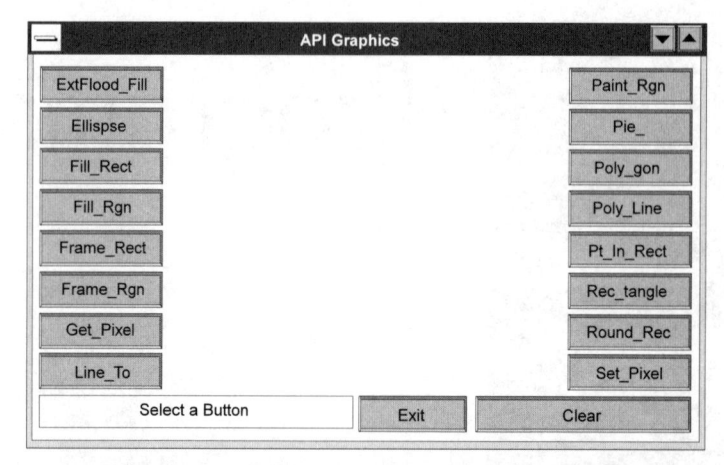

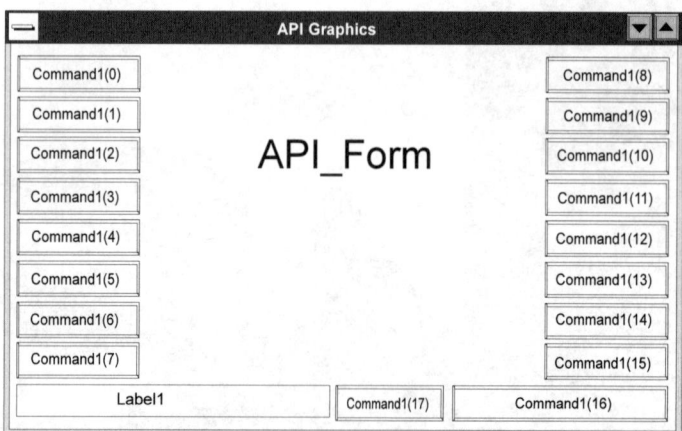

Windows 32-bit operating systems use the GDI32 file to handle 32-bit (Long) API functions. To convert most 16-bit API functions to 32-bit, you usually need to change its declaration to a 32-bit (Long) value. Some argument values that you pass to the 32-bit function will have to be sent as Long (&) data types.

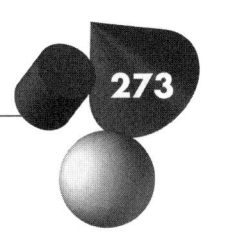

The following is an example of a 16-bit declaration:

```
Declare Function Polyline Lib "GDI" (ByVal hDC As Integer,
↪lpPoints As POINTAPI, ByVal nCount As Integer) As Integer
```

The following example is a 32-bit declaration. Take note that the hDC and nCount arguments are also Long (&) in this example.

```
Declare Function Polyline Lib "GDI32" (ByVal hDC As Long,
↪lpPoints As POINT, ByVal nCount As Long) As Long
```

Some of commonly used 32-bit API drawing functions are listed at the end of this chapter.

You must declare a DLL procedure in the Declaration section of the form that will be using the function, or in a module form so it is available to all forms in your program. A sample Declaration follows. The following must be typed as one continuous line.

```
Declare Function LineTo Lib "GDI" (ByVal hDC As Integer,
↪ByVal X As Integer, ByVal Y As Integer) As Integer
```

To shorten a function call, use the suffixes for the data types:

```
Declare Function LineTo% Lib "GDI" (ByVal hDC%, ByVal X%, ByVal Y%)
```

> Declare Function or Declare Sub: The Visual Basic command that states that a function or subroutine is being declared.
>
> LineTo%: The name of the sample API function being used. The name inserted here will be the actual library name of the function.
>
> Lib "User": The name of the DLL library file in which the function resides. An alias keyword is another option available to this field. See Visual Basic's programmer's guide, "Calling Procedures in DLLs."

The second part of the API function declaration (which is in parentheses) could have these parts:

> ByVal hDC%: The window, control, or object on which to focus. Most functions require this information.

The hDC is considered the **h**andle of a **d**evice **c**ontext. The device context usually is your Visual Basic form or control. For example, Artwork.hDC tells the API to search for an handle that identifies a picture box window called Artwork. It will look for a device context that is a properties chart (not unlike Visual Basic) that holds all the information about this picture box. There are other handle identifiers, such as hBITMAP (bitmap) and hWnd (window).

> ByVal X%, ByVal Y%: An example of this is that values and/or option settings are considered the arguments to pass to the function. The ByVal clause is needed to pass any argument parameter as a value. Visual Basic passes an argument by reference unless it is an expression or constant.

# API Drawing Programs

Some arguments need a user-defined Type structure placed in a module form in order to be processed. See Visual Basic's reference guide for more details. You can find more information on API functions in your Visual Basic documentation. Visual Basic 3.0 includes API copy and paste tools.

The APIdraw program's form and control properties are listed in Table 8.1.

**Table 8.1.** The properties of the APIdraw form and controls.

*Object: Form*
*Object Name: API_Form*

| | | | |
|---|---|---|---|
| BackColor | = &H00FFFFFF& | Left | = 450 |
| Caption | = "API Graphics" | ScaleMode | = 3 'Pixel |
| DrawMode | = 6 'Invert | Top | = 1305 |
| Height | = 4320 | Width | = 7935 |

*Object: Command Button*
*Object Name: Command1   18 indexed controls*

| | | | |
|---|---|---|---|
| Height | = 375 | Width | = 1245 |
| Caption | = "ExtFloodFill" : Index 0 | Caption | = "Pie" : Index 9 |
| Caption | = "Ellipse" : Index 1 | Caption | = "Polygon" : Index 10 |
| Caption | = "FillRect" : Index 2 | Caption | = "Polyline" : Index 11 |
| Caption | = "FillRgn" : Index 3 | Caption | = "PtIn_Rect" : Index 12 |
| Caption | = "FrameRect" : Index 4 | Caption | = "Rectangle" : Index 13 |
| Caption | = "FrameRgn" : Index 5 | Caption | = "RoundRect" : Index 14 |
| Caption | = "GetPixel" : Index 6 | Caption | = "SetPixel" : Index 15 |
| Caption | = "LineTo" : Index 7 | Caption | = "Clear Screen" : Index 16 |
| Caption | = "PaintRgn" : Index 8 | Caption | = "Exit" : Index 17 |

*Object: Label*
*Object Name: Label1*

| | | | |
|---|---|---|---|
| Alignment | = 2 'Center | Left | = 105 |
| BorderStyle | = 1 'Fixed Single | Top | = 3465 |
| Height | = 330 | Width | = 3690 |

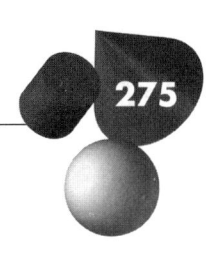

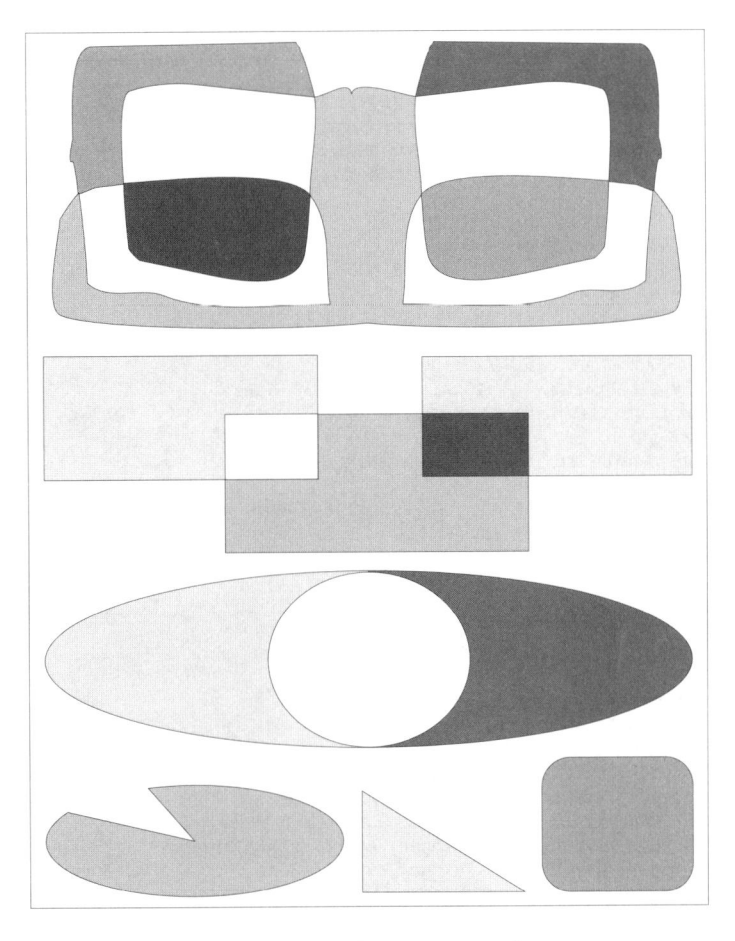

## The Declaration Section of the APIdraw Program

The following declarations are for Windows operating systems that can define 16-bit values. You may want to change the 16-bit API functions to 32 GDI functions for future use in 32-bit Windows operating systems.

**Listing 8.1. The variable names used in the API program.**

```
Declaration
Dim BoundingBox As Rectangle
Dim BoundingBox2 As Rectangle
Dim B As Integer
Dim W(1 To 20) As Integer
Dim N(1 To 20) As Integer
Dim E(1 To 20) As Integer
```

*continues*

## API Drawing Programs

**L**isting 8.1. continued

```
Dim S(1 To 20) As Integer
Declare Function ExtFloodfill% Lib "GDI" (ByVal hDC%,
➥ByVal X%, ByVal Y%, ByVal crColor As Long,ByVal wFillType%)
Declare Function Ellipse% Lib "GDI" (ByVal hDC As Integer,
➥ByVal X1 As Integer, ByVal Y1 As Integer,ByVal X2 As Integer,
➥ByVal Y2 As Integer)
Declare Function FillRect% Lib "User" (ByVal hDC%,
➥R As Rectangle, ByVal hBrush%)
Declare Function FillRgn% Lib "GDI" (ByVal hDC%,
➥ByVal hrgn%, ByVal hBrush%)
Declare Function FrameRect% Lib "User" (ByVal hDC%,
➥R As Rectangle, ByVal hBrush%)
Declare Function FrameRgn% Lib "GDI" (ByVal hDC%,
➥ByVal hrgn%, ByVal hBrush%, ByVal nWidth%,ByVal nHeight%)
Declare Function GetPixel& Lib "GDI" (ByVal hDC%,
➥ByVal X%, ByVal Y%)
Declare Function LineTo% Lib "GDI" (ByVal hDC As Integer,
➥ByVal X As Integer, ByVal Y As Integer)
Declare Function PaintRgn% Lib "GDI" (ByVal hDC%, ByVal hrgn%)
Declare Function Pie% Lib "GDI" (ByVal hDC%, ByVal X1%,
➥ByVal Y1%, ByVal X2%, ByVal Y2%, ByVal X3%, ByVal Y3%,
➥ByVal X4%, ByVal Y4%)
Declare Function Polygon% Lib "GDI" (ByVal hDC%,
➥P As PointXY, ByVal N%)
Declare Function Polyline% Lib "GDI" (ByVal hDC%,
➥P As PointXY, ByVal N%)
Declare Function PtInRectBynum% Lib "User"
➥Alias "PtInRect" (R As Rectangle, ByVal Pnt&)
Declare Function Rectangle Lib "GDI" (ByVal hDC As Integer,
➥ByVal X1 As Integer, ByVal Y1 As Integer,
➥ByVal X2 As Integer, ByVal Y2 As Integer) As Integer
Declare Function RoundRect Lib "GDI" (ByVal hDC As Integer,
➥ByVal X1 As Integer, ByVal Y1 As Integer, ByVal X2 As Integer,
➥ByVal Y2 As Integer, ByVal X3 As Integer, ByVal Y3 As Integer) As Integer
Declare Function SetPixel& Lib "GDI" (ByVal hDC%, ByVal X%,
➥ByVal Y%, ByVal crColor&)
'''Other calls needed to preform above functions''''
Declare Function MoveTo Lib "GDI" (ByVal hDC As Integer,
➥ByVal X As Integer, ByVal Y As Integer)As Long
Declare Function GetCurrentPosition&
➥Lib "GDI" (ByVal hDC As Integer)
Declare Function CreateEllipticRgn%
➥Lib "GDI" (ByVal X1%, ByVal Y1%, ByVal X2%, ByVal Y2%)
Declare Function CreateRectRgn%
➥Lib "GDI" (ByVal X1%, ByVal Y1%, ByVal X2%, ByVal Y2%)
Declare Function CreateSolidBrush% Lib "GDI" (ByVal crColor&)
Declare Function DeleteObject% Lib "GDI" (ByVal hObject%)
Declare Function SelectObject%
➥Lib "GDI" (ByVal hDC%, ByVal hObject%)
Const INVERTMODE = 6
Const Left_Mouse = 1
Dim Toggle As Integer
Dim X1 As Single, Y1 As Single, X2 As Single, Y2 As Single
Dim CurrentButton As Integer
```

The ArtAPI program stores the dimensions of a bounding box using Type Rect data structures. Chapter 2, "The Artisan Program," covers the Type variable structure in the introduction of the Artisan program.

> **Dim BoundingBox As Rectangle**: The API FrameRect function uses a Type Rect structure to display the outline of a rectangular shape. The left, top, right, and bottom dimensions of this object are defined using the Type Rect data structure located in the APIDRAW.BAS file. The BoundingBox variable is then used to store the dimensions. An example is as follows:
>
> ```
> BoundingBox.Left = 10 : BoundingBox.Top = 15
> BoundingBox.Right = 150 : BoundingBox.Bottom = 100
> ```

Most API drawing functions require the dimensions or coordinates to be in pixel units.

> **Dim BoundingBox2 As Rectangle**: Used in the Pt_In_Rect example for this program.
>
> **Dim B As Integer**: Used to store the number of the rectangles drawn.
>
> **Dim W(1 To 20) As Integer**: Used to store the west or left coordinate of the object drawn. N(index), E(index), and S(index) are used to store the north (top), east (right), and south (bottom) coordinates of the object. The total number of coordinates values that can be stored in each W, N, E, and S array is 20.
>
> **Declare Function ExtFloodfill%**: One of several API drawing functions used within this program. There are more than 1,000 API functions available in programming.

### API Drawing Functions

The following list shows the most commonly used Windows 3.11 API drawing functions. Additionally, there are pen, brush, metafile, and bitmaps API functions. The 32-bit Windows operating system includes enhanced line and metafiles functions, as well as enabling the programmer to create Bézier curves.

| | | | |
|---|---|---|---|
| Arc | FrameRect | GetROP2 | PolyLine |
| Chord | FrameRgn | GetROP2 | PolyPolygon |
| DrawFocusRect | GetBkColor | LineTo | Rectangle |
| Ellipse | GetBkMode | MoveTo | RoundRect |
| ExtFloodFill | GetCurrentPosition | MoveToEx | SetBkColor |
| FillRect | GetNearestColor | PaintRgn | SetPixel |
| FillRgn | GetPixel | Pie | SetPoly |
| FloodFill | GetPolyFillMode | PolyGon | SetROP2 |

# API Drawing Programs

**Figure 8.2.**
*The available drawing functions.*

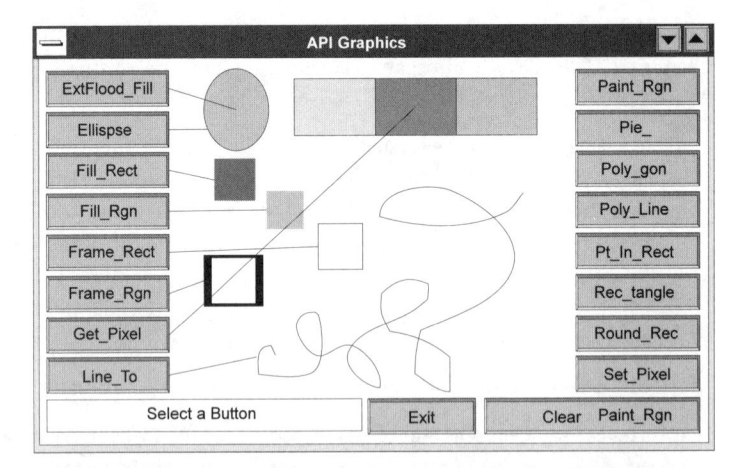

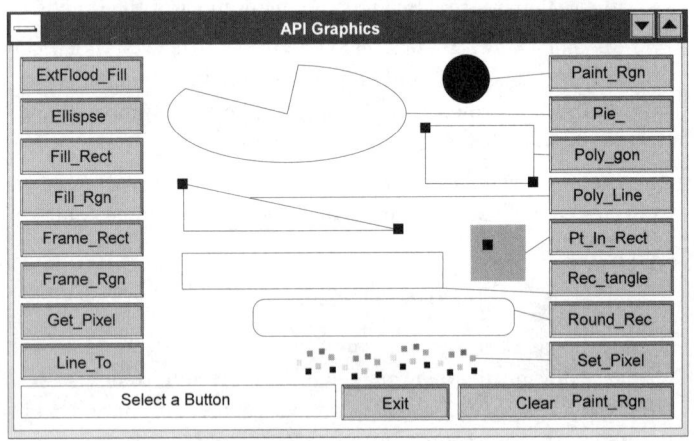

Listing 8.2 illustrates the Form_Load event starting up default values.

**Listing 8.2.** Form_Load event starts up default values.

```
Sub Form_Load ()
 Command1_Click (16)
 Toggle = True
End Sub
```

**Command1_Click (16):** Triggers the Clear Screen button (index button 16).

**Toggle:** Used in the Poly_gon and Poly_line procedures to switch each new line segment's start and end positions. Switches X1, Y1 to X2, Y2, and vice versa.

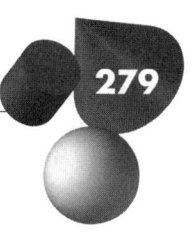

## Clicking an API Function Button

Each of the 17 indexed Command1 buttons on the form performs an API drawing function. Most of these functions are only performed when you click the form. The button you select stores its assigned index number to the variable named CurrentButton. The form events will know which button was selected by checking the value of CurrentButton. The CommandButton_Click event, for the most part, displays messages in the Label1 control instructing you what to do next.

**Listing 8.3. Displaying the action to take for each button.**

```
Sub Command1_Click (Index As Integer)
CurrentButton = Index

Select Case CurrentButton
  Case 0 'ExtFloodFill
    Label1.Caption = "Fill Area With Color"
  Case 1 'Ellipse
    Label1.Caption = "Drag to Draw Circle"
  Case 2 To 5 'Fill Rgn To Frame Rgn
    Label1.Caption = "Mouse Down"
  Case 6 'Get Pixel
    Label1.Caption = "Click Color Palette"
    Cls: DrawMode = 13
    Line (180, 50)-(230, 100), QBColor(1), BF
    Line (230, 50)-(280, 100), QBColor(2), BF
    Line (280, 50)-(330, 100), QBColor(3), BF
    DrawMode = 6
  Case 7 'Line_To
    Label1.Caption = "Drag to Draw Lines"
  Case 8 'Paint_Rgn
    Label1.Caption = "Mouse Down"
  Case 9 'Pie_
    Label1.Caption = "Drag to Draw Pie Shape"
  Case 10 'Poly_gon
    Label1.Caption = "Pick two Corner Points"
  Case 11 'Poly_Line
    Label1.Caption = "Pick two Angle Points"
  Case 12 'Pt_In_Rect
    Label1.Caption = "Draw Some Rectangles First"
  Case 13 To 14 'Rec_Tangle to Set_Pixel
    Label1.Caption = "Drag Mouse"
  Case 15 'Rec_Tangle to Set_Pixel
    Label1.Caption = "Drag Mouse"
    Line (0, 0)-(ScaleWidth, ScaleHeight \ 2), , BF
  Case 16 'CLS
    Label1.Caption = "Select a Button": Cls
  Case 17
    End
End Select
End Sub
```

# API Drawing Programs

**CurrentButton:** Keeps track of which indexed button you have selected.

**Select Case:** Depending on which button you selected, do the one of the following Case expressions:

**Case 0:** You have selected the button titled Flood_Fill.

**Case 1 To 17:** As in Case 0, you have selected a button whose caption matches the name of the API function. In most cases, a message will be displayed in the label control telling you what to do next. In Case 6, a three-panel palette is drawn in order to better demonstrate the GetPixel API function. In Case 15, a rectangle is drawn to enhance the SetPixel API function example.

### API Pen and Brush Functions

The following list shows the most commonly used Windows 3.11 API pen and brush functions.

| | | |
|---|---|---|
| CreatHatchBrush | CreatePenIndirect | DeleteObject |
| SelectObject | CreatPatternBrush | CreateSolidBrush |
| GetBrushOrg | SetBrushOrg | CreatePen |
| CreatBrushIndirect | GetStockObject | UnrealizeObject |

### API Rectangle and Region functions (bounding box)

The following list shows some of the most commonly used Windows 3.11 API Rect and Rgn functions.

| | | | |
|---|---|---|---|
| CopyRect | FillRgn | GetRgnBox | SetRect |
| CreateRectRgn | FrameRect | InfateRect | SetRectRgn |
| EqualRect | FrameRgn | OffsetRect | SetRectEmpty |
| FillRect | GetBoundsRect | Rectangle | SubtractRect |

## The Form's Mouse Events

The Form_MouseDown event in Listing 8.4 creates the default dimensions of the rectangular shapes used by API functions that require a Type Rect structure. The Select Case statement uses the value of CurrentButton to go to the Case that contains the proper procedure to branch off to. The CurrentButton value is the index of the button you have selected.

**Listing 8.4. Setting the first action or procedure call.**

```
Sub Form_MouseDown (Button%, Shift%, X As Single, Y As Single)
If CurrentButton = 2 Or CurrentButton = 4 Then 'needed for FillRect or FrameRect
    BoundingBox.Left = X - 20
    BoundingBox.Top = Y - 20
    BoundingBox.Right = X + 20
    BoundingBox.Bottom = Y + 20
End If
Select Case CurrentButton
    Case 2 'FillRect
        hndBrush% = CreateSolidBrush(RGB(0, 0, 255))
        R = FillRect(API_Form.hDC, BoundingBox, hndBrush%)
        R = DeleteObject(hndBrush%)
    Case 3 'FillRgn
        DrawMode = 13
        hrgn% = CreateRectRgn(X - 20, Y - 20, X + 20, Y + 20)
        hndBrush% = CreateSolidBrush(RGB(255, 0, 255))
        R = FillRgn(API_Form.hDC, hrgn%, hndBrush%)
        R = DeleteObject(hndBrush%)
        R = DeleteObject(hrgn%)
    Case 4 'FrameRect
        hndBrush% = CreateSolidBrush(RGB(0, 0, 255))
        R = FrameRect(API_Form.hDC, BoundingBox, hndBrush%)
        R = DeleteObject(hndBrush%)
    Case 5 'FrameRgn
        DrawMode = 13
        hrgn% = CreateRectRgn(X - 20, Y - 20, X + 20, Y + 20)
        hndBrush% = CreateSolidBrush(RGB(255, 0, 0))
        nWidth% = 8: nHeight% = 2
        R = FrameRgn(API_Form.hDC, hrgn%, hndBrush%, nWidth%, nHeight%)
        R = DeleteObject(hndBrush%)
        R = DeleteObject(hrgn%)
    Case 6
        Get_Pixel Button, Shift, X, Y
    Case 8 'PaintRgn
        hrgn% = CreateEllipticRgn(X - 20, Y - 20, X + 20, Y + 20)
        R = PaintRgn(API_Form.hDC, hrgn%)
        R = DeleteObject(hrgn%)
    Case 10 'Polygon
        DrawWidth = 4: PSet (X, Y): DrawWidth = 1
        Poly_gon Button, Shift, X, Y: Exit Sub
    Case 11 'Polyline
        DrawWidth = 4: PSet (X, Y): DrawWidth = 1
        Poly_Line Button, Shift, X, Y: Exit Sub
    Case 12 'Pt In Rect
        Pt_In_Rect Button, Shift, X, Y: Exit Sub
End Select
        X1 = X: Y1 = Y: X2 = X: Y2 = Y
        R = MoveTo(API_Form.hDC, X, Y)
End Sub
```

**If CurrentButton:** If you have selected the Fill_Rect or Frame_Rect buttons, you need to define the size of the rectangle using a Type data structure.

**BoundingBox.Left (Top, Right, Bottom):** The Type structure as defined in the DRAWAPI.BAS file.

# API Drawing Programs

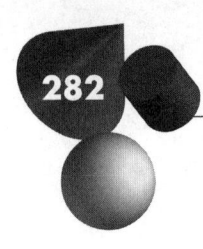

**CurrentButton:** Keeps track of which one of the 17 indexed buttons you have selected.

**Select Case:** Depending on which button you selected, do the one of the following Case expressions:

**Case 2:** API `FillRect` function.

> **CreateSolidBrush:** Creates a color to fill the rectangle with.
>
> **FillRect:** The API `FillRect` function has the following arguments: 1. The control to draw into, 2. The four screen position points, 3. the fill color.
>
> **DeleteObject:** You must kill the fill color brush so other events can use it.

**Case 3:** The API `FillRgn` function.

> **CreateRectRgn:** Manually creates the four screen points of a rectangle.
>
> **CreateSolidBrush:** Creates a color to fill the rectangle.
>
> **FillRgn:** The API `FillRgn` function has the following arguments: 1. What control to draw into, 2. The four screen position points, 3. the fill color.
>
> **DeleteObject:** You must kill the fill color and custom rectangle when you're finished.

**Case 4:** The API `FrameRect` function.

> **CreateSolidBrush:** Creates a color with which to boarder the rectangle.
>
> **FrameRect:** The API `FrameRect` function has the following arguments: 1. Control to draw into, 2. The four screen position points, 3. the fill color.
>
> **DeleteObject:** You must kill the fill color brush so other events can use it.

**Case 5:** The API `FrameRgn` function.

> **CreateRectRgn:** Manually creates the four screen points of a rectangle.
>
> **CreateSolidBrush:** Creates a color with which to boarder the rectangle.
>
> **nWidth:** This equals the thickness of the side borders.
>
> **nHeight:** This equals the thickness of the top and bottom borders.
>
> **FrameRgn:** The API `Frame Rect` function has the following arguments: 1. What control to draw into, 2. the four screen position points, 3. the border color, 4. the side border thickness, 5. the top and bottom border thickness.
>
> **DeleteObject:** You must kill the fill color and custom rectangle when you're finished.

**Case 6:** Go directly to the procedure `Get_Pixel`.

**Case 8:** The API `PaintRgn` function.

> **CreateEllipticRgn:** Manually creates the four points of an ellipse.
>
> **PaintRgn:** What control to draw into, the structured object to paint.
>
> **DeleteObject:** You must kill the custom object so other events can use it.

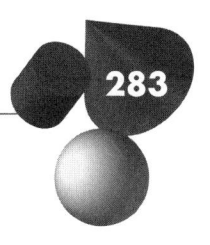

**Case 10:** Go directly to the procedure Poly_gon.

**Case 11:** Go directly to the procedure Poly_Line.

**Case 12:** Go directly to the procedure Pt_In_Rect.

Finally, assign the current X and Y positions of the mouse pointer so drawing a stretching bounding box can be achieved during the form's MouseMove events.

**X1, Y1, X2, Y2:** The standard MouseDown routine for drawing objects.

**R = MoveTo(API_Form.hDC, X, Y):** The API MoveTo function is used to indicate the starting coordinates of the scribbled line drawing used in the Line_To procedure.

The Form_MouseMove procedure in Listing 8.5 branches off to procedures that require the X and Y coordinates of the mouse pointer in order to draw moving objects.

**Listing 8.5. The API drawing operations.**
```
Sub Form_MouseMove (Button%, Shift%, X As Single, Y As Single)
If Button = Left_Mouse Then
Select Case CurrentButton
    Case 1 'Ellipse
        Ellipse_ Button, Shift, X, Y
    Case 7 'Line To
        Line_To Button, Shift, X, Y
    Case 9 'Pie
        Pie_ Button, Shift, X, Y
    Case 13 'Rectangle
        Rec_tangle Button, Shift, X, Y
    Case 14 'RoundRec
        Round_Rect Button, Shift, X, Y
    Case 15 'Set Pixel
        Set_Pixel Button, Shift, X, Y
End Select
End If
End Sub
```

**If Button = Left_Mouse Then:** If the left mouse button (1) is held, continue.

**Select Case CurrentButton:** The Select Case statement uses the value of CurrentButton to go to the Case that contains the proper procedure to branch off to. The CurrentButton value is the button you selected (the button's index number).

**Case 1 To 15:** Branches off to the procedure indicated in the Case. All procedures are passed the values of the mouse button, shift key, and the X and Y coordinates of the mouse pointer as it is being moved.

# Painting via the *FloodFill* Function

The Form_MouseUp event in Listing 8.6 is used to fill the entire form with a random color when you have selected the FloodFill button. The MouseUp event also counts the number of rectangles you have drawn on the form.

# API Drawing Programs

**Listing 8.6. Setting or resetting any needed values.**

```
Sub Form_MouseUp (Button%, Shift%, X As Single, Y As Single)
Select Case CurrentButton
    Case 0 'FloodFill
        DrawMode = 13
        color% = (14 * Rnd) + 1
        FillColor = QBColor(color%)
        R = ExtFloodfill(API_Form.hDC, X, Y, &H8, FloodFillBorder)
    Case 13 'Rectangle
        If B < 20 Then B = B + 1
        W(B) = X1: N(B) = Y1: E(B) = X2: S(B) = Y2
End Select
DrawMode = 6: FillStyle = 1
End Sub
```

**Select Case CurrentButton:** The Select Case statement uses the value of CurrentButton to go to the Case that contains the proper procedure to branch off to. The CurrentButton value is the index of the button you have selected.

**Case 0:** The API FloodFill function.

**DrawMode = 13: FillStyle = 0:** The drawing mode is set to 13, which is normal (copy_pen). In order to see the color used in a FloodFill, you must change the default FillStyle of transparent (1) to solid (0) or a pattern FillStyle (2 through 7).

**FillColor:** Selects a random color from the 16 available forms of the QBasic color values, excluding black (0). The chosen random color is used to paint the form's background.

**R = ExtFloodfill:** The API ExtFloodFill function has the following arguments: 1. what control to draw into, 2. the X, Y screen position to start the color fill, 3. the border color to use, 4. the type of fill style to perform.

**Case 13:** Stores a rectangle's coordinate points that are used with the Pt_In_Rect function. The maximum number of rectangles you can draw is 20.

## The API Drawing Functions

The variable used to call an API procedure represents a dummy value holder. The dummy variable can be named anything you want; for example, you can use API, dummy, or R, as long as the variable conforms to Visual Basic's variable naming standards. The dummy variable in most cases returns a value that tells you wheather the function was sucessful at performing the API function or not. An example follows:

```
API = LineTo(API_Form.hDC, X, Y)
```

If the API ToLine function was a sucess the return value in the API variable would be nonzero (for example, -1). If the function failed the return value would be zero (0).

Sometimes a successful API function returns the assigned numbers of window (handle) or other useful information. You can use ADD Watch, debug, print, or format$(*dummy name*) in a Visual Basic statement immediately after calling the API function to view the return values. An example follows:

Print *dummy name*, Label1.Caption = Format$(*dummy name*)

The following sections deals with the procedures that contain the API drawing functions.

## The *Ellipse* Function

You can draw a circle or ellipse with the Ellipse function. Listing 8.7 presents this function.

**Listing 8.7. The subroutine to draw an expandable circle or ellipse.**
```
Sub Ellipse_ (Button As Integer, Shift As Integer, X As Single, Y As Single)
R = Ellipse%(API_Form.hDC, X1, Y1, X2, Y2)
    X2 = X
    Y2 = Y
R = Ellipse%(API_Form.hDC, X1, Y1, X2, Y2)
End Sub
```

**Ellipse%:** The Ellipse% function needs to know the control to draw into (API_Form.hDC) and the four screen points of the ellipse (X1, Y1, X2, and Y2) as parameters. The circle or ellipse is within a bounding box from point X1, Y1 to X2, Y2.

**X2 = X: Y2 = Y:** Makes a corner position of the bounding box equal to the current mouse pointer's coordinate. You are drawing in Inverse mode, which draws the first image the reverse color of the background (white to black). If any of the next image drawn lands on a black pixel of the first image, it is drawn white (and vice versa). This gives the illusion of movement.

**Ellipse%:** Calls the ellipse procedure again for the illusion of movement.

## The *Get_Pixel* Function

The Get_Pixel function returns the color value of a pixel. This is a **hexidecimal** value. Listing 8.8 presents the Get_Pixel function, which uses the GetPixel API function.

**Listing 8.8. Get_Pixel returns the red, green, and blue values of a pixel.**
```
Sub Get_Pixel (Button As Integer, Shift As Integer, X As Single, Y As Single)
    RGB_Value = GetPixel(API_Form.hDC, X, Y)
    Msg$ = "RGB Value = "
    Label1.Caption = Msg$ + RGB_Value
End Sub
```

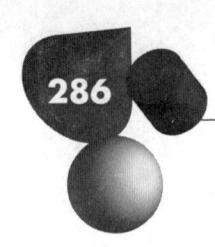

# API Drawing Programs

**RGB_Value:** The red, green, and blue values of the pixel on which you have clicked. The API GetPixel function has the following arguments: 1. The control you click the mouse on. 2. The X and Y coordinate of the mouse. On sucess, the return value is a hexadecimal RGB color value.

**Label1.Caption:** This is the caption displayed in Label1. For example, RGB value = 255 is a caption.

## The *Line_To* Function

The Line_To function is similar to Basic's PSet and Step Line statements and to the Postscript printer language in which you get the program to move to a stated coordinate within your drawing page.

**Listing 8.9. The Line_To procedure draws a continuous line.**

```
Sub Line_To (Button As Integer, Shift As Integer, X As Single, Y As Single)
    R = LineTo(API_Form.hDC, X, Y)
End Sub
```

**LineTo(hDC, X, Y):** The API LineTo function needs to know the control (API_Form.hDC) to start or move a coordinate point. This procedure draws a scribbled line as you move and hold down the mouse button.

## API *Pie* Function

The API Pie function found in the Pie_ procedure of Listing 8.10 is rather inept for drawing a moving pie shape since the pie's side wedges leave traces of pixels if the x3, y3, x4, y4 values change as the mouse is moved. This is also true for the x3, y3 values used in the API RoundRect function.

If the pie's side wedges remain a constant value as the pie is being moved, the shape will display correctly. Refer to the MetaFile program in the 16MISC directory of the companion disk for an example of a pie using constant side wedge values.

I suggest using a manual drawing routine using the standard Visual Basic Circle statements to display moving pie shapes. An example of moving an object with both straight and curved line segments is demonstrated in Chapter 11, "The Rounded Corners Program."

The pie's wedge shape is drawn independently from the circles arc shape. The sides of the wedge are lines connected to the center of the circle. Where you place the end points of these two lines determines the angle of each wedge line.

In the following API Pie function in Listing 8.10, one wedge line follows the mouse pointer. The opposite side's wedge line is drawn at a random location. You should move the mouse slowly across the desktop in order to view the changing pie shape.

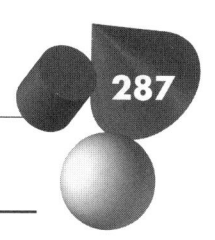

**Listing 8.10.** Drawing an expandable pie shape.

```
Sub Pie_ (Button As Integer, Shift As Integer, X As Single, Y As Single)
    ForeColor = BackColor
    R = Pie(API_Form.hDC, X1, Y1, X2, Y2, X3, Y3, X4, Y4)
        X2 = X
        Y2 = Y

        X3 = X2             'wedge side follow mouse
        Y3 = Y2
        X4 = X2 * Rnd       'wedge side is random
        Y4 = Y2 * Rnd
    BackColor = ForeColor
    R = Pie(API_Form.hDC, X1, Y1, X2, Y2, X3, Y3, X4, Y4)
End Sub
```

**ForeColor = BackColor:** Since the API Pie function plays havoc with the draw mode, reverse this action. However, switching the ForeColor and BackColor is not recommended and you may want to manually draw pie shapes. Refer to Chapter 11, "The Rounded Corners Program."

**Pie:** The API Pie function needs to know the control (API_Form.hDC) it draws into and the eight points of the pie shape (X1, Y1, X2, Y2, X3, Y3, X4, and Y4).

**X2 = X, Y2 = Y:** Makes the corner position of the bounding box equal to the current mouse pointer's coordinate. This will give the illusion of movement.

**X3, Y3:** The side of the pie's wedge line that follows the mouse pointer.

**X4, Y4:** Side of the pie's wedge line that is placed at a random screen coordinate.

**BackColor = ForeColor:** Reverses the drawing color again.

**Pie:** Calls the Pie procedure again for the illusion of movement.

## Polygons

Polygons are shapes made of lines connected end to end in a closed loop. This is referred to as a **closed** polygon shape. A triangle is an example of a polygon shape with three points. Listing 8.11 presents the Polygon function being used to draw a rectangular, polygon shape.

**Listing 8.11.** Drawing a rectangular, polygon shape.

```
Sub Poly_gon (Button As Integer, Shift As Integer, X As Single, Y As Single)
Dim N As Integer
Static POINTS(1 To 5) As PointXY
    If Toggle = True Then
        X1 = X: Y1 = Y
    Else
        X2 = X: Y2 = Y
POINTS(1).X = X1  'Draw a Star shape
POINTS(1).Y = Y1
POINTS(2).X = X1 - (X2 - X1)
POINTS(2).Y = Y2
POINTS(3).X = X2
POINTS(3).Y = Y1 + ((Y2 - Y1) \ 3)
```

*continues*

**Listing 8.11.** continued

```
POINTS(4).X = X1 - (X2 - X1)
POINTS(4).Y = Y1 + ((Y2 - Y1) \ 3)
POINTS(5).X = X2
POINTS(5).Y = Y2
N = 5
R = Polygon(API_Form.hDC, POINTS(1), N)
End If
Toggle = Not Toggle
End Sub
```

**Dim N As Integer:** N represents the total number of points in the polygon.

**Static POINTS(1 To 5) As PointXY:** POINTS represents an array that holds the polygon's screen position points. The X and Y coordinates must be in pixel units. A Type structure in the APIDRAW.BAS file is used to define the X and Y screen points. This example uses five X, Y values (1 to 5). To draw a polygon that has more points, increase the array's size.

**If Toggle = True Then:** On the first mouse click, the variable Toggle equals True, which will make the variables X1 and Y1 equal the mouse pointer's current X and Y coordinate. On the second mouse click, the variable Toggle equals False, and the POINT variables 2, 3, 4, and 5 have their X and Y values set which will create a polygon star shape on the desktop.

**POINT(1).X: POINT(1).Y:** The first X and Y points of the polygon shape.

**POINT(2).X: POINT(2).Y:** The second X and Y points of the polygon shape.

**POINT(3).X: POINT(3).Y:** The third X and Y points of the polygon shape.

**POINT(4).X: POINT(4).Y:** The fourth X and Y points of the polygon shape.

**POINT(5).X: POINT(5).Y:** The fifth X and Y points of the polygon shape.

**N = 5:** There are five coordinate points in this drawing. If there were more points in the polygon, you would increase this number accordingly.

**R = Polygon:** This API function needs to know the control (.hDC) to draw into, the starting point for drawing (POINTS(1)), and the total number of X, Y coordinates to draw. For example:

```
API = Polygon(API_Form.hDC, POINTS(1), N)
```

The polygon's first point uses the values stored in the index specified (Point(index)). The drawing then uses the values in the next highest index number (and so forth) until it reaches the index number specified by N. If you set the starting point to an index higher than the total of the array, you will get an error.

**Toggle = Not Toggle:** At startup, the toggle variable equals True. The Not operator switches the True value to False. The next time this statement is executed, False becomes True (and so forth).

## The *Polyline* Function

The API `Polyline` function is relatively the same as the API `Polygon` function except that the start and end points are not connected automatically and is referred to as an **open** poly shape. The API `Polyline` function is the same as Visual Basic's `Line` statements using the `Step` option to connect lines together. Sometimes, Visual Basic's `Line` statement is easier to work since less code is needed. Listing 8.12 presents the code to draw a triangular polyline shape.

**Listing 8.12. Drawing a triangular polyline shape.**

```
Sub Poly_Line (Button As Integer, Shift As Integer, X As Single, Y As Single)
Dim N As Integer
Static POINTS(1 To 5) As PointXY
    If Toggle = True Then
        X1 = X: Y1 = Y
    Else
        X2 = X: Y2 = Y
POINTS(1).X = X1    'Draw a Star shape
POINTS(1).Y = Y1
POINTS(2).X = X1 - (X2 - X1)
POINTS(2).Y = Y2
POINTS(3).X = X2
POINTS(3).Y = Y1 + ((Y2 - Y1) \ 3)
POINTS(4).X = X1 - (X2 - X1)
POINTS(4).Y = Y1 + ((Y2 - Y1) \ 3)
POINTS(5).X = X2
POINTS(5).Y = Y2
FirstPoint = 1: TotalPoints = 5
R = Polyline(API_Form.hDC, POINTS(FirstPoint), TotalPoints)
End If
Toggle = Not Toggle
End Sub
```

> **R = Polyline:** The API `Polyline` function is relatively the same as the API `Polygon` function except that the start and end points are not connected automatically. Refer to the `Poly_gon` procedure in Listing 8.11 for explanations on how a polygon shape is created.

## The *Pt_In_Rect* Function

The `Pt_In_Rect` routine presented in Listing 8.13 is very important in drawing programs. The API `PtInRect` function can automatically search an array of bounding boxes to determine whether the mouse pointer's coordinate is within one of the bounding boxes.

The Artisan program stores the bounding box positions of each object drawn in separate arrays (`W(B)`, `N(B)`, `E(B)`, `S(B)`), and then searches through all four arrays to find the object. However, you could store each bounding box in a single `Type` structure or multi-array and call the API `PtInRect` function to determine whether the mouse pointer is within any bounding box object or `Rect` structure. The Artisan program uses the API `PtInRect` function to locate objects that the mouse pointer touches.

# API Drawing Programs

**Listing 8.13. Determining whether the mouse pointer is within a bounding box.**

```
Sub Pt_In_Rect (Button As Integer, Shift As Integer, X As Single, Y As Single)
LastB = B
For B = 1 To 20
    BoundingBox2.Left = W(B)
    BoundingBox2.Top = N(B)
    BoundingBox2.Right = E(B)
    BoundingBox2.Bottom = S(B)
    XY& = X + CLng(Y) * &H10000
        If PtInRectBynum%(BoundingBox2, XY&) Then
            DrawWidth = 4: PSet (X, Y): Exit For
        End If
Next B
B = LastB
    If DrawWidth = 4 Then
        Label1.Caption = "Point is in Rectangle": DrawWidth = 1
    Else
        Label1.Caption = "Point is not in Rectangle"
    End If
End Sub
```

**For B = 1 To 20:** You can draw up to 20 rectangles on this program, The For...Next statement loops 20 times so the API PtInRect function can check all possible bounding box coordinates.

**BoundingBox.Left (Top, Right, Bottom):** This is the Type structure as defined in the ARTAPI.BAS file. The API PtInRect functions needs the left, top, right, and top coordinates of the rectangle to be passed as a Rect structure.

**XY& = X + CLng(Y) * &H10000:** Remember this formula; it is used to send the X and Y coordinate positions as one LONG data value. This formula splices the two 16-bit values together, placing the X position is the low order and the Y position is the high order of a 32-bit value. The variable XY& contains the value of X plus the value of Y converted to a (CLng) Long value times 65,536.

**PtInRectBynum%:** The API PtInRectBynum function receives the bounding box that you are searching for (BoundingBox2) and any X, Y point that falls within the inside dimensions of the bounding box (XY&).

**If PtInRect%:** When you click a mouse down event and if the mouse pointer is within the bounding box, the Pset statement draws a big dot, which indicates that the bounding box has been found. The Label.Caption then reads Point is inside rectangle.

## The Rec_tangle Function

The Rec_tangle procedure shown in Listing 8.14 is similar to Visual Basic's Line statement using the B option, which tells the Line statement to draw a box shape.

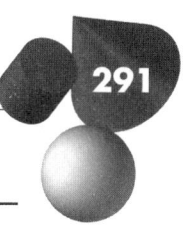

**Listing 8.14.** Drawing a expandable rectangle or box.
```
Sub Rec_tangle (Button As Integer, Shift As Integer, X As Single, Y As Single)
    R = Rectangle(API_Form.hDC, X1, Y1, X2, Y2)
        X2 = X
        Y2 = Y
    R = Rectangle(API_Form.hDC, X1, Y1, X2, Y2)
End Sub
```

**R = Rectangle:** The API Rectangle function needs to know the control to draw into (API_Form.hDC) and the four screen points of the rectangle (X1, Y1, X2, and Y2).

**X2 = X, Y2 = Y:** Makes the corner position of the bounding box equal to the current mouse pointer's coordinate. This will give the illusion of movement.

**R = Rectangle:** Calls the API Rectangle function again for the illusion of movement.

## The *Round_Rect* Function

The Round_Rect procedure presented in Listing 8.15 draws an expanded rectangle with rounded corners. The API RoundRec function draws a rounded rectangle using a rectangle and four ellipses at each corner. See the Pie procedure in Listing 8.10 for an explanation on why you must set ForeColor equal to BackColor.

**Listing 8.15.** Drawing an expandable rectangle with rounded corners.
```
Sub Round_Rect (Button%, Shift%, X As Single, Y As Single)
ForeColor = BackColor
    R = RoundRect(API_Form.hDC, X1, Y1, X2, Y2, X3, Y3)
        X2 = X
        Y2 = Y
        X3 = 50
        Y3 = 50
        BackColor = ForeColor
    R = RoundRect(API_Form.hDC, X1, Y1, X2, Y2, X3, Y3)
End Sub
```

**R = RoundRec:** The RoundRec API function needs to know the control (API_Form.hDC) to draw into and the six screen position points (X1, Y1, X2, Y2, X3, and Y3).

**X2 = X, Y2 = Y:** Makes a corner position of the bounding box equal to the current mouse pointer's coordinate. This will give the illusion of movement.

**X3:** The width of the ellipse (each of the four rounded corners).

**Y3:** The height of the ellipse (each of the four rounded corners).

**R = RoundRec:** Calls the API RoundRec function again for the illusion of movement.

## The *SetPixel* Function

The `Set_Pixel` procedure presented in Listing 8.16 is basically the same as Visual Basics `PSet` statement.

**Listing 8.16. Spray-painting a rainbow of pixels.**

```
Sub Set_Pixel (Button As Integer, Shift As Integer, X As Single, Y As Single)
    DrawMode = 13
    crColor& = QBColor(15 * Rnd)
    R = SetPixel(API_Form.hDC, X, Y, crColor&)
End Sub
```

**DrawMode = 13:** Sets the drawing of pixels mode to normal (`Copy_Pen`).

**crColor&:** The red, green, and blue values of the pixel to draw.

**SetPixel:** The API `SetPixel` function needs to know the control (`API_Form.hDC`) drawn into, the X, Y position of the pixel (X and Y), and the color to use (`crColor&`).

# 32-Bit API Drawing Functions

The following are some commonly used 32-bit API functions for Windows operating systems that can define 32-bit API functions.

| | | | |
|---|---|---|---|
| AngleArc* | FillRect | Polyline | SetBkMode |
| AnimatePalette | FillRgn | PolyPolygon | SetDIBitsToDevice |
| Arc | FloodFill | PolyPolyline | SetPixel |
| ArcTo* | GetDIBits | RealizePalette | SetPolyFillMode |
| BeginPath* | GetPath* | Rectangle | SetROP2 |
| BitBlt | IntersectClipRect | RestoreDC | SetStretchBltMode |
| Chord | LineTo | RoundRect | SetTextColor |
| CloseFigure* | MakePath* | PtInRegion | SetTextJustification |
| CopyEnhMetaFile* | MaskBlt* | SaveDC | SetViewportExt |
| CreatBrushIndirect | MoveToEx | ScaleViewportExt | SetWindowExt |
| CreateDIBitmap | OffsetClipRgn | ScaleWindowExt | SetWindowOrg |
| CreateDIBPatternBrush | OffsetViewportOrg | SelectClipPath* | StretchBlt |
| CreateEnhMetaFile* | OffsetWindowOrg | SelectClipRgn | StrokeAndFillPath* |
| CreateFontIndirect | PatBlt | SelectFont | StrokePath* |
| CreatePatternBrush | PathToRegion* | SelectObject | StretchDIBits |
| DeleteObject | Pie | SelectPalette | TextOut |

| | | | |
|---|---|---|---|
| Ellipse | PlayEnhMetaFile* | SetArcDirection* | WidenPath* |
| EndPath* | PlgBlt* | SetBkColor | |
| EnumEnhMetaFile* | PolyBezier* | SetMapMode | |
| ExcludeClipRect | PolyBezierTo* | SetWindowExtEx | |
| ExtTextOut | PolyDraw* | SetViewportExtEx | |
| FillPath* | Polygon | SetViewportOrgEx | |

*New to the Windows API library.

# Summary

The API drawing functions can be used to replace Line, Circle, and PSet statements in Visual Basic. In some cases, though, Visual Basic graphical statements can out-perform the output created by APIs, and you also have the bonus of typing less code. On the other hand, there are graphical operations that cannot be easily performed in Visual Basic because they are not featured as methods or functions, or statements within the language. An example is the DOS Basic language Paint statement that paints an area of the screen. Visual Basic, however, has to rely on the API FloodFill or ExtFloodFill functions to achieve the same effect.

The ArtAPI program in Chapter 15 is a reconstruction of the Artisan program found in Chapter 2. The Artisan program uses basic graphical statements to draw object shapes onto the desktop. The ArtAPI program replaces these basic graphical statements with API functions to draw the same object shapes on the desktop. When drawing a line, box, or circle shapes, you don't have to use the API LineTo, Rectangle, or Ellipse functions since Visual Basic's Line and Circle statements do the job just as efficiently. You will, however, need the API graphical functions when you paint complex object shapes. The Join Nodes program in Chapter 13 demonstrates painting a polygon-shaped object using API graphical functions.

# CHAPTER 9

# Fountain Blends

# Fountain Blends

Fountain fills are sometimes called *gradient fills*. A fountain fill blends two colors defined at opposite ends of a bounding box, resulting in smooth gradiation of colors between the two. This can give an object an air brush or shading effect. The Palette program uses vertical bands of color to create the fountain fills. Each band of color consists of a `Line` statement using the box fill option (`BF`). In order to create fountain fills that are at an angle, you need to manually draw each side of an angled box shape and then fill the shape with color. In DOS versions of the Basic language, the `Draw` statement had an angle option that made this relatively easy to achieve. However, in Visual Basic, you need to use a combination of an API polyline or line drawing method with the API `FloodFill` function.

The Palette program shows two ways to blend shades of color between two color ranges. Figure 9.1 presents the main screen of the Palette program. The `Fill_Button` control, with the Fountain Fill caption, uses the `PicBlend` picture box control to display each range of color by using the Visual Basic `Line` statement to draw boxes filled with the appropriate color. The `Line` statement's color description uses the Palette program's procedure called `RGBcolor&` to assign each new color, which creates the fountain fill blend effect. (See Figure 9.2.)

Create the fountain fill by using the formula within the Palette program's `RGBcolor&` function to find the difference between each red, green, and blue color element of the two colors you selected in the `PicRGB` picture box palettes. The `Pic_Blend` picture box is then scaled into palette-like sections (strips) to hold each new color of the fountain fill.

The second fountain fill method in this program uses the API library functions to manually separate each of the red, green, and blue elements of a color. The methods used to draw each color blend are relatively the same as the `RGB` method. The `DitherBtn` button control, with the API Dithered caption calls the `Draw_Blends` function to draw the fountain fill colors directly on the form.

The Palette program's `APIcolor&` function then uses a formula to separate the individual red, green, and blue elements of the color. Finally, the `CreateCustomPalette` procedure indexes each range of color between the two colors you selected from the `PicRGB` picture box palettes.

**Figure 9.1.**
*The Palette program.*

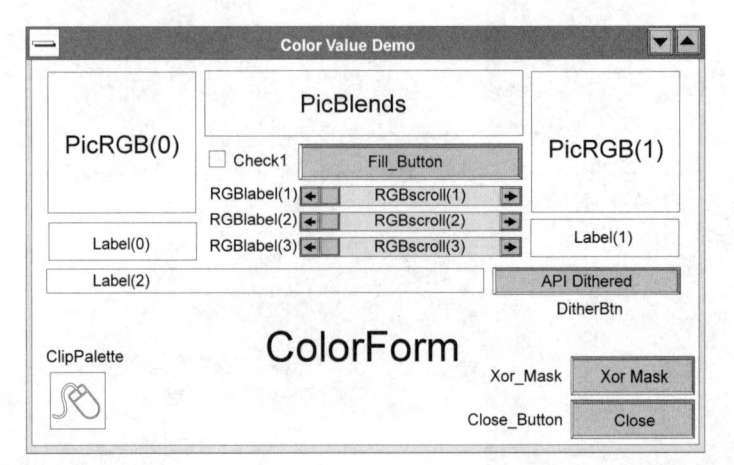

**F**igure 9.2.
*Screen shot in the Palette program.*

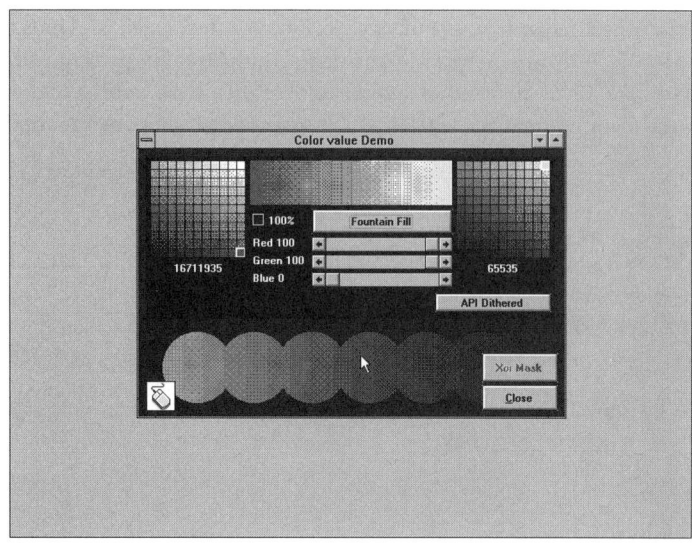

## Structures to Hold the Colors

The Type structures LOGPALETTE and PALETTEENTRY defined in the PALETTE.BAS file locate and separate each red, green, and blue color element much in the same way the Visual Basic RGB statement does.

Using LOGPALETTE and PALETTEENTRY type structures to define color elements lets you use API palette functions. In the Fountain Fill program, use the API CreatePalette function to copy a palette to the clipboard and use this palette information as a Picture property to load into the main form. If you have a VGA display card capable of displaying 256 colors or more, you will get a stunning display of pure blended colors. To see the same representation of colors in a plain dithered format (various dot patterns made up of the basic 16 colors to simulate pure colors), select the fountain fill button.

> **NOTE** This program assumes you are using a driver with a display of 256. If you are using a display driver higher than 256 colors, dithered pattern effects will not be visible. For instance, some 65,536+ display drivers display only pure colors in Visual Basic. If you are using a VGA card that only supports 16 colors, you will not be able to build a custom clipboard palette; thus, the icon with a picture of a mouse pointing device will have a visual palette effect in this program.

Use the Xor_Mask button control with the Xor Mask caption to fill an object of any shape or size with a fountain fill blend.

# Fountain Blends

Use the scrollbars to display a single color. Each red, green, and blue color has a range from values 0 to 25. When the Check1 `Label` control displays 255 percent, each scroll label will show red, green, and blue elements of a given color. When the Check1 `Label` control displays 100 percent, each color element is divided by 2.55 to show the values in a range between 0 and 100 percent.

Table 9.1 lists the Palette program's form and control properties.

**Table 9.1. The properties of the Palette form and controls.**

*Object: Form*
*Object Name: Colorform*

| | | | |
|---|---|---|---|
| BackColor | = &H00FF0000& | Caption | = "Color value Demo" |
| Height | = 4920 | Left | = 1245 |
| ScaleMode | = 3 'Pixel | Top | = 1230 |
| Width | = 7530 | | |

*Object: Picture Box*
*Object Name: ClipPalette*

| | | | |
|---|---|---|---|
| AutoSize | = -1 'True | Enabled | = 0 'False |
| Height | = 510 | Left | = 120 |
| Picture | = Mouse icon | Top | = 3960 |
| Width | = 510 | | |

*Object: Command Button*
*Object Name: Close_Button*

| | | | |
|---|---|---|---|
| Caption | = "&Close" | Height | = 435 |
| Left | = 6000 | Top | = 4020 |
| Width | = 1335 | | |

*Object: Command Button*
*Object Name: Xor_Mask*

| | | | |
|---|---|---|---|
| Caption | = "Xor Mask" | Enabled | = 0 'False |
| Height | = 495 | Left | = 6000 |
| Top | = 3480 | Width | = 1335 |

*Object: Frame*
*Object Name: Frame1*

| | | | |
|---|---|---|---|
| BackColor | = &H00000000& | Height | = 2775 |
| Left | = 120 | Top | = 120 |
| Width | = 7155 | | |

*Object: Command Button*
*Object Name: DitherBtn*

| | | | |
|---|---|---|---|
| Caption | = "API Dithered" | Enabled | = 0 'False |
| Height | = 315 | Left | = 5040 |
| Top | = 2340 | Width | = 2055 |

*Object: HScrollBar*
*Object Name: RGBscroll   3 indexed control*

| | | | |
|---|---|---|---|
| Height | = 255 | Index | = 0 To 3 |
| LargeChange | = 35 | Max | = 255 |
| SmallChange | = 4 | Width | = 2475 |

*Object: Picture Box*
*Object Name: PicBlend*

| | | | |
|---|---|---|---|
| BackColor | = &H000000FF& | Height | = 795 |
| Left | = 1800 | MousePointer | = 2 'Cross |
| Top | = 60 | Width | = 3555 |

*Object: Picture Box*
*Object Name: PicRGB*

| | | | |
|---|---|---|---|
| Height | = 1680 | Index | = 0 |
| Left | = 60 | ScaleHeight | = 110 |
| ScaleMode | = 3 'Pixel | ScaleWidth | = 110 |
| Top | = 60 | Width | = 1680 |

*Object: Picture Box*
*Object Name: PicRGB*

| | | | |
|---|---|---|---|
| Height | = 1680 | Index | = 1 |
| Left | = 5400 | ScaleHeight | = 110 |
| ScaleMode | = 3 'Pixel | ScaleWidth | = 110 |
| Top | = 60 | Width | = 1680 |

*Object: Command Button*
*Object Name: Fill_Button*

| | | | |
|---|---|---|---|
| Caption | = "Fountain Fill" | Enabled | = 0 'False |
| Height | = 435 | Left | = 2880 |
| Top | = 900 | Width | = 2475 |

*continues*

**T**able 9.1. continued

*Object: Check Box*
*Object Name: Check1*

| | | | |
|---|---|---|---|
| BackColor | = &H00000000& | Caption | = "100%" |
| ForeColor | = &H00FFFFFF& | Height | = 375 |
| Left | = 1860 | Top | = 900 |
| Width | = 915 | | |

*Object: Label*
*Object Name: Label1*

| | | | |
|---|---|---|---|
| Alignment | = 2 'Center | BackColor | = &H00FFFFFF& |
| BorderStyle | = 1 'Fixed Single | ForeColor | = &H00FFFFFF& |
| Height | = 315 | Index | = 2 |
| Left | = 60 | Top | = 2340 |
| Width | = 4875 | | |

*Object: Label*
*Object Name: RGBlabel*

| | | | |
|---|---|---|---|
| BackColor | = &H00000000& | Caption | = "Red 0" |
| ForeColor | = &H00FFFFFF& | Height | = 255 |
| Index | = 1 | Left | = 1860 |
| Top | = 1380 | Width | = 1035 |

*Object: Label*
*Object Name: RGBlabel*

| | | | |
|---|---|---|---|
| BackColor | = &H00000000& | Caption | = "Green 0" |
| ForeColor | = &H00FFFFFF& | Height | = 255 |
| Index | = 2 | Left | = 1860 |
| Top | = 1680 | Width | = 1035 |

*Object: Label*
*Object Name: RGBlabel*

| | | | |
|---|---|---|---|
| BackColor | = &H00000000& | Caption | = "Blue 0" |
| ForeColor | = &H00FFFFFF& | Height | = 195 |
| Index | = 3 | Left | = 1860 |
| Top | = 1980 | Width | = 1035 |

*Object: Label*
*Object Name: Label1*

| | | | |
|---|---|---|---|
| Alignment | = 2 'Center | BackColor | = &H00FFFFFF& |
| BorderStyle | = 1 'Fixed Single | ForeColor | = &H00FFFFFF& |
| Height | = 435 | Index | = 0 |
| Left | = 60 | Top | = 1800 |
| Width | = 1695 | | |

*Object: Label*
*Object Name: Label1*

| | | | |
|---|---|---|---|
| Alignment | = 2 'Center | BackColor | = &H00FFFFFF& |
| BorderStyle | = 1 'Fixed Single | ForeColor | = &H00FFFFFF& |
| Height | = 435 | Index | = 1 |
| Left | = 5400 | Top | = 1800 |
| Width | = 1695 | | |

## The Palette Program's Declarations

Listing 9.1 presents the default variables used in the Palette program.

### Listing 9.1. The default variables used in this program.

```
Declarations
Dim ColorIndex&(0 To 120) 'stores each color value
Dim Pic1Red, Pic1Green, Pic1Blue As Integer 'RGB of PicRGB(0)
Dim Pic2Red, Pic2Green, Pic2Blue As Integer 'RGB of PicRGB(1)
```

**Dim ColorIndex&(0 To 120):** There are two PicRGB picture box controls, each containing 121 colors. The ColorIndex& array stores each color's values for the currently selected PicRGB picture box color palette. The PicRGB_Paint event updates this array each time the user selects a color.

**Dim Pic1Red, Pic1Green, Pic1Blue:** Store the red, green, and blue color elements from the PicRGB (index 0) picture box control located on the left side. When the user selects a color from the PicRGB palette, the MouseDown event contains a formula to separate the red, green, and blue elements of the color. These values are then saved in the Pic1Red, Pic1Green, and Pic1Blue variables to use in forthcoming procedures.

**Dim Pic2Red, Pic2Green, Pic2Blue:** Same as the Pic1Red, Pic1Green, and Pic1Blue variables except you are using the second PicRGB (index 1) picture box control.

## The *Form_Resize* Routine

The Palette program's `Form_Resize` routine is used to set the color of the label control's background to black. This routine is presented in Listing 9.2.

**Listing 9.2. Setting the label control's back color to black.**

```
Sub Form_Resize ()
    Label1(0).BackColor = Frame1.BackColor
    Label1(1).BackColor = Frame1.BackColor
    Label1(2).BackColor = Frame1.BackColor
End Sub
```

**`Label1(index).BackColor = Frame1.BackColor`:** Set the background color for each `Label` control to black to match the form's background color. This is to help you see the label's captions better.

## The Two Main Color Palettes

The two `PicRGB` picture box palettes display the 121 colors using the `PicRGB_Paint` event. The first palette ((`PicRGB(0)`) uses a constant 255 value of blue for each color, and the second palette ((`PicRGB(1)`) uses a constant 0 value of blue for each color. The paint events are executed first for the `PicRGB(0)` then `PicRGB(1)`. Using an `If...Else` statement enables you to change the constant blue values used by both picture boxes.

The next step is to evenly divide the color ranges that you'll display in each palette. The first `PicRGB(0)` palette's prime colors are pure cyan, white, blue, and magenta. Evenly scaled amounts of red and green are then subtracted or added to graduate the shade of between `PicRGB(0)`'s four prime colors. The second `PicRGB(1)` palette's prime colors are represented by pure green, yellow, black, and red. Even graduated shades make up the colors between these prime colors. Evenly scaled amounts of red and green are then subtracted or added to graduate the shade of between `PicRGB(1)`'s four prime colors. (See Figure 9.3.)

**Figure 9.3.**
*The order in which the prime colors are generated.*

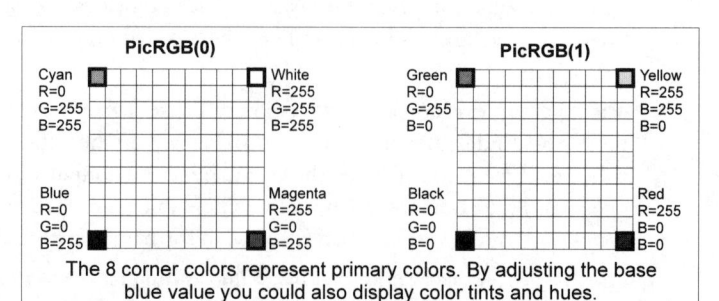

PicRGB(0)

Cyan — R=0, G=255, B=255
White — R=255, G=255, B=255
Blue — R=0, G=0, B=255
Magenta — R=255, G=0, B=255

PicRGB(1)

Green — R=0, G=255, B=0
Yellow — R=255, G=255, B=0
Black — R=0, G=0, B=0
Red — R=255, G=0, B=0

The 8 corner colors represent primary colors. By adjusting the base blue value you could also display color tints and hues.

Chapter **9**

With eight ranges of prime colors, you can display most colors within a relatively small grid. Furthermore, by increasing or decreasing amounts of blue (which are preset at 255 or 0), you can createhues of yellow, white, blue, and black to display any one of 16,777,216 color combinations.

By scaling both `PicRGB` picture boxes to 11 by 11 units, you get an even distribution of colors between each color cell in the palettes. (See Listing 9.3.)

**Listing 9.3. Drawing the 121 colors within each `PicRGB` picture box control.**

```
Sub PicRGB_Paint (Index As Integer)
    PicRGB(Index).Scale (0, 0)-(11, 11)
    colordown = 100: Colorup = 0 'color start values
    If Index = 0 Then BaseColor = 100 * 2.55 Else BaseColor = 0 'base color blue
For Y1 = 0 To 10
    For X1 = 0 To 10
        Red1 = Colorup * 2.55: Green2 = colordown * 2.55: Blue3 = BaseColor
        ''Label1(2).Caption = "Red " + Format$(Red1) + " Green " +
            ➥Format$(Green2) + " Blue " + Format$(Blue3)
        PicRGB(Index).Line (X1, Y1)-(10 + X1, 10 + Y1), RGB(Red1, Green2, Blue3), BF
        ColorIndex(i) = RGB(Red1, Green2, Blue3): i = i + 1
        PicRGB(Index).Line (X1, Y1)-(10 + X1, 10 + Y1), , B
        Colorup = Colorup + 10
    Next X1 'next column to the right
        Colorup = 0: colordown = colordown - 10
Next Y1 'next row below
End Sub
```

**`PicRGB(Index).Scale (0, 0)-(11, 11)`:** Scale the internal dimension of each picture box to an 11-by-11 grid in order to draw each palette cell.

**`colordown = 100: Colorup = 0`:** This represents the starting point from which to add or subtract even amounts of either red or green color.

**`If Index = 0 Then BaseColor = 100 * 2.55 Else BaseColor = 0`:** There are two `PicRGB` picture box palettes. The first palette (index 0) has a constant blue element value of 255. The second palette (index 0) has a constant blue element value of 0.

**`For Y1 = 0 To 10`:** Used to set each new row of color in the palette.

**`For X1 = 0 To 10`:** Used to set 11 colors within each row.

**`Red1 = Colorup * 2.55: Green2 = colordown * 2.55: Blue3 = BaseColor`:** The red and green elements are added or subtracted to the last values used to set the correct color within each cell.

**`Label1(2).Caption = "Red " + Format$(Red1) + etc.`:** To view the drawing of each cell, remove the `ReMark Out` (') and add a `Stop` just before this statement. Use the F5 key after each stop to quickly view the color cell drawn.

# Fountain Blends

`PicRGB(Index).Line (X1, Y1)-(1 + X1, 1 + Y1), RGB(Red1, Green2, Blue3), BF:` This statement draws each cell and inserts a color. The `ScaleHeight` and `ScaleWidth` of each `PicRGB` picture box control are set to 110 units each. You could reset the value of 1 used in the `Line` Statement to 10 and then change the loop statement to read `For Y1 = 0 To 100 Step 10 : For X1 = 0 To 100 Step 10` since the internal pixel dimensions are at scale to the formula already.

`ColorIndex(i) = RGB(Red1, Green2, Blue3):` Stores the 121 hexadecimal color values of the current palette being drawn. The `PicRGB_Paint` event is triggered every time you use the mouse to select a color. The 121 indexes correspond with the 121 color values of the current palette. The `i = i + 1` code increases the index count by 1 for each of the 121 loops.

`PicRGB(Index).Line (X1, Y1)-(1 + X1, 1 + Y1), , B:` Draw the black border lines around each cell.

`Colorup = Colorup + 10:` `Colorup` equals 0 at the start of this event and works its way up to the 255. When the `Y1` value in the loop equals 10, `Colorup` will equal 100. The `Colorup` variable (100) times 2.55 will then equal the highest color element value of any RGB color.

`Next X1:` Continue the inside loop to draw the next cell across the control.

`Colorup = 0: Colordown = Colordown - 10:` After each row is complete, the `Colorup` variable is reset to 0, and the `Colordown` variable is decreased by 10 to graduate the block of colors.

`Next Y1:` The next row of colors starts, and the inside loop repeats again.

## Selecting a Color from the Palette

The `PicRGB_MouseDown` in Listing 9.4 draws a white box around the selected color and then grabs the hexadecimal color value that was stored in the `ColorIndex` array that matches the cell number. You then manually extract the red, green, and blue elements of the selected color and display these values in the corresponding `RGBscroll` label controls.

**Listing 9.4. Highlighting the selected color and setting the index color value.**

```
Sub PicRGB_MouseDown (Index As Integer, Button As Integer, Shift As Integer, X As
Single, Y As Single)
Xor_Mask.Enabled = False
    PicRGB_Paint Index
    X = Fix(X): Y = Fix(Y)
PicRGB(Index).DrawWidth = 2
PicRGB(Index).Line (X, Y)-(X + 1, Y + 1), QBColor(15), B
PicRGB(Index).DrawWidth = 1
    Temp = X + (Y * 11)
    Label1(Index).Caption = ColorIndex(Temp)
R1 = (ColorIndex(Temp) And &HFF)
G2 = (ColorIndex(Temp) And &HFF00&) \ 256
B3 = (ColorIndex(Temp) And &HFF0000) \ 65536
```

```
'R1 = ColorIndex(Temp) Mod 256
'G2 = ColorIndex(Temp) \ 256 Mod 256
'B3 = ColorIndex(Temp) \ 65536 Mod 256
If Index = 0 Then Pic1Red = R1: Pic1Green = G2: Pic1Blue = B3
If Index = 1 Then Pic2Red = R1: Pic2Green = G2: Pic2Blue = B3
        RGBScroll(1).Value = Val(R1)
        RGBScroll(2).Value = Val(G2)
        RGBScroll(3).Value = Val(B3)
End Sub
```

**PicRGB_Paint Index:** Rather than using Xor drawing methods to erase the last white box displayed in the PicRGB picture box control, this redraws all the color cells.

**X = Fix(X): Y = Fix(Y):** The PicRGB palettes are scaled (0, 0) to (11, 11) units. However, the X and Y arguments are declared as Single (decimal numbers). The Fix statement will round these X and Y decimal values to the next whole number.

**PicRGB(Index).DrawWidth = 2:** Change the drawing width in order to draw a thick white box.

**PicRGB(Index).Line (X, Y)-(X + 1, Y + 1), QBColor(15), B:** Draw a white box around the color cell that you have selected.

**PicRGB(Index).DrawWidth = 1:** Reset the drawing width to back to the default of 1 unit.

**Temp = X + (Y * 11):** This simple formula finds the number cell of any grid that runs left to right from top to bottom. The value 11 equals the number of rows in the grid.

**Label1(Index).Caption = ColorIndex(Temp):** Each ColorIndex array index value matches the cell number so the Label1(Index).Caption will display the correct hexadecimal number for that cell.

---

The following formula is used to extract each red, green, and blue element value from a hexadecimal color number. A hexadecimal color value is a long integer containing spliced-together hexadecimal values of red, green, and blue. *Hexa* means six, and *decimal* means 10, totaling 16. The hexadecimal system uses the characters: 0, 1, 2, 3, 4, 5, 6, 7, 8, 9, A, B, C, D, E, and F to represent 16 numeric values, where A equals 10, B equals 11, C equals 12, D equals 13, E equals 14, and F equals 15. An &H symbol (for example, &H255) in front of a numeric value tells the program that the number after it represents a long hexadecimal value.

The basic theory of hexadecimal representation is as follows: The total value of any digit is its value multiplied by its position value.

Position values starting from the right digit are 1, 16, 256, 4096, 65536, and so forth, where 16 is raised to the power of the next position (for example, 16 ^ 0, 16 ^ 1, 16 ^ 2, and 16 ^ 3). The value of FF would equal 255 since each F character is multiplied by its position value. Hence, the far-right F equal 15 times 1 (15) while the next F equals 15 times 16 (240). Add 15 and 240, and you get 255. The value FF00 equals 65,280, or (0 * 1) + (0 * 16) + (15 * 256) + (15 * 4096). The value FF0000 would equal 16,711,680 (0 * 1) + (0 * 16) + (0 * 256) + (0 * 4096) + (15 * 1,048,576) + (15 * 65,536).

**F**ountain Blends

As you can see, very large decimal numbers can be represented by the shorter hexadecimal values. The decimal range of each red, green, and blue element in a color can be between 0 and 255. In hexadecimal values, the number 255 can be abbreviated to FF. The hexadecimal value &HFF equals red (255), &HFF00 equals green (65280), and &HFF0000 equals blue (16,711,680). Any RGB values spliced together will be six digits long at the most, so the hexadecimal color value is &Hrrggbb.

To separate these combined color element values, use the And bitwise operator. Refer to Visual Basic's language reference guide, *Operators*, for details on the AND logical operator. Colors are assigned decimal values between 0 and 16,777,216. When you use the AND bitwise operator, a color value with the red, green, or blue hexadecimal or decimal value enables you to extract the correct amount of RGB element in the color. The green and blue elements also need to divide (shift) the sum by their hexadecimal positions in order to retrieve the decimal equivalent. It may be best to remember the following formula rather than get too involved with binary manipulation:

```
R1 = (ColorIndex(Temp) AND &HFF)
G2 = (ColorIndex(Temp) AND &HFF00&) \ 256
B3 = (ColorIndex(Temp) AND &HFF0000) \ 65536
```

As an alternative method, you can use the Visual Basic Mod operator, as shown in the following example:

```
'R1 = ColorIndex(Temp) Mod 256
'G2 = ColorIndex(Temp) \ 256 Mod 256
'B3 = ColorIndex(Temp) \ 65536 Mod 256
```

**If Index = 0 Then Pic1Red = R1:** These variables temporarily store the red, green, and blue elements of the color selected in the left PicRGB(0) picture box. The PicRed1, PicGreen1, and PicBlue1 variables are used as the first color of the fountain fill blend.

**If Index = 1 Then Pic2Red = R1:** These variables temporarily store the red, green, and blue elements of the color selected in the right PicRGB(1) picture box. The PicRed2, PicGreen2, and PicBlue2 variables are used for the last color of the fountain fill blend.

**RGBScroll(i).Value = Val(R1), Val(G2), Val(B3):** By changing the Value property of each of the three RGB scrollbars, the correct color you selected will also be displayed in the PicBlend picture box. Each scrollbar's Min value property is set to 0, and the Max value property is set to 255.

## Enabling the Fountain Fill Controls

The Fill_Button, DitherBtn, and Picture1 controls are activated only after one color from each of the palettes is selected. Listing 9.5 presents the PicRGB_MouseUp routine, which turns various buttons on or off.

**Listing 9.5.** Turning various buttons on or off.
```
Sub PicRGB_MouseUp (Index As Integer, Button As Integer, Shift As Integer,
    ↪X As Single, Y As Single)
    If Label1(0).Caption <> "" And Label1(1).Caption <> "" Then
        Fill_Button.Enabled = True: DitherBtn.Enabled = True
        ClipPalette.Enabled = True
    Else
        Fill_Button.Enabled = False: DitherBtn.Enabled = False
        ClipPalette.Enabled = False
    End If
End Sub
```

> **If Label1(0).Caption <> "":** When a color is selected in either palette, the label controls below each palette will show the hexadecimal value of the color. If a label control's caption is blank, the Fill_Button, DitherBtn, and Picture1 controls are disabled.

## The API Color Palette

The APIcolor& function in Listing 9.6 is used only with events that use the Draw_Blends procedure to draw an API color palette. When an API palette is created, each color is stored in an array called CustomPalette. This palette is defined in a Type structure called LOGPALETTE (PALETTE.BAS), which then uses a subentry called palPalEntry to define each of the red, green, and blue element of the color. The palPalEntry array needs a Type structure called PALETTEENTRY (PALETTE.BAS) in order to define each of the red, green, and blue elements in a color.

**Listing 9.6.** Splicing the red, green, and blue elements of a color together.
```
Function APIcolor& (cell)
    Dim Color As PALETTEENTRY
    Color = customPalette.palPalEntry(cell)
    RGBcolors& = Asc(Color.peRed)
    RGBcolors& = RGBcolors& Or (Asc(Color.peGreen) * 256&)
    RGBcolors& = RGBcolors& Or (Asc(Color.peBlue) * 256& * 256&)
    APIcolor& = RGBcolors&
End Function
```

After the palette array is loaded with color value entries, you can examine an individual color by using the statement CustomPalette.palPalEntry(cell). The cell variable represents the index number within the array that holds the color value.

Each color cell value is stored in an ANSI string format, so you must use the Visual Basic Asc statement to convert the ANSI string to a numeric value. Each numeric value must then be spliced together to use as a RGB color value. This is similar to the routine used to separate each red, green, and blue element, as shown in Listing 9.4. Rather than using the AND operator and the dividing operator to separate each color element, use the Or operator and multiply each result to group the color elements together.

# Fountain Blends

The final result will be a decimal color value that is then stored in the `APIcolor&` variable. This value is used by the `Line (Startcell, 0)-(Endcell, ScaleHeight), APIcolor&((r)), BF` statement in the `Draw_Blends` procedure (Listing 9.12) to draw each of the fountain fill color blends.

## Viewing the Range of a Color's Value

The `Check1` `CheckBox` control in Listing 9.7 triggers the `RGBscroll_Scroll` event to display either a 100- or 255-percent value of each color element in each of the `RGBlabel` label captions.

**Listing 9.7. Switching the scrollbar percentage values to either 100 or 255 percent.**

```
Sub Check1_Click ()
    For r = 1 To 3
        RGBscroll_Change (r)
    Next r
End Sub
```

`RGBscroll_Change (r)`: There are three horizontal scrollbar controls that can be used to view a single color. Each scrollbar adds or subtracts either a red, green, or blue (`RGB`) color value in order to display a particular color. Each `RGB` color element has a value range from 0 to 255. An `RGB` color of 0 red, 0 green, and 0 blue would display black; an `RGB` color of 255 red, 255 green, and 255 blue would display white. Changing any of the three color element values would add a percentage of the element color to the base color.

Use the `Check1_Click` procedure to display each `RGB` color percentage used in a color either in its 255-percent or in a 100-percent range. All calculations are performed in the `RGBscroll_Change` event in Listing 9.15.

## Displaying a Pure Color Palette

You can use Visual Basic's clipboard properties to copy a custom API palette into a form or picture box control. If you have a 256 or greater VGA graphics card, you can display pure fountain fills color blends as opposed to dithered colors. Listing 9.8 presents the `ClipPalette_MouseDown` routine, which copies a custom palette to the clipboard.

**Listing 9.8. Copying a custom palette to the clipboard.**

```
Sub ClipPalette_MouseDown (Button As Integer, Shift As Integer, X As Single,
➥Y As Single)
    ColorForm.DrawMode = 13
            CreateCustomPalette
    API = OpenClipboard(ColorForm.hWnd)
If API = 0 Then MsgBox "clipboard error": End
    API = SetClipboardData(CF_PALETTE, CreatePalette1(customPalette))
    API = CloseClipboard()
    ColorForm.Picture = Clipboard.GetData(CF_PALETTE)
    Xor_Mask.Enabled = True
End Sub
```

**CreateCustomPalette:** You must first define a new custom palette that will hold the range of colors you want to blend. The CreateCustomPalette procedure creates 20 evenly divided shades of color between the two colors selected from the PicRGB picture box controls.

**API = OpenClipboard(ColorForm.hWnd):** After a palette is defined in the CustomPalette array, open the Windows Clipboard. You are going to copy the CustomPalette array to your main form. This is similar to loading a 256-color, Visual Basic device-independent bitmap (.DIB file) into your form.

**If API = 0 Then MsgBox "clipboard error": End:** If the clipboard fails to open, the API OpenClipboard function will return the value 0 to the variable called API. This procedure will then close.

**API = SetClipboardData(CF_PALETTE, CreatePalette1(customPalette)):** If the clipboard was successfully opened, it will copy the 20 colors defined in the CustomPalette array using the API CreatePalette function (aliased as CreatePalette1). The CF_PALLETE tag tells the clipboard that the following API CreatePalette information should be formatted as palette data.

**API = CloseClipboard():** Always close the clipboard after you use clipboard functions.

**ColorForm.Picture = ClipBoard.GetData(CF_PALETTE):** The palette can now be loaded as a standard Visual Basic picture property. You should indicate that the picture is a palette by using the CF_PALETTE tag (since the clipboard could also be holding text), bitmap, or metafile information from other applications.

**Xor_Mask.Enabled = True:** The Xor Mask button is now enabled if you want to fountain fill a complex object using pure colors.

After a custom palette has been pasted from the clipboard into a form or picture box, any future drawing within these containers will use the palette's custom colors. The Draw_Blends procedure uses the Visual Basic Line statement to draw the fountain fill blends onto the main ColorForm form. (See Listing 9.9.)

**Listing 9.9. Drawing the pure color palette supplied by the clipboard.**

```
Sub Clip_Button_MouseUp (Button As Integer, Shift As Integer, X As Single, Y As Single)
    Draw_Blends
End Sub
```

## Creating a Custom Palette

The CreateCustomPalette function presented in Listing 9.10 is used to index each range of color between the two colors you selected using the PicRGB picture box palettes. The CreateCustomPalette function stores an array of color values using the same type of formula used in the RGBcolor& function. The Type structures LOGPALETTE and PALETTEENTRY, defined in the PALETTE.BAS file, locate and separate each red, green, and blue color element much in the same way the Visual Basic RGB statement does.

# Fountain Blends

**Listing 9.10.** Creating a custom palette using the fountain fill blend colors.

```
Sub CreateCustomPalette ()
Temp1 = Pic1Red: Temp2 = Pic1Green: Temp3 = Pic1Blue
customPalette.palVersion = &H300 'Window version
customPalette.palNumEntries = APIcells 'total number of colors
For cellnumber = 0 To APIcells - 1
    Distance = Pic1Red - Pic2Red
    Red1 = Temp1 - ((Distance) \ (APIcells)): Temp1 = Red1

    Distance = Pic1Green - Pic2Green
    Green1 = Temp2 - ((Distance) \ (APIcells)): Temp2 = Green1

    Distance = Pic1Blue - Pic2Blue
    Blue1 = Temp3 - ((Distance) \ (APIcells)): Temp3 = Blue1

    customPalette.palPalEntry(cellnumber).peRed = Chr$(Red1)
    customPalette.palPalEntry(cellnumber).peGreen = Chr$(Green1)
    customPalette.palPalEntry(cellnumber).peBlue = Chr$(Blue1)
    customPalette.palPalEntry(cellnumber).peFlags = Chr$(0)
Next cellnumber
End Sub
```

**Temp1 = Pic1Red: Temp2 = Pic1Green: Temp3 = Pic1Blue:** Store the original red, green, and blue elements of the color you selected in the left PicRGB picture box control.

**CustomPalette.palVersion = &H300:** The LOGPALETTE type structure requires the Windows version you are using for compatibility reasons.

**CustomPalette.palNumEntries = APIcells:** The LOGPALETTE type structure requires the total number of color cells that will be registered in your custom palette.

**For cellnumber = 0 To APIcells - 1:** For every color cell starting at index 0 and continuing up to the value of APIcells minus one cell, do the following code statements.

**Distance = Pic1Red - Pic2Red:** Find the decimal color value difference between the color you selected in the left PicRGB(0) and right PicRGB(1) picture boxes.

**Red1 = Temp1 - ((Distance) \ (APIcells)):** Subtract the original color element value from the percentage of color between the start and end of the palette. The Red1 variable increases or decreases the amount of red color that will be displayed.

**Temp1 = Red1:** Make the Temp1 variable the new color element value. The next cell color assigned increases or decreases further in value using the Red1 = Temp1 - ((Distance) \ (APIcells)) code line.

**Next cellnumber:** Repeat the loop until the custom palette is completed.

# PALETTE and PALETTEENTRY

The new palette is called CustomPalette and is stored as a Type LOGPALETTE structure in the PALETTE.BAS file. The third and last subheading of the LOGPALETTE type structure stores each of the red, green, and blue elements of each color. Each of the RGB color elements of a color are separated using the PALETTEENTRY type structure, which is also in the PALETTE.BAS file. The Type

PALETTEENTRY structure stores each value as an ANSI character value. Therefore, use the Visual Basic `Chr$` statement to convert the decimal value to an ANSI character value. The following code line shows the Red1 color decimal value being stored in ANSI character form:

```
customPalette.palPalEntry(cellnumber).peRed = Chr$(Red1)
```

## Using Dithered Colors in the Palette

When you press the API Dither button, the form will use a dither color palette. A dithered color uses various dot patterns, made up of the basic 16 colors, to simulate pure colors. Listing 9.11 contains the code for the `DitherBtn_Click` routine.

**Listing 9.11. Displaying a dithered color palette.**

```
Sub DitherBtn_Click ()
    ColorForm.Picture = LoadPicture()
    Xor_Mask.Enabled = True
        ColorForm.BackColor = QBColor(0)
    DrawMode = 7 'Xor pixel on a black background
    Draw_Blends  'will restore original color
    DrawMode = 13 'restore
End Sub
```

**ColorForm.Picture = LoadPicture():** The main `ColorForm` form may contain a pure clipboard palette. You can erase this clipboard palette by loading a blank picture into the form.

**Xor_Mask.Enabled = True:** The `Xor Mask` button is now enabled if you want to fountain fill a complex object using dithered colors.

**ColorForm.BackColor = QBcolor(0):** You will use the Visual Basic `Line` statement to draw a series of side-by-side boxes as high as the form they will be displayed in. Each box will be filled with the color used to make up the fountain fill. However, the `Line` statement also draws each box with a pixel-wide border. Erasing this border or the fountain fill will cause lines to appear between each color displayed.

> The trick to erasing unwanted border lines displayed by the `Line` statement is to use a combination of `Xor DrawMode` (7) and `Transparent DrawStyle` (5) on a black background. The border is erased because of the order in which Visual Basic draws a filled box with a border and a combination of the transparent drawing mode reacting to the bitwise properties of the `Xor Pen`. Refer to the Visual Basic Programmer's Guide for more information.

**DrawMode = 7:** Change the drawing mode to `Xor_Pen`.

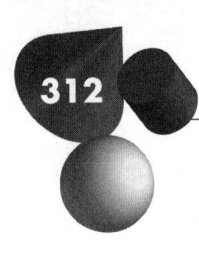

**Draw_Blends:** The `Draw_Blends` procedure (Listing 9.12) uses the Visual Basic `Line` statement to draw the fountain fill blends onto the main `ColorForm` control.

**DrawMode = 13:** Restore the drawing mode to normal (`Copy_Pen`).

## Painting Each Palette Color

After all the palette arrays have been assigned palette colors, it is time to paint the form, as shown in Listing 9.12.

**Listing 9.12. Drawing the fountain fill blend effects using API type structures.**

```
Sub Draw_Blends ()
CreateCustomPalette
Scale (0, 0)-(APIcells, 1)
For r = 0 To APIcells - 1
        'For RR = 1 To 15000: Next RR
StartCell = (ScaleWidth * r) \ APIcells
EndCell = (ScaleWidth * (r + 1)) \ APIcells
    ColorForm.FillStyle = 0
    ColorForm.DrawStyle = 5 'Transparent
    ColorForm.FillColor = APIcolor&(r)
    Line (StartCell, 0)-(EndCell, ScaleHeight), , B
    'PX = Screen.TwipsPerPixelX
    'StartCell = ((Width \ PX) * r) \ APIcells
    'EndCell = ((Width \ PX) * (r + 1)) \ APIcells
    'API = Rectangle(ColorForm.hDC, StartCell - 1, 0, EndCell, Height)
Next r
ColorForm.DrawStyle = 0 'Reset to Solid
End Sub
```

**CreateCustomPalette:** This function is used to index each color of the fountain fill. The colors are blends between the two colors you selected in the `PicRGB` picture box. The `CreateCustomPalette` procedure (Listing 9.10) stores the array of color values using a similar type of formula that is used in the `RGBcolor&` function (Listing 9.14).

**Scale (0, 0)-(APIcells, 1):** Scale the main `ColorForm` form control as one big palette.

**For R = 0 To APIcells - 1:** Start the loop that will draw each color cell of the fountain fill blend.

**'For RR = 1 To 20000: Next RR:** To see each cell as it is being drawn, use this statement.

**Startcell = (ScaleWidth * r) \ APIcells:** Because of the scale being used on the form, use this formula to determine the starting point of each color cell you are about to draw.

**Endcell = (ScaleWidth * (r + 1)) \ APIcells:** Because of the scale being used on the form, use this formula to determine the ending point of each color cell you are about to draw.

**ColorForm.FillStyle = 0:** Make sure the current file style is set to solid.

**`ColorForm.DrawStyle = 5`:** Set the drawing mode to transparent. See the `DitherBtn_Click` event in Listing 9.11 for details on why the drawing mode is set to transparent.

**`ColorForm.FillColor = APIcolor&(r)`:** Calls the `APIcolor&` procedure (Listing 9.6) to assign the correct fountain fill color to the following `Line` statement.

**`Line (Startcell, 0)-(Endcell, ScaleHeight), APIcolor&((r)), BF`:** The Visual Basic `Line` statement is used to draw each palette color cell as a box shape. The fill color of each cell box is determined by calling the `APIcolor&` function (Listing 9.6) within this `Line` statement.

**`'API = Rectangle`:** Use the remarked out (`'`) statements in this procedure to display the fountain fill using the API `Rectangle` function. However, the fountain fill is drawn slower when using the API function. You must remark out the `Line` statement in order to use the API routine.

**`Next R`:** Repeat the loop until all colors are produced.

## The Fountain Fill Button

The `Fill_Button_Click` event in Listing 9.13 uses a formula similar to the one found in the `Draw_Blends` procedure (Listing 9.12). The difference between the two procedures is the color value used in the Visual Basic `Line` statement that assigns each fountain fill color.

**Listing 9.13.** Drawing the fountain fill blend effects using Visual Basic's `RGB` statement.

```
Sub Fill_Button_Click ()
If Label1(0).Caption = "" Or Label1(1).Caption = "" Then Exit Sub
        PicBlend.Scale (0, 0)-(numcolors, 1)

    For r = 0 To numcolors - 1
        'For RR = 1 To 30000: Next RR
        Startcell = (PicBlend.ScaleWidth * r) / numcolors
        Endcell = (PicBlend.ScaleWidth * (r + 1)) / numcolors
        PicBlend.Line (Startcell, 0)-(Endcell, PicBlend.ScaleHeight), RGBcolor&(), BF
    Next r
End Sub
```

**`PicBlend.Scale (0, 0)-(numcolors, 1)`:** The `PicBlend` picture box is scaled to the number of fountain fill colors you want to display (`numcolors`). The `numcolor` value is a constant defined as 20 in PALETTE.BAS file.

**`For r = 0 To numcolors - 1`:** Starting at 0 and continuing up to 19, draw each color in the fountain fill that will be displayed in the top picture box, called `PicBlend`.

**`Startcell = (PicBlend.ScaleWidth * r) / numcolors`:** The left position of each box that will contain a color.

**`Endcell = (PicBlend.ScaleWidth * (r + 1)) / numcolors`:** The right position of each box that will contain a color.

# Fountain Blends

`PicBlend.Line (Startcell, 0)-(Endcell, PicBlend.ScaleHeight)`: Draw each box side by side within the `PicBlend` picture box. Each box is filled with a color assigned by the `RGBcolor&` function (Listing 9.14). The `RGBcolor` function uses a manual routine using only the RGB values to create a fountain fill blend.

`Next r`: Repeat the process to draw the next color within the `PicBlend` picture box.

## Using *RGB* Color Values to Build a Palette

The `RGBcolor&` function is one of two ways described in this chapter to assign a color to a fountain fill. Listing 9.14 shows a manual routine to calculate the 18 shades of color between the first color selected in the `PicRGB(0)` palette and the color selected in the `PicRGB(1)` palette. The second method used in this program to assign colors to a fountain fill is detailed in the `CreateCustomPalette` procedure (Listing 9.10 ).

**Listing 9.14. Using the Visual Basic RGB statement to blend color.**

```
Function RGBcolor& ()
Static counter, Temp1, Temp2, Temp3
counter = counter + 1
Select Case counter
  Case 1
    ColorCell& = Val(Label1(0).Caption)
    Temp1 = Pic1Red: Temp2 = Pic1Green: Temp3 = Pic1Blue
  Case numcolors
    ColorCell& = Val(Label1(1).Caption)
    counter = 0: Temp1 = 0: Temp2 = 0: Temp3 = 0
  Case Else
    Distance = Pic1Red - Pic2Red
    Red1 = Temp1 - ((Distance) \ (numcolors - 2)): Temp1 = Red1
    Distance = Pic1Green - Pic2Green
    Green1 = Temp2 - ((Distance) \ (numcolors - 2)): Temp2 = Green1
     Distance = Pic1Blue - Pic2Blue
    Blue1 = Temp3 - ((Distance) \ (numcolors - 2)): Temp3 = Blue1
    ColorCell& = RGB(Red1, Green1, Blue1) 'color of cell
End Select
RGBcolor& = ColorCell&
End Sub
```

`counter = counter + 1`: The counter variable counts each color as it is added to the fountain fill.

`Select Case counter`: This goes to the `Case` statement that matches the counter's current value.

`Case 1`: The first color to use is the same color that was selected in the `PicRGB(0)` picture box.

`ColorCell& = Val`: The RGB value displayed below the `PicRGB(0)` picture box is the correct color value to use as the first color in the fountain fill.

**Temp1 = Pic1Red: Temp2 = Pic1Green: Temp3 = Pic1Blue:** Store the original red, green, and blue elements of the color you selected in the PicRGB(0) picture box control. The Pic1Red, Pic1Green, and Pic1Blue values are the individual RGB elements that were calculated in the PicRGB_MouseDown event when you first selected the color.

**Case numcolors:** The last color to use is the same color that was selected in PicRGB(1) picture box.

**ColorCell& = Val:** The RGB value displayed below the PicRGB(1) picture box is the correct color value to use as the last color in the fountain fill.

**counter = 0: Temp1 = 0 : etc,:** The fountain fill is painted, so reset all values to their defaults.

**Case Else:** Every color between Case 1 and Case numcolors is assigned in the following group of code statements.

**Distance = Pic1Red - Pic2Red**: Find the decimal color value difference between the color you selected in the left PicRGB(0) and right PicRGB(1) picture boxes.

**Red1 = Temp1 - ((Distance) \ (APIcells))**: Subtract the original color element value from the percentage of color between the start and end of the palette. The Red1 variable increases or decreases the amount of red color that will be displayed.

**Temp1 = Red1:** Make the Temp1 variable the new color element value. The next cell color assigned further increases or decreases in value using the Red1 = Temp1 - ((Distance) \ (APIcells)) code line.

**ColorCell& = RGB:** Assign the new shade of color to the ColorCell& variable.

**RGBcolor& = ColorCell&:** The function name returns the correct color to assign the RGBcolor variable used in the Visual Basic Line statement.

## Changing Colors with the Scrollbars

The RGBscroll_Scroll event uses the values of each of the three scrollbars to display a color in the PicBlend picture box and shows the decimal value of each color element in the RGBlabel label controls. The RGBscroll_Scroll routine presented in Listing 9.16 is called from the RGBscroll_Change routine (Listing 9.15).

**Listing 9.15. The scrollbars displaying individual colors.**

```
Sub RGBscroll_Change (Index As Integer)
    RGBscroll_Scroll Index
End Sub
```

**RGBscroll_Scroll Index:** This branches off to the scroll event to display a color.

## Fountain Blends

**Listing 9.16.** Displaying the red, green, or blue values of a color.

```
Sub RGBscroll_Scroll (Index As Integer)
    PicBlend.BackColor = RGB(RGBScroll(1).Value,
        ➥RGBScroll(2).Value, RGBScroll(3).Value)
    If Check1.Value = 1 Then
        ScaleValue = RGBScroll(Index).Value
        Check1.Caption = "255%"
    Else
        ScaleValue = Int(RGBScroll(Index).Value / 2.55)
        Check1.Caption = "100%"
    End If
RGBlabel(Index).Caption = Choose(Index, "Red ", "Green ", "Blue ")
        ➥+ ScaleValue
End Sub
```

**PicBlend.BackColor = RGB:** The single color is displayed automatically by way of the scrollbar's Value properties. The scrollbar's values are as follows: Min = 0, and Max = 255 (which is the maximum RGB color value allowed).

**If Check1.Value = 1 Then:** If the checkbox control is checked, the ScaleValue variable will equal the current Value property of the scrollbar. This will make the RGBlabels display the colors elements in a range from 0 to 255 percent.

**Else:** The checkbox is not checked, so the ScaleValue variable equals the current Value property of the scrollbar divided by 2.55. This makes the RGBlabel display the colors elements in a range from 0 to 100 percent.

**RGBlabel(Index).Caption:** Display the color value in the RGBlabel.

## Painting a Complex Object with a Fountain Fill

Use the Xor_Mask button to fill any shaped object with a fountain fill blend. (See Listing 9.17.) The current dithered colors are drawn in Xor mode first, and then five overlapping circles are drawn atop in solid black. When you apply the same dithered colors again in Xor mode, the black circle mask will absorb the true blended colors while the outlying colors disappear.

**Listing 9.17.** Filling shapes with a fountain fill.

```
Sub Xor_Mask_Click ()
    BackColor = &HFF0000 'remake out if you wish
    DrawMode = 7 'Xor dithered colors
            Draw_Blends
    Scale
    DrawMode = 1 'draw any shape solid black
    FillStyle = 0
        For r = 0 To 5000 Step 1000
            Circle (1000 + r, Height - 1200), 600
        Next r
```

```
    DrawMode = 7 'Xor again it fill shape with blends
            Draw_Blends
    DrawMode = 13 'restore
End Sub
```

**BackColor = &HFF0000:** Change the form's background color to erase old background patterns. You can remark out (') this statement or use the `Cls` statement.

**DrawMode = 7:** Change the drawing mode to `Xor`. Refer to the `DitherBtn_Click` event in Listing 9.11 for details on how the `Xor` mode is used within this program.

**Draw_Blends:** This procedure uses Visual Basic's `Line` statement to draw the fountain fill blends onto the `ColorForm` form.

**Scale:** Set the drawing scale mode to twip units, enabling you to place the circles within the form.

**DrawMode = 1:** Set the pen and fill color to solid black.

The following `For...Next` statement draws five overlapping circles on the form:

```
For r = 0 To 5000 Step 1000
    Circle (1000 + r, Height - 1200), 600
Next r
```

**DrawMode = 7:** Reset the drawing mode to `Xor` again.

**Draw_Blends:** Use Visual Basic's `Line` statement to draw the fountain fill blends again.

**DrawMode = 13:** The shape is now filled with a fountain fill, so reset the original drawing mode.

## Summary

This chapter showed several basic ways to select custom colors within your application. The `RGBcolor&` method of fountain fill blends is best-suited for working with dithered colors or Visual Basic Palette (PAL) files. This method does not create a custom palette but uses the current palette of the system or Visual Basic container palette, if preset. The order in which this program generates an RGB fountain fill blend is as follows:

1. The `PicRGB_Paint` event draws the two 121-color palettes at startup using Visual Basic `RGB` statement.

2. The `RGB_MouseDown` event finds the color you selected from the `ColorIndex` array and then separates the red, green, and blue elements of the color using either the hexadecimal or `Mod` dividing formulas.

3. The `Fill_Button_Click` event (the fountain fill button) draws the fountain fill blend using Visual Basic's `Line` statement, which then calls the `RGBcolor&` procedure to insert each fill color.

The `APIcolor&` method of fountain fill blends is best-suited for working with pure colors (256 +) or self-made custom palettes. This method requires `Type` structures and/or API palette functions.

# Fountain Blends

The order in which this program generates an API fountain fill blend is as follows:

1. `PicRGB_Paint` draws the two 121-color palettes at startup using Visual Basic `RGB` statement.
2. `RGB_MouseDown` finds the color you selected from the `ColorIndex` array and then separates the red, green, and blue elements of the color using either the hexadecimal or `Mod` dividing formulas.
3. `DitherBtn_Click` (the API dithered button) calls the `Draw_Blends` procedure.
4. `Draw_Blends` calls the `CreateCustomPalette` procedure, which uses the `LOGPALETTE` and `PALETTEENTRY` type structures to make a palette array called `CustomPalette`.
5. `Draw_Blends` then draws the fountain fill using the Visual Basic `Line` statement, which then calls the `APIcolor&` procedure to insert each color fill.

The `APIcolor&` method basically performs the same routine as the `RGBcolor&` method. However, it creates a new custom palette array using API palette functions in the `CreateCustomPalette` procedure. The custom palette array now contains the colors that were already defined in the `ColorIndex` array at startup (minus the first and last color).

After the custom palette is defined in a structured array, you can access the palette via the clipboard. The clipboard method can be used to paste a pure (non-dithered) palette onto the form.

# CHAPTER 10

# The Mini-Bézier Curve Program

## The Mini-Bézier Curve Program

The Mini-Bézier program is a stand-alone Bézier curve application that shows the basic structure you use to plot Bézier curve points. The Mini-Bézier program uses the same Bézier routines that are present in both the Artisan program in Chapter 3 and ArtAPI program in Chapter 15. The variable names used to build the Bézier curve also are identical to the ones found in the `Declaration` section of the Artisan program in Chapter 2. The Mini-Bézier program has been supplied so you have an application in which to test alternative methods to generate Bézier curves. If you are using a Windows 32-bit operating system, you have access to the new GDI32 file library. The GDI32 library contains about a dozen new API drawing functions that are available to the Visual Basic 32-bit application platform. Among the new GDI32 APIs are two Bézier curve functions called `PolyBézier` and `PolyBézierTo`.

You can use the `PolyBézier` function to generate a curve by issuing it the four curve points needed to create a Bézier curve. The four curve points are the two handle and two end points of the curve illustrated in Chapter 2. You use the `PolyBézierTo` function to connect a curve's end point to another object or coordinate point.

When using the API PolyBézier you no longer require the `BezDivide` (see Listing 10.2) or `BezDraw` procedure (see Listing 10.3) to calculate the *deCasteljau* dividing formula to draw a curve. The `PolyBézier` function does not generate the Bézier's handles, levers, or nodes. Any changes to the node and handles' event routines are minimal and require only that the reference to `BezDraw` be changed to the single line GDI32 `PolyBézier` function.

Some professional illustration packages allow you to control the Bézier curve by pushing or dragging the actual curve. This method automatically moves the Bézier's handle controls to conform with the new location of the curve as it is being moved. The Mini-Bézier program is an ideal candidate to experiment with curve and node editing features.

The Mini-Bézier program's form and control properties are listed in Table 10.1.

**Table 10.1. The properties of the Mini-Bézier form and controls.**

*Object: Form*
*Object Name: Form1*

| | | | |
|---|---|---|---|
| BackColor | &H0000FFFF& | Caption | "Bézier Curves" |
| Height | 4830 | Left | 180 |
| Top | 765 | Width | 6180 |

*Object: Command Button*
*Object Name: Exit*

| | | | |
|---|---|---|---|
| Caption | "Exit" | Height | 375 |
| Left | 135 | Top | 3960 |
| Width | 1050 | | |

*Object: Textbox*
*Object Name: Text1*

| | | | |
|---|---|---|---|
| Height | 375 | Left | 1260 |
| Top | 3960 | Width | 915 |

*Object: Textbox*
*Object Name: Text2*

| | | | |
|---|---|---|---|
| Height | 375 | Left | 2205 |
| Top | 3960 | Width | 915 |

*Object: Command Button*
*Object Name: ClearBtn*

| | | | |
|---|---|---|---|
| Caption | "Clear" | Height | 375 |
| Left | 3195 | Top | 3960 |
| Width | 1215 | | |

*Object: Picture Box*
*Object Name: Picture1*

| | | | |
|---|---|---|---|
| DrawMode | 6 'Invert | Height | 3795 |
| Left | 135 | Top | 90 |
| Width | 5835 | | |

*Object: Picture Box*
*Object Name: Node1*

| | | | |
|---|---|---|---|
| BackColor | &H00C00000& | BorderStyle | 0 'None |
| Height | 105 | Left | 0 |
| ScaleHeight | 105 | ScaleWidth | 105 |
| Top | 495 | Width | 105 |

*Object: Picture Box*
*Object Name: Node2*

| | | | |
|---|---|---|---|
| BackColor | &H00C00000& | BorderStyle | 0 'None |
| Height | 105 | Left | 0 |
| ScaleHeight | 105 | ScaleWidth | 105 |
| Top | 720 | Width | 105 |

*continues*

**T**able 10.1. continued

*Object: Picture Box*
*Object Name: Handle1*

| | | | |
|---|---|---|---|
| BackColor | &H00FF00FF& | BorderStyle | 0 'None |
| DrawMode | 6 'Invert | Height | 105 |
| Left | 0 | ScaleHeight | 105 |
| ScaleWidth | 105 | Top | 0 |
| Width | 105 | | |

*Object: Picture Box*
*Object Name: Handle2*

| | | | |
|---|---|---|---|
| BackColor | &H00FF00FF& | BorderStyle | 0 'None |
| DrawMode | 6 'Invert | Height | 105 |
| Left | 0 | ScaleHeight | 105 |
| ScaleWidth | 105 | Top | 240 |
| Width | 105 | | |

*Object: Picture Box*
*Object Name: Shape1*

| | | | |
|---|---|---|---|
| Height | 105 | Left | 0 |
| Top | 1200 | Width | 105 |

*Object: Shape*
*Object Name: Shape2*

| | | | |
|---|---|---|---|
| Height | 105 | Left | 0 |
| Top | 1320 | Width | 105 |

*Object: Command Button*
*Object Name: Nodehandle*

| | | | |
|---|---|---|---|
| Caption | "nodes" | Height | 375 |
| Left | 4500 | Top | 3960 |
| Width | 1455 | | |

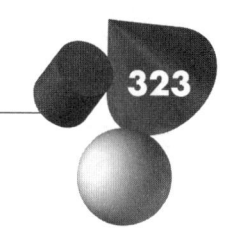

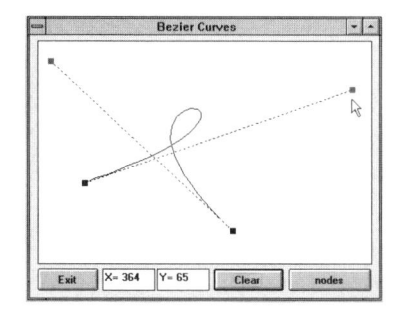

# Variable Names for the 16-Bit Bézier Curve Program

The Mini-Bézier program in Listing 10.1 demonstrates manual routines you can use to construct a Bézier curve utilizing the *deCasteljau* formula to pre-plot Bézier curve points. When you use the PolyBézier function on 32-bit operating systems, the D1, D2, D3, E1, E2, and C1 array variables in this listing are not required.

**Listing 10.1. Generating the default values at startup.**

```
Declaration
Declare Function Polyline Lib "GDI" (ByVal hDC%, P As POINTS,
➥ByVal NUM_PTS%) As Integer
Const MAX_POINTS = 33
Dim P_Index(1 To MAX_POINTS) As POINTS
Dim P As Integer
Dim X1 As Integer
Dim Y1 As Integer
Dim X2 As Integer
Dim Y2 As Integer

Dim P1 As POINTS
Dim H1 As POINTS
Dim H2 As POINTS
Dim P2 As POINTS

Dim D1(1 To MAX_POINTS) As POINTS
Dim D2(1 To MAX_POINTS) As POINTS
Dim D3(1 To MAX_POINTS) As POINTS
Dim E1(1 To MAX_POINTS) As POINTS
Dim E2(1 To MAX_POINTS) As POINTS
Dim C1(1 To MAX_POINTS) As POINTS
Const Yellow = &HFFFF&
Dim PixelX As Integer
Dim PixelY As Integer
```

# The Mini-Bézier Curve Program

**Declare Function Polyline:** An API procedure to draw a line, similar to Visual Basic's Line statement.

**Const MAX_POINTS:** The total number of points to store on a Bézier curve.

**Dim P_Index(1 To MAX_POINTS) As POINTS:** The index that holds the Bézier points. You store it using the type structure POINTS, which can point the X and Y coordinates to a single array name.

**Dim P As Integer:** Represents the starting point of the index.

**X1, X2, Y1, Y2:** Temporary screen coordinates used primarily to erase the last position of an object when moved to another location.

**P1, H1, H2, P2:** The four control points of a Bézier curve. P1 = Bézier node Point 1. H1 = Bézier handle 1. H2 = Bézier handle 2. P2 = Bézier node Point 2.

**D1, D2, D3, E1, E2, C1:** The actual dividing points of a Bézier curve. The C1 variable is an actual point on the curve after the *deCasteljau* dividing formula BezDivide is performed.

**Const Yellow:** The hexadecimal number for the color yellow. The dotted lines you see when moving a curve handle are cyan. The yellow changes to cyan when you set the DrawMode to drawing pixels in Xor mode. The Xor mode restores any background color the dotted line may pass over as it is being moved.

Figure 10.1 illustrates the structure of the formula created in Listing 10.1.

**Figure 10.1.**
*The structure of the deCasteljau formula.*

```
D1(P).X = (P1.X + h1.X) \ 2
D1(P).Y = (P1.Y + h1.Y) \ 2
D2(P).X = (h1.X + h2.X) \ 2
D2(P).Y = (h1.Y + h2.Y) \ 2
D3(P).X = (p2.X + h2.X) \ 2
D3(P).Y = (p2.Y + h2.Y) \ 2
E1(P).X = (D1(P).X + D2(P).X) \ 2
E1(P).Y = (D1(P).Y + D2(P).Y) \ 2
E2(P).X = (D2(P).X + D3(P).X) \ 2
E2(P).Y = (D2(P).Y + D3(P).Y) \ 2
C1(P).X = (E1(P).X + E2(P).X) \ 2
C1(P).Y = (E1(P).Y + E2(P).Y) \ 2
```

deCasteljau algorithm

```
p1  h1  h2  p1
 └┬┘ └┬┘ └┬┘
  D1  D2  D3
  └┬─┘ └─┬┘
    E1    E2
    └──┬──┘
       C1
```

## Calculating the Curve's Points

You can simplify the calculation of a Bézier curve by using the *deCasteljau* algorithm. (See Listing 10.2.) If you simply divide the four Bézier curve control points (P1, P2, H1, and H2) in half repeatedly, you will eventually end up with a plot coordinate that represents a point on a curve.

**Listing** 10.2. The *deCasteljau* dividing formula.

```
Sub BezDivide (P1 As POINTS, H1 As POINTS,
↳                          H2 As POINTS, P2 As POINTS)
D1(P).X = (P1.X \ 2 + H1.X \ 2)
D1(P).Y = (P1.Y \ 2 + H1.Y \ 2)
D2(P).X = (H1.X \ 2 + H2.X \ 2)
D2(P).Y = (H1.Y \ 2 + H2.Y \ 2)
D3(P).X = (P2.X \ 2 + H2.X \ 2)
D3(P).Y = (P2.Y \ 2 + H2.Y \ 2)
E1(P).X = (D1(P).X \ 2 + D2(P).X \ 2)
E1(P).Y = (D1(P).Y \ 2 + D2(P).Y \ 2)
E2(P).X = (D2(P).X \ 2 + D3(P).X \ 2)
E2(P).Y = (D2(P).Y \ 2 + D3(P).Y \ 2)
C1(P).X = (E1(P).X \ 2 + E2(P).X \ 2)
C1(P).Y = (E1(P).Y \ 2 + E2(P).Y \ 2)
'Picture1.DrawWidth = 4 : Picture1.DrawMode = 6
'Picture1.PSet (C1(P).X, C1(P).Y)
'Picture1.DrawWidth = 1
End Sub
```

**D1(P).X = (P1.X \ 2 + H1.X \ 2):** Long division is used in this code only to force the answers to integer values. You can shorten the statement (P1.X \ 2 + H1.X \ 2) to (p1.X + H1.X) \ 2, which works well in Pixel mode. In twips, P1.X + H1.X could surpass the maximum value that an integer can store ( -32,768 to 32,767). You can see the actual curve points (C1) using the PSet statement. Remove the ReMark Out ( ' ) on the last three lines of the BezDivide procedure code. For a full explanation of how you produce a Bézier curve, see the Artisan program in Chapter 2.

> **CAUTION** Always divide by integers (whole numbers) using the Shift right slash (\) dividing operator when using the *deCasteljau* formula. Serious performance slowdown occurs if you use the floating-point (decimal number) division (/) operator.

## Plotting the Curve Points

The variable P used in the BezDraw procedure (Listing 10.2) represents the index number that stores each value generated by the *deCasteljau* algorithm in the BezDivide procedure (Listing 10.1).

# The Mini-Bézier Curve Program

The P variable also represents the number given to the plotted points that make up the curve. Beginning from the curve's starting point (P1) and stopping at the curve's end point (P2), the points are numbered 2 through 32. Therefore, the curve point indexed as 17 is the center mark, halfway through the curve.

In Listing 10.3, you plot the left side of the curve first, using the same dividing formula for each new curve point. This creates the curve points 2 through 16. Next, you plot the right side, which is basically a mirror of the left side. This then creates the curve points 18 through 32.

**Listing 10.3. Plotting each curve point manually.**

```
Sub BezDraw ()
P = 17: BezDivide P1, H1, H2, P2
Left Side
P = 13: BezDivide P1, D1(17), E1(17), C1(17)
P = 9: BezDivide P1, D1(13), E1(13), C1(13)
P = 5: BezDivide P1, D1(9), E1(9), C1(9)
P = 3: BezDivide P1, D1(5), E1(5), C1(5)
P = 2: BezDivide P1, D1(3), E1(3), C1(3)
P = 4: BezDivide C1(3), E2(3), D3(3), C1(5)
P = 7: BezDivide C1(5), E2(5), D3(5), C1(9)
P = 6: BezDivide C1(7), D1(7), E1(7), C1(5)
P = 8: BezDivide C1(7), E2(7), D3(7), C1(9)
P = 11: BezDivide C1(9), E2(9), D3(9), C1(13)
P = 10: BezDivide C1(11), D1(11), E1(11), C1(9)
P = 12: BezDivide C1(11), E2(11), D3(11), C1(13)
P = 15: BezDivide C1(13), E2(13), D3(13), C1(17)
P = 14: BezDivide C1(15), D1(15), E1(15), C1(13)
P = 16: BezDivide C1(15), E2(15), D3(15), C1(17)
Right Side
P = 21: BezDivide C1(17), E2(17), D3(17), P2
P = 25: BezDivide C1(21), E2(21), D3(21), P2
P = 29: BezDivide C1(25), E2(25), D3(25), P2
P = 31: BezDivide C1(29), E2(29), D3(29), P2
P = 32: BezDivide C1(31), E2(31), D3(31), P2
P = 30: BezDivide C1(29), D1(31), E1(31), C1(31)
P = 27: BezDivide C1(25), D1(29), E1(29), C1(29)
P = 28: BezDivide C1(29), E2(27), D3(27), C1(27)
P = 26: BezDivide C1(25), D1(27), E1(27), C1(27)
P = 23: BezDivide C1(21), D1(25), E1(25), C1(25)
P = 24: BezDivide C1(25), E2(23), D3(23), C1(25)
P = 22: BezDivide C1(21), D1(23), E1(23), C1(23)
P = 19: BezDivide C1(17), D1(21), E1(21), C1(21)
P = 20: BezDivide C1(21), E2(19), D3(19), C1(19)
P = 18: BezDivide C1(17), D1(19), E1(19), C1(19)

Picture1.DrawMode = 6: Picture1.DrawStyle = 0
 P_Index(1).X = P1.X \ PixelX
 P_Index(1).Y = P1.Y \ PixelY
 For P = 2 To 32
  P_Index(P).X = C1(P).X \ PixelX
  P_Index(P).Y = C1(P).Y \ PixelY
 Next P
```

```
P_Index(33).X = P2.X \ PixelX
P_Index(33).Y = P2.Y \ PixelY
NUM_PTS = 33
R = Polyline(Picture1.hDC, P_Index(1), NUM_PTS)
End Sub
```

**Left side:** P is a temporary integer that passes the index number of arrays D1, D2, D3, E1, E2, and C1. It also represents the order in which the points are placed on a curve. They start at BezNode1 (p1) and count up 32 more points; they finally connect to point 33, which is BezNode2 (p2).

You fool Sub BézierDivide into thinking that the four arguments you pass to it are the Bézier's node points P1 and P2, and the Bézier's handle points H1 and H2.

The first block of six calculations divides the left side of the curve, as shown in the Figure 10.2 (the black nodes starting from 17). These curve points are stored as C1(*index number*). Hence, the first six points are stored in C1(17), C1(13), C1(9), C1(5), C1(3), and C1(2).

**Figure 10.2.**
*The order of plotted points for the left side of the curve.*

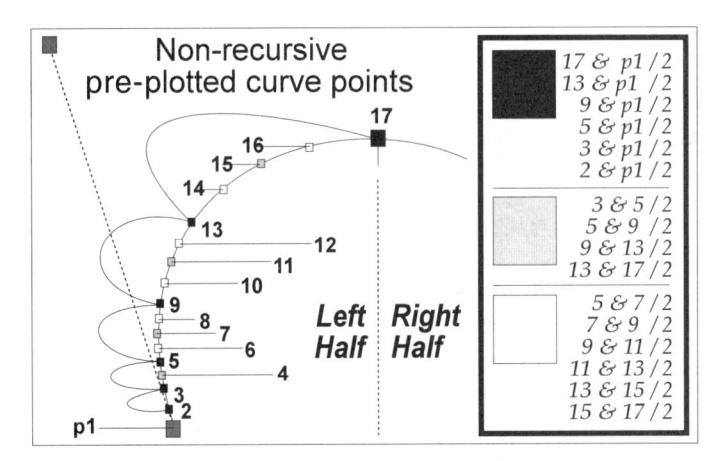

Non-recursive pre-plotted curve points

17 & p1/2
13 & p1/2
9 & p1/2
5 & p1/2
3 & p1/2
2 & p1/2

3 & 5/2
5 & 9/2
9 & 13/2
13 & 17/2

5 & 7/2
7 & 9/2
9 & 11/2
11 & 13/2
13 & 15/2
15 & 17/2

Left Half | Right Half

Now you plot the remaining 10 points for the left side by finding the halfway point between the black nodes; you start with points 3 and 5 (C1(3) and C1(5)) and work your way back up. (See the gray nodes in Figure 10.2.) If a visual gap appears between a gray node and black node, you find the halfway point between each of these points and plot yet another point. (See the white nodes in Figure 10.2.)

Look at the second block of statements starting with P = 4. Notice that the first argument, C1, and the fourth argument, also C1, are pretending to be two Bézier node points, and the two middle arguments are pretending to be the Bézier's control handles. Here, you are creating a vortex of the same pattern used to create the first point (17) and swirling counterclockwise to make the left side of the curve. You create the right side by repeating this vortex pattern but having it swirl clockwise starting from point (17). Each repeated pattern gets smaller and smaller as you near the end points. p1 is the start point for the left side, and p2 is the end point for the right side.

# The Mini-Bézier Curve Program

You draw Bézier curves in *controls* that have their `ScaleMode` turn set to the `Twip` scale (1,440 units per inch). Using `Pixel` mode, for instance, causes the Bézier curve to appear crooked near the Bézier's control points (`Node1` and `Node2`). Because you are using the *deCastlejau* formula for dividing, the curve points (`C1`) get closer together as they near each node point. The `Form_Load` event in Listing 10.4 uses Visual Basic's `TwipPerPixel` function to convert twip units to pixel units.

**Listing 10.4. The default values at startup.**
```
Sub Form_Load ()
    PixelX = Screen.TwipsPerPixelX
    PixelY = Screen.TwipsPerPixelY
End Sub
```

> **PixelX, PixelY:** Converts `Twips` units to `Pixel` units. You need to convert internal scales for two reasons: (1) The API `Polyline` function accepts only `X` and `Y` values in pixel coordinates. (2) The `Text1` and `Text2` textbox controls display the `X` and `Y` pixel positions when you move the mouse.

The `Form_Resize` event in Listing 10.5 centers the form on the screen.

**Listing 10.5. Positioning the main form on the screen.**
```
Sub Form_Resize ()
    Form1.Left = (Screen.Width - Form1.Width) \ 2
    Form1.Top = (Screen.Height - Form1.Height) \ 2
End Sub
```

> **Form1.Left (Top):** Resizes the form to be centered on your screen.

In the `Picture1_MouseDown` event in Listing 10.6 any line or curve image is raised and the nodes are reset to their original values. The `Line_MouseDown` procedure code could be placed within this event, however, the Mini-Bézier program is simulating the same event and procedure order used in the Artisan program in Chapter 3.

**Listing 10.6. The `Picture1_MouseDown` event.**
```
Sub Picture1_MouseDown (Button%, Shift%, X!, Y!)
    ClearBtn_Click
    Line_MouseDown X, Y
End Sub
```

> **ClearBtn:** Triggers the Clear button on the form to clear the `Form`.
>
> **Line_MouseDown:** Call this procedure to set the line's start point. You can put this code here, but more complicated programs may need this space in future.

Chapter **10**

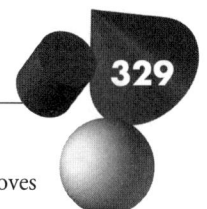

The `Picture1_MouseMove` event in Listing 10.7 tracks the position of the mouse pointer as it moves across the picture box.

**Listing 10.7. Moving the mouse over the form.**
```
Sub Picture1_MouseMove (Button%, Shift%, X!, Y!)
    Text1.Text = "X= " + Format(X) \ PixelX
    Text2.Text = "Y= " + Format(Y) \ PixelY
    Line_MouseMove Button, X, Y
End Sub
```

**Text1.Text, Text2.Text:** Displays the current X and Y mouse positions.

**Line_MouseMove:** Calls the procedure that draws the moving line.

The `Picture1_MouseUp` event in Listing 10.8 calls the `Line_MouseUp` procedure, which will calculate the final coordinates of the line.

**Listing 10.8. The `Picture1 MouseUp` event.**
```
Sub Picture1_MouseUp (Button%, Shift%, X!, Y!)
    Line_MouseUp X, Y
End Sub
```

**Line_MouseUp:** Calls the procedure that sets the finished line.

Figure 10.3 shows a line being converted to a curve.

**Figure 10.3.**
*A line being converted to a curve.*

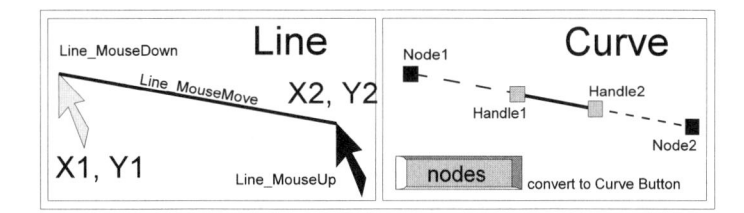

## Drawing the Line on the Form

You must first draw a line in the `Picture1` picture box control so the line can be converted to a curve. Simply click the mouse button and hold the mouse pointer at the position you want the line to start. Next, drag the mouse to draw the line; then let go of the mouse button.

The `Line_MouseDown` event in Listing 10.9 initiates the starting coordinates of the line.

**Listing 10.9. Setting the start position of a line.**
```
Sub Line_MouseDown (X As Single, Y As Single)
    X1 = X : Y1 = Y
    X2 = X1 : Y2 = Y1
End Sub
```

# The Mini-Bézier Curve Program

**X1, Y1, X2, Y2:** Sets all the line-drawing positions to the current X and Y.

The `Line_MouseMove` event in Listing 10.10 draws the line as you drag the mouse pointer.

### Listing 10.10. Drawing a movable line.

```
Sub Line_MouseMove (Button As Integer, X!, Y!)
    If Button Then
        Picture1.Line (X1, Y1)-(X2, Y2), QBColor(4)
            X2 = X
            Y2 = Y
        Picture1.Line (X1, Y1)-(X2, Y2), QBColor(4)
    End If
End Sub
```

**If Button Then:** Continues only if a mouse button is held down.

**Picture1.Line:** Draws a line.

**X2, Y2:** Makes a corner position of the line equal to the current mouse pointer's coordinate. You are drawing in `Inverse` mode, which draws the first image the reverse color of the background (white to black). If any of the next images drawn land on a black-pixel image of the first image, then the image is drawn white, and vice versa. This gives the illusion of movement.

**Picture1.Line:** Redraws the line to erase the line drawn previously.

The `Line_MouseUp` event in Listing 10.11 saves the line's coordinates. As soon as you release the mouse button, two nodes are then positioned at either end of the line. The X and Y coordinates of the curves start and end points are then saved in the variables P1 and P2.

### Listing 10.11. Setting the line's final node positions.

```
Sub Line_MouseUp (X As Single, Y As Single)
    If X1 = X Or Y1 = Y Then Exit Sub
        Node1.Move X1 - 45, Y1 - 45
        Node2.Move X - 45, Y - 45
        Node1.ScaleLeft = Node1.Left
        Node1.ScaleTop = Node1.Top
        Node2.ScaleLeft = Node2.Left
        Node2.ScaleTop = Node2.Top
    P1.X = X1
    P1.Y = Y1
    P2.X = X2
    P2.Y = Y2
End Sub
```

**If X1 = X Or Y1 = Y:** The line's length isn't longer than one pixel width, so exit this procedure.

**Node1(i).Move:** Relocates the two nodes to either end of the line.

**Node1(i).ScaleLeft (Top):** Scales the nodes so that they reflect the form's internal scale.

**P1.X, P1.Y, P2.X, P2.Y:** Sets the curve's two main control points (Node1, Node2) to be that of the line's start and end points.

Figure 10.4 illustrates the form and its controls.

**F**igure 10.4.
*The layout of the form and its controls.*

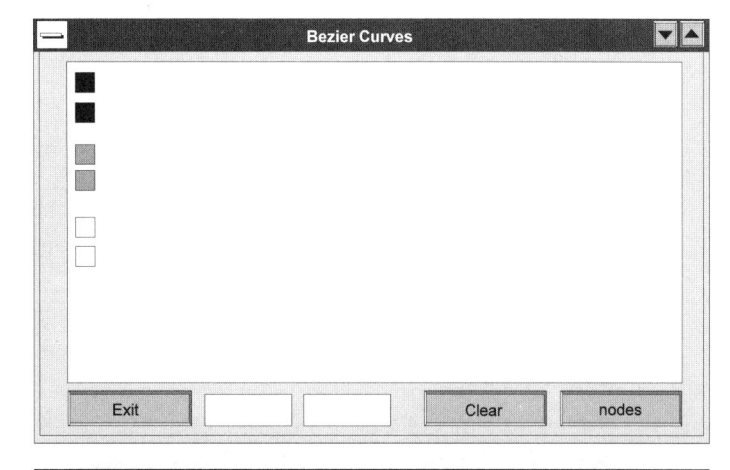

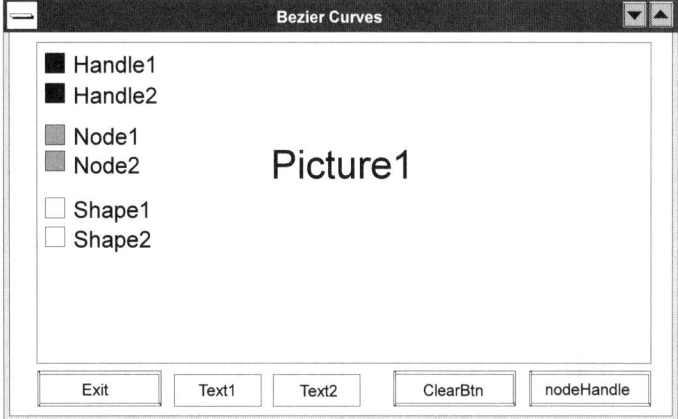

## Erasing the Curve's Image Before a Move

You call the routine in Listing 10.12 to draw the first Bézier curve when a handle or node is moved. In the Mini-Bézier program, you are not preserving the image of the curve by using the AutoRedraw property. You need only to erase the old image of the line before it was converted to a curve.

## The Mini-Bézier Curve Program

**Listing 10.12. Erasing the old line image.**

```
Sub BezMove ()
    Picture1.DrawMode = 7: Picture1.DrawStyle = 2
    Picture1.Line (P1.X, P1.Y)-(H1.X, H1.Y), Yellow
    Picture1.Line (P2.X, P2.Y)-(H2.X, H2.Y), Yellow
    If P = 0 Then
        Picture1.DrawStyle = 0: Picture1.DrawMode = 13
        Picture1.Line (X1, Y1)-(X2, Y2), QBColor(15)
        BezDraw
    End If
    Picture1.DrawMode = 7: Picture1.DrawStyle = 2
    Picture1.Line (P1.X, P1.Y)-(H1.X, H1.Y), Yellow
    Picture1.Line (P2.X, P2.Y)-(H2.X, H2.Y), Yellow
End Sub
```

**Picture1.DrawMode:** Dotted-lever lines connect the Bézier nodes to the Bézier handles. Because they can be drawn over the top or passed through a curved line that was originally drawn in Copy_Pen mode (13), you must change modes.

**Picture1.DrawStyle:** Because the lines you are going to draw are dotted, change the DrawStyle to Dot (2).

**Picture1.Line:** Draws each of the dotted-lever lines.

**If P = 0:** The variable P equals 0 when each line object is first drawn. You must now erase this line because you have converted the line object to a curve. Drawing a white line over the top of the black line image erases the image.

**Picture1.DrawStyle:** Resets the drawing style back to Solid (0 normal).

**Picture1.DrawMode:** Resets the drawing mode to Copy_Pen (13 normal) so that you can erase the line using the color White. You also can use DrawMode 16 (Whiteness) to achieve this effect.

**Picture1.Line:** Draws a white line over the top of the current line to erase it.

**BezDraw:** Calls the BezDraw procedure to draw the Bézier curve where the line used to be.

## Resetting Values to Start a New Curve

The ClearBtn_Click event in Listing 10.13 resets all controls to their original form values. Rather than hide the nodes and handles, as in the Artisan program of Chapter 2, you just move them to the side of the form.

To begin, draw a line on the middle of the desktop; then click the mouse on the desktop. The line image disappears, but the line's start and end value coordinates are still present at the location. Now, move a node or handle while it is still positioned at the side of the form. This procedure illustrates how nodes and handles are positioned and aligned on a curved object. It also demonstrates how you move a curve from an offset point when using the blue Node1 and Node2 picture box controls.

Chapter **10**

**Listing 10.13. Resetting all values to begin a new line.**
```
Sub ClearBtn_Click ()
If Node1.Left = 0 Then Exit Sub
    Picture1.Cls
    Handle1.Move 0, 150
    Handle2.Move 0, 300
    Node1.Move 0, 450
    Node2.Move 0, 600
    Shape1.Move 0, 900
    Shape2.Move 0, 1200
        P = 0
        Picture1.ForeColor = QBColor(1)
        Picture1.DrawMode = 6
        Picture1.DrawStyle = 0
End Sub
```

**If Node1.Left = 0 Then:** Your controls are already at their startup position, so exit.

**Picture1.Cls:** Clears Picture1 of any drawings that are present.

**Handle1.Move:** Moves this control back to the default startup position.

**Node1.Move:** Moves this control back to the default startup position.

**Shape1.Move:** Moves this control back to the default startup position.

**P = 0:** Resets the erase line flag variable back to 0.

**Picture1.DrawMode:** Resets the drawing mode to Inverse mode (6).

**Picture1.DrawStyle:** Resets the drawing style to Solid (0).

# Bézier Handle #1

The Handle1_MouseDown event in Listing 10.14 starts the process of redrawing the curve to give the illusion of movement as the curve is being reshaped.

**Listing 10.14. Preparing the curve when clicking a Bézier handle.**
```
Sub Handle1_MouseDown (Button%, Shift%, X!, Y!)
    Handle1.Visible = False
    BezMove
End Sub
```

**BezHandle1:** First makes the current Bézier handle invisible. The Bézier nodes and handles are really picture box controls; the dotted-lever line that joins the Bézier's node to a handle has one of its end points centered in the middle of each node and handle picture box. To redraw the lever lines correctly as the curve is being moved, you must hide the handle control that is being used to move the curve.

**BezMove:** Calls the BezMove procedure (Listing 10.12) to draw the first curve.

# The Mini-Bézier Curve Program

## Redrawing Levers for Handle #1

The *lever* is a dotted line that is attached to the handle and the curve's ending point. When you reshape a curve using one of its two handles, you also must redraw the levers, as shown in Listing 10.15.

**Listing 10.15. Drawing the Bézier curve as Handle #1 is moved.**

```
Sub Handle1_MouseMove (Button%, Shift%, X!, Y!)
Text1.Text = "X= " + Format$(X)
Text2.Text = "Y= " + Format$(Y)
    If Button Then
        BezDraw
        Picture1.DrawMode = 7
        Picture1.DrawStyle = 2
        Picture1.Line (P1.X, P1.Y)-(H1.X, H1.Y), Yellow
            H1.X = X
            H1.Y = Y
        Shape1.Left = H1.X - 45
        Shape1.Top = H1.Y - 45
        Picture1.Line (P1.X, P1.Y)-(H1.X, H1.Y), Yellow
    BezDraw
End If
End Sub
```

**Text1.Text:** Displays the current X coordinate of the picture box control.

**Text2.Text:** Displays the current Y coordinate of the picture box control.

**If Button then:** Continues only if the mouse button is held down.

**BezDraw:** Calling the BezDraw procedure draws the Bézier curve.

**ArtWork.DrawMode:** Changes DrawMode to Xor (7) so that dotted-lever lines can pass through other objects without erasing their images on the desktop.

**ArtWork.Line:** Draws the dotted lines. Yellow lever lines appear cyan when drawn in Xor mode.

**H1.X = X:** Makes a corner position of the lever line equal to the current mouse pointer's coordinate. You are drawing in Xor mode, which restores any images the lever lines pass over when the lever lines are redrawn again. This gives the illusion of movement.

**H1.Y = Y:** The same as H1.X = X, except for the Y coordinate of the lever line.

**Shape1.Left, Shape1.Top:** A Shape control replaces the Bézier Handle1 picture box control. If you try to move the Handle1 picture box using its Left and Top properties, the control bounces back and forth repeatedly. The Shape control acts as though you had drawn the handle manually.

**ArtWork.Line:** Draws the dotted-lever lines again to restore any images the lever line passes over. To animate a moving object, set the drawing mode to Xor (7) and draw the object twice. The Xor mode restores the background images.

**BezDraw:** Redraws the curve so that the illusion of movement is achieved.

## Rescaling Handle #1

After you move the Bézier handles to a new location, you must rescale the `Handle1` picture box control. The `Handle1` picture box is within the `Picture1` picture box, which acts as a container. Rescaling makes the internal coordinates of the `Handle1` picture box align to the internal coordinates of the `Picture1` container. (See Listing 10.16.)

**Listing 10.16. Rescaling the Bézier's handles to the new location.**
```
Sub Handle1_MouseUp (Button%, Shift%, X!, Y!)
    Handle1.Move X - 45, Y - 45
    Handle1.ScaleLeft = Handle1.Left
    Handle1.ScaleTop = Handle1.Top
    Handle1.Visible = True
End Sub
```

> **Handle1.Move:** Repositions `Handle1` so that it appears attached to the dotted-lever line.
>
> **Handle1.ScaleLeft (Top):** Rescales the handle so that it reflects the internal scale of the container.
>
> **Handle1.Visible:** Shows the handle only after you have repositioned it.

## Bézier Handle #2

The `Handle2_MouseDown` event in Listing 10.17 starts the process of redrawing the curve to give the illusion of movement as the curve is being reshaped.

**Listing 10.17. Setting the Bézier curve when clicking Handle #2.**
```
Sub Handle2_MouseDown (Button%, Shift%, X!, Y!)
    Handle2.Visible = False
    BezMove
End Sub
```

> **BezHandle2:** First makes the current Bézier handle invisible. The Bézier nodes and handles are really picture box controls; the dotted-lever line that joins the Bézier's node to a handle has one of its end points centered in the middle of each node and handle picture box. To redraw the lever lines correctly as the curve is being moved, you must hide the handle control that is being used to move the curve.
>
> **BezMove:** Calls the `BezMove` procedure (Listing 10.12) to draw the first curve.

## Redrawing Levers for Handle #2

The lever is a dotted line that is attached to the handle and the curve's ending point. When you reshape a curve using one of its two handles, you also must redraw the levers. (See Listing 10.18.)

## The Mini-Bézier Curve Program

**Listing 10.18. Redrawing the Bézier curve when Handle #2 is moved.**

```
Sub Handle2_MouseMove (Button %, Shift%, X!, Y!)
Text1.Text = "X= " + Format$(X)
Text2.Text = "Y= " + Format$(Y)
    If Button Then
        BezDraw
        Picture1.DrawMode = 7
        Picture1.DrawStyle = 2
        Picture1.Line (P2.X, P2.Y)-(H2.X, H2.Y), Yellow
            H2.X = X
            H2.Y = Y
        Shape2.Left = H2.X - 45
        Shape2.Top = H2.Y - 45
        Picture1.Line (P2.X, P2.Y)-(H2.X, H2.Y), Yellow
        BezDraw
    End If
End Sub
```

**Text1.Text:** Displays the current X coordinate of the picture box control.

**Text2.Text:** Displays the current Y coordinate of the picture box control.

**If Button then:** Continues only if the mouse button is held down.

**BezDraw:** Calling the BezDraw procedure draws the Bézier curve.

**ArtWork.DrawMode:** Changes DrawMode to Xor (7) so that dotted-lever lines can pass through other objects without erasing their images on the desktop.

**ArtWork.Line:** Draws the dotted lines. Yellow lever lines appear cyan when drawn in Xor mode.

**H2.X = X:** Makes a corner position of the lever line and curve's handle equal to the current mouse pointer's coordinate. You are drawing in Xor mode, which restores any images the lever lines pass over when the lever lines are redrawn again. This gives the illusion of movement.

**H2.Y = Y:** The same as H2.X = X, except for the Y coordinate of the lever line and curve's handle.

**Shape2.Left, Shape2.Top:** A Shape control replaces the Bézier Handle2 picture box control. If you try to move the Handle2 picture box using its Left and Top properties, the control bounces back and forth repeatedly. The Shape control acts as though you had drawn the handle manually.

**ArtWork.Line:** Draws the dotted-lever lines again to restore any images the lever line passes over. To animate a moving object, set the drawing mode to Xor (7) and draw the object twice. The Xor mode restores the background images.

**BezDraw:** Redraws the curve so that the illusion of movement is achieved.

Chapter **10**  337

## Rescaling Handle #2

After you move the Bézier's handle to a new location, you must rescale the `Handle2` picture box control. The `Handle2` picture box is within the `Picture1` picture box, which acts as a container. Rescaling makes the internal coordinates of the `Handle2` picture box align to the internal coordinates of the `Picture1` container, as shown in Listing 10.19.

**Listing 10.19. Rescaling the Bézier's handles to the new location.**

```
Sub Handle2_MouseUp (Button%, Shift%, X!, Y!)
    Handle2.Move X - 45, Y - 45
    Handle2.ScaleLeft = Handle2.Left
    Handle2.ScaleTop = Handle2.Top
    Handle2.Visible = True
End Sub
```

**Handle2.Move:** Repositions `Handle2` so that it looks attached to the dotted line.

**Handle2.ScaleLeft (Top):** Rescales the handle so that it reflects the internal scale of the container.

**Handle2.Visible:** Shows the handle only after you have repositioned it.

## Grabbing a Curve by Its Nodes

The nodes located on either end of a curve object are called `Node1` and `Node2`. You can move a curve using either one of these two Bézier nodes.

The `Node1` mouse event routines are based on the `Handle` routines (starting at Listing 10.14), except you also have to move `Handle1`, which is attached to `Node1`, while moving the curve. Listing 10.20 shows how to set the curve.

**Listing 10.20. Setting the curve when clicking Bézier's Node #1.**

```
Sub Node1_MouseDown (Button%, Shift%, X!, Y!)
    If P = 0 Then Nodehandle_Click
        BezMove
        Picture1.Line (P1.X, P1.Y)-(H1.X, H1.Y), Yellow
        Node1.Visible = False
        Handle1.Visible = False
End Sub
```

**If P = 0 Then Nodehandle_Click:** The nodes are placed on either end of the line as soon as you finish drawing a line. The handles are not visible until you click the button marked Nodes (`NodeHandle_Click`). If you want to move the line using either node before clicking the Nodes button, however, you must trigger the `Node1_MouseDown` event. You use the P variable as a flag to trigger the Nodes button.

## The Mini-Bézier Curve Program

**BezMove:** Draws the first Bézier curve that erases the current line.

**Picture1.Line:** Draws the dotted-lever line.

**Node1.Visible:** Hides the node you are moving.

**Handle1.Visible:** Hides the handle that is attached to the node by the dotted-lever line.

The Node_MouseMove event in Listing 10.21 draws the circle whenever the first node is manually moved by the mouse pointer.

**Listing 10.21. Redrawing the Bézier curve when Node #1 is moved.**

```
Sub Node1_MouseMove (Button%, Shift%, X!, Y!)
Text1.Text = "X= " + Format$(X)
Text2.Text = "Y= " + Format$(Y)
    If Button Then
        BezDraw
        P1.X = X
        P1.Y = Y
        H1.X = (X - X1) + Handle1.Left + 45
        H1.Y = (Y - Y1) + Handle1.Top + 45
        Shape1.Left = P1.X - 45
        Shape1.Top = P1.Y - 45
        BezDraw
    End If
End Sub
```

**Text1.Text:** Displays the current X coordinate of the picture box control.

**Text2.Text:** Displays the current Y coordinate of the picture box control.

**If Button then:** Continues only if the mouse button is held down.

**BezDraw:** Calling the BezDraw procedure (Listing 10.3) draws the first Bézier curve.

**P1.X = X:** Makes a corner position of the lever line and curve's end point equal to the current mouse pointer's coordinate. You are drawing in Xor mode, which restores any images the lever lines pass over when the lever lines are redrawn again. This gives the illusion of movement.

**P1.Y = Y:** The same as P1.X = X, except for the Y coordinate of the lever line and curve end point.

**H1.X, H1.Y:** Moves the curve's handle, keeping the same distance and angle between the original Node1 and Handle1 positions.

**Shape1.Left, Shape1.Top:** A Shape control replaces the Bézier Node1 picture box control. If you try to move the Node1 picture box using its Left and Top properties, the control bounces back and forth repeatedly. The Shape control acts as though you had drawn the node manually.

**BezDraw:** Redraws the curve so that the illusion of movement is achieved.

## Rescaling Node #1

Now that you've moved the Bézier's node and handle to a new location, you must rescale both picture box controls. The node and handle picture boxes are within the Picture1 picture box, which acts as a container. Rescaling makes the internal coordinates of the node and handle picture boxes align to the internal coordinates of the Picture1 container. (See Listing 10.22.)

**Listing 10.22. Rescaling the Bézier's Node #1.**

```
Sub Node1_MouseUp (Button%, Shift%, X!, Y!)
Node1.Move X - 45, Y - 45
Node1.ScaleLeft = Node1.Left
Node1.ScaleTop = Node1.Top
Node1.Visible = True
    Handle1.Move (X - X1) + Handle1.Left, (Y - Y1) + Handle1.Top
    Handle1.ScaleLeft = Handle1.Left
    Handle1.ScaleTop = Handle1.Top
    Handle1.Visible = True
X1 = P1.X
Y1 = P1.Y
    Picture1.DrawMode = 7: Picture1.DrawStyle = 2
    Picture1.Line (P1.X, P1.Y)-(H1.X, H1.Y), Yellow
End Sub
```

**Node1.Move:** Relocates Node1 to the new coordinates.

**Node1.ScaleLeft** (Top): Resets the scales so that they reflect the Picture1's internal scale.

**Node1.Visible:** Makes the Node1 picture box visible.

**Handle1.Move:** Relocates Handle1 to the new coordinates.

**Handle1.ScaleLeft** (Top): Scales Handle1's interior so that it reflects the Picture1 internal scale.

**Handle1.Visible:** Makes the Handle1 picture box visible.

**X1, Y1:** Stores the curve's end point coordinates.

**Picture1.Line:** Redraws the dotted-lever line that connects Node1 to Handle1.

## Moving the Curve's Node #2

The Node2 MouseDown events in Listing 10.23 are the same as the Node1 MouseDown, MouseMove, and MouseUp events, except you change each reference to the node and handle control names to reflect Node2 or Handle2. (See Listings 10.23 through 10.25.) For example, you change any reference to P1.X, P1.Y H1.X, H1.Y to P2.X, P2.Y, H2.X, H2.Y. You change the Node1, Handle1, and Shape1 references to Node2, Handle2, and Shape2, respectively.

# The Mini-Bézier Curve Program

**Listing 10.23. Setting the curve when clicking Node #2.**

```
Sub Node2_MouseDown (Button%, Shift%, X!, Y!)
    If P = 0 Then Nodehandle_Click
        BezMove
    Picture1.Line (P2.X, P2.Y)-(H2.X, H2.Y), Yellow
    Node2.Visible = False
    Handle2.Visible = False
End Sub
```

Refer to the `Node1_MouseDown` event (Listing 10.20) for details on how to structure the preceding code.

**Listing 10.24. Moving the curve when using Node #2.**

```
Sub Node2_MouseMove (Button%, Shift%, X!, Y!)
Text1.Text = "X= " + Format$(X)
Text2.Text = "Y= " + Format$(Y)
    If Button Then
            BezDraw
        Picture1.DrawMode = 7
            P2.X = X
            P2.Y = Y
        H2.X = (X - X2) + Handle2.Left + 45
        H2.Y = (Y - Y2) + Handle2.Top + 45
        Shape2.Left = P2.X - 45
        Shape2.Top = P2.Y - 45
            BezDraw
    End If
End Sub
```

Refer to the `Node1_MouseMove` event (Listing 10.21) for details on how to structure the preceding code.

**Listing 10.25. Rescaling the Bézier's nodes to the new location.**

```
Sub Node2_MouseUp (Button%, Shift%, X As Single, Y As Single)
    Node2.Move X - 45, Y - 45
    Node2.ScaleLeft = Node2.Left
    Node2.ScaleTop = Node2.Top
    Node2.Visible = True
Handle2.Move (X - X2) + Handle2.Left, (Y - Y2) + Handle2.Top
    Handle2.ScaleLeft = Handle2.Left
    Handle2.ScaleTop = Handle2.Top
    Handle2.Visible = True
            X2 = P2.X
            Y2 = P2.Y
    Picture1.DrawMode = 7: Picture1.DrawStyle = 2
    Picture1.Line (P2.X, P2.Y)-(H2.X, H2.Y), Yellow
End Sub
```

Refer to the `Node1_MouseUp` event (Listing 10.22) for details on how to structure the preceding code.

## Converting a Line to a Curve

After you draw a line on the desktop, you can click the Nodes button, which converts a line to a curve using the `NodeHandle_Click` event. The `Nodehandle_Click` routine places the two Bézier handles a quarter distance from either end of the two nodes that are attached to line. (See Listing 10.26.) It then draws two dotted-lever lines that are attached to each of the two nodes and two handles.

**Listing 10.26. Placing the handles on the line.**

```
Sub Nodehandle_Click ()
If Node1.Left = 0 Then Exit Sub
    Picture1.Enabled = True
    Picture1.DrawMode = 7: Picture1.DrawStyle = 2
        MoveLeft = (X2 + X1) \ 2
        MoveTop = (Y2 + Y1) \ 2
    Handle1.Left = (X1 + MoveLeft) \ 2 - 45
    Handle1.Top = (Y1 + MoveTop) \ 2 - 45
    Handle2.Left = (X2 + MoveLeft) \ 2 - 45
    Handle2.Top = (Y2 + MoveTop) \ 2 - 45
    Handle1.ScaleLeft = Handle1.Left
    Handle1.ScaleTop = Handle1.Top
    Handle2.ScaleLeft = Handle2.Left
    Handle2.ScaleTop = Handle2.Top
        H1.X = Handle1.Left + 45
        H1.Y = Handle1.Top + 45
        H2.X = Handle2.Left + 45
        H2.Y = Handle2.Top + 45
    Picture1.Line (X1, Y1)-(H1.X, H1.Y), Yellow
    Picture1.Line (X2, Y2)-(H2.X, H2.Y), Yellow
End Sub
```

**If Node1.Left = 0 Then:** If the node is located at coordinate 0, a line has not been drawn yet, so exit this event.

**MoveLeft, MoveTop:** Variables that represent the halfway mark of the line drawn.

**Handle1 (2), Left (Top):** Moves each handle a quarter distance from the end of each node. The -45 is the center position of the handle picture box controls in twips.

**Handle1 (2), ScaleLeft (Top):** Scales the controls to reflect the scale of the form.

**H1.X = Handle1.Left + 45:** Sets the curve's handle coordinates to reflect the middle position of each Bézier handle.

**Picture1.Line:** Draws the dotted lines that connect each node to a handle.

## Summary

You can generate a four-point Bézier curve by supplying the start and end points of the curve and two handle points to a mathematical formula. The two handles control the elasticity of the left and right halves of the curve. If you are designing Bézier curves in a 16-bit Windows operating system, you require a procedure that can calculate and draw the curve onto the screen or printer.

# The Mini-Bézier Curve Program

If you are designing Bézier curves on a 32-bit Windows operating system, you can use the API `PolyBézier` function to calculate the curve by issuing the four curve points required.

There are several varieties of Bézier curves besides the four-point spline curve demonstrated in this chapter. Another popular Bézier curve is a three-point spline, which is used widely in creating the outline of text characters. A three-point spline curve is similar to the four-point Bézier. The calculation is slightly different, however, because it requires the start and end points of the curve to be drawn but needs only a handle to control the curve's elasticity. You can look at the single-handle approach as welding together the two handles of a four-point Bézier curve. The 32-bit API Bézier functions use the four-point Bézier curves method.

Refer to the Artisan program in Chapter 3 for more details on the construction of Bézier curves.

# CHAPTER 11

# The Rounded Corners Program

## The Rounded Corners Program

The Rounded Corners program shows three ways to use the Visual Basic Line and Circle statements to connect and draw a rectangle with rounded corners. The three options to choose from are CurrentXY, Basic, and Stretcher. Each draws a rounded rectangle using a slightly different procedure. (See Figure 11.1 for a screen shot of the Rounded Corners program.)

**Figure 11.1.**
*Screen shot of the Rounded Corners program.*

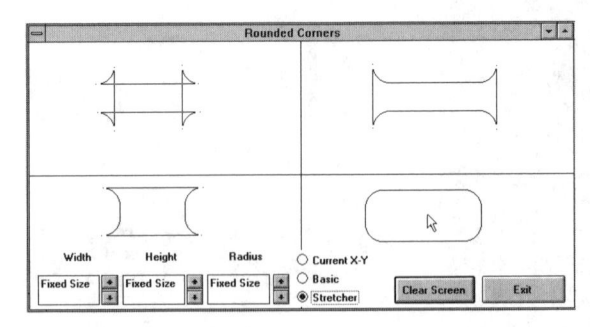

The three drawing routines are as follows:

1. CurrentXY: Draws a line that starts at the current X and Y positions of the MouseDown event. The procedure then uses the Pset statement to update the CurrentX and CurrentY positions before connecting the line to a quarter circle. It continues this pattern, moving counter-clockwise until it has drawn all four lines and quarter circles that make up a rounded rectangle. The CurrentXY procedure works best for rounded rectangles that need to be placed with a MouseDown event but that do not need to be stretched or resized.

2. Basic: Draws a line that starts the X and Y positions of the MouseDown event. It then draws a quarter circle and continues moving counter-clockwise until the rounded rectangle is drawn. The Basic procedure works best for rounded rectangles that you want to resize by using a MouseDown event.

3. Stretcher: Draws all lines and quarter circles counter-clockwise using the MouseMove X1, Y1, X2, and Y2 coordinate values. A rounded corner rectangle is enlarged or reduced when you use the mouse. The Stretcher procedure is best suited for rounded rectangles you need to resize by dragging the mouse pointer.

## How to Use the Program

Now you're ready to start using the Rounded Corners program. In this section, you learn the properties for the form and controls that you need to create or edit a rectangle with round corners. In particular, the following three scrollbar controls are used to control the shape and appearance of the rounded rectangle you create:

Width Scroll bar: Used to change the length of the two horizontal lines that make up a rounded rectangle.

Height Scroll bar: Used to change the length of the two vertical lines that make up a rounded rectangle.

## Chapter 11

    `Radius Scroll bar`: Used to change the size of the quarter circles that make up a rounded rectangle. Setting this value to 0 causes an error.

The `CurrentXY` and `Basic` procedures draw the same rounded rectangle shape. However, each uses a different routine to create the shape.

The Rounded Corners program's form and control properties are listed in Table 11.1.

**Table 11.1. The properties of the Rounded Corners form and controls.**

*Object: Form*
*Object Name: Form1*

| Caption | = "Rounded Corners" | ScaleMode | = 3 'Pixel |
| Height | = 4920 | Top | = 1125 |
| Left | = 60 | Width | = 9615 |

*Object: Command Button*
*Object Name: Exit*

| Caption | = "Exit" | Top | = 4005 |
| Height | = 465 | Width | = 1455 |
| Left | = 7920 | | |

*Object: Option Button*
*Object Name: Option1*

| Caption | = "Stretcher" | Left | = 4680 |
| Height | = 330 | Top | = 4185 |
| Index | = 2 | Width | = 1500 |

*Object: Option Button*
*Object Name: Option1*

| Caption | = "Basic" | Left | = 4680 |
| Height | = 330 | Top | = 3870 |
| Index | = 1 | Width | = 1500 |

*Object: Option Button*
*Object Name: Option1*

| Caption | = "Current X-Y" | Top | = 3555 |
| Height | = 330 | Value | = -1 'True |
| Index | = 0 | Width | = 1500 |
| Left | = 4680 | | |

*continues*

**T**able 11.1. continued

*Object: Command Button*
*Object Name: Cls*

| | | | |
|---|---|---|---|
| Caption | = "Clear Screen" | Left | = 6390 |
| Default | = -1'True | Top | = 4005 |
| Height | = 465 | Width | = 1410 |

*Object: Textbox*
*Object Name: Text1*

| | | | |
|---|---|---|---|
| Height | = 510 | Width | = "40" |
| Index | = 0 | Top | = 3960 |
| Left | = 135 | Text | = 1095 |

*Object: Textbox*
*Object Name: Text1*

| | | | |
|---|---|---|---|
| Height | = 510 | Text | = "10" |
| Index | = 1 | Top | = 3960 |
| Left | = 1620 | Width | = 1095 |

*Object: Textbox*
*Object Name: Text1*

| | | | |
|---|---|---|---|
| Height | = 510 | Text | = "26" |
| Index | = 2 | Top | = 3960 |
| Left | = 3105 | Width | = 1095 |

*Object: Vscroll Bar*
*Object Name: VScroll1*

| | | | |
|---|---|---|---|
| Height | = 510 | SmallChange | = 6 |
| Index | = 2 | Top | = 3960 |
| Left | = 4260 | Value | = 25 |
| Max | = 1 | Width | = 285 |
| Min | = 600 | | |

*Object: VScroll Bar*
*Object Name: VScroll1*

| | | | |
|---|---|---|---|
| Height | = 510 | SmallChange | = 10 |
| Index | = 1 | Top | = 3960 |

| | | | | | |
|---|---|---|---|---|---|
| Left | = | 2745 | Value | = | 10 |
| Max | = | 0 | Width | = | 285 |
| Min | = | 600 | | | |

*Object: VScroll Bar*
*Object Name: VScroll1*

| | | | | | |
|---|---|---|---|---|---|
| Height | = | 510 | SmallChange | = | 10 |
| Index | = | 0 | Top | = | 3960 |
| Left | = | 1260 | Value | = | 40 |
| Max | = | 0 | Width | = | 285 |
| Min | = | 600 | | | |

*Object: Label*
*Object Name: Label1*

| | | | | | |
|---|---|---|---|---|---|
| Alignment | = | 2 'Center | Left | = | 3105 |
| Caption | = | "Radius" | Top | = | 3555 |
| Height | = | 285 | Width | = | 1365 |
| Index | = | 2 | | | |

*Object: Label*
*Object Name: Label1*

| | | | | | |
|---|---|---|---|---|---|
| Alignment | = | 2 'Center | Left | = | 1620 |
| Caption | = | "Height" | Top | = | 3555 |
| Height | = | 285 | Width | = | 1365 |
| Index | = | 1 | | | |

*Object: Label*
*Object Name: Label1*

| | | | | | |
|---|---|---|---|---|---|
| Alignment | = | 2 'Center | Left | = | 135 |
| Caption | = | "Width" | Top | = | 3555 |
| Height | = | 285 | Width | = | 1410 |
| Index | = | 0 | | | |

# The Rounded Corners Program

Figure 11.2 shows the form you create using the properties from Table 11.1.

**Figure 11.2.**
*The form and its controls.*

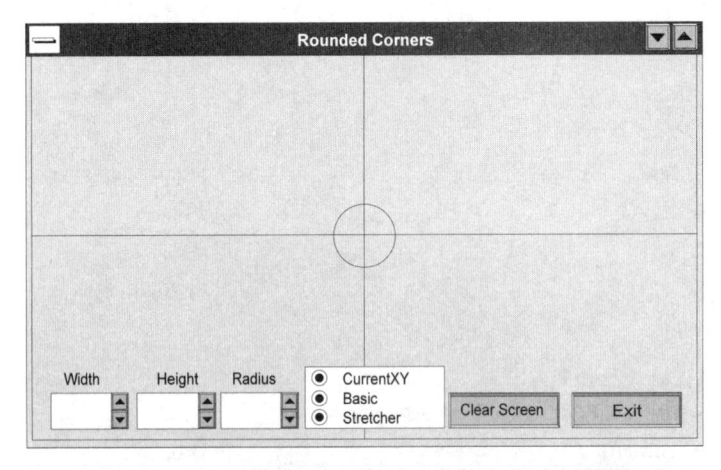

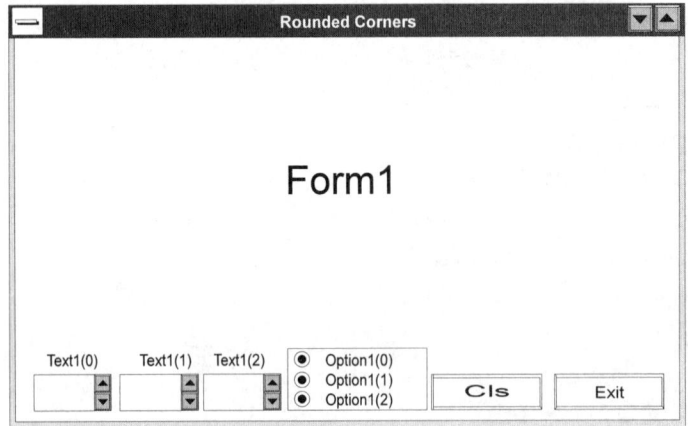

## Declarations and Startup Values

The declaration section of the form (Listing 11.1) uses eight integers to store the coordinates' values needed to draw each rounded rectangle.

**Listing 11.1. Variable names at startup.**

```
Dim X1, Y1, X2, Y2, Wide, High, PI, Radius As Integer
```

> **Dim X1, Y1, X2, Y2:** Variables used to store each rounded corner's start and end coordinates.
>
> **Wide, High:** Stores the length and height values of the rectangles.
>
> **PI, Radius As Integer:** Stores the value of PI (3.14159265) and the radius of each circle.

The `Form_Paint` event (Listing 11.2) draws a vertical and horizontal line to divide the form into four sections when using the stretch routine in this program.

**Listing 11.2. Drawing the crosshair lines on the form.**

```
Sub Form_Paint ()
    Line (0, ScaleHeight \ 2)-(ScaleWidth, ScaleHeight \ 2)
    Line (ScaleWidth \ 2, 0)-(ScaleWidth \ 2, ScaleHeight)
End Sub
```

**Line:** Displays two lines that intersect at the middle position of the form.

The `Form_Resize` event (Listing 11.3) positions the form in the middle of the screen.

**Listing 11.3. Centering the form.**

```
Sub Form_Resize ()
    Form1.Left = (Screen.Width - Width) \ 2
    Form1.Top = (Screen.Height - Height) \ 2
End Sub
```

**Form1.Left:** Centers the form horizontally on the screen.

**Form1.Top:** Centers the form vertically on the screen.

## The Form's Mouse Events

The `Form_MouseDown` event (Listing 11.4) calls a drawing routine that matches the option button selected.

**Listing 11.4. Drawing a rounded rectangle.**

```
Sub Form_MouseDown (Button%, Shift%, X As Single, Y As Single)
    Select Case True
        Case Option1(0)
            DrawMode = 13: Cls
            CurrentXY Button, Shift, X, Y
        Case Option1(1)
            DrawMode = 13: Cls
            Basic Button, Shift, X, Y
        Case Option1(2)
            DrawMode = 6
            X1 = X: Y1 = Y
            X2 = X1: Y2 = Y1
            Stretcher Button, Shift, X, Y
    End Select
End Sub
```

**Select Case True:** Depending on the value of the three `Option` controls (`True`, the option is selected; or `False`, the option is not currently selected), go to one of the following `Case` blocks that matches the true expression:

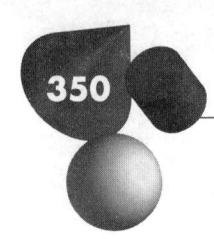

## The Rounded Corners Program

**Case Option1(0):** You have selected the `CurrentXY` option button.

**DrawMode = Copy_Pen:** Start drawing in normal pen mode (13).

**CLS:** Clear the form of any current drawings.

**CurrentXY:** Call the `CurrentXY` procedure (Listing 11.8), which draws a rectangle with rounded corners using the `CurrentX` and `CurrentY` and `Step` values of a `Line` statement.

**Case Option1(1):** You have selected the `Basic` option button.

**DrawMode = Copy_Pen:** Start drawing in normal pen mode (13).

**CLS:** Clear the form of any current drawings.

**Basic:** Call the `Basic` procedure (Listing 11.6) to draw a rectangle with rounded corners using the precise X and Y coordinates when drawing a line or circle.

**Case Option(2):** You have selected the `Stretcher` option button.

**DrawMode = 6 (Inverse):** Change to `Inverse` drawing mode because you are moving the object.

**X1, Y1, X2, Y2:** Store the current mouse pointer's X and Y coordinates. You need these coordinates to move the rounded rectangle object.

**Stretcher:** You call this procedure to draw a moving rounded rectangle. This procedure uses the same `Line` and `Circle` statements as the `Basic` procedure (Listing 11.6), except the X and Y values are replaced with X1, Y1, X2, and Y2 variables. This makes the grouped lines and curves appear to move as one object.

The `Form_MouseMove` event (Listing 11.5) draws a stretching rounded rectangle only if the option button marked Stretch is selected.

### Listing 11.5. Moving the rounded rectangle object.

```
Sub Form_MouseMove (Button%, Shift%, X As Single, Y As Single)
If Button And Option1(2).Value Then
    Stretcher Button, Shift, X, Y
        X1 = X
        Y1 = Y
        X2 = X1 'remark out for skew effect
        Y2 = Y1 'remark out for skew effect
    Stretcher Button, Shift, X, Y
End If
End Sub
```

**If Button And Option(2):** The only procedure that uses the `MouseMove` event is the `Stretcher` procedure (Listing 11.10), which draws the moving object. Only if the mouse button is held and the option button marked as Stretcher is currently selected, do the following block of code.

**Stretcher Button, Shift, X, Y:** Draw the rounded rectangle object.

**X1, Y1, X2, Y2:** Make a start and end position of the line equal to the current mouse pointer's coordinate. You are drawing in `Inverse` mode, which draws the first image the reverse color of the background (white to black). If any of the next image that is drawn lands on a black pixel image of the first image, then it is drawn white, and vice versa. Redrawing gives the illusion of movement.

Remark out (') the X2 and Y2 code lines to view how any Line statements that are included these values remain stationary. This way, you learn how to perform *skewing* on an object. Skewing is a form of stretching an object only on its vertical or horizontal axis. This example, however, skews obstruct points, giving the illusion that the object is breaking apart.

**Stretcher Button, Shift, X, Y:** Redraw the rounded rectangle object to erase the last one drawn.

## Drawing a Rounded Rectangle Using the *Basic* Procedure

The Basic procedure in Listing 11.6 uses the Pset statement to fill in gaps that are caused by the Line statement removing the last pixel point of a line object. However, a Pset pixel image is square only up to a four-pixel width; then the Pset pixel image is round. The round shape is calculated from the center pixel out. Evenly numbered pixel image widths could add an undesirable extra row of pixels where the line and circle objects join.

The Stretcher procedure (Listing 11.10) replaces the Pset statement by using the values specified by the p1 and p2 variables. Another possible problem may result if you use large drawing width values. All line and circle start and end points are rounded. This makes objects that are joined in Inverse mode appear to have gaps in between them.

**Listing 11.6.** The Basic **option button procedure.**

```
Sub Basic (Button As Integer, Shift As Integer, X As Single, Y As Single)
    Const PI = 3.14159265
    Wide = Val(Text1(0).Text)
    High = Val(Text1(1).Text)
    Radius = Val(Text1(2).Text)
X = X - (Val(Text1(0).Text) \ 2) 'offsets from mouse pointer
Y = Y - Val(Text1(2).Text)
'''''''''''''''''''
Line (X, Y)-(X + Wide, Y): PSet (X + Wide, Y)
Circle (X + Wide, Y + Radius), Radius, , 0, PI / 2
'''''''''''''''''''
Line (X + Wide + Radius, Y + Radius)-(X + Wide + Radius, Y + Radius + High)
PSet (X + Wide + Radius, Y + Radius + High)
Circle (X + Wide, Y + High + Radius), Radius, , 3 * PI / 2, 0
'''''''''''''''''''
Line (X + Wide, Y + Radius + High + Radius)-(X, Y + Radius + High + Radius)
PSet (X, Y + Radius + High + Radius)
Circle (X, Y + Radius + High), Radius, , PI, 3 * PI / 2
'''''''''''''''''''
Line (X - Radius, Y + Radius + High)-(X - Radius, Y + Radius)
PSet (X - Radius, Y + Radius)
Circle (X, Y + Radius), Radius, , PI / 2, PI
End Sub
```

# The Rounded Corners Program

**Const PI:** This represents the value of PI (3.14159265).

**Wide, High:** Change the rectangle's width and length measurements.

**Radius:** Change the radius length of each rounded corner.

Here's how the rectangle with rounded corners is constructed using the `Line` and `Circle` statements for Listing 11.6. The rounded rectangle travels in a clockwise direction as each line and circle element is added.

1. **Line:** The starting X and Y screen positions; the line then travels horizontally to the right.
2. **Pset:** The last pixel point can be truncated in Visual Basic graphics methods, so draw a single pixel point.
3. **Circle:** (Top-right corner.) The circle starts at the twelve o'clock position and ends at the three o'clock position.
4. **Line:** Connects to the circle's three o'clock position. The line then travels vertically downward.
5. **Pset:** The last pixel point can be truncated in Visual Basic graphic methods, so draw a single pixel point.
6. **Circle:** (Bottom-right corner.) The circle starts at the three o'clock position and ends at the six o'clock position.
7. **Line:** Connects to the circle's six o'clock position; the line then travels horizontally to the left.
8. **Pset:** The last pixel point can be truncated in Visual Basic graphic methods, so draw a single pixel point.
9. **Circle:** (Bottom-left corner.) The circle starts at the six o'clock position and ends at the nine o'clock position.
10. **Line:** Connects to the circle's nine o'clock position; the line then travels vertically upward.
11. **Pset:** The last pixel point can be truncated in Visual Basic graphics methods, so draw a single pixel point.
12. **Circle:** (Top-left corner.) The circle starts at the nine o'clock and ends at the twelve o'clock position.

Listing 11.7 shows the routine for erasing images on the form.

### Listing 11.7. Erasing the images on the form.

```
Sub CLS_Click ()
    Cls
    Form_Paint
End Sub
```

**Cls:** Erase any images by clearing the screen.

**Form_Paint:** Force the form's paint event to redraw the horizontal and vertical dividing lines.

## Using the *Step* Keyword to Round a Shape

The CurrentXY procedure in Listing 11.8 uses the Step statement in conjunction with the Pset statement to position each starting coordinate of a line or circle. The Pset statement fills in any possible gaps between the connection of a line and circle. The Pset statement also changes the CurrentX and CurrentY drawing coordinates to match the last graphical pixel point drawn on the screen.

**Listing 11.8.** The CurrentXY option button procedure.

```
Sub CurrentXY (Button As Integer, Shift As Integer, X As Single, Y As Single)
    Const PI = 3.14159265
    Wide = Val(Text1(0).Text)
    high = Val(Text1(1).Text)
    Radius = Val(Text1(2).Text)
    CurrentX = X: CurrentY = Y
''''''''''''''''''''''''''''
Line -(CurrentX, CurrentY - high)
Circle Step(-Radius, 0), Radius, , 0, PI / 2
''''''''''''''''''''''''''''
PSet Step(0, -Radius)
Line -(CurrentX - Wide, Y - high - Radius)
Circle Step(0, Radius), Radius, , PI / 2, PI
''''''''''''''''''''''''''''
PSet Step(-Radius, 0)
Line -(CurrentX, CurrentY + high)
Circle Step(Radius, 0), Radius, , PI, 3 * PI / 2
''''''''''''''''''''''''''''
PSet Step(0, Radius)
Line -(CurrentX + Wide, CurrentY)
Circle Step(0, -Radius), Radius, , 3 * PI / 2, 0
End Sub
```

**Const PI:** This represents the value of PI (3.14159265).

**Wide, High:** Change the rectangle's width and length measurements.

**Radius:** Change the radius length of each rounded corner.

**CurrentX = X: CurrentY = Y:** Position the X and Y coordinates for the next drawing method you apply.

Here's how you construct a rectangle with rounded corners using the form's CurrentX and CurrentY values. This example travels in a counter-clockwise direction:

**Line - :** The hyphen (-) indicates that the line starts at the last CurrentX and CurrentY coordinate and connects to the top-right circle (three o'clock position).

**Circle Step:** The Step keyword indicates that the next X and Y coordinates are offset from the CurrentX and CurrentY positions by the distances indicated (top right-hand corner twelve o'clock to three o'clock position). You are drawing each of the four line and circle objects in a counter-clockwise fashion. However, the Circle statement always draws in a clockwise direction. You may want to switch values to position and draw all objects in a clockwise direction.

*continues*

## The Rounded Corners Program

**PSet Step(0, -Radius):** The Step keyword indicates that the next X and Y coordinates are offset from the CurrentX and CurrentY positions by the distances indicated. The last object drawn was a circle, so the CurrentX and CurrentY are the center coordinate of the circle. (Do not get tricked into thinking that the last pixel point drawn on the circle's arc is the CurrentX, CurrentY position.)

An alternative to the CurrentX, CurrentY method shown in Listing 11.8 is to use the Line, Circle, and Pset statements' Step keyword options, as demonstarted in the following code example:

```
CurrentX = X: CurrentY = Y
    ''''''''''''''''''''''''''
Line -Step(0, -high)
Circle Step(-Radius, 0), Radius, , 0, PI / 2
    '''''''''''''''''''''''''
PSet Step(0, -Radius)
Line -Step(-wide, 0)
Circle Step(0, Radius), Radius, , PI / 2, PI
    '''''''''''''''''''''''
PSet Step(-Radius, 0)
Line -Step(0, high)
Circle Step(Radius, 0), Radius, , PI, 3 * PI / 2
    '''''''''''''''''''''''
PSet Step(0, Radius)
Line -Step(wide, 0)
Circle Step(0, -Radius), Radius, , 3 * PI / 2, 0
```

The Step keyword option specifies that the starting coordinates are relative to the current graphics position, given by the CurrentX and CurrentY values. The CurrentX and CurrentY coordinates change when a line, circle, or pixel point is drawn. The Line statement's CurrentX and CurrentY would be the last pixel drawn on the line. The Circle statements CurrentX and CurrentY would be the center point of the circle and the Pset statement's CurrentX and CurrentY would be the pixel drawn.

## Choosing a Drawing Option

When you choose an option button marked Basic or CurrentXY, the wide, high, and radius values of the rounded rectangle are displayed in the three text boxes on the form. If you choose the option button marked Stretcher, the three text boxes display the word "Fixed," which indicates that the wide, high, and radius values cannot be changed. See Listing 11.9.

**Listing 11.9. Choosing one of the three option buttons.**

```
Sub Option1_Click (Index As Integer)
    If Index = 2 Then
        Cls: Form_Paint
        Text1(0).Text = "Fixed Size"
        Text1(1).Text = "Fixed Size"
        Text1(2).Text = "Fixed Size"
    Else
        Text1(0).Text = Vscroll1(0).Value
        Text1(1).Text = Vscroll1(1).Value
        Text1(2).Text = Vscroll1(2).Value
    End If
End Sub
```

**If Index = 2 Then:** The width, high, and radius values of the object cannot be changed.

**Else:** The width, high, and radius value of the object can be changed.

## Using the *Stretcher* Procedure to Draw a Rounded Rectangle

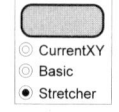

The Stretcher procedure in Listing 11.10 uses the p1 and p2 variables' values to fill in gaps that are caused by the Line statement removing the last pixel point of a line object. A problem may result if you use large drawing width values because line and circle start and end points are always rounded. This makes objects that are joined in Inverse mode appear to have gaps in between them.

Listing 11.10. The Stretcher option button procedure.

```
Sub Stretcher (Button As Integer, Shift As Integer, X As Single, Y As Single)
Const PI = 3.14159265
Wide = X1 - (Form1.ScaleWidth \ 2)
high = Y1 - (Form1.ScaleHeight \ 2)
Radius = X2 - (X2 - 20)
If DrawWidth = 1 Then
  p1 = DrawWidth: p2 = DrawWidth 'offset pixel
Else
  p1 = DrawWidth: p2 = -DrawWidth 'offset pixel
End If
'''''''''''''''''''''
Line (X1 + p1, Y1)-(X2 + Wide + p2, Y2)
Circle (X1 + Wide, Y1 + Radius), Radius, , 0, PI / 2
'''''''''''''''''''''
Line (X1 + Wide + Radius, Y1 + Radius + p1)- [IC:CCC]
          (X2 + Wide + Radius, Y2 + Radius + high + p2)
Circle (X1 + Wide, Y1 + high + Radius), Radius, , 3 * PI / 2, 0
'''''''''''''''''''''
Line (X1 + Wide - p1, Y1 + Radius + high + Radius)- [IC:CCC]
          (X2 - p2, Y2 + Radius + high + Radius)
Circle (X1, Y1 + Radius + high), Radius, , PI, 3 * PI / 2
'''''''''''''''''''''
Line (X1 - Radius, Y1 + Radius + high - p1)- [IC:CCC]
          (X2 - Radius, Y2 + Radius - p2)
Circle (X1, Y1 + Radius), Radius, , PI / 2, PI
End Sub
```

**Const PI:** This represents the value of PI (3.14159265).

**Wide, High:** Change the rectangle's width and length measurements. For this example, the width and height of the object is changed as you move the mouse pointer. The 0 width and 0 height dimensions are at the form's dead center point.

Positioning the mouse point at the center coordinate creates a perfect circle. You use negative width values to the left of center, and you use positive width values to the right of center. Negative height values are within the top half of the form, and positive height values are within the bottom half of the form.

# The Rounded Corners Program

**Radius:** A fixed radius length of each rounded corner.

**If DrawWidth = 1 Then:** When you're using a drawing width of one pixel, both the p1 and p2 offset values are positive. For any other drawing width value, the p1 value is positive and the p2 value is negative.

The steps for the construction of a rectangle with rounded corners are the same ones you use in the Basic procedure in Listing 11.6. However, the Stretcher procedure replaces the Pset statements by adding or subtracting extra pixel points to fill in any gaps that the Line statement may have created.

## Using the Scrollbar Controls

The scrollbar's Value property indicates the width, height, and radius of the rounded rectangle. (See Listing 11.11.)

### Listing 11.11. Changing the size of the object.

```
Sub VScroll1_Change (Index As Integer)
If Text1(0).Text = "Fixed Size" Then Exit Sub
    Select Case Index
        Case 0
            Text1(0).Text = Vscroll1(0).Value
        Case 1
            Text1(1).Text = Vscroll1(1).Value
        Case 2
            Text1(2).Text = Vscroll1(2).Value
    End Select
End Sub
```

**Case 0:** You are changing the width of the rounded rectangle. The minimum value is 600, and the maximum value is 0. This makes the values increase when you press the top scrollbar arrow.

**Case 1:** You are changing the height of the rounded rectangle. The minimum value is 600, and the maximum value is 0. This makes the values increase when you press the top scrollbar arrow.

**Case 2:** You are changing the radius of the four circles at each corner of the rectangle. The minimum value is 600, and the maximum value is 1. This makes the values increase when you press the top scrollbar arrow. You cannot have a circle's radius equal less than one unit of measurement. The maximum value must not be less than 1; otherwise, an error occurs.

## Summary

The `Basic`, `CurrentXY`, and `Stretcher` procedures draw rectangles with rounded corners when you click the mouse button on the form. You may want to consider adding eight small picture box controls at the corner positions of the rectangle. You then can use the `MouseMove` event of the picture box to trigger code statements that round the corners of the rectangle object. You may also need to add eight variable arrays to store each new coordinate because a rounded rectangle has eight screen position points.

You should also experiment with changing the order in which each line and circle is drawn (clockwise or counter-clockwise). It is important to remember that a circle is always drawn clockwise when you use the Visual Basic `Circle` statement.

For using Visual Basic programs that can access the GDI32 API functions in Windows operating systems that support such features, use the API `ArcTo` and/or API `PolyDraw` functions to shorten the code routines shown in this chapter. Refer to Appendix B, "Windows NT, Windows 95 and Higher," for details about the GDI32 API functions.

There are as many ways to connect the lines to lines, circles to circles, or lines to circles as there are options to place the `CurrentX` and `CurrentY` coordinates when using graphical methods. Refer to the section titled "Summary," in Chapter 1 for possible current steps, last moves, or next-step combinations available for the `Line`, `Circle`, and `Pset` statements.

# CHAPTER 12

# The Text Alignment Program

# The Text Alignment Program

Chapter 12 covers text alignment, attributes, and drawing. Many illustrators and desktop publishers use text to not only enhance graphics, but graphical statements themselves.

The TxtAlign, APItext, and DrawText programs use Visual Basic's Print statements and a limited variety of API font functions to align and format text characters. If you were to build a complete word processing or page publishing program, you would need to use advanced API font functions within more sophisticated procedures. To display true print previews (*WYSIWYG*), you need a thorough knowledge of advanced font technology.

Windows uses a measurement of logical units to display text on your monitor. These logical units are about 40 percent larger in monitor display size than the actual point size of the font when printed. This size compensates for monitors with low screen resolution. You can view resolution sizing values by using the API GetDeviceCaps function to retrieve the physical and logical dimensions of devices such as monitors and printers.

To get a font's typographical information, use the API OutLineTextMetrics and GetTextMetrics functions, which retrieve the correct letter spacing, line spacing (leading), character placement, aspect ratios, and so on.

To convert typographic point sizes (72 points per inch) to your monitor, you retrieve the LOGPIXELSY dimensions of your monitor (vertical pixels per inch) using the API GetDeviceCaps function. Then you apply the following formula:

```
API = GetDeviceCaps(ArtWork.hDC, 90)
ifHEIGHT = -1 * ( API * point size ) / 72 )
```

1. The value 90 represents the LOGPIXELSY index.
2. The ifHEIGHT value is part of the LOGFONT structure that stores all the font's attributes you are about to draw onto the screen.
3. The negative value (-1) tells the GDI to use the height of the character rather than the height of the invisible bounding box (cell) in which each text character resides.
4. The value (point size) can be a number you enter into a textbox. For example:

```
ifHeight = -1 * ( API * Text1.Text ) / 72
```

## Line Spacing (Leading)

*Line spacing* (or leading) is the blank space between each line of text you type. In word processing programs, you usually can change the line spacing by values of 1 line, 1.5 lines, 2 lines, and so on, of blank space. You also can achieve additional typographical effects by calculating the fractional amounts of spacing before and after each paragraph.

To use a default line-spacing value (or leading) on multiline text, use the following formula:

```
Leading = tmHeight + tmExternalLeading
```

Then multiply this value by each line number added to the text. For example, (3 * Leading) correctly places the Y text position for the third line of text.

Here's an example of TextOut leading:

```
LineCounter = LC
Leading = tmHeight + tmExternalLeading
Storedtext = Label1.Caption
TxtLength = Len (Label1.Caption)
API = TextOut(form1.hDC, X, LineCounter * Leading, Storedtext, TxtLength)
```

You can use the API SendMessage function to get the EM_LINECOUNT on some Visual Basic controls or make your own code to count each line of text entered or deleted. The Artisan program in Chapter 2 uses the latter method by detecting the Enter and Backspace keys; however, this approach does not utilize the deletion of a block of text.

## Letter Spacing (Width)

Notice that certain text strings print out longer or shorter on the printer than what you see displayed on the monitor. In this case, you need to adjust the "ABC" dimensions of each character using the API GetCharABCWidths function. The "ABC" widths are, in the simplest of terms, the margins of the character. Remember that each character is within an invisible bounding box: "A" is the left margin, "B" is the character width, and "C" is the right margin. If you make the "A" and/or "C" widths negative, the characters' margins get smaller, allowing the characters' spacing to come closer together or appear tighter.

You can think of the tmInternalLeading value as the top and bottom margins of the bounding box (or cell). The internal leading is the difference between the height of the character's glyph and the height of the character's bounding box (cell). The glyph is the height of the actual character as viewed on the monitor.

The leading or white space between each line of text is called the tmExternalLeading. External leading is not part of the character's bounding box cell. When you're not directly specifying a font character cell, you can calculate the leading for a font by adding the external leading plus the internal leading of the font.

The TxtAlign program's form and control properties are listed in Table 12.1.

**Table 12.1. The properties of the TxtAlign form and controls.**

*Object: Form*
*Object Name: Form1*

| | | | | | |
|---|---|---|---|---|---|
| Caption | = | "Alignment" | Height | = | 2730 |
| Left | = | 645 | ScaleMode | = | 3 'Pixel |
| Top | = | 1215 | Width | = | 4920 |

*continues*

## The Text Alignment Program

**Table 12.1. continued**

*Object: Frame*
*Object Name: Frame1*

| | | | | |
|---|---|---|---|---|
| Caption | = "Alignment" | Height | = | 1320 |
| Left | = 3330 | Top | = | 90 |
| Width | = 1410 | | | |

*Object: Option Button*
*Object Name: Option1*

| | | | | |
|---|---|---|---|---|
| Caption | = "Right" | Height | = | 240 |
| Index | = 2 | Left | = | 90 |
| Top | = 990 | Width | = | 1230 |

*Object: Option Button*
*Object Name: Option1*

| | | | | |
|---|---|---|---|---|
| Caption | = "Center" | Height | = | 240 |
| Index | = 1 | Left | = | 90 |
| Top | = 675 | Value | = | -1 'True |
| Width | = 1230 | | | |

*Object: Option Button*
*Object Name: Option1*

| | | | | |
|---|---|---|---|---|
| Caption | = "Left" | Height | = | 240 |
| Index | = 0 | Left | = | 90 |
| Top | = 315 | Width | = | 1230 |

*Object: Picture Box*
*Object Name: Picture1*

| | | | | |
|---|---|---|---|---|
| Height | = 2130 | Left | = | 120 |
| MousePointer | = 'Cross | ScaleMode | = | 3 'Pixel |
| Top | = 120 | Width | = | 3120 |

*Object: Label*
*Object Name: Label1*

| | | | | |
|---|---|---|---|---|
| AutoSize | = -1 'True | BorderStyle | = | 'Fixed Single |
| Caption | = "Type something" | Height | = | 225 |
| Left | = 810 | Top | = | 540 |
| Width | = 1500 | | | |

*Object: Command Button*
*Object Name: SetTextBtn*

| Caption | = "Set Text" | Height | = 690 |
| Left | = 3375 | Top | = 1485 |
| Width | = 1365 | | |

## The TxtAlign Program

The TxtAlign program uses Visual Basic's `Print` statement and manual alignment calculation to place text on the `Picture1` picture box control.

Figure 12.1 shows a screen shot of the TxtAlign program.

**Figure 12.1.**
*A screen shot of the TxtAlign program.*

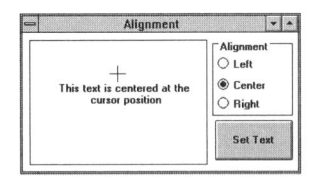

Listing 12.1 shows how to initiate the default variables used in the TxtAlign program.

**Listing 12.1. Variable names at startup.**
```
Declaration
Dim TextX As Integer
Dim TextY As Integer
```

> **Dim TextX, TextY:** Store the values of the `CurrentX` and `CurrentY` coordinates of the `Picture1` picture box control. These values indicate at what coordinate the first line of text starts printing.

The `Form_Resize` event in Listing 12.2 centers the form on the screen and initates the coordinate position where the text will be placed.

**Listing 12.2. Centering the form and text cursor (caret).**
```
Sub Form_Resize ()
  Left = (Screen.Width - Width) \ 2
  Top = (Screen.Height - Height) \ 2

  TextX = Label1.Left
  Picture1.CurrentY = Label1.Top + 1
  Label1.FontSize = Picture1.FontSize
  Picture1.SetFocus
End Sub
```

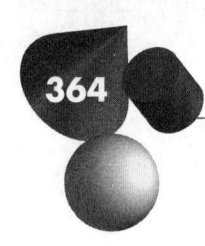

# The Text Alignment Program

**Left, Top:** Center the form on the screen.

**TextX = Label1.Left:** As you type text, it is placed within a label control. When you click an Alignment Option button or the Set Text button, the text is transferred to the underlying `Picture1` picture box. The TxtAlign program uses the Visual Basic `Print` statement to draw the text. The `TextX` variable acts as the `CurrentX` coordinate for the `Print` statement. For the text from the label control to match the same coordinate position as the `Picture1` picture box, simply make the `Text1` variable equal to the label's `Left` property.

**Picture1.CurrentY = Label1.Top + 1:** Basically the same as `TextX`, except that you add one pixel unit to compensate for the label's border width.

**Label1.FontSize = Picture1.FontSize:** Makes the label's font size match `Picture1`'s font size.

The `Option1_Click` event in Listing 12.3 forces the Set Text button to execute the aligning and drawing of the text.

### Listing 12.3. Using the option buttons to align the text.

```
Sub Option1_Click (Index As Integer)
    SetTextBtn_Click
End Sub
```

**SetTextBtn_Click:** Forces the `TextBtn_Click` (Listing 12.6) event to execute in order to draw the text.

The `Picture1_KeyPress` event in Listing 12.4 displays each character typed in the label control.

### Listing 12.4. Typing text within the label control.

```
Sub Picture1_KeyPress (KeyAscii As Integer)
    If Label1.Caption = " Type something " Then Label1.Caption = ""
    Label1.Caption = Label1.Caption + Chr(KeyAscii)
End Sub
```

**If Label1:** Informs you that you can start typing.

**Label1.Caption:** Whatever you type is displayed in the label control.

The `Picture1_MouseDown` event in Listing 12.5 clears the picture box of any text and moves the label control to the mouse pointer coordinate.

### Listing 12.5. Positioning the starting point of the text.

```
Sub Picture1_MouseDown (Button%, Shift%, X!, Y!)
    Picture1.AutoRedraw = True
    Picture1.Cls
    Picture1.AutoRedraw = False
```

```
    TextX = X: Picture1.CurrentY = Y
    Label1.Left = X: Label1.Top = Y - 1
    Label1.Height = 15: Label1.Width = 2: Label1.Visible = True
End Sub
```

**Picture1.AutoRedraw:** To draw multiline text, you set the AutoRedraw property to True. You should erase the old text image using Cls (the clear screen method).

**TextX, CurrentY:** The text starts to display at the current mouse pointer position.

**Label1.Left (Top):** Move the label control to the text start position (the mouse pointer position).

**Label.Height, Label.Width:** Makes the label look as though it is a text cursor.

**Label1.Visible:** Displays the label control.

Figure 12.2 illustrates the TxtAlign form and its controls.

**Figure 12.2.**
*The TxtAlign form and its controls.*

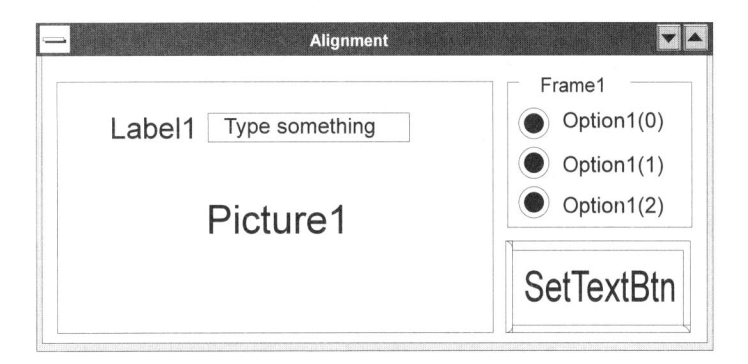

## Manually Setting Text in Visual Basic

The SetTextBtn_Click event in Listing 12.6 extracts each line of text typed into the label control. The TextWidth method calculates the length of each line, and an offset is added to compensate for left, center, or right alignment of the text. The extracted line is then printed on the Picture1 picture box. Finally, the next CurrentX and CurrentY text positions are calculated to position the next line of text. The routine is repeated for each line of text present in the label control.

**Listing 12.6. Extracting text from the label control.**

```
Sub SetTextBtn_Click ()
    If Label1.Caption = "" Then Exit Sub
    Dim LineCount As Integer
    LabelWidth = Label1.Width
    Label1.Visible = False
For R = 1 To 100    'LineCount Maximum
    Labeltext$ = Label1.Caption + Chr(13)
    CR = InStr(Labeltext$, Chr(13))
    TopLine = Left(Labeltext$, CR - 1)
```

*continues*

## The Text Alignment Program

**Listing 12.6. continued.**

```
    Select Case True
        Case Option1(0).Value
            Picture1.CurrentX = TextX
        Case Option1(1).Value
            Picture1.CurrentX = TextX - (TextWidth(TopLine) \ 2)
        Case Option1(2).Value
            Picture1.CurrentX = TextX - (TextWidth(TopLine))
    End Select
Picture1.AutoRedraw = True
Picture1.Print TopLine
Picture1.AutoRedraw = False
    txtLength = Len(Labeltext$)
    If txtLength = LineCount Then Label1.Caption = "":
    Picture1.SetFocus : Exit Sub
    LineCount = LineCount + 1
    Scroll = Mid(Labeltext$, CR + 1, txtLength)
    Label1.Caption = Scroll
Next R
End Sub
```

**If Label1.Caption:** Nothing was typed, so exit this event.

**Dim LineCount As Integer:** Represents the number of times to loop through the For/Next statement block. You can modify this statement to equal the total number of lines present in the label control.

**Label1.Visible:** Hides the label control because you are about to print its caption to Picture1.

**For R = 1 To 100:** For every number of text lines starting at 1 and going to the 100 text line, do the following block of code statements. (The value 100 is for this example only.)

**Labeltext$:** Represents all the text typed in the label caption. You add a carriage return (Chr(13)) to the end of the text so that you have a "search for" flag when using the InStr function.

**CR = InStr:** Returns the character position of the carriage return (Chr(13)). The syntax for the InStr function is as follows:

   InStr *(the text we are searching in, the character we are looking for)*

**TopLine = Left(Labeltext$, CR - 1):** Returns the top line of text in the label's caption (minus the Chr(13)).

**Select Case True:** Depending on the value of the three option controls (True, the option is selected; or False, the option is not currently selected), go to the Case expression that is true:

**Case Option1(0):** You selected the Left Align option button.

**Picture1.CurrentX:** Text is left-aligned to the CurrentX screen position.

**Case Option(1):** You selected the Center Align option button.

**Picture1.CurrentX:** The text is center aligned above or below the longest line of text.

**Case Option(2):** You selected the Right Align option button.

**Picture1.CurrentX:** The text is right aligned above or below the longest line of text.

**Picture1.AutoRedraw:** Set to True so that each new line of text is not erased when you're sending repeated Print statements.

**Picture1.Print:** Prints the top line of text in the caption.

**Picture1.AutoRedraw:** Resets AutoRedraw to off; otherwise, double images of each text line appear.

**txtLength:** Represents the length of the caption text in characters.

**If txtLength:** When the line count reaches the end, erases the caption and then exits the sub.

**LineCount:** Increases the line count by one.

**Scroll:** Reprints all the caption text that is beneath the first line of text.

**Label1.Caption:** Eliminates the first line of text you have already printed to the Picture1 picture box control. You then make the next line of text appear to be the first line of text.

**Next R:** Repeats the process until every line of text is printed.

## Summary of the TxtAlign Program

If you do not want to use API text-alignment functions in your programs, then the routines shown in the TxtAlign program should be adequate for simple text-placement tasks. Note the way the Scroll variable (SetTextBtn_Click in Listing 12.6) uses the Mid$ string function to simulate scrolling text. As each line of text is printed, the line is then deleted, causing the label's caption to move all following text up one line space automatically.

The SetTextBtn_Click event is just one example of extracting a label's caption and then using Visual Basic's Print statement to redraw the caption onto another control. You may want to experiment with alternative combinations of Visual Basic string functions such as Instr$, Left$, LTrim, RTrim, Mid$, and Right$.

## Using the APItext Program

The APItext program incorporates both API text-drawing features and the Basic language Print statements. The APItext program uses a standard API text-formatting function. For professional font manipulation, however, you need a thorough knowledge of advanced font technology.

The API GlyphOutLine function is one example of an API that you can use in conjunction with advanced procedures to manipulate text characters as if they were graphical objects. You use the API GlyphOutLine function to extract information on the outline structure of each text character. Follow these steps to create data type structures required to manipulate a font:

# The Text Alignment Program

1. Type `POINTAPI (X, Y)`.
2. Type `FIXED (fract, value)`.
3. Type `mat2 (FIXED)`.
4. Type `POINTFX (X, Y)`.
5. Type `GLYPHMETRICS`.
6. Type `TTPOLYGONHEADER`.
7. Type `TTPOLYCURVE`.

Additional elements required to retrieve the character's outline are

- A B-spline Bézier curve procedure
- Management of polygon headers and poly-curves

To advance your knowledge of the inner workings of TrueType fonts, you may need additional references. Because of the numerous procedures needed to extract a TrueType character's structure, no example is supplied with this chapter. The FONT.BAS file lists the majority of the text Type structures.

The APItext program's form and control properties are listed in Table 12.2.

**Table 12.2. The properties of the APItext form and controls.**

*Object: Form*
*Object Name: TextEditor*

| | | | |
|---|---|---|---|
| BorderStyle | = 1 'Fixed Single | Caption | = "Text Editor" |
| Height | = 5955 | Left | = 225 |
| ScaleMode | = 3 'Pixel | Top | = 1185 |
| Width | = 8625 | | |

*Object: Check Box*
*Object Name: Check1*

| | | | |
|---|---|---|---|
| Caption | = "Rotation" | Height | = 195 |
| Index | = 5 | Left | = 6780 |
| Top | = 4890 | Width | = 1230 |

*Object: Check Box*
*Object Name: Check1*

| | | | |
|---|---|---|---|
| Caption | = "Weight" | Height | = 195 |
| Index | = 4 | Left | = 6780 |
| Top | = 4665 | Width | = 1230 |

*Object: Check Box*
*Object Name: Check1*

| Caption | = "Width" | Height | = 195 |
|---|---|---|---|
| Index | = 3 | Left | = 5520 |
| Top | = 4890 | Width | = 1230 |

*Object: Check Box*
*Object Name: Check1*

| Caption | = "Underline" | Height | = 195 |
|---|---|---|---|
| Index | = 2 | Left | = 5520 |
| Top | = 4665 | Width | = 1230 |

*Object: Check Box*
*Object Name: Check1*

| Caption | = "StrikeThru" | Height | = 195 |
|---|---|---|---|
| Index | = 1 | Left | = 4215 |
| Top | = 4890 | Width | = 1230 |

*Object: Check Box*
*Object Name: Check1*

| Caption | = "Italic" | Height | = 195 |
|---|---|---|---|
| Index | = 0 | Left | = 4215 |
| Top | = 4665 | Width | = 1230 |

*Object: Command Button*
*Object Name: FontLogBtn*

| Caption | = "Font Log" | Enabled | = 0 'False |
|---|---|---|---|
| Height | = 360 | Left | = 5580 |
| Top | = 5160 | Width | = 1320 |

*Object: Command Button*
*Object Name: APICRLF*

| Caption | = "API CR/LF" | Height | = 360 |
|---|---|---|---|
| Left | = 2820 | Top | = 5160 |
| Width | = 1320 | | |

*Object: Command Button*
*Object Name: TextMex*

| Caption | = "Text Metrics" | Enabled | = 0 'False |
|---|---|---|---|
| Height | = 360 | Left | = 4200 |
| Top | = 5160 | Width | = 1320 |

*continues*

**T**able 12.2. continued

*Object: Picture Box*
*Object Name: Artwork*

| | | | | | |
|---|---|---|---|---|---|
| Height | = | 3435 | Left | = | 60 |
| MousePointer | = | 2 'Cross | ScaleMode | = | 3 'Pixel |
| Top | = | 60 | Width | = | 5535 |

*Object: Textbox*
*Object Name: Text1*

| | | | | | |
|---|---|---|---|---|---|
| FontSize | = | 9.75 | Height | = | 3435 |
| Left | = | 5700 | MultiLine | = | -1 'True |
| ScrollBars | = | 3 'Both | Top | = | 60 |
| Width | = | 2775 | | | |

*Object: Command Button*
*Object Name: APItext*

| | | | | | |
|---|---|---|---|---|---|
| Caption | = | "API text" | Height | = | 360 |
| Left | = | 1440 | Top | = | 5160 |
| Width | = | 1320 | | | |

*Object: Combo Box*
*Object Name: Style_Combo*

| | | | | | |
|---|---|---|---|---|---|
| Height | = | 300 | Left | = | 4260 |
| Style | = | 2 'Dropdown List | Top | = | 3720 |
| Width | = | 1905 | | | |

*Object: Frame*
*Object Name: Frame1*

| | | | | | |
|---|---|---|---|---|---|
| Caption | = | "Alignment" | Height | = | 1485 |
| Left | = | 2460 | Top | = | 3600 |
| Width | = | 1695 | | | |

*Object: Option Button*
*Object Name: Option1*

| | | | | | |
|---|---|---|---|---|---|
| Caption | = | "Right" | Height | = | 375 |
| Index | = | 2 | Left | = | 120 |
| Top | = | 1020 | Width | = | 1095 |

*Object: Option Button*
*Object Name: Option1*

| | | | |
|---|---|---|---|
| Caption | = "Center" | Height | = 375 |
| Index | = 1 | Left | = 120 |
| Top | = 660 | Width | = 1095 |

*Object: Option Button*
*Object Name: Option1*

| | | | |
|---|---|---|---|
| Caption | = "Left" | Height | = 330 |
| Index | = 0 | Left | = 120 |
| Top | = 360 | Value | = -1 'True |
| Width | = 1215 | | |

*Object: Command Button*
*Object Name: Option1 CloseBtn*

| | | | |
|---|---|---|---|
| Caption | = "Close" | Height | = 360 |
| Left | = 7080 | Top | = 5160 |
| Width | = 1335 | | |

*Object: Command Button*
*Object Name: BasicPrint*

| | | | |
|---|---|---|---|
| Caption | = "Basic print" | Height | = 360 |
| Left | = 60 | Top | = 5160 |
| Width | = 1335 | | |

*Object: VScroll Bar*
*Object Vscroll1*

| | | | |
|---|---|---|---|
| Height | = 1365 | LargeChange | = 10 |
| Left | = 8145 | Max | = 4 |
| Min | = 400 | Top | = 3690 |
| Value | = 12 | Width | = 300 |

*Object: List Box*
*Object Name: FontList*

| | | | |
|---|---|---|---|
| Height | = 1470 | Left | = 60 |
| Sorted | = -1 'True | Top | = 3600 |
| Width | = 2295 | | |

*continues*

## The Text Alignment Program

**Table 12.2. continued**

*Object: Label*
*Object Name: SizeBox*

| | | | |
|---|---|---|---|
| Alignment | = 1 'Right Justify | BorderStyle | = 1 'Fixed Single |
| Height | = 315 | Left | = 7080 |
| Top | = 3720 | Width | = 975 |

*Object: Label*
*Object Name: ViewFont*

| | | | |
|---|---|---|---|
| Height | = 480 | Left | = 4260 |
| Top | = 4095 | Width | = 3735 |

*Object: Label*
*Object Name: Label3*

| | | | |
|---|---|---|---|
| Alignment | = 1 'Right Justify | Caption | = "Size:" |
| Height | = 255 | Left | = 6240 |
| Top | = 3690 | Width | = 50 |

## Declarations and Structures for the APItext Program

The APItext program deals with standard font placement and alignment of text characters using standard API text functions. The program uses API functions to align, rotate, underline, and perform several other text-formatting procedures. The API `GetTextMetrics` and `CreateFontIndirect` functions are used in this program to supply information about the current font or to apply special attributes to a font.

Listing 12.7 initiates the default variables used in the APItext program.

**Listing 12.7. Variable names at startup.**

```
Declaration
Dim Align As Integer
Dim APIcr As FontLog
Dim TextX, TextY As Single
```

**Dim Align:** Informs the API `SetTextAlign` function to the text justification value.

**Dim APIcr:** Stores the API font attributes using a `Type` structure called `FontLog`. You can find the `FontLog` structure in the FONT.BAS file.

**Dim TextX, TextY:** Stores the starting position of the text, which is then sent to the API `TextOut` function.

Chapter **12** 373

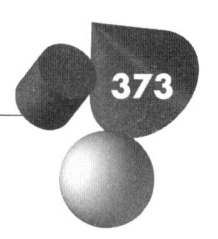

Figure 12.3 shows a screen shot of the APItext program.

**F**igure 12.3.
*A screen shot of the APItext program.*

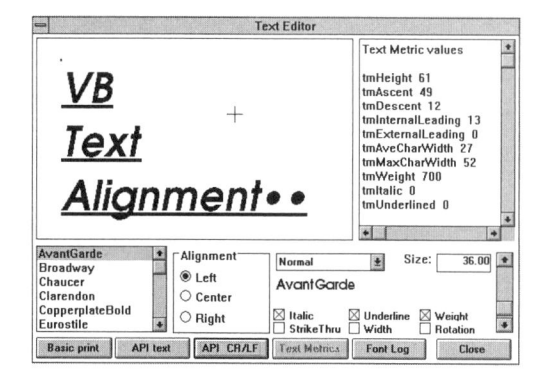

## Default Startup Values

The startup values load a list box with the first 10 screen fonts that are installed in your system. (See Listing 12.8.) If, for some reason, you do not have 10 screen fonts installed, you must change the value accordingly.

**L**isting 12.8. Loading the font list and default values.

```
Sub Form_Load ()
    Style_Combo.AddItem "Normal"
    Style_Combo.AddItem "Bold"
    Style_Combo.AddItem "Italic"
    Style_Combo.AddItem "Bold-Italic"
    SizeBox.Caption = "12.00"
    ViewFont.FontSize = 12
For R = 0 To 10
    FontNames$ = Screen.Fonts(R)
    FontList.AddItem FontNames$
Next R
  FontList.ListIndex = 0
  Style_Combo.ListIndex = 0
End Sub
```

**Style_Combo.AddItem:** Adds the normal, italic, and bold attributes' names to the combo list.

**SizeBox.Caption = "12.00":** The default font point size with which you draw text.

**ViewFont.FontSize = 12:** The ViewFont label control displays an image of the font currently selected.

**For R = 0 To 10:** Adds 10 screen fonts to the FontList list box control.

**FontList.ListIndex = 0:** Highlights the first screen font name in the list box control.

**Style_Combo.ListIndex = 0:** Selects the first font attribute (normal) in the Style combo box.

## The Text Alignment Program

Figure 12.4 illustrates the APItext form.

The `Form_Resize` event in Listing 12.9 centers the form on the screen.

### Listing 12.9. Centering the form on the screen.

```
Sub Form_Resize ()
    TextEditor.Move (Screen.Width - Width) / 2, [IC:CCC]
            (Screen.Height - Height) / 2
End Sub
```

**TextEditor.Move:** Positions the form exactly in the center of the screen.

**Figure 12.4.**
*The APItext form and its controls.*

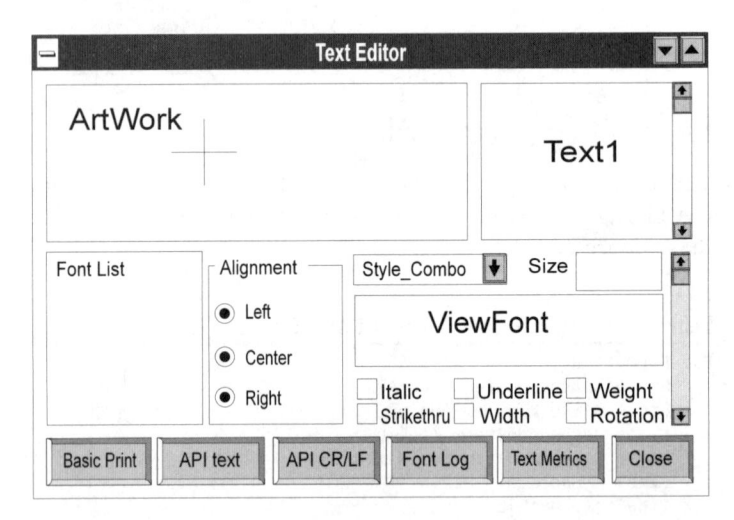

Listing 12.10 shows how the `Form_Unload` event deletes the font changes made when using API text functions.

### Listing 12.10. Deleting changed device context attributes before quitting.

```
Sub Form_Unload (Cancel As Integer)
    R = DeleteObject(FontSelection%)
End Sub
```

**DeleteObject:** When an API function creates a font, it is assigned as the primary font object of the control in which it resides. You must delete this object when it is no longer needed.

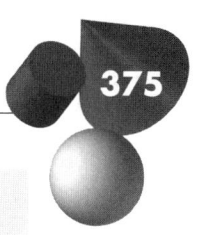

> **CAUTION:** In this example, you are using three different font functions that could easily mess up the GUI. You should not have other applications running while you're running this example. If the order in which API font objects are deleted clashes with Visual Basic's internal handling of fonts, you can easily make a Type Manager program go out of control.

## Adding Carriage Returns to API Text

The `APICRLF_Click` event is triggered when the API CR/LF button is pressed. This routine is basically the same text printing routine used in the previous TxtAlign program, except that the API text functions are being used.

First, the `APIcr` variables are loaded with the font attributes you assign with the check buttons. The `APIcr` points to the `Type FontLog` structure (FONT.BAS) to get data types. Then it takes the following steps to draw the text:

1. The API `CreateFontIndirect` builds the font, and the API `SelectObject` sets the device context attributes.
2. The API `GetTextMetrics` retrieves the line spacing needed for each line of text.
3. The API `SetTextAlign` function calculates the justification of the text.
4. The API `SendMessage` function counts the total number of text lines in the `Text1` textbox control.
5. The API `TextOut` function draws the text. (See Listing 12.11.)

**Listing 12.11. Using the API `TextOut` function to draw the text.**

```
Sub APICRLF_Click ()
    TextX = ArtWork.CurrentX
    TextY = ArtWork.CurrentY
If FontList.ListCount = 0 Then Exit Sub
''''''''''''''''''''''
FontLogBtn.Enabled = True
APIcr.FontCharSet = Chr$(DEFAULT_CHARSET)
APIcr.FontClipPrecision = Chr$(OUT_DEFAULT_PRECIS)
APIcr.FontFaceName = FontList.Text + Chr$(0)
API = GetDeviceCaps(ArtWork.hDC, 90)
APIcr.FontHeight = -1 * (API * Val(SizeBox.Caption)) \ 72
APIcr.FontItalic = Chr$(Check1(0).Value)
APIcr.FontOutPrecision = Chr$(OUT_DEFAULT_PRECIS)
APIcr.FontPitchFamily = Chr$(DEFAULT_PITCH Or FF_DONTCARE)
APIcr.FontQuality = Chr$(DEFAULT_QUALITY)
APIcr.FontStrikeThru = Chr$(Check1(1).Value)
```

*continues*

## The Text Alignment Program

**Listing 12.11. continued**

```
APIcr.FontUnderLine = Chr$(Check1(2).Value)
If Check1(3).Value = 1 Then APIcr.FontWidth = 20 Else APIcr.FontWidth = 0
If Check1(4).Value = 1 Then APIcr.FontWeight = 700 Else APIcr.FontWeight = 0
If Check1(5).Value = 1 Then APIcr.FontRotate = 1800 Else APIcr.FontRotate = 0
''''''''''''''''''''''''''''''
FontSelection% = CreateFontIndirect(APIcr)
NewFont% = SelectObject(ArtWork.hDC, FontSelection%)
  Dim tm As TEXTMETRIC
  API = GetTextMetrics(ArtWork.hDC, tm)
  Leading = tm.tmHeight + tm.tmExternalLeading
Select Case True
    Case Option1(0).Value
      R = SetTextAlign(ArtWork.hDC, TA_LEFT)
    Case Option1(1).Value
      R = SetTextAlign(ArtWork.hDC, TA_CENTER)
    Case Option1(2).Value
      R = SetTextAlign(ArtWork.hDC, TA_RIGHT)
End Select
''''''''''''''''''''''''''''''
Const WM_USER = 1024
Const EM_GETLINECOUNT = WM_USER + 10
TotalLines = SendMessage(Text1.hWnd, EM_GETLINECOUNT, 0, 0&)
For B = 1 To TotalLines
  textStr$ = Text1.Text + Chr(13)
  CR = InStr(textStr$, Chr(13))
    If B = CarriageCount Then
      TopLine$ = Left(textStr$, CR - 3)
    Else
      TopLine$ = Left(textStr$, CR - 1)
    End If
R = TextOut(ArtWork.hDC, TextX, TextY + Cursor, (TopLine$), Len(TopLine$))
  Cursor = (B * Leading)
  TxtLength = Len(textStr$)
  LineCount = LineCount + 1
  Scroll = Mid(textStr$, CR + 2, TxtLength)
  Text1.Text = Scroll
Next B
    R = SelectObject(ArtWork.hDC, NewFont%)
    R = DeleteObject(FontSelection%)
End Sub
```

**TextX, TextY:** Store the picture box's CurrentX and CurrentY to send to the API TextOut function. The first text character is positioned here. You set TextX and TextY using the MouseDown coordinates.

**If FontList.ListCount = 0 Then:** Although it is unlikely, you may have no fonts installed. If this is the case, exit this event.

**FontLogBtn.Enabled:** Shows the attributes of the current font.

Here is a rough outline of the API LogFont structure, which you find in the FONT.BAS file:

APIcr.**FontCharSet** = ANSI_Charset or Default_Charset or Symbol_Charset or OEM_Charset.

APIcr.**FontClipPrecision** = See FONT.BAS file listing.

APIcr.**FontFaceName** = The font name, or default device font name if not used.

APIcr.**FontHeight** = Character cell height in positive numbers, or Glyph if negative.

APIcr.**FontItalic** = 0 for no italic, or any number for an italic face.

APIcr.**FontOutPrecision** = See FONT.BAS file listing.

APIcr.**FontPitchFamily** = default_Pitch or fixed_Pitch or variable_Pitch family: FF_Decorative, FF_Modern, FF_Roman, FF_Script, FF_Swiss, or FF_Dontcare.

APIcr.**FontQuality** = Default_Quality or Draft_Quality or Proof_Quality.

APIcr.**FontRotate** = Escapement or rotation of the font.

APIcr.**FontStrikeThru** = 0 for no strikethrough, or any number for a strikethrough face.

APIcr.**FontUnderLine** = 0 for no underline, or any number for an underlined face.

APIcr.**FontWidth** = Character cell width in positive numbers, or Glyph if negative.

APIcr.**FontWeight** = Value 100 through 900, where 100 is light, 400 is normal, and 700 is bold.

The API function GetDeviceCaps (ArtWork.hDC, 90) in this procedure returns LogPixelsY value for your screen. This value equals the logical pixel per inch of your monitor vertically. You use this value to display fonts in a true WYSIWYG point size. In typography measurement units, there are 72 unit points per inch.

The APIcr.FontHeight equals the following formula:

`-1 * (API * Val(SizeBox.Text)) \ 72`

This formula gives you the correct screen font size.

**If Check1(index).Value = 1:** Bolds, italicizes, widens, underlines, strikes through, or rotates the fonts. Using the example in Listing 12.11, you can change the first value (20) to increase or decrease the font's attributes. You use the last value to turn off or set the font to its normal properties. For example:

`If Check1(3).Value = 1 Then APIcr.FontWidth = 20 Else APIcr.FontWidth = 0`

**FontSelection%, NewFont:** Builds the font and sets the device context attributes.

**API = GetTextMetrics(ArtWork.hDC, tm):** Retrieves the Artwork picture box's font attributes. Now you want to know the current font's height and leading values. A font character is centered within its own bounding box cell, and the bounding box has left, top, right, and bottom margins. The placement of these margins defines the white space around the character. The leading, however, is not part of the bounding box cell and is the distance between each row of cells.

# The Text Alignment Program

**Leading = tm.tmHeight + tm.tmExternalLeading:** Calculates the correct amount of leading to provide to each new line of text by adding the height and external leading values that the `TextMetrics` provides.

**Select Case True:** Selects the alignment option button currently highlighted.

**R = SetTextAlign(ArtWork.hDC, TA_LEFT):** Sets the text's alignment.

**TotalLines = SendMessage:** Retrieves the total number of text lines within the `Text1` textbox.

**For B = 1 To TotalLines:** The rest of the procedure is similar to the `SetTextBtn_Click` procedure found in the TxtAlign program at the beginning of this chapter. The `Artwork.Print` statement is replaced with the API `TextOut` function.

**R = TextOut:** One of many API text functions that draws text on the window. In this example, the text draws to the picture box called `Artwork`, drawing the first line of text at the value's `TextX` (X coordinate) and `TextY + Cursor` (Y coordinate).

The API `TextOut` function draws text similar to the `Print` statement. Its properties are as follows:

    TextOut ( 1, 2, 3, 4, 5)

    *1* is the control (`hDC`) to draw into.
    *2* is the starting X point of text.
    *3* is the starting Y point of text.
    *4* is the string of text to draw.
    *5* is the length of the text string.

The API `TextOut` function prints all characters including carriage returns and line feeds.

**SelectObject:** Replaces the previous object type.

## Adding Attributes to the *TextOut* Function

In Listing 12.12, the button marked API Text is basically the same as the `APICRLF_Click` event in Listing 12.11, except that it does not strip the embedded carriage return and line feeds from the text. Take note that the carriage return (`Chr(13)` and line feed (`Chr(10)`) characters are printed when you use the API `TextOut` functions. They may appear as square or dot symbols in some fonts.

**Listing 12.12. Drawing embedded CR/LF text.**

```
Sub APItext_Click ()
    TextX = ArtWork.CurrentX
    TextY = ArtWork.CurrentY
If FontList.ListCount = 0 Then Exit Sub
''''''''''''''''''''''
TextMex.Enabled = True
APIcr.FontCharSet = Chr$(DEFAULT_CHARSET)
APIcr.FontClipPrecision = Chr$(OUT_DEFAULT_PRECIS)
APIcr.FontFaceName = FontList.Text + Chr$(0)
API = GetDeviceCaps(ArtWork.hDC, 90)
```

```
APIcr.FontHeight = -1 * (API * Val(SizeBox.Caption)) \ 72
APIcr.FontItalic = Chr$(Check1(0).Value)
APIcr.FontOutPrecision = Chr$(OUT_DEFAULT_PRECIS)
APIcr.FontPitchFamily = Chr$(DEFAULT_PITCH Or FF_DONTCARE)
APIcr.FontQuality = Chr$(DEFAULT_QUALITY)
APIcr.FontStrikeThru = Chr$(Check1(1).Value)
APIcr.FontUnderLine = Chr$(Check1(2).Value)
If Check1(3).Value = 1 Then APIcr.FontWidth = 20 Else APIcr.FontWidth = 0
If Check1(4).Value = 1 Then APIcr.FontWeight = 700 Else APIcr.FontWeight = 0
If Check1(5).Value = 1 Then APIcr.FontRotate = 1800 Else APIcr.FontRotate = 0
'''''''''''''''''''''''''''''''''
FontSelection% = CreateFontIndirect(APIcr)
Focus% = SelectObject(ArtWork.hDC, FontSelection%)
R = SetTextAlign(ArtWork.hDC, Align)
''''''''''''
R = TextOut(ArtWork.hDC, TextX, TextY, (Text1.Text), Len(Text1.Text))
R = SelectObject(ArtWork.hDC, Focus%)
R = DeleteObject(FontSelection%)
End Sub
```

**APIcr.FontCharSet:** The FontLog attribute setting is the same as in the APICRLF_Click event in Listing 12.11. You can use any of these values to change the appearance of text when it is displayed. Refer to Listing 12.11 for an explanation of what each FontLog entry does.

**R = TextOut:** This example of the API TextOut function is as simple as it gets. It draws all the text that is displayed in the Text1 textbox including embedded carriage returns and line feeds.

The Artwork_MouseDown event in Listing 12.13 initiates the starting coordinate of the text that is to be drawn.

**Listing 12.13. Setting the text coordinates.**

```
Sub ArtWork_MouseDown (Button%, Shift %, X As Single, Y As Single)
    ArtWork.Cls
    ArtWork.DrawWidth = 4
    ArtWork.PSet (X, Y)
    ArtWork.DrawWidth = 1
    ArtWork.CurrentX = X
    ArtWork.CurrentY = Y
    TextX = X: TextY = Y
End Sub
```

**ArtWork.Cls:** Erases the text displayed in the picture box.

**ArtWork.PSet (X, Y):** Draws a dot to indicate the CurrentX and CurrentY positions.

**TextX = X: TextY = Y:** Saves the CurrentX and CurrentY coordinates.

## The Text Alignment Program

## Placing Text Using the *ScaleLeft* Property

Pressing the button marked Basic Print triggers the `BasicPrint_Click` event. When Visual Basic's `Print` statement encounters a carriage return embedded in text, the `CurrentX` is set to `0`. (See Listing 12.14.) Therefore, the next line of text is printed at the far left side of the form or picture box. If you change the `ScaleLeft` property of the form or picture box, you can align text correctly. You do so by making the `0` coordinate match the starting `X` position of the first line of text. The `SetTextAlign(ArtWork.hDC, Align)` statement in the option button's click event left-, center-, and right-justifies the text.

**Listing 12.14. Drawing text using the `Print` statement.**

```
Sub BasicPrint_Click ()
    ArtWork.Cls
    ArtWork.CurrentX = TextX
    ArtWork.CurrentY = TextY
If Text1.Text > "" Then 'print attributes
    Select Case Style_Combo.Text
        Case "Normal"
            ArtWork.FontBold = False: ArtWork.FontItalic = False
        Case "Bold"
            ArtWork.FontBold = True: ArtWork.FontItalic = False
        Case "Italic"
            ArtWork.FontItalic = True: ArtWork.FontBold = False
        Case "Bold-Italic"
            ArtWork.FontBold = True: ArtWork.FontItalic = True
    End Select
 ArtWork.FontName = ViewFont.FontName
 ArtWork.FontSize = Val(SizeBox.Text)
    Select Case Align 'Scale Aligning
        Case 0, 6, 2'Left
            ArtWork.ScaleLeft = -ArtWork.CurrentX
    End Select
End If
    ArtWork.Print Text1.Text
    ArtWork.ScaleLeft = ArtWork.CurrentX 'reset ScaleLeft
End Sub
```

`ArtWork.ScaleLeft = -ArtWork.CurrentX:` If you assign a negative `CurrentX` value to the `ScaleLeft` property, you make the text left-align to the `MouseDown` X and Y coordinates. The `BasicPrint_Click` event is the same routine used in the Artisan program of Chapter 2. The main trick here is changing the picture box's `ScaleLeft` to set the `CurrentX` and then have the API `SetTextAlign` function take care of justifying the text.

The `FontList_Click` event in Listing 12.15 changes the font's normal, italic, and bold attribute styles, and then displays the font in the `ViewFont` label control.

**Listing 12.15. Setting the font's style type.**
```
Sub FontList_Click ()
ViewFont.FontName = FontList.Text
    Select Case Style_Combo.Text
        Case "Normal"
            ViewFont.FontBold = False: ViewFont.FontItalic = False
        Case "Bold"
            ViewFont.FontBold = True: ViewFont.FontItalic = False
        Case "Italic"
            ViewFont.FontItalic = True: ViewFont.FontBold = False
        Case "Bold-Italic"
            ViewFont.FontBold = True: ViewFont.FontItalic = True
    End Select
    ViewFont.Caption = FontList.Text
End Sub
```

**ViewFont.FontName = FontList.Text**: When you select a font name from the font list, the name appears in the ViewFont label control using its own font style.

**Select Case Style_Combo.Text**: The ViewFont display matches the font attribute (normal, italic, or bold) you selected for the Style_Combo list box.

## Displaying the *FontLog* Attributes

Pressing the button marked Font Log triggers the FontLogBtn_Click event. This event, in turn, simply displays attributes currently stored in APIcr. (See Listing 12.16.)

**Listing 12.16. Showing the current attributes of the control's font.**
```
Sub FontLogBtn_Click ()
r = Chr(13) + Chr(10)
M$ = "Font Log values" + r + r
M$ = M$ + "FontCharSet " + Format$(Val(APIcr.FontCharSet)) + r
M$ = M$ + "FontClipPrecision " + Format$(Val(APIcr.FontClipPrecision)) + r
M$ = M$ + "FontHeight " + Format$(APIcr.FontHeight) + r
M$ = M$ + "FontItalic " + Format$(Val(APIcr.FontItalic)) + r
M$ = M$ + "FontOutPrecision " + Format$(Val(APIcr.FontOutPrecision)) + r
M$ = M$ + "FontPitchFamily " + Format$(Val(APIcr.FontPitchFamily)) + r
M$ = M$ + "FontQuality " + Format$(Val(APIcr.FontQuality)) + r
M$ = M$ + "FontRotate " + Format$(APIcr.FontRotate) + r
M$ = M$ + "FontStrikeThru " + Format$(Val(APIcr.FontStrikeThru)) + r
M$ = M$ + "FontUnderLine " + Format$(Val(APIcr.FontUnderLine)) + r
M$ = M$ + "FontWidth " + Format$(APIcr.FontWidth) + r
M$ = M$ + "FontWeight " + Format$(APIcr.FontWeight) + r
M$ = M$ + "FontFaceName " + r + Format$(APIcr.FontFaceName) + r
    Text1.Text = M$
        FontLogBtn.Enabled = False
End Sub
```

**Text1.Text = M$**: Displays the current attributes of the font.

## Using the API Text Alignment Function

Selecting an option button sets the alignment value for the API `SetTextAlign` function. (See Listing 12.17.) You can use Visual Basic's `Choose` statement to replace the `Select Case` blocks, thus shortening the routine.

**Listing 12.17. Setting the font's Align property.**

```
Sub Option1_Click (Index As Integer)
    Select Case Index
        Case 0 'Align Left
            Align = 0
        Case 1 'Align Center
            Align = 6
        Case 2 'Align Right
            Align = 2
    End Select
    API = SetTextAlign(ArtWork.hDC, Align)
End Sub
```

`API = SetTextAlign(ArtWork.hDC, Align):` Sets the justification of the text.

The `Style_Combo_Change` event in Listing 12.18 forces the `FontList_Click` event to execute, which will change the font's attribute style.

**Listing 12.18. Setting the font's style.**

```
Sub Style_Combo_Change ()
    FontList_Click
End Sub
```

`FontList_Click:` Selecting either the normal, italic, or bold text items in the `Style_Combo` list triggers execution of the `FontList_Click` event. (See Listing 12.15.) The `FontList_Click` event contains a routine to change the style of the font currently in use.

## Displaying the Text Metrics of a Font

Pressing the button marked Text Metrics triggers the `TextMex_Click` event. This event, in turn, displays the current font's characteristics. (See Listing 12.19.)

**Listing 12.19. Displaying the current font's characteristics.**

```
Sub TextMex_Click ()
    Dim tm As TEXTMETRIC
    Dim textbuffer As String * 20
    r = Chr(13) + Chr(10)
If FontSelection% = 0 Then Exit Sub
FontSelection% = CreateFontIndirect(APIcr)
Focus% = SelectObject(ArtWork.hDC, FontSelection%)
```

```
     API = GetTextMetrics(ArtWork.hDC, tm)
     API = GetTextFace(ArtWork.hDC, 19, textbuffer)
     M$ = "Text Metric values" + r + r
     M$ = M$ + "tmHeight " + Str$(tm.tmHeight) + r
     M$ = M$ + "tmAscent " + Str$(tm.tmAscent) + r
     M$ = M$ + "tmDescent " + Str$(tm.tmDescent) + r
     M$ = M$ + "tmInternalLeading " + Str$(tm.tmInternalLeading) + r
     M$ = M$ + "tmExternalLeading " + Str$(tm.tmExternalLeading) + r
     M$ = M$ + "tmAveCharWidth " + Str$(tm.tmAveCharWidth) + r
     M$ = M$ + "tmMaxCharWidth " + Str$(tm.tmMaxCharWidth) + r
     M$ = M$ + "tmWeight " + Str$(tm.tmWeight) + r
     M$ = M$ + "tmItalic " + Str$(Val(tm.tmItalic)) + r
     M$ = M$ + "tmUnderlined " + Str$(Val(tm.tmUnderlined)) + r
     M$ = M$ + "tmStruckOut " + Str$(Val(tm.tmStruckOut)) + r
     M$ = M$ + "tmFirstChar " + Str$(Asc(tm.tmFirstChar)) + r
     M$ = M$ + "tmLastChar " + Str$(Asc(tm.tmLastChar)) + r
     M$ = M$ + "tmDefaultChar " + Str$(Val(tm.tmDefaultChar)) + r
     M$ = M$ + "tmBreakChar " + Str$(Val(tm.tmBreakChar)) + r
     M$ = M$ + "tmPitchAndFamily " + Str$(Val(tm.tmPitchAndFamily)) + r
     M$ = M$ + "tmCharSet " + Str$(Val(tm.tmCharSet)) + r
     M$ = M$ + "tmOverhang " + Str$(tm.tmOverhang) + r
     M$ = M$ + "tmDigitizedAspectX " + Str$(tm.tmDigitizedAspectX) + r
     M$ = M$ + "tmDigitizedAspectY " + Str$(tm.tmDigitizedAspectY) + r
     M$ = M$ + "Font name" + r + textbuffer
        Text1.Text = M$
            API = SelectObject(ArtWork.hDC, Focus%)
            API = DeleteObject(FontSelection%)
            TextMex.Enabled = False
End Sub
```

**Dim tm As TEXTMETRICS:** Stores each characteristic in the variable structure called tm.

**Dim textbuffer As String:** Stores the font name by using the API GetTextFace function. This line is not part of the TEXTMETRIC structure.

**CRLF$:** The carriage returns, and a line feeds needed to display the message.

**GetTextMetrics:** Retrieves all the characteristics of the current font and stores them in the tm variable structure. The following is a list of the data types used by the TEXTMETRIC structure:

    **tmHeight** = Height of character cell
    **tmAscent** = Ascent of character cell
    **tmDescent** = Descent of character cell
    **tmInternalLeading** = Internal leading of cell
    **tmExternalLeading** = External leading of cell
    **tmAveCharWidth** = Average character width
    **tmMaxCharWidth** = Maximum character width
    **tmWeight** = 100–900 / light, normal, bold
    **tmItalic** = 0 if not an italic font character
    **tmUnderlined** = 0 if not an underlined character
    **tmStruckOut** = 0 if not a struckout character
    **tmFirstChar** = First character in the font set

tm**LastChar** = Last character in the font set
tm**DefaultChar** = Default character to use
tm**BreakChar** = Character used to define justification
tm**PitchAndFamily** = See the APICRLF_Click event (Listing 12.11).
tm**CharSet** = Character set of the font
tm**Overhang** = Spacing between synthesized fonts
tm**DigitizedAspectX** = The X aspect ratio of the font
tm**DigitizedAspectY** = The Y aspect ratio of the font

## Summary of the APItext Program

Probably the easiest way to align text in Visual Basic is by using the BasicPrintBtn_Click routine, which is executed when you press the Basic Print button. The BasicPrintBtn_Click event uses the standard built-in text function of Visual Basic and only one API function to align the text either left, right, or center. If you need to adjust text in any way, however, you are limited when using Visual Basic's text functions.

When you press either of the two API Text buttons, you invoke the API TextOut function, which is the most basic of the API text functions. The API TextOut function is best suited for situations in which you do not require tabbing, word wrapping, or other word processing features when drawing the text. You may find that Visual Basic's Print statement is better equipped for printing text. However, the Print statement may fall short in some formatting areas; in this case, the following DrawText program introduces you to the robust API DrawText function.

## The DrawText Program

The DrawText program uses the API DrawText function to place text on a form or picture box control. The API DrawText function is really a small text processing program that you can use to simulate the same properties as a textbox or label control.

All API calls return a value after you call the API function. In most cases, the return value equals True (non-zero, such as -1) on successful completion of the function, or zero (0) if it failed to work. In the following example, the variable R holds the return value:

```
R = DrawText(ArtWork.hDC, KeyBoard, -1, BB, DT_CalCrect)
```

The API DrawText function returns the text height, which you can use to space the next line of text when you apply a carriage return.

The DrawText program's form and control properties are listed in Table 12.3.

Chapter **12**

**T**able 12.3. *The properties of the* DrawText *form and controls.*

*Object: Form*
*Object Name: TextEditor*

| | | | |
|---|---|---|---|
| Caption | = "Draw Text" | Height | = 5040 |
| Left | = 165 | Top | = 1215 |
| Width | = 7935 | | |

*Object: Command Button*
*Object Name: Keyboard*

| | | | |
|---|---|---|---|
| Caption | = "Keyboard" | Height | = 420 |
| Left | = 4380 | Top | = 4140 |
| Width | = 2115 | | |

*Object: Command Button*
*Object Name: Draw_Text*

| | | | |
|---|---|---|---|
| Caption | = "Draw Text" | Height | = 420 |
| Left | = 2100 | Top | = 4140 |
| Width | = 2115 | | |

*Object: Picture Box*
*Object Name: Artwork*

| | | | |
|---|---|---|---|
| Height | = 3930 | Left | = 2070 |
| MousePointer | = 2 'Cross | ScaleMode | = 3 'Pixel |
| Top | = 90 | Width | = 5685 |

*Object: Label*
*Object Name: Txt*

| | | | |
|---|---|---|---|
| AutoSize | = -1 'True | BorderStyle | = 1 'Fixed Single |
| Caption | = "Txt" | Height | = 225 |
| Left | = 2070 | Top | = 1080 |
| Width | = 255 | | |

*Object: Combo Box*
*Object Name: Style_Combo*

| | | | |
|---|---|---|---|
| Height | = 300 | Left | = 45 |
| Style | = 2 'Dropdown List | Top | = 3735 |
| Width | = 1905 | | |

*continues*

# The Text Alignment Program

**T**able 12.3. continued

*Object: Frame*
*Object Name: Frame1*

| Caption | = "Alignment" | Height | = 1500 |
| Left | = 45 | Top | = 1710 |
| Width | = 1920 | | |

*Object: Option Button*
*Object Name: Option1*

| Caption | = "Right" | Height | = 375 |
| Index | = 2 | Left | = 135 |
| Top | = 990 | Width | = 1095 |

*Object: Option Button*
*Object Name: Option1*

| Caption | = "Center" | Height | = 375 |
| Index | = 1 | Left | = 135 |
| Top | = 630 | Width | = 1095 |

*Object: Option Button*
*Object Name: Option1*

| Caption | = "Left" | Height | = 330 |
| Index | = 0 | Left | = 135 |
| Top | = 315 | Value | = -1 'True |
| Width | = 1215 | | |

*Object: Command Button*
*Object Name: CloseBtn*

| Caption | = "Close" | Height | = 420 |
| Left | = 6720 | Top | = 4140 |
| Width | = 1020 | | |

*Object: VScroll Bar*
*Object Name: VScroll1*

| Height | = 420 | LargeChange | = 10 |
| Left | = 1665 | Max | = 4 |
| Min | = 400 | Top | = 3240 |
| Value | = 14 | Width | = 300 |

*Object: List Box*
*Object Name: FontList*

| | | | | |
|---|---|---|---|---|
| Height | = 1590 | Left | = 45 |
| Sorted | = -1 'True | Top | = 90 |
| Width | = 1935 | | |

*Object: Label*
*Object Name: SizeBox*

| | | | | |
|---|---|---|---|---|
| Alignment | = 1 'Right Justify | BorderStyle | = 1 'Fixed Single |
| Height | = 375 | Left | = 900 |
| Top | = 3240 | Width | = 735 |

*Object: Label*
*Object Name: ViewFont*

| | | | | |
|---|---|---|---|---|
| Alignment | = 2 'Center | AutoSize | = -1 'True |
| BackColor | = &H00FFFFFF& | Height | = 375 |
| Left | = 45 | Top | = 4095 |
| Width | = 1890 | | |

*Object: Label*
*Object Name: Label3*

| | | | | |
|---|---|---|---|---|
| Alignment | = 1 'Right Justify | Caption | = "Size:" |
| FontBold | = -1 'True | Height | = 255 |
| Left | = 90 | Top | = 3285 |
| Width | = 750 | | |

## Variable Names and Startup Values

The events in the following listings (Listings 12.20 through 12.23) are basically the same as those used in the APItext program. For this reason, some events have no explanation following the code listing. Refer to the APItext program for any further explanation or details on the following control events.

**L**isting 12.20. Variable names at startup.

```
Declarations
Dim Align , DT As Integer
```

## The Text Alignment Program

**Dim Align, DT:** Both of these variables store alignment values.

**Dim BB As Rect:** Stores the coordinates of the text's bounding box.

Figure 12.5.
*A screen shot of the DrawText program.*

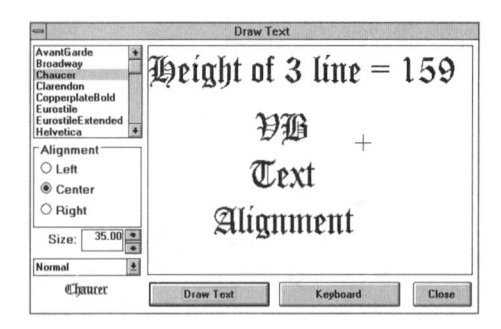

### Listing 12.21. Loading the font list.

```
Sub Form_Load ()
    Style_Combo.AddItem "Normal"
    Style_Combo.AddItem "Bold"
    Style_Combo.AddItem "Italic"
    Style_Combo.AddItem "Bold-Italic"
For R = 0 To 10
    FontNames$ = Screen.Fonts(R)
    FontList.AddItem FontNames$
Next R
    FontList.ListIndex = 0
    Style_Combo.ListIndex = 0
SizeBox.Text = "14.00"
ViewFont.FontSize = 14
Txt.FontSize = 14
Txt.FontName = FontList.Text
ArtWork.FontSize = 14
ArtWork.FontName = FontList.Text
    ResetLabelText
End Sub
```

**Form_Load:** Refer to the `Form_Load` event (Listing 12.8) in the APItext program for details.

Figure 12.6 illustrates the `TextDraw` form.

**Figure 12.6.**
*The* TextDraw *form and its controls.*

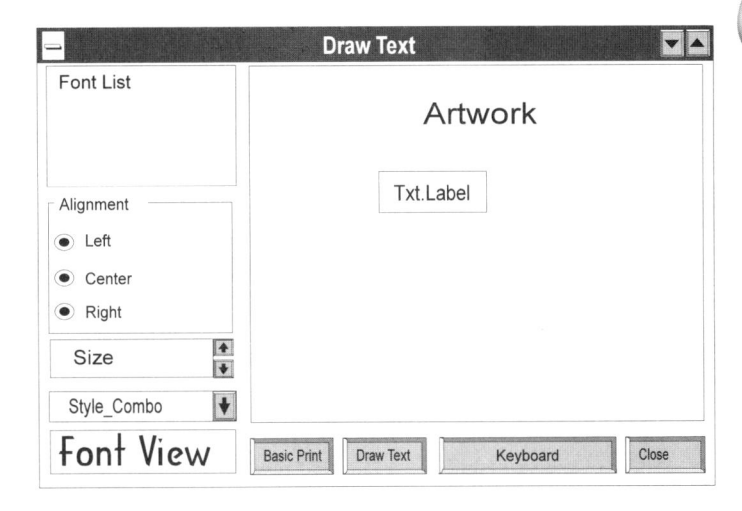

[Figure showing Draw Text form with Font List, Alignment options (Left, Center, Right), Size, Style_Combo, Font View, and buttons Basic Print, Draw Text, Keyboard, Close, plus Artwork area with Txt.Label]

**Listing 12.22. Centering the form on the screen.**

```
Sub Form_Resize ()
    TextEditor.Move (Screen.Width - Width) / 2, [IC:CCC]
            (Screen.Height - Height) / 2
End Sub
```

**TextEditor.Move:** Positions the form exactly in the center of the screen.

**Listing 12.23. Setting the font's style.**

```
Sub Style_Combo_Change ()
    FontList_Click
End Sub
```

**FontList_Click:** Selecting either the normal, italic, or bold text items in the Style_Combo list triggers the execution of the FontList_Click event (Listing 12.28). The FontList_Click event contains the routine to change the style of the font currently in use.

## Drawing Text Using the *DrawText* Function

When you type characters at the keyboard, the API DrawText function displays text in the picture box control. The API DrawText function requires a Type Rect structure to enclose the text within a bounding box. The DT_CalCrect flag in the API DrawText function indicates that the bounding box expands automatically as you type each new character.

# The Text Alignment Program

Here is a list of available `DrawText` flags:

**DT_BOTTOM:** Aligns text to the bottom of the bounding box (single line).

**DT_CALCREST:** The bottom of the bounding box is extended as more text is inserted (multiline) or the right of the bounding box is extended (single line). The bounding box dimensions are processed only, and no text is drawn into the container.

**DT_CENTER:** Text is center aligned.

**DT_EXPANDTABS:** Tabs are moved to correspond with the text being drawn. The default tab stop is eight characters. Change tab settings using the `DT_TABSTOP` flag.

**DT_EXTERALLEADING:** You can use the external leading of the character to calculate line height.

**DT_LEFT:** Text is left-aligned.

**DT_NOCLIP:** Does not clip the bounding box when text expands.

**DT_NOPREFIX:** When you use the & character, it underlines the next character much like the menu controls in Visual Basic. This flag turns off that feature.

**DT_RIGHT:** Text is right aligned.

**DT_SINGLELINE:** Draws a single line of text only.

**DT_TABSTOP:** Changes the tab stop spacing.

**DT_TOP:** Aligns text to the top of the bounding box (single line).

**DT_VCENTER:** Aligns text to the center of the bounding box (single line).

**DT_WORDBREAK:** Wraps text to the next line when the characters meet the bounding box borders or when a carriage return is used.

The `Artwork_KeyPress` event in Listing 12.24 calls the API `Drawtext` function whenever a character is typed, thus simulating a label control.

**Listing 12.24. Setting the text within a bounding box.**

```
Sub ArtWork_KeyPress (KeyAscii As Integer)
    BB.Left = Txt.Left: BB.Top = Txt.Top
    Txt.Visible = False: ArtWork.Cls

Static KeyBoard As String
KeyBoard = KeyBoard + Chr(KeyAscii)
API = DrawText(ArtWork.hDC, KeyBoard, -1, BB, DT_CalCrect)
API = DrawText(ArtWork.hDC, KeyBoard, -1, BB, DT)
End Sub
```

**BB.Left, BB.Top:** Makes the bounding box's left and top coordinates match the label control's top and left coordinates. You can use `CurrentX` and `CurrentY` positions of the `MouseDown` event.

**KeyBoard:** Stores all the characters typed so far in the `KeyBoard` variable.

**API = DrawText #1:** When you use the `DT_CalCrect` flag, no text is drawn; only the new bounding box dimensions are calculated.

**API = DrawText #2:** The DT variable holds the DT_Alignment flag value. The alignment flag variable is set in the Option1_Click event (Listing 12.30). The text is then aligned within the bounding box.

Listing 12.25. Changing the button's caption.

```
Sub ArtWork_LostFocus ()
    KeyBoard.Caption = "Keyboard"
End Sub
```

**KeyBoard.Caption:** The keyboard button currently displays the caption "Type Something." When you click another control, the button's caption is changed to "Keyboard."

Listing 12.26. Placing the label control at the MouseDown position.

```
Sub ArtWork_MouseDown (Button%, Shift%, X!, Y!)
    ArtWork.Cls
    Txt.Left = X
    Txt.Top = Y
End Sub
```

**Txt.Left, Txt.Top:** The Txt label is moved to the coordinates of the mouse pointer when you click the desktop.

# API Text Drawing and Text Height

Pressing the button marked Draw Text triggers the Draw_Text_Click event. It is basically the same routine as used in the APICRLF_Click event (Listing 12.11) of the APItext program. However, in the Draw_Text_Click event in Listing 12.27, the return value of the API DrawText function calculates the combined text height of the three lines displayed.

Listing 12.27. Using the DrawText function to draw the text.

```
Sub Draw_Text_Click ()
    Txt.Visible = False: ArtWork.Cls
    ArtWork.FontSize = Val(SizeBox.Caption)
    ArtWork.FontName = ViewFont.FontName
Txt.FontSize = Val(SizeBox.Caption)
Txt.FontName = ViewFont.FontName
    BB.Left = Txt.Left
    BB.Top = Txt.Top
    BB.Right = Txt.Left + Txt.Width
    BB.Bottom = Txt.Top + Txt.Height
''''''''''''''''''''
Labeltext = Txt.Caption
API = DrawText(ArtWork.hDC, Labeltext, -1, BB, DT)
ArtWork.Print "Height of 3 line = " + API
    ResetLabelText
End Sub
```

**BB.Left = Txt.Left:** The API DrawText function requires a Type Rect structure to enclose the text within a bounding box. The label control is already the correct size because it contains the same text you want to extract. Simply make BB equal to the label control's dimensions.

**Labeltext = Txt.Caption:** Gets the label control's text.

**API = DrawText(ArtWork.hDC, Labeltext, -1, BB, DT):** Draws the text on the Artwork picture box control. The text string to draw is stored in Labeltext. The -1 value indicates that every character within the string is used. The value of DT equals an alignment value (left-align = &H0, center-align = &H1, and right-align = &H2).

**ArtWork.Print "Height of 3 line = " + API:** The API DrawText function returns the text height. You called the function using a dummy variable named API. You can now print the dummy value.

### Listing 12.28. Setting the font's style property.

```
Sub FontList_Click ()
ViewFont.FontName = FontList.Text
    Select Case Style_Combo.Text
        Case "Normal"
            ViewFont.FontBold = False: ViewFont.FontItalic = False
        Case "Bold"
            ViewFont.FontBold = True: ViewFont.FontItalic = False
        Case "Italic"
            ViewFont.FontItalic = True: ViewFont.FontBold = False
        Case "Bold-Italic"
            ViewFont.FontBold = True: ViewFont.FontItalic = True
    End Select
    ViewFont.Caption = FontList.Text
    ArtWork.FontName = FontList
    Txt.FontName = FontList
End Sub
```

**FontList_Click:** Refer to the FontList event (Listing 12.8) in the APItext program for details.

### Listing 12.29. Changing the button's caption.

```
Sub Keyboard_Click ()
    Txt.Visible = False
    KeyBoard.Caption = "Type something"
    ArtWork.SetFocus
End Sub
```

**KeyBoard.Caption:** The keyboard button currently displays the caption "Keyboard." Change the button's caption to "Type something."

**Listing 12.30. Setting the font's alignment.**
```
Sub Option1_Click (Index As Integer)
    Select Case Index
        Case 0 'Align Left
            Align = 0: DT = DT_Left
        Case 1 'Align Center
            Align = 6: DT = DT_Center
        Case 2 'Align Right
            Align = 2: DT = DT_Right
        End Select
End Sub
```

**Option1_Click:** Refer to the Option1 event (Listing 12.17) in the APItext program for details.

**Listing 12.31. Resetting the display text in the label control.**
```
Sub ResetLabelText ()
    CRLF$ = Chr(13) + Chr(10)
    Txt.Caption = "VB" + CRLF$ + "Text" + CRLF$ + "Alignment"
End Sub
```

**Txt.Caption:** The Txt label's caption reads "VB Text Alignment."

# Summary of the DrawText Program

The API DrawText function has several optional flag settings you can use to align, set tabs, clip the displayed text, and word-wrap characters automatically. The TextOut function also returns a value indicating the height of the text drawn.

You can use the API DrawText function to bypass the use of label controls in some instances. The Tabs program in the 16MISC directory of the companion disk is a good example of using the API TextOut function as an alternative to label controls.

# Summary

Visual Basic has limited built-in functions to control the manipulation of font characters. The three program examples in this chapter show you several ways to align text manually or use API text functions.

The API text functions can be used when you need to find the leading values to correctly align text on a vertical axis, as well as to add or subtract spacing between characters. The Visual Basic TextHeight function combines the font set's maximum character height and the normal leading space above and below the text string. You can use a combination of Visual Basic's TextHeight

# The Text Alignment Program

and `FontSize` properties of the font to adjust the leading between text lines. The following example would place the first "T" character flush to the top of the form unless another character within the font set was taller. The tallest character can vary from font to font, thus affecting the `FontSize` and `TextHeight` values. For this reason, the API text functions can be used for more accurate font placement.

Following is an example of a Visual Basic leading method:

```
PixelY = Screen.TwipsPerPixely: CurrentY = 0
CurrentY = -(TextHeight ("") - (FontSize * PixelY)) / 2
Print "This text is aligned at the top of the form"
```

The Windows API text functions can easily retrieve any font attribute you require. Changing some of the font's attributes, such bold and italic, are better suited to be changed by the control's property list, so API text functions would be required.

# CHAPTER 13

# The Join Nodes Program

## The Join Nodes Program

The Join Nodes program demonstrates how to use nodes as controlling points for editing complex object shapes. Each node is an indexed Visual Basic picture box control. You use only one such node picture box because you use the Load statement to create additional nodes. After you position all the nodes around the object, you can use any node to edit the shape of the object. You edit the shape by dragging a node picture box control to a new coordinate location.

After you finish editing the object, you use the Unload statement to remove the nodes from the object. You load and unload each node rather than hide it. If you were to continue creating more nodes (picture boxes) for each new shape, you could easily exceed the limit of 470 controls allowed per form.

To know how many nodes you need to connect to each line segment of a shape, you must keep a continuous count. You also need to keep track of the start and end node points of each object so that the UpdateObjects procedure (Listing 13.17) can correctly redraw each shape. Array variables are used to hold the first and last node positions of each object that is drawn. Each group of polyshaped objects is assigned an object number so that the object can be located easily.

You should keep track of each line segment of the polyshaped object in case you want to add code in the future to break a shape in pieces, convert one or more line segments to curves, or simply erase a line segment. You can get deep into code when you start to add breakable node object and Bezier curve connections. The ArtAPI program in Chapter 15 can connect line and curve segments to nodes but does not deal with breakable node connections or other advanced node features.

## How the Program Works

To begin working with the Join Nodes program, simply drag the mouse to draw a line. A blue node and a black node appear at both ends of the line. Continue drawing line segments starting from the black node. After you form a shape, connect the last line segment to the blue node. (See Figure 13.1.) A polyshape object with a random color fill is then formed. Refer to Figure 13.2 also.

**Figure** 13.1.
*The connection between lines.*

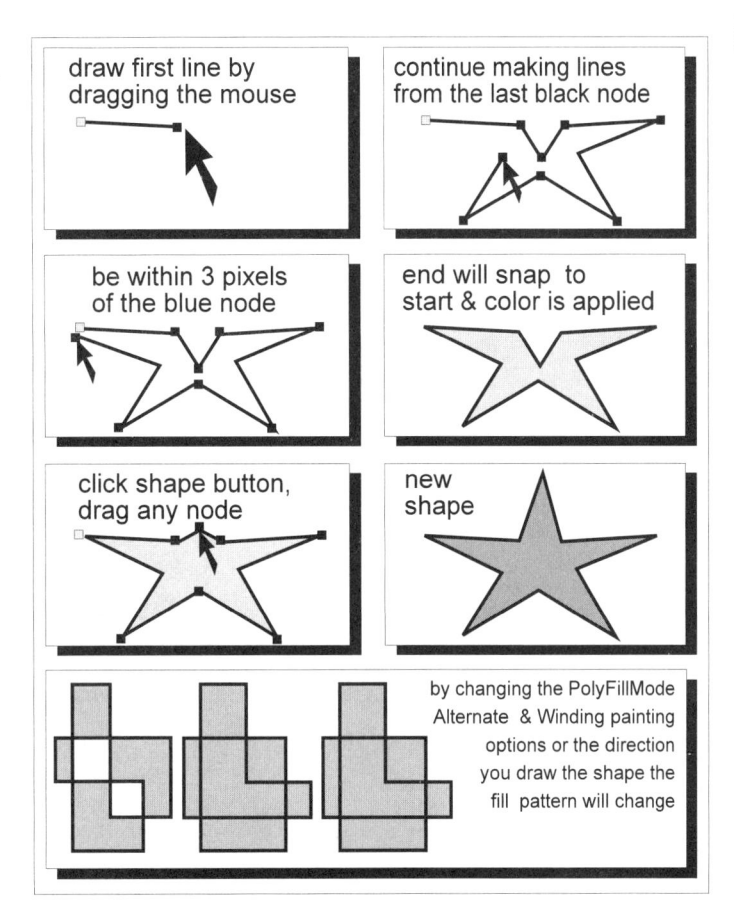

# The Join Nodes Program

**F**igure 13.2.
*The Join Nodes connecting procedures.*

The Join Nodes program's form and control properties are listed in Table 13.1.

**T**able 13.1. The properties of the Join Nodes form and controls.

*Object: Form*
*Object Name: Main1*

| | | | |
|---|---|---|---|
| Caption | = "Join & Fill" | Height | = 4485 |
| Left | = 405 | Top | = 825 |
| Width | = 6855 | | |

*Object: Check Box*
*Object Name: Main1 Check1*

| | | | |
|---|---|---|---|
| Caption | = "Alternate" | Height | = 195 |
| Left | = 5265 | Top | = 3285 |
| Width | = 1320 | | |

*Object: Command Button*
*Object Name: Shapebtn*

| Caption | = "Shape" | Enabled | = 0 'False |
| Height | = 465 | Left | = 5220 |
| Top | = 3555 | Width | = 1365 |

*Object: Command Button*
*Object Name: FloodFillBtn*

| Caption | = "PolyFill" | Height | = 375 |
| Index | = 2 | Left | = 3465 |
| Top | = 3285 | Width | = 1590 |

*Object: Command Button*
*Object Name: FloodFillBtn*

| Caption | = "ExtFloodFill" | Height | = 375 |
| Index | = 1 | Left | = 1755 |
| Top | = 3285 | Width | = 1590 |

*Object: Picture Box*
*Object Name: Artwork*

| DrawMode | = 6 'Invert | Height | = 3120 |
| Left | = 90 | Top | = 90 |
| Width | = 6540 | | |

*Object: Picture Box*
*Object Name: node*

| BackColor | = &H00FF0000& | BorderStyle | = 0 'None |
| Height | 90 | Index | 0 |
| Left | 0 | ScaleHeight | 90 |
| ScaleWidth | 90 | TabIndex | 2 |
| Top | 0 | Width | 90 |

*Object: Command Button*
*Object Name: FloodFillBtn*

| Caption | "FloodFill" | Height | 375 |
| Index | 0 | Left | 90 |
| Top | 3285 | Width | 1590 |

*Object: Label*
*Object Name: Label1*

| Alignment | 2 'Center | BorderStyle | 1 'Fixed Single |
| Height | 285 | Left | 135 |
| Top | 3735 | Width | 4965 |

# The Join Nodes Program

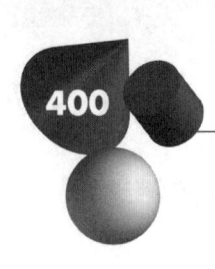

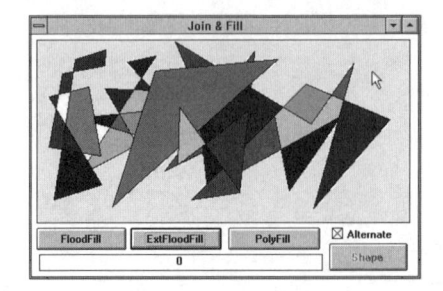

## Variable Names and Startup Values

The Join Nodes program demonstrates how to join a single line to form a polyshape object. Each line object is within its own bounding box.

The declaration section in Listing 13.1 initiates the variables used in the Join Nodes program.

**Listing 13.1. Variable names at startup.**

```
Declarations
Dim X1, Y1, X2, Y2, X3, Y3 As Integer
Dim B As Integer 'Object Number
Dim Total As Integer 'Total objects
Dim PixelX, PixelY As Integer
Const Limit = 100 'Limit of objects you can draw
Dim W(Limit) As Integer 'Line Start Points
Dim N(Limit) As Integer
Dim E(Limit) As Integer 'Line End Points
Dim S(Limit) As Integer
Dim NodeTotal As Integer 'Number of nodes per object
Dim PolyShape(0 To 100) As Integer 'PolyShape number
Dim FlagPoly(Limit) As Integer 'Object Redraw Flag
Dim PolyPts As Integer 'API number of points
Dim Npt(1 To 101) As POINTAPI 'API address of each point
Dim FirstPolyPt(Limit) As Integer 'First Point of each object
Dim LastPolyPt(Limit) As Integer 'Last point of each object
Dim TotalPolyPts(Limit) As Integer 'Total points of each object
Dim FP, LP, ZZ, Counter As Integer 'calculate above to pass to API
```

**X1, Y1, X2, Y2, X3, Y3:** Temporarily stores the start and end points of each line drawn. The X3 and Y3 variables store the node's coordinates of joining lines. These coordinates are needed so that both connected lines can be redrawn when the node is moved to another coordinate to edit the polyshape.

**Dim B:** Holds the object number of the current line.

**Dim Total:** Stores the total number of lines drawn to date.

**Dim PixelX, PixelY:** Holds the conversion value of the twips per pixel screen dimensions. When you're using twips as a form or picture box's scale mode, you must convert any API Polygon to pixel coordinates.

**Const Limit = 100:** Represents the limit of line objects that can be placed on the desktop.

**Dim W, N, E, S:** Represents the four arrays that store the X1, Y1, X2, and Y2 line start and end points (west, north, east, and south).

**Dim NodeTotal:** Holds the total number of nodes that are present around the object's shape.

**Dim PolyShape:** Because an object is made up of several individual lines, you need to assign them as a polyshape group of lines so that the API Polygon function knows what group of line segments to "close" to create the polygon.

**Dim FlagPoly:** The flag used by the UpdateObject procedure (Listing 13.17) to know what drawing functions to use to draw the shape. Because polygon shapes are the only type of objects redrawn in this program, this flag is not really needed; it has been added for future considerations.

**Dim PolyPts:** Holds the number of Poly points to pass to the API Polygon function.

**Dim Npts:** Holds the X and Y coordinates of each point to pass to the API Polygon function.

**Dim FirstPolyPt:** Stores the index number to retrieve from Npts to start each object drawing.

**Dim LastPolyPt:** Stores the index number to retrieve from Npts to end each object drawing.

**Dim FP, LP, ZZ:** Temporary holders of the first poly point (FP), last poly point (LP), and PolyShape(ZZ).

### Listing 13.2. Setting the default values at startup.

```
Sub Form_Load ()
    PixelX = Screen.TwipsPerPixelX
    PixelY = Screen.TwipsPerPixelY
    Total = 0: B = 0
    NodeTotal = 1: Counter = 1
End Sub
```

**PixelX, PixelY:** Converts the ScaleMode of Twips to pixels so that the API drawing functions work.

**Total = 0: B = 0:** Sets the current line and total number of line objects to 0.

## The Join Nodes Program

**NodeTotal = 1:** You use the Load control statement to add additional nodes (picture boxes) as needed for the shape you are drawing. To add additional controls, you must have at least one similarly named control on your form. Because you are counting the number of nodes, NodeTotal at startup equals the one node you have on the form.

**Counter = 1:** The node count equals the one node on the form at startup.

### The Mouse Events

You must take two possible MouseDown scenarios into consideration in this program. The first scenario is when you click the desktop while a polyshape's nodes are visible (Listing 13.3). The second scenario is when you use the MouseDown event to start a new polyshape object by creating the first line segment (Listing 13.4).

**Listing 13.3. Removing nodes from a polyshape.**

```
Sub ArtWork_MouseDown (Button%, Shift%, X!, Y!)
    If NodeTotal > 1 Then
        Node(0).Visible = False
        On Error GoTo NoNode:
            For R = 1 To NodeTotal
                Unload Node(R)
            Next R
NoNode:
    UpdateObjects
    Counter = 1: ShapeBtn.Enabled = False: NodeTotal = 1
End If
ArtWork.DrawMode = 6
    If Button = 1 Then
        BoundingBox_Down Button, Shift, X, Y
    End If
Exit Sub
End Sub
```

**If NodeTotal > 1 Then:** Scenario #1—nodes are visible on the desktop.

**Node(0).Visible:** Hides the original blue node.

**On Error GoTo NoNode:** You are about to remove any loaded nodes that appear around the polyshape object. If you try to unload more nodes than are present on the form, you get a fatal error. For safety purposes, if this error occurs, you can escape by jumping to the line called NoNode.

**For R = 1 To NodeTotal:** For every node starting at 1 and continuing up to the total number of nodes.

**Unload Nodes(R):** Removes all the nodes as you count up using the For/Next statement.

Chapter **13**

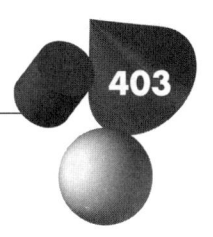

**NoNodes:** The escape label used by the `On Error Goto` statement.

**UpdateObjects:** Call this procedure to redraw all polyshape objects on the desktop.

**Counter = 1:** Resets node counter to the default of 1.

**ShapeBtn.Enabled = False:** Disables the Shape button temporarily.

**NodeTotal = 1:** Resets the total number of nodes back to the default of 1.

**ArtWork.DrawMode = 6:** If the draw mode has changed due to a routine in the `UpdateObject` procedure, then this line resets the mode to the default `Inverse` mode.

**If Button = 1 Then:** Scenario #2—drawing the first line of a polyshape. Only if the left button is pressed, do the following block of code statements.

**BoundingBox_Down:** You are about to draw a new line, so branch off to the `BoundingBox_Down` procedure, which draws the line segment.

**Exit Sub:** If an `Error` occurred by removing the nodes, then the `On Error Goto` statement expects a `Resume Next` statement. You bypass this statement by simply adding the `Exit Sub` statement.

The `Artwork_MouseMove` event in Listing 13.4 calls the `BoundingBox_Move` procedure, which draws each polyline segment.

**Listing 13.4. Drawing a new line object.**

```
Sub ArtWork_MouseMove (Button%, Shift%, X!, Y!)
    If Button = 1 Then
        BoundingBox_Move Button, Shift, X, Y
            X2 = X
            Y2 = Y
        BoundingBox_Move Button, Shift, X, Y
    End If
End Sub
```

**If Button = 1 Then:** Only if the left mouse button is held, then continue.

**BoundingBox_Move:** Go to this procedure to draw a new line segment.

**X2, Y1:** Standard formula to reverse the line's start and end points for the illusion of movement.

**BoundingBox_Move:** Go to this procedure again to erase the first line drawn.

**Listing 13.5. Setting the new line object.**

```
Sub ArtWork_MouseUp (Button%, Shift%, X!, Y!)
    If MoveMouse() = True Then
        BoundingBox_Up Button, Shift, X, Y
    End If
End Sub
```

## The Join Nodes Program

**If MoveMouse() = True Then:** Only if the mouse has moved the distance specified in the `MoveMouse` function (Listing 13.10), then continue to set the final values of the new line object. The current setting for the `MoveMouse` function = 45 twips or three pixels in any direction.

## Drawing the Polyline Segments

You draw all lines using the three following bounding box procedures, as shown in Listings 13.6 through 13.8.

**Listing 13.6. Initializing the line's start and end coordinates.**

```
Sub BoundingBox_Down (Button%, Shift%, XI, YI)
    X1 = X
    Y1 = Y
    X2 = X1
    Y2 = Y1
End Sub
```

**X1, Y2, X1, Y2:** Sets the line's start and end points to the current X and Y MouseDown position.

**Listing 13.7. Drawing a line or polyline segment.**

```
Sub BoundingBox_Move (Button%, Shift%, XI, YI)
    If MoveMouse() = False Then Exit Sub
        If Button Then
            ArtWork.Line (X1, Y1)-(X2, Y2)
        End If
End Sub
```

**If MouseMove() = False Then Exit Sub:** The mouse has not moved the distance specified in the `MouseMove` function. The current distance is 45 twip or 3 pixels in any direction.

**If Button then:** Only if a mouse button is held down, then continue.

**ArtWork.Line:** Draws the new line or polyline segment.

**Listing 13.8. Snapping a polyshape closed.**

```
Sub BoundingBox_Up (Button%, Shift%, XI, YI)
    Total = Total + 1: B = Total
    W(B) = X1: N(B) = Y1: E(B) = X2: S(B) = Y2
If Counter = 1 Then FirstPolyPt(B) = B: FlagPoly(B) = B: ZZ = B
    Snap = 120 'Distance from mouse pointer to blue node
If X2 > Node(0).Left - Snap And X2 < Node(0).Left + 90 + Snap [IC:CCC]
And Y2 > Node(0).Top - Snap And Y2 < Node(0).Top + 90 + Snap [IC:CCC]
Then E(B) = Node(0).Left + 45: S(B) = Node(0).Top + 45
    For r = 1 To NodeTotal - 1
        Unload Node(r)
```

```
        Next r
        NodeTotal = 1: LastPolyPt(ZZ) = B: TotalPolyPts(ZZ) = Counter
        PolyShape(B) = ZZ: ShapeBtn.Enabled = True
        UpdateObjects
    End If
        Nodes 'Load new nodes
End Sub
```

**Total = Total +1:** If the mouse has moved the 45-twip distance, a line is drawn on the form. Add 1 to the total to represent this new line object.

**B:** The line is then assigned a number, which at this point is equal to the total.

**W(B), N(B), E(B), S(B):** Stores the line's start (X1, Y1) and end (X2, Y2) coordinates in these indexed arrays for future reference.

**If Counter = 1:** The counter represents each node that is added to an object. The coordinates of the first node are needed to pass to the API Polygon function.

**FlagPoly = B:** So that the UpdateObject procedure knows what type of drawing function to use, you store the type of object you are drawing. At present, there is only one type of drawing action in this program; it is a polyobject drawing.

**ZZ = B:** Temporarily stores the line number in ZZ. As each new line segment is added, ZZ is increased until the last line segment is connected to the first line segment to form a polygon shape.

**Snap = 120:** You can make the last line segment's node snap to the first line segment's node. You do so by stating the maximum twip distance that the two nodes must be apart from each other before they are snapped together. At present, the snap is 120 twips or 8 pixels in any direction. Change this number to suit your needs.

**If X2 > Node(0).Left - Snap And:** If the first and last node are within 120 twips of each other, connect the two points to create a polygon object.

**E(B) = Node(0).Left + 45: S(B) = Node(0).Top + 45:** The E(B) and S(B) values equal the last line segment's node. You simply connect the center of this node to the center of the first node in the polyshape (which is always the blue node).

**For R = 1 To NodeTotal - 1:** For every node starting at 1 and continuing up to the total number of nodes minus 1, do the following block of code statements.

**Unload Node(R):** Unloads all the nodes that appear on every line segment.

**NodeTotal = 1:** Resets the total number of nodes to the default of 1.

**LastPolyPts(ZZ) = Counter:** Saves the total number of points in this shape so that you can pass it to the API Polygon function.

**PolyShape(B) = ZZ:** The polyshape group number is equal to the last point drawn.

**UpdateObjects:** Redraws all the Polyline shapes that appear on the desktop.

**Nodes:** After each polygon shape is redrawn, call the Nodes procedure to hide the blue node.

## The Join Nodes Program

# Filling a Complex Object with Color

You use the `FloodFillBtn_Click` event in Listing 13.9 to color all polygon shapes. You can color individual sections if you use the mouse pointer to click an area and then choose either the FloodFill or ExtFloodFill buttons.

**Listing 13.9. Three painting (fill) methods.**

```
Sub FloodFillBtn_Click (Index As Integer)
    ArtWork.DrawMode = 13
    ArtWork.FillStyle = 0
    ArtWork.FillColor = QBColor(15 * Rnd)
If ArtWork.FillColor = QBColor(0) [IC:CCC]
        Then ArtWork.FillColor = QBColor(1)
    X = X1 \ PixelX: Y = Y1 \ PixelY
Select Case Index
    Case 0 'FloodFill
        r = FloodFill(ArtWork.hDC, X, Y, &H8)
    Case 1 'ExtFloodFill
        r = ExtFloodFill(ArtWork.hDC, X, Y, &H8, FLOODFILLBORDER)
    Case 2 'PolyFillMode
        If Check1.Value = 1 Then PolyMode = 1 Else PolyMode = 2
        r = SetPolyFillMode(ArtWork.hDC, WINDING)
        r = Polygon(ArtWork.hDC, Npt(FP), PolyPts)
End Select
End Sub
```

**ArtWork.DrawMode = 13:** You are going to paint a shape or area with color. You must change the current line drawing mode from Inverse to normal (copy_pen 13).

**ArtWork.FillStyle = 0:** You first must set the type of fill you want to use. In this case, it is 0, or Solid.

**Artwork.FillColor:** Because this short program doesn't use a palette bar so that you can choose color, you use randomly selected colors: QBcolor (a color number 0 through 15 randomly selected).

**If ArtWork.FillColor = 0:** This is black. Because black isn't a good example of color, change it.

**X = X1 \ PixelX: Y = Y1 \ PixelY:** If you are going to use the Floodfill or ExtFloodFill buttons to color a selected area on the form, you must change the X and Y scale. Most API drawing functions must use pixel coordination values in order for them to work. X1 and Y1 equal the current X and Y MouseDown position, and PixelX, PixelY convert the twips to pixels.

**Select Case Index:** Depending on which button you choose, do the following Case expression that matches the index of the button you selected.

**Case 0:** You selected the FloodFill button.

FloodFill ( hDC, X, Y, Color )

FloodFill = (The object to draw into, the X, Y screen position to start painting from, and the color of the border to paint up to).

**Case 1:** You selected the ExtFloodFill button.

ExtFloodFill ( hDC, X, Y, Color, Option )

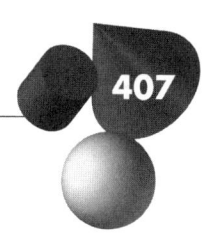

ExtFloodFill = (The object to draw into, the X, Y screen position to start painting from, and the color of the border to paint up to or the pixel color to paint onto; one of two options for painting).

**Option 1: FLOODFILLBORDER**: Paints until the border color is found. Same as the FloodFill function.

**Option 2: FLOODFILLSURFACE**: Paints only on top of the color specified and up to any surrounding pixel with the same color.

**Case 2:** You selected the PolyFill button:

SetPolyFillMode ( hDC, Option )

SetPolyFillMode = (The object to which you are setting plus one of two options).

**Option 1: ALTERNATE**: Fills by coloring every other closed intersection from left to right.

**Option 2: WINDING**: Depending on which direction you draw the object's segments, the fill can be either solid or open. See Figure 13.2.

The MoveMouse function in Listing 13.10 determines whether the mouse pointer has moved a given distance when the mouse has been dragged.

**Listing 13.10. Determining whether the mouse has moved a given distance.**

```
Function MoveMouse ()
    If X1 > X2 + 45 Or X1 < X2 - 45 Or Y1 > Y2 + 45 Or [IC:CCC]
            Y1 < Y2 - 45 Then
        MoveMouse = True
    Else
        MouseMouse = False
    End If
End Function
```

**If X1 > X2 + 45 Or etc.:** When the user clicks the mouse, triggering a MouseDown event, the X1, Y1, X2, and Y2 values equal the X and Y coordinates of the mouse pointer. You can then add a value to this position to determine whether the mouse has moved a specified distance. The distance in this case is 45 twips, which is 3 pixels in any direction. You can change this value to suit yourself.

# Using a Node to Edit the Shape

The order in which nodes are placed around the object is controlled by the index assigned to the node when it was loaded. The Join Nodes program uses Node(1) as the first line segment's node of the polyshape. The original Node(0) is hidden beneath Node(1).

# The Join Nodes Program

In the ArtAPI program in Chapter 15, the first line segment's node is `Node(0)` and then continues up in index numbers. The starting index number for the first node on the first line segment is a decision you must make. (See Listing 13.11.) When you start to add more complex segments and node editing features, you may find one routine better suited than the other.

**Listing 13.11. Setting additional line segments' start points.**

```
Sub node_MouseDown (Index%, Button%, Shift%, X!, Y!)
    ArtWork.DrawMode = 6
    X1 = Node(Index).Left + 45
    Y1 = Node(Index).Top + 45
    X2 = X1
    Y2 = Y1
End Sub
```

**`ArtWork.DrawMode = 6`:** If the drawing mode has changed, reset the mode to `Inverse`.

**`X1, Y1`:** Places the line's starting coordinate to the center of the previous node.

**`X2, Y1`:** Starts the line drawing from the center of the previous node.

The `Node_MouseMove` event in Listing 13.12 draws the two polyline segments that attach to the node when the node is moved.

**Listing 13.12. Moving polyshape line segments.**

```
Sub node_MouseMove (Index%, Button%, Shift%, X!, Y!)
Label1.Caption = Format$(Index)
    If Button = 1 Then
        If ShapeBtn.Enabled = True Then NodeMove Index, [IC:CCC]
            Button, Shift, X, Y: Exit Sub
        BoundingBox_Move Button, Shift, X, Y
        X2 = X
        Y2 = Y
    BoundingBox_Move Button, Shift, X, Y
End If
End Sub
```

**`Label1.Caption`:** When the mouse pointer passes over a node, the label displays the node number assigned to it. Node number 1 is located underneath node number 0 at this point.

**`If Button =1 Then`:** Only if the mouse button is held, then continue.

**`If ShapeBtn.Enabled`:** The Shape button is enabled only after a polygon shape is made. You then go to the `NodeMove` procedure (Listing 13.14) to edit the shape of the object you have just drawn.

**`BoundingBox_Move`:** If the Shape button is disabled, you are still drawing line segments for your object. The `BoundingBox_Move` procedure (Listing 13.7) takes over from here.

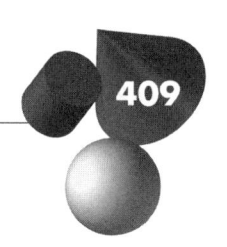

**X2, Y2:** Reverses the line's end or start points.

**BoundingBox_Move:** Repeats this procedure to erase the first line that was drawn.

The `Node_MouseUp` event in Listing 13.13 recalculates the node's coordinates after the polyshape has been edited. The polyshape is then redrawn by calling the `UpdateObjects` procedure.

**Listing 13.13. Setting each new line segment of the shape.**

```
Sub node_MouseUp (Index%, Button%, Shift%, X!, Y!)
    If ShapeBtn.Enabled = True Then
        Node(Index).Left = X - 45: Node(Index).Top = Y - 45
        Node(Index).ScaleLeft = X - 45: Node(Index).ScaleTop = Y - 45
        Node(1).Left = Node(0).Left: Node(1).Top = Node(0).Top
        Node(1).ScaleLeft = Node(0).ScaleLeft:
        Node(1).ScaleTop = Node(0).ScaleTop
            UpdateObjects
    Exit Sub
End If
    ArtWork_MouseUp Button, Shift, X, Y
End Sub
```

**If ShapeBtn.Enabled = True Then:** This button is enabled after the polygon object is drawn. This relocates the node you started to move to the new screen position. Unlike the Artisan program in Chapter 2 that drags a line node (Shape control) as you move a line, this program draws the box that looks like the node control.

**Node(1).Left = Node(0).Left:** You need this line only to place the first node under the blue node after the Shape button has been pressed. To save code space, it was placed here. The blue `Node(0)` on a "closed" polygon acts as the polygon's end node, and `Node(1)` acts as the start node. When you break a polygon shape at a node junction, you can use the blue node to jump to the break point to act again as the end node. The breaking of nodes, however, is not covered in this example.

**Node(1).ScaleLeft = Node(0).ScaleLeft:** When you move a node to a new location, you must rescale the interior dimension to reflect the scale of the `Artwork` picture box desktop.

**UpdateObjects:** Redraws all the objects that are displayed to date and then exits this event.

**ArtWork_MouseUp:** If the Shape button was disabled, you are still drawing line segments. By forcing a `MouseUp` event in the `Artwork` picture box, you automatically draw one line segment.

# Moving Connected Line Segments

When you move a node, the two lines that are connected to the node must follow. You use the `NodeMove` procedure in Listing 13.14 to move two connecting line segments at the same time. You need a formula to find what index the node's X and Y points are stored in so that you can safely redraw all the polygon shapes.

# The Join Nodes Program

**Listing 13.14. Editing the node positions of a polyshape.**

```
Sub NodeMove (Index%, Button%, Shift%, XI, YI)
    If Button Then
        Z = PolyShape(B)
        r = FirstPolyPt(Z) + Index - 2
        rr = FirstPolyPt(Z) + Index
If rr > LastPolyPt(Z) Then rr = FirstPolyPt(Z)
If Index = 0 Then r = FirstPolyPt(Z) + 1: rr = LastPolyPt(Z)
    X1 = W(r): Y1 = N(r): X3 = W(rr): Y3 = N(rr)
ArtWork.Line (X1, Y1)-(X2, Y2): ArtWork.Line -(X3, Y3)
ArtWork.Line (X2 - 45, Y2 - 45)-(X2 + 45, Y2 + 45), , B
    X2 = X
    Y2 = Y
ArtWork.Line (X1, Y1)-(X2, Y2): ArtWork.Line -(X3, Y3)
ArtWork.Line (X2 - 45, Y2 - 45)-(X2 + 45, Y2 + 45), , B
    If Index = 0 Then
        W(r - 1) = X: N(r - 1) = Y
    Else
        W(r + 1) = X: N(r + 1) = Y
    End If
End If
End Sub
```

**If Button Then:** Only if the button is held down, then continue.

**Z = PolyShape(B):** The value of B equals the last line segment number. The `PolyShape()` indexed number matching the B value indicates the first coordinate index for the group of line segments that make up the polyshape.

**r = FirstPolyPt(Z) + Index - 2:** In this program, the blue node is always index 0, and the following nodes are indexed 2, 3, 4, and so on. Because `Node(1)` is hidden under the blue node, it makes the process a little tricky. You need to find the two nodes at the opposite sides of the node you are moving. The r variable gives you the next lowest index number from the node you are moving.

**rr = FirstPolyPt(Z) + Index:** You have to move two line segments at one time. The rr variable gives you the next highest index number from the node you are moving.

**If rr > LastPolyPt(Z) Then:** The last node on the polyshape presents a problem because the next highest indexed node is really the first indexed node number on a "closed" polygon shape. This statement accommodates the needed change if you move the last node in the chain.

**If Index = 0 Then:** The first node on the polyshape presents a problem also. The next lowest node is really the last node on a "closed" polygon shape. This statement accommodates the change needed if you move the first node.

**X1 = W(r): Y1 = N(r):** Equals the preceding node to the one you are moving.

**X3 = W(rr): Y3 N(rr):** Equals the subsequent node in the one you are moving.

**ArtWork.Line (X1, Y1)-(X2, Y2): ArtWork.Line -(X3, Y3):** Draws two joining lines.

**ArtWork.Line (X2 - 45, Y2 - 45)-(X2 + 45, Y2 + 45), , B:** Draws a little black node.

**X2 = X : Y2 = Y:** Reverses the values to give the illusion of a movable line and node.

**ArtWork.Line:** Redraws the two lines and little black node to erase the first ones drawn.

**If Index = 0 Then W(r - 1) = X: N(r - 1) = Y Else W(r + 1) = X: N(r + 1) = Y:** Finally, stores the new line segment's start points in the proper indexed arrays.

## Adding More Picture Box Nodes

The Nodes procedure in Listing 13.15 simply adds new nodes to the end points of each new line you draw. Each node is a picture box control. To add new controls at runtime, you use the Load statement along with the name of the control plus an index number to assign to it. You must already have at least one control of the same name on your form before you can load additional controls. After you load a new node, you reposition it to the end of the previous line segment. You then rescale the interior of the node so that it reflects the scale of the Artwork picture box desktop.

**Listing 13.15. Loading new nodes as they are needed.**

```
Sub Nodes ()
    If Counter = 1 Then 'First blue node
        Node(0).Visible = False
        Node(0).Left = W(B) - 45: Node(0).Top = N(B) - 45
        Node(0).ScaleLeft = Node(0).Left:
        Node(0).ScaleTop = Node(0).Top
        Node(0).Visible = True
    End If
r = NodeTotal 'add new node
Load Node(r): Node(r).BackColor = &HF&
    Node(r).Left = E(B) - 45: Node(r).Top = S(B) - 45
    Node(r).ScaleLeft = Node(r).Left:
    Node(r).ScaleTop = Node(r).Top
NodeTotal = NodeTotal + 1
Counter = Counter + 1
    Node(r).Visible = True
End Sub
```

**If Counter = 1:** If the Counter variable equals 1, you are drawing the first line segment of your polygon object. This line hides the first node, which is blue, and then moves it to the starting point of the first line. After it is moved, the node is made visible again.

**NodeTotal = NodeTotal + 1:** The node total and counter are advanced by 1. The next r variable then equals the index number to use with the next node.

**Load Node(r): Node(r).BackColor = &HF&:** A new picture box control is loaded onto the form. Make the node black and then scale and reposition the node to the end of the last line drawn.

**Node(r).Visible = True:** You must make the new control visible. By default, all new controls are invisible when you first load them.

## The Join Nodes Program

# Loading All Nodes Around an Object

When you press the Shape button, it reloads nodes (picture boxes) onto the newly drawn polyshape. See Listing 13.16.

**Listing 13.16. Positioning the nodes around the polyshape.**

```
Sub ShapeBtn_Click ()
    If nodetotal > 2 Then Exit Sub
g = PolyShape(B): rr = 2
    For r = FirstPolyPt(g) + 1 To LastPolyPt(g) 'add new nodes
        Load Node(rr): Node(rr).BackColor = BLACK
        Node(rr).Left = W(r) - 45: Node(rr).Top = N(r) - 45
        Node(rr).ScaleLeft = Node(rr).Left:
        Node(rr).ScaleTop = Node(rr).Top
        Node(rr).Visible = True: rr = rr + 1
    Next r
    NodeTotal = rr - 1: Node(0).Visible = True
End Sub
```

**g = PolyShape(B): rr = 2:** The B variable holds the index number of the last line segment drawn. The PolyShape() array holds the corresponding index to send to the FirstPolyPt and LastPolyPt arrays to find the first and last node position points of the polygon shape.

**rr = 2:** Equals the index number to assign the first new node. Node(0) index 0 and Node(1) index 1 are never unloaded in this program; you start by loading nodes at index 2.

**For R = FirstPolyPt(g) + 1 To LastPolyPt(g):** For every value of node starting at the first line segment point plus 1 one and continuing to the last line segment point, do the following block of code statements.

**Load Node(rr):** Loads a new node picture box control.

**Node(rr).BackColor = BLACK:** The original Node(0) is blue. If you do not change the BackColor of each new node, it also becomes blue.

**Node(rr).Left:** Positions each new node to the start of the proper line segment in the shape.

**Node(rr).ScaleLeft:** Rescales each new node so that its interior scale reflects that of the Artwork's desktop.

**Node(rr).Visible = True:** When you add new controls at runtime, they are invisible by default.

**rr = rr + 1:** Increases the index number by 1.

**NodeTotal = rr - 1:** Stores the number of nodes that now appear around the object.

**Node(0).Visible = True:** Makes the blue node visible again.

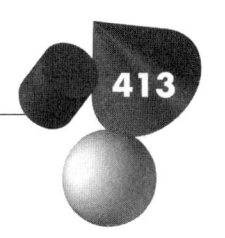

# Drawing the Final Shape

Listing 13.17 is a shortened version of the same `UpdateObject` procedures in the Artisan program in Chapter 5 and the ArtAPI program in Chapter 15. All `UpdateObject` procedures draw the final object shapes.

**Listing 13.17. Redrawing the polyshapes.**

```
Sub UpdateObjects ()
    ArtWork.Cls: LastB = B: B = 1
Do While B < Total + 1
    Select Case B
        Case FlagPoly(B)
            FP = FirstPolyPt(B): LP = LastPolyPt(B)
            Npt(1).X = W(FP) \ PixelX: Npt(1).Y = N(FP) \ PixelY
    For BB = FP To LP
        Npt(BB).X = W(BB) \ PixelX: Npt(BB).Y = N(BB) \ PixelY
    Next BB
        PolyPts = TotalPolyPts(B): Counter = 0
        FloodFillBtn_Click 2
End Select
    B = B + 1
Loop
    B = LastB
End Sub
```

**ArtWork.Cls:** Clears the screen and erases any objects drawn.

**LastB = B: B = 1:** Temporarily stores the last line segment number and makes B equal to 1.

**Do While B < Total + 1:** Continues looping through the following block of statements until all line segments are redrawn onto Artwork's desktop.

**Select Case B:** Goes to the drawing function that matches the flag. There is only one flag in this program.

**Case FlagPoly(B):** Redraws each polygon shape to date.

The API `Polygon` function is as follows:

        Polygon(ArtWork.hDC, Npt(FP), PolyPts)

**FP = FirstPolyPt(B):** Represents the index number to use to look up the first X and Y points of the polyshape.

**LP = LastPolyPt(B):** Represents the index number to use to look up the last X and Y points of the shape.

**Npt(1).X = W(FP) \ PixelX:** Sets the first X and Y points of the polygon shape. This is similar to using the `Pset` statement to start a line with the `Step` statement. You convert the twips values to pixels because the API `Polygon` function is drawn in this mode.

## The Join Nodes Program

**For BB = FP To Lp:** Loops through the array starting at the first line segment points to the last.

**Npt(BB).X = W(BB) \ PixelX:** Converts each additional X and Y value to pixel coordinates.

**PolyPts = TotalPolyPts(B):** Value sent to the API Polygon function to indicate the total number of points to draw on the polyshape.

**FloodFillBtn_Click 2:** Forces a FloodFillBtn event, which in turn draws the polygon shape. The argument 2 causes execution of the Select Case Index 2 routine.

## API Functions in the Join Nodes Program

Listing 13.18 illustrates the Type structure and API drawing functions you use in the Join Nodes program.

### Listing 13.18. The API functions used in the Join Nodes program.

```
Bas Module file declarations.
Type POINTAPI
    X As Integer
    Y As Integer
End Type
Declare Function FloodFill% Lib "GDI" (ByVal hDC As Integer, [IC:CCC]
ByVal X As Integer, ByVal Y As Integer, ByVal crColor As Long)
Declare Function ExtFloodFill% Lib "GDI" (ByVal hDC As Integer, [IC:CCC]
ByVal X As Integer, ByVal Y As Integer, ByVal crColor As Long, [IC:CCC]
ByVal wFillType As Integer)
Declare Function SetPolyFillMode% Lib "GDI" (ByVal hDC As [IC:CCC]
Integer ByVal nPolyFillMode As Integer)
Declare Function Polygon% Lib "GDI" (ByVal hDC As Integer, [IC:CCC]
lppoints As POINTAPI, ByVal nCount As Integer)
Global Const FLOODFILLSURFACE = 1
Global Const FLOODFILLBORDER = 0
Global Const ALTERNATE = 1
Global Const WINDING = 2
Global Const BLACK = &H0&
Global Const RED = &HFF&
Global Const GREEN = &HFF00&
Global Const YELLOW = &HFFFF&
Global Const BLUE = &HFF0000
Global Const MAGENTA = &HFF00FF
Global Const CYAN = &HFFFF00
Global Const WHITE = &HFFFFFF
These are the Windows API functions that the Join Nodes program uses.
FloodFill (hDC, X, Y, Color)
ExtFloodFill (hDC, X, Y, Color, FillType)
SetPolyFillMode (hDC, PolyFillMode) ALTERNATE = 1 : WINDING = 2
Polygon (hDC, POINTAPI, Count)
```

# Summary

The Join Nodes program shows the basic structure for joining line objects together. You can use several varieties of array structures to store and find node points around polyline objects. Some programs use data structures similar to 3-D modeling to store and find node points. You must decide the way in which you store and retrieve the coordinate points of nodes. This decision is also important if you intend to build complex graphical editing programs.

In Chapter 15, "The ArtAPI Program," you use the same technique you use in this chapter to connect line objects to curve objects. This process can get complicated at times, so you should fully understand the array structures used in the Join Nodes program.

If you don't need to have editable connecting line and curve segments in your programs, you may want to build the procedure's outline in this chapter to enhance other types of programs. Some possible alternatives are line charts that you can edit directly using the mouse pointer. Another suggestion is creating connecting line paths for 2-D bitmap animation.

# CHAPTER 14

# The Scaling and Printing Program

# The Scaling and Printing Program

Visual Basic provides two methods, called Printer object and `PrintForm`, for printing graphics and text to your printer. The Printer object method is used to send `Circle`, `Line`, `Print`, and `Pset` statement directly to the printer (similar to way you would send the objects to a form or picture box). When you have finished sending the graphical and text objects to the printer, you use the `EndDoc` statement to print the page. The Visual Basic `NewPage` keyword also can be used to print multiple pages. The `PrintForm` method takes a snapshot of your form and prints the resulting picture in the resolution of your monitor. The majority of monitors have less resolution than your advance printer, which can result in disappointing printed images.

You also can send API graphical and text functions to the printer. In some cases, however, you must perform addition scaling calculations in order to place the API graphics and text correctly.

The Windows API graphical functional requires that all coordinates sent to the API functions be in pixel units. The Art picture box in the PrintAPI program uses twip units as its scale mode property. All internal picture box coordinates must be converted form twips to pixel units before being sent to the API graphical function to be rendered.

The PrintAPI program draws two boxes, a circle, and a diagonal line object onto the picture box control. The larger box object represents the printable margin areas of the printer's page. You use this program to test the manual scale setting between the image areas on two devices (the picture box and the printer's page).

To correctly scale an image that is sent via API functions to the printer, you must calculate the differnce between the pixel resolution used by the API and the DPI resolution used by the printer. Two formulas you can use to convert API pixel resolution to the printer resolution are shown in the following examples:

1. `Npt(Z).X = (Npt(Z).X * HPrinterDPI) - LeftM`

   `Npt(Z).Y = (Npt(Z).Y * VPrinterDPI) - TopM`

2. `Npt(Z).X = (Npt(Z).X - LeftM) * HPrinterDPI`

   `Npt(Z).Y = (Npt(Z).Y - TopM) * VPrinterDPI`

The `Npt` array holds the X coordinate to send to the API graphical functions.

`HPrinterDPI` and `VPrinterDPI` are variables that represent the printer's pixel per inch values. When using twips as the scale mode on the form or picture box, you must convert these values to pixel units. (Refer to the `Print_API_Click` event in Listing 14.5.)

You use the `HPrinterDPI` and `VPrinterDPI` values to multiply the difference between horizontal scale width and vertical height of the two devices.

`LeftM` is the starting left margin image area that represents the page. If you use the first formula, `LeftM` is an offset to add for the 0, 0 coordinate of the control. If you use the second formula, `LeftM` is the difference between the 0, 0 coordinate and any negative or positive `Scaleleft` property of the control. In this example, the `Scaleleft` of the picture box control is zero, so `LeftM` equals 0.

You use the `TopM` and `PrintDPI` values for the `Npt(Z).Y` coordinate. You use the `VPrinterDPI` value to multiply the difference between vertical scale widths of the two devices.

**Figure 14.1.**
*The PrintAPI form and its controls.*

[Figure 14.1: The PrintAPI form titled "test print API patern" with three buttons: Draw1, Manual Print, and Print API]

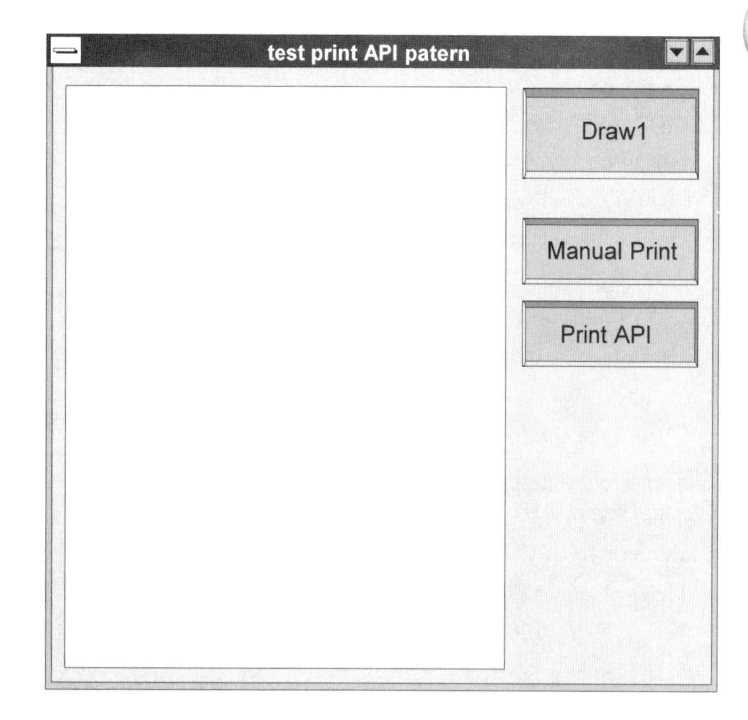

Figure 14.1 illustrates the `PrintAPI` form.

The PrintAPI program's form and control properties are listed in Table 14.1.

**Table 14.1. The properties of the `PrintAPI` form and controls.**

*Object: Form*
*Object Name: Form1*

| | | | |
|---|---|---|---|
| BackColor | = &H00FF0000& | Left | = 390 |
| Caption | = "test print API pattern" | Top | = 1185 |
| Height | = 5865 | Width | = 6255 |

*Object: Command Button*
*Object Name: Print_API*

| | | | |
|---|---|---|---|
| Caption | = "PrintAPI" | Left | = 4380 |
| Enabled | = 0  'False | Top | = 2040 |
| Height | = 615 | Width | = 1635 |

*continues*

# The Scaling and Printing Program

**T**able 14.1. continued

*Object: Command Button*
*Object Name: Manual_print*

| | | | |
|---|---|---|---|
| Caption | = "Manual Print" | Left | = 4380 |
| Enabled | = 0  'False | Top | = 1320 |
| Height | = 615 | Width | = 1680 |

*Object: Command Button*
*Object Name: Draw1*

| | | | |
|---|---|---|---|
| Caption | = "Draw1" | Top | = 60 |
| Height | = 960 | Width | = 1725 |
| Left | = 4365 | | |

*Object: Picture Box*
*Object Name: Art*

| | | | |
|---|---|---|---|
| BorderStyle | = 0 None | ScaleWidth | = 4095 |
| Height | = 5285 | Top | = 120 |
| Left | = 120 | Width | = 4090 |
| ScaleHeight | = 5280 | | |

Figure 14.2 shows a screen shot of the PrintAPI program.

**F**igure 14.2.
*A screen shot of the PrintAPI program.*

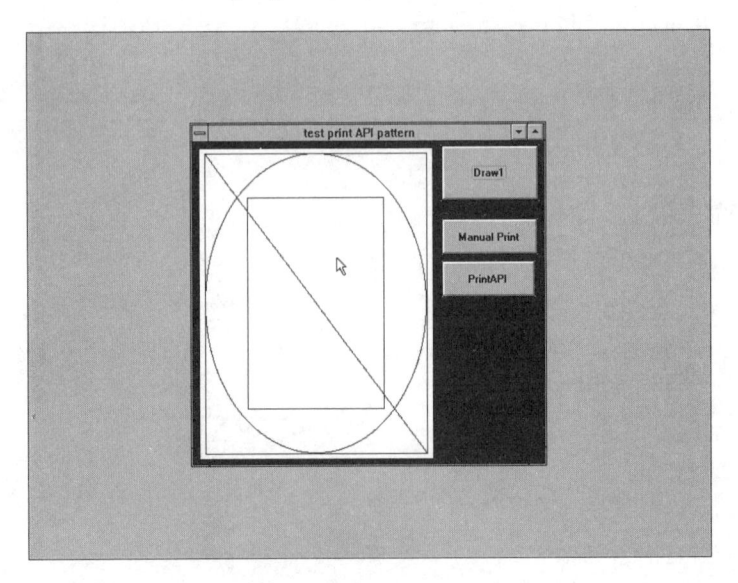

## Variable Names and API Functions

The PrintAPI program is set up to print on an 8.5- by 11-inch letter page to a 300 dpi printer. You have to change scaling values manually if your printer does not conform to these default values. The declaration section in Listing 14.1 includes extra API functions if you want to add additional printing features. Your printer driver controls the escape codes needed to print Windows graphical commends. Nearly all laser printers today are capable of printing the test page in the PrintAPI program. Some dot matrix and jet ink printers will print the test page if their print drivers were designed for graphical use for Windows 3.0 and higher.

**Listing 14.1. The API graphical functions to test.**

```
Declaration:
Declare Function EscapeBynum% Lib "GDI" Alias "Escape"
➥(ByVal hDC%, ByVal nEscape%, ByVal nCount%,
➥ByVal lpInData&, ByVal lpOutData&)
Declare Function DPtoLP Lib "GDI" (ByVal hDC As Integer,
➥lpPoints As POINTAPI, ByVal nCount As Integer) As Integer
Declare Function CreateDC% Lib "GDI"
➥(ByVal lpDriverName As String, ByVal lpDeviceName As String,
➥ByVal lpOutput As String, ByVal lpInitData As String)
Declare Function DeleteDC% Lib "GDI" (ByVal hDC As Integer)
Declare Function CreateMetaFile% Lib "GDI" (lpString As Any)
Declare Function LPtoDP% Lib "GDI"
➥(ByVal hDC As Integer, lpPoints As POINTAPI,
➥ByVal nCount As Integer)
Declare Function IsRectEmpty% Lib "User" (lpRect As Rect)
Declare Function Polygon% Lib "GDI"
➥(ByVal hDC As Integer, lpPoints As POINTAPI,
➥ByVal nCount As Integer)
Declare Function Polyline% Lib "GDI"
➥(ByVal hDC As Integer, lpPoints As POINTAPI,
➥ByVal nCount As Integer)
Declare Function SetPolyFillMode% Lib "GDI"
➥(ByVal hDC As Integer, ByVal nPolyFillMode As Integer)
Declare Function Rectangle% Lib "GDI"
➥(ByVal hDC As Integer, ByVal X1 As Integer, ByVal Y1 As Integer,
➥ByVal X2 As Integer, ByVal Y2 As Integer)
Declare Function Ellipse% Lib "GDI"
➥(ByVal hDC As Integer, ByVal X1 As Integer, ByVal Y1 As Integer,
➥ByVal X2 As Integer, ByVal Y2 As Integer)
Const HORZRES = 8: Const VERTRES = 10
Declare Function GetDeviceCaps% Lib "GDI"
➥(ByVal hDC As Integer, ByVal nIndex As Integer)
Dim HPrinterDPI As Single
Dim VPrinterDPI As Single
Dim PixelX, PixelY As Integer
Dim Npt(10) As POINTAPI
Dim Npt2(10) As POINTAPI
Dim OS As Integer
```

**Dim HPrinterDPI:** Holds the horizontal pixel resolution difference between the picture box and the printer.

## The Scaling and Printing Program

**Dim VPrinterDPI:** Holds the vertical pixel resolution difference between the picture box and the printer.

**Dim PixelX, PixelY:** Converts twip units to pixel units of measurement (`TwipPerPixel`).

**Dim Npt(10) As POINTAPI:** Stores the dimensions of the smaller of two box objects.

**Dim Npt2(10) As POINTAPI:** Stores the bounding box dimensions of the page (margins).

**Dim OS:** Holds an offset value to position the smaller of two box objects.

## Drawing the Shapes on the Picture Box

Pressing the button marked Draw1 draws the box, circle, and line shapes onto the Art picture box control. The `Npt(index)` values in the `Draw1_Click` event of Listing 14.2 represent the margin area within the printer's page.

**Listing 14.2. Assigning the drawing coordinates of the four objects.**

```
Sub Draw1_Click ()
    Npt(1).X = 100 \ PixelX: Npt(1).Y = 75 \ PixelY
    Npt(2).X = 100 \ PixelX: Npt(2).Y = 5200 \ PixelY
    Npt(3).X = 4000 \ PixelX: Npt(3).Y = 5200 \ PixelY
    Npt(4).X = 4000 \ PixelX: Npt(4).Y = 75 \ PixelY
Device% = Art.hDC
OS = 50: HPrinterDPI = 0: VPrinterDPI = 0
DrawObjects Device%
    Manual_Print.Enabled = True
    Print_API.Enabled = True
End Sub
```

**Npt(1).X = 100 \ PixelX:** Assigns the box's and line object's bounding boxes (the margins) and converts the `Twip` values to pixel units. The `Form_Load` event includes the code lines:

```
PixelX = Screen.TwipsPerPixelX
PixelX = Screen.TwipsPerPixelX
```

**Device% = Art.hDC:** Makes it easier to pass the name of the device into which you draw the API drawing functions. This program draws into either the Art picture box or the printer's page.

**OS = 50: HPrinterDPI = 0: VPrinterDPI = 0:** Sets default values for drawing coordinates.

**DrawObjects Device%:** Calls the `DrawObjects` procedure (Listing 14.3) and passes the procedure the name of the device into which you are going to draw. In this case, the device is the Art picture box control.

## Drawing the Objects

The `DrawObjects` procedure in Listing 14.3 draws each object to the device after you press any of the three main buttons on the `PrintAPI` form. The `Device As Integer` argument equals the name of the `hDC` device (picture box or printer).

## Listing 14.3. Drawing the four objects onto a device.

```
Sub DrawObjects (Device As Integer)
    API1 = Ellipse(Device, Npt(1).X, Npt(1).Y, Npt(3).X, Npt(3).Y)
    API2 = Polygon(Device, Npt(1), 4)
    API3 = Rectangle(Device, Npt(1).X + OS, Npt(1).Y + OS,
        ↪Npt(3).X - OS, Npt(3).Y - OS)
    Npt2(1).X = Npt(1).X: Npt2(1).Y = Npt(1).Y
    Npt2(2).X = Npt(3).X: Npt2(2).Y = Npt(3).Y
    Api4 = Polyline(Device, Npt2(1), 2)
End Sub
```

**API1 = Ellipse:** Draws the ellipse attached to the edges of the margins.

**API2 = Polygon:** Draws a box around the margin area of the page.

**API3 = Rectangle:** Draws a smaller rectangle within the page. The OS value equals an added offset from the margins.

**API4 = Polyline:** Draws a diagonal line across the page.

## Manually Scaling the Printer's Page

The Manual_print_Click event in Listing 14.4 uses preset HPrinterDPI and VPrinterDPI values to adjust the differences between the picture box and printer's scales. This routine is the same one used in the Print_API_Click event (see Listing 14.5). The APIH and APIV values are the same values that the API GetDeviceCaps functions calculates, as demonstarted in Listing 14.5.

## Listing 14.4. Testing printer scaling values.

```
Sub Manual_print_Click ()
    Screen.MousePointer = 11
    Form1.Caption = "Printing page, please wait."
        Printer.PSet (0, 0) 'start printer
        LeftM = 0: TopM = 0 'adjust Margins

        APIH = Printer.ScaleWidth / Printer.TwipsPerPixelX
        APIV = Printer.ScaleHeight / Printer.TwipsPerPixelY
        HPrinterDPI = APIH / (Art.Width / Screen.TwipsPerPixelX)
        VPrinterDPI = APIV / (Art.Height / Screen.TwipsPerPixelX)
    For Z = 1 To 4
        Npt(Z).X = (Npt(Z).X * HPrinterDPI) - LeftM
        Npt(Z).Y = (Npt(Z).Y * VPrinterDPI) - TopM
    Next Z
Device% = Printer.hDC
OS = 50 * HPrinterDPI
DrawObjects Device%
    Printer.EndDoc : Art.Cls
    Manual_Print.Enabled = False: Print_API.Enabled = False:
    Form1.Caption = "test print API pattern"
    Screen.MousePointer = 0
End Sub
```

**Screen.MousePointer = 11:** Changes the mouse pointer to an hourglass shape.

**Printer.PSet (0, 0):** Sometimes you might find that API graphical functions do not immediately start drawing into a Visual Basic control or a printer's page. To correct this situation, you need to get a handle on the device context of the control into which you are drawing. Visual Basic does this automatically when you issue a Basic language graphic, font, or print statement. By placing a single pixel point on the control, you now have a device context reference to the control. You use the 0, 0 coordinate because you never see this single pixel at this location.

**LeftM = 0: TopM = 0 :** Adjusts the margins if images are not centered.

**APIH: APIV:** The logical number of pixels per inch that reflect the printer's page size can be retrieved by dividing the printer's ScaleWidth and ScaleHeight by the number of twip per pixels. This is the same as using the API GetDeviceCaps function to query the printer's LogPixelSX (8) and LogPixelSY (10) capability.

**HPrinterDPI:** You can change this value to manually stretch the image horizontally. On some printers, you may need to multiply the value for a higher dot per inch (DPI) printer (for example, HPrinterDPI * 2 for 600 dpi printers).

**VPrinterDPI:** You can change this value to manually stretch the image vertically. On some printers, you may need to multiply the value for a higher dot per inch (DPI) printer (for example, HPrinterDPI * 2 for 600 dpi printers).

**Npt(Z).X = (Npt(Z).X * HPrinterDPI) - LeftM:** The X coordinate for each object.

**Npt(Z).Y = (Npt(Z).Y * VPrinterDPI) - TopM:** The Y coordinate for each object.

**Device% = Printer.hDC:** Assigns the name of the device into which you draw.

**OS = 50 * HPrinterDPI:** An offset from the margins to draw the smaller of the two box objects.

**DrawObjects Device%:** Calls the DrawObject procedure (Listing 14.3), which draws the object onto the device (the picture box or printer's page).

**Printer.EndDoc:** Tells the printer to send (print) the page.

**Screen.MousePointer = 0:** Resets the mouse pointer to an arrow.

## API Printing

Pressing the button marked Print API triggers the Print_API_Click event in Listing 14.5. You can use the API GetDeviceCaps to get information about the capabilities of a device. To print images displayed on the monitor to the printer, you must calculate the resolution difference between the two devices. You may want to add additional API printing device calls to retrieve everything about the particular printer into which you are drawing. This list of possible API functions to retrieve or send information to a printer is quite extensive; you should refer to the Windows SDK reference guide.

**Listing 14.5.** Using API `GetDeviceCaps` when printing.

```
Sub Print_API_Click ()
    Screen.MousePointer = 11
    Form1.Caption = "Printing page, please wait."
Printer.PSet (0, 0) 'start printer
APIH = GetDeviceCaps(Printer.hDC, 8)
APIV = GetDeviceCaps(Printer.hDC, 10)
HPrinterDPI = APIH / (Art.Width \ PixelX)
VPrinterDPI = APIV / (Art.Height \ PixelY)
LeftM = 0: TopM = 0 'adjust Margins
    For Z = 1 To 4
        Npt(Z).X = (Npt(Z).X - LeftM) * HPrinterDPI
        Npt(Z).Y = (Npt(Z).Y - TopM) * VPrinterDPI
    Next Z
Device% = Printer.hDC
OS = 50 * HPrinterDPI
DrawObjects Device%
    Printer.EndDoc : Art.Cls
    Print_API.Enabled = False: Manual_Print.Enabled = False
    Form1.Caption = "test print API pattern"
    Screen.MousePointer = 0
End Sub
```

**Screen.MousePointer = 11:** Changes the mouse pointer to an hourglass shape.

**Printer.PSet (0, 0):** Gets the printer's attention by sending a graphical statement.

**APIH = GetDeviceCaps(Printer.hDC, 8):** Retrieves the horizontal resolution of the printer.

**APIV = GetDeviceCaps(Printer.hDC, 10):** Retrieves the vertical resolution of the printer.

**HPrinterDPI = APIH / (Art.Width \ PixelX):** Adjusts the horizontal scaling differences between the picture box and printer. Adding or subtracting from this value scales the page images horizontally.

**VPrinterDPI = APIV / (Art.Height \ PixelY):** Adjusts the vertical scaling differences between the picture box and printer. Adding or subtracting from this value scales the page images vertically.

**LeftM = 0: TopM = 0 :** Adjusts the margins if images are not centered correctly.

**Npt(Z).X = (Npt(Z).X - LeftM) * HPrinterDPI:** The X coordinate for each object.

**Npt(Z).X = (Npt(Z).X - TopM) * VPrinterDPI:** The Y coordinate for each object.

**Device% = Printer.hDC:** Assigns the name of the device (printer) into which you draw.

**OS = 50 * HPrinterDPI:** An offset from the margins to draw the smaller of the two box objects.

**DrawObjects Device%:** Calls the `DrawObject` procedure (Listing 14.3), which draws the object onto the device (the picture box or printer's page).

**Printer.EndDoc:** Tells the printer to send (print) the page.

**Screen.MousePointer = 0:** Resets the mouse pointer to an arrow.

## Summary of the PrintAPI Program

Using the PrintAPI program should give you a general idea of how to print API graphical images to a printer's page. Although you also have to include more procedures to determine the capabilities of the printer to which you are printing, this small sacrifice is better than using Visual Basic's `PrintForm` statement to print your images only as screen shots.

Resizing the Art picture box and then print the images. Whatever image is visible within the picture box's interior will be stretched or reduced to fit the printer's page. When using twip scale units, you can use the Art picture box's `ScaleWidth` property to replace the `Art.Width` value in the `HPrinterDPI` and `VPrinterDPI` formulas. This should give you more freedom to test scaling effects on the images you print.

## The Scaltest Program

You use the Scaltest program to test different scaling formulas within a Visual Basic picture box control. In the following sections, you find two examples to adjust Zoom In and Zoom Out tool features. The `Zoom_Basic` menu uses Visual Basic scaling statements, and the `Zoom_API` menu uses API functions. Mixing and matching these two methods can be disastrous to your applications and is not recommended. The zoom percentage values stated in the `Zoom_Basic` menu are bogus and do not represent the true percentage of scaling.

You must remember to check if the ruler guidelines align to the mouse pointer when you drag them in different settings. In the `Zoom_API` scaling mode, the guidelines do not align because the `Ruler` events do not use the API `DLtoLP` function to convert the mouse's X and Y coordinates. You also should note the mouse's current X and Y values displayed in the label control when you're using the API scaling functions.

You can find the program RULER.MAK in the 14SCALE directory of the companion disk. The Ruler program is basically a copy of the Scaltest program, except different formulas are used to draw the rulers in each program. The two picture boxes that contain the ruler images in each of the Artisan, ArtAPI, and Scaltest programs are moved when you use the horizontal or vertical scrollbars. In the Ruler program, the two rulers remain stationary.

Another smaller scaling program called ScaleAPI, which is located in the 16MISC directory on the companion disk, demonstrates zooming into a selected area of a form or picture box.

> **NOTE** The Scaltest program uses the Visual Basic scaling properties method and the API scaling function. You should not mix and match these two methods. Doing so can lead to frustration when one method competes with the other during execution of the scaling routine. The Visual Basic scale properties or form and picture boxes use a completely different mapping method than their API counterparts.

Figure 14.3 illustrates the Scaltest form.

**Figure 14.3.**
*The* Scaltest *form and its controls.*

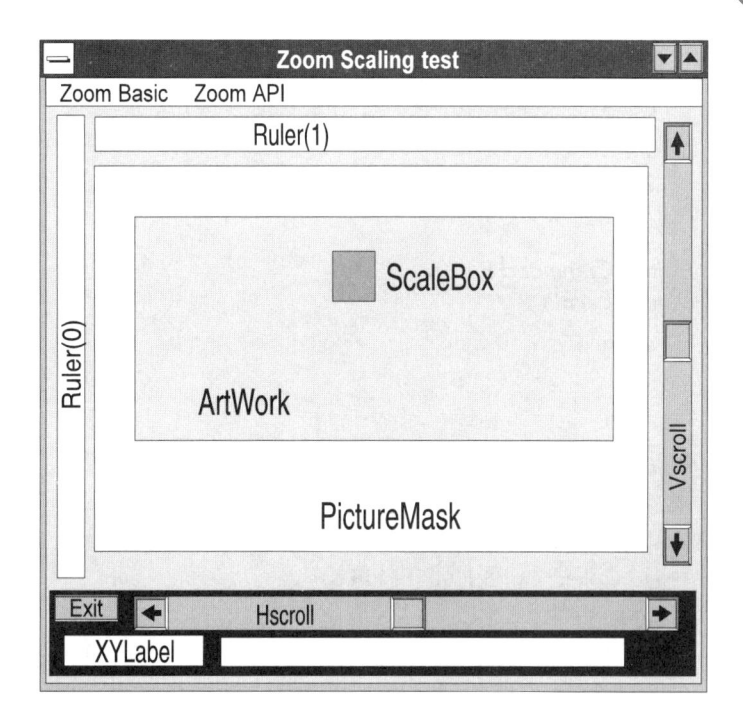

The Scaltest program's form and control properties are listed in Table 14.2.

**Table 14.2. The properties of the Scaltest form and controls.**

*Object: Form*
*Object ZoomTest*

| | | | |
|---|---|---|---|
| BackColor | = &H00FFFFFF& | ScaleMode | = 3 'Pixel |
| Caption | = "Zoom Scaling Test" | Top | = 1125 |
| Height | = 5925 | Width | = 7245 |
| Left | = 105 | | |

*Object: Picture Box*
*Object StatusArea*

| | | | |
|---|---|---|---|
| BackColor | = &H00FF0000& | ScaleMode | = 3 'Pixel |
| Height | = 750 | Top | = 4440 |
| Left | = 60 | Width | = 7035 |

*continues*

**T**able 14.2. continued

*Object: HScroll Bar*
*Object  HScroll*

| | | | |
|---|---|---|---|
| Height | = 285 | Min | = -200 |
| LargeChange | = 100 | SmallChange | = 10 |
| Left | = 810 | Top | = 0 |
| Max | = 200 | Width | = 6135 |

*Object: Command Button*
*Object  ExitBtn*

| | | | |
|---|---|---|---|
| Caption | = "Exit" | Top | = 0 |
| Height | = 270 | Width | = 645 |
| Left | = 90 | | |

*Object: Label*
*Object  StatusLabel*

| | | | |
|---|---|---|---|
| AutoSize | = -1 'True | Height | = 285 |
| BackColor | = &H00FFFFFF& | Left | = 1800 |
| BorderStyle | = 1 'Fixed Single | Top | = 360 |
| ForeColor | = &H00FFFFFF& | Width | = 4485 |

*Object: Label*
*Object  XYLabel*

| | | | |
|---|---|---|---|
| Alignment | = 2 'Center | Left | = 180 |
| BorderStyle | = 1 'Fixed Single | Top | = 405 |
| Height | = 285 | Width | = 1500 |

*Object: VScroll Bar*
*Object  VScroll*

| | | | |
|---|---|---|---|
| Height | = 4245 | Min | = -200 |
| LargeChange | = 100 | SmallChange | = 10 |
| Left | = 6720 | Top | =0 |
| Max | = 200 | Width | = 285 |

*Object: Picture Box*
*Object  Ruler*

| | | | |
|---|---|---|---|
| BackColor | = &H00C0C0C0& | ScaleHeight | = 300 |
| DrawMode | = 7 'Xor Pen | ScaleWidth | = 6060 |
| Height | = 330 | Top | = 90 |
| Index | = 1 | Left | = 540 |
| Width | = 6090 | | |

*Object: Picture Box*
*Object  Ruler*

| | | | |
|---|---|---|---|
| BackColor | = &H00C0C0C0& | Left | = 120 |
| DrawMode | = 7 'Xor Pen | Top | = 120 |
| Height | = 4245 | Width | = 330 |
| Index | = 0 | | |

*Object: Picture Box*
*Object  PictureMask*

| | | | |
|---|---|---|---|
| BorderStyle | = 0 'None | ScaleMode | = 3 'Pixel |
| Height | = 3480 | Top | = 540 |
| Left | = 540 | Width | = 6000 |

*Object: Picture Box*
*Object  ArtWork*

| | | | |
|---|---|---|---|
| BackColor | = &H0000FFFF& | Left | = 420 |
| BorderStyle | = 0 'None | Top | = 660 |
| Height | = 1770 | Width | = 5235 |

*Object: Picture Box*
*Object  ScaleBox*

| | | | |
|---|---|---|---|
| BackColor | = &H000000FF& | ScaleWidth | = 300 |
| Height | = 330 | Top | = 270 |
| Left | = 2565 | Width | = 330 |
| ScaleHeight | = 300 | | |

*Menu ZoomBasic*

    Caption = "Zoom &Basic"

*Menu Z_Basicsub*

    Caption = " 25 %"
    Index = 0

*Menu Z_Basicsub*

    Caption = " 50 %"
    Index = 1

*Menu Z_Basicsub*

    Caption = " 75 %"
    Index = 2

*continues*

## The Scaling and Printing Program

**T**able 14.2. continued

| | | | |
|---|---|---|---|
| Menu Z_Basicsub | | | |
| Caption | = "100 %" | Index | = 3 |
| Menu Z_Basicsub | | | |
| Caption | = "125 %" | Index | = 4 |
| Menu Z_Basicsub | | | |
| Caption | = "150 %" | Index | = 5 |
| Menu Z_Basicsub | | | |
| Caption | = "175 %" | Index | = 6 |
| Menu Z_Basicsub | | | |
| Caption | = "200 %" | Index | = 7 |
| Menu Z_Basicsub | | | |
| Caption | = "Full Page" | Index | = 8 |
| Menu ZoomAPI | | | |
| Caption | = "Zoom &API " | | |
| Menu Z_APIsub | | | |
| Caption | = " 2000" | Index | = 0 |
| Menu Z_APIsub | | | |
| Caption | = " 4000" | Index | = 1 |
| Menu Z_APIsub | | | |
| Caption | = "-6000" | Index | = 2 |
| Menu Z_APIsub | | | |
| Caption | = "Full Page" | Index | = 3 |

Figure 14.4 shows a screen shot of the Scaltest program.

**F**igure 14.4.
*A screen shot of the* ScalTest *program.*

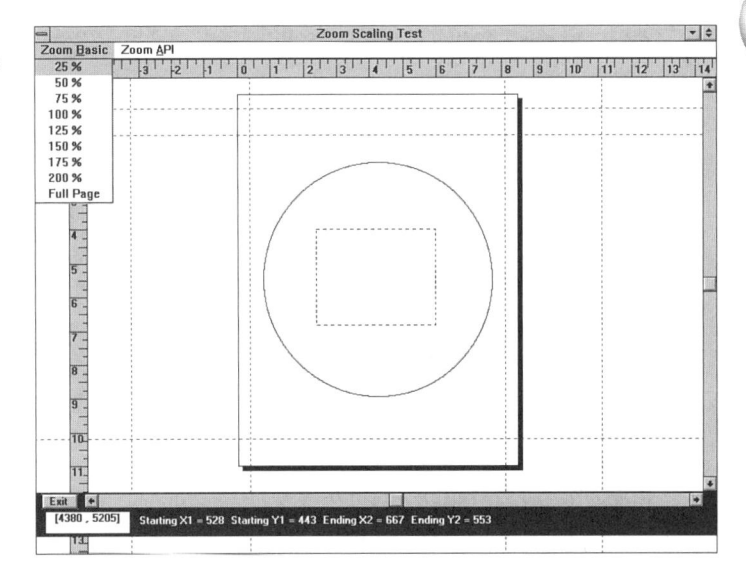

## Declarations and Startup Values

The declaration section in Listing 14.6 uses the same variable names and values used by the Artisan program in Chapter 2.

**Listing 14.6.** The variable names at startup.

```
Declaration:
Dim WIDE, HIGH As Integer
Dim PixelX, PixelY As Integer
Dim BSM, SSM As Single
Dim StartPt As Integer
Dim ASL, AST, ASW, ASH As Integer
Dim Ruler0X, Ruler0Y As Long
Dim Ruler1X, Ruler1Y As Long
Dim X1, Y1, X2, Y2 As Long
Dim XX1, YY1, XX2, YY2 As Long
Dim OldSW As Long
Dim OldSH As Long
Dim OldRH As Long
Dim OldRW As Long
Dim PerSW As Single
Dim PerSH As Single
Dim XY(1 To 4) As POINTAPI
```

# The Scaling and Printing Program

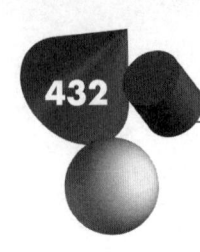

**WIDE and HIGH:** Switch monitor resolution. VGA and SVGA are usually 96 pixels per inch.

**PixelX and PixelY:** Represent the TwipsPerPixelX and TwipsPerPixelY values as defined in the Visual Basic Reference language guide.

**BBM** (bottom scroll move) and **SSM** (side scroll move): Offsets used for scrollbars when you're moving the Artwork picture box and the Rulers picture boxes.

**StartPt:** Initializes the starting coordinate when you're drawing a marquee box on the screen.

**Dim ASL, AST, ASW, ASH As Integer:** Stores the values of Artwork's ScaleLeft, ScaleTop, ScaleWidth, and ScaleHeight.

**Ruler0X, Ruler0Y, Ruler1X, and Ruler1Y:** Temporary line coordinate points when drawing a ruler guideline. They are the X1, Y1, X2, and Y2 values used in each ruler's Line statement.

**OldSW, OldSH, OldRH, OldRW:** Stores the previous ScaleLeft and ScaleHeight of the Artwork and Ruler picture boxes.

**PerSW, PerSH:** Manual offsets used to rescale controls after a zoom.

## The Picture Box Mouse Events

The Artwork picture box mouse events simply draw a dotted outline box shape on the desktop. The Scaltest program demonstrates two completely different scaling methods (API scaling and Visual Basic scaling). Because API functions require drawing coordinates to be in pixel units, you must adjust coordinate values because the Artwork desktop is using custom user-defined scaling. One way to retrieve devices to logical point coordinates is to use the API DPtoLP function, as explained in Listing 14.8.

The ArtWork_MouseDown event in Listing 14.7 saves the present scaling dimension of the Artwork picture box. Any drawing you perform is in pixel units, and any redrawing of scaled images is in user-defined units.

**Listing 14.7. Setting the scale mode of the picture box.**

```
Sub ArtWork_MouseDown (Button%, Shift%, X!, Y!)
    ASL = ArtWork.ScaleLeft
    AST = ArtWork.ScaleTop
    ASW = ArtWork.ScaleWidth
    ASH = ArtWork.ScaleHeight
    ArtWork.DrawMode = 6: ArtWork.DrawStyle = 2
    ArtWork.ScaleMode = 3
    StartPt = True
End Sub
```

**ASL = ArtWork.ScaleLeft:** Saves all the current scale dimensions of the picture box.

**ArtWork.DrawMode :** Changes the drawing mode to Inverse (6).

**ArtWork.DrawStyle:** Changes the drawing style to Dots (2) to draw a dotted outline of a box.

**ArtWork.ScaleMode = :** Changes the drawing scale mode to Pixel (3) units.

**StartPt = True:** Rather than initialize the starting point of the box in the MouseDown, you use the StartPt variable as a flag in the MouseMove event to set the coordinates.

The Artwork_MouseMove event in Listing 14.8 draws a dotted rectangle on the picture box. Because the program is using two scaling methods (API scaling and Visual Basic scaling), the API DPtoLP function converts the X and Y coordinates so the correct screen coordinates are used.

**Listing 14.8. Using devices to logical point conversions.**

```
Sub Artwork_MouseMove (Button%, Shift%, X!, Y!)
    Xstr = Format$(X, "000"): Ystr = Format$(Y, "000")
    XYLabel.Caption = "[" + Xstr + " , " + Ystr + "]"
RulerGuides Index%, Button, Shift, X, Y
    If SideRuler = True Or TopRuler = True Then
        GuideLines Index%, Button, X, Y
    End If
    If Button Then
        XY(1).X = X
        XY(1).Y = Y
        API = DPtoLP(ArtWork.hDC, XY(1), 1)
        XX = XY(1).X
        YY = XY(1).Y

If StartPt = True Then StartPt = False: W = XX: N = YY: E = XX: S = YY
  API = Rectangle(ArtWork.hDC, W, N, E, S)
    E = XX: S = YY
  API = Rectangle(ArtWork.hDC, W, N, E, S)

  Msg$ = "Starting X1 = " + Format$(W) + "  "
  Msg$ = Msg$ + "Starting Y1 = " + Format$(N) + "  "
  Msg$ = Msg$ + "Ending X2 = " + Format$(E) + "  "
  Msg$ = Msg$ + "Ending Y2 = " + Format$(S) + "  "
  StatusLabel.Caption = Msg$
End IfEnd Sub
```

**XY(1).X = X:** Puts the current X coordinate of the mouse pointer in the Npt array.

**XY(1).Y = Y:** Puts the current Y coordinate of the mouse pointer in the Npt array.

**API = DPtoLP(ArtWork.hDC, XY(1), 1):** The API DPtoLP function converts device points to logical points. In this case, you can consider Device points the Artwork picture box control, which uses pixel units of measurement with the coordination system starting at the upper-left corner of the control. The Logical points are any new API internal scaling dimensions when the picture box has been scaled. When you use Visual Basic's

## The Scaling and Printing Program

`ScaleWidth` and `ScaleHeight` to change the internal scale of the control manually, device and logical points are converted automatically for you. When you're using the API scaling functions to change the internal scaling, the control's `ScaleWidth` and `ScaleHeight` are not changed from the original settings. You use the `DPtoLP` function to set the proper coordinates manually. This capability emulates Visual Basic's scale width and scale height statements.

**XX = XY(1).X:** Stores the new X coordinate.

**YY = XY(1).Y:** Stores the new Y coordinate.

**If StartPt = True Then:** You are initializing the box's start and end points in the `MouseMove` event rather than the `MouseDown` event. The start points are initialized in this event because the *arguments* X As Single and Y As Single remain as pixel units until the API `DPtoLP` functions convert them.

**StartPt = False:** The starting point of the box need only be set once during the `MouseMove`.

**W = XX: N = YY:** Assigns the box's start and end coordinate points.

**API = Rectangle:** Draws the box shape using the API function.

**E = XX: S = YY:** Makes a corner position of the bounding box equal to the current mouse pointer's coordinate.

**API = Rectangle:** Redraws the image to erase the last rectangle image.

The Artwork_MouseUp event in Listing 14.9 resets the picture box's original Visual Basic dimensions.

### Listing 14.9. Restoring the desktop scaling.

```
Sub ArtWork_MouseUp (Button%, Shift%, X!, Y!)
    ArtWork.DrawMode = 6: ArtWork.DrawStyle = 0
    ArtWork.ScaleLeft = ASL
    ArtWork.ScaleTop = AST
    ArtWork.ScaleWidth = ASW
    ArtWork.ScaleHeight = ASH
End Sub
```

**ArtWork.ScaleLeft:** Resets the scale so that the rulers work properly. This line does not work correctly if you use the Visual Basic Scale (1, 2)-(3, 4) statement. You must set each scale property individually.

## Aligning Scaling Values at Startup

The `ScaleBox` picture box is within the Artwork picture box control. When Artwork's internal scale is changed with a zoom value, then the `ScaleBox` automatically repositions itself to the new internal scale. The Ruler_Paint event assigns the correct internal scaling for the guidelines and rulers using the new position of the `ScaleBox`.

The `Form_Activate` event in Listing 14.10 saves the original scale width and scale height values of the Artwork picture box so they can be reset after the API scaling function is performed.

**Listing 14.10. Saving scale values at startup.**

```
Sub Form_Activate ()
    ScaleBox.Top = 3750
    ScaleBox.Left = 3600
    ScaleBox.Width = 330
    ScaleBox.Height = 330
    OldSW = ArtWork.ScaleWidth: OldSH = ArtWork.ScaleHeight
    OldRW = 300
    OldRH = 300
        Ruler(0).Scale: Ruler(1).Scale
End Sub
```

**ScaleBox.Top = 3750:** The `ScaleBox` is a picture box control that has its `Visible` property set to `False`. You use the `ScaleBox`'s designated position on the desktop to align the pull-away guidelines of the rulers correctly. Because the rulers are separate picture boxes, you have to change the internal scale of each to reflect the correct scale of the Artwork's picture box internal scale. The `ScaleBox` is located directly underneath the intersection point of the two rulers. At startup, the `Left` property of the control equals the starting `Scaleleft` property of `Ruler(0)`, and the `Top` property equals the starting `ScaleTop` property of `Ruler(1)`.

**OldSW = ArtWork.ScaleWidth:** Stores the last scale width value before using a zoom.

**OldSH = ArtWork.ScaleHeight:** Stores the last scale height value before using a zoom.

**OldRW = 300:** Stores the last scale width value of `Ruler(0)` before using a zoom.

**OldRH = 300:** Stores the last scale height value of `Ruler(1)` before using a zoom.

## The Zoom API Menu

Selecting a sub-menu item from the Zoom API menu item triggers the `Z_APIsub_Click` event. The Zoom API routine in Listing 14.11 uses API scaling functions (Viewports) to emulate Visual Basic's scaling methods. The advantage to using API scaling functions is their capability to rescale images that are drawn using API graphical functions. For instance, if a box object with a one pixel outline width is enlarged (zoomed in) using API scaling functions, then the box's outline is increased automatically to reflect the new viewport scale.

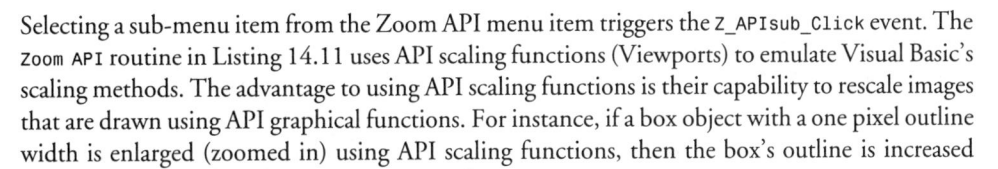

**Listing 14.11. Zooming in using API functions.**

```
Sub Z_APIsub_Click (Index As Integer)
ArtWork.Scale 'reset original size
    Select Case Index
        Case 0
            Area = 2000
```

*continues*

## The Scaling and Printing Program

**Listing 14.11. continued**

```
            Case 1
                Area = 4000
            Case 2
                Area = -6000
            Case 3

                HScroll.Value = 0: VScroll.Value = 0
                PerSW = 1: PerSH = 1
                UpdateObjects
                Exit SubEnd Select
ArtWorkScale% = SaveDC%(ArtWork.hDC)
    SW = ArtWork.ScaleWidth
    SH = ArtWork.ScaleHeight
API = SetMapMode(ArtWork.hDC, 8)
API = SetWindowOrg(ArtWork.hDC, 0, 0)
API = SetWindowExt(ArtWork.hDC, SW, SH)
API = SetViewportExt(ArtWork.hDC, SW - Area, SH - Area)

API = SetViewportOrg(ArtWork.hDC, (Area \ 2) \ PixelX, (Area \ 2) \ PixelY)
        UpdateObjects
    API = RestoreDC%(ArtWork.hDC, ArtWorkScale%)
End Sub
```

**ArtWork.Scale:** Resets the scale to `Twips` to compensate for the two different scale methods used in this program.

**Select Case Index:** Depending on the menu item selected, do the following `Case` block the matches the menu index selected:

**Case 0, 1, 2, Area = 2000, 4000, -6000:** Assigns the width to apply to the viewport of the Artwork picture box.

**Case 3:** Restores the original startup scale and page size.

**HScroll.Value = 0: VScroll.Value = 0:** Resets the scrollbars to the center positions.

**PerSW = 1: PerSH = 1:** Resets the percentage value of any scrollbar movement.

**UpdateObjects:** Redraws the page on the desktop.

**ArtWorkScale% = SaveDC%(ArtWork.hDC):** Saves the previous device context of the Artwork picture box.

**API = SetMapMode(ArtWork.hDC, 8):** Sets the scale mode to use. `MM_ANISOTROPIC` is value `8` and is similar to `ScaleMode` "0" in Visual Basic.

**API = SetWindowOrg(ArtWork.hDC, 0, 0):** Previous `ScaleLeft`, `ScaleTop` of the picture box control.

**API = SetWindowExt(ArtWork.hDC, SW, SH):** Previous `ScaleWidth`, `ScaleHeight` of the picture box control.

**API = SetViewportExt:** New `ScaleWidth`, `ScaleHeight`.

**API = SetViewportOrg:** New `ScaleLeft`, `ScaleTop`.

**UpdateObjects:** Redraws the page on the desktop to the new API scale dimensions.

Chapter **14**

# The Zoom Basic Menu

Selecting a sub-menu item from the Zoom Basic menu item triggers the `Z_Basicsub_Click` event. The `Zoom Basic` routine in Listing 14.12 uses standard Visual Basic scaling properties of the picture box to zoom in or out of the desktop images. The new `ScaleLeft`, `ScaleTop`, `ScaleWidth`, and `ScaleHeight` properties of the picture box are initialized here, and the actual scaling changes are performed in the `Zoom` procedure (see Listing 14.13).

**L**isting 14.12. Scaling in using Visual Basic statements.

```
Sub Z_Basicsub_Click (Index As Integer)
ArtWork.Scale 'restore scale or scaling will be infinite
''''''Index, ZLeft, ZTop, ZWidth, ZHeight
    Select Case Index
        Case 0 '25
            Zoom 2, -5000, -5000, 10000, 8500
        Case 1 '50
            Zoom 2, -4000, -4000, 8000, 6800
        Case 2 '75
            Zoom 2, -3000, -3000, 6000, 5100
        Case 3 '100
            Zoom 2, -2000, -2000, 4000, 3400
        Case 4 '125
            Zoom 2, 2000, 2000, -4000, -3400
        Case 5 '150
            Zoom 2, 3000, 3000, -6000, -5100
        Case 6 '175
            Zoom 2, 3750, 3750, -7500, -6375
        Case 7 '200
            Zoom 2, 5000, 5000, -10000, -8500
        Case 8 'Full Page
            ArtWork.Scale
            HScroll.Value = 0: VScroll.Value = 0
            PerSW = 1: PerSH = 1
            UpdateObjects
            Ruler(0).ScaleTop = ArtWork.ScaleTop
            Ruler(0).ScaleHeight = ArtWork.ScaleHeight
            Ruler(1).ScaleLeft = ArtWork.ScaleLeft
            Ruler(1).ScaleWidth = ArtWork.ScaleWidth
End Select
Ruler(0).Refresh
End Sub
```

**Select Case Index:** Depending on which Menu item you choose, do the following Case block the matches the menu items index value:

**Case 0 to 7:** Rescales the picture box control by using Visual Basic scaling values. Zoom is the name of the procedure that changes the scaling values (Listing 14.13). The *arguments* to pass are

1. Index of the menu you choose.
2. The ScaleLeft property.

## The Scaling and Printing Program

3. The `ScaleTop` property.
4. The `ScaleWidth` property.
5. The `ScaleHeight` property.

**`Case 8`:** Resets the original values used at startup.

**`ArtWork.Scale`:** Resets the scale mode to `Twips`.

**`HScroll.Value = 0: VScroll.Value = 0`:** Resets the scrollbars to the center positions.

**`PerSW = 1: PerSH = 1`:** Resets the percentage value of any scrollbar movement.

**`UpdateObjects`:** Redraws the page on the desktop.

**`Ruler(0).ScaleTop, Height, Left, Width`:** Resets the ruler's internal scales.

**`Ruler(0).Refresh`:** Paints the rulers to show the inch-mark images.

## Rescaling the Picture Box Control

The `Zoom` procedure in Listing 14.13 takes the arguments passed by the `Z_Basicsub_Click` event in Listing 14.12 to rescale the picture box. This method simply takes the current scale of the picture box and then adds or subtracts the scaling values passed by the `Z_Basicsub_Click` event. The new scaling dimensions are then saved and adjustments are made to values used by both ruler picture boxes.

**Listing 14.13. Rescaling the desktop using Visual Basic statements.**

```
Sub Zoom (Index%, ZLeft%, ZTop%, ZWidth%, ZHeight%)
    ArtWork.ScaleLeft = ArtWork.ScaleLeft + ZLeft
    ArtWork.ScaleTop = ArtWork.ScaleTop + ZTop
    ArtWork.ScaleWidth = ArtWork.ScaleWidth + ZWidth
    ArtWork.ScaleHeight = ArtWork.ScaleHeight + ZHeight
NewSW = ArtWork.ScaleWidth: NewSH = ArtWork.ScaleHeight
PerSW = NewSW / OldSW: PerSH = NewSH / OldSH
    BSM = BSM * PerSW: SSM = SSM * PerSH
''''''''''
        UpdateObjects
    Ruler(0).ScaleTop = ArtWork.ScaleTop
    Ruler(0).ScaleHeight = ArtWork.ScaleHeight
    Ruler(1).ScaleLeft = ArtWork.ScaleLeft
    Ruler(1).ScaleWidth = ArtWork.ScaleWidth
End Sub
```

**`ArtWork.ScaleLeft, Top, Width, Height`:** Rescales the internal dimensions of the Artwork picture box control.

**`NewSW : NewSH`:** Saves the new `ScaleWidth` and `ScaleHeight` values.

**`PerSW = NewSW / OldSW`:** Calculates the difference between the new `ScaleWidth` and the old `ScaleWidth`.

**`PerSH = NewSH / OldSH`:** Calculates the difference between the new `ScaleHeight` and the old `ScaleHeight`.

**BSM = BSM * PerSW:** Calculates the Bottom Scrollbar Movement times the PerSH value from above. BSM is calculated in the scrollbar's Change event ((HScroll.Value * PixelX) * PerSW) to offset any desktop scrolling that the user may use.

**SSM = SSM * PerSH:** Calculates the Side Scrollbar Movement.

**UpdateObjects:** Redraws the page onto the desktop.

**Ruler(0).ScaleTop, Height:** Resets the ruler's internal scaling.

# Summary

The Visual Basic ScaleMode and API scaling functions can have different effects on how a graphic is displayed on your monitor. API scaling functions usually inform the GUI to adjust API drawing attributes to reflect the current scaling dimension. If you draw a box with a one-pixel-width border, for instance, and then call the API SetViewPortOrg and SetViewportExt to zoom in, the box's outline width is increased automatically to reflect the new scaling dimensions. However, changing the Visual Basic ScaleMode in conjunction with the API scaling functions preserves the original width, similar to the wireframe mode in drawing packages.

The Visual Basic scaling feature makes it simple and easy to change internal scaling if you use the Scale, ScaleLeft, ScaleTop, ScaleWidth, and ScaleHeight keywords. However, you may notice that the drawing width remains the same. You can place the actual drawing accurately and easily enough, but you have to devise your own formula to change the drawing width for each object that may have different outline widths. Using the API scaling functions has an advantage in that they can do the job for you, but using the functions may require converting device points to logical points.

If you decide just to use Pixel scale mode for all controls, be warned that you must make several changes to the Rulers, Guidelines, Scalebox, and scrollbars to reflect the Pixel mode. Also, remember that manually drawn Bezier curves need a Twips or higher scale mode to place each pixel curve point accurately when you use the *deCasteljau* dividing formula.

# CHAPTER 15

# ArtAPI

# ArtAPI

The ArtAPI program uses a routine similar to one that was discussed in Chapter 13 ("The Join Nodes Program") to connect line segments and Bézier curves to form polyline or polygon shapes. So things are easier for you to understand, most of the procedures are reworks of those found in the Artisan program of Chapter 2. The layout of the ArtAPI form is considerably different than the Artisan form. Refer to the `Form Resize` event for a listing of the new controls and their positions on the form. The biggest form appearance change is the addition of the PicClip.VBX control that is used to hold all the bitmap tool images within a single picture box container. The `MenuBitmaps` procedure (see the ARTAPI1.FRM source code) extracts each bitmap cell within the picture box container and places each image in the assigned submenu of the form's menubar.

## Handles and Nodes

The original Artisan handle and node picture boxes are replaced with `Image` controls to increase the performance of the program. The image controls do not have an interior scaling property, so all scaling functions have been removed from this program. As such, the Zoom tool is basically useless unless you want to write a procedure to relocate all visible handles and nodes when you rescale the `Artwork` picture box desktop. However, doing so will prove to be time-consuming and unpractical when using many nodes on a complex object shape. One solution is to use the API `Rect` functions (for example, `SetRect`, `SetRectEmpty`, `CopyRect`, or `PtInRect`) to draw and locate all the handles and nodes; then use the mouse events of the Artwork picture box control to control the movement of the nodes and handles.

## Scaling and the Zoom Tool

Drawing nodes and handles directly on the desktop (picture box) may seem rather tedious, but by using the approach mentioned previously, you are one step ahead in understanding the fundamentals of programming Windows in C. Rather than writing long rescaling routines to reposition each handle and node when zooming in and out, use the custom `Rect` structures, which are part of the desktop's interior dimension. Thus, when you rescale any section of the desktop, the handles, nodes, and any other graphics images are automatically scaled to the new viewport or scale dimensions. However, if you do not need zooming features or need just a limited number of graphics in your programs, you should just stick to the manual routines discussed in this book.

## Desktop and Printer API Graphics

Most of the Basic language graphical statements for the screen and printer have been replaced with API graphical functions in the ArtAPI program.

Visual Basic uses its own scaling routines to position `Line` and `Circle` statements within a form or picture box. Graphics can thus be rescaled rather easily by using device-to-device scale offsets.

However, when using API graphics functions, you are faced with a greater challenge: placing the correct coordinates within a given device (picture box or printer), because the API does not use the same scaling properties present in Visual Basic controls.

As explained at the beginning of the Chapter 2, the API function GetDeviceCaps is essential for correctly displaying API graphics on unknown devices, such as monitors or printers. Each device can have various internal scaling and resolution output.

## The Graphical API Functions in the ArtAPI Program

The ArtAPI program uses many API functions. Some of them are explained in the following list.

**Polyline:** Replaces the Line statement to draw single or multiple connecting lines.

**Polygon:** Draws and fills complex shapes that are closed (attached) at the start and end points of the shape.

**Ellipse:** Replaces the Circle statement. However, the ellipse or circle is drawn within an invisible bounding box that you stretch to size. If you want the mouse pointer to attach to the edges of the shape as you draw it, you must manually offset the mouse pointer.

**Rectangle:** Replaces the Line statement's B and BF options. With all API graphics, you need additional code lines to set the Pen and Brush colors. Visual Basic can automatically use the ForeColor and FillStyle properties to change Pen and Brush attributes for you.

## Major Changes in this ArtAPI Program

There are 18 new procedures to the ArtAPI version of the Artisan program from Chapter 2. In addition, several controls once found in the original Artisan program have been moved to procedure calls to deal with multiple Bézier curve segments. Examples of this are the BezNode1 and BezNode2 controls, and their mouse events.

Rather than duplicating procedures and controls from the Artisan program, this chapter lists only the procedures that have had major changes. Some events have had minor changes to conform with the new variable listings. You should double-check all code against the codes printed in Chapters 2 through 5.

The code routines in some of these procedures are long because they use Visual Basic Image controls to simulate on-screen placement of nodes and handles. Figure 15.3, presented later in this chapter, helps you understand the procedures used to load, unload, and move the node and handles.

## New Picture Box Control

Several new controls and procedures are used to deal with polyshape object drawings using API graphical statements. These include the ArtMask picture box and Pnode image control.

**ArtMask:** A picture box used to find each object on screen. In the original Artisan program, you could find an object by using a bubble type array to search through every bounding box. When you found the object (directly over the mouse pointer), that object was highlighted. This method was not feasible if several bounding boxes (objects) were located on top of each other. This made it impossible to pick or move the desired object if another object overlapped a bounding box.

Use the `ArtMask` picture box to select any object by just touching the object's outline. This is done by simulating an off-screen drawing using a picture box with its `AutoRedraw` property (set to `True`) and its `Visible` property (set to `False`).

**Pnode:** A single image control that represents all the nodes you add or remove from a complex polyshape object. A `Pnode` reacts similarly to the original node controls that are still present in this program. `Pnode`s are placed around polyshaped objects only. All of `Pnode`'s mouse-event routines could have been placed within the original node control's mouse events, but this would have made for extremely large event codes.

## Old Controls Switched to Procedures

Several controls in the original Artisan program from Chapter 2 have been switched to procedures. Some of these are explained in the following list.

**BezNode1, BezNode2** (picture boxes): These two picture box controls, which were in the Artisan program of Chapter 2, have been deleted in the ArtAPI program. The `BezNode1` and `BezNode2` mouse events were moved to the following control's events.

**BezNode_Down:** Handles the `MouseDown` events for poly-Bézier curves.

**BezNode_Move:** Handles the `MouseMove` events for poly-Bézier curves.

**BezNode_Up:** Handles the `MouseUp` events for poly-Bézier curves.

## Other Changes

Several of the procedures in the original Artisan program from Chapter 2 have been modified. These include the following:

**Find_Object:** This procedure now uses the API `PtInRect` function to locate an object's bounding box. The `Find_Object` procedure now processes a copy of the object into the `ArtMask` image control.

**MenuBitmaps:** Loads bitmap pictures into the form's `Menu`.

**mnuFileOpen:** Four additional lines of code are added in order to open polyshapes saved in a file.

**mnuFileSave:** Four additional lines of code are added in order to save polyshapes to a file.

**UpdateArtMask:** Similar to the `UpdateObject` procedure, except the `UpdateArtMask` procedure draws only a single object into the `ArtMask` image control.

**UpdateObjects:** Similar to the original `UpdateObject` procedure in Chapter 5, except all objects are now drawn using API graphical functions.

**WinPrint:** Uses a manual scaling method to place API graphics onto a printer's page. You adjust the `LeftM`, `RightM`, `TopM`, and `BottomM` variables to suit your printer's output.

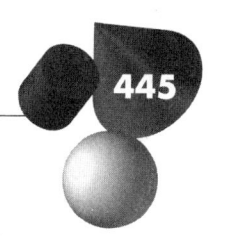

# New Polyshape Procedures

There are 12 new procedures used to manipulate polyline or polygon images. All these procedures deal with the fact that nodes and handles are image controls that must be positioned around the image. To position image controls (nodes and handles) around a complex shape requires a great deal of coding. The best way to examine what happens when you move a node or stretch a polyshape is to use the F8 key or Visual Basic's Single Step button. What seems like a simple procedure to move a polycurve section of an image can require up to eight different procedure and event calls.

All polyshape procedures are coded in sections so you can better understand how each routine used. If you have Window's 32-bit operating system, you could exclude several procedures in the preceding list. The 32-bit GDI library file includes API functions that can create Bézier curves with little code, as well as several new move object to functions. Refer to the APIdraw program in Chapter 8 for 32-bit API function names.

The 12 new polyshape procedures are as follows:

**Poly_CurveMove1:** Moves curve segments wihin a closed polyshape.

**Poly_CurveMove2:** Moves curve segments within an open polyshape.

**Poly_curves:** Three separate scaling routines to draw a Bézier curve to the screen, ArtMask, or printer.

**Poly_gon:** Initiates a polygon line segment.

**Poly_Handles:** Places stretch handles around a polyshape.

**Poly_LineMove1:** Moves line segments wihin a closed polyshape.

**Poly_LineMove2:** Moves line segments within an open polyshape.

**Poly_Lines:** Draws the polyline shape if the user switches the focus away from the drawing.

**Poly_Nodes:** Loads new nodes as each line segment is added to the polyshape.

**Poly_Reload:** Reloads the exact number of nodes when you select a polyshape object.

**Poly_Stretch:** Stretches or flips a polyshape.

**Poly_Update:** Resets the visible property of nodes.

The previous polyshape routines are limited in their capabilities to manipulate polyshapes. Additional coding is needed to break or delete node connects. Only a single node can be moved at one time. Polyline or polygon shapes can be drawn only in a continuous path; you cannot switch start and end points to continue line segments in these routines. Poly-Bézier curves are limited to cusp connecting points and do not feature smooth or symmetrical connections. Figure 15.1 illustrates the construction of a polyshape.

**Figure 15.1.**
*The construction of a polyshape.*

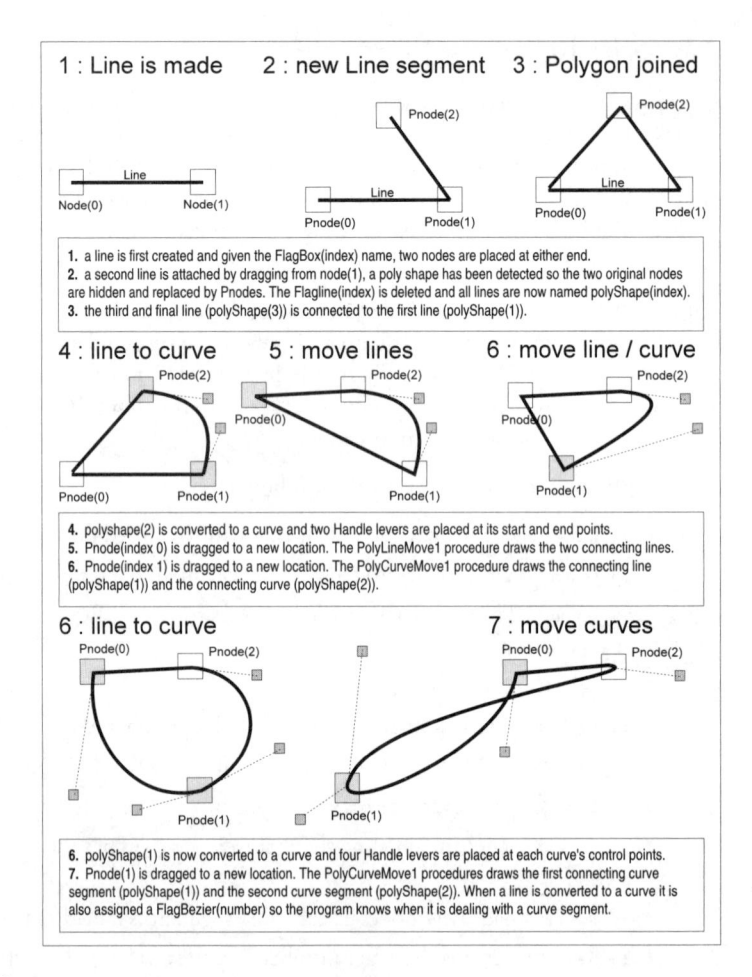

1 : Line is made
2 : new Line segment
3 : Polygon joined

1. a line is first created and given the FlagBox(index) name, two nodes are placed at either end.
2. a second line is attached by dragging from node(1), a poly shape has been detected so the two original nodes are hidden and replaced by Pnodes. The Flagline(index) is deleted and all lines are now named polyShape(index).
3. the third and final line (polyShape(3)) is connected to the first line (polyShape(1)).

4 : line to curve
5 : move lines
6 : move line / curve

4. polyshape(2) is converted to a curve and two Handle levers are placed at its start and end points.
5. Pnode(index 0) is dragged to a new location. The PolyLineMove1 procedure draws the two connecting lines.
6. Pnode(index 1) is dragged to a new location. The PolyCurveMove1 procedure draws the connecting line (polyShape(1)) and the connecting curve (polyShape(2)).

6 : line to curve
7 : move curves

6. polyShape(1) is now converted to a curve and four Handle levers are placed at each curve's control points.
7. Pnode(1) is dragged to a new location. The PolyCurveMove1 procedures draws the first connecting curve segment (polyShape(1)) and the second curve segment (polyShape(2)). When a line is converted to a curve it is also assigned a FlagBezier(number) so the program knows when it is dealing with a curve segment.

## *To_Front_Back* Routines

The `To_Front_Back` procedure moves an object to the front or back of all other objects. The original Artisan program did this by changing the order of every object and each object's associated attributes. You can now perform this procedure by using a short and simple loop routine that changes the order in which objects are drawn on the desktop. This requires only one additional array, called `DrawOrder`, to hold and keep track of the drawing order. The `UpdateObjects` procedure uses a `For/Next` statement, which draws each object according to the order stated in the `DrawOrder` variable array.

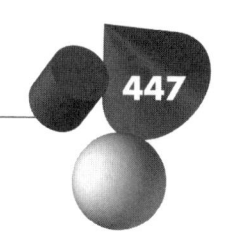

# API Scaling and Winprint

This program uses three different scaling routines to draw API graphics to the Artwork picture box, ArtMask picture box, and the printer. The API graphical functions draw into a device (Visual Basic control or printer's page) using the upper-left corner as the 0,0 start coordinate. Using Visual Basic's Scale properties to change these settings will have no effect on the coordinates. The API library includes several functions to change internal scaling or for converting logical- and device-coordination points. The ArtAPI program, however, uses manual techniques to position each object in a picture box or on the printer's page.

## The Test Button

The Test button has a short routine that redraws a polyshape using the Visual Basic Line statement. When doing so, it makes each line segment of the shape a different color. Draw the curve segments by using the BezDraw procedure.

## The Zoom Tool

This tool is disconnected in this program because you are using Visual Basic image controls as nodes. Having a zoom tool would require too many manual scaling and placement routines. Refer to Chapter 14 for possible ways to incorporate a zoom tool within your program.

The ArtAPI program's form and control properties are listed in Table 15.1.

**T**able 15.1. The properties of ArtAPI's form and controls.

*Object: Form*
*Object Name: ArtAPI*

| | | | |
|---|---|---|---|
| BackColor | = &H00404040& | Caption | = "Mini API Graphic Shell" |
| ClipControls | = 0 'False | ForeColor | = &H00FFFFFF& |
| Height | = 6735 | Left | = 60 |
| ScaleMode | = 3 'Pixel | Top | = 1065 |
| Width | = 7110 | WindowState | = 2 'Maximized |

*Object: PictureBox*
*Object Name: ToolButtons*

| | | | |
|---|---|---|---|
| Align | = 1 'Align Top | AutoSize | = -1 'True |
| BackColor | = &H00C0C0C0& | BorderStyle | = 0 'None |
| ClipControls | = 0 'False | DrawMode | = 6 'Invert |
| Height | = 540 | Left | = 0 |

*continues*

**Table 15.1. continued**

| | | | |
|---|---|---|---|
| Picture | = ToolButton.BMP | ScaleMode | = 3 'Pixel |
| Top | = 0 | Visible | = 0 'False |

*Object: ComboBox*
*ObjectName: Combo1*

| | | | |
|---|---|---|---|
| BackColor | = &H00FFFFFF& | Height | = 300 |
| Left | = 4380 | Style | = 2 'Dropdown List |
| TabIndex | = 20 | Top | = 240 'within ToolButtons |
| Width | = 1815 | | |

*Object: PictureBox*
*Object Name: StatusColor*

| | | | |
|---|---|---|---|
| Height | = 450 | Left | = 6300 |
| ScaleMode | = 3 'Pixel | Top | = 60 'within ToolButtons |
| Visible | = 0 'False | Width | = 630 |

*Object: PictureBox*
*Object Name: StatusPaint*

| | | | |
|---|---|---|---|
| Height | = 315 | Left | = 120 |
| Top | = 60 'within StatusColor | Visible | = 0 'False |
| Width | = 345 | | |

*Object: Label*
*Object Name: StatusLabel*

| | | | |
|---|---|---|---|
| Alignment | = 2 'Center | BackColor | = &H00FFFF00& |
| BorderStyle | = 1 'Fixed Single | Height | = 255 |
| Left | = 4380 | Top | = 0 'within ToolButtons |
| Visible | = 0 'False | Width | = 1575 |

*Object: CommonDialog*
*Object Name: CMDialog1*

| | | | |
|---|---|---|---|
| CancelError | = -1 'True | Left | = 0 |
| Top | = 4320 | | |

*Object: PictureBox*
*Object Name: StatusArea*

| | | | |
|---|---|---|---|
| Align | = 2 'Align Bottom | BackColor | = &H00000000& |
| BorderStyle | = 0 'None | ForeColor | = &H00FFFFFF& |
| Height | = 915 | Left | = 0 |

|  |  |  |  |
|---|---|---|---|
| ScaleMode | = 3 'Pixel | Top | = 5160 |
| Visible | = 0 'False | Width | = 7020 |

*Object: PictureBox*
*Object Name: ColorMask*

|  |  |  |  |
|---|---|---|---|
| ClipControls | = 0 'False | Height | = 435 |
| Left | = 45 | ScaleMode | = 3 'Pixel |
| Top | = 405 'within StatusArea | Visible | = 0 'False |
| Width | = 5895 |  |  |

*Object: PictureBox*
*Object Name: ColorBar*

|  |  |  |  |
|---|---|---|---|
| ClipControls | = 0 'False | Height | = 270 |
| Left | = 135 | Picture | = Visual Basic 256 Palette |
| ScaleMode | = 0 'User | Top | = 90 'within ColorMask |
| Visible | = 0 'False |  |  |

*Object: HScrollBar*
*Object Name: ColorScroll*

|  |  |  |  |
|---|---|---|---|
| Height | = 240 | LargeChange | = 96 |
| Left | = 6240 | Max | = 0 |
| Min | = -800 | SmallChange | = 32 |
| Top | = 540 'within StatusArea | Visible | = 0 'False |
| Width | = 510 |  |  |

*Object: CommandButton*
*Object Name: No_Fill*

|  |  |  |  |
|---|---|---|---|
| Caption | = "X" | Height | = 240 |
| Left | = 6180 | Top | = 180 'within StatusArea |
| Visible | = 0 'False | Width | = 585 |

*Object: CommandButton*
*Object Name: TestButton*

|  |  |  |  |
|---|---|---|---|
| Caption | = "test" | Height | = 285 |
| Left | = 45 | Top | = 90 'within StatusArea |
| Visible | = 0 'False | Width | = 780 |

*continues*

**Table 15.1. continued**

*Object: Label*
*Object Name: XYLabel*

| | | | |
|---|---|---|---|
| Alignment | = 2 'Center | BackColor | = &H00FFFF00& |
| BorderStyle | = 1 'Fixed Single | Height | = 315 |
| Left | = 900 | Top | = 60 'within StatusArea |
| Visible | = 0 'False | Width | = 5055 |

*Object: PictureBox*
*Object Name: PictureMask*

| | | | |
|---|---|---|---|
| BackColor | = &H00008000& | BorderStyle | = 0 'None |
| ClipControls | = 0 'False | Height | = 3975 |
| Left | = 780 | ScaleMode | = 3 'Pixel |
| Top | = 720 | Visible | = 0 'False |
| Width | = 4245 | | |

*Object: PictureClip*
*Object Name: PicClip1*

| | | | |
|---|---|---|---|
| Cols | = 8 | Location | = "3840,1365,2475,240" |
| Picture | = ClipAPI.BMP | Rows | = 3 |

*Object: PictureBox*
*Object Name: ArtWork*

| | | | |
|---|---|---|---|
| AutoRedraw | = -1 'True | BackColor | = &H00FFFFFF& |
| BorderStyle | = 0 'None | FontBold | = 0 'False |
| FontItalic | = 0 'False | FontName | = "Arial" |
| FontSize | = 12 | FontStrikethru | = 0 'False |
| FontUnderline | = 0 'False | Height | = 2145 |
| Left | = 180 | ScaleMode | = Twips |
| Top | = 120 'within PictureMask | Visible | = 0 'False |
| Width | = 3840 | | |

*Object: PictureBox*
*Object Name: ArtMask*

| | | | |
|---|---|---|---|
| AutoRedraw | = -1 'True | BackColor | = &H00FFFFFF& |
| ClipControls | = 0 'False | DrawStyle | = 6 'Inside Solid |
| DrawWidth | = 4 | Height | = 870 |

| | | | |
|---|---|---|---|
| Left | = 2220 | ScaleMode | = Twips |
| Top | = 180 'within Artwork | Visible | = 0 'False |
| Width | = 1425 | | |

*Object: PictureBox*
*Object Name: ScaleBox*

| | | | |
|---|---|---|---|
| BackColor | = &H00FFFFFF& | Height | = 330 |
| Left | = 1395 | ScaleHeight | = 300 |
| ScaleWidth | = 300 | TabIndex | = 14 |
| Top | = 45 | Visible | = 0 'False |
| Width | = 330 | | |

*Object: PictureBox*
*Object Name: BezHandle1*

| | | | |
|---|---|---|---|
| BackColor | = &H00FF00FF& | BorderStyle | = 0 'None |
| ClipControls | = 0 'False | DrawMode | = 6 'Invert |
| Height | = 105 | Left | = 45 |
| ScaleHeight | = 105 | ScaleWidth | = 105 |
| Top | = 270 'within Artwork | Visible | = 0 'False |
| Width | = 105 | | |

*Object: PictureBox*
*Object Name: BezHandle2*

| | | | |
|---|---|---|---|
| BackColor | = &H00FF00FF& | BorderStyle | = 0 'None |
| ClipControls | = 0 'False | DrawMode | = 6 'Invert |
| Height | = 105 | Left | = 45 |
| ScaleHeight | = 105 | ScaleWidth | = 105 |
| Top | = 495 'within Artwork | Visible | = 0 'False |
| Width | = 105 | | |

*Object: PictureBox*
*Object Name: Bezhandle3*

| | | | |
|---|---|---|---|
| BackColor | = &H00FF00FF& | BorderStyle | = 0 'None |
| ClipControls | = 0 'False | DrawMode | = 6 'Invert |
| Height | = 105 | Left | = 45 |
| ScaleHeight | = 105 | ScaleWidth | = 105 |
| Top | = 675 'within Artwork | Visible | = 0 'False |
| Width | = 105 | | |

*continues*

**T**able 15.1. continued

*Object: PictureBox*
*Object Name: Bezhandle4*

| | | | |
|---|---|---|---|
| BackColor | = &H00FF00FF& | BorderStyle | = 0 'None |
| ClipControls | = 0 'False | DrawMode | = 6 'Invert |
| Height | = 105 | Left | = 45 |
| ScaleHeight | = 105 | ScaleWidth | = 105 |
| Top | = 855 'within Artwork | Visible | = 0 'False |
| Width | = 105 | | |

*Object: Image*
*Object Name: Node  4 indexed controls*

| | | | |
|---|---|---|---|
| BorderStyle | = 1 'Fixed Single | Height | = 90 |
| Index | = 0 to 3 | Left | = 840 |
| MousePointer | = 2 'Cross | Top | = 'within Artwork |
| Visible | = 0 'False | Width | = 90 |

*Object: Image*
*Object Name: handle  8 indexed controls*

| | | | |
|---|---|---|---|
| Height | = 120 | Index | = 7 |
| Left | = 'within Artwork | MousePointer | = 2 'Cross |
| Picture | = Handle.BMP | Top | = 1170 |
| Visible | = 0 'False | Width | = 120 |

*Object: Image*
*Object Name: Pnode*

| | | | |
|---|---|---|---|
| BorderStyle | = 1 'Fixed Single | Height | = 510 |
| Index | = 0 | Left | = 'within Artwork |
| MousePointer | = 2 'Cross | Top | = 45 |
| Visible | = 0 'False | Width | = 615 |

*Object: Label*
*Object Name:  Txt*

| | | | |
|---|---|---|---|
| AutoSize | = -1 'True | BackColor | = &H00FFFFFF& |
| BackStyle | = 0 'Transparent | BorderStyle | = 1 'Fixed Single |
| Height | = 480 | Left | = 'within Artwork |
| TabIndex | = 5 | Top | = 945 |
| Visible | = 0 'False | Width | = 15 |

*Object: Shape*

*Object Name: Shape2*

| | | | |
|---|---|---|---|
| BackColor | = &H00FF0000& | BackStyle | = 1 'Opaque |
| BorderStyle | = 0 'Transparent | Height | = 105 |
| Left | = 45 | Top | = 'within Artwork |
| Visible | = 0 'False | Width | = 105 |

*Object: Shape*
*Object Name: Shape1*

| | | | |
|---|---|---|---|
| BackColor | = &H00FF0000& | BackStyle | = 1 'Opaque |
| BorderStyle | = 0 'Transparent | Height | = 105 |
| Left | = 60 | Top | = 'within Artwork |
| Visible | = 0 'False | Width | = 105 |

*Object: Menu*
*Object Name: Menu_File*

Caption = "&File"

*Object: Menu*
*Object Name: Menu_FileSelection*

| Caption | = "&New" | Index | = 0 |
|---|---|---|---|

*Menu_FileSelection*

| Caption | = "&Open..." | Index | = 1 |
|---|---|---|---|

*Menu_FileSelection*

| Caption | = "&Save" | Index | = 2 |
|---|---|---|---|

*Menu_FileSelection*

| Caption | = "Save &As..." | Index | = 3 |
|---|---|---|---|
| Shortcut | = {F12} | | |

*Menu_FileSelection*

| Caption | = "-" | Index | = 4 |
|---|---|---|---|

*Menu_FileSelection*

| Caption | = "&Print" | Index | = 5 |
|---|---|---|---|

*Menu_FileSelection*

| Caption | = "-" | Index | = 6 |
|---|---|---|---|

*Menu_FileSelection*

| Caption | = "E&xit" | Index | = 7 |
|---|---|---|---|

*Object: Menu*

*continues*

**T**able 15.1. continued

*Object Name: Menu_Arrange*
 Caption  = "&Arrange"

*Object: Menu*
*Object Name: Menu_ArrangeSelection*
 Caption  = "To &Front"  Index  = 0

*Menu_ArrangeSelection*
 Caption  = "To &Back"  Index  = 1

*Menu_ArrangeSelection*
 Caption  = "Delete"  Index  = 2

*Object: Menu Menu_ArrangeSelection*
 Caption  = "POPUP MENU"  Checked  = -1 'True
 Index  = 3

*Menu_ArrangeSelection*
 Caption  = "ShowArtMask"  Index  = 4

*Object: Menu*
*Object Name: Menu_Lines*
 Caption  = "&Lines"

*Object: Menu*
*Object Name: Menu_SubLines*
 Index  = 0 to 7 blank captions

*Object: Menu*
*Object Name: Menu_Paint*
 Caption  = "&Paint"

*Object: Menu*
*Object Name: Menu_SubPaint*
 Index  = 0 to 7 blank captions

*Object: Menu*
*Object Name: Menu_Text*
 Caption  = "&Text"

*Object: Menu*
*Object Name: Menu_SubText*
 Index  = 0 to 2 blank captions

Figure 15.2 shows a screen shot of the ArtAPI form.

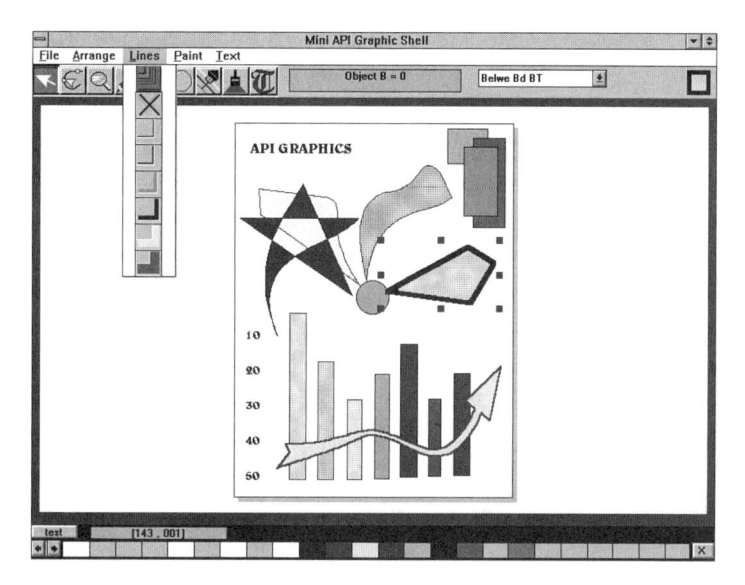

## New Declaration for the ArtAPI Program

To save space, the ArtAPI declaration section has only a partial listing of all variables and arrays. The Dim statements not shown are exactly the same as those found in the declaration section of the Artisan program in Chapter 2. Only the new variables and arrays are shown in Listing 15.1.

**Listing 15.1. A listing of new variable names at startup.**

```
Declarations
DefInt A-Z
Dim FlagPrinter As Integer
Dim FlagArtMask As Integer
Dim Foundcolor As Integer
Dim EraseOldImage As Integer
Dim UpdateMove As Integer
Dim MaskForeColor As Long
Const Limit = 100 'maximum number of objects you can draw
Dim B As Integer ' Current Object (bounding box)
Dim Total As Integer ' Total Number of Objects
Dim DrawOrder(Limit) As Integer
Dim Draw As Integer
Dim FillValue(Limit) As Integer 'No Fill
Dim LineValue(Limit) As Integer 'No Line
Dim OFFSETx, OFFSETy As Integer
Dim WIDE, HIGH As Integer 'Monitor Type
Dim PixelX, PixelY As Integer
Dim SSM As Single 'Side Scroll Move
Dim BSM As Single 'Bottom Scroll Move
Dim LastMove As Integer
```

*continues*

## ArtAPI

**Listing 15.1. continued**

```
Dim LastMenu As Integer
Dim FlagMove As Integer
''''Poly-shape variables''''
Dim NodeTotal As Integer 'Number of nodes per object
Dim FlagPoly(Limit) As Integer 'Polygon Redraw Flag
Dim FlagPolyLine(Limit) As Integer 'PolyLine Redraw Flag
Dim PolyPts As Integer 'API number of points
Dim Npt(0 To 300) As POINTAPI 'API address of each point
Dim FirstPolyPt(Limit) As Integer 'First Point of each object
Dim LastPolyPt(Limit) As Integer 'Last point of each object
Dim PolyShape(Limit) As Integer
Dim fp, LP, ZZ, Counter As Integer 'calculate above to pass to API
Dim Toggle As Integer
Dim PolyClose As Integer
Dim PolyCurveNode As Integer
Dim CountPolyPts As Integer
Dim WB, NB, SB, EB As Integer
Dim X1 As Long : Dim Y1 As Long : Dim X2 As Long : Dim Y2 As Long
Dim X3 As Long : Dim Y3 As Long : Dim X4 As Long : Dim Y4 As Long
Dim PtSize As Single
```

**Dim FlagArtMask:** Used to redraw Bézier curves in the ArtMask control. (See the Poly_Curves procedure in Listing 15.22).

**Dim Foundcolor:** Determines whether the Find_Object procedure should continue its search.

**Dim EraseOldImage:** Erases the old image position of a polyshape after it has been moved.

**Dim MaskForeColor:** States what color the ArtMask redraws the object's outline.

**Dim DrawOrder(Limit):** Redraws all objects in the order of array count. See the Front_to_Back procedure.

**Dim NodeTotal:** Counts each new node that is added to a polyshape as it is drawn.

**Dim FlagPoly(Limit):** Used in the UpdateObjects procedure to draw a closed polygon shape.

**Dim FlagPolyLine(Limit):** Used in the UpdateObjects procedure to draw an open polyshape.

**Dim PolyPts:** Used in the API Polygon and Polyline functions to specify the number of X, Y points to draw.

**Dim Npt(0 To 300):** Used in the API Polygon and Polyline functions to specify the *X* and *Y* positions. An example follows:

```
API = Polyline(Artwork.hDC, Npt(1), PolyPts)
```

The polylines are drawn on the Artwork picture box control. Npt(1) is the first index position of a group of X and Y coordinate points stored in a type POINTAPI structure defined as Npt. PolyPts represents the number of indexed X and Y points to draw.

**Dim FirstPolyPt(Limit):** First node point of each polyobject. This is needed to locate other nodes.

**Dim LastPolyPt(Limit):** Last node point of each polyobject. This is needed to locate other nodes.

**Dim PolyShape(Limit):** Checks to see if the current object is a polyshape or another object (such as text or a box).

**Dim fp, LP, ZZ, Counter:** Variables to keep tab on how the polyshape is formed.

**Dim Toggle:** Checks to see when it is safe to start drawing a polyline.

**Dim PolyClose:** Tells the poly-procedures that the polyshape has been closed and that the shape needs updated. A closed polyshape is used when the last node and line segment is attached to the first node and line segment (polygon). A triangle shape is an example of a closed polyshape.

**Dim PolyCurveNode:** Tells the Pnode procedure the polyshape has Bézier curves attached.

**Dim CountPolyPts:** Flags the Poly_Curves procedure (Listing 15.22) to erase the first image when moving a polynode.

**Dim X1, Y1, X2, Y2:** Used mostly to hold the start and end point positions of a line or two polylines.

**Dim X3, Y3, X4, Y4:** Additional X and Y points required when moving the center node between two polyline segments.

**Dim PtSize As Single:** Stores the font size used when the point size of the current font is changed. The PtSize value is stored during the TxtSize_MouseUp event. The ReDrawText procedure places the PtSize value into the TextSize array, which assigns the current font point size to each text string during screen redraws and printing.

## Converting a Polyline to Curves

In most ArtAPI events and procedures, only slight changes are needed when incorporating the original code from the Artisan program in Chapters 2 through 5. The one change that becomes apparent most often are the new variable flags called PolyShape() and FlagPolyLine. Since you have incorporated the capability to draw connecting line and curve segments in the form of polyshapes, a flag is needed to tell the program to treat polyshapes as special objects. For other types of objects, use variable flags, such as FlagBox, FlagCircle, and FlagText.

FlagPolyLine is the main variable assigned to the first segment of a polyshape. A triangle is an example of three separate polyline segments. Each of the triangle's polyline segments are assigned a variable name tag called PolyShape().

The PolyShape() flag is necessary in order for the program to assign the proper values when converting a polyline to a curve. The program also uses the PolyShape() flag to place handles around the polyshape or to move a polyshape object to a new screen location.

# ArtAPI

A polyshape always starts out as a line (`Flagline`) and is changed to a polyshape (`FlagPolyLine`) when an additional line segment is added. If the polyshape is closed to form a polygon, the `FlagPolyLine` flag is deleted, and a `FlagPoly` flag is added to the object's attribute list.

The `Artwork_DblClick` event in Listing 15.2 determines whether you have double-clicked a line, Bézier curve, or polyline. The first `Select Case True` block enables the conversion buttons that you will be selecting. After you make a button selection, the object is converted to a line or curve. The next `Select Case True` block assigns the new flag name to the object. You delete the old flag name by setting its value to 0.

**Listing 15.2. Converting a curve to a line, and vice versa.**

```
Sub Artwork_DblClick ()
    If StatusLabel.Caption = "No Object Found" Then Exit Sub
    If StatusLabel.Caption = "No color Found" Then Exit Sub
If B = FlagBox(B) Or FlagCircle(B) Or FlagText(B) Or 0 Then
    Message$ = "Convert to curves is set for Poly-shapes and Lines only."
    Message$ = Message$ + Chr(13) + "Skewing and rotation not available"
    MsgBox Message$
    Exit Sub
End If
Select Case True
    Case FlagLine(B) = B
        NodeEdit!To_Line.Enabled = False
    Case FlagBézier(B) = B
        NodeEdit!To_Curve.Enabled = False
    Case PolyShape(B) = FlagBézier(B)
        NodeEdit!To_Curve.Enabled = False
    Case Else
        NodeEdit!To_Line.Enabled = False
End Select
    If CurrentTool = 1 Then NodeEdit.Show Modal Else Exit Sub
    StatusLabel.Caption = "Object B = " + Format$(B)
Select Case True
    Case Convert_Curve
        FlagLine(B) = 0: FlagBézier(B) = B
        BezErase = True: BezHandles
        BezHandle1.Visible = True: BezHandle2.Visible = True
        Convert_Curve = False: NodeEdit!To_Line.Enabled = True
    Case Convert_Line
        W(B) = p1X(B): N(B) = p1Y(B): E(B) = p2X(B): S(B) = p2Y(B)
        p1X(B) = 0: p1Y(B) = 0: p2X(B) = 0: p2Y(B) = 0
        If PolyShape(B) = B Then FlagLine(B) = 0 Else FlagLine(B) = B
        FlagBézier(B) = 0
        Nodes
        Convert_Line = False: NodeEdit!To_Curve.Enabled = True
        UpdateObjects
    End Select
End Sub
```

**Select Case True:** When an object is selected, it returns an object number (B). If the object is not of the type specified in the Case expression, the value equals False.

**Case FlagLine, FlagBézier, PolyShape, Else:** Enables or disables the correct To Curve or To Line buttons on the popup Node Edit form.

**Select Case True:** Depending on which button you selected, do the following Case block that matches the index of the button you selected.

**Case Convert_Curve:** A single line and a polyline segment require the FlagBézier variable flag when converting to a curve.

**Case Convert_Line:** Converting a curve to a line needs special treatment, depending on whether the curve is a single Bézier curve or a Bézier curve within a polyshape object. If the curve is within a polyshape, it still retains its FlagPolyline status and does not receive a new FlagLine variable flag. All four of the old curve's control points are erased when you set the values to 0.

Figure 15.3 shows the effects of various text attributes.

**F**igure 15.3.
*The effects of different text attributes.*

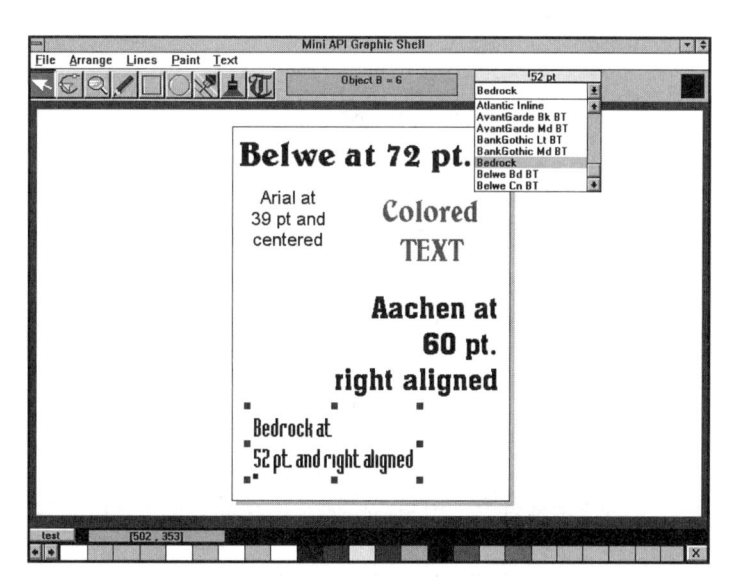

## The Artwork Mouse Events

The code explanation following Listing 15.3 has been condensed. The code explanations show only the new code statements added to the original Artisan MouseDown event from Chapter 2.

**Listing 15.3. Finding a polyshape on the desktop.**

```
Sub Artwork_MouseDown (Button As Integer, Shift As Integer, X As Single, Y As Single)

If PolyClose = True Then Pnode(0).Visible = False: PolyClose = False: Poly_Lines
If BezHandle3.Visible = False Then X1 = 0: Y1 = 0: X2 = X1: Y2 = Y1
' ' ' ' ' ' '
If Button = Left_Button Then
  ArtWork.DrawStyle = 0: ArtWork.DrawMode = 6
  N_H_Clear

Select Case CurrentTool
    Case PointerTool
      Find_Object X, Y
      BoundingBox_Down X, Y
    Case BézierTool
      If BezHandle1.Visible = True Then ShowDotted = False: BezUpdate
      If BezHandle3.Visible Then BezHandleMove Index
      Find_Object X, Y
      If B > 0 And PolyShape(B) = B Then Poly_Reload
      BoundingBox_Down X, Y
    Case LineTool To CircleTool
      BoundingBox_Down X, Y
    Case TextTool
      If txt.Caption > "" Then RedrawText': Align = 0
      If Button = Left_Button Then
        txt.BorderStyle = 0
        Dim tm As TEXTMETRIC
        API = GetTextMetrics(ArtWork.hDC, tm)
        Leading = (tm.tmExternalLeading + tm.tmInternalLeading) * PixelY
        txt.Left = X: txt.Top = Y - (txt.Height - Leading)
      End If

End Select
End IfEnd Sub
```

**If PolyClose = True Then:** You have just drawn an open polyline shape and clicked the mouse pointer down on the desktop area. This calls the `Poly_Lines` procedure to hide the nodes and redraw the new open polyline shape.

**Case Béziertool:** This new routine loads the `Pnode` controls onto a polyshape object when the user touches the polyshape's outline with the mouse pointer.

**Find_Object X, Y:** This procedure (Listing 15.11) determines whether the mouse pointer touched a polyshape object's outline.

**If B > 0 And PolyShape(B) = B Then:** If the mouse pointer touched a polyshape object, B will be greater than 0, and the polyshape's object number will match the object the `Find_Object` procedure located. You then call the `Poly_Reload` procedure to load nodes around the polyshape.

## Redrawing the Polyshape on the Desktop

The code explanation following Listing 15.4 has been condensed. The code explanations show only the new code statements that were added to the original Artisan MouseUp event from Chapter 2.

**Listing 15.4.** Drawing objects using API graphical functions.

```
Sub Artwork_MouseUp (Button As Integer, Shift As Integer, X As Single, Y As Single)


If CurrentTool <> 8 Then ArtWork.MousePointer = 0
PX = PixelX: PY = PixelY

If Button = Left_Button Then
Select Case CurrentTool

 Case PointerTool
  If UpdateMove = True Then
    MoveObject_Up Button, Shift, X, Y
    UpdateObjects
    UpdateMove = False: FlagMove = False: Exit Sub
  End If

  If MoveMouse() = True Then
    ArtWork.DrawStyle = Dot: ArtWork.ForeColor = Yellow
    API = Rectangle(ArtWork.hDC, X1 \ PX, Y1 \ PY, X2 \ PX, Y2 \ PY)
    FindAllObjects X1, Y1, X2, Y2, X, Y: Exit Sub
  Else
    If B > 0 Then Handles
  End If

 Case BézierTool
  If MoveMouse() = True Then
    ArtWork.DrawStyle = Dot: ArtWork.ForeColor = Yellow:
    API = Rectangle(ArtWork.hDC, X1 \ PX, Y1 \ PY, X2 \ PX, Y2 \ PY)
  End If
 Case LineTool To CircleTool
  If MoveMouse() = True Then
    BoundingBox_Up X1, Y1, X2, Y2
    If B = Total Then Draw = True: UpdateObjects
  End If
 Case TextTool
   txt.BorderStyle = 1: txt.Width = 15: txt.Visible = True
End Select

  ArtWork.DrawWidth = 1: ArtWork.DrawStyle = Solid
  UpdateMove = False: FlagMove = False
End If

If Button = 2 And Menu_ArrangeSelection(3).Checked And CurrentTool = 0 Then
  Dim X_Y As POINTAPI
  GetCursorPos X_Y: TPM_CENTERALIGN = &H4: TPM_RIGHTBUTTON = &H2
  API = TrackPopupMenu(GetSubMenu(GetMenu(hWnd), LastMenu),
      ➥TPM_CENTERALIGN, X_Y.X, X_Y.Y, 0, hWnd, 0)
End If
End Sub
```

**PX = PixelX: PY = PixelY:** The API graphical functions in the `PointerTool` and `BézierTool` Case expressions require coordinates in pixel units. `PixelX` and `PixelY` used the `Screen.TwipsPerPixel` method to retrieve the correct conversion value during the `Form_Load` event.

**If Button = Left_Button Then:** If the left mouse button is being used, do the following Case block that matches the current tool being used.

**Select Case CurrentTool:** Go to the `Case` statement that matches the current tool being used.

**Case PointerTool:** If the pointer tool (tool number 1) is selected, do the following block of code statements.

**If UpdateMove = True Then:** The `UpdateMove` variable is true only when you have moved an object from one location to another. If this is the case, you need to redraw only the object that was moved.

**MovePoly_Up Button, Shift, X, Y:** If you moved a polyshape to a new location on the desktop, the `MoveObject_Up` procedure updates all the object's `X` and `Y` coordinate positions.

**Case BézierTool, LineTool, etc.:** In all other cases, an object is drawn according to the tool that created the object. What is new to this procedure are the API graphical functions that replace the Visual Basic's graphical statements. In some cases, the API graphical statements are executed in the `BoundingBox_Up` procedure.

Figures 15.4 through 15.10 illustrate the steps to construct a polyshape.

**Figure 15.4.**
*To start a polyshape, select the line tool and draw a line.*

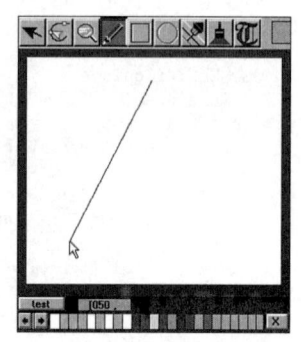

Chapter **15**

**F**igure 15.5.
*Form a polyshape by continuing lines from the end node of each line segment.*

**F**igure 15.6.
*Connect the last line segment to the first node and select a color to fill the polyshape.*

**F**igure 15.7.
*Select the shape tool and double-click a line to convert the line to a curve.*

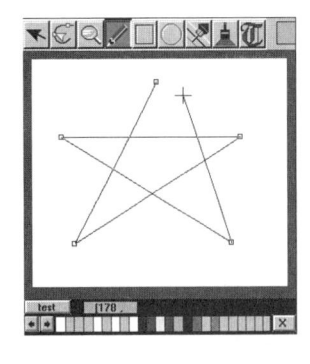

**Figure 15.8.**
*Use the Bézier handles to edit the polyshape.*

**Figure 15.9.**
*Two Bézier handles have been used to give a star shape.*

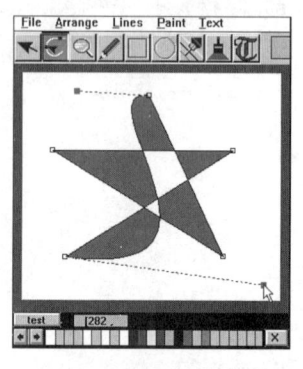

**Figure 15.10.**
*Select the test button to draw the correct path outline of a polyshape.*

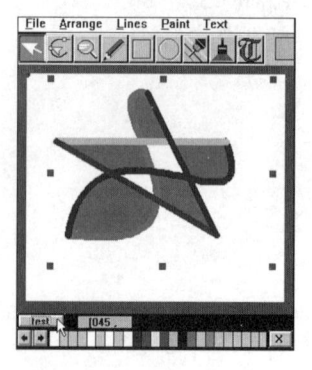

# The *Pnode* Image Control's *Tag* Properties

Nearly all Visual Basic controls have a Tag property. A Tag is a string (character) expression that you assign to each control on the form or to the form itself. You can use this string expression to identify the control or carry information about the control or form to other procedures, events, controls, or forms. See the Visual Basic language reference guide for more details.

In the ArtAPI program, you have two types of nodes. The first type is an image control called Node, which is used only on lines, boxes, circles, and text objects. The second control is also an image control, called Pnode (short for polynode), and is used exclusively for connecting segment points of polyshapes.

You can group all code from the Node's mouse events into the Pnode's mouse events. However, this can call for some rather lengthy Select Case statements.

The following explains the three possible tag names a Pnode could be assigned in the ArtAPI program:

> **Pnode(Index).Tag:** A Tag is assigned to the Pnode image control if the Pnode is connected to a Bézier curve. If the Pnode connects a line segment to a Bézier curve (left to right), the Pnode is tagged "Rightcurve." If the Pnode connects a line segment to a Bézier curve (right to left), the Pnode is tagged "Leftcurve." Finally, if the Pnode connects two Bézier curves together, the Pnode is tagged "2curves."

Use this information to properly redraw the two poly-segments (line-curve, curve-line, or curve-curve) that are connected to each Pnode.

> **Pnode(Index).Tag = "Leftcurve":** A Bézier curve connected to the left side of the Pnode.
>
> **Pnode(Index).Tag = "Rightcurve":** A Bézier curve connected to the right side of the Pnode.
>
> **Pnode(Index).Tag = "2curves":** Two Bézier curves connected to the Pnode.

In the Artisan program (from Chapter 3), two picture box controls named BezNode1 and BezNode2 were used to move a Bézier curve's end points. These controls have been deleted from this program, and their event codes have been placed into the preceding three procedures called BezNode_Down, BezNode_Move, and BezNode_Up.

The BezNode_Down procedure is triggered from the Pnode MouseDown event. The Pnode image control must be connected to a curve segment within a polyshape in order to call the BezNode_Down procedure.

**Listing 15.5. A subprocedure of the Pnode MouseDown event.**

```
Sub BezNode_Down (Index%, Button%, Shift%, Lever%,
                                  r%, rr%, rrr%, FCP%, LCP%, X!, Y!)
    Artwork.DrawMode = 7: Artwork.DrawStyle = 2
    If BezHandle1.Visible = True Then
        Artwork.Line (p1.X, p1.Y)-(h1.X, h1.Y), Yellow
        Artwork.Line (p2.X, p2.Y)-(h2.X, h2.Y), Yellow
    End If
If BezHandle3.Visible = True Then
    X2 = BezHandle3.Left + 45: Y2 = BezHandle3.Top + 45
    X4 = BezHandle4.Left + 45: Y4 = BezHandle4.Top + 45
    Artwork.Line (X1, Y1)-(X2, Y2), Yellow
    Artwork.Line (X3, Y3)-(X4, Y4), Yellow
End If
```

*continues*

## Listing 15.5. continued

```
BezHandleMove Index 'remove Bézier Handle if visible
''''redraw the dotted handle lines for Xor movement''''
LastIndex = (LastPolyPt(B) - FirstPolyPt(B)) - 1
    If Index = 0 Then ii = LastIndex Else ii = Index - 1
    If Index = LastIndex Then I = 0 Else I = Index + 1
    If FlagPolyLine(FCP) = FirstPolyPt(B) Then I = Index + 1
Select Case Pnode(Index).Tag
    Case "Leftcurve"
 X1 = Pnode(Index).Left + 45: Y1 = Pnode(Index).Top + 45
 X2 = BezHandle1.Left + 45: Y2 = BezHandle1.Top + 45
 X3 = Pnode(I).Left + 45: Y3 = Pnode(I).Top + 45
 X4 = BezHandle2.Left + 45: Y4 = BezHandle2.Top + 45
    Case "Rightcurve"
 X1 = Pnode(Index).Left + 45: Y1 = Pnode(Index).Top + 45
 X2 = BezHandle2.Left + 45: Y2 = BezHandle2.Top + 45
 X3 = Pnode(ii).Left + 45: Y3 = Pnode(ii).Top + 45
 X4 = BezHandle1.Left + 45: Y4 = BezHandle1.Top + 45
    Case "2curves"
 X1 = Pnode(Index).Left + 45: Y1 = Pnode(Index).Top + 45
 X2 = BezHandle3.Left + 45: Y2 = BezHandle3.Top + 45
 X3 = Pnode(Index).Left + 45: Y3 = Pnode(Index).Top + 45
 X4 = BezHandle4.Left + 45: Y4 = BezHandle4.Top + 45
End Select
Artwork.DrawMode = 6: Artwork.DrawStyle = 0
If FlagPolyLine(FCP) = FirstPolyPt(B) Then Poly_CurveMove2
                ➥Index, Button, Shift, Lever, X, Y
If FlagPoly(FCP) = FirstPolyPt(B) Then Poly_CurveMove1
                ➥Index, Button, Shift, Lever, X, Y
    Artwork.DrawMode = 7: Artwork.DrawStyle = 2
    Artwork.Line (X1, Y1)-(X2, Y2), Yellow
    Artwork.Line (X3, Y3)-(X4, Y4), Yellow
End Sub
```

**If Beznode1.Visible: If BezHandle3.Visible:** The dotted lever lines connecting the Bézier curve's control points to the handles are visible, so erase them.

**BezHandleMove Index:** Call this procedure (see the ARTAPI1.FRM source code) to move, rescale, and make visible the Bézier curve's two handles. The Tag name of the Pnode image control determines which BezHandle controls will be used.

Now redraw the dotted handle lines again so they can be Xored for the illusion of movement.

**LastIndex, FlagPolyLine(FCP), etc.:** When each polyline segment was first drawn, the program issued an object number for the first and last point of the polyshape. These numbers were stored in two arrays called FirstPolyPt and LastPolyPt. Using this stored information, you can tell the computer which Pnode you are currently moving, or in this case, drawing a dotted line to. Each loaded Pnode has an index number. The index is 0 for the very first Pnode loaded and continues counting up until the last Pnode is placed on the polyshape. By adding or subtracting the index number for either the FirstPolyPt or LastPolyPt object number, you can find any Pnode image control within the polyshape.

The `FlagPolyLine(FCP)` tells the computer whether the object is a closed or open polyshape so it can adjust the index variable accordingly. Otherwise, an open polyshape object would incorrectly have dotted lever handles at the start and end points of the shape.

FCP is a variable that represents the **F**irst **C**ontrol **P**oint, which is (`FirstPolyPt(object #)`).

**If FlagPolyLine(FCP) - Then Poly_CurveMove2:** Call this procedure to calculate the number of polypoints to pass to the API `Polyline` function, which erases the old image segments. Use the `Poly_CurveMove2` procedure only if the object is an open polyshape. (For example, the letter W is an open polyshape consisting of four line segments.)

**If FlagPoly(FCP) - Then Poly_CurveMove1:** This is almost identical to the `PolyLineMove2` procedure. The difference is that a few lines of code work on closed polyshape objects only. (For example, a triangle is a closed polyshape consisting of three line segments.) Since the `Poly_CurveMove2` and `Poly_CurveMove1` procedures use many of the same code routines, you may want to combine them into a single procedure at a later date.

The `BezNode_Move` procedure in Listing 15.6 is used to draw the handle levers of a Bézier curve when a Pnode is moved. The `BezNode_Move` Procedure then branches off to another procedure that will draw the polyshape as it is being edited (moved).

**Listing 15.6.** A subprocedure of the `Pnode MouseMove` event.

```
Sub BezNode_Move (Index%, Button%, Shift%, Lever%,
                                ↪r%, rr%, rrr%, FCP%, LCP%, X!, Y!)
If Button Then
    Artwork.DrawMode = 7: Artwork.DrawStyle = 2
Select Case Pnode(Index).Tag
    Case "Leftcurve", "Rightcurve"
        Artwork.Line (X1, Y1)-(X2, Y2), Yellow
        X1 = X + Pnode(Index).Left
        Y1 = Y + Pnode(Index).Top
    Case "2curves"
        Artwork.Line (X1, Y1)-(X2, Y2), Yellow
        Artwork.Line (X3, Y3)-(X4, Y4), Yellow
        X1 = X + Pnode(Index).Left
        Y1 = Y + Pnode(Index).Top
        X3 = X + Pnode(Index).Left
        Y3 = Y + Pnode(Index).Top
End Select
'''''''''''''''''''''''''''''''''''''''''
If FlagPolyLine(FCP) = FirstPolyPt(B) Then Poly_CurveMove2
                ↪Index, Button, Shift, Lever, X, Y
If FlagPoly(FCP) = FirstPolyPt(B) Then Poly_CurveMove1
                ↪Index, Button, Shift, Lever, X, Y
'''''''''''''''''''''''''''''''''''''''''
    Artwork.DrawMode = 7: Artwork.DrawStyle = 2
    Artwork.Line (X1, Y1)-(X2, Y2), Yellow
    If Pnode(Index).Tag = "2curves" Then Artwork.Line
                ↪(X3, Y3)-(X4, Y4), Yellow
End If
End Sub
```

# ArtAPI

**Artwork.DrawMode: Artwork.DrawStyle:** Changes to `Xor` drawing mode to set the drawing style to dotted lines so you can draw and move the levers connected to the Bézier's handles.

**Select Case Pnode(Index).Tag:** Checks to see what the current `Pnode`'s tag string is and then selects the `Case` block that matches the string expression.

**Case "Leftcurve", "Rightcurve":** The `Pnode` you are about to move has either a line (first) and then a curve connected to it, or a curve (first) and then a line connected to it. You need to draw only one moving dotted lever line connecting to a `BezHandle` image control (since there is only one Bézier curve being moved).

**Artwork.Line (X1,Y1,-(X2,Y2), Yellow:** Draws a single dotted lever line in `Xor` `Yellow`. The dotted line will appear to be a light blue (cyan) in color.

**X1 = X + Pnode(Index).Left: Y1 = Y + Pnode(Index).Top:** You are going to move the X1, Y1 coordinates of the dotted lever line to make it appear to be moving in the direction you the drag the mouse pointer. The `Pnodes` are image controls that do not have a `Scaleleft` or `Scaletop` property, so you cannot use the same method you used in the `BezNode1` and `BezNode2` events in the Artisan program. The internal measurements of each `Pnode` image control starts at coordinate 0, 0 at the top-left corner of the control. Each `Pnode` is located within the `Artwork` picture box control so its `Left` and `Top` properties correspond with the desktop coordinates. Add the internal X coordinate of the `Pnode` to its `Left` property value and the internal Y coordinate to the `Pnode`'s `Top` property to get the accurate drawing locations.

**Case "2curves":** The `Pnode` you are about to move has two curves connected to it. Draw two moving lever lines that connect to two `BezHandle` image controls (since there are two Bézier curves being moved).

**ArtworkLine (X1,Y1)-(X2,Y2), Yellow:** Draws the first dotted lever line.

**ArtworkLine (X3,Y3)-(X4,Y4), Yellow:** Draws the second dotted lever line.

**X1, Y1, X3, Y3:** Moves the two dotted lever lines.

FCP is a variable that represents the **F**irst **C**ontrol **P**oint, which is (`FirstPolyPt(object #)`). This is a flag that tells the program what type of shape the object is. It can be either an open or closed polyshape.

**If FlagPolyLine(FCP) - Then Poly_CurveMove2:** Call this procedure to draw the two polysegments connected to the moving `Pnode`. The `Poly_CurveMove2` procedure is used only if the object is an open polyshape. (For example, the letter W is an open polyshape consisting of four line segments.)

**If FlagPoly(FCP) - Then Poly_CurveMove1:** This is almost identical to the `PolyCurveMove2` procedure. The difference is that the code that works on the closed polyshape object only. (For example, a triangle is a closed polyshape consisting of three line segments.)

`ArtworkDrawMode: Artwork.DrawStyle:` The `Poly_CurveMove2` and `Poly_CurveMove1` procedures draw the two polysegments in `Solid Inverse` mode. Therefore, change back to the `Xor` dotted mode to redraw the dotted lever lines.

`Artwork.Line (X1,Y1)-(X2,Y2), Yellow:` Redraw the dotted lever line.

`If Pnode(Index).Tag = "2curves" Then:` Redraw the second dotted lever line.

## Updating a Curve's Coordinates

The `BezNode_Up` procedure in Listing 15.7 is divided into two sections. The first section deals with updating the coordinates of a `Pnode` that had one or two curves attached and was moved to a new location. The second part deals with `Pnodes` that had polylines attach on either a closed or open polyshape.

After the `Pnode` is moved, you'll have a long list of coordinates and variable flags, as well as a general clean-up to perform in the `Beznode_Up` procedure. There are five actions you must execute:

1. Store the object's new positions in the correct array. For example, if you moved a Bézier curve, you would update the curve start and end points (`P1X`, `P1Y`, and `P2X`, `P2Y`). If one of the polysegments were a line, you would also update the `W`, `N`, and `S`, `E` start and end points of each line segment.

2. Use the `BézierStore` procedure to calculate the new coordinates of the polyshape, including the positions of `BezHandles`, so the handles can be placed around the bounding box of the polyshape.

3. Call the `Poly_Handles` procedure to set the bounding box dimensions. The `Poly_Handles` procedure erases the underlying image area before redrawing the shapes.

4. Redraw the objects with the `UpdateObjects` procedure.

5. Redraw the dotted line's lever lines that connect to any Bézier's handles.

Figure 15.11 illustrates a polyshape's nodes and handle names and the order in which they are placed. The top illustration shows a polyshape consisting of four polylines (1 through 4) and the `Pnodes` that would be attached to each line segment. The middle illustration shows the location of the Bézier curve's control points (P1, P2) and the Bézier curve's handles (H1, H2) that would be attached to the dotted lever lines after polylines 2 and 4 had been converted to curves. The bottom illustration shows the locations of the curve control, and handle points and lever lines after all the polylines had been converted to curves.

**Figure 15.11.**
*Line and curve nodes and handles on a polyshape.*

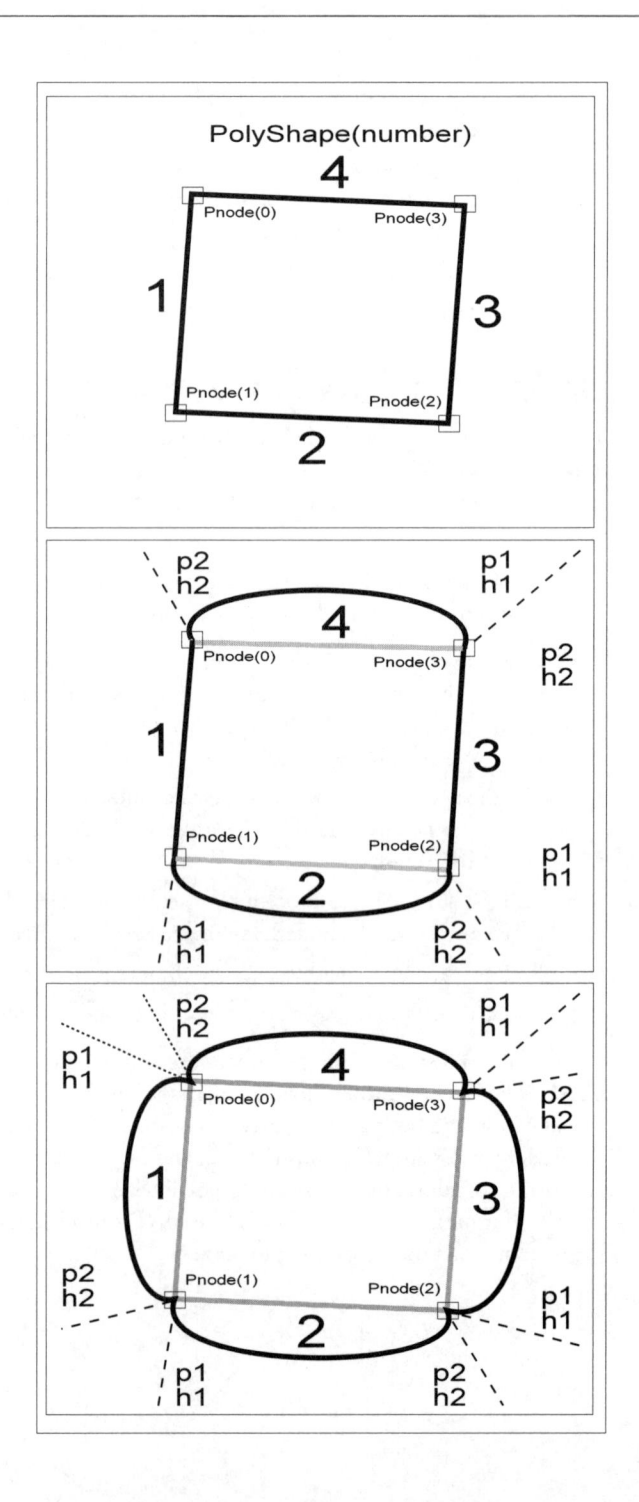

**Listing 15.7.** A subprocedure of the Pnode MouseUp event.

```
Sub BezNode_Up (Index%, Button%, Shift%, Lever%, X!, Y!)
    CountPolyPts = 0: PolyPts = 0
    Pnode(Index).Left = X + Pnode(Index).Left - 45
    Pnode(Index).Top = Y + Pnode(Index).Top - 45
r = FirstPolyPt(B) + Index 'Index +1
rr = FirstPolyPt(B) + Index - 1 'Index
rrr = FirstPolyPt(B) + Index - 2 'Index -1
FCP = FirstPolyPt(B) 'First object
LCP = LastPolyPt(B) - 1 'last object
LastIndex = (LastPolyPt(B) - FirstPolyPt(B)) - 1
''''''''''''''''''''''''''''''''''''''''''''''
If Pnode(Index).Tag = "2curves" Then
    Select Case Index
        Case 0
            p1X(FCP) = Pnode(Index).Left + 45
            p1Y(FCP) = Pnode(Index).Top + 45
            p2X(LCP) = Pnode(Index).Left + 45
            p2Y(LCP) = Pnode(Index).Top + 45
                B = FCP
                BézierStore
            B = LCP
p1.X = p1X(B): p1.Y = p1Y(B): p2.X = p2X(B): p2.Y = p2Y(B)
h1.X = h1X(B): h1.Y = h1Y(B): h2.X = h2X(B): h2.Y = h2Y(B)
            BézierStore
    Case Else
            p1X(r) = Pnode(Index).Left + 45
            p1Y(r) = Pnode(Index).Top + 45
            p2X(rr) = Pnode(Index).Left + 45
            p2Y(rr) = Pnode(Index).Top + 45
            B = r
        BézierStore
        B = rr
p1.X = p1X(B): p1.Y = p1Y(B): p2.X = p2X(B): p2.Y = p2Y(B)
h1.X = h1X(B): h1.Y = h1Y(B): h2.X = h2X(B): h2.Y = h2Y(B)
            BézierStore
End Select
```

The following is a line-by-line explanation of the `BezNode_Up` procedure's first code section:

**CountPolyPts = 0:** This variable held the flag that erased the original poly-segments. Set it back to 0.

**PolyPts = 0:** This variable held the number of X and Y points to draw using the API Polyline statement. Set it back to 0.

**Pnode(Index).Left, Pnode(Index).Top:** Reposition the Pnode image control to its new coordinate.

**r , rr, rrr, FCP, LCP, LastIndex:** These variables find the index number of the Pnode you have just moved. They also take into consideration closed and open polyshapes.

**If Pnode(Index).Tag = "2curves" Then**: You have moved a Pnode that connects two Bézier curves. You must do the following:

**Select Case Index:** If the Pnode index was 0, update both the P1 (first control point) index points and the P2 (last control point) index points of the two connecting Bézier curves.

**B = FCP:** You have two Bézier curves to update, so assign B the first control point (FCP), which is the Bézier curve to the left of Pnode(0).

**BézierStore:** This procedure finds the position of the first Bézier curve's bounding box. This is necessary because the ArtMask picture box control relies on knowing all individual polyshape and bounding box dimensions. Otherwise, you could not find or move any object in the ArtAPI program.

**B = LCP:** Having found the first Bézier curve's bounding box, you now look for the second Bézier curve's bounding box. The second curve is located to the right of Pnode(0) and is the last control point (LCP) object.

**p1.X = p1X(B), etc.:** Since the BézierStore procedure uses these variables to find a Bézier curve's bounding box, you must switch values to reflect the second Bézier curve's control points.

**BézierStore:** Stores the bounding box dimensions of the second Bézier curve.

**Case Else:** This is exactly the same as the Case 0 code block, except you have just moved a Pnode with an index greater than 0. The r and rr variables will know which indexed Pnode you have just moved.

All you have to do now is update the drawing, place a bounding box around the entire polyshape, and redraw the dotted lever lines.

Listing 15.8 shows the second code section of the BezNode_Up procedure:

### Listing 15.8. The BezNode_Up procedure, continued.

```
    Pnode(Index).Tag = ""
    EraseOldImage = True
       Poly_Handles
       UpdateObjects
    Artwork.DrawMode = 7: Artwork.DrawStyle = 2
X1 = Pnode(Index).Left + 45: Y1 = Pnode(Index).Top + 45
X2 = BezHandle3.Left + 45: Y2 = BezHandle3.Top + 45
X3 = Pnode(Index).Left + 45: Y3 = Pnode(Index).Top + 45
X4 = BezHandle4.Left + 45: Y4 = BezHandle4.Top + 45
    Artwork.Line (X1, Y1)-(X2, Y2), Yellow
    Artwork.Line (X3, Y3)-(X4, Y4), Yellow
Exit Sub
End If
'''''''''''''''''''''''''''''''
If Index = 0 Then
    If FlagPolyLine(B) = B Then
    W(FCP) = Pnode(Index).Left + 45 : N(FCP) = Pnode(Index).Top + 45
  Else
    W(FCP) = Pnode(Index).Left + 45 : N(FCP) = Pnode(Index).Top + 45
    E(LCP) = Pnode(Index).Left + 45 : S(LCP) = Pnode(Index).Top + 45
  End If
```

```
    Else
        If FlagPolyLine(FCP) = FCP And LastPolyPt(B) = B + 1 Then
            E(rr) = Pnode(Index).Left + 45
            S(rr) = Pnode(Index).Top + 45
        Else
            W(r) = Pnode(Index).Left + 45
            N(r) = Pnode(Index).Top + 45
            E(rr) = Pnode(Index).Left + 45
            S(rr) = Pnode(Index).Top + 45
End If
Select Case Lever
    Case 1 'Beznode1_Up
                BezHandle1.ScaleLeft = BezHandle1.Left
        BezHandle1.ScaleTop = BezHandle1.Top
    Case 2
        BezHandle2.ScaleLeft = BezHandle2.Left: BezHandle2.ScaleTop = BezHandle2.Top
End Select
p1X(B) = p1.X: p1Y(B) = p1.Y: p2X(B) = p2.X: p2Y(B) = p2.Y
h1X(B) = h1.X: h1Y(B) = h1.Y: h2X(B) = h2.X: h2Y(B) = h2.Y
    EraseOldImage = True
        Poly_Handles
        UpdateObjects
p1.X = p1X(B): p1.Y = p1Y(B): p2.X = p2X(B): p2.Y = p2Y(B)
h1.X = h1X(B): h1.Y = h1Y(B): h2.X = h2X(B): h2.Y = h2Y(B)
        Artwork.DrawMode = 7: Artwork.DrawStyle = 2
Artwork.Line (p1.X, p1.Y)-(h1.X, h1.Y), Yellow
    Artwork.Line (p2.X, p2.Y)-(h2.X, h2.Y), Yellow
        BézierStore
End Sub
```

**Pnode(Index).Tag = "":** Erases the Pnode's 2curve tag. Since Pnodes are always reloaded to save memory, the correct tag name is assigned at each Pnode_MouseDown event.

**EraseOldImage = True:** This variable tells the Poly_Handle procedure that the old image's bounding box must be erased and to assign the new bounding box dimensions to W(0), N(0), E(0), and S(0).

**Poly_Handles:** Assigns the coordinates for the new bounding box of the polyshape.

**UpdateObjects:** Redraws all the objects on the desktop.

**Artwork.DrawMode: Artwork.DrawStyle:** Now you redraw the dotted lever lines to the new positions and change to the Xor dotted line draw mode.

**X1, X2, X3, X4:** Set the dotted lever lines start and end points.

**Artwork.Line:** Draw both of the dotted lever lines.

**Exit Sub:** A Pnode with two curves attached has been updated, so exit the procedure.

The last part of the code deals with Pnodes that have only one curve attached. The following code also takes into account whether the curve belongs to open or closed polyshapes. Also, the procedure checks to see whether the curve is located on the first or last Pnode, in which case additional routines are performed.

**If Index = 0 Then:** The first `Pnode` in the polyshape is a special case. The `If/Then` code block must check to see whether the first `Pnode` is on an open or closed polyshape.

**If FlagPolyLine(B) = B Then:** The first `Pnode` on an open polyshape has no end points (E, S) to update (since the coordinates E and S remain stationary when dragging `Pnode(0)`).

**Else:** The first `Pnode` is connected to the start and end segments of a closed polyshape. Update all possible line segments' start or ends points (W, N, E, and S).

**Else:** You are updating a `Pnode` whose index is greater than 0.

**If FlagPolyLine(FCP) = FCP And LastPolyPt(B) = B + 1:** The last `Pnode` on an open polyshape has no start point (W, N) to update (since coordinates W and N remain stationary when dragging the last `Pnode`).

**Else:** You are updating a `Pnode` whose index is greater then 0 and is located on a closed polyshape.

**W(r), N(r), E(rr). S(rr):** Update the line segments that are connected to a `Pnode` indexed greater than 0 and is located on a closed polyshape.

**Select Case Lever:** The lever is made up of the dotted handle lines attached to the ends of a Bézier curve. Lever 1 is usually assigned to the left side of the `Pnode` image control or the first control point of the Bézier curve. Lever 2 is usually assigned to the right side of the `Pnode` image control or end control point of a Bézier curve. The lever works like the `BezNode1` and `BezNode2` controls found in the Artisan program, in Chapter 3. The lever identifies on which side of the curve the `P1X`, `P1Y`, and the `P2X`, `P2Y` points are located.

**Case 1:** You have moved a `Pnode` that has a single Bézier curve attached to it. This is usually connected by the starting point of the curve. The `Lever` number (1) is assigned in the Pnode_MouseMove event.

**BezHandle1.ScaleLeft, ScaleTop, Visible:** Reset the proper `BezHandle` associated with `Lever 1`.

**Case 2:** You have moved a `Pnode` that has a single Bézier curve attached to it. This is usually connected to the ending point of the curve. `Lever 2` is also assigned in the Pnode_MouseMove event.

**BezHandle2.ScaleLeft, ScaleTop, Visible:** Reset the proper `BezHandle` associated with `Lever 2`.

**p1X(B) = p1.X, etc.:** The `Pnode` had only one Bézier curve attached to it. Therefore, you can update the curve's points very simply. The p1.X, p1.Y, p2.X, and p2Y variables hold the curve's start and end points, so store these values in the appropriate arrays.

**EraseOldImage: Poly_Handles: UpdateObjects:** Erase the old image area, calculate the bounding box coordinates, and redraw the polyshape.

**p1.X = p1X(B), etc.:** When the UpdateObjects procedure redraws all the objects on the desktop, it can change the values of p1.X, p1Y, p2.X, and p2.Y, so restore their original values.

**BézierStore:** Stores the new bounding box position of the polyshape.

## Moving the Objects

The BoundingBox_Down procedure in Listing 15.9 is similar to the procedure of the same name found in the Artisan program from Chapter 2. The main difference is that in the BoundingBox_Down procedure in the ArtAPI program, you calculate the movable polyshape bounding box and the erasable bounding box area.

The BoundingBox_Down procedure in Listing 15.9 shows another way to move an object. The Movetest (Chapter 1) and Artisan programs (Chapter 2) use a formula to move objects by calculating each position move on the fly (variables are changed as the object moved). This is the same structure as the previously mentioned formulas, but you can shorten the codes by calculating the new positions after the MouseUp event.

See Listing 15.9 for a subprocedure of the Artwork_MouseDown event.

**Listing 15.9. A subprocedure of the Artwork_MouseDown event.**

```
Sub BoundingBox_Down (X As Single, Y As Single)
    X1 = X: Y1 = Y: X2 = X1: Y2 = Y1
    Artwork.DrawMode = Inverse
If CurrentTool = 0 And ArtMask.Point(X - 15, Y - 15) = MaskForeColor Then
    If PolyShape(B) = B Then
        Poly_Handles 'Find Poly-shape bounding box
        XX1 = W(0): YY1 = N(0): XX2 = E(0): YY2 = S(0)
        WB = W(0): NB = N(0): EB = E(0): SB = S(0)
    Else
        XX1 = W(B): YY1 = N(B): XX2 = E(B): YY2 = S(B)
        WB = W(B): NB = N(B): EB = E(B): SB = S(B)
    End If
    FlagMove = True: Foundcolor = False
End If
End Sub
```

The MoveObject (Listing 15.16) and MoveObject_Up procedures (Listing 15.17) take care of repositioning all of the objects' new X and Y coordinate points as the object is dragged (MouseMove) and released (MouseUp).

**If CurrentTool = 0 And ArtMask.Point(X - 15, Y - 15):** The current tool must be the pointer tool, and the pixel located in a memory bitmap called ArtMask must match the current X and Y positions of the mouse. The memory bitmap X, Y point must be the ArtMask.ForeColor, which is 0 (black).

**If PolyShape(B) = B Then:** The object is a polyshape.

**Poly_Handles:** Calculate the dimensions of a polyshape's bounding box. Handles are usually placed around a bounding box so the object can be stretched.

**XX1 = W(0): WB = W(0):** Stores a polyshape's bounding box position.

**Else XX1 = W(B): WB = W(B):** Stores a rectangle's, line's, circle's, or text's bounding box position.

**FlagMove = True:** Tells the program it is ready to move an object if the user wants to drag it.

**Foundcolor = False:** Reset to False since the Find_Object procedure has already found an object.

## API Drawing Functions

The `BoundingBox_Move` procedure (See Listing 15.10) differs from the Artisan program in that it uses API graphical functions to draw lines, boxes, and circles. By replacing the Basic language graphical statements, you must adhere to certain rules that govern API functions. The main rule is that API graphics require that the coordinates be given in pixel dimensions. Also, Visual Basic uses its own custom scaling routines, which may have an effect on the placement of graphics when you switch scale modes or set internal scaling dimensions within your form or picture box. For this reason, this program has eliminated the zoom and scaling routines. It may be best to first experiment with the Scaltest program in Chapter 14 before adding zoom features.

**Listing 15.10.** A subprocedure of the `Artwork_MouseMove` event.

```
Sub BoundingBox_Move (Shift As Integer, X As Single, Y As Single)
If CurrentTool = 0 And FlagMove = True And MoveMouse() = True
              ➥Then MoveObject Button, Shift, X, Y: Exit Sub
    PX = PixelX: PY = PixelY
If MoveMouse() = True Then
    Select Case CurrentTool
        Case PointerTool To BézierTool
            Artwork.DrawMode = Xor_Pen
            Artwork.DrawStyle = Dot: Artwork.ForeColor = Yellow
            r = Rectangle(Artwork.hDC, X1 \ PixelX, Y1 \ PixelY,
                     ➥X2 \ PixelX, Y2 \ PixelY)
        Case LineTool
            Npt(1).X = X1 \ PX: Npt(1).Y = Y1 \ PY
            Npt(2).X = X2 \ PX: Npt(2).Y = Y2 \ PY: PolyPts = 2
            r = Polyline(Artwork.hDC, Npt(1), PolyPts)
        Case BoxTool
            r = Rectangle(Artwork.hDC, X1 \ PixelX, Y1 \ PixelY,
                     ➥X2 \ PixelX, Y2 \ PixelY)
        Case CircleTool
            r = Ellipse(Artwork.hDC, X1 \ PixelX, Y1 \ PixelY,
                     ➥X2 \ PixelX, Y2 \ PixelY)
    End Select
End If
End Sub
```

**If CurrentTool = 0 - Then MoveObject Button:** If you are moving an object to a new screen location, you do not need to draw any object.

**Select Case CurrentTool:** Go to the API graphical function that draws the object associated with the tool currently being used.

You also may want to also use the API LineTo and MoveTo functions to draw lines when using the LineTool Case block. You can find most of Windows 3.1 API drawing function examples in Chapter 8.

The API graphical calls in this program use the PixelX and PixelY values to convert twips to pixels. The PixelX and PixelY values are set in the Form_Load event (see the ARTAPI1.FRM source code) by using the TwipsperPixelX and TwipsPerPixelY screen values. On most VGA monitors, the pixels per inch are 96 both vertically and horizontally. Divide 1,440 twips per inch by 96 pixels per inch, and the TwipPerPixel value would be 15.

This number can vary depending on the type of monitor you have. You also can use the API GetDeviceCaps functions to view your monitor's pixels-per-inch resolution values.

The BoundingBox_Up procedure in Listing 15.11 keeps track of how many objects have been drawn and also assigns flag names to the line, box, and circle objects.

**Listing 15.11. A subprocedure of the Artwork_MouseUp event.**

```
Sub BoundingBox_Up (X1&, Y1&, X2&, Y2&)
If MoveMouse() = True Then
    Total = Total + 1: B = Total
    DrawOrder(B) = Total
    StatusLabel.Caption = "Object B = " + Format$(B)
    LineWidth(B) = Artwork.DrawWidth
    W(B) = X1: E(B) = X2: N(B) = Y1: S(B) = Y2
Select Case CurrentTool
    Case LineTool 'Lineto
        FlagLine(B) = B : Nodes
    Case BoxTool 'Rectangle
        FlagBox(B) = B : FillValue(B) = 1 : Nodes
    Case CircleTool 'Ellipse
        FlagCircle(B) = B : FillValue(B) = 1 : Nodes
End Select
End If
End Sub
```

**If MoveMouse() = True Then:** Continues only if the mouse has moved a given distance.

**Total = Total + 1: B = Total:** Increases the object count by 1.

**DrawOrder(B) = Total:** Inserts the current object's assigned number in the DrawOrder array. The To_Front_Back procedure (Listing 15.31) retrieves the numbers assigned to the DrawOrder array to shuffle the drawing order so the UpdateObject procedure can place an object to the front or back of all other objects.

**Select Case CurrentTool:** Assigns a number to the new object and then place the nodes around the object.

## Finding the Outline of an Object

In the Artisan program, you could not select an object that was directly behind another. The mouse pointer selected the bounding box rather than the object's outline. This made it very difficult to highlight the current object. The Find_Object procedure in Listing 15.12 shows one of many ways to select an object by touch.

The FindObject procedure uses two searching features not found in the Artisan program of Chapter 2. The first feature is the API PtinRect function, which replaces the manual search for the object's bounding box. The second search feature uses a hidden picture box called ArtMask. If the mouse pointer is clicked on the bounding box of an object, a masked outline image of the object is created in ArtMask. If the mouse pointer is at the same coordinate that the masked outline of the object is, the object is selected.

**Listing 15.12. Finding a guideline or the outline of any object on the desktop.**

```
Sub Find_Object (X As Single, Y As Single)
For r = -90 To 90 Step 15: For rr = -90 To 90 Step 15
If Artwork.Point(X - r, Y - rr) = Artwork.BackColor
                        ➥Then Z = Z + 1 Else Foundcolor = True
If Z = 169 Then StatusLabel.Caption = "No color Found": B = 0: Exit Sub
Next rr: Next r
''''''''''Find bounding box
I = Total
XY& = X + CLng(Y) * &H10000
Do While I > 0
Dim BB1 As Rect: Dim BB2 As Rect: Dim BB3 As Rect: Dim BB4 As Rect
BB1.Left = W(I) - 30: BB1.Top = N(I) - 30
BB1.Right = E(I) + 30: BB1.Bottom = S(I) + 30
BB2.Left = W(I) - 30: BB2.Top = S(I) - 30
BB2.Right = E(I) + 30: BB2.Bottom = N(I) + 30
BB3.Left = E(I) - 30: BB3.Top = S(I) - 30
BB3.Right = W(I) + 30: BB3.Bottom = N(I) + 30
BB4.Left = E(I) - 30: BB4.Top = N(I) - 30
BB4.Right = W(I) + 30: BB4.Bottom = S(I) + 30
If PtInRectBynum%(BB1, XY&) Or PtInRectBynum%(BB2, XY&)
    ➥Or PtInRectBynum%(BB3, XY&) Or PtInRectBynum%(BB4, XY&) Then
B = I: ArtMask.Cls
If N(I) <= S(I) Then AT = N(I): AH = S(I) Else AT = S(I): AH = N(I)
If W(I) <= E(I) Then AL = W(I): AW = E(I) Else AL = E(I): AW = W(I)
ArtMask.Top = AT - 150 : ArtMask.Left = AL - 150
ArtMask.Width = (AW - AL) + 300 : ArtMask.Height = (AH - AT) + 30
ArtMask.ScaleLeft = ArtMask.Left : ArtMask.ScaleTop = ArtMask.Top
UpdateArtMask
    If ArtMask.Point(X - 15, Y - 15) = MaskForeColor Then Exit Do
End If
    If I = 0 Then Exit Do Else I = I - 1
Loop
        B = I: StatusLabel.Caption = "Object B = " + Format$(B)
        ArtApi.StatusColor.BackColor = OutLineColor(B)
        ArtApi.StatusPaint.BackColor = PaintColor(B)
    Nodes
End Sub
```

**For r = -90 To 90 Step 15:** Since the `Find_Object` procedure is called for each `MouseDown` event, determine whether the mouse pointer is on top of any object; if not, exit this procedure.

**ArtWork.Point (X-r, Y-rr):** Scans a block of 169 pixels around the mouse pointer and searches for a color other than the desktop's back color of white. If it does not find an object color, it will exit the procedure.

The second part of this procedure looks for any vertical or horizontal guidelines that may be on the desktop. If it finds a guideline, it erases it in anticipation that you are going to move it to a new location.

The following is the section of code used to find a bounding box:

**XY& = X +CLng(Y) * &H1000:** Splices the X and Y (high and low 16-bit values) to a 32-bit combined value. The API `PtInRect` function needs both values connected as a `Long` data type.

**Dim BB1, BB2, BB3, BB4 As Rect:** The API `PtInRect` function looks for bonding boxes defined as `Rect Type` structures (left, top, right, and bottom). If an object is flipped using the handles, the bounding box coordinates are also flipped. Four `Rect` bounding box structures are thus needed to check every possible bounding box position.

**If PointInRectBynum%:** If the mouse pointer is over a bounding box, you must find which object has been touched. Take note that you use an `Alias` name for the API `PtInRect` function to pass the 32-bit value as `Long`.

**If (N(I) <= S(I) Then AT = N(I):** You redraw every object that could be within this area to a hidden picture box called `ArtMask`. If the current X and Y coordinates of Artwork match the `ArtMask`'s X and Y coordinates and the pixel color in `ArtMask` is indeed black, the object is found.

**ArtMask.ScaleLeft, Top, Width, Height:** To save memory when using a persistent bitmap, resize each picture box to the actual size of each object it looks for. The `UpdateArtMask` procedure draws the object into the hidden `ArtMask` picture box. To see this in action, click the Show ArtMask submenu option from the main menubar.

# Calculating a Bounding Box for a Polyshape

The only change to the `Handle` events in the ArtAPI program is an added `Poly_Handles` call if the object happens to be a polyshape. If the object is indeed a polyshape, the `Poly_Handles` procedure in Listing 15.13 scans for the dimensions of all polyline and polycurve segments to form a single bounding box for the polyshape. Once a bounding box is created for a polyshape, the eight handles used to resize a polyshape are placed around the bounding box.

**Listing 15.13. Combining polyshapes as a whole.**

```
Sub Poly_Handles ()
    StoreB = B: ii = FirstPolyPt(B)
WB = W(ii): NB = N(ii): EB = E(ii): SB = S(ii)
    For I = FirstPolyPt(ii) To LastPolyPt(ii) - 1
        If WB > W(I) Then WB = W(I)
        If NB > N(I) Then NB = N(I)
        If EB < E(I) Then EB = E(I)
        If SB < S(I) Then SB = S(I)
    Next I
    For I = FirstPolyPt(B) To LastPolyPt(B) - 1
        If WB > E(I) Then WB = E(I)
        If NB > S(I) Then NB = S(I)
        If EB < W(I) Then EB = W(I)
        If SB < N(I) Then SB = N(I)
    Next I
If Artwork.DrawStyle = Dot Then W(0) = WB: N(0) = NB:
                               ↪E(0) = EB: S(0) = SB : Exit Sub
If EraseOldImage = True Then
    EraseOldImage = False
    XX1 = WB: YY1 = NB: XX2 = EB: YY2 = SB: Exit Sub
Else
    W(0) = WB: N(0) = NB: E(0) = EB: S(0) = SB
    B = 0
    If CurrentTool = 0 Then Handles
    B = StoreB
    End If
End Sub
```

**WB = W(ii), etc.:** Stores the original object numbers since they are about to scanned.

**For I = FirstPolyPt(ii) To LastPolyPt(ii) -1:** The first object of every polyshape drawn holds the first and last Pnode position. With this information, you can find the first and last objects, as well as all the objects between.

**If WB > W(I) Then WB = W(I):** Compares each west dimension of each polyobject within the polyshape. Once the procedure has looped through each coordinate, the furthest point to the left will equal W(I), the furthest to the right will equal E(I), the furthest to the top will equal N(I), and the furthest to the bottom will equal S(I).

**If WB > E(I) Then WB = E(I):** If the object has been flipped, switch values.

The rest of the procedure stores the old image areas so they'll be erased after a stretch or move.

## Opening and Saving a Polyshape File

Listing 15.14 shows a condensed listing of the menuFileOpen procedure. For an entire list of file open and save commands, refer to the mnuFileOpen and mnuFileSave procedures in ARTAPI1.FRM source code file. In the ArtAPI program, only five additional variables are needed to redraw any polyshape. This number can reduced further if certain poly-routines are combined. The sixth variable stores the drawing order, since you are using a new To_Front_Back procedure. The DrawOrder(B) value is used in the UpdateObject procedure.

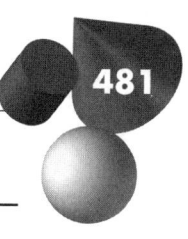

**Listing 15.14. New file read commands to open files.**

```
Sub mnuFileOpen ()
Line Input #1, B1: FlagPoly(B) = B1
Line Input #1, B1: FirstPolyPt(B) = B1
Line Input #1, B1: LastPolyPt(B) = B1
Line Input #1, B1: PolyShape(B) = B1
Line Input #1, B1: FlagPolyLine(B) = B1
Line Input #1, B1: DrawOrder(B) = B1
'see ARTAPI.FRM file for addition values
End Sub
```

**Line Input #1, B1:** This program uses Visual Basic's Input# statement to save object attributes and coordinates. You may want to use other available Visual Basic file I/O methods.

Listing 15.15 shows a condensed listing of the mnuFileSave procedure. For an entire list of file open and save commands, see the Artisan program in Chapter 4.

**Listing 15.15. New file write commands to save a file.**

```
Sub mnuFileSave ()
31 : Print #1, FlagPoly(B)
32 : Print #1, FirstPolyPt(B)
33 : Print #1, LastPolyPt(B)
34 : Print #1, PolyShape(B)
35 : Print #1, FlagPolyLine(B)
36 : Print #1, DrawOrder(B)
'see ARTAPI.FRM file for additional values
End Sub
```

**Print #1, FlagPoly(B):** This program uses Visual Basic's Print# statement to open object attributes and coordinates. You may want to use other available Visual Basic file I/O methods.

# Moving a Polyshape Object

The BoundingBox_Down and MoveObject procedures have been greatly reduced in size by including an additional Move_Object_Up procedure. Although the Artisan program in Chapter 2 used on-the-fly coordinate changes, it also called for extra variables. You have eliminated these by updating all coordinate points after the move.

The BoundingBox_Down procedure (Listing 2.12) in Chapter 2 calculated the center of the object and then offset it by the X and Y positions of the mouse. This formula is as follows:

```
XCenter = X - ((W(B) \ 2) + (E(B)) \ 2)
YCenter = Y - ((N(B) \ 2) + (S(B)) \ 2)
OFFSETx = XCenter: OFFSETy = YCenter
```

# ArtAPI

In the `MoveObject` procedure (Listing 4.25) of the Artisan program, Chapter 4, the `OffsetX` and `OffsetY` values remain constant since they are set in the `MouseDown` event. During the `MouseMove` event, the following formula shifts all the bounding box points away from the center and offsets the mouse's `currentX` and `currentY` positions:

```
W(B) = (W(B) - OFFSETx) + XCenter : N(B) = (N(B) - OFFSETy) + YCenter
E(B) = (E(B) - OFFSETx) + XCenter : S(B) = (S(B) - OFFSETy) + YCenter
```

No updating of the bounding box position was necessary since the values were changed as the object was dragged.

In the ArtAPI program, the `MoveObject` and `MoveObject_Up` procedures significantly reduce the amount of code needed to move an object by adding an additional `MouseUp` procedure. By subtracting X and Y from the X1 and Y1 values at the `BoundingBox_MouseDown` event, you can determine the distance moved by the mouse. Then subtract the distance traveled by the mouse from the coordinates of the bounding box's original positions. The `MoveObject` procedure in Listing 15.16 calculates the offset coordinates needed to move an object using the mouse pointer.

**Listing 15.16. Moving an object to a new screen location.**

```
Sub MoveObject (Button As Integer, Shift As Integer, X As Single, Y As Single)
If PolyShape(B) = B Then i = 0 Else i = B
    If Artwork.MousePointer = 0 Then
        Artwork.DrawMode = 7: Artwork.DrawWidth = 1
        N_H_Clear
        Artwork.Line (W(i), N(i))-(E(i), S(i)), Yellow, B
        UpdateMove = True: Artwork.MousePointer = 5
    End If
XCenter = X1 - X : YCenter = Y1 - Y
Artwork.Line (WB, NB)-(EB, SB), Yellow, B
    WB = W(i) - XCenter
    NB = N(i) - YCenter
    EB = E(i) - XCenter
    SB = S(i) - YCenter
Artwork.Line (WB, NB)-(EB, SB), Yellow, B
End Sub
```

**If PolyShape(B) = B Then i = 0 :** Determines whether the object being moved is a polyshape. If the object is a polyshape, its bounding box coordinates are temporarily stored as object number 0.

**If Artwork.MousePointer = 0 :** You have to initiate certain values only once in order to give the illusion the object is moving. This procedure is called constantly as the mouse moves, so the picture box's mouse pointer icon property will act as a flag to bypass the If/Then statement after the first movement of the mouse.

**UpdateMove = True: Artwork.MousePointer = 5 :** The UpdateMove flag tells other mouse events that an object is being moved. The mouse pointer in then changed to a four-arrow direction icon.

**XCenter = X1 - X : YCenter = Y1 - Y:** If the object is a circle, the center coordinates will change to reflect the new coordinates.

`Artwork.Line (WB, NB)-(EB, SB):` Draws the object's bounding box outline as you move the mouse.

The `MoveObject_Up` procedure in Listing 15.17 stores the new coordinate positions of an object after it has been moved and the mouse button has been released.

**Listing 15.17. Changing all coordinates of an object after a move.**

```
Sub MoveObject_Up (Button As Integer, Shift As Integer, X As Single, Y As Single)
    If PolyShape(B) = B Then
        First = FirstPolyPt(B): Last = LastPolyPt(B) - 1
    Else
        First = B: Last = B
    End If
For i = First To Last
    XCenter = X - X1 : YCenter = Y - Y1
    W(i) = W(i) + XCenter
    N(i) = N(i) + YCenter
    E(i) = E(i) + XCenter
    S(i) = S(i) + YCenter
If FlagBézier(i) = i Then
    p1X(i) = p1X(i) + XCenter
    p1Y(i) = p1Y(i) + YCenter
    p2X(i) = p2X(i) + XCenter
    p2Y(i) = p2Y(i) + YCenter
    h1X(i) = h1X(i) + XCenter
    h1Y(i) = h1Y(i) + YCenter
    h2X(i) = h2X(i) + XCenter
    h2Y(i) = h2Y(i) + YCenter
End If
Next i
    If FlagText(B) = B Then OFFSET(B) = (OFFSET(B) - OFFSETx) + XCenter
End Sub
```

**If PolyShape(B) = B Then:** The moving object is a polyshape, so you must change every polyline and curve coordinate within the polyshape. Every polyshape object node coordinate starts at `FirstPolyPt(poly-shape #)` and ends at `LastPolyPt(poly-shape #)`.

**First = B: Last = B:** If the object is not a polyshape, the For/Next statement executes only once.

**For i = First To Last:** If the object is a polyshape, you loop through and change all the polyshape's bounding box coordinates and any curve's control points within the polyshape.

# The Polyshape's Nodes (*Pnodes*)

There are two types of nodes in this program. The first is the `Image` control, which is used to connect and move only a single-line object. The second node is called a `Pnode`, which is used to connect and move polyline or polycurve objects. A polyshape always starts out as a single-line object with two node controls on either end. After the user continues a secondary line from the last node on a single-line object, the shape is converted to a polyline shape. The two original node controls are hidden and replaced with Pnodes when the polyshape is updated.

Error handlers have not been included in the Node image control events. Continuing a line from a node after a polyobject has been drawn can connect the two, and possibly group all, objects as one. This can give an altered perspective of moving and combining groups. It is not recommended.

The Pnode_MouseDown procedure in Listing 15.18 determines what type of object is connected to the Pnode (for example, polyline or Bézier curve). The Pnode's tag name is then changed to indicate what side of the Pnode the curve is attached to (Leftcurve, Rightcurve), or if two curves are attached. The information will then be sent to the BezNode_Down procedure to begin the process of drawing the polyshape as it is being edited (moved). If no curves are attached to the Pnode, the procedure prepares to draw the attached polyline(s).

**Listing 15.18. Setting the polynode coordinates for a move.**

```
Sub Pnode_MouseDown (Index%, Button%, Shift%, X As Single, Y As Single)
If CurrentTool = 3 And Index < NodeTotal - 1 Then Beep: Exit Sub
If CurrentTool = 3 And Index < LastPolyPt(B) Then Beep: Exit Sub
StatusLabel.Caption = "Node " + Format$(Index) + " ( " +
            ➥Format$(Pnode(Index).Left \ PixelX) + " - " +
                ➥Format$(Pnode(Index).Top \ PixelY) + " )"
Artwork.DrawStyle = 0: Artwork.DrawMode = Inverse
XX2 = E(0): YY2 = S(0): XX1 = W(0): YY1 = N(0)
'''''''''''''''''''''''''''''''''''''''''''''
r = FirstPolyPt(B) + Index 'Index +1
rr = FirstPolyPt(B) + Index - 1 'Index
rrr = FirstPolyPt(B) + Index - 2 'Index -1
FCP = FirstPolyPt(B) 'First object
LCP = LastPolyPt(B) - 1 'last object
'''''''''''''''''''''''''''''''''''''''''''''
PIL = Pnode(Index).Left + 45
PIT = Pnode(Index).Top + 45
BezErase = False
Select Case CurrentTool 'tools is either Bézier or Line tool
    Case BézierTool
Select Case Index 'Find the object number first
    Case 0
If p1X(FCP) = PIL And p1Y(FCP) = PIT Then B = FCP: Pnode(Index).Tag = "Leftcurve"
If p2X(LCP) = PIL And p2Y(LCP) = PIT Then B = LCP: Pnode(Index).Tag = "Rightcurve"
If p1X(FCP) = PIL And p2X(LCP) = PIL Then B = LCP: Pnode(Index).Tag = "2curves"
    Case Else
If p1X(r) = PIL And p1Y(r) = PIT Then B = r: Pnode(Index).Tag = "Leftcurve"
If p2X(rr) = PIL And p2Y(rr) = PIT Then B = rr: Pnode(Index).Tag = "Rightcurve"
If p1X(r) = PIL And p2X(rr) = PIL Then Pnode(Index).Tag = "2curves"
End Select
Select Case Pnode(Index).Tag
    Case "Leftcurve", "2curves"
 Pnode(Index).Visible = False: PolyCurveNode = True
 BezNode_Down Index, Button, Shift, 1, r, rr, rrr, FCP, LCP, X, Y
 Exit Sub
    Case "Rightcurve"
```

```
    Pnode(Index).Visible = False: PolyCurveNode = True
  BezNode_Down Index, Button, Shift, 2, r, rr, rrr, FCP, LCP, X, Y
  Exit Sub
End Select
If PolyShape(B) = B Then 'set for line move
BezHandleMove Index
Toggle = True: P = 1: Pnode(Index).Visible = False
    X1 = Pnode(Index).Left + 45: Y1 = Pnode(Index).Top + 45
    X2 = X1: Y2 = Y1: Exit Sub
End If
    Case LineTool 'Set start of new line segment
        X1 = Pnode(Index).Left + 45: Y1 = Pnode(Index).Top + 45
        X2 = X1: Y2 = Y1
End Select
End Sub
```

The Pnode image controls are used for edit segments of polyshape objects. A Pnode connects lines or acts as a control point of Bézier curves.

> **If CurrentTool = 3:** This program uses a scaled-down version of polynode editing. It does not enable you to add any additional segments to open or closed polyshapes. You can start a polyline shape in only one direction. For instance, you cannot draw a line and then try to continue a new line segment from the Pnode located on the line's opposite end. You would need additional array shuffling code to perform that.
>
> **XX2 = E(0): YY2 = S(0):** These values are the polyshape's bounding box dimensions and are later used to erase the old image area after a polysegment has been moved.

The following variables tell the routine events what Pnode is connected to a given polysegment shape. Each polysegment within a polyshape is given a number. Each of these individual polysegment's start and end points are indexed according to their (polyshape) numbers.

> **r** = FirstPolyPt(B) + Index  'Index +1
>
> **rr** = FirstPolyPt(B) + Index - 1 'Index
>
> **rrr** = FirstPolyPt(B) + Index - 2 'Index -1
>
> **FCP** = FirstPolyPt(B) 'First object
>
> **LCP** = LastPolyPt(B) - 1 'last object

To save memory, the Pnodes are reloaded for every polyshape you highlight. The Pnode control's index starts at 0 and ends with the last Pnode within the polyshape. You know the number of the Pnode by the index property assigned to it. You also know the start and end polyshape segment numbers that were stored in the variable arrays FirstPolyPt and LastPolyPt when the object was being drawn. By adding or subtracting to these known values, you can find any polysegment's connecting points using r, rr, rrr, FCP, or LCP.

You can put the r, rr, rrr, FCP, and LCP variables in a Declaration or Module file as constants to save space. The r, rr, rrr, FCP, and LCP variables are repeated throughout the Pnode events and several procedures for quick reference.

**PIL and PIT** (PnodeIndex.Left and PnodeIndexTop): The center point of each Pnode. You will compare the Pnode's position with that of the polysegment's indexed X and Y coordinates. If the center point of the Pnode equals the X and Y value of r, rr, rrr, FCP, and LCP, you will have a match. Otherwise, the r, rr, rrr, FCP, and LCP index values will be 0, and the program will skip that line of code.

**If p1X(FCP) = PIL:** Each polycurve has a start (p1.X and p1.Y) and end point (p2.X and p2.Y). If the p1s match, you tag the Pnode with the name Leftcurve; if the p2s match, you tag that Pnode with the name Rightcurve. If the Pnode has two Bézier curves attached, one connection will be a p1 and the other is always a p2; the Pnode would then be tagged as 2curves.

**Select Case (Pnode(Index).Tag:** Depending on what the Pnode's tag name is, do the Case block that matches the Pnode's tag name.

**Case "Leftcurve" , "2curves":** If the Pnode has one of these tags, assign the Pnode a Lever argument value of 1 in the BezNode_Down procedure (Listing 15.5). The Lever value (the third argument) represents one side of the curve that the handle or node is connected to. In upcoming events and procedures, the Lever value will flag which side of the curve is being moved; so one of the dotted lines (the levers) that is connected to a handle and node is placed accordingly.

**Case "Rightcurve":** Changes the third BezNode_Down argument to the value 2. This represents the second dotted line (lever) attached to the opposite handle and node of the Bézier curve.

**If PolyShape(B) = B Then:** The Pnode being moved has one or two lines connected to it and no curves. Use a separate procedure in the Pnode_MouseMove event (Listing 15.18) to move these types of polyline connections.

**BezHandleMove:** Erases and resets dotted lever lines, and relocates the attached handles.

**Toggle = True: P = 1:** The variable Toggle is used as a flag in the Pnode_MouseMove event to trigger the Poly_LineMove procedures that redraw the moving line segments. The P variable is another flag used to loop a drawing routine that must be reset to the value 1 at the start of each move.

**Pnode(Index).Visible:** You hide the Pnode that you are moving so it will not interfere with the drawing of the moving line segments.

**X1, Y1, X2, Y2:** You set the starting positions of the line segments you are about to draw so the illusion of a moving line can be achieved.

**Case LineTool:** If this tool were selected, you would not move a Pnode, but you would draw a new line segment from it. This is similar to how the Join Nodes program (Chapter 13) makes each new line segment of a polyshape object.

**X1, Y1, X2,Y2:** You set the starting positions of the line segments that you are about to draw so you can achieve the illusion of a moving line.

It takes several procedures and events to calculate and draw the polyshape objects attached to a Pnode. Figure 15.12 illustrates the chain of events that occurrs when you move a Pnode to a new coordinate. Listing 15.18 shows how you can reference the each procedure call as you continue on through this chapter.

**F**igure 15.12.
*The procedure chain of* Pnodes.

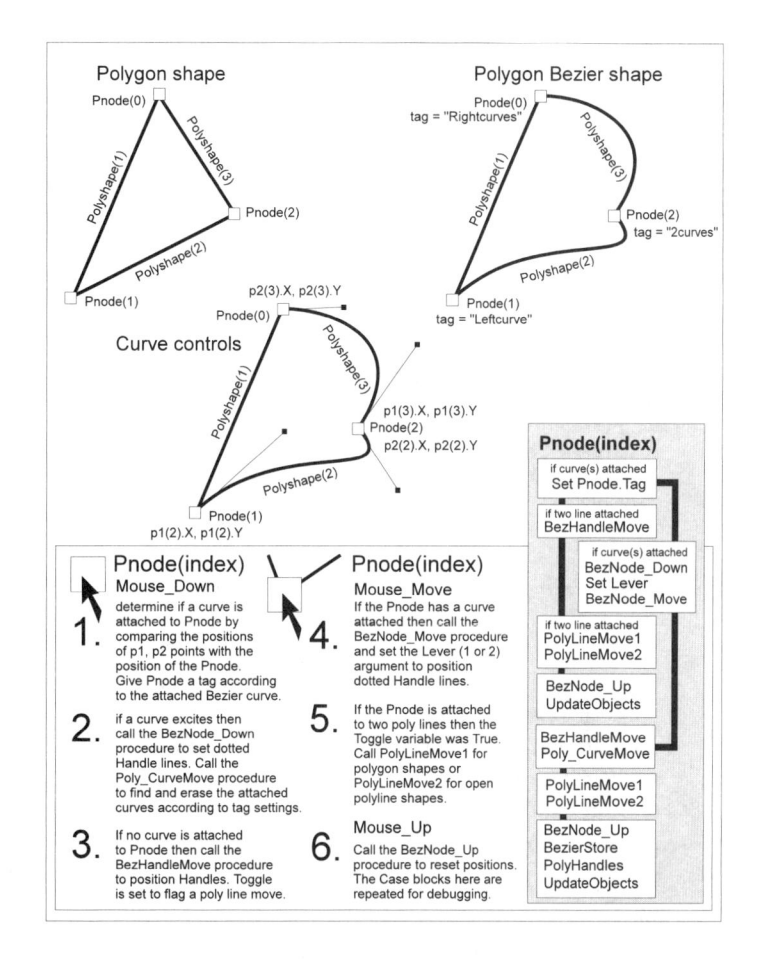

**L**isting 15.18. Moving a poly-segment to new location.

```
Sub Pnode_MouseMove (Index%, Button%, Shift%, X As Single, Y As Single)
PL = (X + Pnode(Index).Left): PT = (Y + Pnode(Index).Top)
Xstr = Format$(PL \ PixelX, "000"): Ystr = Format$(PT \ PixelY, "000")
XYLabel.Caption = "[" + Xstr + " , " + Ystr + "]"
If CurrentTool = 3 And Index < NodeTotal - 1 Then Exit Sub
If CurrentTool = 3 And Index < LastPolyPt(B) Then Exit Sub
''''''''''''''''''''''''''''''''''''''''''''
r = FirstPolyPt(B) + Index   'Index +1
rr = FirstPolyPt(B) + Index - 1  'Index
```

*continues*

## Listing 15.18. continued

```
rrr = FirstPolyPt(B) + Index - 2 'Index -1
FCP = FirstPolyPt(B) 'First object
LCP = LastPolyPt(B) - 1 'last object
'........................................
If Button Then
If CurrentTool <> 1 And Index < NodeTotal - 1 Then Exit Sub
Select Case CurrentTool
    Case BézierTool
If PolyCurveNode = True Then
Select Case Pnode(Index).Tag
    Case "Leftcurve", "2curves"
BezNode_Move Index, Button, Shift, 1, r, rr, rrr, FCP, LCP, X, Y: Exit Sub
    Case "Rightcurve"
BezNode_Move Index, Button, Shift, 2, r, rr, rrr, FCP, LCP, X, Y: Exit Sub
End Select
End If
If Toggle = True And FlagPolyLine(FCP) = FirstPolyPt(B)
        ➥Then Poly_LineMove2 Index, Button, Shift, X, Y: Exit Sub
If Toggle = True And FlagPoly(FCP) = FirstPolyPt(B)
        ➥Then Poly_LineMove1 Index, Button, Shift, X, Y:
Exit Sub
    Case LineTool 'Draw new Line segment
        Artwork.Line (X1, Y1)-(X2, Y2)
            X2 = X + Pnode(Index).Left: Y2 = Y + Pnode(Index).Top
        Artwork.Line (X1, Y1)-(X2, Y2)
End Select
End If
End Sub
```

**PL, PT:** This gives the current X and Y coordinates within each Pnode control.

**If CurrentTool = 3:** This program is not set up to draw additional polylines from a polyshape that has already been set. You also cannot continue a line segment from the opposite end of a polyshape. To achieve this, you would need to add a routine that shuffles the index numbers around to accommodate the new path of Pnodes in the drawing. Additional coding would be necessary for routines that would break a polyshape's path into subpaths or into separate polyobjects.

**r, rr, rrr, FCP, LCP:** Refer to the Pnode_MouseDown event for a description of these variables.

**If Button Then:** Only if the mouse button is held in, continue this procedure.

**If CurrentTool <>1:** This stops you from drawing if the wrong tool is being used.

**Select Case CurrentTool:** Depending on which tool you are using, do the following Case block that matches the tool currently being used:

> **Case BézierTool:** You are about to move a polyshape segment with the Bézier (shape) tool.
>
> **If PolyCurveNode = True Then:** The Pnode_MouseDown procedure made this flag True if the Pnode was connected to one or more Bézier curves.

**Select case Pnode(Index).Tag:** If the `Pnode` has been tagged as `Leftcurve` or `Rightcurve`, you must assign it a `Lever` argument value of 1 in the `BezNode_Move` procedure (Listing 15.6). The `Lever` value (the third argument) represents one side of the curve that a handle or node is connected to. In upcoming events and procedures, the `Lever` value will flag which side of the curve is being moved; so one of the dotted lines (the levers) connecting the handle and node are placed accordingly.

**Case "Rightcurve":** This changes the third `BezNode_Move` argument to the value 2. This represents the second dotted line (lever) attached to the opposite handle and node of the Bézier curve.

**If Toggle = True:** The `FlagPolyLine` variable tells the program that the object is an open polyshape. An open polyshape occurs when the start and end points do not connect (as they do in the W character).

**If Toggle = True:** The `FlagPoly` variable tells the program that the object is a closed polyshape. A closed polyshape occurs when the start and end points are connected (as in a triangular shape).

Use the `Poly_LineMove2` (see the ARTAPI1.FRM source code) and `PolyLineMove1` procedures to draw the moving lines of an open or closed polyobject. These procedures are similar to each other except for a few lines of code that prohibit the drawing of a closing line segment on an open polyshape. You may want to combine these two procedures into one by adding additional code in order to accomplish both tasks.

**Poly_LineMove2:** Draws the line segments of an open polyshape.

**Poly_LineMove1:** Draws the line segments of a closed polyshape.

**Case LineTool:** If you are using the line drawing tool, do the following block of code statements.

You are using the `LineTool` to draw a new line segment from the current `Pnode` control:

**ArtWork.Line:** Draws the new line segment.

**X2, Y2:** Reverses the start and end points for the illusion of movement.

**ArtWork.Line:** Redraws the line to erase the old image.

The `Pnode_MouseUp` event in Listing 15.20 does a general clean-up after the `Pnode` is moved to a new coordinate. The `BezNode_Up` procedure is called and will store all new coordinate points. Then the `Pnode`'s tag name is deleted, and variable flags are reset to their original values.

**Listing 15.20. Setting the new coordinates of a moved polyshape.**

```
Sub Pnode_MouseUp (Index%, Button%, Shift%, X As Single, Y As Single)
If CurrentTool = 3 And Index < NodeTotal - 1 Then Exit Sub
If CurrentTool = 3 And Index < LastPolyPt(B) Then Exit Sub
'''''''''''''''''''''''''''''''''''''''''
r = FirstPolyPt(B) + Index    'Index +1
rr = FirstPolyPt(B) + Index - 1  'Index
rrr = FirstPolyPt(B) + Index - 2 'Index -1
```

*continues*

# ArtAPI

**Listing 15.20. continued.**

```
FCP = FirstPolyPt(B) 'First object
LCP = LastPolyPt(B) - 1 'last object
'''''''''''''''''''''''''''''''''''''''''''''
Select Case CurrentTool
    Case BézierTool
If PolyCurveNode = True Then
    Select Case Pnode(Index).Tag
    Case "Leftcurve", "2curves"
        BezNode_Up Index, Button, Shift, 1, X, Y
        PolyCurveNode = False: Pnode(Index).Visible = True
        Pnode(Index).Tag = "": Exit Sub
    Case "Rightcurve"
        BezNode_Up Index, Button, Shift, 1, X, Y
        PolyCurveNode = False: Pnode(Index).Visible = True
        Pnode(Index).Tag = "": Exit Sub
    End Select
End If
If Toggle = True Then Poly_Update Index, Button, Shift, X, Y: Exit Sub
    Case LineTool 'set new line segments
        Poly_gon Index
End Select
End Sub
```

**If CurrentTool = 3:** This program is not set up to draw additional polylines from a polyshape that has already been set. You are also not allowed to continue a line segment from the opposite end of a polyshape.

**r, rr, rrr, FCP, LCP:** Refer to the Pnode_MouseDown event for a description of these variables.

**Select Case CurrentTool:** Depending on which tool you are using, do the following Case block that matches the tool's name currently been used:

**Case BézierTool:** You are using the Bézier (shape) tool.

**If PolyCurveNode = True Then:** The Pnode_MouseDown procedure made this flag True if the Pnode was connected to one or more Bézier curves.

**Select case Pnode(Index).Tag:** If the Pnode has one of the Select Case Tags, you must assign it a Lever argument value of 1 in the BezNode_Up procedure (Listing 15.7). The Lever value (the third argument) represents one side of the curve that a handle or node is connected to. In upcoming events and procedures, the Lever value will flag which side of the curve is being moved; so one of the dotted lines (levers) connecting the handle and node is placed accordingly.

**Case "Rightcurve":** Changes the third BezNode_Up argument to the value 2. This represents the second dotted line (lever) attached to the opposite handle and node of the Bézier curve.

**If Toggle = True:** The Pnode is connected to polyline segments, not curves. The Poly_Update procedure resets the current Pnode's X and Y coordinates and values.

**Case LineTool:** You are using the line drawing tool to add new line segments.

**Poly_gon Index:** This procedure adds the Pnodes to the new polyobject once it is completed. If the last polyline segment is near the first line segment of the object, the lines will snap together to form a polygon shape.

> **NOTE**
>
> There are 12 polyshape procedures in the ArtAPI program. Most of these procedures could be grouped by adding If/Then or Choose statements to combine similar procedures together. The Poly_CurveMove1 and Poly_CurveMove2, as well as the PolyLineMove1 and PolyLineMove2 procedures are examples of routines that can be combined as single procedures. These procedures are separated to demonstrate separate polyline and polygon drawing routines.
>
> The Poly_gon, Poly_Lines, and Poly_Update procedures deal draw the object while the Poly_Nodes and Poly_Reload perform the duties of positioning the Pnodes within the polyshape.
>
> The following list shows related procedures that are branched off from the Pnode image control:
>
> Moving a Pnode with a curve attached to a polygon: Poly_CurveMove1.
>
> Moving a Pnode with a curve attached to a polyline: Poly_CurveMove2.
>
> Moving a Pnode with a line attached to a polygon: Poly_LineMove1 .
>
> Moving a Pnode with a line attached to a polyline: Poly_LineMove2 (see the ARTAPI1.FRM source code).
>
> Drawing the finished polyshape: Poly_gon (Listing 15.24), Poly_Lines (Listing 15.25), Poly_Curves (Listing 15.23), and Poly_Update (Listing 15.29).
>
> Adding or reloading Pnodes onto the polyshape: Poly_Nodes (Listing 15.27) and Poly_Reload (Listing 15.28).
>
> Calculating the polyshape's bounding box and resizing features: Poly_Handles (Listing 15.13) and Poly_Stretch (Listing 15.30).

## Editing a Curve on a Polyshape

The Poly_CurveMove1 procedure in Listing 15.21 draws the curve segments attached to the Pnode while the segments are being moved. This routine is used for moving closed polyshape objects and is divided into three primary sections. This should give you a a better understanding of how the Poly_CurveMove1 procedure works.

# ArtAPI

**Listing 15.21.** Drawing movable curves attached to closed polyshapes.

```
Sub Poly_CurveMove1 (Index%, Button%, Shift%, Lever%, X!, Y!)
r = FirstPolyPt(B) + Index 'Index +1
rr = FirstPolyPt(B) + Index - 1 'Index
rrr = FirstPolyPt(B) + Index - 2 'Index -1
FCP = FirstPolyPt(B) 'First object
LCP = LastPolyPt(B) - 1 'last object
LastIndex = (LastPolyPt(B) - FirstPolyPt(B)) - 1
''''''''''''''''''''''''''''''''''''''''''''''''''
Select Case Pnode(Index).Tag
    Case "Leftcurve"
If Index = 0 Then BB = FCP: ii = LastIndex: PT = FCP: Z = 1
If Index > 0 Then BB = rrr: ii = Index - 1: PT = r
    Case "Rightcurve"
If Index = 0 Then BB = LCP: ii = Index + 1: PT = LCP
If Index > 0 Then BB = rr: ii = Index + 1: PT = rr
If Index = LastIndex Then BB = rr: ii = 0: PT = rr
    Case "2curves"
If Index = 0 Then BB = LCP: PT = LCP: Lever = 2
If Index > 0 Then BB = rr: PT = rr: Lever = 2
End Select
```

> **NOTE** This code listing continues after the following explanation of the first section of the `PolyCurveMove1` procedure.

The following variables tell the events what Pnode is connected to a given polyshape. Each polyobject within a polyshape is assigned a number. Each of these individual polyshape's start and end points are indexed according to their polyshape number.

**r** = FirstPolyPt(B) + Index 'Index +1

**rr** = FirstPolyPt(B) + Index - 1 'Index

**rrr** = FirstPolyPt(B) + Index - 2 'Index -1

**FCP** = FirstPolyPt(B) 'First object

**LCP** = LastPolyPt(B) - 1 'last object

**Select Case Pnode(Index).Tag:** Depends on which side the curve is attached to the Pnode.

**Case "Leftcurve"**: **"Rightcurve"** : **"2curves"**: The value BB represents the index number of a Bézier curve's starting point, if one exists.

The value ii represents the index number of a line segment's starting point, if one exists.

The value PT represents the index number of the four Bézier curves' control points.

When the Pnode has 2curves attached, both Levers are used to draw each of the curves.

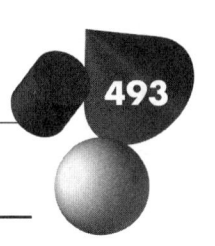

**Listing 15.21.** Drawing movable curves, continued.

```
If CountPolyPts = 1 Then 'calculate the number of PolyPts
    Artwork.DrawMode = 6: Artwork.DrawStyle = 0
If Z = 1 Then fp = 0 Else fp = 1
    API = Polyline(Artwork.hDC, Npt(fp), PolyPts)'draw shape first
End If
i = 1
''''''''''''''''''''
For DrawShape = 1 To 2
If BB = FlagBézier(B + NC) And BB = PolyShape(B + NC) Then
Select Case Lever
    Case 1 'BezNode1
  p1.X = X + Pnode(Index).Left: p1.Y = Y + Pnode(Index).Top
  p2.X = p2X(PT): p2.Y = p2Y(PT)
  h1.X = h1X(PT): h1.Y = h1Y(PT)
  h2.X = h2X(PT): h2.Y = h2Y(PT)
  Poly_curves i
    Case 2 'BezNode2
  p2.X = X + Pnode(Index).Left: p2.Y = Y + Pnode(Index).Top
  p1.X = p1X(PT): p1.Y = p1Y(PT)
  h1.X = h1X(PT): h1.Y = h1Y(PT)
  h2.X = h2X(PT): h2.Y = h2Y(PT)
  Poly_curves i
End Select
'''''''''''''''''''''''''''''''''''''''''''''''''''''''''''
Else 'Draw a line
    Npt(i).X = (Pnode(ii).Left + 45) \ PixelX
    Npt(i).Y = (Pnode(ii).Top + 45) \ PixelY: i = i + 1
End If
''''''''''''
If Z = 1 Then
    Npt(0).X = (Pnode(LastIndex).Left + 45) \ PixelX
    Npt(0).Y = (Pnode(LastIndex).Top + 45) \ PixelY: i = i - 1
End If
BB = BB + 2
If Pnode(Index).Tag = "2curves" Then Lever = 1:
                ↪BB = BB - 1: NC = 1: PT = PT + 1
If Pnode(Index).Tag = "2curves" And Index = 0 Then
    Lever = 1: BB = FCP: NC = -LastIndex: PT = FCP
End If
Next DrawShape
```

> **NOTE** This code listing continues after the following text.

The second part of Listing 15.21 calculates the number of `PolyPts` to send to the API `Polyline` function, so the procedure will draw only the two segments you are moving— not the whole polyobject.

You should draw only the two segments that are connected to the Pnode you are moving. First, calculate the number of index points from the arrays in which all points are stored.

The following procedure statements are descriptions for the second section of the Poly_CurveMove1 procedure in Listing 15.21:

**If CountPolyPts = 1 Then:** The CountPolyPts variable equals 0 at the beginning of each movement. You don't know how many PolyPts to feed the API Polyline function until you look at each segment attached to the Pnode. The procedure skips this If/Then block routine until the second mouse move call is sent.

**API = Polyline:** This draws the first two segments after the PolyPts are calculated.

The next group of procedure statements calculate the number of PolyPts to add to the Npt array:

**For DrawShape = 1 to 2:** You have to loop twice to find both segments connected to the Pnode control.

**If BB = FlagBézier(B + NC):** If the first segment is a Bézier curve, you grab each of the correct curve points and store them in the Npt array. The B variable equals the first curve attached to the Pnode. If a Bézier curve is the second curve attached to the Pnode, NC (the next curve) will equal 1 on the second loop.

**Select Case Lever:** The Lever (1 or 2) was set in the Pnode event. Remember that a Bézier curve is divided in half and is controlled by a handle and node on either side (p1,h1 and p2,h2).

**Case 1:** This is similar to the routine used in the BezNode1 events of the Artisan program in Chapter 3. The p1.X and p1.Y control points are moved along the mouse's dragging path. The three other Bézier control points are grabbed from the array in which they're stored and then passed to the Poly_curves procedure that uses the *de Casteljau* division formula to make the Bézier curve.

**Poly_curves I:** All curve points are stored in the Npt array when in the Poly_curves procedure. The arguments I keep track of each array index placement for the API polyline's Npt array.

**Case 2:** This is similar to the routine used in the BezNode2 events of the Artisan program (Chapter 3) and is basically the same as Case 1, except that you use the curve's left-side coordinates.

**Else:** If the polysegment is not a curve, it has to be a line. The procedure will then execute the following block of Else/Then code statements.

**Npt(i).X = (Pnode(ii).Left +45):** Draws a line from the present Pnode(i) to the next Pnode(ii).

**BB = BB +2:** If a line segment connects to a curve, BB will equal the FlagBézier value on the second pass. This will process the connecting Bézier curve.

**If Pnode(Index).Tag = "2curves" Then:** The procedure has to draw to another curve if the Pnode has two curves attached. This changes all the current values that point to the first curve so that they now point at the second curve.

**If Pnode(Index).Tag = "2curves" And Index = 0 Then:** A special case is needed for the first Pnode in the polyshape. You change all the values to look for the last curve segment in the polyshape.

**Next DrawShape:** Goes back to the For DrawShape statement and calculates the other PolyPts for the second polysegment attached to the Pnode control.

**Listing 15.21. continued.**
```
PolyPts = i - 1
If CountPolyPts = 0 Then
    CountPolyPts = 1
    Artwork.AutoRedraw = True
Artwork.DrawMode = 16: Artwork.DrawWidth = 4: Artwork.DrawStyle = 0
If Z = 1 Then fp = 0 Else fp = 1
    Artwork.AutoRedraw = False
    API = Polyline(Artwork.hDC, Npt(fp), PolyPts)
    Artwork.DrawMode = 6: Artwork.DrawWidth = 1
End If
If Z = 1 Then fp = 0 Else fp = 1
    API = Polyline(Artwork.hDC, Npt(fp), PolyPts)    'redraw shape
End Sub
```

The third and final section of the Poly_CurveMove1 procedure erases the old poly-shape image that is on the screen. It does this only once (at the beginning of the move) and then skips to the last two code statements and actually starts drawing the two polysegments being moved.

**PolyPts = i - 1:** The total number of PolyPts to send to the API Polyline function that makes up the two poly-segments to draw.

**If CounterPolyPts = 0 Then:** This is the first pass of the MouseMove event, so you need to erase the old polyshape image.

**CountPolyPts = 1:** You make CountPolyPts equal to 1; so this block of image-erasing statements is not repeated. For each additional mouse move, the very first API Polyline statement at the start of this procedure will be triggered to work. This finally gives you the two drawing calls that can erase and draw the polyshape while in Inverse drawing mode. The second recursive API Polyline call is located at the bottom of this procedure.

**ArtWork.AutoRedraw = True:** You must erase the image from the memory bitmap. This is a good trick that will not slow down your program when changing AutoRedraw properties. First, set the DrawMode property to 16 (white) and then set AutoRedraw back to False before you start the drawing. By the time the memory bitmap gets the message, you'll be ahead of the procedure and the image will be updated during a MouseMove pause. If you placed a graphical statement between the AutoRedraw = True and AutoRedraw = False, statements, the image would be updated immediately. This freezes all events until the image is processed and causes the next image to jump.

**If Z = 1 Then fp = 0 Else fp = 1:** Pnode(0), which connects the first and last segments together, needs a special case. The Polyline function draws in one continuous line; so you need to reserve the first index of Npt for the last polysegment to draw first. The fp variable is an acronym for First Point.

**API = Polyline:** Draws the polyshape segments in white to erase the old image.

**If Z = 1 Then fp = 0 Else fp = 1:** The fp variable is an acronym for First Point, which the procedure looks at to initiate the first drawing point of the polyshape.

**API = Polyline:** The last API graphics function that redraws the segments constantly in Inverse mode.

Since the Poly_CurveMove2 procedure in Listing 15.24 uses a routine similar to the Poly_CurveMove1 procedure, only the code section (which is different) is listed here.

**Listing 15.22. Drawing movable curves attached to open polyshapes.**

```
Sub Poly_CurveMove2 (Index%, Button%, Shift%, Lever%, X!, Y!)
'Poly_CurveMove2 uses a routine similar to Poly_CurveMove1 (listing 15.20).
'Only the code lines which are different are listed in the preceding.
Else 'Draw a line
Select Case Index
    Case 0, LastIndex
    Case Else
        Npt(i).X = (Pnode(ii).Left + 45) \ PixelX
        Npt(i).Y = (Pnode(ii).Top + 45) \ PixelY: i = i + 1
    End Select
End If
BB = BB + 2
If Pnode(Index).Tag = "2curves" Then Lever = 1: BB = BB - 1:
            ↪NC = 1: PT = PT + 1
If Pnode(Index).Tag = "2curves" And Index = 0 Then
    Lever = 1: BB = FCP: NC = -LastIndex: PT = FCP
End If
Next DrawShape
''''''''''''''
PolyPts = i - 1
If CountPolyPts = 0 Then
    CountPolyPts = 1
    Artwork.AutoRedraw = True
    Artwork.DrawMode = 16: Artwork.DrawWidth = 4: Artwork.DrawStyle = 0
    Artwork.AutoRedraw = False
    API = Polyline(Artwork.hDC, Npt(1), PolyPts)
    Artwork.DrawMode = 6: Artwork.DrawWidth = 1
End If
    API = Polyline(Artwork.hDC, Npt(1), PolyPts) 'redraw shape
End Sub
```

The Poly_CurveMove2 procedure is almost identical to the Poly_CurveMove1 procedure. The difference is in the way it draws the first and last polysegments when using Pnode(0) or the last node, Pnode(LastIndex).

You also must change the three API Polyline functions to start the drawing with an index 1 of array Npt. This eliminates the If Z = 1 Then fp = 0 Else fp = 1 statement found in the Poly_CurveMove1 procedure.

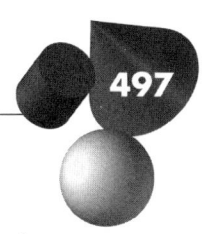

## Drawing each Curve on a Polyshape

The `Poly_curves` procedure's *de Casteljau* dividing formula is omitted to save space. This formula can be viewed in Chapter 3, "Bézier Curves."

The *de Casteljau* algorithm plots the 33 curve points that make up a Bézier curve. The `Poly_curves` procedure then takes these 33 plotted points, which have been stored in array `C1(1 to 33)`, and draws the Bézier curve on `Artwork` picture box desktop, `ArtMask` picture box, or to the printer. Each of the three devices use a completely different internal scale so each device has its own drawing routine.

If you are using a Windows 32-bit operating system, you can replace most of the code lines in Listing 15.23 with the GUI32 API `PolyBézier` and `PolyBézierTo` functions.

Listing 15.23. The *de Casteljau* dividing formula for Bézier curves.

```
Sub Poly_curves (i As Integer)
' the dividing algorithm has been omitted to save space
' refer to the source code or Chapter 2 - Bézier curves.
If FlagPrinter = True Then GoTo Printcurve
If FlagArtMask = True Then GoTo ArtMaskcurve
Npt(I).X = p1.X \ PixelX: Npt(I).Y = p1.Y \ PixelY
    For P = 2 To 32
        Npt(P + I - 1).X = C1(P).X \ PixelX
        Npt(P + I - 1).Y = C1(P).Y \ PixelY
    Next P
Npt(33 + I - 1).X = p2.X \ PixelX
Npt(33 + I - 1).Y = p2.Y \ PixelY
I = I + 33
Exit Sub
'''''''''''''''''''''''''''''''''''''''''
Printcurve:
Dim RightM As Single
Dim BottomM As Single
LeftM = PageX1: TopM = PageY1 'Adjust Margins
APIH = GetDeviceCaps(Printer.hDC, 8)
APIV = GetDeviceCaps(Printer.hDC, 10)
HPrinterDPI! = APIH / (PageX2 - PageX1)
VPrinterDPI! = APIV / (PageY2 - PageY1)
RightM = HPrinterDPI!    'Adjust Scale size
BottomM = VPrinterDPI!
Npt(I).X = (p1.X - LeftM) * RightM: Npt(I).Y = (p1.Y - TopM) * BottomM
    For P = 2 To 32
        Npt(P + I - 1).X = (C1(P).X - LeftM) * RightM
        Npt(P + I - 1).Y = (C1(P).Y - TopM) * BottomM
    Next P
Npt(33 + I - 1).X = (p2.X - LeftM) * RightM
Npt(33 + I - 1).Y = (p2.Y - TopM) * BottomM
I = I + 33
Exit Sub
'''''''''''''''''''''''''''''''''''''''''
ArtMaskcurve:
Npt(I).X = (p1.X - ArtMask.Left) \ PixelX
```

*continues*

# ArtAPI

### Listing 15.23. continued

```
        Npt(I).Y = (p1.Y - ArtMask.Top) \ PixelY
        For P = 2 To 32
            Npt(P + I - 1).X = (C1(P).X - ArtMask.Left) \ PixelX
            Npt(P + I - 1).Y = (C1(P).Y - ArtMask.Top) \ PixelY
        Next P
    Npt(33 + I - 1).X = (p2.X - ArtMask.Left) \ PixelX
    Npt(33 + I - 1).Y = (p2.Y - ArtMask.Top) \ PixelY
    I = I + 33
    Exit Sub
End Sub
```

> **If Flagprinter:** You are sending the curve to be drawn on the printer's page.
>
> **If FlagArtMask:** You have touched a curve segment with the mouse pointer.

The curve's plot points are stored in array C1 and are then assigned to the Npt (next point) array so the API Polyline or Polygon functions can draw the curve. Chapter 3 has a full description on how curve points are plotted.

There are three devices on which to draw the Bézier curves. The device you need to draw into can be either one of the two Visual Basic picture box controls (Artwork and ArtMask) or the Printer.

The Artwork picture box control represents the desktop. You need to convert the X and Y coordinates from twip measurements to pixel units in order to draw into this device.

The other picture box control to draw into is called ArtMask, which is hidden and acts as a memory bitmap image of individual objects and segments of polyshapes. The dimensions of the ArtMask control are resized every time you touch an object or segment of a polyshape with the mouse pointer. The ArtMask picture box's purpose is to find the outline of the object so you can select or move the polyshape. Every time the ArtMask picture box control is resized, the interior twip scale always starts at the 0,0 coordinate of the upper-left corner. To draw the curve, you need to subtract the ArtMask picture box's Left value position and Top value position with the corresponding X and Y coordinates of the curve's plotted points.

Another device onto which you can draw a curve is a printer. A printer's internal page size is different from manufacturer to manufacturer, so the values used might have to be adjusted to suit your model. You can use the APIprint program in Chapter 14 to test manual and API printing methods and functions.

To place the curve on the printer's page, adjust the margin differences. Artwork's desktop page is placed halfway from the Left and Top property values of the control. The printer's page starts at the 0,0 coordinates of the defined page. Then, multiply by a scaling factor to compensate for the printer's internal dots-per-inch (DPI) scale mode.

The following code statements from the Poly_Curves procedure correctly place points of a Bézier curve onto a printer's page:

**APIH = GetDeviceCaps(Printer.hDC, 8):** Retrieves the horizontal resolution (in pixel units) of the printer.

**APIV = GetDeviceCaps(Printer.hDC, 10):** Retrieves the vertical resolution (in pixel units) of the printer.

**HPrinterDPI! = APIH / (PageX2 - PageX1):** Calculates the difference between the printer's page width and the horizontal area of the Artwork picture box control that you want to print. PageX1 and PageX2 represent the width of the page image drawn on the desktop in the UpdateDesktop procedure. (See the ARTAPI1.FRM source code.)

**VPrinterDPI! = APIV / (PageY2 - PageY1):** Calculates the difference between the printer's page height and the vertical area of the Artwork picture box control that you want to print. PageY1 and PageY2 represent the height of the page image drawn on the desktop in the UpdateDesktop procedure. (See the ARTAPI.FRM source code.)

**RightM = HPrinterDPI!    'Adjust Scale size:** Adding or subtracting percentages from these values scales the objects being printed to the page.

**BottomM = VPrinterDPI!:** Adding or subtracting percentages from these values scales the objects being printed to the page.

## Closing a Polygon Shape

The Poly_gon procedure in Listing 15.26 adds additional nodes to the line segments you are currently drawing. If the line segment you are dragging comes within eight pixel units of the first Pnode in the polyshape, the two Pnodes will snap together and form a polygon shape.

**Listing 15.24.** Adding Pnodes to new polysegments or closing a polygon.

```
Sub Poly_gon (Index)
If Counter = 1 Then FlagLine(B) = 0: ZZ = B: PolyShape(B) = ZZ:
            ↪FirstPolyPt(B) = ZZ: Snap = 120
If X2 > Node(0).Left - Snap And X2 < Node(0).Left + 90 + Snap And
        ↪Y2 > Node(0).Top - Snap And Y2 < Node(0).Top + 90 + Snap Then
 Total = Total + 1: B = Total : DrawOrder(B) = Total
 FlagLine(B) = 0: PolyShape(B) = B: FirstPolyPt(B) = ZZ: FlagPoly(ZZ) = ZZ
 W(B) = X1: E(B) = X2: N(B) = Y1: S(B) = Y2
 LineWidth(B) = Artwork.DrawWidth
    E(B) = Node(0).Left + 45: S(B) = Node(0).Top + 45
    NodeTotal = 2: PolyClose = False
    For r = FirstPolyPt(B) To B + 1
        LastPolyPt(r) = B + 1
    Next r
    FillValue(B) = 1
    UpdateObjects
    Exit Sub
Else
    PolyClose = True
    Poly_Nodes Index 'Load new nodes
End If
End Sub
```

**If Counter = 1:** The counter represents each Pnode that is added to an object. The first node's coordinates are needed to pass to the API Polyline or Polygon functions as the starting point to which to draw the object.

**FlagLine(B) = 0:** The original line object is now a polyline segment, so erase the index flag.

**ZZ = B:** You temporarily store the first polyline segment number in the ZZ variable. As each new line segment is added, ZZ is increased until the last line segment is connected to the first line segment to form a polygon shape.

**PolyShape(B) = ZZ:** The original line object is now a polyshape object, so store the index.

**FlagPoly = ZZ:** You store the type of object that you are drawing so the UpDateObject procedure (Listing 15.33) knows what type of drawing action to take.

**FirstPolyPt(B) = ZZ:** Tag the first line segment (first Pnode) so you can find all points in between the first and last Pnode on the polyshape.

**Snap = 120:** You can make the last line segment's node snap to the first line segment's node by stating the maximum twip distance that the two nodes must be from each other before they can snap together. At present, the snap is set at 120 twips, or 8 pixels, in any direction. Change this number to suit your needs.

**If X1 > Node(0).Let Snap And X2 <(0).Left + 90 + Snap And etc., etc., :** This is the formula for calculating the distance for both nodes in order for them to snap together.

**Total = Total +1: B = Total:** You added a new segment, so increase the total number of objects by 1.

**FlagLine(B) = 0:** This sets all the values for the last line segment after the snap forms a polygon.

**W(B) = X1:** Stores the bounding box positions of the line segment.

**LineWidth(B) = ArtWork.DrawWidth:** Stores the current width of the line segment.

**E(B) = Node(0).Left + 45: S(B) = Node(0).Top + 45:** The E(B) and S(B) values equal the last line segment's end coordinates. You connect these to the first node of the original line that you started with.

**NodeTotal = 2:** Resets the number of nodes to a default of 2.

**PolyClose:** This flag tells the program that the polygon is completed.

**For R = FirstPolyPt(B) To B + 1:** You assign every polyshape segment the index value of the last polypoint in the polygon. This way, you can determine what any shape's last point is.

**LastPolyPts(r) = B + 1:** This statement reflects the last point in this shape; so you can pass it to the API Polygon function.

**Fillvalue(B) = 1:** The shape is transparent until you fill it in with a color. The Fillvalue variable flags the FillStyle to 1 (transparent) when the polyshape is redrawn in the UpdateObject procedure.

**UpdateObjects:** Redraws all the objects that appear on the desktop.

**Else:** You are still adding new line segments to the polyshape; so don't close the polyshape.

**PolyClose:** The object is still an open polyshape, so keep this flag set to `True`.

**Poly_Nodes:** The shape is still being drawn, so add another `Pnode` to the new line segment.

## Drawing a Polyline Shape

The `Poly_Lines` procedure sets final values needed to draw an open polyshape. This procedure is executed in either the `Artwork MouseDown` (Listing 15.3) or the `Artwork Lost_Focus` event (see ARTAPI.FRM source code) and draws the polyshape if the user clicks the mouse on the desktop or selects another program control (such as a toolbar or color palette). A polyobject always begins as an open polyshape. If you connect the last `Pnode` to the first, the object automatically closes as a polygon shape. If, while drawing each line segment of the open polyshape, you change the focus to another task, the `Poly_Lines` procedure in Listing 15.25 unloads the current `Pnodes` and sets the shape in its present `Polyline` form.

**Listing 15.25. Setting an open polyline shape and unloading the** `Pnodes`.

```
Sub Poly_Lines ()
    FlagPolyLine(ZZ) = ZZ
    On Error GoTo No_Node:
For r = 1 To NodeTotal - 1
    If NodeTotal > 0 Then Unload Pnode(r)
Next r
No_Node: Resume Next
NodeTotal = 2
    For R = FirstPolyPt(B) To B + 1
        LastPolyPt(r) = B + 1
    Next R
    FillValue(B) = 1
    UpdateObjects
End Sub
```

**FlagPolyLine(ZZ) = ZZ:** The object (by default) is an open polyline shape. The ZZ variable holds the first segment's assigned number, which will be added to the `FlagPolyLine` index, so the `UpdateObjects` procedure (Listing 15.33) can then draw the shape using the open `Polyline` drawing routine.

**On Error GoTo No_Node:** Occasionally, unloading and loading nodes get mixed up. To safeguard from an "Index already exists" or "Index does not exist" error message, skip the `Unload` statement when the error occurs.

**For R = 1 To NodeTotal - 1:** Starting at `Pnode(1)` and continuing up until the last `Pnode` index, do the following block of `For/Next` statements.

# ArtAPI

> **CAUTION:** Never unload the original Pnode control, which is indexed as Pnode(0). You must always have one of these image controls on your form in order to duplicate (Load) it.

**If NodeTotal > 0 Then Unload Pnode(r):** unload the Pnodes from the poly-shape.

**No_Node: Resume Next:** If an error occurred, the procedure jumps to this code line.

**NodeTotal = 2:** Resets the default value of total nodes when starting a new line.

**For r = FirstPolyPt(B) To B + 1:** Starting at the first segment and continuing up to the last, do the following block of For/Next code statements:

**LastPolyPt(r) = B + 1:** Assigns the last segment point index to every segment in the polyshape.

**FillValue(B) = 1:** Gives each segment a transparent fill so no color is applied.

**UpdateObjects:** Redraws all the objects on the desktop.

## Editing a Polyline Shape

Use the Poly_LineMove1 procedure in Listing 15.26 to move two connecting line segments that are attached to a Pnode control on a closed polyshape. The Poly_LineMove2 procedure (see the ARTAPI.FRM source code) is similar but is used for moving two line segments on an open polyshape. You may want to add additional code to combine the two into one procedure.

**Listing 15.26. Moving two polyline segments to a new location.**

```
Sub Poly_LineMove1 (Index%, Button%, Shift As Integer, X As Single, Y As Single)
If Button Then
        LastIndex = (LastPolyPt(B) - FirstPolyPt(B)) - 1
        r = FirstPolyPt(B) + Index - 1
        rr = FirstPolyPt(B) + Index + 1
        If rr > LastIndex Then rr = FirstPolyPt(B)  ' Last node point
    If Index = 0 Then r = FirstPolyPt(B) + 1: rr = LastPolyPt(B) - 1

Select Case Index
    Case 0
 X1 = Pnode(LastIndex).Left + 45: Y1 = Pnode(LastIndex).Top + 45
 X3 = Pnode(Index + 1).Left + 45: Y3 = Pnode(Index + 1).Top + 45
    Case LastIndex
 X1 = Pnode(Index - 1).Left + 45: Y1 = Pnode(Index - 1).Top + 45
 X3 = Pnode(0).Left + 45: Y3 = Pnode(0).Top + 45
    Case Else
 X1 = Pnode(Index - 1).Left + 45: Y1 = Pnode(Index - 1).Top + 45
 X3 = Pnode(Index + 1).Left + 45: Y3 = Pnode(Index + 1).Top + 45
End Select
'Erase in whiteness mode
If P = 1 Then    Artwork.AutoRedraw = True: Artwork.DrawMode = 16
    Artwork.DrawWidth = 2 :
```

```
Artwork.AutoRedraw = False
        Artwork.Line (X1, Y1)-(X2, Y2): Artwork.Line -(X3, Y3)
        Artwork.Line (X2 - 45, Y2 - 45)-(X2 + 45, Y2 + 45), , B
        Artwork.DrawMode = 6: Artwork.DrawWidth = 1: P = 0
        Artwork.Line (X1, Y1)-(X2, Y2): Artwork.Line -(X3, Y3)
        Artwork.Line (X2 - 45, Y2 - 45)-(X2 + 45, Y2 + 45), , B
End If
'Draw in inverse mode
Artwork.Line (X1, Y1)-(X2, Y2): Artwork.Line -(X3, Y3)
Artwork.Line (X2 - 45, Y2 - 45)-(X2 + 45, Y2 + 45), , B
    X2 = X + Pnode(Index).Left
    Y2 = Y + Pnode(Index).Top
Artwork.Line (X1, Y1)-(X2, Y2): Artwork.Line -(X3, Y3)
Artwork.Line (X2 - 45, Y2 - 45)-(X2 + 45, Y2 + 45), , B

If Index = 0 Then
  W(r - 1) = X + Pnode(Index).Left: N(r - 1) = Y + Pnode(Index).Top
  E(rr) = X + Pnode(Index).Left: S(rr) = Y + Pnode(Index).Top
Else
  W(r + 1) = X + Pnode(Index).Left: N(r + 1) = Y + Pnode(Index).Top
  E(r) = X + Pnode(Index).Left: S(r) = Y + Pnode(Index).Top
End IfEnd If
End Sub
```

**If Button Then:** If the mouse button is held in, continue.

**LastIndex = (LastPolyPT(B) - FirstPolyPt(B)) - 1:** By subtracting the last segment's number from the first segment's assigned number, you will get the correct index value of the last Pnode in the chain.

**r = :** The Pnode that is to the left of the Pnode you are moving.

**rr = :** The Pnode that is to the right of the Pnode you are moving.

**If rr > LastIndex Then:** A special case is needed for the last Pnode in the polyshape chain. When moving a Pnode in this procedure, you need to have a line segment connected to a Pnode on either side of the control. The last Pnode in the chain would have the last line segment connected to the first Pnode, which is indexed as 0. Change the rr variable to point to the first polypoint segment.

**If Index = 0 Then:** A special case is also needed for the first Pnode in the polyshape chain. The first Pnode needs the last line segment connected to the last Pnode.

**Select Case Index:** Depending on the index number of the Pnode, do the Case block that matches the Pnode's index number.

**Case 0:** You are dragging Pnode (0).

**X1 = Pnode(LastIndex).Left + 45:** Connects and draws a line to the last Pnode.

**X3 = Pnode (Index + 1).Left + 45:** Connects and draws a line to Pnode(1).

**Case LastIndex:** You are dragging the last Pnode in the polyshape chain.

**X1 = Pnode(Index - 1).Left + 45:** Connects and draws a line to the preceding Pnode.

**X3 = Pnode(0).Left + 45:** Connects and draws a line to Pnode(0).

**Case Else:** You are dragging a `Pnode` between `Pnode(0)` and the last `Pnode`.

**X1 = Pnode(Index - 1).Left + 45:** Connects and draws a line to the left of the `Pnode`.

**X3 = Pnode(Index + 1).Left + 45:** Connects and draws a line to the right of the `Pnode`.

The following If/Then statement will only be executed once to erase the two old line segment images for the bitmap memory image.

**If P = 1 Then:** The first call by the `MouseMove` event triggers the following block of If/Then code statements.

**ArtWork.AutoRedraw:** This is a trick used to stop screen flashes and image jumps when using the `AutoRedraw` property. Turn the `AutoRedraw` on so it will point to the memory bitmap image of your picture box control. Set the `DrawMode` to 16 (white) and then turn the `AutoRedraw` off so you can draw directly into the picture box control.

**ArtWork.Line (X1, Y1)-(X2, Y2): -(X3, Y3):** This erases the two line segments.

**ArtWork.Line (X2 - 45, Y2 - 45)-(X2 + 45, Y2 + 45), , B:** This erases any `Pnode` mouse droppings (the little specks of pixels that are left after an image is moved by the mouse).

**ArtWork.DrawMode = 6:** Resets the drawing mode back to `Inverse`.

**P = 0:** Resets the erasing flag back to 0 so this block of code is not repeated.

**ArtWork.Line:** Draw the two lines and then draw the node shape using `Line` statement's box option (B).

**X2, Y2:** Changes the end points to give the effect of movement.

**ArtWork.Line:** Redraws the lines using the new mouse pointer positions.

**If Index = 0 Then:** You are going to store the new bounding box positions of both line segments. You need a special case for `Pnode(0)` because one of the lines is connected to the last polyshape segments.

**W(r - 1) = X + Pnode(Index).Left:** Only one corner of the original line's bounding box is being changed, so you need to change just the west and north values for the first line segment.

**E(rr) = X +Pnode(Index).Left:** Only the opposite corner of the second line's bounding box is being changed, so you need to change just the east and south values for last line segment.

**Else:** You are dragging a `Pnode` other than index 0.

**W(r + 1) , N(r + 1), E(r), S(r):** This reflects the same principles described above except it uses different index values to calculate the new bounding box coordinates of each line.

## Loading and Positioning *Pnodes* on a Polyshape

The `Poly_Nodes` procedure in Listing 15.27 loads new `Pnode` image controls for every polyline segment you add to the polyshape.

Chapter **15**   505

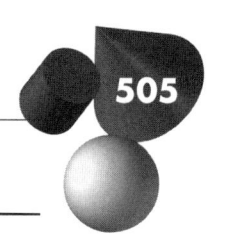

**L**isting 15.27. Loading new Pnodes on a polyshape.

```
Sub Poly_Nodes (Index)
If Counter = 1 Then
    FillValue(B) = 1
    Node(0).Visible = False: Node(1).Visible = False
    Pnode(0).Left = Node(0).Left: Pnode(0).Top = Node(0).Top
    Pnode(0).Visible = True
    Load Pnode(1):
    Pnode(1).Left = Node(1).Left: Pnode(1).Top = Node(1).Top
    Pnode(1).Visible = True
End If
Total = Total + 1: B = Total
DrawOrder(B) = Total
FlagLine(B) = 0: PolyShape(B) = B: FirstPolyPt(B) = ZZ
W(B) = X1: E(B) = X2: N(B) = Y1: S(B) = Y2
LineWidth(B) = Artwork.DrawWidth
r = NodeTotal 'add new node
If NodeTotal > 1 Then Load Pnode(r)
Pnode(r).Left = E(B) - 45: Pnode(r).Top = S(B) - 45
    NodeTotal = NodeTotal + 1
    Counter = Counter + 1
    Pnode(r).Visible = True
End Sub
```

**If Counter = 1 Then:** The counter will count the number of Pnodes you add to the polyshape. The first time you add a new line segment to the original line object you must convert this line to a polyshape segment. The original line had two normal nodes (Node(0), Node(1)) on either end of it. You must hide these nodes and replace them with Pnodes.

**FillValue(B) = 1:** Make the object's fill value transparent.

**Node(0).Visible = False : Node(1).Visible = False:** Hide the original Node image controls.

**Pnode(0).Left = Node(0).Left:** Replace the first Node image control with Pnode(0).

**Pnode(0).Visible = True:** Make the hidden Pnode visible.

**Load Pnode(1):** Load a new Pnode to replace the second Node image control.

**Pnode(1).Left = Node(1).Left:** Position the second Pnode.

**Pnode(1).Visible = True:** By default, all new controls are invisible when loaded so make the new Pnode visible.

**Total = Total + 1: B = Total:** Increase the object count by one for each new polyline segment.

**DrawOrder(B) = Total:** Increase the drawing order array by one.

**FlagLine(B) = 0:** Make sure that no polyline segment is flagged as a line object.

**PolyShape(B) = B:** Assign a number to the new polyline segment.

**FirstPolyPt(B) = ZZ:** Assign the number of the first polypoint segment to each new line segment.

**W(B) = X1: E(B) = X2:** Give each new line segment a bounding box.

**LineWidth(B) = ArtWork.DrawWidth:** Assign the line's drawing width.

**r = NodeTotal:** This will keep track of the number of Pnodes loaded to date.

The following If/Then code block adds additional Pnode image controls to the polyshape.

**If NodeTotal > 1 Then Load Pnode(r):** Load a new Pnode.

**Pnode(r).Left = E(B) - 45:** Position the Pnode at the correct location.

**NodeTotal = NodeTotal + 1:** Increase the Pnode count by 1.

**Counter = Counter + 1:** Increase the Counter by 1.

**Pnode(r).Visible = True:** After positioning the newly loaded Pnode image control, make the new Pnode visible.

## Reloading *Pnodes* on a Polyshape

The Poly_Reload procedure in Listing 15.28 will reposition the Pnodes around any poly-object that you select. You have to take into consideration that a polyshape could have a mixture of a polyline and curve segments. The Pnodes are placed using the values stored in the bounding box (W, N, E, S) arrays for line segments, while curve segments are placed using the values in the curve control point (p1, p2) arrays.

Listing 15.28. Reloads Pnodes on a polyshape when selected.

```
Sub Poly_Reload ()
    If StatusLabel.Caption = "No color Found" Then Exit Sub
    If StatusLabel.Caption = "No Object Found" Then Exit Sub
    I = FirstPolyPt(B): rr = 1
On Error GoTo AlreadyLoaded
If FirstPolyPt(B) = FlagBézier(I) Then
    Pnode(0).Left = p1X(I) - 45: Pnode(0).Top = p1Y(I) - 45
Else
    Pnode(0).Left = W(I) - 45: Pnode(0).Top = N(I) - 45
End If
For r = FirstPolyPt(I) + 1 To LastPolyPt(I) - 1 'add new nodes
    Load Pnode(rr)
If FlagBézier(r) = r Then
    Pnode(rr).Left = p1X(r) - 45: Pnode(rr).Top = p1Y(r) - 45
Else
    Pnode(rr).Left = W(r) - 45: Pnode(rr).Top = N(r) - 45
End If
Pnode(rr).Visible = True: rr = rr + 1
Next r
NodeTotal = rr - 1: Pnode(0).Visible = True
Toggle = True
AlreadyLoaded:
    FCP = FirstPolyPt(B)
    LCP = LastPolyPt(B) - 1
    If FlagPolyLine(FCP) = FCP Then
    Load Pnode(rr)
```

```
If FlagBézier(LCP) = LastPolyPt(LCP) - 1 Then
    Pnode(rr).Left = p2X(LCP) - 45: Pnode(rr).Top = p2Y(LCP) - 45
Else
    Pnode(rr).Left = E(LCP) - 45: Pnode(rr).Top = S(LCP) - 45
End If
        Pnode(rr).Visible = True
    End If
Exit Sub
End Sub
```

**If StatusLabel.Caption:** During the Find_Object procedure (Listing 15.11) the StatusLabel.Caption will indicate whether or not an object has been found. If no object has been found you do not have to go any further, so exit the procedure.

**I = FirstPolyPt(B): rr = 1:** The variable I will equal the first segment of the polyshape. The variable rr equals the first Pnode index to load.

**On Error GoTo AlreadyLoaded:** If you try to load a new control that is already loaded and displayed on the desktop, you will cause an error in the program. To safeguard the program from shutting down, the procedure will skip to the AlreadyLoaded code line if an error occurs.

**If FirstPolyPt(B) = FlagBézier(I) Then:** The first poly-segment is a Bézier curve, so use the curve arrays.

**Pnode(0).Left = p1X(I) - 45:** Position the first Pnode using the curve's control point values.

**Else:** The first poly-segment is a line segment, so use the bounding box arrays.

**Pnode(0).Left = W(I) - 45:** Position the Pnode using the line segment's corner positions.

You now are ready to load the remaining Pnode image controls onto the polyshape.

**For r = FirstPolyPt(I) + 1 To LastPolyPt(I) - 1:** Starting at the second polyshape segment and continuing up to the beginning of the last segment's point begin to add Pnodes.

**Load Pnode(rr):** Load a new Pnode beginning with Pnode(1).

**If FlagBézier(r) = r Then:** If the segment is a curve then use the curve's array values.

**Pnode(rr).Left = p1X(r) - 45:** Position the Pnode at the curve's control points.

**Else:** The poly-segment is a line, so use the bounding box array values.

**Pnode(rr).Left = W(r) - 45:** Position the Pnode using the line segment's corner positions.

**Pnode(rr).Visible = True: rr = rr + 1:** By default all new controls are invisible so make them visible.

**Next r:** Repeat the For\Next code block again until all the Pnodes are loaded and positioned correctly.

**NodeTotal = rr - 1:** Store the number of Pnodes you just loaded.

**Toggle = True:** This flag will tell the Pnode Mouse_Move event (Listing 15.18) that the ArtAPI program is ready to move any polysegments.

**AlreadyLoaded:** If an error occurred then you will skip the previous code and continue from this point in the code.

The following code statements deal with open polyshapes. Because an open polyshape does not have a closing segment found in Polygon shapes it does not have a reference for placing the last Pnode in the chain. You must manually assign the Pnode to the last segment of an open polyshape.

**FCP = FirstPolyPt(B):** This will equal the first segment's starting point.

**LCP = LastPolyPt(B) - 1:** This will equal the last segment's starting point.

**If FlagPolyLine(FCP) :** This flag can tell the program if the object is an open polyshape.

**Load Pnode(rr):** If it is indeed an open polyshape then load a Pnode.

**If FlagBézier(LCP):** If the last segment of an open polyshape is a curve, do the following code statement.

**Pnode(rr).Left = p2X(LCP) - 45:** Position the Pnode at the curve's end control point.

**Else:** The last open poly-segment is a line, so do the following instead:

**Pnode(rr).Left = E(LCP) - 45:** Position the Pnode at the line's end point.

**Pnode(rr).Visible = True:** Make the new Pnode control visible.

## After a Polyshape Segment is Edited

When you edit the shape of the polyshape the Pnode is hidden during the mouse move events. In Listing 15.29 you call the Poly_Update to position the Pnode to its new location.

**Listing 15.29.** Positions the hidden Pnode to its new location.

```
Sub Poly_Update (Index%, Button%, Shift%, X As Single, Y As Single)
    XXX = (X + Pnode(Index).Left) - 45
    YYY = (Y + Pnode(Index).Top) - 45
    Pnode(Index).Left = XXX
    Pnode(Index).Top = YYY
    Pnode(Index).Visible = True
StatusLabel.Caption = "Node " + Format$(Index) + " ( " +
            ↪Format$(Pnode(Index).Left \ PixelX) + " - " +
                    ↪Format$(Pnode(Index).Top \ PixelY) + " )"
    UpdateObjects
End Sub
```

**XXX = (X + Pnode(Index).Left) - 45:** Reposition the Pnode to the new X coordinate.

**YYY = (Y + Pnode(Index).Top) - 45:** Reposition the Pnode to the new Y coordinate.

**UpdateObjects:** Redraw all objects on the desktop.

## Resizing and Stretching a Polyshape

The `Poly_Stretch` procedure in Listing 15.30 repositions all the X and Y coordinates of all polyline and curve segments belonging to the polyshape object. This routine is identical to the Bézier stretch procedure in the Artisan program discussed in Chapter 3, "Bézier Curves." However, you must include the For/Next statements so the procedure can loop through all the poly-segments.

The `Poly_Stretch` procedure is shown in Listing 15.27. Once you are familiar with how it works, you can easily combine the sections or even add nested loops to shorten the code's procedure.

**Listing 15.30. Resizing or flipping a polyshape object.**

```
Sub Poly_Stretch (Index%, Button%, Shift %, X As Single, Y As Single)
Select Case Index
    Case 0, 1, 2
      percentage! = (Y - YY1) / (YY2 - YY1): ANCHOR = YY2
    Case 3
      percentage! = (X - XX2) / (XX1 - XX2): ANCHOR = XX1
    Case 4, 5, 6
      percentage! = (Y - YY2) / (YY1 - YY2): ANCHOR = YY1
    Case 7
      percentage! = (X - XX1) / (XX2 - XX1): ANCHOR = XX2
End Select
'''''''''''''''''''''''''''''''''''''''''''''''
For i = FirstPolyPt(B) To LastPolyPt(B) - 1
Select Case Index
  Case 0, 1, 2, 4, 5, 6
    Bouy1 = N(i): Bouy2 = S(i)
    p1XY = p1Y(i): p2XY = p2Y(i)
    h1XY = h1Y(i): h2XY = h2Y(i)
  Case 3, 7
    Bouy1 = W(i): Bouy2 = E(i)
    p1XY = p1X(i): p2XY = p2X(i)
    h1XY = h1X(i): h2XY = h2X(i)
End Select
  Bouy1 = ((ANCHOR - Bouy1) * percentage!) + Bouy1
  Bouy2 = ((ANCHOR - Bouy2) * percentage!) + Bouy2
  Boat1 = p1XY: Boat2 = p2XY
  Boat3 = h1XY: Boat4 = h2XY
  Boat1 = ((ANCHOR - Boat1) * percentage!) + Boat1
  Boat2 = ((ANCHOR - Boat2) * percentage!) + Boat2
  Boat3 = ((ANCHOR - Boat3) * percentage!) + Boat3
  Boat4 = ((ANCHOR - Boat4) * percentage!) + Boat4

Select Case Index
  Case 0, 1, 2, 4, 5, 6
    N(i) = Bouy1: S(i) = Bouy2
    p1Y(i) = Boat1: p2Y(i) = Boat2
    h1Y(i) = Boat3: h2Y(i) = Boat4
  Case 3, 7
    W(i) = Bouy1: E(i) = Bouy2
    p1X(i) = Boat1: p2X(i) = Boat2
    h1X(i) = Boat3: h2X(i) = Boat4
End Select
```

*continues*

## Listing 15.30. continued

```
Next i
''''' corners
Select Case Index
    Case 0, 6 'Left corners
        percentage! = (X - XX1) / (XX2 - XX1): ANCHOR = XX2
    Case 2, 4 'Right corners
        percentage! = (X - XX2) / (XX1 - XX2): ANCHOR = XX1
    Case Else
        Exit Sub
End Select
'''''''''''''''''''''''''''''''''''''''''''''''''
For i = FirstPolyPt(B) To LastPolyPt(B) - 1
  Bouy1 = W(i): Bouy2 = E(i)
  Bouy1 = ((ANCHOR - Bouy1) * percentage!) + Bouy1
  Bouy2 = ((ANCHOR - Bouy2) * percentage!) + Bouy2
  Boat1 = p1X(i): Boat2 = p2X(i)
  Boat3 = h1X(i): Boat4 = h2X(i)
  Boat1 = ((ANCHOR - Boat1) * percentage!) + Boat1
  Boat2 = ((ANCHOR - Boat2) * percentage!) + Boat2
  Boat3 = ((ANCHOR - Boat3) * percentage!) + Boat3
  Boat4 = ((ANCHOR - Boat4) * percentage!) + Boat4

  W(i) = Bouy1: E(i) = Bouy2
  p1X(i) = Boat1: p2X(i) = Boat2
  h1X(i) = Boat3: h2X(i) = Boat4
Next i
End Sub
```

Refer to the Artisan program in Chapter 3, "Bézier Curves," for details on the Poly_Stretch routine's inner workings.

## Using the Test Button

The TestButton_Click procedure in Listing 15.31 will redraw the polyshape that is currently selected. This routine uses the Visual Basic Line statement to draw polyshapes and can be used to replace the API polyline statement to the same degree. However, you will not be able to fill the polyshape with color because the Visual Basic language does not support the Paint statement. In this case you would still need to use API Floodfill functions to paint an area of screen.

### Listing 15.31. Drawing an outline of a polyshape's path.

```
Sub TestButton_Click ()
Artwork.DrawWidth = 8: Artwork.DrawMode = 13
Artwork.DrawStyle = 0: rr = 1
For r = FirstPolyPt(B) To LastPolyPt(B) - 1
    X1 = W(r): Y1 = N(r): X2 = E(r): Y2 = S(r)
If FlagBézier(r) = r Then
    p1.X = p1X(r): p1.Y = p1Y(r): p2.X = p2X(r): p2.Y = p2Y(r)
    h1.X = h1X(r): h1.Y = h1Y(r): h2.X = h2X(r): h2.Y = h2Y(r)
    BezDraw
    GoTo SkipLine:
```

```
End If
    Artwork.Line (X1, Y1)-(X2, Y2), QBColor(Rnd * 14)
SkipLine:
Next r
    Artwork.DrawWidth = 1: Artwork.DrawMode = 6
End Sub
```

> **For r = FirstPolyPt(B) To LastPolyPt(B) - 1:** Starting at the first poly-segment and continuing up to the beginning of the last poly-segment, do the following:
>
> **X1 = W(r): Y1 = N(r): X2 = E(r): Y2 = S(r):** Get each line segment's start and end points.
>
> **If FlagBézier(r) = r Then:** If the segment is a curve, then do the following:
>
> **p1.X = p1X(r):** Get all four control points for the curve.
>
> **BezDraw:** Call this procedure to draw the Bézier curve.
>
> **GoTo SkipLine:** The curve segment has been drawn, so do not draw the following Line statement by jumping the SkipLine code statement.
>
> **ArtWork.Line:** If the segment is a polyline then draw it.
>
> **SkipLine:** The procedure jumps to this point if the polysegment is a curve.
>
> **Next r:** Go back to the top and repeat everything for the next polyshape segment.

## Moving an Object to the Front or Back

The To_Front_Back procedure in Listing 15.32 is used to move an object to the front or back of all other objects. The original Artisan program in Chapter 4 did this by changing the order of every object and its associated attributes. It is now performed by using a short and simple loop routine. You bypass switching every object number and its attributes by simply changing the order in which the objects were initially drawn. This requires only one additional array, called DrawOrder, to hold and keep track of the drawing order. The UpdateObjects procedure (Listing 15.35) uses a For/Next statement to draw each object according to the order stated in the DrawOrder variable array.

**Listing 15.32. Sending an object to the front or back of all other objects.**

```
Sub To_Front_Back (Index As Integer)
If B = 0 Then Beep: Exit Sub
If PolyShape(B) = B Then B = FirstPolyPt(B)
Select Case Index
    Case 0 'To Front
        For Objectnumber = 1 To Total
            Z = DrawOrder(Objectnumber)
            If Z = B Then Exit For
        Next Objectnumber 'Objectnumber will highlighted object
    Temp = DrawOrder(Objectnumber)
    For Repeat2 = Objectnumber To Total
        NextA = Repeat2 + 1
        DrawOrder(Repeat2) = DrawOrder(NextA)
```

*continues*

# ArtAPI

**Listing 15.32. continued**

```
     Next Repeat2
DrawOrder(Total) = Temp
    Case 1 'To back
        For Objectnumber = 1 To Total
            Z = DrawOrder(Objectnumber)
            If Z = B Then Exit For
        Next Objectnumber 'Objectnumber will highlighted object
Temp = DrawOrder(Objectnumber)
    For Repeat2 = Objectnumber To 2 Step -1
        NextA = Repeat2 - 1
        DrawOrder(Repeat2) = DrawOrder(NextA)
        Next Repeat2
DrawOrder(1) = Temp
End Select
        UpdateObjects
End Sub
```

**If B = 0 Then Beep:** If you have not selected an object, then exit this procedure.

**If PolyShape(B) = B Then:** If the object is a polyshape, then you must grab the first polysegment in order to point to the entire object.

**Select Case Index:** Depending on which Menu selection you made, do the following:

**Case 0:** You have selected to move the object to the front of all other objects.

**For Objectnumber = 1 To Total:** For every object do the following:

**Z = DrawOrder(Objectnumber):** The variable Z represents the object number assigned to each index in the DrawOrder array. Each value is the number assigned to the object. If you chose not to use this procedure, then the object numbers would be in order (each index number in the array would match the object's assigned number). You shuffle the array's values each time you move an object to the front or back.

**If Z = B Then Exit For:** The currently selected object's number equals B. If the array values are shuffled you do not know what index this number is placed in. Loop through the array's indexes. If you find the object number, then you have what you are looking for.

**Next Objectnumber:** Loop through the indexes until you find the current object's assigned number.

**Temp = DrawOrder(Objectnumber):** You have found the object's number so store the array index number that holds the object's number.

**For Repeat2 = Objectnumber To Total:** Starting at the index number you just found, and continuing to the last index in the DrawOrder array, do the following:

**NextA = Repeat2 + 1:** Store the number of the next highest index.

**DrawOrder(Repeat2) = DrawOrder(NextA):** Put the object number from the next highest index into the present index.

**Next Repeat2:** Continue grabbing the next index's object number.

**DrawOrder(Total) = Temp:** By the time you get to the top of the index, the next highest index will hold nothing. Luckily, you are moving the currently selected object number here. Believe it or not the object will always be on top. If you're good at stacking cards you can make additional shuffle variations to move any object backward or forward any number of spaces.

**Case 1:** You have selected to move the object to the back of all other objects.

This is exactly the same routine as the previous `Case 0` block of codes; the only difference is that you loop backward.

**For Repeat2 = Objectnumber To 2 Step -1:** Only go back to the second index position to leave space to drag the current object into the first index position. The `Step -1` keyword makes the count go backward.

**NextA = Repeat2 - 1:** Take the object number from the next lowest index in this routine.

**UpdateObjects:** Redraw the newly shuffled deck of objects.

## Selecting an Object by Its Outline Image

The `UpdateArtMask` procedure in Listing 15.33 is similar to the `UpdateObject` procedure (Listing 15.35) except you draw a single object into the `ArtMask` image control using a four-pixel draw width. The `Find_Object` procedure (Listing 15.11) will size the control to save memory, then search for the outline of the object, selecting the object if found. You are able to do this by simulating off-screen drawings by setting the `ArtMask`'s `AutoRedraw` property to `True` and its visible property to `False`.

In the original `Artisan` program in Chapter 3 each object was found by using a bubble type array to search through every bounding box until the one located over the mouse was found. This method was not feasible if several bounding boxes (objects) were placed on top of each other in a pile. This made it impossible to pick or move one object that overlapped the object you wanted to select.

**Listing 15.33. Drawing an object into a memory bitmap.**

```
Sub UpdateArtMask ()
    ArtMask.PSet (0, 0)
        If PolyShape(B) = B Then
            If FlagBézier(B) = 0 Then FlagLine(B) = B
        End If
ArtMask.DrawWidth = 4 : FlagArtMask = True
X1 = W(B) - ArtMask.Left: Y1 = N(B) - ArtMask.Top
X2 = E(B) - ArtMask.Left: Y2 = S(B) - ArtMask.Top
Select Case B
    Case FlagCircle(B) 'Ellipse
        r = Ellipse(ArtMask.hDC, X1 \ PixelX, Y1 \ PixelY, X2
                    ➥\ PixelX, Y2 \ PixelY)
    Case FlagLine(B) 'Single polyline
        Npt(1).X = X1 \ PixelX: Npt(1).Y = Y1 \ PixelY
        Npt(2).X = X2 \ PixelX: Npt(2).Y = Y2 \ PixelY: PolyPts = 2
        r = Polyline(ArtMask.hDC, Npt(1), PolyPts)
```

*continues*

## ArtAPI

**Listing 15.33. continued**

```
        Case FlagBox(B) 'rectangle
            API = Rectangle(ArtMask.hDC, X1 \ PixelX, Y1
                         ↪\ PixelY, X2 \ PixelX, Y2 \ PixelY)
        Case FlagBézier(B) 'Bézier curve
            I = 1: BB = B
p1.X = p1X(B): p1.Y = p1Y(B): p2.X = p2X(B): p2.Y = p2Y(B)
h1.X = h1X(B): h1.Y = h1Y(B): h2.X = h2X(B): h2.Y = h2Y(B)
            Poly_curves I
            API = Polyline(ArtMask.hDC, Npt(1), 33)
            SkipaCurve:
        Case FlagText(B) 'text
            ArtMask.CurrentX = OFFSET(B) - 15: ArtMask.CurrentY = N(B) - 15
            SaveScaleLeft = ArtMask.ScaleLeft
            ArtMask.ScaleLeft = ArtMask.Left - ArtMask.CurrentX
            ArtMask.FontName = TextFont(B)
            ArtMask.ForeColor = 0
            ArtMask.FontSize = TextSize(B)
            ArtMask.FontBold = TextBold(B)
            ArtMask.FontItalic = TextItalic(B)
            wFlag = FlagAlign(B)
            TA = SetTextAlign(ArtMask.hDC, wFlag)
            ArtMask.Print StoredText(B)
            ArtMask.ScaleLeft = SaveScaleLeft
End Select
' ' ' ' '
            FlagArtMask = False
        If PolyShape(B) = B Then FlagLine(B) = 0
End Sub
```

**ArtMask.PSet (0, 0):** Sometimes you might find that API graphical functions will not immediately start drawing into a Visual Basic control. To correct this you need to get a handle on the device context of the control you are drawing into. Visual Basic does this automatically when you issue a Basic language graphic, font, or print statement. By placing a single pixel point on the control, you now have a device context reference to the control. Use the 0,0 coordinate because you will never see this single pixel at this location.

**If PolyShape(B) = B Then:** If the object you are drawing is a polyshape segment, do the following:

**If FlagBézier(B) = 0 Then FlagLine(B) = B:** The UpdateObject procedure draws the entire polyshape using either the FlagPoly or FlagPolyline routines. However, you only want to draw the individual polyline segment. Rather than use a long code routine to pick and choose the correct segment to draw, reassign any polyline as a Flagline object. After the single polyline segment is drawn you will again delete this Flagline object by setting it to 0.

**ArtMask.DrawWidth = 4 :** The mouse pointer only looks for the outline of the object, so make the masked object four pixels wide so the mouse pointer can easily find it within a few pixels.

**FlagArtMask = True:** This will tell the `Poly_Curves` procedure (Listing 15.22) that the curve is to be drawn on the ArtMask picture box control.

**X1 = W(B) - ArtMask.Left: Y1, X2, Y2:** All of these values will place the graphic at the correct internal location of the ArtMask control and will precisely match the position of the graphic displayed on the desktop.

**Select Case B:** Refer to the preceding `UpdateObjects` procedure (Listing 15.37) for details on the API graphical statements found within the Select/Case code statements in this procedure. The following line of code is the last statement in this procedure and is used to reset the object flag that was changed earlier.

**If PolyShape(B) = B Then FlagLine(B) = 0:** Delete the line object flag.

## Drawing all Objects onto the Desktop

The `UpdateObject` procedure in Listing 15.34 is basically the same as the `UpdateObject` procedure found in Chapter 4 of the Artisan program. The main difference in the ArtAPI program is the use of API drawing functions to draw each of objects onto the desktop.

**Listing 15.34. Drawing all objects onto the desktop.**

```
Sub UpdateObjects ()
StoreB = B: Artwork.DrawStyle = Solid
Artwork.DrawMode = Copy_Pen: Artwork.AutoRedraw = True
If Draw = True Then GoTo SkipErase
    Artwork.DrawWidth = 20
    Artwork.Line (W(B), N(B))-(E(B), S(B)), White, BF
    Artwork.Line (XX1, YY1)-(XX2, YY2), White, BF
If B > 0 And PolyShape(B) = B Then
    Artwork.Line (W(0), N(0))-(E(0), S(0)), White, BF
    Poly_Handles
    Artwork.Line (W(0), N(0))-(E(0), S(0)), White, BF
End If
UpdateDeskTop
For Repeat = 1 To Total
    B = DrawOrder(Repeat)
    If B = 0 Then B = Repeat
If LineValue(B) > 0 Then Artwork.DrawStyle = 5 Else
                ➥Artwork.DrawStyle = Solid
SkipErase:
X1 = W(B): Y1 = N(B): X2 = E(B): Y2 = S(B)
Artwork.FillColor = PaintColor(B): Artwork.FillStyle = FillValue(B):
➥Artwork.DrawWidth =LineWidth(B)
rr& = Artwork.ForeColor: Artwork.ForeColor = OutLineColor(B)
```

> **NOTE** The code listing continues after the following.

**StoreB = B:** You are going to use a For/Next statement to loop through all the objects. The value of B will change because of the loop so you will temporarily store the current object value in variable StoreB.

**ArtWork.DrawStyle:** You also start drawing in default Solid mode.

**ArtWork.DrawMode:** Redraw in default Copy_Pen drawing mode.

**If Draw:** Whenever this flag is set to True you have just drawn or stretched an object that is the on top of all other layers, and there is no need to redraw all objects. You can skip the For/Next statement and only draw the top object by going to SkipErase:

The next 3 lines are used to erase the last position of an object's bounding box.

**ArtWork.DrawWidth:** You set the bounding box border width to 20 pixels in case this object has a wide outline; otherwise, this padded area would not be erased.

**ArtWork.Line (W(B), N(B))-(E(B), S(B)):** These are the current bounding box dimensions, so you erase this area by filling the inside with White.

**ArtWork.Line (XX1,YY1)-(XX2,YY2):** The last positions of the bounding box before an object has been moved or stretched. You also erase this area by filling the area with White.

The next three lines are used to erase the last position of a polyshape's bounding box.

**If B > 0 And PolyShape(B) = B Then:** If the current object is a polyshape, do the following:

**ArtWork.Line (W(0), N(0))-(E(0), S(0)):** These are the current bounding box dimensions of a polyshape that you will erase. The "0" index of the W, N, E, S arrays are reserved for any polyshape bounding box.

**Poly_Handles:** Calculates the new bounding box area after it has been stretched.

**ArtWork.Line (W(0), N(0))-(E(0), S(0)):** Erase the area beneath the new image of the polyshape.

**UpdateDeskTop:** The white page that is centered on the desktop at the start of the program is actually two boxes: The first is filled black, the next is filled white and is shifted slightly to the left. You redraw these by calling the procedure UpdateDeskTop.

The next three lines are used to draw all the objects in the order specified in the DrawOrder array.

**For Repeat = 1 To Total:** You replaced the Do/While Loop statement from the Artisan program in Chapter 4 with a For/Next statement, which will loop through all drawing routines.

**B = DrawOrder(Repeat):** The variable B equals the object that is to be drawn. The DrawOrder array is indexed from "0" up to the total number of objects. Each index will hold the object's assigned number, which could been in any order depending on if you used the To_Front_Back procedure (Listing 15.31).

**If B = 0 Then B = Repeat:** A safeguard in case the DrawOrder array is corrupt.

## Chapter 15

**If LineValue(B):** Having an object's LineValue equal to 0 makes an object outline invisible. You cannot set the DrawWidth to 0. If you want an object with no outline, make the LineValue variable equal to -0, which will then flag the Artwork picture box's DrawStyle to transparent (1) when drawing the outline.

**SkipErase:** This skips the For/Next loop if the flag Draw was set to TRUE.

**X1 = W(B): Y1 = N(B):** Assign the coordinates to be used with circle and box objects.

**ArtWork.FillColor, etc.:** Assign the correct brush and drawing width values for the object to be drawn.

**rr& = ArtWork.ForeColor:** Store the current pen (ForeColor) of the desktop so you can reset the original color after the objects are drawn.

**Listing 15.35. Drawing objects onto the desktop, continued.**

```
Select Case B
    Case FlagCircle(B) 'Ellipse
        r = Ellipse(Artwork.hDC, X1 \ PixelX, Y1 \ PixelY, X2 \
                    ➥PixelX, Y2 \ PixelY)
    Case FlagLine(B) 'Single polyline
        Npt(1).X = X1 \ PixelX: Npt(1).Y = Y1 \ PixelY
        Npt(2).X = X2 \ PixelX: Npt(2).Y = Y2 \ PixelY: PolyPts = 2
        r = Polyline(Artwork.hDC, Npt(1), PolyPts)
    Case FlagPolyLine(B) 'Open multi-Polyline Shape
        fp = FirstPolyPt(B): LP = LastPolyPt(B) - 1: I = 1
For BB = fp To LP
    If BB = FlagBézier(BB) And BB = PolyShape(BB) Then
        p1.X = p1X(BB): p1.Y = p1Y(BB): p2.X = p2X(BB): p2.Y = p2Y(BB)
        h1.X = h1X(BB): h1.Y = h1Y(BB): h2.X = h2X(BB): h2.Y = h2Y(BB)
        Poly_curves I
    Else
        Npt(I).X = W(BB) \ PixelX: Npt(I).Y = N(BB) \ PixelY: I = I + 1
    End If
Next BB
Npt(I).X = E(BB - 1) \ PixelX: Npt(I).Y = S(BB - 1) \ PixelY
If FlagBézier(BB - 1) = BB - 1 Then Npt(I).X = p2.X \ PixelX:
                    ➥Npt(I).Y = p2.Y \ PixelY
        PolyPts = I
        API = Polyline(Artwork.hDC, Npt(1), PolyPts)
'''''''''''''''''''''''''''''''''''''''''''
    Case FlagPoly(B) 'Closed polygon shape
        fp = FirstPolyPt(B): LP = LastPolyPt(B) - 1: I = 1
For BB = fp To LP
    If BB = FlagBézier(BB) And BB = PolyShape(BB) Then
        p1.X = p1X(BB): p1.Y = p1Y(BB): p2.X = p2X(BB): p2.Y = p2Y(BB)
        h1.X = h1X(BB): h1.Y = h1Y(BB): h2.X = h2X(BB): h2.Y = h2Y(BB)
        Poly_curves I
    Else
        Npt(I).X = W(BB) \ PixelX: Npt(I).Y = N(BB) \ PixelY: I = I + 1
    End If
Next BB
        API = SetPolyFillMode(Artwork.hDC, 1): PolyPts = I - 1
        API = Polygon(Artwork.hDC, Npt(1), PolyPts)
```

*continues*

## ArtAPI

**Listing 15.35. continued**

```
    Case FlagBox(B) 'rectangle
        API = Rectangle(Artwork.hDC, X1 \ PixelX, Y1 \ PixelY, X2 \
                        ➥PixelX, Y2 \ PixelY)
    Case FlagBézier(B) 'Bézier curve
        If FlagBézier(B) = PolyShape(B) Then GoTo SkipCurve
p1.X = p1X(B): p1.Y = p1Y(B): p2.X = p2X(B): p2.Y = p2Y(B)
h1.X = h1X(B): h1.Y = h1Y(B): h2.X = h2X(B): h2.Y = h2Y(B)
        Artwork.ForeColor = OutLineColor(B)
        BezDraw
        SkipCurve:
    Case FlagText(B) 'text
        ArtWork.CurrentX = OFFSET(B): ArtWork.CurrentY = N(B)
        SaveScaleLeft = ArtWork.ScaleLeft
        ArtWork.ScaleLeft = -ArtWork.CurrentX

        ArtWork.FontSize = TextSize(B) * TextPoint
        ArtWork.FontName = TextFont(B)
        ArtWork.FontSize = TextSize(B) * TextPoint 'SMALL FONT CALL
        ArtWork.ForeColor = PaintColor(B)
        ArtWork.FontBold = TextBold(B)
        ArtWork.FontItalic = TextItalic(B)
        wFlag = FlagAlign(B)
        TA = SetTextAlign(ArtWork.hDC, wFlag)
        ArtWork.Print StoredText(B)
        ArtWork.ScaleLeft = SaveScaleLeft
End Select
```

> **NOTE:** The code listing continues after the following.

**Select Case B:** The variable B represents the current bounding box of the object.

**Case FlagCircle:** If the current bounding box contains a circle then:

**X1, Y1, X2, Y2:** The bounding box positions to pass to API `Ellipse` function.

**Case FlagLine(B):** The object is a line. Draws a line

Use a fixed `PolyPts` value of 2 because you only need to two X and Y coordinates to the API `Polyline` function. The `Npt` array holds each X and Y coordinate to pass to the function.

**Case FlagPolyLine(B):** Draw any open `Polyline` object.

**For BB = fp To LP:** Starting at the first polyline segment and continuing up to the start of the last polyline segment, do the following:

**If BB = FlagBézier(BB) -Then:** The segment is a Bézier curve so get the curve's four control points.

**p1.X = p1X(BB), etc.,:** Grab the four curve control points.

**Poly_curves I:** Calculate and draw the Bézier curve. The argument I will keep track of the number of index arrays to assign to the Npt array the API Polyline function uses.

**Else:** The segment is a line so get its start and end points.

**Npt(I).X = W(BB) \ PixelX:** Assign the correct X and Y coordinates to the Npt array. The stored values are in twips, so convert them to pixel units. Finally, increase the Npt index count (I) by one.

**Next BB:** Repeat the process for all segments within the polyshape.

**Npt(I).X = E(BB - 1) \ PixelX:** An "open" polyshape does not have the same pleasure as a polygon shape in automatically closing its end point. You must manually assign the last X and Y coordinate to the open Polyline shape.

**If FlagBézier(BB - 1) = BB - 1 Then:** If the last point in the shape connects to a Bézier curve, execute the If/Then code statement.

**PolyPts = I:** The I variable will equal the total number of indexed X and Y points to draw.

**API = Polyline(ArtWork.hDC, Npt(1), PolyPts):** Draw the open polyline shape.

**Case FlagPoly(B):** Draw any closed polygon shape.

This routine is exactly like the FlagPolyline case except for the PolyPts count. The last segment is automatically connected to the first segment to close the shape and form a polygon.

**API = SetPolyFillMode(ArtWork.hDC, 1):** You have a choice between "Alternate or Winding" modes in how you want polygon shapes to fill with color. Refer to the Join Nodes program (Listing 13.9) in Chapter 13 for details.

**PolyPts = I - 1:** Subtract the last index point because it is not needed to form a polygon.

**API = Polygon(Artwork.hDC, Npt(1), PolyPts):** Draw the closed polygon shape.

**Case FlagBox(B):** Draw a rectangular box object.

**X1, Y1, X2, Y2:** The bounding box positions to pass to API Rectangle function.

**Case FlagBézier:** The object is a Bézier curve, so get the four stored control points then change Artwork's Forecolor to the curve's outline color. The BezDraw procedure uses this property to color and draw the Bézier curve. This routine draws only single Bézier curves and could be combined with the FlagPolyline routine.

**Case FlagText(B):** No API text functions have been included in this program. All text is formatted manually using Basic language statements. See the UpdateObjects procedure in Chapter 5 for details on this. Refer to the APItext program in Chapter 12 for standard API text formatting procedures. Artwork's text size is placed twice, once before the font name and once after. Windows uses bitmap fonts when displaying fonts less than 8 points in size. Recalling the font size (or font name) will reset the controls original font properties.

# ArtAPI

**Listing 15.35. Drawing objects onto the desktop, continued.**

```
Artwork.ForeColor = rr&: Artwork.FillColor = 0: Artwork.FillStyle = 1
If Draw = True Then Draw = False: Artwork.AutoRedraw = False:
                        ➥B = StoreB: Exit Sub
    B = B + 1
Next Repeat
    B = StoreB
    Artwork.AutoRedraw = False
    Artwork.DrawWidth = 1: Artwork.DrawStyle = Solid
If DeleteObject = True Then Exit Sub
If CurrentTool = 1 Or CurrentTool = 2 Or CurrentTool = 10 Then Exit Sub
If SideRuler = True Or TopRuler = True Then Exit Sub
        Handles
        Nodes
End Sub
```

Refer to the Artisan program, Chapter 5, the UpdateObjects procedures (Listing 5.16) for details on the remaining code in Listing 15.33.

## Printing all Objects

The WinPrint procedure in Listing 15.36 is identical to the previous UpdateObjects procedure in Listing 15.35 except it will use manual scaling values to print the graphics to the printer's page.

**Listing 15.36. Prints all objects to a printer's page.**

```
Sub WinPrint ()
    On Error GoTo PrintErr:
CMDialog1.Flags = &H2& Or &H4& Or &H8& Or &H100000
CMDialog1.Action = 5
NumCopies = CMDialog1.Copies
Screen.MousePointer = 11
For r = 1 To NumCopies
    Dim RightM As Single
    Dim BottomM As Single
LeftM = PageX1: TopM = PageY1 'Adjust Margins
APIH = GetDeviceCaps(Printer.hDC, 8)
APIV = GetDeviceCaps(Printer.hDC, 10)
HPrinterDPI! = APIH / (PageX2 - PageX1)
VPrinterDPI! = APIV / (PageY2 - PageY1)
PageScale! = Printer.ScaleWidth / (PageX2 - PageX1)
RightM = HPrinterDPI!  'Adjust Margins
BottomM = VPrinterDPI!
    FlagPrinter = True
    Printer.PSet (0, 0)
''''''''''''''''''''
For Repeat = 1 To Total
    B = DrawOrder(Repeat)
    If B = 0 Then B = Repeat
If LineValue(B) > 0 Then Printer.DrawStyle = 5 Else
                    ➥Printer.DrawStyle = Solid
X1 = (W(B) - LeftM) * RightM: Y1 = (N(B) - TopM) * BottomM
X2 = (E(B) - LeftM) * RightM: Y2 = (S(B) - TopM) * BottomM
```

```
    Printer.FillColor = PaintColor(B): Printer.FillStyle = FillValue(B)
If LineWidth(B) > 1 Then Printer.DrawWidth = LineWidth(B) * 5 Else
                        ➥Printer.DrawWidth = LineWidth(B)
    rr& = Printer.ForeColor: Printer.ForeColor = OutLineColor(B)
Select Case B
    Case FlagCircle(B) 'Ellipse
r = Ellipse(Printer.hDC, X1, Y1, X2, Y2)
    Case FlagLine(B) 'Single polyline
Npt(I).X = X1: Npt(I).Y = Y1: FLP = I: I = I + 1
Npt(I).X = X2: Npt(I).Y = Y2: I = I + 1
    r = Polyline(Printer.hDC, Npt(FLP), 2)
'''''''''''''''''''''''''''''''''''''''
    Case FlagPolyLine(B) 'Open multi-Polyline Shape
fp = FirstPolyPt(B): LP = LastPolyPt(B) - 1: I = 1
For BB = fp To LP
    If BB = FlagBézier(BB) And BB = PolyShape(BB) Then
        p1.X = p1X(BB): p1.Y = p1Y(BB): p2.X = p2X(BB): p2.Y = p2Y(BB)
        h1.X = h1X(BB): h1.Y = h1Y(BB): h2.X = h2X(BB): h2.Y = h2Y(BB)
        Poly_curves I
    Else
        Npt(I).X = (W(BB) - LeftM) * RightM
        Npt(I).Y = (N(BB) - TopM) * BottomM: I = I + 1
    End If
Next BB
        Npt(I).X = (E(BB - 1) - LeftM) * RightM
        Npt(I).Y = (S(BB - 1) - TopM) * BottomM
If FlagBézier(BB - 1) = BB - 1 Then Npt(I).X = (p2.X - LeftM) * RightM
                        Npt(I).Y = (p2.Y - TopM) * BottomM
    PolyPts = I
        API = Polyline(Printer.hDC, Npt(1), PolyPts)
'''''''''''''''''''''''''''''''''''''''
    Case FlagPoly(B) 'Closed polygon shape
fp = FirstPolyPt(B): LP = LastPolyPt(B) - 1: I = 1
    For BB = fp To LP
        If BB = FlagBézier(BB) And BB = PolyShape(BB) Then
            p1.X = p1X(BB): p1.Y = p1Y(BB): p2.X = p2X(BB): p2.Y = p2Y(BB)
            h1.X = h1X(BB): h1.Y = h1Y(BB): h2.X = h2X(BB): h2.Y = h2Y(BB)
            Poly_curves I
        Else
            Npt(I).X = (W(BB) - LeftM) * RightM
            Npt(I).Y = (N(BB) - TopM) * BottomM: I = I + 1
        End If
Next BB
        API = SetPolyFillMode(Printer.hDC, 1): PolyPts = I - 1
            API = Polygon(Printer.hDC, Npt(1), PolyPts)
'''''''''''''''''''''''''''''''''''''''
    Case FlagBox(B) 'rectangle
        API = Rectangle(Printer.hDC, X1, Y1, X2, Y2)
    Case FlagBézier(B) 'Bézier curve
        If FlagBézier(B) = PolyShape(B) Then GoTo SkipCurve2
    p1.X = p1X(B): p1.Y = p1Y(B): p2.X = p2X(B): p2.Y = p2Y(B)
    h1.X = h1X(B): h1.Y = h1Y(B): h2.X = h2X(B): h2.Y = h2Y(B)
        Printer.ForeColor = OutLineColor(B)
        BezDraw
        SkipCurve2:
         Case FlagText(B) 'text
```

*continues*

# ArtAPI

**Listing 15.38. continued**

```
            Printer.FontSize = TextSize(B) * PageScale!
            Printer.FontName = TextFont(B)
            Printer.FontSize = TextSize(B) * PageScale!
            Printer.ForeColor = PaintColor(B)
            Printer.FontBold = TextBold(B)
            Printer.FontItalic = TextItalic(B)
            If FlagAlign(B) = TA_LEFT Then DT_FLAG = DT_LEFT
            If FlagAlign(B) = TA_CENTER Then DT_FLAG = DT_CENTER
            If FlagAlign(B) = TA_RIGHT Then DT_FLAG = DT_RIGHT
            Dim TextRect As Rect
            TextRect.Left = (W(B) - LeftM) * RightM
            TextRect.Top = (N(B) - TopM) * BottomM
            TextRect.Right = (E(B) - LeftM) * RightM
            TextRect.Bottom = (S(B) - TopM) * BottomM
            API = DrawText(Printer.hDC, StoredText(B), -1, _
                    TextRect, DT_FLAG Or DT_NOCLIP)
    End Select
'''''
    Printer.ForeColor = rr&: Printer.FillColor = 0: Printer.FillStyle = 1
    B = B + 1
Next Repeat
''''''''''''''''
        Printer.EndDoc
Next r
    FlagPrinter = False
    Screen.MousePointer = 0
    FlagPrinter = 0
    Exit Sub
PrintErr:
    FlagPrinter = False
    Screen.MousePointer = 0
    FlagPrinter = 0
    Printer.EndDoc
Exit Sub
End Sub
```

By changing the `RightM` and `BottomM` variables you can have graphics print correctly to 600, 1200, or other PostScript printers with higher DPI (dots per inch) scaling . You should also note that not all printers are capable of printing Windows GUI functions, or even Visual Basic graphic statements.

**`APIH = GetDeviceCaps(Printer.hDC, 8):`** Retrieve the horizontal resolution of the printer in pixel units.

**`APIV = GetDeviceCaps(Printer.hDC, 10):`** Retrieve the vertical resolution of the printer in pixel units.

**`HPrinterDPI! = APIH / (PageX2 - PageX1):`** Calculate the difference between the printer's page width and the horizontal area of the `Artwork` picture box control you want to print. `PageX1` and `PageX2` represent the width of the page image drawn on the desktop in the `UpdateDesktop` procedure (see source code).

**VPrinterDPI! = APIV / (PageY2 - PageY1):** Calculate the difference between the printer's page height and the vertical area of the Artwork picture box control you want to print. PageY1 and PageY2 represent the height of the page image drawn on the desktop in the UpdateDesktop procedure (see source code).

**RightM = HPrinterDPI!:** Adding or subtracting percentages from these values will scale the objects being printed to the page.

**BottomM = VPrinterDPI!:** Adding or subtracting percentages from these values will scale the objects being printed to the page.

The LeftM and TopM variables are measured in the current ScaleMode you are using on the form. To manually adjust the images printed on the page do the following:

**LeftM = :** The left margin of the images. Changing this number will move all the images left or right on the printer's page.

**TopM = :** The top margin of the images. Changing this number will move all the images higher or lower on the printer's page.

The RightM and BottomM variables are multiple differences between the scales used by both devices.

**RightM = :** The right margin of the images. Changing this number will enlarge or shrink all the images horizontally on the printer's page.

**BottomM = :** The bottom margin of the images. Changing this number will enlarge or shrink all the images vertically on the printer's page.

# Summary

The ArtAPI program shows the basic fundamentals of graphical drawing procedures combining Visual Basic image and picture box controls with API drawing functions. Most of the polyshape procedures have a simple underlying node construction structure. Some of these polyshape procedures tend to be rather long due to the extra line coding needed to reposition the Visual Basic image and picture box controls (nodes). What you may want to consider doing is combining some of the 12 polyshape procedures into single procedures and moving all Visual Basic control positioning within a separate function call.

The basic principle of line and curve node construction can be broken down as follows:

A node is a coordinate point that can connect one of the following:

- A line object to either side of the node's X and Y coordinate.
- A curve object to either side of the node's X and Y coordinate.
- A line and curve object to either side of the node's X and Y coordinate.
- A line or curve object to either the start or end coordinate of the object.

Because Visual Basic controls only have `Left`, `Top`, `Width`, and `Height` position properties you will either have to add offset coordinate values from the node's X and Y points or include a small function to calculate an image or picture box's center point and then position the node accordingly. If your current application only requires nodes for limited polyline or polygon design construction then you may want to eliminate Visual Basic controls altogether and use a `Pset` statement to represent the node points. This would greatly reduce the amount of polyshape procedures and events your application would require. Many 2-D and 3-D architectural and virtual games let the user define polyshape node configurations using simple `Pset` points as nodes and line statements to construct floor plans and interior designs.

Sooner or later, the 16-bit API for Windows will be sent to the pasture. You should consider rebuilding the programs provided in this book to conform with the new GUI32 standard (refer to Appendix B, "Windows NT, Windows 95, and Higher"). In most cases, only simple declaration changes will be necessary to have programs up and running in a 32-bit operating environment. If you have read this book from start to finish, you will have a good idea of how to manually create most graphical drawing routines. However, when you incorporate GDI32 polyshape and path functions, a few of these routines will no longer be required. You will still have to structure your arrays and manually code drawing routines that enhance certain functions. Some obvious GDI32 functions that could replace the manual code calculations shown in this book are the `PolyBézier` and `PolyBézierTo` functions. However, you will still be required to code routines to create Bézier handles and nodes.

I hope this book has given you some insight into the fundamentals of graphical programming, and can further be used to enhance your programs to new visual heights.

# APPENDIX A

# Artisan .BAS File

# Artisan .BAS File

## The ART3_7.BAS File

Appendix A contains the global declarations for variables, constants, and procedures used by the Artisan (Chapters 2 through 5) and ArtAPI programs (Chapter15). The ART3_7.BAS file is the main module file for the Artisan program. The ARTAPI.BAS is the main module file for the ArtAPI program and is basically identical to the ART3_7.BAS file.

## The ART3_7.BAS file Global Declarations

Listing A.1 contains the global variables used by all forms in both the Artisan and ArtAPI project. It also contains two global procedures called `Display_Color_Palette` and `Update_Mouse_Colors`, which are modified versions of the procedures found in Visual Basic's IconWorks program example and used to create and select colors from the color palettes found in both the Artisan and ArtAPI programs.

Appendix A also contains the APIFONT.BAS global variable listings used by the Text form in the Artisan project. This file is also used by other programs, so you may want to save this file under another name before editing it.

**Listing A.1. The global declarations of the Artisan program.**

```
DefInt A-Z

'Text Labels
Global Align As Integer
Global TextPoint As Single
Global CarriageCount(1000) As Integer
Global crCounter As Integer

'Zoom Bar Flags
Global Zoom_In, Zoom_Out  As Integer

' Bezier Curves
Global Convert_Curve%
Global Convert_Line%
Global FlagPrinter%

Type POINTS
 X As Integer
 Y As Integer
End Type

Type Rect
    Left As Integer
    Top As Integer
    Right As Integer
    Bottom As Integer
End Type
```

```
Declare Sub GetCursorPos Lib "User" (lpPoint As POINTAPI)
Declare Function GetMenu Lib "User" (ByVal hWnd)
Declare Function GetPrivateProfileString Lib "Kernel" (ByVal Appname$,
➥ByVal KeyName$, ByVal DEFAULT$, ByVal ReturnedString$,
➥ByVal MaxSize, ByVal FileName$)
Declare Function GetSubMenu Lib "User" (ByVal hWnd, ByVal Position)
Declare Function SendMessageByNum% Lib "User" Alias "PostMessage" (ByVal
➥hWnd%, ByVal wMsg%, ByVal wParam%, ByVal lParam&)
Declare Function TrackPopupMenu Lib "User" (ByVal hMenu, ByVal E2,
➥ByVal X, ByVal Y, ByVal r2, ByVal hWnd, ByVal r3&)
Declare Function WritePrivateProfileString Lib "Kernel" (ByVal Appname$,
➥ByVal KeyName$, ByVal NewString$, ByVal FileName$)

'odds & ends
Global Const SRCCOPY = &HCC0020
Global Const SRCAND = &H8800C6
Global Const SRCINVERT = &H660046
Global Const Blackness = &H42&
Global Const MF_BYPOSITION = &H400
Global Const BITSPIXEL = 12
Global Const HELP_CONTEXT = &H1
Global Const HELP_QUIT = &H2
Global Const HELP_HELPONHELP = &H4


'KeyWord Names
Global Const KEY_NAME = "Artisan"
Global Const KEY_ENTRY = "Colors Row"
Global Const INI_FILENAME = "Artisan.INI"

'Default Color palette values
Global Const BAS_PALETTE1 = "16777215 14737632 12632319 12640511 14745599
➥12648384 16777152 16761024 16761087 00000192
➥00016576 00049344 00049152 12632064 12582912 12583104"
Global Const BAS_PALETTE2 = "12632256 04210752 08421631 08438015 08454143
➥08454016 16777088 16744576 16744703 00000128
➥00016512 00032896 00032768 08421376 08388608 08388736"
Global Const BAS_PALETTE3 = "08421504 00000000 00000255 00033023 00065535
➥00065280 16776960 16711680 16711935 00000064
➥04210816 00016448 00016384 04210688 04194304 04194368"

'Default value for Artisan Filename field
Global Const UNTITLED = "[Untitled]"

'Artisan's ToolPalette ID's
Global Const PointerTool = 0
Global Const BezierTool = 1
Global Const ZoomTool = 2
Global Const LineTool = 3
Global Const BoxTool = 4
Global Const CircleTool = 5
Global Const OutLineTool = 6
Global Const PaintTool = 7
Global Const TextTool = 8
Global Const Poly_line = 9
```

*continues*

# Artisan .BAS File

### Listing A.1. continued

```
'Artisan's ZoomBar  ID's
Global Const ZoomIn = 0
Global Const ZoomOut = 1
Global Const ZoomAll = 2
Global Const ZoomPage = 3

'Artisan's ToolLine ID's
Global Const LineColor = 0
Global Const NoLine = 1
Global Const HairLine = 2
Global Const OnePt = 3
Global Const TwoPt = 4
Global Const FourPt = 5
Global Const EightPt = 6
Global Const TwelvePt = 7

'Artisan ToolFill ID's
Global Const Palette = 0
Global Const NoFill = 1
Global Const WhiteBrush = 2
Global Const Brush10 = 3
Global Const Brush20 = 4
Global Const Brush50 = 5
Global Const Brush70 = 6
Global Const BlackBrush = 7

'Index's into the ColorPalettes' Scrl_RGB()
Global Const RED_ELEMENT = 0
Global Const GREEN_ELEMENT = 1
Global Const BLUE_ELEMENT = 2

' Color palette array
Global Colors(47)   As Long
Global PenColor As Long
Global BrushColor As Long

'Artisan global variables
Global Opaque%
Global CurrentTool%
Global LastToolUsed%
Global CurrentLine%
Global CurrentBrush%
Global CurrentZoom%
Global ColorIndex%
Global ColorString        As String
' Miscellaneous
Global Text               As String
Global CRLF               As String * 2
Global A_TAB              As String * 1
' WindowState
Global Const MINIMIZED = 1
' Clipboard formats
Global Const CF_BITMAP = 2
' Show parameters
```

# Appendix A

```
Global Const MODAL = 1
Global Const MODELESS = 0
' Colors
Global Const BLACK = &H0&
Global Const DARKBLUE = &H800000
Global Const DARKGREEN = &H8000&
Global Const DARKCYAN = &H808000
Global Const DARKRED = &H80&
Global Const DARKPURPLE = &H800080
Global Const DARKYELLOW = &H8080&
Global Const DARKGRAY = &H808080
Global Const GRAY = &HC0C0C0
Global Const BLUE = &HFF0000
Global Const GREEN = &HFF00&
Global Const CYAN = &HFFFF00
Global Const RED = &HFF&
Global Const PURPLE = &HFF00FF
Global Const YELLOW = &HFFFF&
Global Const WHITE = &HFFFFFF
' MousePointer
Global Const DEFAULT = 0
Global Const CROSSHAIR = 2
Global Const SIZE = 5
Global Const UP_ARROW = 10
Global Const HOURGLASS = 11
' DrawMode Values
Global Const Black_Pen = 1
Global Const INVERSE = 6
Global Const Xor_Pen = 7
Global Const COPY_PEN = 13
' DrawStyle property Values
Global Const SOLID = 0
Global Const DOT = 2
' FillStyle Values
Global Const TRANSPARENT = 1
' Key Codes
Global Const KEY_BACK = &H8
Global Const KEY_SHIFT = &H10
Global Const KEY_CONTROL = &H11
Global Const KEY_INSERT = &H2D
Global Const KEY_DELETE = &H2E
Global Const KEY_SPACE = &H20
Global Const KEY_F1 = &H70
' Shift parameter masks
Global Const SHIFT_MASK = 1
Global Const CTRL_MASK = 2
Global Const ALT_MASK = 4
' Button parameter masks
Global Const LEFT_BUTTON = 1
Global Const RIGHT_BUTTON = 2
Global Const MIDDLE_BUTTON = 4
' ScaleModes
Global Const TWIPS = 1
Global Const PIXELS = 3
' MsgBox return values
Global Const MBYES = 6
```

*continues*

```
Global Const MBNO = 7
' PageSize
Global PageX1 As Integer
Global PageY1 As Integer
Global PageX2 As Integer
Global PageY2 As Integer
```

# The ARTFONT.BAS File Global Declarations

```
Type FontLog
    FontHeight As Integer
    FontWidth As Integer
    FontRotate As Integer
    FontOrientation As Integer
    FontWeight As Integer
    FontItalic As String * 1
    FontUnderLine As String * 1
    FontStrikeThru As String * 1
    FontCharSet As String * 1
    FontOutPrecision As String * 1
    FontClipPrecision As String * 1
    FontQuality As String * 1
    FontPitchFamily As String * 1
    FontFaceName As String * 20
End Type
''''''''
Type TEXTMETRIC
    tmHeight As Integer
    tmAscent As Integer
    tmDescent As Integer
    tmInternalLeading As Integer
    tmExternalLeading As Integer
    tmAveCharWidth As Integer
    tmMaxCharWidth As Integer
    tmWeight As Integer
    tmItalic As String * 1
    tmUnderlined As String * 1
    tmStruckOut As String * 1
    tmFirstChar As String * 1
    tmLastChar As String * 1
    tmDefaultChar As String * 1
    tmBreakChar As String * 1
    tmPitchAndFamily As String * 1
    tmCharSet As String * 1
    tmOverhang As Integer
    tmDigitizedAspectX As Integer
    tmDigitizedAspectY As Integer
End Type
''''''''
Type POINTAPI
    x As Integer
    y As Integer
End Type
''''''''
```

```
Type GLYPHMETRICS
    gmBlackBoxX As Integer
    gmBlackBoxY As Integer
    gmptGlyphOrigin As POINTAPI
    gmCellIncX As Integer
    gmCellIncY As Integer
End Type

Type Fixed
   fract As Integer
   value As Integer
End Type

Type Mat2
   eM11 As Fixed
   eM12 As Fixed
   eM21 As Fixed
   eM22 As Fixed
End Type

Type POINTFX
   x As Fixed
   y As Fixed
End Type

Type TTPOLYGONHEADER
   cb As Long
   dw As Long
   pfxStart As POINTFX
End Type

Type TTPOLYCURVE
   wType As Integer
   cpfx As Integer
   pfx(0 To 2) As POINTFX
End Type

Declare Function CreateFontIndirect% Lib "GDI" (lpFontLog As FontLog)
Declare Function DeleteObject% Lib "GDI" (ByVal hObject%)
Declare Function GetTextMetrics% Lib "GDI" (ByVal hDC%,
➥lpMetrics As TEXTMETRIC)
Declare Function GetTextFace% Lib "GDI" (ByVal hDC%, ByVal nCount%,
➥ByVal lpFacename$)
Declare Function GetGlyphOutLine& Lib "GDI" (ByVal hDC%, ByVal uChar%,
➥ByVal fuFormat%, lpgm As GLYPHMETRICS, ByVal cbBuffer&,
➥lppt As POINTAPI, lpmat2 As Mat2)
Declare Function GlobalUnlock% Lib "Kernel" (ByVal hMem%)
Declare Function GlobalFree% Lib "Kernel" (ByVal hMem%)
Declare Function PolyPolygon% Lib "GDI" (ByVal hDC%, lpPoints As POINTAPI,
➥lpPolyCounts%, ByVal nCount%)
Declare Function SelectObject% Lib "GDI" (ByVal hDC%, ByVal hObject%)
Declare Function SetTextAlign% Lib "GDI" (ByVal hDC%, ByVal wFlags%)
Declare Function TextOut% Lib "GDI" (ByVal hDC%, ByVal x%, ByVal y%, ByVal
➥lpString$, ByVal nCount%)

Global FontSelection%

Global Const ANSI_CHARSET = 0
```

# Artisan .BAS File

```
Global Const CLIP_CHARACTER_PRECIS = 1
Global Const CLIP_DEFAULT_PRECIS = 0
Global Const CLIP_EMBEDDED = &H80
Global Const CLIP_LH_ANGLES = &H10
Global Const CLIP_STROKE_PRECIS = 2
Global Const CLIP_TT_ALWAYS = &H20

Global Const DEFAULT_QUALITY = 0
Global Const DEFAULT_CHARSET = 1
Global Const DEFAULT_PITCH = 0

Global Const DEVICE_FONTTYPE = 2

Global Const DRAFT_QUALITY = 1

Global Const DT_TOP = &H0
Global Const DT_LEFT = &H0

Global Const DT_BOTTOM = &H8
Global Const DT_CALCRECT = &H400
Global Const DT_CENTER = &H1
Global Const DT_EXPANDTABS = &H40
Global Const DT_EXTERNALLEADING = &H200
Global Const DT_INTERNAL = &H1000
Global Const DT_NOCLIP = &H100
Global Const DT_NOPREFIX = &H800
Global Const DT_RIGHT = &H2
Global Const DT_SINGLELINE = &H20
Global Const DT_TABSTOP = &H80
Global Const DT_VCENTER = &H4
Global Const DT_WORDBREAK = &H10

Global Const FIXED_PITCH = 1

Global Const FF_DECORATIVE = 80
Global Const FF_DONTCARE = 0
Global Const FF_MODERN = 48
Global Const FF_ROMAN = 16
Global Const FF_SCRIPT = 64
Global Const FF_SWISS = 32

Global Const FW_BOLD = 700
Global Const FW_DONTCARE = 0
Global Const FW_EXTRABOLD = 800
Global Const FW_EXTRALIGHT = 200
Global Const FW_HEAVY = 900
Global Const FW_LIGHT = 300
Global Const FW_MEDIUM = 500
Global Const FW_NORMAL = 400
Global Const FW_SEMIBOLD = 600
Global Const FW_THIN = 100

Global Const LF_FULLFACESIZE = 64

Global Const NTM_BOLD = &H20&
Global Const NTM_ITALIC = &H1&
Global Const NTM_REGULAR = &H40&
```

```
Global Const OEM_CHARSET = 255

Global Const OUT_CHARACTER_PRECIS = 2
Global Const OUT_DEFAULT_PRECIS = 0
Global Const OUT_DEVICE_PRECIS = 5
Global Const OUT_RASTER_PRECIS = 6
Global Const OUT_STRING_PRECIS = 1
Global Const OUT_STROKE_PRECIS = 3
Global Const OUT_TT_ONLY_PRECIS = 7
Global Const OUT_TT_PRECIS = 4

Global Const PROOF_QUALITY = 2

Global Const RASTER_FONTTYPE = 1

Global Const SHIFTJIS_CHARSET = 128

Global Const SYMBOL_CHARSET = 2

Global Const TA_CENTER = 6
Global Const TA_BOTTOM = 8
Global Const TA_BASELINE = 24
Global Const TA_LEFT = 0
Global Const TA_NOUPDATECP = 0
Global Const TA_RIGHT = 2
Global Const TA_TOP = 0
Global Const TA_UPDATECP = 1

Global Const TMPF_DEVICE = 8
Global Const TMPF_FIXED_PITCH = 1
Global Const TMPF_TRUETYPE = 4
Global Const TMPF_VECTOR = 2

Global Const TRUETYPE_FONTTYPE = 4

Global Const VARIABLE_PITCH = 2
```

## Assigning Color to the Palette

The Display_Color_Palette procedure in Listing A.2 is used by the main Artisan form and the color palette form. It draws each color cell and the dividing lines in the ColorBar picture box control (main palette at bottom of the Artisan and ArtAPI main forms).

**Listing A.2. The Artisan palette color values.**

```
Sub Display_Color_Palette (ColorBar As Control)
    ColorBar.Scale (0, 0)-(48, 1)

    For I = 0 To 47
        ColorBar.Line (I, 0)-(I + 1, 1), Colors(I), BF
        If I Then ColorBar.Line (I, 0)-(I, 3)
    Next I

End Sub
```

# Artisan .BAS File

**ColorBar.Scale:** Use a custom scale to divide the picture box controls into 48 sections. The height is defined as one unit, so no matter what size you make the ColorBar, the 48 colors will run in one straight row the length of the control.

**For I = 0 to 47:** For every color starting at 0 and continuing to 47, do the following.

**ColorBar.Line:** Draw each color palette entry one at a time, advancing one color cell for each loop.

**Color(I):** This is an indexed array that holds each color value. The array holds index colors 0 to 47.

**If I Then ColorBar.Line:** This draws a line between each color for better visual effect.

Note that the height is stated a three units. This is because the main ColorPalette form (edit the palette) also uses the Display_ColorPalette procedure, but each color displayed is sent to a picture box that is three color rows high.

## Assigning Colors to Objects

The Update_Mouse_Colors procedure in Listing A.3 assigns a fill color to the object if the left mouse button is clicked on a palette color. An outline color for the object is assigned if the right mouse button is clicked on a palette color.

**Listing A.3. Clicking the mouse to assign a color.**

```
Sub Update_Mouse_Colors (Button, X As Single, Y As Single)
Dim color As Long

    ColorIndex = Fix(X) + Fix(Y) * 47
 color = Colors(ColorIndex)


If Button = RIGHT_BUTTON Or CurrentTool = 6 Then
PenColor = color

Artisan.StatusColor.BackColor = color :
Exit Sub

End If


BrushColor = color

Artisan.StatusPaint.BackColor = color

End Sub
```

**Dim color:** The color value is stated as a hexadecimal value that needs a Long data type to store the value.

**ColorIndex:** This returns the CurrentX and CurrentY positions of the MouseDown event, which also represents the indexed color number to retrieve. X and Y values are in decimal form, so the FIX method rounds them off.

**If Button = RIGHTBUTTON:** This sets the outline color of the object when the right mouse button is clicked.

**ArtisanStatusColor:** This is the small picture box color indicator located on the bottom-right corner of the form. Use the BackColor property instead of the BorderColor property since dithered colors would not be visible.

**BrushColor:** This sets the fill color of the object if the left mouse button is clicked.

**Artisan.StatusPiantColor:** This is a small color indicator within the StatusColor picture box. It represents the present fill color of the object. The picture box control is made smaller so you can see the underlying StatusColor picture box that represents the outline color of the object.

# Artisan1 *Text* Form

The Text form uses Basic text placement rather than API functions. You may find the API text placement functions a better choice. For professional text manipulation, however, you may want to read up on True Type font technology before getting too involved with changing this form.

The controls and their codes are very straightforward and easy to understand. The ReDrawText procedure performs the actual text drawing within the main Artisan form.

You cannot change a text box control's alignment properties at runtime. The text box control you see on this form really consists of three text box controls, one on top of the other. This is done so you can see the alignment of the text as you type. What is shown is the text box that uses the correct alignment; the other two text boxes are hidden.

One of the hardest things to achieve when placing text using Visual Basic's Print statement is the proper scaling of the text's point size when using the zoom tool. Visual Basic likes to round the point size automatically when using scaling fonts to under 8 points in size. You have to either called the font size or font names properties twice since Visual Basic simulates a small font using a bitmap font image. This plays havoc on point sizes defined in decimal form (for example, 4.37-point text). For this reason, no attempt was made to advance the zoom tool features of the Artisan program. The values used to size the text when the Artwork desktop is in the Zoom In or Zoom Out mode are approximate values only. Therefore, some text will not appear as the true WYSIWYG text point size. Figure A.1 illustrates what the Text form look like.

The declarations in Listing A.4 contain the start variables used by the Text form.

# Artisan .BAS File

**F**igure A.1.
*The text editing form of the Artisan program.*

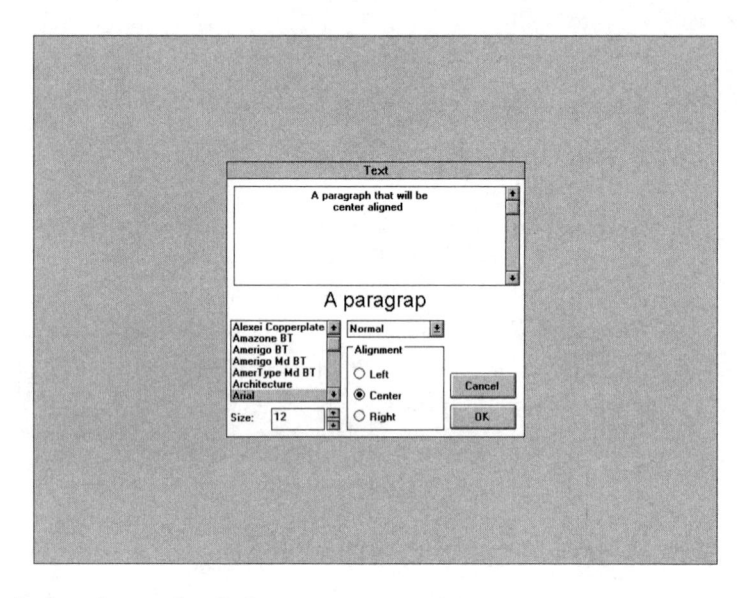

## Listing A.4. Values used when form is loaded.

**Declaration**

```
Dim Z As Integer
Dim LastFontSize As Integer
Dim LastFontName As String
```

> **Dim Z:** Stores the current text box index number.
>
> **Dim LastFontSize:** Stores the current font size if user cancels text size changes.
>
> **Dim LastFontName:** Stores the current font name if the user cancels the font change operation.

The Form_Load event in Listing A.5 initiates the default settings used by the Text form.

## Listing A.5. Setting the default values.

```
Sub Form_Load ()
TextForm.Move (Screen.Width - TextForm.Width) / 2,
                         ↪(Screen.Height - TextForm.Height) / 2
    Style_Combo.AddItem "Normal"
    Style_Combo.AddItem "Bold"
    Style_Combo.AddItem "Italic"
    Style_Combo.AddItem "Bold-Italic"

Text1(1).Visible = False
Text1(2).Visible = False

    Sizebox.Text = ARTISAN.ArtWork.FontSize
    LastFontName = ARTISAN.ArtWork.FontName
    LastFontSize = Sizebox.Text
    ViewFont.FontSize = 18
```

## Appendix A

```
For R = 0 To 20 'Printer.FontCount - 1
    FontNames$ = Printer.Fonts(R)
    FontList.AddItem FontNames$
Next R

For i = 0 To FontList.ListCount - 1
    If FontList.List(i) = ARTISAN.ArtWork.FontName Then FontList.ListIndex = i
Next i

    Style_Combo.ListIndex = 0
  crCounter = 0

End Sub
```

**TextForm.Move:** Centers the text form on the screen.

**Style_Combo.AddItem "Normal":** Adds the font attribute names to the combo list.

**Text1(1).Visible = False:** Hides the center- and right-aligned text boxes.

**Sizebox.Text:** Makes the current font size equal the last font size used in the program.

**LastFontName:** Saves the current font name if the user cancels text changes.

**LastFontSize:** Saves the current font size if the user cancels text changes.

**ViewFont.FontSize:** Displays the preview of the font in the label control.

**For R = 0 To 20 'Printer.FontCount - 1:** Loads only 20 printer fonts to save time. You will have to change this value if you do not have at least 20 fonts installed in your system. If you do not want to use a printer, change Printer.Font(R) to Screen.Fonts(R). The Printer.FontCount -1 or Screen.FontCount -1 causes all the printer or screen fonts in your system to display.

**FontList.AddItem FontNames$:** Adds each font name to the list box control.

**For i = 0 To FontList.ListCount - 1:** Searches though every font name that appears in the list box and highlights the current font being used in the program.

**Style_Combo.ListIndex = 0:** Sets the font attribute to normal style.

**crCounter = 0:** This program saves the number of carriage returns you type. This is only for extracting text lines when you save or open a file using the Print# or Write# I/O file methods.

The Cancel_Btn_Click event in Listing A.6 resets the initial values if the user cancels the text editing operation.

### Listing A.6. Cancelling the text edit functions.

```
Sub Cancel_Btn_Click ()
    ARTISAN.ArtWork.FontName = LastFontName
    ARTISAN.ArtWork.FontSize = LastFontSize
    ARTISAN.ArtWork.FontBold = False
    ARTISAN.ArtWork.FontItalic = False
```

*continues*

## Artisan .BAS File

**Listing A.6. continued**

```
    ARTISAN.Txt.FontName = LastFontName
    ARTISAN.Txt.FontSize = LastFontSize
    ARTISAN.Txt.FontBold = False
    ARTISAN.Txt.FontItalic = False
    ARTISAN.Txt.Width = 15
    Align = 0

    Unload TextForm

End Sub
```

**ARTISAN.ArtWork.FontName:** You have selected the Cancel button, which will reset all text attributes to the their default settings.

**Unload TextForm:** Unloads the text form. Hiding the form would not update the attributes automatically because the update code is in the Form_Load event (Listing A.5).

The CarriageReturns procedure in Listing A.7 counts each time the user presses the Enter key. A carriage return flag is needed to save text strings to a file.

**Listing A.7. Calculating carriage returns in the text string.**

```
Sub CarriageReturns ()
    Static curindex As Long
    Dim Find As String
    Find = Chr(13)

Do
    curindex = InStr(curindex + 1, Text1(Z).Text, Find)
    If curindex > 0 Then

    Text1(Z).SelStart = curindex - 1
    Text1(Z).SelLength = Len(Find)
    CR_LF = CR_LF + 1
  End If

Loop While curindex > 0

    crCounter = CR_LF
End Sub
```

**Find = Chr(13):** This program saves the number of carriage returns you type. This is only for extracting text lines when you save or open a file using the Print# or Write# I/O file methods. The method used here is exactly the same routine as used in the Multi-Search and Replace program in Chapter 7. Refer to that chapter for a detailed explanation of the code used in Listing A.7.

The FontList_Click event in Listing A.8 is used to select a new font for the list box.

## Listing A.8. Selecting a new font form a list box.

```
Sub FontList_Click ()
    ViewFont.FontName = FontList.Text
    ARTISAN.ArtWork.FontName = ViewFont.FontName
    ARTISAN.Txt.FontName = ViewFont.FontName
    ARTISAN.Txt.Width = 15

End Sub
```

**ViewFont.FontName:** You have selected a new font name for the list box. Change all font name properties accordingly. The Artisan.Txt label control is set to resize automatically, which will expand when the font name is changed. The Txt label acts as the cursor, so change the width to 15 twips wide (1 pixel width).

The OK_Btn_Click event in Listing A.9 accepts text changes when the user selected the OK button on the Text form.

## Listing A.9. Printing your edited text to the desktop.

```
Sub OK_Btn_Click ()
If Text1(Z).Text > "" Then 'print attributes

    ARTISAN.ArtWork.FontName = ViewFont.FontName
    ARTISAN.ArtWork.FontBold = ViewFont.FontBold
    ARTISAN.ArtWork.FontItalic = ViewFont.FontItalic

ARTISAN.Txt.Visible = False
ARTISAN.Txt.FontName = ViewFont.FontName
ARTISAN.Txt.FontSize = Val(Sizebox.Text)
If Zoom_In = True Then ARTISAN.Txt.FontSize = ARTISAN.Txt.FontSize * TextPoint
If Zoom_Out = True Then ARTISAN.Txt.FontSize = ARTISAN.Txt.FontSize * TextPoint

ARTISAN.Txt.Caption = Text1(Z).Text
ARTISAN.StatusLabel.Caption = ViewFont.FontName

    Select Case True
        Case Option1(0)
            Align = 0 'left
        Case Option1(1)
            Align = 6 'center
        Case Option1(2)
            Align = 2 'right
    End Select

End If
        Unload TextForm

End Sub
```

## Artisan .BAS File

**If Text1(Z).Text > "" Then:** You have selected the OK button. If you have typed characters in the text box, they will be redrawn on the desktop. If no characters appear in the text box, any attribute changes will take effect typing occurs on the desktop.

The `Option1_Click` event in Listing A.10 changes the alignment of the text to left, center, or right alignment.

**Listing A.10. Aligning the text within a text box.**

```
Sub Option1_Click (Index As Integer)
Select Case Index
    Case 0 'Align Left
Text1(0).Text = Text1(Z).Text
Text1(0).Visible = True: Z = Index: Text1(0).SetFocus
Text1(1).Visible = False: Text1(2).Visible = False
    Case 1 'Align Centre
Text1(1).Text = Text1(Z).Text
Text1(1).Visible = True: Z = Index: Text1(1).SetFocus
Text1(0).Visible = False: Text1(2).Visible = False
    Case 2 'Align Right
Text1(2).Text = Text1(Z).Text
Text1(2).Visible = True: Z = Index: Text1(2).SetFocus
Text1(0).Visible = False: Text1(1).Visible = False
End Select
End Sub
```

**Select Case Index:** Depending on which alignment option button you selected, do the following:

**Text1(0).Text = Text1(Z).Text:** Switch the text from one alignment text box to another.

**Text1(0).Visible = True: Z = Index:** Show the new alignment text box and store the new index number.

**Text1(1).Visible = False:** Hide the old alignment text box.

The `SizeBox_Change` event in Listing A.11 changes the point size of the font.

## Listing A.11. Manually typing in a new font size.

```
Sub SizeBox_Change ()
On Error GoTo BadInput
    Pts = Val(Sizebox.Text)
    Pt2 = Fix(Pts)
    VScroll1.Value = Pt2: Exit Sub

BadInput:
    Sizebox.Text = "12"
    Exit Sub
End Sub
```

**On Error GoTo BadInput:** You can type a font size into the text box that is equal to or between the minimum and maximum values of the VScroll1 scrollbar control. If you type a letter character or exceed the minimum and maximum values, the font size gets set to the default of 12.

The Style_Combo_Click event in Listing A.12 changes the font's normal, italic, or bold attributes.

## Listing A.12. Selecting a new font attribute.

```
Sub Style_Combo_Click ()
Select Case Style_Combo.Text
  Case "Normal"
    ViewFont.FontBold = False: ViewFont.FontItalic = False
  Case "Bold"
    ViewFont.FontBold = True: ViewFont.FontItalic = False
  Case "Italic"
    ViewFont.FontItalic = True: ViewFont.FontBold = False
  Case "Bold-Italic"
    ViewFont.FontBold = True: ViewFont.FontItalic = True
End Select

End Sub
```

**Select Case Style_Combo.Text:** Change the font attributes according to which combo item you selected.

The Text1_Change event in Listing A.13 display a formatted text example of the first 10 characters of the text the user types.

## Listing A.13. Displaying an example of the text.

```
Sub Text1_Change (Index As Integer)

Z = Index: ViewFont.Caption = Left$(Text1(Z).Text, 10)

End Sub
```

**Z = Index: ViewFont.Caption:** If you typed text into a text box, display the first 10 characters in the font preview label.

The `VScroll_Change` event in Listing A.14 changes the current font size when the user uses the vertical scrollbar control.

**Listing A.14. Changing the font size using a scrollbar control.**
```
Sub VScroll1_Change ()
   Sizebox.Text = Format$(VScroll1.Value)
   ARTISAN.ArtWork.FontSize = Sizebox.Text

   ARTISAN.Txt.Visible = False
   ARTISAN.Txt.FontSize = Sizebox.Text
   ARTISAN.Txt.Width = 15
   ARTISAN.Txt.Visible = True

End Sub
```

**Sizebox.Text = Format$(VScroll1.Value):** Display the current font size changes in the font size text box. Change all font sizes for currently being used by the program.

## Summary of the *Text* Form

The text edit form for the Artisan program has limited text features, but it can be modified quite easily. To display and edit text already on the desktop, make the `StoredText(B)` array global by placing it into one of the two module files. All text strings are stored in the `StoredText` array, where B represents the object number assigned to the string. During the `Form_Load` event, you can add code that would determine whether the currently selected object on the desktop has a `FlagText` attribute. If so, place the `StoredText` string that matches the objects assigned number into a text edit box.

## Artisan *NodeEdit* Form

The `NodeEdit` form is a simple dialog box used to convert a line to a curve, or vice versa. The global variables `Convert_Curve` and `Convert_Line` are used to flag the `Artwork_DblClick` event and determine what conversion action to take. Figure A.2 illustrates the `NodeEdit` form.

The `Cancel_Click` event in Listing A.15 hides the `NodeEdit` form if the Cancel button is selected.

**Listing A.15. Pressing the Cancel button.**
```
Sub Cancel_Click ()
    NodeEdit.Hide

End Sub
```

**NodeEdit.Hide:** Cancel the conversion operation and hide the node edit form.

**F**igure A.2.
*The node editing form of the Artisan program.*

When the To Curve button is selected, the `To_Curve_Click` event tells the `Artwork_DblClick` event to change the line to curve:

**Sub To_Curve_Click ()**

Convert_Curve = True: NodeEdit.Hide

End Sub

> **Convert_Curve = True:** You selected the Convert to Curve button, which will make the Artwork double click event convert a line object to a Bézier curve.

When the To Line button is selected, the `To_Line_Click` event tells the `Artwork_DblClick` event to change the curve to line.

**Sub To_Line_Click ()**

Convert_Line = True: NodeEdit.Hide
End Sub

> Convert_Line = True: You selected the Convert to Line button, which will make the Artwork_DlbClick event convert a Bézier curve to a line object.

# Artisan *ColorPalette* Form

The `ColorPalette` form is a very simple palette editor. It has some additional features, such as drag-and-drop color changes. You can use the RGB scrollbars to create a custom color, and then drag the new color to the main palette display area. Any changes to the secondary palette are saved in a file called ARTISAN.INI.

## Artisan .BAS File

After you have changed the default color palette, the program will use the ARTISAN.INI palette information every time you start this program. To have the Artisan program use the default palette again at startup, you must erase or `Kill` the ARTISAN.INI file. Figure A.3 illustrates the Palette form.

**Figure A.3.**
*The color palette form of the Artisan program.*

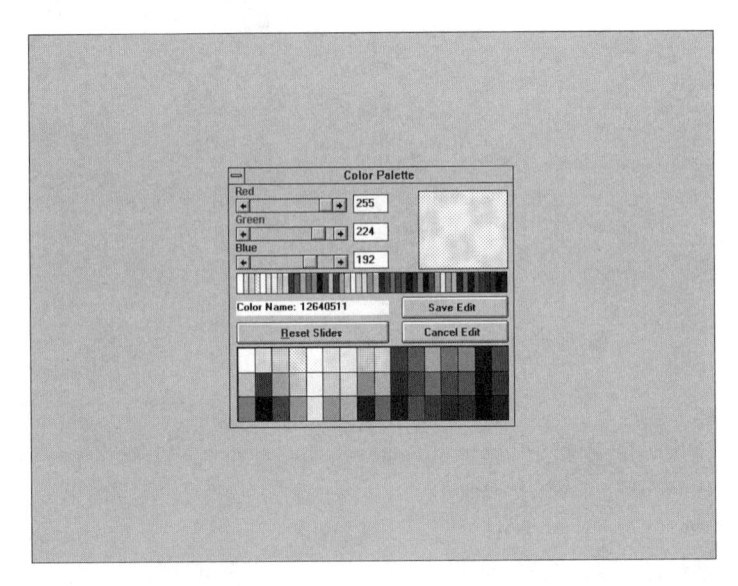

## Values Used in the Palette Form

The palette form is a simple editor you can use to change the available colors within the Artisan program. Do this by dragging and dropping a newly defined color onto the palette display area.

The `Form_Load` event in Listing A.16 centers the palette form on the screen and then loads the current color palette into the palette editing picture box.

**Listing A.16. The default values at startup.**

```
Sub Form_Load ()
    ColorPalette.Left = (Screen.Width - Width) / 2
    ColorPalette.Top = (Screen.Height - Height) / 2

 BrushColor = Artisan.StatusPaint.BackColor
 RGBscroll(0).Value = BrushColor And &HFF&
 RGBscroll(1).Value = (BrushColor And &HFF00&) \ 256
 RGBscroll(2).Value = (BrushColor And &HFF0000) \ 65536

    For i = 0 To 47
        PaletteColors(i) = Colors(i)
    Next I

End Sub
```

# Appendix A

**ColorPalette.Left:** Centers the form on the screen.

**BrushColor = Artisan.StatusPaint.BackColor:** The fill color of the currently selected object on the desktop.

**RGBscroll(0).Value:** The hexadecimal red color element of the RGB color.

**RGBscroll(1).Value:** The hexadecimal green color element of the RGB color.

**RGBscroll(2).Value:** The hexadecimal blue color element of the RGB color.

**For i = 0 To 47:** Stores Artisan's current 48-color palette.

**PaletteColors(i) = Colors(i):** Each Artisan palette color is stored in array Color(i), so temporarily store the current palette values into the PaletteColors(i) array.

The OKbtn_Click event in Listing A.17 accepts the edit changes to the color palette when the OK button is selected.

### Listing A.17. Saving or canceling palette color edits.

```
Sub OKbtn_Click ()
    If Index = 0 Then
        For i = 0 To 47
            Colors(i) = PaletteColors(i)
        Next i
    End If

    Unload ColorPalette

End Sub
```

**Colors(i) = PaletteColors(i):** You selected the Save Edit button, so reassign all 48 of Artisan's palette colors the new palette entries.

**Unload ColorPalette:** You have selected the Save Edit or Cancel Edit button, so unload the form.

The Cmd_Reset_Click event in Listing A.18 resets the RGB scrollbars to the last color value before the edit.

### Listing A.18. Resetting the scrollbars to their previous values.

```
Sub Cmd_Reset_Click ()
    GetRGBcolors

End Sub
```

**GetRGBcolors:** Resets the color element's values to their original settings.

The ColorBar_MouseUp event in Listing A.19 places the selected color from the small palette into the color display picture box for editing.

# Artisan .BAS File

**Listing A.19.** Selecting a color from the Artisan program's palette.

```
Sub ColorBar_MouseUp (Button As Integer, Shift As Integer, X As Single, Y As Single)
Dim color As Long
X = Fix(X): Y = Fix(Y)
ColorIndex = X + Y * 47

    If X >= 0 And X < 48 And Y >= 0 And Y < 2 Then
        color = Colors(ColorIndex)
        GetRGBcolors
        ColorName.Caption = "Color Name: " + Format$(DragColor.BackColor)
    End If

End Sub
```

> **Dim color As Long:** All colors are stored as hexadecimal values that require `Long` data types.
>
> **X = Fix(X): Y = Fix(Y):** The `ColorBar` picture box is scaled as 48 whole units wide and 1 unit high. The `X` and `Y` arguments of the `MouseUp` event are declared as `Single` (decimal units). The `Fix` statement rounds the `X` and `Y` mouse coordinates to whole numbers.
>
> **ColorIndex = X + Y * 47:** The Artisan palette colors are stored in a array called `Colors`, which has 48 index entries. The mouse's coordinates will return a value between 0 and 47 that will match the array index of the colors palette array.
>
> **If X >= 0 And X < 48 And Y >= 0 And Y < 2 Then:** Make sure the mouse cannot exceed the 0 to 47 scale width and 1 unit scale height of the `ColorBar` picture box.
>
> **Color = Colors(ColorIndex):** Make the variable `Color` equal the hexadecimal color value returned by Artisan's `Colors( X+Y * 47 )` palette array.
>
> **GetRGBcolors:** Extracts each `RGB` color element, thus changing the scrollbars—which in turn will display the color within the `DragColor` picture box control.

The `ColorBar_Paint` event in Listing A.20 displays the small color palette.

**Listing A.20.** Drawing each color of the Artisan program's palette.

```
Sub ColorBar_Paint ()
    Display_Color_Palette ColorBar
End Sub
```

> **Display_Color_Palette ColorBar:** Draws each of the 48 Artisan palette colors into the `ColorBar` picture box.

The `DragColor_DragOver` event in Listing A.21 displays a "DRAG COLOR" message when the mouse is clicked on the edit picture box.

**Listing A.21. Assigning a new color to the Artisan color palette.**

```
Sub DragColor_DragOver (Source As Control, X As Single, Y As Single, State As Integer)
    If State = 0 Then DragColor.Cls
    DragColor.ForeColor = (QBColor(15 * Rnd))
    DragColor.CurrentX = 6
    DragColor.Print "DRAG COLOR"
    If DragColor.CurrentY > 100 Then DragColor.CurrentY = 0
End Sub
```

**If State = 0 Then DragColor.Cls:** Holding the mouse over the DragColor picture box makes the mouse pointer change to a felt marker icon. You can now drag the color form over to the main PaletteBox picture box control. Releasing the mouse button then drops the color into the main palette. The DragMode property is set to automatic when ever you click the control with the mouse pointer.

The GetRGBcolors procedure in Listing A.22 extracts each red, green, and blue element from a color so the color can be edited.

**Listing A.22. Extracting the RGB color elements.**

```
Sub GetRGBcolors ()
    R1 = (Colors(ColorIndex) And &HFF)
    G2 = (Colors(ColorIndex) And &HFF00&) \ 256
    B3 = (Colors(ColorIndex) And &HFF0000) \ 65536

'R1 = Colors(ColorIndex) Mod 256            'same as above
'G2 = Colors(ColorIndex) \ 256 Mod 256
'B3 = Colors(ColorIndex) \ 65536 Mod 256

'R1 = Colors(ColorIndex) And &HFF&
'G2 = (Colors(ColorIndex) \ 2 ^ 8) And &HFF&
'B3 = (Colors(ColorIndex) \ 2 ^ 16) And &HFF&

    RGBscroll(RED_ELEMENT).Value = R1
    RGBscroll(GREEN_ELEMENT).Value = G2
    RGBscroll(BLUE_ELEMENT).Value = B3
End Sub
```

**R1 = (Colors(ColorIndex) And &HFF):** Extracts the hexadecimal red color element of the RGB color.

**G2 = (Colors(ColorIndex) And &HFF00&) \ 256:** Extracts the hexadecimal green color element of the RGB color.

**B3 = (Colors(ColorIndex) And &HFF0000) \ 65536:** Extracts the hexadecimal blue color element of the RGB color. The two blocks of code statements that are remarked out are alternative methods you can use to extract RGB color elements from a hexadecimal color value.

## Artisan .BAS File

**RGBscroll(RED_ELEMENT).Value = R1:** Changes the scrollbar that controls the display of the red color element.

**RGBscroll(GREEN_ELEMENT).Value = G2:** Changes the scrollbar that controls the display of the green color element.

**RGBscroll(BLUE_ELEMENT).Value = B3:** Changes the scrollbar that controls the display of the blue color element.

The `PaletteBox_DragDrop` event in Listing A.23 places the color from the editing picture box into the main palette picture box.

### Listing A.23. Dropping a new color into the main palette.

```
Sub PaletteBox_DragDrop (Source As Control, X As Single, Y As Single)
X = Fix(X) 'will return the location
If Fix(Y) = 1 Then X = Fix(X) + 15
If Fix(Y) = 2 Then X = Fix(X) + 32

    PaletteColors(X) = Val(DragColor.BackColor)
    PaletteBox_Paint 'Update Color in Palette Box

End Sub
```

**If Fix(Y) = 1 Then X = Fix(X) + 15:** Drops the color into the second row of the main palette display.

**If Fix(Y) = 2 Then X = Fix(X) + 32:** Drops the color into the third row of the main palette display.

**PaletteColors(X) = Val(DragColor.BackColor):** Updates the form's palette array entry.

**PaletteBox_Paint:** Redraws the new color in main palette.

The `PaleteBox_DragOver` event in Listing A.24 displays a "DROP COLOR" message when the edited color is dragged over the main palette.

### Listing A.24. Printing the drag-and-drop instructions.

```
Sub PaletteBox_DragOver (Source As Control, X As Single, Y As Single, State As Integer)
    If State = 0 Then DragColor.Cls
    DragColor.ForeColor = (QBColor(15 * Rnd))
    DragColor.CurrentX = 6
    DragColor.Print "DROP COLOR"
    If DragColor.CurrentY > 100 Then DragColor.CurrentY = 0
End Sub
```

**If State = 0 Then DragColor.Cls:** When the mouse enters into the main `PaletteBox` picture box, the drop color is displayed in the `DragColor` picture box control.

The `PaletteBox_Paint` event in Listing A.25 displays three rows of the main palette's colors.

**Listing A.25.** Drawing each color into the three-row color palette.
```
Sub PaletteBox_Paint ()
    PaletteBox.Scale (0, 0)-(16, 3)

  For R = 1 To 3

    For i = 0 To 15
        PaletteBox.Line (i, R - 1)-(i + 1, R), PaletteColors(i + NR), BF
        PaletteBox.Line (i, R - 1)-(i + 1, R), QBColor(0), B
    Next i
    NR = NR + 16 'Next row of color values
  Next R

End Sub
```

> **PaletteBox.Scale (0, 0)-(16, 3):** Scales the `PaletteBox` picture box to 16 color cells wide by 3 color cell rows.
>
> **PaletteBox.Line (I, R-1)-(I + 1, R), Colors(I), BF:** Displays each color in the specified row of the picture box.
>
> **PaletteBox.Line (i, R - 1)-(i + 1, R), QBColor(0), B:** Draws a black border around each color displayed.

The `RGB_Scroll_Change` event in Listing A.26 initiates the scrollbar's scrolling event to change the red, green, or blue elements of a color.

**Listing A.26.** Changing a color's element using a scrollbar.
```
Sub RGB_Scrolls_Change (Index As Integer)
    RGBscroll_scroll Index
End Sub
```

> **RGBscroll_scroll Index:** Triggers the `scroll` event of this control to execute.

The `RGBscroll_Change` event in Listing A.27 displays the new red, green, or blue elements of a color in the editing picture box.

**Listing A.27.** Displaying a color using a scrollbar control.
```
Sub RGBscroll_scroll (Index As Integer)
    DragColor.BackColor = RGB(RGBscroll(0).Value, RGBscroll(1).Value,
➥RGBscroll(2).Value)

  For i = 0 To 2
      RGB_TextBox(i).Text = Format$(RGBscroll(i).Value)
  Next i

End Sub
```

`DragColor.BackColor = RGB:` Displays the new color element in the `DragColor` picture box.

`RGB_TextBox(i).Text = Format$:` Displays the numeric value of the color element in the text box.

The `RGB_Textbox_Change` event in Listing A.28 displays the values of each red, green, and blue element of a color.

**Listing A.28. Manually typing a color element value into a text box control.**

```
Sub RGB_TextBox_Change (Index As Integer)
On Error GoTo BadInput
    RGBscroll(Index).Value = RGB_TextBox(Index).Text: Exit Sub
BadInput:
    RGB_TextBox(Index).Text = RGBscroll(Index).Value: Exit Sub

End Sub
```

`On Error GoTo BadInput:` A red, green, or blue color element can only be defined as 0 through 255. The `RGB_TextBox_Change` event ensures that you don't enter any lower or higher value.

# Summary of the *Palette* Form

The palette edit form for the Artisan program has limited color-enhancement features. You may want to consider adding optional color settings, such as web-press values of cyan, magenta, yellow, and black, as well as hue and saturation color combinations. Refer to the Fountain Fill Palette program in Chapter 9 for alternative palette creation methods.

# Appendix B

# Windows NT, Windows 95, and Higher

# Windows NT, Windows 95, and Higher

This book was published prior to the release of Visual Basic 4.0 and Windows 95. The 32-bit API drawing functions currently available in Windows NT will most likely be subject to the Windows 95 platform. For all intents and purposes, the following GUI32 drawing function descriptions are intended for Visual Basic versions that can run on WIN32 or WIN32's operating platforms.

The GDI32 (Graphical Device Interface/32-bit) is an API library that contains 32-bit application functions. In Windows 3.1, the majority of API functions were stored in the GDI.EXE, USER.EXE, and KRNL386.EXE files. The API drawing functions available in Windows 3.1 are adequate to perform standard drawing operations but lack somewhat behind third-party illustration applications, which tend to use their own routines for more complex imaging and drawing tasks. The GUI32 now contains more robust features, which can save you from coding advanced routines and which can be used to replace some of the manual coding methods described in this book. For instance, the API path, stroke, and region functions can be incorporated to automatically collect coordinate points and build a bounding box around single or several objects. API path, clipping, and fill functions can be used to extract the outline of text characters and fill the text strings with custom patterns or colors. Advance metafile and bitmap functions enable editing and rotating—just to name few new features.

The list of new API features in the GDI32 are too numerous to mention in this appendix. The following subsections describe some of the commonly used new API drawing functions.

## GDI32 Paths

A *path* refers to an outline of a graphics object. An *object* can be a single (or several) group of lines or curves connected to each other either as a whole or by object starting coordinates. This is similar to the way PostScript printers interpret graphics; that is, all objects being drawn are really connected by one long scribble line. Once the end coordinate of one object is set, an imaginary line moves to the next object in the order. Paths can collect the coordinate points of the object being drawn and can use this information to find the points furthest left, top, right, and bottom of the object. Knowing this information, a bounding box (region) can be calculated for the object or group of objects. Sizing or moving this bounding box will size or move the object or objects contained within. If you increase the drawing width of the pen, you can automatically widen the bounding box dimensions.

The following API functions can be used as path outlines:

```
AngleArc      LineTo       Polyline
Arc           MoveToEx     PolylineTo
ArcTo         Pie          PolyPolygon
Chord         PolyBezier   PolyPolyline
CloseFigure   PolyBezier   ToRectangle
Ellipse       PolyDraw     RoundRect
ExtTextOut    Polygon      TextOut
```

To start a path, call the API `BeginPath` function stating the control that you will be drawing into. For example:

```
API32 = BeginPath(Picture1.hDC)
```

To end a path, call the API `EndPath` function stating the control that you have be drawn into. For example:

```
API32 = EndPath(Picture1.hDC)
```

## GDI32 *StrokePath*

You can draw the path by calling the API `StrokePath` function. To draw the path, use the current pen and state the control that you want to draw into. For example:

```
API32 = StrokePath(Picture1.hDC)
```

Once the API `StrokePath` function is called, the buffer holding the path coordinates is destroyed. You should only use this method when you no longer require changes to the path.

## GDI32 *StrokeAndFillPath*

The API `StrokeAndFillPath` automatically closes the figure, draws the path's outline, and fills the outline of the path with a pattern or the current brush color. For example:

```
API32 = StrokeAndFillPath(Picture1.hDC)
```

## GDI32 *FillPath*

The API `FillPath` function paints the path's interior using the current brush color or a pattern. The painting method is defined by the polygon fill mode, which can be either alternate or winding. For example:

```
API32 = FillPath(Picture1.hDC)
```

## GDI32 *GetPath*

The API `GetPath` function can retrieve the coordinate points of a path that has not been automatically destroyed by a stroke function. When the API `GetPath` is used in conjunction with the API `PolyDraw` function, you can mirror or copy objects on the desktop. Following is an example of the API `GetPath` function:

```
API32 = GetPath(Picture1.hDC, lpPoints, lpTypes, nSize)
```

## GDI32 *SelectClipPath*

The API `SelectClipPath` function can change the path's outline to a clipping region. This is great for filling complex objects with any type of fill. Chapter 9 demonstrates how to use Xor mode to mask and fill complex object shapes. The API `SelectClipPath` can be used as an alternative to mask an object. A path's clipping area enables you to fill character or polyshapes with bitmaps, patterns, fountain fills, and so on, or change a character or polyshape to a hollow shape. Following is an example of the API `SelectClipPath` function:

```
API32 = SelectClipPath(Picture1.hDC, RGN)
```

## GDI32 *PathToRegion*

Use the API `PathToRegion` function to create a bounding box region around an object or a group of objects. Use a region to keep track of an object you draw, similar to the Artisan program in Chapter 2. Chapter 2 manually calculated an objects bounding box and then assigned the figure within an object number. Use the API `PathToRegion` function to move one or several objects to new screen locations via API region functions. You also can group single objects together or scuffle the bounding box regions around to switch the drawing laying order. You must still maintain an array of some sort to collect paths and regions since the `BeginPath`, `FillPath`, `PathToRegion`, `StrokePath`, `StrokeAndFillPath`, and `SelectClipPath` function calls will destroy the previous path.

An example of an API `PathToRegion` call is as follows:

```
API32 = PathToRegion(Picture1.hDC)
```

## GDI32 *WidenPath*

Calling the API `WidenPath` function expands the path's width by the current width of the pen. The following is an example of calling the `WidenPath` API function:

```
API32 = WidenPath(Picture1.hDC)
```

# GDI32 Drawing Functions

There are several new API polyshape functions, as well as new bitmap and metafile calls and structures. The following descriptions merely touch the full abilities of the GDI32 drawing functions.

## GDI32 *AngleArc*

The API `AngleArc` draws an angle line and an arc. For the most part, the Visual Basic `Circle` statement can do the same by using negative values in the start and end keyword arguments. Following is an example of a call to the API `AngleArc` function:

```
API32 = AngleArc(Picture1.hDC, X, Y, Radius, StartAngle, SweepAngle)
```

## GDI32 *ArcTo*

The API `ArcTo` function can update the last point set as the current X and Y coordinate. The Visual Basic `Circle` statement makes the circle's center point the current position. You can use the API `ArcTo` function to create the rounded corners on a rectangular shape. Refer to the Rounded Corners program in Chapter 11. Following is an example of the API `ArcTo` function:

```
API32 = ArcTo(Picture1.hDC, X1, Y1, X2, Y2, X3, Y3, X4, Y4)
```

## GDI32 *SetArcDirection*

Use the API `SetArcDirection` function to set the direction the arc is drawn (clockwise or counterclockwise). The Visual Basic `Circle` statement always draws in a clockwise direction. Following is an example of the API `SetArcDirection` function:

```
API32 = SetArcDirection(Picture1.hDC, AD)
```

## GDI32 *CloseFigure*

The API `CloseFigure` function is similar to the polygon functions except the shape of the figure can be made up of several objects connected together. The end point is automatically closed to the starting point of the figure. Following is an example of the API `CloseFigure` function:

```
API32 = CloseFigure(Picture1.hDC)
```

## GDI32 *PolyBezier*

The API `PolyBezier` function is a built-in algorithm that calculates the curve points needed to generate a Bézier curve. The function works on the same principle as the `BezierDivide` procedures found in the Artisan and Mini-Bézier programs in Chapter 10. Use the API `PolyBezier` function to draw several Bézier curves connected to each; thus, the `PolyBezier` function could be used to shorten or eliminate some of the polyshape procedures demonstrated in the ArtAPI program in Chapter 15. Following is an example of the API `PolyBezier` function:

```
API32 = PolyBezier(Picture1.hDC, starting address, Count)
```

## GDI32 *PolyBezierTo*

This function takes care of connecting a Bézier curve's node coordinate to the start of another graphical object. The API `PolyBezierTo` function, when used with the API `PolyBezier` function, is best suited for manually drawing the outline of text characters or connecting Bézier curves to another object. Following is an example of the API `PolyBezierTo` function:

```
API32 = PolyBezierTo(Picture1.hDC, starting address, Count)
```

# Windows NT, Windows 95, and Higher

## GDI32 *PolyDraw*

Use the API `PolyDraw` function to draw a series of line and curve objects similar to the way the ArtAPI program in Chapter 15 draws polyshapes. However, you cannot change the pen attributes used to draw each individual line or curve object in the polyshape. Refer to the Test Button command control in the ArtAPI program in Chapter 15. The Test Button manually strings each line and curve together so it is possible to change the attributes of each line and curve before it is drawn. Following is an example of the API `PolyDraw` function:

```
API32 = PolyDraw(Picture1.hDC, lpPoints, lpTypes, nSize)
```

## GDI32 *EnumEnhMetaFile*

The previous API Metafile functions used in Windows have had major overhauls. There are several new enhancements to the metafile formats in the GDI32 system. One of new features is the API `EnumEnhMetaFile` function that can extract individual metafile records so you can edit the objects contained in the file. Since most drawing programs use their own structures to save illustrations and since OLE2 now supports most of these programs, the metafile may have had its day. Following is an example of a call using the `EnumEnhMetaFile` API function:

```
API32 = EnumEnhMetaFile(Picture1.hDC, EMFhandle, callback, lpData, lpRect)
```

## GDI32 *MaskBlt*

Use the API `MaskBlt` function to mask a bitmap image in order to make the background transparent. This saves having to create two bitmap images and then inverting specific areas in order to simulate animated effects. Following is an example call using the API `MaskBlt` function:

```
API32 = MaskBlt(Picture1.hDC, Destination, X, Y, Width, Height, Source, X, Y, ROP)
```

## GDI32 *PlgBlt*

Use the API `PlgBlt` function to mirror or rotate a bitmap image. Following is an example call using the API `PlgBlt` function:

```
API32 = PlgBlt(Picture1.hDC lpPoints, Source, X, Y, Width, Height, OptionalMask, X, Y)
```

Table B.1 shows a select few of GDI32 drawing functions.

**T**able B.1. Some of the common GDI32 graphical functions.

| AngleArc* | FillRect | Polyline | SetBkMode |
|---|---|---|---|
| AnimatePalette | FillRgn | PolyPolygon | SetDIBitsToDevice |
| Arc | FloodFill | PolyPolyline | SetPixel |
| ArcTo* | GetDIBits | RealizePalette | SetPolyFillMode |

# Appendix B

| | | | |
|---|---|---|---|
| BeginPath* | GetPath* | Rectangle | SetROP2 |
| BitBlt | IntersectClipRect | RestoreDC | SetStretchBltMode |
| Chord | LineTo | RoundRect | SetTextColor |
| CloseFigure* | MakePath* | PtInRegion | SetTextJustification |
| CopyEnhMetaFile* | MaskBlt* | SaveDC | SetViewportExt |
| CreatBrushIndirect | MoveToEx | ScaleViewportExt | SetWindowExt |
| CreateDIBitmap | OffsetClipRgn | ScaleWindowExt | SetWindowOrg |
| CreateDIBPatternBrush | OffsetViewportOrg | SelectClipPath* | StretchBlt |
| CreateEnhMetaFile* | OffsetWindowOrg | SelectClipRgn | StrokeAndFillPath* |
| CreateFontIndirect | PatBlt | SelectFont | StrokePath* |
| CreatePatternBrush | PathToRegion* | SelectObject | StretchDIBits |
| DeleteObject | Pie | SelectPalette | TextOut |
| Ellipse | PlayEnhMetaFile* | SetArcDirection* | WidenPath* |
| EndPath* | PlgBlt* | SetBkColor | |
| EnumEnhMetaFile* | PolyBezier* | SetMapMode | |
| ExcludeClipRect | PolyBezierTo* | SetWindowExtEx | |
| ExtTextOut | PolyDraw* | SetViewportExtEx | |
| FillPath* | Polygon | SetViewportOrgEx | |

*New to the Windows API library.

# APPENDIX C

# The Companion Disk

# The Companion Disk

The companion the disk for *Graphics Programming with Visual Basic* contains

- All the source code for creating executable programs presented in the book
- Picture files (.BMP files) that some of the programs require
- Icon files (.ICO files) that some of the programs require
- .VBX files, stamp-dated when the programs were developed

## Installing the Companion Disk Files

You should copy all programs to, and run them from, your hard drive. Any program that requires Visual Basic .VBX files has its Visual Basic .MAK file pointing to the C:\WINDOWS\SYSTEM directory. If you have the required .VBX files located on another directory, use a text editor (such as Notepad in Windows) to change the file pointers in the appropriate .MAK file.

All files are 16-bit and were compiled using Visual Basic 3.0. All custom controls are in .VBX format and can be converted to .OCX custom controls. The `PicClip` control by Microsoft and Thuridion Software Engineering Inc., requires the VB.LIC file (Visual Basic professional version) in order to load. All programs were designed in 800 by 600 video resolution (256 colors) using Visual Basic 3.0 for Windows 3.1 and 3.11.

Figure C.1 shows the directory structure of disk that accompanies this book.

**Figure C.1.**
*Directory structure of this book's disk.*

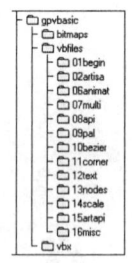

The following are the directory names and descriptions of the files or programs contained within each directory:

*BITMAPS:* Contains all the bitmap images used in the programs. All images in the BITMAPS directory are saved in 16-color format.

*.VBXs:* All .VBX files are stamp-dated 4/28/93. However, there have been several updates since then. The .VBX files are included on disk to guarantee compatibility with the programs. You may want to use newer Visual Basic .VBX- or .OCX-compatible custom controls. The ArtAPI program located in the 15ARTAPI directory uses the `PicClip` control supplied with the professional version of Visual Basic. If your Visual Basic product does not include the VB.LIC file, you will either have to upgrade or use the ArtAPI_s program in Chapter 15 (which does not use the `PicClip` control).

# Appendix C

The VBFILES directory contains the following subdirectories and the programs within each subdirectory:

*01BEGIN:* The Begin, Pset, and Movetest programs from Chapter 1.

*02ARTISA:* The Artisan program, starting at Chapter 2 and finishing with Chapter 5.

*06ANIMAT:* The Animate program from Chapter 6.

*07MULTI:* The Multi-Search and Replace (MULTISR.MAK) program from Chapter 7.

*08API:* The APIdraw program from Chapter 8.

*09PAL:* The palette program from Chapter 9.

*10BÉZIER:* The Mini-Bézier program from Chapter 10.

*11CORNER:* The Rounded Corners program from Chapter 11.

*12TEXT:* The TxtAlign, APItext, and DrawText programs from Chapter 12.

*13NODES:* The Join Nodes program from Chapter 13.

*14SCALE:* The PrintAPI and Scaltest programs from Chapter 14 (plus the Ruler Test program).

*15ARTAPI:* The ArtAPI program from Chapter 15 and the ArtAPI_s program for standard versions of Visual Basic (similar to the ArtAPI program, minus the PicClip control and the associated MenuBitMap procedure).

*16MISC:* Twelve miscellaneous programs that show various examples of Visual Basic graphics, data, and other tidbits. The programs in the 16MISC directory have no chapters dedicated to their source code. Most of the programs have short explanations within their .FRM files. The following describes each program:

*APISCALE:* Shows how to create a custom magnifying glass mouse pointer for use with Visual Basic programs later than version 4.0. The APIscale program uses API viewport functions to scale a selected area of the desktop by using the magnifying glass mouse pointer to marquee the area to enlarge (zoom in).

*ARRAY:* Shows a standard text book example of a nested loop that sorts the values in an array in either ascending or descending order.

*BOUNDING:* Illustrates the principles behind a Bézier curve's bounding box as described in the Chapter 3.

*BUTTON:* Shows three alternative methods to build custom pushbuttons. The first method demonstrates single or multirow pushbuttons. The second method shows how to build a custom region that accepts mouse events within its borders. The third method uses the foreground color of a bitmap icon to trigger mouse events.

*DATA1:* Shows how to store .BMP, .WMF, and .ICO files into an Access 1.0 data file, and simulates a data bound list box for Visual Basic versions later than 4.0. Requires the MSAJT110.DLL, MSAES110.DLL, and VBDB300.DLL from the .VBX directory to be copied to your WINDOWS\SYSTEM directory. The DataBaseName property of the DATA1 control should read as follows:

## The Companion Disk

*C:\GPVBASIC\VBFILES\16MISC\PICDATA.MDB:* If you have copied the PICDATA.MDB file to another directory or drive, change the DATA1 `DataBaseName` property to reflect the new path.

*DIGITAL:* Demonstrates the API `FloodFill` function used on bitmap images. Rather than using True Type or graphical methods to draw digital numbers, the Digital program paints selected areas of a bitmap image to simulate a digital clock interface.

*ELASTIC:* This example demonstrates resizing controls at runtime.

*GAMEBMP:* A bit of everything thrown into a simple bitmap viewer. The Game256 and Master1 bitmap images are very large screen shots of illustrations I created in CorelDRAW. The GAMEBMP shows how to open a file without the use of the CMDIALOG.VBX. It also shows how to scroll an image without the use of scrollbar controls.

> **CAUTION** I needed a PCI 64 video accelerator and a Pentium computer to scroll the large images without flickering or any noticeable repainting of the images when using the Gamebmp program. The Master1 bitmap image is in 256-color resolution and is approximately 1 MB in size.

*INVERT:* Demonstrates using the API bitmap functions to build a custom toolbar.

*MENUTEST:* The Menutest program shows how to add a menu item using Visual Basic 2.0 and 3.0. A menu item can be added or removed from any application (not to be confused with ADD-INs for Visual Basic 4.0).

*TABS:* The Tabs program uses simple `Line` statements to build a custom tab dialog box. The tab names are printed using the API `Drawtext` function, eliminating the need for label controls.

*VB-CLIP:* This is for use with Visual Basic 2.0 and 3.0. It saves you desktop space when using a small monitor. In order for the program to work with future releases of Visual Basic, you will have to change the `Parent`, `Child`, and `Module` handles. You can build your own Spy program or get a Visual Basic spy program from the MSbasic modem library in order to quickly view the window handles in Windows.

# Index

## SYMBOLS

**32-bit API Drawing functions, 292-293**

## A

**Add button (list boxes), 261**
**Addbtn_Click event, 251**
**Addbtn_GotFocus event, 251**
**adding picture box nodes, Join Nodes program, 411**
**algorithms**
    Bresenham, 27
    deCasteljau, 104
**Align property, fonts, 382**
**aligning text, 360**
    with option buttons (listing 12.3), 364
    within text boxes (listing A.10) Artisan program, 540
**AngleArc function, 554**
**angular slopes, drawing with Bresenham algorithm, 27**
**ANIMATE#.BAS file, Animator program, 219**
**Animator program, 210-219**
    form and control properties, 213-218
    startup default values, 220
    variable names (listing 6.1), 219
**API (Application Programming Interface), 50**
    AngleArc function, 554
    ArcTo function, 555
    BeginPath function, 553
    CloseFigure function, 555
    drawing functions, ArtAPI program, 476-477
    DrawText function, 389-391
    EndPath function, 553
    EnumEnhMetaFile function, 556
    FillPath function, 553
    functions in Join Nodes program (listing 13.18), 414
    GetCharABCWidths function, 361
    GetDeviceCaps function, 360
        *printing (listing 14.5), 425*
    GetPath function, 553
    GetTextMetrics function, 360
    graphical functions, testing with PrintAPI program, 421
    MaskBlt function, 556
    OutLineTextMetrics function, 360
    PathToRegion function, 554
    PlgBlt function, 556
    PolyBezier function, 555
    PolyDraw function, 556
    Polyline function, 112
    printing with PrintAPI program, 424
    PtInRect function, 141
    SelectClipPath function, 554
    SendMessage function, 159, 361
    SetArcDirection function, 555
    SetTextAlign function, 382
    StrokeAndFillPath function, 553
    StrokePath function, 553
    TextOut function drawing text (listing 12.11), 375-376
    WidenPath function, 554
**API color palette, Palette program, 307-308**
**API Drawing functions, 272**
    buttons, 279-280
    Form_Load event, 278
    Form_MouseDown event, 280-283
    functions
        *32-bit, 292-293*
        *bounding box, 280*
        *brush, 280*
        *declarations, 275-278*
        *Ellipse, 285*
        *FloodFill, 283-284*
        *Get_Pixel, 285-286*
        *Line_To, 286*
        *pen, 280*
        *Pie, 286-287*
        *Polyline, 289*
        *Pt_In_Rect, 289-290*
        *Rec_tangle, 290-291*
        *rectangle, 280*
        *Round_Rect, 291*
        *Set_Pixel, 292*
    polygons, 287-288
    drawing operations, 283
    hDC (handle of a Device Context), 273
**API functions, ArtAPI program, 443**
**APICRLF_Click event, 375, 378**
**APItext program, 367-384**
    carriage returns, 375
    setting text coordinates (listing 12.13), 379
    startup variables (listing 12.7), 372
**arcs, calculating radians, 14-15**
**ArcTo function, 555**
**Arrange menu, Artisan program, 62**
**arrays, defining for Artisan program, 70**
**ART3_7.BAS file, 526-535**
**ArtAPI program, 442**
    API drawing functions, 476-477
    API functions, 443
    form/control properties, 447-454
    handles/nodes, 442
    picture box control, 443-444
    Pnode image control, 464-469
    polyshape procedures, 445
    procedures, 444
    scaling and zoom tool, 442
    scaling routines, 447
    startup variables (listing 15.1), 455-456
    Test button, 447
    To_Front_Back procedure, 446
    zoom tool, 447
**ARTFONT.BAS file, global declarations, 530-533**
**Artisan palette color values, 533**
**Artisan program, 50**
    Arrange menu, 62
    array definition, 70
    assigning new colors to palette, 547
    calculating carriage returns, 538
    Cancel button press (listing A.15), 542
    changing font sizes with scroll bars, 542
    color bar palette, 56
    Color menu, 62, 166
    Color Palette submenu, 62
    ColorPalette form, 543-550
    data types, 71
    declarations, 73
    default values, 536
    displaying text examples, 541
    drawing each color of palette, 546

dropping new colors into main palette, 548
Edit menu, 61
extracting RGB color elements, 547
File menu, 61
file menu options, 164
font attributes (listing A.12), 541
global declarations (listing A.1), 526-530
main menu selections, 162-163
menu area, 58
mouse events, 62
NodeEdit form, 542-543
palette form, 544
procedures, 136
scrollbar control, 58
selecting colors from palette, 546
startup values (listing 2.7), 82
status area frame, 58
Text form, 535-542
typing characters, 94
variable definitions, 70
Zoom tool, 54
ARTISAN.INI file, 138-139
  extracting color values, 182
  writing color values to, 192
ArtMask picture box, ArtAPI program, 443
Artwork picture box control, Artisan program, 53
Artwork_DlbClick event (listing 2.15), 94
Artwork_KeyPress event, 95, 390
Artwork_LostFocus event (listing 2.17), 95
ArtWork_MouseDown event, 88-89, 379, 432
Artwork_MouseMove event, 90, 433
ArtWork_MouseUp event, 91-92, 434
assigning drawing coordinates to objects, PrintAPI program, 422
assigning new colors to Artisan palette, (listing A.21), 547
attributes adding to TextOut function, 378
AutoRedraw property, Artwork picture box control, 53

## B

B-spline curves, 104
**Basic option button procedure (listing 11.6), 351**
**BasicPrint_Click event, 380**
**Begin program, 2-4**
  Circle statement, 16-17
  circles, calculating radians, 14
  ColorBar, 9
  control properties, 5-7
  drawing objects, 12-14
  form
    *clearing*, 9
    *properties*, 5-7
    *variable declarations*, 7-8, 22
  Line statement, 15-16
  selecting drawing options, 11
  setting start position for drawing, 10
**BeginPath function, 553**
**BezDivide procedure, 107**
**BezDraw procedure, 107, 325**
**BezHandle1 procedure, 146**
**BezHandle1_MouseDown event, 114**
**BezHandle2 mouse event, 117**
**BezHandle2 procedure, 146**
**Bézier curves, 54, 104-108**
  calculating new bounding box (listing 3.14), 125
  calculating new coordinates of curves when stretched (listing 3.16), 131
  drawing with MouseDown event using handle #1, 114
  erasing old image of curve and handle lines (listing 3.13), 124
  flipping, 129
  moving when using node #2, 340
  placing handles and dotted lines on line (listing 3.9), 119-120
  plotting points, 109, 320
  redrawing when Bézier node #1 is moved, 122
  redrawing when handle #1 is moved, 114-115
  redrawing when Handle #2 is moved, 336
  redrawing when handle #2 is moved, 118
  redrawing when node #1 is moved, 338
  rescaling handles to new location, 118, 123, 337
  rescaling handles to new locations, 116
  rescaling node #1, 339
  rescaling nodes to new location, 340
  resetting scaling and dotted handle lines of curves, 126-127
  setting when clicking Bézier node #1, 337
  setting when clicking handle #2, 117
  setting when clicking handle #2 (listing 10.17), 335
  setting when clicking node #2 (listing 10.23), 340
  standard attributes for drawing, 79
  stretching, 129
**Bézier handle #1, 333-335**
**Bézier handle #2, 335-337**
**Bézier tool, Artisan program, 55**
**BézierStore procedure, 119**
**BézierTool, Artisan program, 93**
**BezNode_Move procedure, 467**
**BezNode_Up procedure, 469**
**BezNode1 event, 121**
**BezNode1_Mouse_Up event, 123**
**BezStretch procedure, 129**
**BezUpdate procedure, 128**
borders, erasing, 311
**bounding box functions, API Drawing function, 280**
**Bounding Box_Down procedure, 96**
bounding boxes, 45
  calculating for polyshapes, 480-481
  dragging/stretching for objects (listing 4.13), 156
  handle positions, 157
**bounding boxes of curves, 125**
**BoundingBox _Down event (listing 2.18), 96**
**BoundingBox_Down procedure, 475, 481**
**BoundingBox_move event (listing 2.19), 98**

BoundingBox_Up event, 99
BoundingBox_Up procedure, 72, 477
box tool, Artisan program, 56
Box_Pset event, 26-27
Box_Pset event (listing 1.13), 26
Bresenham procedure (listing 1.14), 27
Bresenham_360 procedure (listing 1.15), 28-29
brush functions, API Drawing function, 280
BUIF picture box, Multi-Search and Replace program, 269
BUIF_MouseDown event, 267
BUIF_MouseUp event, 268
BUIF_Paint event, 268
button captions, DrawText program, 392
buttons
  Add (list boxes), 261
  API Drawing function, 279-280
  command, Pset program, 18-19, 23
  Command1_Click, 9
  Multi-Search and Replace program, 251
  Replace, list boxes, 261-262

## C

calculating
  Bézier curves, 104
  bounding boxes for polyshapes, 479-480
  carriage returns, Artisan program, 538
  curve points, deCasteljau algorithm, 325
  mouse movements, 167-168
  new bounding box of curve (listing 3.14), 125
  new coordinates of curves when stretched, 131
  new coordinates of guideline (listing 5.11), 187-188
  predefined argument curve, plots to be divided, 109-110
  radians, 14-15
  radius of circles, 11
  radius of moving circle, 183
  with cosine, 26
  with sine, 25-26
Cancel button press (listing A.15), Artisan program, 542
Cancel_Btn_Click event, Artisan program, 537
Cancel_Click event, Artisan program, 542
canceling palette form color edits, 545
CarriageReturns procedure, Artisan program, 538
centering DrawText form (listing 12.22), 389
centering form, Rounded Corners program, 349
centering form and text cursor, 363
centering form on screen, APItext program, 374
characters, typing in Artisan program, 94
Circle statement, 2, 16-17
circle tool, Artisan program, 56
Circle_Pset procedure, 29-30
Circle_sin_cos procedure, 30
Circle_Sqr procedure (listing 1.18), 31
circles
  calculating radius, 11, 14-15
  drawing, 8-14
  moving, calculating radius, 183
  perfectly drawn, 183
  radius, 4-5
ClearBtn_Click event, 332
clearing Begin program form, 9
clicking mouse on objects, 141-144
ClipPalette_MouseDown routine, Palette program, 308-309
CloseFigure function, 555
closing polygon shapes, 499-501
ClsBtn_Click event (listing 1.25), 41
Cmd_Reset_Click event, 545
CodeLst1_Click event, 252
codelst2_click list box event, 252
color
  Palette program
    changing with scrollbar, 315-316
    dithered, 311-312
    hexidecimal numbers, 305-306
    pure, 308-309
    selecting, 304-306
    viewing range, 308
color bar palette, Artisan program, 56
Color menu, Artisan program, 62, 166
color palette, resetting default version, 167
color palette bar, editing, 166
Color Palette submenu, Artisan program, 62
color values
  ColorBar_MouseDown procedure, 137
  extracting from .INI file, 138-139, 182
  writing to ARTISAN.INI file, 192
color values for pixels, 35
Color_INI procedure, 138
ColorBar, drawing (Begin program), 9
Colorbar_MouseDown event, 8-9
ColorBar_MouseDown procedure, 136
ColorBar_MouseUp event, 545
ColorBar_MouseUp procedure, 137
ColorBar_Paint event, 9, 546
ColorBar_Paint procedure, repainting colors (listing 4.3), 138
ColorPalette form, 166, 543-550
colors
  changing element using scrollbar, 549
  displaying using scrollbar control, 549
  drawing each one of Artisan palette, 546
  drawing into three-row color, palette, 549
  dropping into Artisan main palette, 548
  extracting from arrays, 192
  manually typing element values into text box controls, 550
  selecting for drawing circles/lines, 8-9
  selecting from Artisan program palette, 546
  setting pixels to, 17

storage/display,
ColorBar_MouseUp
procedure, 137
**ColorScroll_Change event, 138**
**command buttons, Pset program,
18-19, 23**
**Command1_Click button, 9**
**Command1_Click event (listing
1.26), 42**
Begin program, 9
Pset program, 23
**control attributes, displaying with
Font Log button, 381**
**control properties**
ArtAPI program, 447-454
Artisan program, 63
Join Nodes program, 398-399
Mini-Bézier program, 320-322
Multi-Search and Replace
program, 243-249
PrintAPI program, 419-420
Rounded Corners program,
345-347
Scaltest program, 427-430
TxtAlign program, 361-363
**controls**
Begin program properties, 5-7
color bar picture box, 57
forms, 250
Palette program, 298-301
positioning in Artisan program, 84
properties for Animator program,
213-218
Pset program properties, 19
rescaling for container after
Zoom, 186
scrollbar, Artisan program, 58
**converting**
lines to curves, 119, 341, 458
polylines to curves, 457-459
twips to pixels, 328
**copying text, 255-256**
**cosine, calculating with, 26**
**CreateCustomPalette function,
309-310**
**crosshair lines, drawing on
form, 349**
**CurrentXY option button procedure, 353**

**cursors, advancing position,
266-267**
**curve objects, 54**
**curves**
Bézier type, 104-108
calculating points, deCasteljau
algorithm, 325
calculating predefined argument
plots to be divided, 109-110
converting lines to, 341
converting polylines to, 457-459
converting to lines (listing
15.2), 458
drawing lines on forms to create
curves, 329-331
editing on polyshapes, 491-496
erasing images, 124, 331-332
grabbing by nodes, 337-340
moving, 121
moving node #2, 339-340
moving when using node #2 (listing 10.24), 340
plotting points, 320, 325-329
plotting points manually (listing
10.3), 326-327
recalculating bounding
boxes, 125
redrawing, 114
*Bézier handle #1, 333-335*
*Bézier handle #2, 335-337*
rescaling nodes to new location, 340
resetting scaling, 126
resetting values for new curves,
332-333
restoring coordinate points, 116
setting when clicking node
#1, 337
setting when clicking node
#2 , 340
stretching, 129
*see also* Bézier curves
**cutting text, 255-256**

# D

**Dash_Pset procedure (listing
1.19), 31**
**dashed line styles, 31**
**data types, Artisan program, 71**

**DATABANK.DAT file, Animator
program, 211**
**deCasteljau algorithm, 104**
calculating curve points, 325
dividing formula (listing
10.2), 325
**deCasteljau formula demonstration, 113**
**declarations**
API drawing function, 275-278
Begin program form variables,
7-8, 22
**default values**
loading, APItext program, 373
Mini-Bézier program startup, 323
**default values, Artisan program,
536**
**default values, palette form, Artisan
program, 544**
**defining arrays/variables for Artisan
program, 70**
**deleting**
list boxes, 253
objects, 59, 163-165
changed device context attributes, 374
**desktop**
changing scale, 206
deleting objects from, 163-165
dragging/moving mouse on, 89
drawing text objects on, 183-184
executing drawing on, 97
initiating drawing,
Artwork_MouseDown event,
88-89
moving objects on, 168-169
placing text on, 183-185
redrawing objects, 195
redrawing text, 95
removing nodes/handles
from, 171
rescaling, 206
*with Visual Basic statements, 438*
resetting default width, 162
restoring scaling, 434
scaling for zoom effect, 203-204
scrolling, 158-160
updating nodes and handles, 164

## desktop/printer graphics

desktop/printer graphics, 442-443
device points, conversion to logical point, 433
dialog boxes and fonts, 268
directories on companion disk, 560-562
Display_Color_Palette ColorBar procedure, 138
Display_Color_Palette procedure, 137, 533
dithered color, Palette program, 311-312
dividing formula for deCasteljau algorithm, 325
dotted/dashed line styles, 31
drag-and-drop instructions, printing in Artisan program, 548
DragColor_DragOver event, 546
dragging/stretching object bounding box, 156
Draw_Blends procedure, Palette program, 307-308
Draw_Text_Click event, 391
drawing
    all objects onto desktop, 515-520
    assigning coordinates objects, 422
    basic shapes, Begin program, 2-4
    Bézier curves, 111
    circles, 12-14
        colors, 8-9
        drawing options, 11
        start position, 10
    ColorBar, Begin program, 9
    colors into three-row color palette, 549
    crosshair lines on form, 349
    curves on polyshapes, 497-499
    each color of Artisan palette, 546
    embedded CR/LF text, 378-379
    execution on desktop, Artisan program, 97
    finalized shapes with Join Nodes program, 413-414
    four objects onto a device, 423
    functions
        ArtAPI program, 476-477
        GDI32, 554-557
    GDI32 function paths, 552-553
    GUI32 function descriptions, 552
    guidelines (listing 5.10), 187

    handles manually, 150
    initiating on desktop, Artwork_MouseDown event, 88-89
    line/polyline segments, 404
    lines, 12-14
        colors, 8-9
        drawing options, 11
        start position, 10
        slowly expanding, 34
        moving, Node Mouse Move event, 178
        on forms for curves, 329-331
    movable lines (listing 10.10), 330
    new line objects, Join Nodes program, 403
    page guidelines, 144-145
    perfect circles, 183
    polyline segments, 404-405
    polyline shapes, 501-502
    rounded rectangles, 349-356
    ruler slide lines (listing 5.12), 188-189
    ruler inch marks, 189-191
    ruler internal guidelines, 159
    shapes on picture box, 422
    text
        DrawText function (listing 12.27), 391
        on desktop (listing 5.7), 183-184
        with Print statement (listing 12.14), 380
drawing tools, selecting in Artisan program, 86
DrawObjects procedure PrintAPI program, 422-423
DrawText function, 389-391
DrawText program, 384-393
    button captions, 391-392
    centering form onscreen, 389
    loading font list, 388
    startup variables, 387

## E

Edit menu, Artisan program, 61
editing
    color palette bar, 166
    curves on polyshapes, 491-496

list boxes, 254-255
node positions of polyshapes, 410
polyline shapes, 502-504
shapes with nodes, 407-409
text, 253-254
Ellipse functions, 285
ellipse tool, Artisan program, 56
EndPath function, 553
EnumEnhMetaFile function, 556
erasing
    array values and objects, 165
    borders, 311
    curve image before moving, 331-332
    curve images, 124
    images on forms, 352
    old image of curve and handle lines, 124
    old line images, 176-177, 332
events
    Addbtn_Click, 251
    Addbtn_GotFocus, 251
    APICRLF_Click, 375, 378
    Artwork_DlbClick, 94
    Artwork_KeyPress, 95, 390
    Artwork_LostFocus, 95
    ArtWork_MouseDown, 88-89, 379, 432
    Artwork_MouseMove, 90, 433
    Artwork_MouseUp, 434
    BasicPrint_Click, 380
    BezHandle1_MouseDown, 114
    BezHandle2 mouse, 117
    BezNode1, 121
    BezNode1_Mouse_Up, 123
    BoundingBox _Down, 96
    BoundingBox_move, 98
    BoundingBox_Up, 99
    Box_Pset, 26-27
    Box_Pset (listing 1.13), 26
    Bresenham (listing 1.14), 27
    Bresenham_360, 28-29
    BUIF_MouseDown, 267
    BUIF_MouseUp, 268
    BUIF_Paint, 268
    Cancel_Btn_Click, 537
    Cancel_Click, 542
    ClearBtn_Click, 332
    ClsBtn_Click, 41
    Cmd_Reset_Click, 545
    CodeLst1_Click, 252

# fonts 569

codelst2_click list box, 252
Colorbar_MouseDown, 8-9
ColorBar_MouseUp, 545
ColorBar_Paint, 9, 138, 546
ColorScroll_Change, 138
Command1_Click, 9, 23, 42
DragColor_DragOver, 546
Draw_Text_Click, 391
Fill_Button_Click, 313-314
FontList_Click, 380, 538
FontLogBtn_Click, 381
Form_Activate, 435
Form_Load, 9, 536, 544
Form_MouseDown, 10, 23-24, 43-44, 280-283, 349
Form_MouseMove, 45-46, 350
Form_MouseUp, 12-14, 48, 284
Form_Paint, 349
Form_Resize, 84-85, 250, 328, 349, 363, 374
Form_Unload, 374
GetRGBcolors, 547
Handle mouse move, 155
Handle_MouseDown, 152, 333
Handle_MouseMove, 154
Handle_MouseUp, 155, 158
Handle2_MouseDown, 335
Line_MouseDown, 329-330
Line_MouseUp, 330
LineButton_Down, 161
LineButtons_MouseUp, 162
Menu_FindSub_Click, 257
Menu_Insert_Click, 258
Menu_Palette_Click, 166
Menu_txt, 265
mouse, Artisan program, 62
MouseDown, 402-404
MouseMove, 89-90
MouseUp, 91-93
Node Mouse Up, 180
Node_MouseDown, 176
Node_MouseMove, 338
Node1 mouse, 337
Node2 MouseDown, 339
NodeHandle_Click, 341
OK_Btn_Click, 539, 545
Opencom menu, 249
Option1_Click, 11, 364, 540
PaleteBox_DragOver, 548
PaletteBarColors, 182-183
PaletteBox_DragDrop, 548

PaletteBox_Paint, 548
PicRGB_Paint, 302-304
picture box mouse, 432-434
Picture1._MouseUp, 266, 329
Picture1_KeyPress, 266, 364
Picture1_MouseDown, 328, 364
Picture1_MouseMove, 329
Pnode_MouseUp, 489
Poly_Update, 509
Print_API_Click, 424
ReplaceBtn_Click, 261
RGB_Scroll_Change, 549
RGB_Textbox_Change, 550
RGBscroll_Change, 549
RGBscroll_Scroll, 308
Ruler_MouseDown, 186
Ruler_Paint, 189-190, 434
SetTextBtn_Click, 365-367
SineCosine, 24-25
Style_Combo_Change, 382
Style_Combo_Click, 541
Text1_Change, 541
TextMex_Click, 382
Timer1_Timer, 269
To_Curve_Click, 543
To_Line_Click, 543
ToolButton_MouseDown, 86
ToolButtons_Paint, 88
VScroll_Change, 160, 542
Z_APIsub_Click, 435
Z_Basicsub_Click, 437
*see also* procedures
**exporting filters, 51**
**extracting**
    array colors (listing 5.14), 192
    color values from .INI file, 182
    RGB color elements from Artisan program (listing A.22), 547
    text from label control (listing 12.6), 365-366

# F

**File menu, Artisan program, 61, 164**
**files**
    ANIMATE#.BAS, 219
    ART3_7.BAS, 526-535
    ARTFONT.BAS, 530-533

ARTISAN.INI, 138-139
    *extracting color values, 182*
    *writing color values to, 192*
DATABANK.DAT, 211
    importing/exporting with filters, 51
    installing from disk, 560-562
    opening, 256-259
    saving, 256-259
    text
        *opening, 260-261*
        *SaveCom procedure, 263-264*
**fill patterns, Fill_Pset procedure, 33**
**fill tool, Artisan program, 56**
**Fill_Button_Click event, 313-314**
**Fill_Line procedure, 32**
**Fill_Pset procedure, 33**
**filling areas of screen, 32**
**filling complex objects with color, 406-407**
**filling objects, 180-182**
**filling selected object with color, 181**
**FillPath function, 553**
**fills for objects, 136-138**
**filters, importing/exporting, 51**
**Find_Object procedure, 143, 478**
**FindAllObjects procedure, 139**
**finding objects with marquee, 139-141**
**FindObject procedure, 141, 144**
**flags, UpDateObjects procedure, 77-78**
**flipped objects, reversing handle positions, 149-151**
**flipping Bézier curves, 129**
**FloodFill function, 283-284**
**font attributes (listing A.12), 541**
**font lists, loading, 373**
**Font Log button, control attributes, 381**
**font sizes, changing with scroll bars, 542**
**FontList_Click event, 380, 538**
**FontLogBtn_Click event, 381**
**fonts, 267**
    dialog box, 268
    displaying characteristics, 382-383
    loading list, DrawText program, 388

selecting new for list boxes, 539
setting Align property, 382
setting alignment, 393
setting style (listing 12.18), 382, 389
setting style type, 381
showing current attributes for control , 381
style property (listing 12.28), 392

**form properties**
  ArtAPI program, 447-454
  Artisan program, 63
  Join Nodes program, 398-399
  Mini-Bézier program, 320-322
  Multi-Search and Replace program, 243-249
  PrintAPI program, 419-420
  Rounded Corners program, 345-347
  Scaltest program, 427-430
  TxtAlign program, 361-363

**Form_Activate event, 435**
**Form_Load event, 9**
  API Drawing function, 278
  Artisan program, 536, 544
**Form_MouseDown event, 349**
  API Drawing function, 280-283
  Begin program, 10
  listing 1.27, 43-44
  Pset program, 23-24
**Form_MouseMove event, 45-46, 350**
**Form_MouseUp event, 12-14, 48, 284**
**Form_Paint event, 349**
**Form_Resize event, 84-85, 250, 328, 349, 363, 374**
**Form_Resize routine, Palette program, 302**
**Form_Unload event, 374**
**formatting text, 360**
**forms, 265**
  Animator program
    *NodeEdit, 542-543*
    *palette, 544*
    *properties, 213-218*
    *Text, 535-542*
  Begin program
    *clearing, 9*
    *properties, 5-7*
    *variable declarations, 7-8, 22*

centering (listing 11.3), 349
  *in middle of screen, 220*
ColorPalette, 166, 543-550
erasing images (listing 11.7), 352
Movetest properties, 38-40
Multi-Search and Replace program controls, 250
Palette program, 298-301
Pset program properties, 19
scaling dimensions, 149
**fountain fills, 296**
  buttons, 313-314
  painting complex objects, 316-318
  Palette program, 306-307
  palettes, 312-313
**four-point Bézier spline curves, 104**
**functions**
  32-bit API Drawing, 292-293
  AngleArc, 554
  API drawing functions, 277, 280
  ArcTo, 555
  BeginPath, 553
  CloseFigure, 555
  CreateCustomPalette, 309-310
  drawing, GDI32 paths, 552-553
  DrawText, 389-391
  Ellipse, 285
  EndPath, 553
  EnumEnhMetaFile, 556
  FillPath, 553
  FloodFill, 283-284
  Get_Pixel, 285-286
  GetCharABCWidths, 361
  GetDeviceCaps, 360, 425
  GetPath, 553
  GetTextMetrics, 360
  Line_To, 286
  MaskBlt, 556
  MoveMouse, 97, 167
  OutLineTextMetrics, 360
  PathToRegion, 554
  Pie, 286-287
  PlgBlt, 556
  PolyBezier, 320, 555
  PolyBézierTo, 320
  PolyDraw, 556
  Polyline, 112, 289
  Pt_In_Rect, 289-290
  PtInRect, 141
  Rec_tangle, 290-291

RGBcolor&, 314-315
Round_Rect, 291
SelectClipPath, 554
SendMessage, 159, 361
Set_Pixel, 292
SetArcDirection, 555
SetTextAlign, 382
StrokeAndFillPath, 553
StrokePath, 553
TextOut, 375-376
TwipPerPixel, 328
WidenPath, 554

# G

**GDI32**
  API drawing functions, 320
  drawing functions, 554-557
  Graphical Device Interface/32-bit, 552
  paths, 552-553
**Get_Pixel function, 285-286**
**GetCharABCWidths function, 361**
**GetDeviceCaps function, 360, 425**
**GetPath function, 553**
**GetRGBcolors procedure, 547**
**GetTextMetrics function, 360**
**global declarations**
  ARTFONT.BAS file, 530-533
  Artisan program (listing A.1), 526-530
**grabbing curves by nodes, 337-340**
**graphics, scrolling on desktop, 158-160**
**Grid_Pset procedure, 34**
**grids, 34**
**GUI32 drawing function descriptions, 552**
**guidelines**
  calculating new coordinates, 187-188
  drawing (listing 5.10), 187
  drawng pages, 144-145
  pulled away from rulers, 144-145
  redrawing with underlying page, 199-200
  ruler, 186-188
**GuideLines procedure, 145**

## H

Handle mouse move event, 155
Handle procedure, 145
Handle_MouseDown event, 152, 333
Handle_MouseMove event, 154
Handle_MouseUp event, 155, 158
Handle2_MouseDown event, 335
HandleReverse routine, 149-151
handles
   ArtAPI program, 442
   Bézier handle #1, 333-335
   Bézier handle #2, 335-337
   manually drawing, 150
   placing around flipped objects, 149-150
   placing on a line, 341
   positioning around objects, 145-149
   positions on bounding boxes, 157
   removing from desktop, 171
   rescaling, 185-186
   rescaling to new locations, 335
handles of objects, 54
Handles procedure, 145
HandlesReverse procedure, 146
hDC (handle of a Device Context), 273
height of text, 391
hexidecimal color (Palette program), 305-306
Hscroll_Change procedure, 160

## I

images
   erasing on forms (listing 11.7), 352
   sending to printers, 201
importing filters, 51
inch marks on ruler, 189-191
index numbers for objects, 99
initializing line start/end coordinates, 404
inserting text in list boxes, 258-259
installing disk files, 560-562
inverted tool buttons (repainting), 88, 89

## J

Join Nodes program, 396
   API functions, 414
   drawing polyline segments, 404-405
   editing shapes with nodes, 407-409
   filling complex objects with color, 406-407
   form/controls properties, 398-399
   MouseDown events, 402-404
   moving connected line segments, 409-411
   painting (fill) methods, 406
   startup default values, 401
   startup variables (listing 13.1), 400

## K-L

keywords (Step), 12

label controls
   extracting text (listing 12.6), 365-366
   placing at MouseDown position, 391
   resetting display text, 393
   typing text within (listing 12.4), 364
left mouse button events, 62
letter spacing of text, 361-363
levers
   curve handles, reshaping, 114
   redrawing for Bézier handle #2, 335-336
   redrawing for handle #1, 334
line spacing, 360-361
Line statement, 2, 15-16
line tool, Artisan program, 56
Line_MouseDown event, 329
Line_MouseMove event, 330
Line_MouseUp event, 330
Line_Pset procedure, 35
Line_To function, 286
LineButton_Down event, 161
LineButtons procedure, 160
LineButtons_MouseUp event, 162

lines
   converting to Bézier curves, 93
   converting to curves, 119, 341, 458
   dotted/dashed styles, 31
   drawing, 12-14
      as they move (Node Mouse Move event), 178
      selecting colors, 8-9
      selecting drawing options, 11
      setting start position, 10
   drawing on forms for curves, 329-331
   drawing slow expanding, 34
   erasing old images, 332
   initializing start/end coordinates, 404
   movable, 330
   moving by node, 178-179
   moving connected segments, 409-411
   start positions (listing 10.9), 329
   text, 266
   updating after moving, 180
list boxes
   buttons, 261-262
   editing, 254-255
   inserting text, 258-259
   Multi-Search and Replace program, 250-251
      deleting, 253
   searching and replacing, 261-263
   selecting new fonts, 539
listings
   1.1. Declaration section of Begin form, 7
   1.2. Colorbar_MouseDown event, 8
   1.3. ColorBar_Paint event, 9
   1.4. command1_click event, 9
   1.5. Form_Load event, 9
   1.6. Form_MouseDown event, 10
   1.7. Option1_Click event, 11
   1.8. Form_MouseUp event, 12-13
   1.9. Variable names needed for Pset program, 22
   1.10. Command1_Click event, 23

# listings

1.11. Form_MouseDown event, 23-24
1.12. The SineCosine event, 24-25
1.13. The Box_Pset procedure, 26
1.14. The Bresenham procedure, 27
1.15. The Bresenham_360 procedure, 28-29
1.16. The Circle_Pset procedure, 29
1.17. The Circle_sin_cos procedure, 30
1.18. The Circle_Sqr procedure, 31
1.19. The Dash_Pset procedure, 31
1.20. The Fill_Line procedure, 32
1.21. The Fill_Pset procedure, 33
1.22. The Grid_Pset procedure, 34
1.23. The Line_Pset procedure, 35
1.24 Movetest program variables, 41
1.24 Point statement, 35
1.25. The ClsBtn_Click event, 41
1.26. The Command1_Click event, 42
1.27 Form_MouseDown event
1.28. The Form_MouseMove even, 45-46
1.29. The Form_MouseUp event, 48
2.1 deleting objects from desktop, 59
2.2 To_Front_Back procedure, 59-60
2.3 To_Front_Back procedure, 60-61
2.4 BoundingBox_Up procedure, 72
2.5 Artisan program declarations, 73
2.6 UpDateObjects procedure flag names, 77
2.7 Artisan program startup values, 82
2.8 ZoomBar procedure, 83

2.9 Form_Resize event, 84-85
2.10 ToolButton_MouseDown event, 86
2.11 repainting inverted tool buttons, 88
2.12 Artwork_MouseDown event, 88-89
2.13 Artwork_MouseMove event, 90
2.14 ArtWork_MouseUp event, 91-92
2.15 Artwork_DlbClick event, 94
2.16 Artwork_KeyPress event, 95
2.17 Artwork_LostFocus event, 95
2.18 BoundingBox_Down event, 96
2.19 BoundingBox_move event, 98
2.20 BoundingBox_Up event, 99
3.1 calculating predefined argument curve plots to be divided, 109-110
3.2 deCasteljau formula demo, 113
3.3 MouseDown event draws a Bézier curve using handle #1, 114
3.4 redrawing Bézier curve when handle #1 is moved, 114-115
3.5 rescaling Bézier's handles to new locations, 116
3.6 setting Bézier curve when clicking handle #2, 117
3.7 redrawing Bézier curve when handle #2 is moved, 118
3.8 rescaling Bézier's handles to new location, 118
3.9 placing handles and dotted lines on line for, 119-120
3.10 setting curve when clicking Bézier node #1, 122
3.11 redrawing Bézier curve when Bézier node #1 is moved, 122
3.12 rescaling Bézier's handles to new location, 123
3.13 erasing old image of curve and handle lines, 124
3.14 calculating new bounding box of curve, 125
3.15 resetting scaling and dotted handle lines of curves, 126-127

3.16 calculating new coordinates of curves
  *when stretched, 131*
  *Bézier curve, 119-120*
4.1 ColorBar_MouseDown (color values), 137
4.2 ColorBar_MouseUp procedure, 137
4.3 ColorBar_Paint event (repainting colors), 138
4.4 horizontal scrollbar control displaying palette colors, 138
4.5 extracting color value numbers from .INI file, 138-139
4.6 FindAllObjects procedure searching for objects, 139-140
4.7 searching for bounding box under mouse position, 142-143
4.8 guidelines pulled away from either ruler, 144-145
4.9 placing stretch handles around objects, 147
4.10 placing handles around flipped objects, 149-150
4.11 setting stretch handle's moveable bounding box, 152
4.12 redrawing page and objects under stretched object, 152-153
4.13 dragging/stretching object bounding box, 156
4.14 updating object position after stretching, 158
4.15 drawing internal guidelines for ruler, 159
4.16 scrolling desktop horizontally, 159
4.17 scrolling desktop vertically, 160
4.18 LineButton_Down event object outline width, 161
4.19 resetting desktop default width, 162
4.20 moving objects to front/back of others, 162
4.21 deleting objects from desktop, 163
4.22 updating desktop nodes and handles, 164

# listings

4.23 erasing all array values and objects, 165
4.24 editing color palette bar, 166
4.25 resetting default color palette, 167
4.26 mouse movement determination, 168
4.27 moving objects using on-the-fly values, 168-169
4.28 positioning nodes around objects, 170
4.29 rendering nodes/handles invisible, 171
5.1 Node_MouseDown erasing old line image, 176-177
5.2 Node Mouse Move event drawing line as it moves, 178
5.3 Node Mouse Up event, 180
5.4 filling selected object with color, 181
5.5 PaletteBarColors event extracting color values from .INI file, 182-183
5.6 calculating radius of moving circle, 183
5.7 drawing text objects on desktop, 183-184
5.8 rescaling container controls after Zoom, 186
5.9 Ruler_MouseDown event, 186
5.10 drawing guidelines, 187
5.11 calculating new coordinates of guideline, 187-188
5.12 drawing ruler slide lines, 188-189
5.13. Ruler_Paint event, 189-190
5.14. extracting array colors, 192
5.15 sending objects to front/back of others, 193-194
5.16 redrawing underlying page and objects, 196-197
5.17 redrawing guidelines and underlying page, 199-200
5.18 WinPrint procedure, 201-202
5.19 scaling desktop for zoom effect, 203-204
5.20 changing desktop scale, 206
6.1 Animator program variable names, 219

6.2 startup default values Animator program, 220
6.3 centering form in middle of screen Animator program, 220
6.4 closing data file on exiting Animator program, 220
7.1 variable declarations Multi-Search and Replace, 249-250
7.2 form controls Multi-Search and Replace program, 250
7.3 list boxes Multi-Search and Replace program, 250-251
7.4 buttons Multi-Search and Replace program, 251
7.5 matching search word and replace word, 252
7.6 matching replace word and search word, 252
7.7 deleting items from list boxes, 253
7.8 finding word in text, 254-270
7.9 editing a search or replace list, 254-255
7.10 cutting, copying, pasting text into Notepad, 255-256
7.11 opening or saving a file, 256-257
7.12 finding text within text, 257-258
7.13 inserting text into list boxes, 258-259
7.14 opening a file, 260
7.15 Add button for list boxes, 261
7.16 Replace button, 261-262
7.17 ReplaceCom procedure, 262-263
7.18 SaveCom procedure, 263-264
7.19 changing form appearance, 265
7.20 calculating text line spacing, 266
7.21 advancing text cursor position, 266-267
7.22 changing font style, 267
7.23 displaying font dialog box, 268
7.24 BUIF picture box, 269
8.1 variable names used in API program, 275-276

8.2 Form_Load event, 278
8.3 buttons, 279
8.4 Form_MouseDown, 281
8.5 API drawing operations, 283
8.6 Form_MouseUp, 284
8.7 drawing ellipses and circles, 285
8.8 Get_Pixel function, 285
8.9 Line_Tp function, 286
8.10 Pie function, 287
8.11 polygons, 287-288
8.12 triangular polyline shape, 289
8.13 mouse in bounding box (Pt_In_Rect), 290
8.14 drawing a rectangle, 291
8.15 rectangle with rounded corners, 291
8.16 Set_Pixel function, 292
9.1 Palette program default variables, 301
9.2 Form_Resize routine, 302
9.3 PicRGB_Paint event, 303
9.4 selecting colors and setting value, 304-305
9.5 Palette program buttons, 307
9.6 splicing colors together (APIcolor & function), 307
9.7 scrollbar percentage values, 308
9.8 ClipPalette_MouseDown, 308
9.9 drawing pure color palette (Clipboard), 309
9.10 creating custom palettes, 310
9.11 dithered color palette, 311
9.12 fountain fill blend effects, 312
9.13 fountain fills with RGB statement, 313
9.14 RGB statement blending color, 314
9.15 scrollbars displaying colors, 315
9.16 displaying the values of a color, 316
9.17 filling shapes with fountain fills, 316-317
10.1 generating startup default values Mini-Bézier program, 323

## listings

10.2 deCasteljau dividing formula, 325
10.3 plotting curve points manually 326-327
10.4 converting twips to pixels, 328
10.5 positioning main form onscreen, 328
10.6 Picture1_MouseDown event, 328
10.7 moving mouse over form, 329
10.8 Picture1 MouseUp event, 329
10.9 setting start position of a line, 329
10.10 drawing movable lines, 330
10.11 setting final node position for line, 330
10.12 erasing old line images, 332
10.13 resetting values for new lines, 333
10.14 Handle_MouseDown event, 333
10.15 drawing Bézier curve while moving handle #1, 334
10.16 rescaling handles to new locations, 335
10.17 setting Bézier curve when clicking handle #2, 335
10.18 redrawing Bézier curve when Handle #2 is moved, 336
10.19 rescaling Bézier handles to new location, 337
10.20 setting curve when clicking Bézier node #1, 337
10.21 redrawing Bézier curve when node #1 is moved, 338
10.22 rescaling Bézier node #1, 339
10.23 setting curve when clicking node #2, 340
10.24 moving curve when using node #2, 340
10.25 rescaling Bézier nodes to new location, 340
10.26 placing handles on a line, 341
11.1 startup variables Rounded Corners program, 348-349

11.2 drawing crosshair lines on form Rounded Corners program, 349
11.3 centering form (Rounded Corners program), 349
11.4 drawing rounded rectangles, 349
11.5 moving rounded rectangle object, 350
11.6 Basic option button procedure, 351
11.7 erasing images on forms, 352
11.8 CurrentXY option button procedure, 353
11.9 choosing one of three option buttons, 354
11.10 Stretcher option button procedure, 355
11.11 changing size of an object, 356
12.1 startup variables TxtAlign program, 363
12.2 centering form and text cursor, 363
12.3 aligning text with option buttons, 364
12.4 typing text within label control, 364
12.5 positioning starting point of text, 364-365
12.6 extracting text from label control, 365-366
12.7 startup variables APItext program, 372
12.8 loading font list/default values APItext program, 373
12.9 centering form on screen APItext program, 374
12.10 deleting changed device context attributes before quitting APItext, 374
12.11 using API TextOut function to draw text, 375-376
12.12 drawing embedded CR/LF text, 378-379
12.13 setting text coordinates APItext program, 379
12.14 drawing text with Print statement, 380
12.15 setting font style type, 381
12.16 showing current attributes of control font, 381

12.17 setting font Align property, 382
12.18 setting font style, 382
12.19 displaying font characteristics, 382-383
12.20 DrawText program startup variables, 387
12.21 loading font list DrawText program, 388
12.22 centering DrawText form, 389
12.23 setting font style, 389
12.24 setting text within bounding box, 390
12.25 changing button caption, 391
12.26 placing label control at MouseDown position, 391
12.27 DrawText function drawing text, 391
12.28 setting font style property, 392
12.29 changing button caption, 392
12.30 setting font alignment, 393
12.31 resetting display text in label control, 393
13.1 Join Nodes program startup variables, 400
13.2 startup default values (Join Nodes program), 401
13.3 removing nodes from polyshapes, 402
13.4 drawing new line object Join Nodes program, 403
13.5 setting a new line object, 403
13.6 initializing line start/end coordinates, 404
13.7 drawing line/polyline segments, 404
13.8 snapping polyshapes closed, 404-405
13.9 painting (fill) methods (Join Nodes program), 406
13.10 determining mouse movement (Join Nodes program), 407
13.11 setting additional line segments' start points, 408
13.12 moving polyshape line segments, 408

# listings

13.13 setting new line segments of a shape, 409
13.14 editing node positions of polyshapes, 410
13.15 loading new nodes as needed, 411
13.16 positioning nodes around polyshapes, 412
13.17 redrawing polyshapes, 413
13.18 API functions in Join Nodes program, 414
14.1 API graphical functions to test
14.2 assigning drawing coordinates objects PrintAPI program, 422
14.3 drawing four objects onto a device PrintAPI program, 423
14.4 testing printer scaling values, 423
14.5 API GetDeviceCaps for printing, 425
14.6 startup variables Scaltest program, 431
14.7 scale mode of picture box, 432
14.8 device point/logical point conversion, 433
14.9 restoring desktop scaling, 434
4.10 saving scale values at startup (Scaltest program), 435
14.11 zooming using API functions, 435-436
14.12 scaling with Visual Basic statements, 437
14.13 rescaling desktop with Visual Basic statements, 438
15.1 startup variables (ArtAPI program), 455-456
15.2 converting curve to line/line to curve, 458
15.3 finding polyshapes on desktop, 460
15.4 drawing objects with API functions, 461
15.5 subprocedure of Pnode MouseDown event, 465-466
15.6 subprocedure of Pnode MouseMove event, 467
15.7 subprocedure of Pnode MouseUp event, 471

15.8 BezNode_Up procedure continuation, 472-473
15.9 subprocedure of Artwork_MouseDown event, 475
15.10 subprocedure of Artwork_MouseMove event, 476
15.11 subprocedure of Artwork_MouseUp event, 477
15.12 guidelines/outlines of objects, 478
15.13 combining polyshapes as a whole, 480
15.14 new file read commands to open files (ArtAPI program), 481
15.15 new file write commands to save a file (ArtAPI program), 481
15.16 moving object to new screen location, 482
15.17 changing coordinates of object after move, 483
15.18 setting polynode coordinates for moves, 484-485
15.19 moving poly-segment to new location, 487-488
15.20 setting new coordinates of moved polyshape, 489-490
15.21 movable curves attached to closed polyshapes, 492
15.21. Drawing movable curves, continuation, 493
15.22 movable curves attached to open polyshapes, 496
15.23 de Casteljau dividing formula for Bézier curves, 497-498
15.24 adding Pnodes to new polysegments/closing polygons, 499
15.25 setting an open polyline shape/unloading Pnodes, 501
15.26 moving two polyline segments to new location, 502-503
15.27 loading new Pnodes on polyshapes, 505
15.28 reloading Pnodes on polyshapes when selected, 506-507

15.29 positioning hidden Pnode to new location, 508
15.30 resizing/flipping polyshape objects, 509-510
15.31 drawing outline of polyshape path, 510-511
15.32 sending object to front/back of others, 511-512
15.33 drawing object into memory bitmap, 513-514
15.34 drawing all objects onto desktop, 515
15.35 drawing all objects onto desktop, 517-518, 520
15.36 WinPrint procedure, 520-522
A.1 Artisan program global declarations, 526-530
A.2 Artisan palette color values, 533
A.3 clicking mouse to assign color, 534
A.5 setting default values, 535
A.4 start values, Text form, 536
A.6 cancelling text edit functions, 537
A.7 calculating carriage returns, 538
A.8 selecting new fonts for list boxes, 539
A.9 printing edited text to desktop, 539
A.10 aligning text within text boxes , 540
A.11 manually typing in new font size, 541
A.12 selecting new font attributes, 541
A.13 displaying text examples, 541
A.14 changing font size with scrollbar, 542
A.15 Cancel button press, 542
A.16 default values, palette form, 544
A.17 saving/canceling palette color edits, 545
A.18 resetting scrollbars to previous values, 545
A.19 selecting colors from Artisan program palette, 546

## listings

A.20 drawing each color of Artisan palette, 546
A.21 assigning new colors to Artisan palette, 547
A.22 extracting RGB color elements from (Artisan program), 547
A.23 dropping new colors into main palette, 548
A.24 printing drag-and-drop instructions, 548
A.25 drawing each color into three-row color palette, 549
A.26 changing color's element using scrollbar, 549
A.27 displaying color using scrollbar control, 549
A.28 manually typing color element values into text box controls, 550

**loading**
font list/default values (APItext program), 373
nodes around polyshapes (Join Nodes program), 412
Pnodes on polyshapes, 504-506
**logical points (device point conversion to), 433**
**LOGPALETTE (Palette program), 297-301, 310-311**

## M

**main menu selections, 162-163**
**manually**
scaling printer page, 423-424
setting text, 365-367
**marquee, finding objects, 139-141**
**MaskBlt function, 556**
**matching search words, 252**
**measurement/scaling in Artisan program, 52**
**menu area, Artisan program, 58**
**Menu_FindSub_Click event, 257**
**Menu_Insert_Click event, 258**
**Menu_Palette_Click event, 166**
**Menu_txt event, 265**
**methods,** *see* **statements**
**Mini-Bézier program, 320-324**
**mouse**
calculating movements, 167-168

clicking, 23-24
  on Begin program form, 10
  on objects, 141-144
dragging/moving on desktop, 89
moving over form, 329
**mouse events (Artisan program), 62**
**MouseDown event**
drawing Bézier curve using handle #1, 114
Join Nodes program, 402-404
**MouseMove event, 89-90**
**MouseUp event, 91-93**
**MoveMouse function, 97, 167**
**MoveObject procedure, 168**
**Movetest form properties, 38-40**
**Movetest program variables, 41**
**moving**
objects by node, 176-178
circles, calculating radius, 183
connected line segments, 409-411
curves, 121
  when using node #2, 340
lines by nodes, 178-180
mouse on desktop, 89
node #2 for curves, 339-340
objects
  on desktop, 168-169
  onscreen, 37-48
  front/back, 511-513
  front/back of others, 162
polyshape objects, 481-483
**Multi-Search and Replace program, 242-249**
BUIF picture box, 269
buttons, 251
  Replace, 261-262
files, 256-259
fonts, 267-268
form controls, 250
  properties, 243-249
forms, 265
list boxes, 250-251
  deleting items, 253
  editing, 254-255
  inserting text, 258-259
searching and replacing, 261-263
matching
  replace word with search word, 252
  search word and replace word, 252

ReplaceCom procedure, 262-263
SaveCom procedure, 263-264
text
  copying, 255-256
  cursor position, 266-267
  cutting, 255-256
  editing, 253-254
  inserting, 258-259
  line spacing, 266
  pasting, 255-256
  spacing, 265-269
text files, opening, 260-261
variable declarations, 249-250

## N

**N_H_Clear procedure, 171**
**node #1, rescaling, 339**
**node #2, moving, 339-340**
**Node Mouse Move event, 178**
**Node Mouse Up event, 180**
**node procedure, 169**
**Node_MouseDown event, 176**
**Node_MouseMove event, 338**
**Node1 mouse event, 337**
**Node2 MouseDown event, 339**
**NodeEdit form (Artisan program), 542-543**
**NodeHandle_Click event, 341**
**nodes**
ArtAPI program, 442
editing shapes, 407-409
grabbing curves by, 337-340
loading around polyshapes, 412
loading as needed, 411
moving
  lines, 178-179
  objects by, 176-178
removing from desktop, 171
removing from polyshapes, 402
repositioning around objects, 169-171
repositioning objects, 176
rescaling, 185-186
**nodes of objects, 54**

## O

**object handles, 54**
**object nodes, 54**

**objects**
  changing size (listing 11.11), 356
  clicking mouse on, 141-144
  complex, filling with color, 406-407
  curve, 54
  deleting from desktop, 59, 163-165
  dragging/stretching bounding box, 156
  drawing onto desktop, 515-520
  filling
    *popup paint tool, 180-182*
    *with color, 181*
    *with marquee, 139-141*
  flipped, reversing handle positions, 149-151
  index numbers (Artisan program), 99
  moving
    *by node, 176-178*
    *on desktop, 168-169*
    *onscreen, 37-48*
    *to front/back, 511-513*
    *to front/back of others, 162*
    *using on-the-fly values, 168-169*
  outline thickness, 160-162
  outlines/fills, 136-138
  placing to front/back, 193-195
  positioning stretch handles around, 145-149
  preparations for stretching, 151-155
  printing all, 520-523
  redrawing
    *on desktop, 195*
    *underlying page, 199*
  repositioning nodes, 169-171
  repositioning with nodes, 176
  rounded rectangle, moving, 350
  rounding with Step keyword, 353
  selecting by outline image, 513-515
  sending to front/back of others, 193-194
  stretching, 155-158
  updating position after stretching, 158
**OK_Btn_Click event (Artisan program), 539**

**OKbtn_Click event (Artisan program), 545**
**Opencom menu event, 249**
**opening**
  files, 256-259
  text files, 260-261
**opening/saving polyshape files, 480-481**
**option button procedure, 351**
**option buttons, 354**
**Option1_Click event, 11, 364**
  Artisan program, 540
**outline thickness of objects, 160-162**
**outline tool, Artisan program, 56**
**outlines (objects), 136-138**
**OutLineTextMetrics function, 360**

# P-Q

**pages**
  guidelines, 144-145
  redrawing under objects, 199
  setup (Artisan program), 51
**painting**
  areas of screen, 32
  fill methods, 406
  form (Palette program), 312-313
  fountain fills, 316-318
  objects (popup paint tool), 180-182
**PaleteBox_DragOver event, 548**
**palette form, 544-545**
**Palette program**
  API color palette, 307-308
  ClipPalette_MouseDown routine, 308-309
  color
    *changing with scrollbar, 315-316*
    *dithered, 311-312*
    *pure, 308-309*
    *selecting, 304-306*
    *viewing range, 308*
  controls, 298-301
  custom palettes, 308-309
  default variables, 301-318
  Draw_Blends procedure, 307-308
  Fill_Button_Click event, 313-314

Form_Resize routine, 302
forms, 298-301
fountain fills, 296, 306-307
  *buttons, 313-314*
  *painting complex objects, 316-318*
  functions (CreateCustomPalette), 309-310
  hexidecimal color numbers, 305-306
  LOGPALETTE, 297-301, 310-311
  painting form, 312-313
  PALETTE, 297-301, 310-311
  PicRGB_MouseDown, 304-306
  PicRGB_Paint event, 302-304
  RGBcolor& function, 314-315
  RGBscroll_Scroll event, 308
  structures
    *LOGPALETTE, 297-301, 310-311*
    *PALETTEENTRY, 297-301, 310-311*
**PALETTE.BAS file, 297-301, 310-311**
**PaletteBarColors event**
  color values from .INI file, 182-183
  extracting color values from .INI file, 182-183
**PaletteBox_DragDrop event, 548**
**PaletteBox_Paint event, 548**
**pasting text, 255-256**
**paths (GDI32 drawing functions), 552-553**
**PathToRegion function, 554**
**pen functions (API Drawing function), 280**
**PicRGB_MouseDown, 304-306**
**PicRGB_Paint event, 302-304**
**picture box**
  controls
    *ArtAPI program, 443-444*
    *rescaling, 438*
  drawing shapes, 422
  mouse events (Scaltest program), 432-434
  nodes, 411
  scaling dimensions, 149
  Tool Buttons (Artisan program), 54-55
**Picture1 MouseUp event, 329**

Picture1._MouseUp event, 266
Picture1.KeyPress event, 266
Picture1_KeyPress event, 364
Picture1_MouseDown event, 328, 364
Picture1_MouseMove event, 329
Pie function, 286-287
pies, calculating radians, 14-15
pixels
    converting twips to (listing 10.4), 328
    finding color values for, 35
    Set_Pixel function, 292
    setting to specified colors, 17
placing
    handles and dotted lines on lines, 119-120 , 341
    objects to front/back, 193-195
    text on desktop, 183-185
PlgBlt function, 556
plotting
    Bézier curve points, 320
    curve points, 325-329
    points of Bézier curves, 109
Pnode image control (ArtAPI program), 443, 464-469
Pnode_MouseDown procedure, 484
Pnode_MouseUp event, 489
Point statement, 35
pointer tool, Artisan program, 55
points
    Bézier curves, 107
    curves, plotting, 325-329
Poly_CurveMove1 procedure, 491
Poly_gon procedure, 499
Poly_Handles procedure, 479
Poly_Nodes procedure, 504
Poly_Reload procedure, 506
Poly_Stretch procedure, 509
Poly_Update event, 508
PolyBézier function, 320, 555
PolyBézierTo function, 320
PolyDraw function, 556
polygons, 287-288
    closing shapes, 499-501
Polyline function, 112, 289
polylines, 12
    converting to curves, 457-459
    drawing segments, 404-405

polyshapes
    calculating bounding boxes, 480-481
    drawing curves, 497-499
    editing curves, 491-496
    editing node positions, 410
    finding on desktop, 460
    line segments, moving , 408
    loading nodes, 412
    opening/saving, 480-481
    procedures (ArtAPI program), 445
    redrawing (listing 13.17), 413
    reloading Pnodes, 506-508
    removing nodes, 402
    snapping closed, 404-405
    stretching, 509-510
popup paint tool (filling objects), 180-182
positioning
    nodes around polyshapes, 412
    Pnodes on polyshapes, 504-506
    starting point of text, 364-365
positions for handles on bounding boxes, 157
pre-plotted Bézier curves, 108
Print statement (drawing text), 380
Print_API_Click event, 424
PrintAPI program
    drawing shapes on picture boxes, 422
    DrawObjects procedure, 422-423
    form/control properties, 419-420
    manually scaling printer page, 423-424
    variables, 421-422
printer
    graphics (ArtAPI program), 442-443
    pages (manually scaling), 423-424
    sending images to, 201
printing
    all objects, 520-523
    Artisan program, 52
    drag-and-drop instructions, 548
    edited text to desktopArtisan program, 539
    with PrintAPI program, 424
procedures
    ArtAPI program, 444
    Artisan program, 136

BezDivide, 107
BezDraw, 107, 325
BezHandle1, 146
BezHandle2, 146
BézierStore, 119
BezNode_Move, 467
BezNode_Up, 469
BezStretch, 129
BezUpdate, 128
Bounding Box_Down, 96, 475, 481
BoundingBox_Up, 72, 477
Box_Pset (listing 1.13), 26
Bresenham (listing 1.14), 27
Bresenham_360 (listing 1.15), 28-29
CarriageReturns (Artisan program), 538
Circle_Pset, 29-30
Circle_sin_cos, 30
Circle_Sqr (listing 1.18), 31
Color_INI, 138
ColorBar_MouseDown, 136
ColorBar_MouseUp, 137
ColorBar_Paint, repainting colors, 138
ColorScroll_Change, 138
CurrentXY option button, 353
Dash_Pset (listing 1.19), 31
Display_Color_Palette, 137, 533
Display_Color_Palette ColorBar, 138
Draw_Blends, 307-308
DrawObjects (PrintAPI program), 422-423
Fill_Line (listing 1.20), 32
Fill_Pset (listing 1.21), 33
Find_Object, 143, 478
FindAllObjects, 139
FindObject, 141, 144
GetRGBcolors, 547
Grid_Pset, 34
GuideLines, 145
Handle, 145
Handle_MouseDown, 152
HandleReverse, 149-151
Handles, 145
HandlesReverse, 146
Hscroll_Change, 160
Line_Pset, 35

LineButtons, 160
MoveObject, 168
N_H_Clear, 171
node, 169
option button, 351
Pnode_MouseDown, 484
Poly_CurveMove1, 491
Poly_gon, 499
Poly_Handles, 479
Poly_Nodes, 504
Poly_Reload, 506
Poly_Stretch, 509
ReplaceCom, 262-263
RulerGuides, 159
SaveCom, 263-265
Set_Pixel, 292
SineCosine, 24-25
Stretcher option button, 355
TestButton_Click, 510
To_Front_Back, 511
    *ArtAPI program, 446*
To_Front_Back, 59-61
Update Desktop, 51
Update_Mouse_Colors, 534
UpdateArtMask, 513
UpDateObjects, 153
    *flag names (listing 2.6), 77-78*
UpdateObjects, 99
WinPrint, 201-202, 520
Zoom, 438
ZoomBar (listing 2.8), 83
ZoomTool, 203-206
*see also* events

**programs**
Animator, 210-220
APItext, 367-384
ArtAPI, 442
Artisan, 50
    *color bar palette, 56*
    *declarations (listing 2.5), 73*
    *main menu selections, 162-163*
    *startup values (listing 2.7), 82*
Begin, *see* Begin program
DrawText, 384-393
Join Nodes, 396
Mini-Bézier, 320
Movetest variables (listing 1.24), 41
Multi-Search and Replace, 242-249

PrintAPI (form/control properties), 419-420
Pset, 17-25
Rounded Corners, 344
Scaltest, 426-439
Text Alignment, 360
TxtAlign, 363-367

**properties**
Animator program forms/controls, 213-218
Artisan form, 63
AutoRedraw, 53
form and control
    *Begin program, 5-7*
    *Join Nodes program, 398-399*
    *Mini-Bézier program, 320-322*
    *Multi-Search and Replace program, 243-249*
    *Pset program, 19*
Movetest form, 38-40
**Pset program, 17-25**
**Pset statement, 17, 37**
**Pt_In_Rect function, 289-290**
**PtInRect function, 141**
**Pythagorean Theorem, 11**

# R

**radians, 14-15**
**radius, 4-5**
calculating, 11
calculating for moving circle, 183
**Rec_tangle function, 290-291**
**rectangles**
expandable, 290-291
functions, 280
rounded corners, 291, 349
**redrawing**
Bézier curve when Bézier node #1 is moved, 122
Bézier curve when handle #1 is moved, 114-115
Bézier curve when handle #2 is moved, 118, 336
Bézier curve when node #1 is moved, 338
**curves, 114**
    *Bézier handle #1, 333-335*
    *Bézier handle #2, 335-337*

guidelines and underlying page, 199-200
levers for Bézier handle #2, 335-336
levers for handle #1, 334
objects on desktop, 195
page under objects, 199
polyshapes (listing 13.17), 413
shapes on desktop, 461-462
text on desktop, 95
**reference numbers for objects (Artisan program), 99**
**reloading Pnodes on polyshapes, 506-508**
**removing nodes/handles from desktop, 171**
**Replace button (list boxes), 261-262**
**ReplaceBtn_Click event, 261**
**ReplaceCom procedure, 262**
**replacing (Multi-Search and Replace program), 242-249**
**repositioning nodes around objects, 169-171**
**rescaling**
Bézier curve handles, 118
Bézier handle #1, 335
Bézier handle #2, 337
Bézier handles to new location, 337
Bézier node #1, 339
Bézier nodes to new location, 340
Bézier's handles to new locations
    *(listing 3.5), 116*
    *(listing 3.12), 123*
    *(listing 3.8), 118*
container controls after Zoom, 186
desktop, 206, 438
handles to new locations, 335
node #1, 339
nodes/handles, 185-186
picture box control, 438
**resetting**
default color palette, 167
scaling and dotted handle lines of curves, 126-127
scaling for curves, 126
values for new curves, 332-333
values for new lines, 333

**resizing polyshapes, 509-510**
**restoring**
    coordinate points for curves, 116
    desktop scaling, 434
**reversing handle positions on flipped objects, 149-151**
**RGB color elements, 547**
**RGB_Scroll_Change event, 549**
**RGB_Textbox_Change event, 550**
**RGBcolor& function, 314-315**
**RGBscroll_Change event, 549**
**RGBscroll_Scroll event, 308**
**right mouse button events, 63**
**Round_Rect function, 291**
**Rounded Corners program, 344**
    form/control properties, 345-347
    startup variables (listing 11.1), 348-349
**rounded rectangles**
    dimensioning with scrollbar property, 356
    drawing (listing 11.4), 349
    drawing with Basic procedure, 351-352
    drawing with Stretcher procedure, 355-356
    moving (listing 11.5), 350
**rounding shapes with Step keyword, 353**
**routines**
    ClipPalette_MouseDown, 308-309
    Form_Resize, 302
**ruler**
    drawing inch marks, 189-191
    drawing internal guidelines, 159
    drawing slide lines, 188-189
    guidelines, 186-188
    slide lines, 188-189
**Ruler_MouseDown event, 186**
**Ruler_Paint event, 434, 189-190**
**RulerGuides procedure, 159**

## S

**SaveCom procedure, 263-264**
**saving**
    files, 256-259
    palette form color edits, 545
    polyshape files, 480-481
**ScaleLeft property, placing text, 380**
**scaling**
    ArtAPI program, 442
    Artisan program, 52
    desktop, 206
        *zoom effect, 203-204*
    dimensions, forms/picture boxes, 149
    resetting for curves, 126
    routines (ArtAPI program), 447
    with Visual Basic statements, 437
**Scaltest program, 426-439**
    form/control properties, 427-430
    picture box mouse events, 432-434
    saving scale values at startup, 435
    startup variables, 431
**scrollbar**
    colors, changing, 315-316
    controls, Artisan program, 58
**scrollbar property, rounded rectangle dimensions, 356**
**scrolling, 158-160**
**search and replace list boxes, 252**
**searching, 242-249**
**Select/Case statements, 10**
**SelectClipPath function, 554**
**selecting colors, 304-306**
**sending objects to front/back, 193**
**SendMessage function, 159, 361**
**Set_Pixel function, 292**
**SetArcDirection function, 555**
**SetTextAlign function, 382**
**SetTextBtn_Click event, 365, 367**
**setting**
    curves when clicking Bézier node
        #1 (listing 10.20), 337
        #1 (listing 3.10), 122
    curves when clicking node #2, 340
    font style type, 381
    line objects, 403
    text coordinates, 379
    text within bounding box, 390
**shapes**
    drawing finalized versions with Join Nodes program, 413-414
    drawing on picture box, 422
    editing with nodes, 407-409
    redrawing on desktop, 461-462
**sine, 25-26**
**SineCosine event, 24-25**
**slide lines for ruler, 188-189**
**slopes, drawing, 27**
**spacing text, 265-269**
**start positions of lines, 329**
**startup values (Artisan program), 82**
**statements**
    Circle, 2, 16-17
    Line, 2, 15-16
    Point, 35
    Pset, 17, 37
    Select/Case, 10
**status area frame, Artisan program, 58**
**Step keyword, 12, 353**
**stretch handles, 145-149**
**Stretcher option button procedure, 355**
**stretching**
    Bézier curves, 129
    objects, 155-158
        *preparations for, 151-155*
    polyshapes, 509-510
**strings, 242**
**StrokeAndFillPath function, 553**
**StrokePath function, 553**
**structures (Palette program)**
    LOGPALLETTE, 297-301
    PALETTEENTRY, 297-301
**Style_Combo_Change event, 382**
**Style_Combo_Click event, 541**
**subroutines,** *see* **events**
**synchronizing Artisan program, 52**

## T

**Test button (ArtAPI program), 447**
**TestButton_Click procedure, 510**
**testing printer scaling values, 423**
**text**
    aligning with option buttons, 364
    alignment, 360
    copying, 255-256
    cursor position, 266-267

cutting, 255-256
drawing
  *API functions, 391*
  *DrawText function, 391*
editing, 253-254
extracting from label control, 365-366
finding within text, 257-258
formatting, 360
height with API functions, 391
inserting, 258-259
letter spacing, 361-363
line spacing, 266, 360-361
manually setting, 365-367
objects, 183-184
pasting, 255-256
placing on desktop, 183-185
placing using ScaleLeft property, 380
positioning starting point, 364-365
printing edited versions to desktop, 539
redrawing on desktop, 95
setting coordinates, 379
setting within bounding box, 390
spacing, 265-269
strings, 242
**Text Alignment program, 360**
**text boxes**
  aligning text within, 540
  controls, 550
**text cursor, centering, 363**
**text examples (Artisan program), 541**
**text files**
  opening, 260-261
  SaveCom procedure, 263-264
**Text form**
  Artisan program, 535-542
  start values, 536
**Text Metrics button, 382**
**text object attributes (Artisan program), 75**
**text tool (Artisan program), 56**
**Text1_Change event, 541**
**TextMex_Click event, 382**
**TextOut function, 375-378**
**Timer1_Timer event, 269**

**To_Curve_Click event, 543**
**To_Front_Back procedure, 59-61, 511**
  ArtAPI program, 446
**To_Line_Click event 543**
**tool buttons, 89**
**Tool Buttons picture box, 55**
**ToolButton_MouseDown event, 6**
**ToolButtons control, Artisan program, 86**
**ToolButtons_Paint event, 88**
**tools, 54-56**
**TwipPerPixel function, 328**
**twips**
  converting to pixels), 328
  drawing in Artisan program, 82
**TxtAlign program, 363-367**
  form/control properties, 361-363
  startup variables (listing 12.1), 363
**type variables (Artisan program), 72**
**typing characters, Artisan program, 94**
**typing text within label control 364**

## U

**Update Desktop procedure, 51**
**Update_Mouse_Colors procedure, 534**
**UpdateArtMask procedure, 513**
**UpDateObjects procedure, 53, 199**
  flag names (listing 2.6), 77-78
**updating**
  lines after moving, 180
  object position after stretching, 158
**user-defined type variables (Artisan program), 72**

## V

**values, resetting for new curves, 332-333**
**variables**
  Animator program (listing 6.1), 219
  declaring (Begin program form), 7-8, 22

defining for Artisan program, 70
Mini-Bézier program, 323-324
Movetest program, 41
Multi-Search and Replace program, 249-250
Palette program, 301-318
PrintAPI program, 421-422
startup, Rounded Corners program, 348-349
**viewing color range, 308**
**VScroll_Change event, 160, 542**

## W

**WidenPath function, 554**
**WinPrint procedure, 201-202, 520**
**writing color values to ARTISAN.INI file, 192**
**WYSIWYG table, 52**

## X-Y-Z

**Z_APIsub_Click event, 435**
**Z_Basicsub_Click event, 437**
**Zoom procedure, 438**
**zoom tool, 54, 442, 447**
**ZoomBar procedure, 83**
**zooming, 435-436**
**ZoomTool procedure, 203-206**

# Add to Your Sams Library Today with the Best Books for Programming, Operating Systems, and New Technologies

## The easiest way to order is to pick up the phone and call
# 1-800-428-5331

between 9:00 a.m. and 5:00 p.m. EST.
For faster service, please have your credit card available.

| ISBN | Quantity | Description of Item | Unit Cost | Total Cost |
|---|---|---|---|---|
| 0-672-30440-6 | | Database Developer's Guide with Visual Basic 3 (Book/Disk) | $44.95 | |
| 0-672-30517-8 | | CorelDRAW! 5 Unleashed (Book/2 CDs) | $49.99 | |
| 0-672-30160-1 | | Multimedia Developer's Guide (Book/CD ROM) | $49.95 | |
| 0-672-30308-6 | | Tricks of the Graphics Gurus (Book/Disk) | $49.95 | |
| 0-672-30507-0 | | Tricks of the Game-Programming Gurus (Book/CD-ROM) | $45.00 | |
| 0-672-30413-9 | | Multimedia Madness! Deluxe Edition (Book/2 CD-ROMs) | $55.00 | |
| 0-672-30448-1 | | Teach Yourself C In 21 Days, Bestseller Edition | $24.95 | |
| 0-672-30621-2 | | How to Create Real-World Applications with Visual Basic (Book/CD ROM) | $39.99 | |
| 0-672-30362-0 | | Navigating the Internet | $24.95 | |
| 0-672-30604-2 | | Virtual Reality Madness and More! (Book/2 CDs) | $44.95 | |
| 0-672-30492-9 | | 3D Madness! (Book/CD) | $45.00 | |

❑ 3 ½" Disk
❑ 5 ¼" Disk

| | |
|---|---|
| Shipping and Handling: See information below. | |
| TOTAL | |

Shipping and Handling: $4.00 for the first book, and $1.75 for each additional book. Floppy disk: add $1.75 for shipping and handling. If you need to have it NOW, we can ship product to you in 24 hours for an additional charge of approximately $18.00, and you will receive your item overnight or in two days. Overseas shipping and handling adds $2.00 per book and $8.00 for up to three disks. Prices subject to change. Call for availability and pricing information on latest editions.

**201 W. 103rd Street, Indianapolis, Indiana 46290**

1-800-428-5331 — Orders     1-800-835-3202 — FAX     1-800-858-7674 — Customer Service

Book ISBN 0-672-30509-7

# GET CONNECTED
## to the ultimate source of computer information!

## *The MCP Forum on CompuServe*

Go online with the world's leading computer book publisher! Macmillan Computer Publishing offers everything you need for computer success!

*Find the books that are right for you!*
A complete online catalog, plus sample chapters and tables of contents give you an in-depth look at all our books. The best way to shop or browse!

➤ Get fast answers and technical support for MCP books and software

➤ Join discussion groups on major computer subjects

➤ Interact with our expert authors via e-mail and conferences

➤ Download software from our immense library:
  ▷ Source code from books
  ▷ Demos of hot software
  ▷ The best shareware and freeware
  ▷ Graphics files

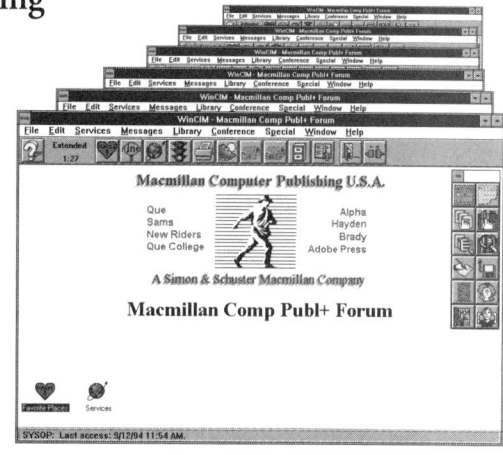

## Join now and get a free CompuServe Starter Kit!

To receive your free CompuServe Introductory Membership, call **1-800-848-8199** and ask for representative #597.

*The Starter Kit includes:*
➤ Personal ID number and password
➤ $15 credit on the system
➤ Subscription to *CompuServe Magazine*

---

*Once on the CompuServe System, type:*

## GO MACMILLAN

*for the most computer information anywhere!*

MACMILLAN COMPUTER PUBLISHING

CompuServe

## PLUG YOURSELF INTO...

# The MCP Internet Site

**Free information and vast computer resources from the world's leading computer book publisher—online!**

### Find the books that are right for you!

A complete online catalog, plus sample chapters and tables of contents give you an in-depth look at *all* our books. The best way to shop or browse!

- ✦ **Stay informed** with the latest computer industry news through discussion groups, an online newsletter, and customized subscription news.
- ✦ **Get fast answers** to your questions about MCP books and software.
- ✦ **Visit** our online bookstore for the latest information and editions!
- ✦ **Communicate** with our expert authors through e-mail and conferences.
- ✦ **Play** in the BradyGame Room with info, demos, shareware, and more!
- ✦ **Download software** from the immense MCP library:
    - Source code and files from MCP books
    - The best shareware, freeware, and demos
- ✦ **Discover hot spots** on other parts of the Internet.
- ✦ **Win books** in ongoing contests and giveaways!

*Drop by the new Internet site of Macmillan Computer Publishing!*

**To plug into MCP:**

**World Wide Web:** http://www.mcp.com/
**Gopher:** gopher.mcp.com  **FTP:** ftp.mcp.com

**GOING ONLINE DECEMBER 1994!**

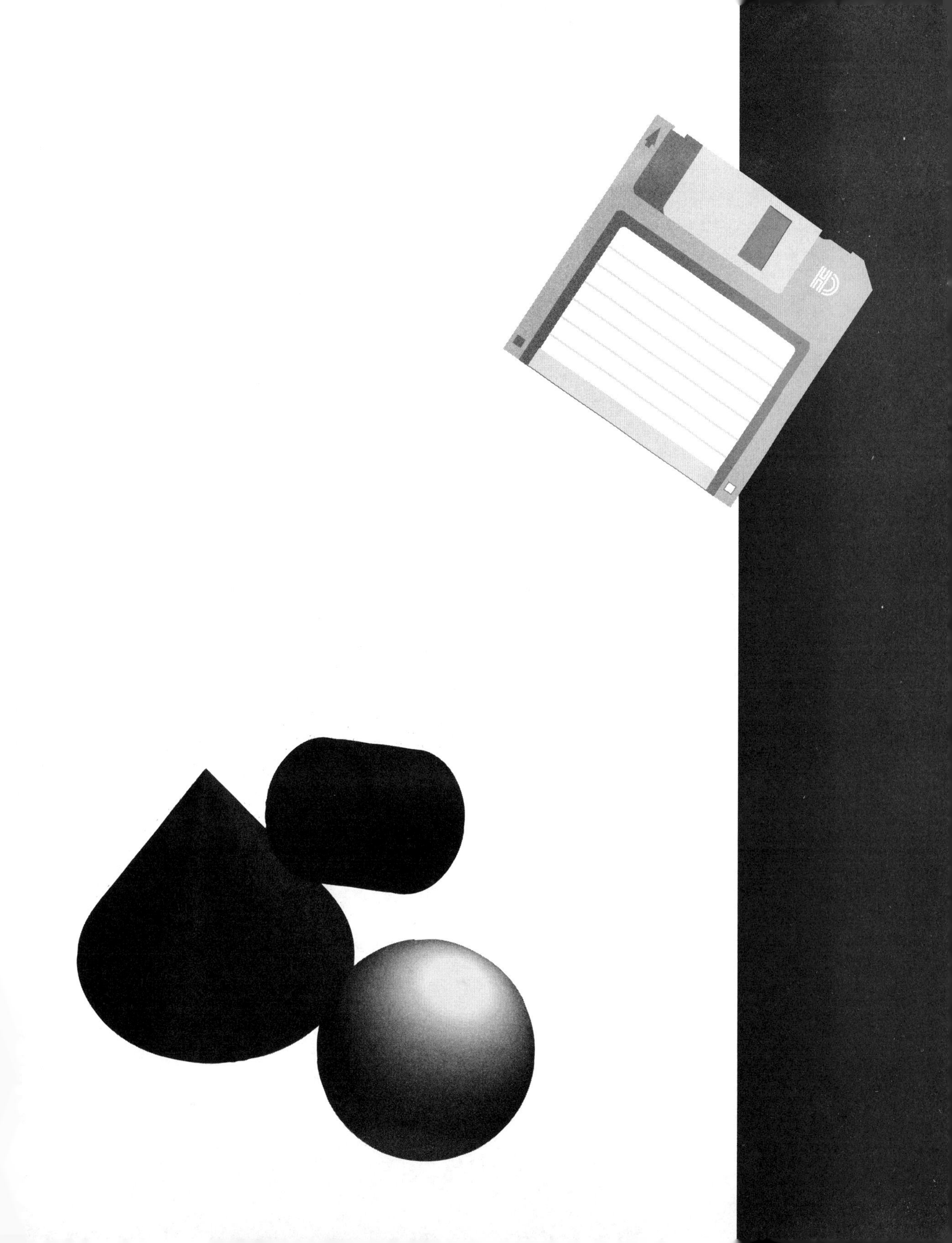

# Installing the Disk

The software on the disk is stored in a compressed form and must be installed to your hard drive using the Windows installation program.

1. From File Manager or Program Manager, choose **R**un from the **F**ile menu.
2. Type `<drive>\SETUP` and press Enter, where `<drive>` is the letter of the drive that contains the installation disk. For example, if the disk is in drive B:, type `B:\SETUP` and press Enter.

Follow the on-screen instructions in the installation program. The files will be installed in the \GPVBASIC directory unless you chose a different directory during installation.